Shiʿi Islam and Sufism

The Institute of Ismaili Studies
Shiʿi Heritage Series, 7

Editorial Board: Farhad Daftary (general editor), Maria De Cillis (managing editor), Gurdofarid Miskinzoda (managing editor), Mohammad Ali Amir-Moezzi, Hermann Landolt, Wilferd Madelung, Orkhan Mir-Kasimov, Andrew Newman, Sabine Schmidtke, Paul E. Walker

Previously published titles:
1. Farhad Daftary. *A History of Shiʿi Islam* (2013).
2. Farhad Daftary, and Gurdofarid Miskinzoda, ed. *The Study of Shiʿi Islam: History, Theology and Law* (2014).
3. Orkhan Mir-Kasimov. *Words of Power: Ḥurūfī Teachings Between Shiʿism and Sufism in Medieval Islam* (2015).
4. Mushegh Asatryan. *Controversies in Formative Shiʿi Islam: The Ghulat Muslims and their Beliefs* (2017).
5. Maria De Cillis. *Salvation and Destiny in Islam: The Shiʿi Ismaili Perspective of Ḥamīd al-Dīn al-Kirmānī* (2018).
6. Orkhan Mir-Kasimov, ed. *Intellectual Interactions in the Islamic World: The Ismaili Thread* (2020).

Shiʿi Islam and Sufism

Classical Views and Modern Perspectives

Edited by
Denis Hermann and Mathieu Terrier

I.B. TAURIS
in association with
THE INSTITUTE OF ISMAILI STUDIES
LONDON, 2020

I.B. TAURIS
Bloomsbury Publishing Plc
50 Bedford Square, London, WC1B 3DP, UK
1385 Broadway, New York, NY 10018, USA

In association with
The Institute of Ismaili Studies
Aga Khan Centre, 10 Handyside Street, London N1C 4DN
www.iis.ac.uk

First published in Great Britain 2020

A catalogue record for this book is available from the British Library.

A catalog record for this book is available from the Library of Congress

HB: 978-0-7556-0227-8
PB: 978-0-7556-0231-5
eISBN: 978-0-7556-0230-8
ePDF: 978-0-7556-0229-2

Series: Shiʿi Heritage Series

Typeset by RefineCatch Limited, Bungay, Suffolk

To find out more about our authors and books visit www.bloomsbury.com and sign up for our newsletters.

The Institute of Ismaili Studies

The Institute of Ismaili Studies was established in 1977 with the object of promoting scholarship and learning on Islam, in the historical as well as contemporary contexts, and a better understanding of its relationship with other societies and faiths.

The Institute's programmes encourage a perspective which is not confined to the theological and religious heritage of Islam, but seeks to explore the relationship of religious ideas to broader dimensions of society and culture. The programmes thus encourage an interdisciplinary approach to the materials of Islamic history and thought. Particular attention is also given to issues of modernity that arise as Muslims seek to relate their heritage to the contemporary situation.

Within the Islamic tradition, the Institute's programmes promote research on those areas which have, to date, received relatively little attention from scholars. These include the intellectual and literary expressions of Shiʿism in general, and Ismailism in particular.

In the context of Islamic societies, the Institute's programmes are informed by the full range and diversity of cultures in which Islam is practised today, from the Middle East, South and Central Asia, and Africa to the industrialized societies of the West, thus taking into consideration the variety of contexts which shape the ideals, beliefs and practices of the faith.

These objectives are realized through concrete programmes and activities organized and implemented by various departments of the Institute. The Institute also collaborates periodically, on a programme-specific basis, with other institutions of learning in the United Kingdom and abroad.

The Institute's academic publications fall into a number of interrelated categories:

1. Occasional papers or essays addressing broad themes of the relationship between religion and society, with special reference to Islam.
2. Monographs exploring specific aspects of Islamic faith and culture, or the contributions of individual Muslim thinkers or writers.
3. Editions or translations of significant primary or secondary texts.
4. Translations of poetic or literary texts which illustrate the rich heritage of spiritual, devotional and symbolic expressions in Muslim history.
5. Works on Ismaili history and thought, and the relationship of the Ismailis to other traditions, communities and schools of thought in Islam.
6. Proceedings of conferences and seminars sponsored by the Institute.
7. Bibliographical works and catalogues which document manuscripts, printed texts and other source materials.

This book falls into category six listed above.

In facilitating these and other publications, the Institute's sole aim is to encourage original research and analysis of relevant issues. While every effort is made to ensure that the publications are of a high academic standard, there is naturally bound to be a diversity of views, ideas and interpretations. As such, the opinions expressed in these publications must be understood as belonging to their authors alone.

Shiʿi Heritage Series

Shiʿi Muslims, with their rich intellectual and cultural heritage, have contributed significantly to the fecundity and diversity of the Islamic traditions throughout the centuries, enabling Islam to evolve and flourish both as a major religion and also as a civilisation. In spite of this, Shiʿi Islam has received little scholarly attention in the West, in medieval as well modern times. It is only in recent decades that academic interest has focused increasingly on Shiʿi Islam within the wider study of Islam.

The principal objective of the *Shiʿi Heritage Series*, launched by The Institute of Ismaili Studies, is to enhance general knowledge of Shiʿi Islam and promote a better understanding of its history, doctrines and practices in their historical and contemporary manifestations. Addressing all Shiʿi communities, the series also aims to engage in discussions on theoretical and methodological issues, while inspiring further research in the field.

Works published in this series include monographs, collective volumes, editions and translations of primary texts, and bibliographical projects, bringing together some of the most significant themes in the study of Shiʿi Islam through an interdisciplinary approach, and making them accessible to a wide readership.

Contents

Contributors xi
Acknowledgements xiii
Transliteration and Dates xv
Abbreviations xvii

Introduction
New Perspectives on Imami Shiʿi–Sufi Relations in the Modern and Pre-Modern Periods 1
Denis Hermann and *Mathieu Terrier*

PART ONE: ALTERNATIVES TO ANTI-SUFI DISCOURSE IN PRE-MODERN AND MODERN SHIʿI LITERATURE

1. The Defence of Sufism among Twelver Shiʿi Scholars of Early Modern and Modern Times: Topics and Arguments 27
   Mathieu Terrier
2. The Limits of 'Orthodoxy'? Notes on the Anti-Abū Muslim Polemic of Early 11th/17th-Century Iran 65
   Andrew Newman

PART TWO: THE SOCIAL HISTORY OF A SHIʿI SUFI BROTHERHOOD: THE NIʿMAT ALLĀHIYYA

3. Between the Spiritual and Material: The Niʿmat Allāhī Order's Institutionalisation and Architectural Patronage in the 9th/15th Century 123
   Peyvand Firouzeh
4. The *mujaddid* and the *majdhūb*: Shāh ʿAlī Riḍā (d. 1215/1801) and the Different Narratives of the Niʿmat Allāhī Renewal 157
   Fabrizio Speziale

5. The Institutionalisation of Niʿmat Allāhī Sufism during the Pahlavi Era: A Study of the Establishment of the Ḥusayniyya of Amīr Sulaymānī as a *waqf* in Tehran 175
Denis Hermann and *Omid Rezai*
6. Text and Contest: Theories of Secrecy, *taqiyya* and Archiving Practices in 20th- and 21st-Century Niʿmat Allāhī Sufism 197
Seema Golestaneh

PART THREE: RELATIONS BETWEEN SHIʿISM AND SUFISM IN OTHER SUFI LITERARY TRADITIONS

7. Sufism and Shiʿism in South Asia: *shahādat* and the Evidence of the Sindhi *marthiya* 225
Michel Boivin
8. Red Sulphur, the Great Remedy and the Supreme Name: Faith in the Twelve Imams and Shiʿi Aspects of Alevi-Bektashi Piety 255
Rıza Yıldırım
9. The Khāksār Shiʿi Sufi Order: An Updated Introduction 291
Alexandre Papas
10. ʿAjam Sufis and Shiʿi Spirituality in 19th-Century Iran 305
Lloyd Ridgeon
11. Two Khāksār Treatises of the 19th Century: The Fourteen Families (*Chahārdah khānawādah*) and The Booklet of Poverty (*Risāla-yi faqīriyya*) 325
Yaser Mirdamadi and *Mehrdad Arabestani*

Index 345

Contributors

Michel Boivin	CNRS-CEIAS, Paris
Peyvand Firouzeh	University of Sydney
Seema Golestaneh	Cornell University, Ithaca, NY
Denis Hermann	CNRS, Mondes Iranien et Indien, Paris / IFRI, Tehran
Andrew Newman	University of Edinburgh
Alexandre Papas	CNRS, CETOBaC, Paris
Omid Rezai	Sāzimān-i Awqāf wa Umūr-i Khayriyya, Tehran
Lloyd Ridgeon	University of Glasgow
Fabrizio Speziale	EHESS, Paris
Mathieu Terrier	CNRS, PSL, Paris
Rıza Yıldırım	Emory University, Atlanta, GA

Treatises in Chapter 11 translated by:

Mehrdad Arabestani	University of Tehran
Yaser Mirdamadi	University of Edinburgh

Acknowledgements

We would like to thank all the contributors for their enthusiasm, commitment and patience during the preparation of this volume. From the start it has been a work of collecting. This volume emerged from various sessions of a seminar organised by Denis Hermann at Institut d'études de l'Islam et des sociétés du monde musulman, l'École des Hautes Études en Sciences Sociales (IISMM/EHESS) between 2011 and 2013. We are indebted to IISMM and to the Centre National de la Recherche Scientifique (CNRS), and in particular to Mondes iranien et indien, who provided an institutional framework and financial support for this event.

Many papers included in this volume were presented at two international workshops. The first, 'Shiʿi Sufism in Modern Times', was held in October 2012 at the University of Edinburgh and was organised by Denis Hermann and Andrew Newman, with the support of the University of Edinburgh, the Institut Français de Recherche en Iran (IFRI), The Institute of Ismaili Studies, London (IIS), the Centre for the Advanced Study of the Arab World (CASAW) and Mondes iranien et indien. The second, 'Shiʿi Spirituality and Sufi Paths in Early Modern and Modern Times', took place in April 2014 at the University Ca' Foscari of Venice and was organised by Denis Hermann, Marco Salati and Mathieu Terrier, with the support of the University Ca' Foscari and the CNRS International Research Group (GDRI) 'New Horizons for the Social and Intellectual History of Shiʿism in Modern Times' (SHIʿISM) conducted by Denis Hermann, in special collaboration with the Centre National de la Recherche Scientifique (CNRS), the Institut d'études de l'Islam et des Sociétés du Monde Musulman, l'École des Hautes Études en Sciences Sociales (IISMM/EHESS), the University Ca' Foscari of Venice, the University of Edinburgh, The Institute of Ismaili Studies (IIS), and Royal Holloway University. We are indebted to all these institutions, without whose generous support these workshops would not have been possible, and we are especially grateful to Andrew Newman and Marco Salati for their friendly hospitality in their cities and universities.

We are grateful to the reviewers, who read the manuscript carefully and made many pertinent suggestions. We extend our special thanks to Anthony Gledhill and Gordon Gledhill for their assistance with the stylistic improvement of the English text of our Introduction.

Last but not least, we would like to express our gratitude to Farhad Daftary, Maria De Cillis and Gurdofarid Miskinzoda, for including this volume in the Shiʿi Heritage Series of The Institute of Ismaili Studies. We are especially indebted to Maria De Cillis, Gurdofarid Miskinzoda and Patricia Salazar for their patience during its long elaboration, their attentive reading of the manuscript, and their assistance through the publishing process.

Finally, we would like to pay tribute to our very esteemed and much lamented colleague, Leonard Lewisohn, who passed away suddenly on 6 August 2018. His work on Persian Sufi literature and Iranian Sufism remains an inestimable resource. His positions on the relations of Shiʿism and Sufism have been a major impetus for our historical and doctrinal research even, and especially, if our conclusions differ somewhat from his. We would like to express our deep gratitude to his memory.

Denis Hermann
Mathieu Terrier

Transliteration and Dates

The system of transliteration used in this book for the Arabic and Persian scripts is based on that adopted in the *Encyclopaedia Islamica*. Dynastic and geographical names have not been transliterated. The lunar years of the Islamic calendar (*hijri*) are followed by the corresponding Gregorian solar years. The Persian solar (*shamsi*) years are abbreviated to Sh.

Abbreviations

The following abbreviations are used for certain periodicals and encyclopaedias cited frequently:

BJMES	*British Journal of Middle East Studies*
BSOAS	*Bulletin of the School of Oriental and African Studies*
EI1	*Encyclopaedia of Islam, First Edition*
EI2	*Encyclopaedia of Islam, Second Edition*
EI3	*Encyclopaedia of Islam, Third Edition*
EIR	*Encyclopaedia Iranica*
EQ	*Encyclopaedia of the Qur'ān*
J. Asiat.	*Journal Asiatique*
JAOS	*Journal of the American Oriental Society*
JNES	*Journal of Near Eastern Studies*
JSAI	*Jerusalem Studies in Arabic and Islam*
JHS	*Journal of the History of Sufism*
JSIS	*Journal of Shiʿa Islamic Studies*
Stud. Islam.	*Studia Islamica*
ZDMG	*Zeitschrift der Deutschen Morgenländischen Gesellschaft*

Introduction

New Perspectives on Imami Shiʿi–Sufi Relations in the Modern and Pre-Modern Periods

Denis Hermann and *Mathieu Terrier*

Despite an extensive and long-standing body of studies on Sufism and the considerable advances made over the past few decades in the field of Shiʿi studies, the relationship between Imami Shiʿism and Sufism has been little explored. Yet the scope of research is vast and of the utmost importance if we are to build a comprehensive historical picture of these two major currents within Islam. The present work will seek to achieve this goal by paving the way to a more systematic exploration of the Shiʿi–Sufi relationship, with a view to developing an intellectual and social history. We intend to show that this lack of study is due not only to the scarce and restricted nature of the primary sources in Shiʿi currents of Sufism, but also to the respective dominant orientations, until recently, of Sufi and Shiʿi studies.

Academic studies have long represented Sufism as a mystical dimension specific to Sunni Islam, when the latter was not indeed conflated with Islam as a whole.[1] The setting aside of Shiʿi doctrines, perhaps because considered too heterodox to warrant attention, and perhaps also because their radical questioning of the majority Sunni 'orthodoxy' was a cause for concern to academic orthodoxy itself, has meant that the specific nature of Sufism has been examined mostly in the context of Sunnism.[2] This ignores the fact that this self-proclaimed Sunni 'orthodoxy' was for a large part created as a reaction and a response to pre-existing Shiʿi ideas: in other words, what was called in retrospect 'heterodoxy' or 'heresy' in fact predates what was later to become established as 'orthodoxy', as is generally the case in the history of religions.[3] As a result, it became difficult to see that many notions, as well as fundamental and distinctive practices within Sufism, had more or less similar equivalents within Shiʿism. We will only mention in passing the notion of *walāya*, 'authority', 'divine love' or 'divine alliance' in Shiʿism, 'sainthood' or 'divine friendship' in Sufism;[4] the embodiment of the *quṭb*, human 'pole' or 'axis' of creation within the Sufism of certain brotherhoods, analogous to that of *imām* within Shiʿism generally, and more specifically within Twelver or Imami Shiʿism;[5] one could also think about the cult of saints, visiting tombs (*ziyāra*) and the request for intercession (*shafāʿa*). Some scholars in oriental studies have sought the origins of Sufism outside Islam, within Christianity, Neoplatonism, Hinduism and Buddhism,[6] rather than within Shiʿism, admittedly a minority current within Islam, despite the fact that its doctrines are arguably the most ancient of this religion.

The links between Sufism and Shiʿism having been thus ignored by most specialists in Sufism, it is paradoxically the theme of their opposition that came to dominate, and finally to become the very *doxa* in the field of Islamic mysticism. Louis Massignon's monumental study of Ḥallāj (d. 309/922), contributed to this development by highlighting the fact that the execution of this mystical figure had been demanded and obtained by the Shiʿi elite of Baghdad, on purely self-interested grounds; and also by considering that 'the doctrine of the sainthood [of Ḥallāj] destroys (. . .) the basis of Shiʿism, of the privileges (*ʿiṣma*) of the ʿAlid Imams as well as of ʿAlid political-theological Mahdism.'[7] On the other hand, the historical-sociological approach to Sufism, focusing as it does on the appearance and development of Sufi orders in the Muslim world since the 5th/11th century, has further consolidated this theoretical frontier between Sufism and Shiʿism, since the vast majority of Sufi orders identify as belonging to the 'People of the Tradition and Majority' (*ahl al-sunna wa'l-jamāʿa*). John Spencer Trimingham, in his classical study *The Sufi Orders in Islam*,[8] puts forward the idea that 'the [Sufi] paths never developed sectarian tendencies. Their founders maintained careful links with the orthodox institution and did not repudiate the formal duties of Islam. One of their functions in Islamic life was to fill the gap left through the suppression of Shiʿi sectarianism.'[9] Such an identification of Sunni Islam with orthodoxy and of Shiʿism with sectarianism is typical of the classical Islamic studies in whose context Sufism was studied. Trimingham rightly draws our attention to the fact that 'the transformation of Sufi companionships into initiatory colleges began with the Sunni triumphs over Shiʿi dynasties (Buyids in Baghdad, 1055; Fatimids in Egypt, 1171), and was settled during the troubled time of the Mongol conquests (Baghdad, 1258)'.[10] From the Mongol Ilkhanate (1256–1353) through to the Safawids (r. 907–1135/1501–1722), the Sufi orders of Iran remained largely Sunni in name. Moreover, after Shāh Ismāʿīl (r. 906–930/1501–1524) became the first ruler of the Safawid dynasty in 907/1501 and established Shiʿism as the state religion, these Sufi orders seem to disappear from their original birthplace, Iran, and especially from the regions of Khurasan and Fars. In the absence of more extensive research on either Iranian Sufism or the 'exaggerating' or 'extremist' movements (*ghulāt*) such as the Ḥurūfiyya and the Mushaʿshaʿa (r. 845–914/1436–1508),[11] the expression 'Sunni Sufism' has in effect become a pleonasm in the field of general studies of Islam and Sufism.

This assumption was radically challenged by the philosopher and Iran specialist, Henry Corbin. Throughout his research, which followed a spiritual purpose as much as a rational or academic programme, he strove to transform the representation of Islamic philosophy and its history – and thereby the representation and practice of philosophy in Western culture. He paid little attention to the socio-historical aspects of Sufism while meditating deeply on some of its mystical and speculative doctrines, such as those of Ibn ʿArabī (d. 638/1240). In so doing, he proposed a genuine and important paradigm shift in the relationship between Sufism and Shiʿism. In his famous book *L'imagination créatrice dans le soufisme d'Ibn ʿArabi* (Creative imagination in the Sufism of Ibn ʿArabī) and in his research on Sayyid Ḥaydar Āmulī (d. after 787/1385), which was synthesised in the third volume of his comprehensive *En Islam iranien* (On Iranian Islam) with studies focused on other thinkers such as ʿAlāʾ al-Dawla al-Simnānī (d. 736/1336) and Ṣāʾin al-Dīn ʿAlī b. Turka Iṣfahānī (d. 830/1427), Henry Corbin stresses the deep links that exist between Sufism and Shiʿism, in terms of both doctrine and spiritual experience, considering the latter to be their ultimate goal.[12] While majority Sunni Islam embodies the exoteric dimension (*ẓāhir*) of Islam, Shiʿism and Sufism share its esoteric dimension (*bāṭin*), even though both also comprise exoteric (Shiʿi legalism, institutionalised Sufism) as well as esoteric dimensions (Shiʿi gnosis, Sufi mysticism) of their own. Opposition between Shiʿism and Sufism only occurs on the inessential plane of the exoteric, giving way to a deep spiritual bond on the essential esoteric plane. Though he refused to apply a historicist approach, Corbin recognised the precedence and influence of Imami Shiʿism on Sufi mysticism, and considered that by integrating the mysticism of Ibn ʿArabī, Shiʿi thinkers between the 14th and 17th centuries had in effect recovered Shiʿism's own essence. True to his phenomenological approach of fully empathising with the ideas of his chosen authors so as better to bring out their full meaning, Corbin was particularly seduced by the theory advanced by Ḥaydar Āmulī, according to which the Sufis are the true Shiʿa, and the true Shiʿa, the Sufis. Moreover, he shared the double purpose of Ḥaydar Āmulī: on the one hand, to reconcile Sufism with what he held to be its Shiʿi origins, and, on the other, to restore to Shiʿism the spiritual dimension of the revelation, the 'gnosis of Islam', of which he believed it was the repositary.[13]

This new conception of Sufism and its fundamental relationship with Imami Shiʿism caused a rift, first of all in France, in the field of the studies of both doctrinal Sufism and of the mysticism of Ibn ʿArabī, between the scholars who sought to corroborate the theory of 'Shiʿi Sufism' and those who categorically rejected the idea.[14] We will only mention here a resolution which consists in declaring the problem not pertinent on the grounds of the ideal transcendence of Sufism, as does William C. Chittick when he writes: 'Being a Sufi certainly has nothing to do with the Sunni/Shiʿi split.'[15] After decades of controversy and in the absence of a decisive argument to the contrary, the theory according to which Sufism has been annexed, however uneasily, by Sunni 'orthodoxy', has itself remained the accepted and 'orthodox' position in the realm of Sufi studies. Whereas the phenomenological, anti-historicist and anti-sociological approach of Henry Corbin overshadowed the role of the Sufi orders in the development of Sufi doctrine,[16] and in this following the Shiʿi scholars who rehabilitated Sufism and its great individual figures, Ḥallāj included, while condemning the orders socially organised around a master (*shaykh*, *pīr* or *quṭb*), the socio-historical approach to Sufism, following Trimingham, has tended to strengthen the commonplace of 'Sunni Sufism'. Tellingly, *Les voies d'Allah* (Paths of God), a quasi-exhaustive survey of all the Sufi orders, only briefly addresses the links between Sufism and Shiʿism, and then only in the context of Iran and the Bektashiyya order, implying that these links only date back to the 10th/16th century, as a consequence of 'Safawid propaganda'.[17] Éric Geoffroy, a specialist on Sufism, summarises this point of view thus: after recognising the 'doctrinal affinities' between Sufism and Shiʿism, he considers them to be 'two rival esoteric traditions' and draws the conclusion that 'Sufism must be defined, in principle as in history, as the mystical or esoteric dimension of Sunni Islam.'[18]

One fact, however, did not go unnoticed by western scholars: the chain of initiation (*silsila*, pl. *salāsil*) of every Sufi order is traced back to ʿAlī b. Abī Ṭālib (d. 41/661), first Shiʿi imam, and first recipient of the esoteric doctrines of the Prophet; and many of these genealogies also trace back to various other imams of Twelver lineage. This reference to ʿAlī and the Shiʿi imams is generally played down by classical scholars in Islamic studies, many of whom believe, with Goldziher, that their borrowing from Shiʿism was a purely opportunistic attempt to gain legitimacy.[19] Such a stance only strengthened, *nolens volens*, the denegation, even self-censorship, which prevailed among certain orders in Ottoman Turkey, during the long war that opposed the Sunni empire to the Shiʿi kingdom. The Khalwatiyya, for example, dissociated itself from Shiʿism to the point of removing the names of the Shiʿi imams from its *silsila*.[20] The exception which proves the rule is the Naqshbandiyya order, whose *silsila* is the only one which starts with Abū Bakr, the first caliph (r. 11–13/632–634), reviled by the Shiʿa for being a usurper, instead of ʿAlī; and nevertheless integrates both Salmān al-Fārsī (d. 35 or 36/655–657), companion and disciple of Imam ʿAlī, and the sixth imam Jaʿfar al-Ṣādiq (d. 148/765). The Naqshbandiyya are without doubt one of the Sufi orders most attached to Sunni obedience, and most opposed to Shiʿism, which is perhaps why they were subjected to intensive and sustained persecution in Safawid Iran.[21]

In this respect, what made possible the gradual acknowledgement of Shiʿi-Sufi relations was the increase in the number of studies on Ilkhanid rule, led notably by Alessandro Bausani, Jean Aubin and later Jean Calmard,[22] which have shown that, concurrently with the development of Sufi orders under the aegis of Sunni authority in Egypt and Syria, following the fall of the Fatimid dynasty (567/1171), Sufism had evolved very differently in the oriental Muslim world. In 656/1258, the Mongol invasion took down, along with the throne of the Abbasid Empire in Baghdad, the Sunni hegemony on the eastern half of the Orient. At this time, two Sunni Sufi orders were particularly powerful within the now defunct frontiers of the Abbasid Empire: the Kubrawiyya (founded by Najm al-Dīn Kubrā, d. 617/1220–1) and the Suhrawardiyya (founded by Shihāb al-Dīn Abū Ḥafṣ ʿUmar Suhrawardī

(d. 632/1234), not to be confused with Shihāb al-Dīn Yaḥyā Suhrawardī, the mystical philosopher executed in 587/1191). As Marijan Molé showed in a major study, the Kubrawiyya played a determining role both in converting the Mongol khans to Islam, and, at a later stage, in progressively introducing Shiʿi doctrine within Iranian Sufism.[23] Though Kubrā was himself a Sunni Shāfiʿī, his eulogies of ʿAlī and the *ahl al-bayt* paved the way for the consequent adoption by the brotherhood of themes specific to Shiʿism, such as the announced Messianic return of the twelfth imam, which was first instigated by his disciple Saʿd al-Dīn Ḥamūya (d. 650/1252). As Mongol power in Iran declined over the following century or so, Shiʿi subgroups whose structure was similar to that of Sufi orders were able to found small autonomous states, such as the Sarbadār in Khurasan (738–783/1337–1381),[24] the Marʿashī in Mazandaran (760/1358–9 to second half of the 10th/16th century),[25] and later the Mushaʿshaʿyān in Khuzistan (840–1092/1436–1681),[26] in which Sufi shaykhs and dervishes played a major role. Founded by Shaykh Ṣafī al-Dīn Isḥāq al-Ardabīlī (d. 735/1334), the Ṣafawiyya, initially of Sunni obedience, switched to a Messianic and 'exaggerated' or 'extremist' (*ghālī*) form of Shiʿism, which included a strong militarised component towards the end of the 9th/15th century.[27] The allegiance of the Qizilbash ('red heads') to the Shiʿitised Safawid shaykhs raises the question of a latent conversion to Shiʿism of the Anatolian Sufi orders.[28] Qizilbash revolts in central and oriental Anatolia had been quashed in blood by the Ottomans prior to the foundation of the Safawid realm in Iran (956/1501). The syncretic doctrines of this period, that became influential through the agency of, and within, the Sufi orders, such as the veneration of ʿAlī and the 'People of the Cloak' (*ahl al-kisāʾ*), Muḥammad, ʿAlī, Fāṭima, Ḥasan and Ḥusayn, and which certain shaykhs sought to accommodate with the veneration of the first two caliphs Abū Bakr and ʿUmar (r. 13–24/634–644),[29] could be described equally as a Sufi adaptation of Twelver Shiʿi tenets, or a Shiʿitisation of Sufism.[30]

Meanwhile, the development and orientation of Shiʿi studies, since the early 1900s, played an equal part in obscuring the links between Shiʿism and Sufism. As already mentioned, scholars have long considered Shiʿism doctrinally heretical, socially legalistic, and, above all, extremely hostile to Sufism. After having long been overlooked by academic circles, Imami Shiʿism became a strong focus of attention following the publications of the aforementioned Henry Corbin, particularly *En Islam iranien* and *Histoire de la philosophie islamique* – in which Corbin identifies Shiʿi esotericism with the 'gnosis of Islam' and advocates representing Shiʿism as essentially spiritual and politically quietist. However, the aftermath of the 1979 Islamic revolution in Iran led to a spectacular increase in the output of Shiʿi studies in the academic world. With a new agenda in mind, scholars sought to explain how the genuine Shiʿism of the imams, initially apolitical and esoteric, could become the rationalised, institutionalised and politicised Shiʿism of the *fuqahāʾ*.[31] According to a paradigm both teleological and regressive, scholars have tended to interpret the whole history of Shiʿism as a gradual alteration of the 'pure doctrine of the source' ending in the political doctrine of the *wilāyat al-faqīh*, literally 'sovereignty of the theologian-jurisconsult', and its putting into practice in Iran.

This recent body of studies has focused particular attention on the Safawid period (906–1134/1501–1722), during which Imami Shiʿism became a state religion, openly dissociated itself from Sunni Islam, established an organised clergy,[32] reassembled and revised its scriptural corpus (the Imami *ḥadīth*) and further developed its doctrines in philosophical gnosis through the teachings of thinkers such as Mīr Dāmād (d. 1041/1630) and Mullā Ṣadrā Shīrāzī (d. 1050/1640).[33] As already mentioned, the Safawiyya order, initially of Sunni obedience, only later turned to an 'extremist' and Mahdist Shiʿism.[34] However, when the young shaykh of the order, at the head of a horde of armed and fanaticised dervishes, the Qizilbash, took Tabriz to become the founder of a dynasty that would reign for over two centuries, he would proclaim Imami Twelver Shiʿism as the official state religion – even though his version of Shiʿism would be better described as a 'Safawid synthesis', to quote Kathryn Babayan, of Qizilbash Mahdism and Imami Shiʿism.[35] The Iranian society of the time, though permeated with veneration for the *ahl al-bayt*, was predominantly Sunni, and, moreover, access to and knowledge of Twelver sources were extremely limited.[36]

Shāh Ismāʿīl called upon Arab Imami scholars from the centres of Shiʿi tradition based in Iraq and Jabal ʿĀmil (present-day South Lebanon) to propagate religious knowledge in his kingdom.[37] His son and successor, Shāh Ṭahmāsp (r. 930–984/1524–1576), accelerated the process of breaking away from the Mahdist Shiʿism of the Qizilbash, routinised the charismatic power of the shaykh, to paraphrase Max

Weber, and instigated the transition towards a rationalised and institutionalised form of Imami Shiʿism, consistent with a long awaiting for the Mahdi, rather than the imminence of his announced return. The great architect of this reform was Shaykh ʿAbd al-ʿAlī al-Karakī (d. 940/1533), who came from Jabal ʿĀmil at the invitation of the Shāh, and was provided by the latter with great means and major religious stature, exemplified by the 'seal of the *mujtahids*' (*khātam al-mujtahidīn*) which he was given in 939/1533, in order to head a clerical administration capable of homogenising society on the religious plane.[38]

As a number of historians have shown, this period was decisive in the development of the relationship between Shiʿism and Sufism in Iran. The founding decision of Shāh Ismāʿīl and its subsequent slow and difficult application, had deep and irreversible impact on the social and doctrinal evolution of not only Imami Shiʿism, but also of Iranian Sufism. The religious policies of the Safawid shahs were initially characterised by violent hostility towards Sufism, whose charismatic leaders were regarded as rivals and represented a potential threat. Upon the conquest of Tabriz, Shāh Ismāʿīl ordered the destruction of all the Sufi tombs and mausoleums. Henceforth, 'Sufi policy' within the realm would oscillate between repression and accommodation, depending on how inclined the various Sufi groups were to recognise the spiritual and temporal authority of the Shāh.[39] A number of orders disappeared or fled under the persecution, others converted to Shiʿism and incorporated the new political-theologian system. Moreover, many Shiʿi *ʿulamāʾ* during this period, whether rationalist *uṣūlī*, as personified by Shaykh ʿAbd al-ʿAlī al-Karakī, or 'scripturalist' *akhbārī*, such as Muḥammad b. al-Ḥasan al-Ḥurr al-ʿĀmilī (d. 1104/1693), declared *fatwas* against Sufis and produced dogmatic treatises which refuted Sufism in the name of orthopraxy and orthodoxy, and condemned, in turn, the antinomianism (*ibāḥiyya*) of the dervishes, the claim to 'divine indwelling' (*ḥulūl*), held by the ecstatic Sufi, the ceremonies of spiritual audition (*samāʿ*) and chants (*ghināʾ*), which were considered 'blameworthy innovations' (*bidʿa*), the dangerous proximity between the pole (*quṭb*) and the imam, and the Sunni affiliation of Sufi orders in general.[40] The broad lines of this reasoning against Sufism persisted and were developed right until the late 19th century by the theological-mystical school of the Shaykhiyya,[41] even though this spiritual school was independent from both Twelver clergy and Iranian state.

By focusing on the anti-Sufi tendency displayed by the Shiʿi *ʿulamāʾ* in Iran during this period, specialists in Imami and Safawid studies have, rather hastily, taken for granted that this hostility was the majority and 'orthodox' position of Imami Shiʿism towards Sufism.[42] Until now, little attention has been paid to an alternative and syncretic discourse which prevailed within a number of Shiʿi circles, during, and even before the Safawid period, which included an apologia for Sufism.[43] This explains, at least in part, how Sufism, though under continuous attack, still managed to hold out, until it re-established itself and revived during the 18th century. Symmetrically, in the whole field of study on the Qajar period (1200–1344/1786–1925), little attention was paid, until recently, to the existence of a judicial tradition, initiated by Sufi and Shaykhi masters, which was deeply rooted in Shiʿi *fiqh*.[44] During this time, the frontiers separating different categories of scholars were more porous than generally portrayed today. For example, the Shiʿi *ʿulamāʾ* of Iran were imbued by the literary tradition of Persia and its mystical poetry of predominantly Sufi origin. Poets like Saʿadī (d. *ca* 690/1291), ʿAṭṭār Nayshābūrī (d. 618 or 627/1221 or 1230) or Jalāl al-Dīn Rūmī (d. 672/1273), were taught within the traditional framework of the *maktab* until the advent of the Pahlavi dynasty (1925–1979); whilst a number of eminent members among the various Sufi orders were also scholars in religious science (*ṭalāba*, pl. of *ṭālib*). These facts, which question the historiographical commonplace of the opposition between Shiʿism and Sufism, suggest that the rationalist clergy has not always had – and maybe still does not – the monopoly on the creation of orthodoxy and orthopraxy in the Imami Shiʿi world.[45]

A thorough investigation of the relationship between Shiʿism and Sufism in the pre-modern and modern times is likely to call into question the traditional and major orientations of Sufi and Shiʿi studies, and offer new perspectives of exploration in these two fields. It is a duty of the editors of the present volume to pay homage to the eminent academics who have led the way in this endeavour and notably to the Iraqi scholar and student of Louis Massignon, Kāmil Muṣṭafā al-Shaybī, whose pioneering work *al-Ṣila bayna'l-taṣawwuf wa'l-tashayyuʿ* (The Connection between Sufism and Shiʿism) has been relatively ignored in Western scholarship, with the exception of S.H. Nasr, notwithstanding the existence of an English translation.[46] In it the author analyses the historical and doctrinal aspects of the relationship between Shiʿism and Sufism, both within the context of collective manifestations such as the Shiʿi messianic movements of the 14th to 15th centuries, e.g. the Mushaʿshaʿa and the Nūrbakhshiyya, and the study of individual thinkers – al-Ḥāfiẓ al-Bursī (d. after 813/1411) and Ibn Abī Jumhūr al-Aḥsāʾī (d. after 901/1496) among others. However, this general survey on the one hand is mainly focused on the Arab-Iranian centre of the Muslim world, and therefore neglects to investigate this same relationship within the Indian subcontinent; and on the other hand, since its publication, new primary sources of Arabic and Persian origin have been made available, which render a number of his conclusions obsolete.

We should also mention Seyyed Hossein Nasr's article, 'Shîʿisme et soufisme. Leurs relations historiques et principelles', published in English as 'Shiʿism and Sufism: Their Relationship in Essence and History', in the proceedings of the notable 1968 Strasbourg colloquium. In this paper, Nasr holds that Shiʿism and Sufism have a common parentage, giving the priority to Shiʿism in its broader sense, by writing 'if we take Sufism and Shiʿism in their historical manifestation in their later period, then neither Shiʿism nor Sunnism nor Sufism within the Sunni world derive from each other (. . .). But if we mean by Shiʿism Islamic esotericism, then it is of course inseparable from Sufism'.[47] However, the author's essentialist rather than historical approach is questionable, especially since he writes in conclusion: 'These historical manifestations have been no more than applications to different moments of time of an essential and principial relationship which belongs to the eternal and integral reality of Islam itself',[48] as is the historical information which he refers to, which comes from authors such as Nūr Allāh Shūshtarī (d. 1019/1610) and Maʿṣūm ʿAlī Shāh (d. 1212/1797–8), who were engaged in Sufi-oriented Shiʿism and Shiʿi-oriented Sufism. Also, let us cite the major work by Richard Gramlich, *Die schiitischen Derwischorden Persiens* (Wiesbaden, 1965–1981), which is devoted to the study of Shiʿi Sufi orders, namely the Niʿmat Allāhiyya, the Dhahabiyya and the Khāksāriyya, although it does not cover their origin and evolution prior to the 19th century. Finally, concerning the two former orders, we have to pay homage to our late lamented colleague Leonard Lewisohn (d. 2018), whose historical approach was engaged in the defence of Sufism against what he considered to be a late and forced Shiʿitisation of the Sufi orders, contrary to the very nature of Sufism, fundamentally neutral in the conflict opposing Shiʿism to Sunnism.[49]

With this in mind, we will mention at this point that another major reason why studies on our theme are so scarce is the paucity of scriptural sources bequeathed by two of the three main branches of Shiʿi Sufism, the Dhahabiyya and the Khāksāriyya. The latter, whose origin, according to the sources, traces back to a subdivision of the Suhrawardiyya called Jalālī, were a group of dervishes of working-class background, sustained by craftsmen and shopkeepers. The poles of this rather informal order saw little interest or virtue in documenting doctrine, which they preferred to transmit orally, while their dervishes were generally not well trained in the classical texts of Sufism.[50] In the third chapter of this volume, some of the rare written material passed on by the Khāksāriyya and recently edited by Mihrān Afshārī,[51] will be introduced and translated. As for the Dhahabiyya, notable progress has been made since the publication of the works of Iranian scholars such as Asad Allāh Khāwarī and ʿAbd al-Ḥusayn Zarrīnkūb, and also the well-documented synthesis of Hamid Algar in the *Encyclopaedia Iranica*, due to two articles by Leonard Lewisohn and the most recent work of Ata Anzali.[52] However we regret not having been able to include any new article on this subject. It is worth recalling that the Dhahabiyya, according to the sources, was the consequence of the secession from the Kubrawiyya in the 9th/15th century, led by ʿAbd Allāh Burzīshābādī (d. *ca* 856/1452) against his master Isḥāq Kuttalānī (d. 826/1423). The order seems to have embraced Shiʿism much later; that is, according to Anzali, in the second century of the Safawid era (11th/17th century), at the same time as it adopted the name *dhahabiyya* (*dhahab* meaning 'gold', i.e. from the golden lineage, *al-silsila al-dhahabiyya*).[53] Under the tutelage of the Safawids, it contributed to the diffusion of Shiʿism in Khurasan.[54] The Dhahabiyya profess to be faithful to Shiʿi orthodoxy and orthopraxy – whilst insistently condemning antinomianism as did Sufi-oriented Shiʿi authors, faithful to the master of Safawid times, Muḥammad ʿAlī Muʾadhdhin Khurāsānī (d. 1078/1667), whose work *Tuḥfa-yi ʿAbbāsī* was dedicated to Shāh ʿAbbās II (r. 1052–1077/1642–1666).[55] However, this conformist attitude, or perhaps this art of compromise, was not enough to avoid condemnation and eventually persecution under Shāh Sulṭān Ḥusayn (r. 1105–1135/1694–1722), when the master of the order fled from Iran to Najaf.[56] The order survived only in the city of

Shiraz, and peacefully integrated itself into the collective religious life under the Qajar dynasty, without suffering the hostility faced by the Niʿmat Allāhiyya following their re-establishment in Iran during the 12th/18th centuries, probably in consequence of their lack of interest in proselytising. In recent decades, the Dhahabiyya have published some of their sources, hitherto available only in manuscript form, however, the order belongs mainly to the world of the bazaar.[57]

In summary, an overview of all the research pertaining to the relationship between Sufism and Shiʿism might raise the following questions: are opposition and rivalry between the two always the rule, and conciliation and interaction, the exception? Must one take at face value the 'orthodox' character of the Sunni affiliation characteristic of most Sufi orders, or indeed the 'orthodox' character of the anti-Sufism common to so many of the Shiʿi *ʿulamā*'? Could one not rather interpret these claims to authority and normative definitions as the sign that a discreet but persistent alternative has existed for some time? Is it now necessary to analyse and deconstruct the 'essentialist' discourse on 'Shiʿi Sufism' to separate historical facts from reconstructed collective memories, to shed light on parallels and distinctions, and attempt to clarify how Sufism might have influenced Shiʿism and vice versa?

In order to answer these questions, to fill some gaps in the research, and to initiate a new and converging orientation of Shiʿi studies and Sufi studies, whilst taking the former pioneering studies into account, our project is to lay down some simple methodological principles. First, the relationship between Shiʿism and Sufism should be studied in a geographical area broader than that of the Iranian plateau to which it has long been confined. Even though Iran remains central to this historical issue, we believe it is necessary to consider both the Indian subcontinent and Anatolia to complete our understanding of it. The articles of Fabrizio Speziale, Michel Boivin and Rıza Yıldırım, fulfil this need. Our second principle has been to study the relationship between Twelver Shiʿism and Sufism over a longer period than is usual in this context, widening current boundaries and focusing not only upon, but also upstream and downstream of the Safawid period in order to better understand its importance. The articles of Peyvand Firouzeh and of Mathieu Terrier thus address the pre-modern period. Our third resolution was to not confine our examination to the sphere of the *'ulamā'*, but to question the relationship between Twelver Shi'ism and Sufism throughout different strata of society. The articles of Denis Hermann and Omid Rezai, as of Seema Golestaneh on the Ni'mat Allāhiyya, the essay of Lloyd Ridgeon on the tradition of the 'Ajam, the general presentation of the Khāksār order by Alexandre Papas and the translations of two epistles of the Khāksāriyya by Mehrdad Arabestani and Yaser Mirdamadi, illustrate this methodology.

Whilst developing these innovative approaches, our volume also proposes two new topics in historical and doctrinal research: first, Shi'i Imami Sufism, embodied by the beliefs and practices of the Sufi orders manifestly connected to the lineage of the twelve imams, such as the Ni'mat Allāhiyya, the Bektāshiyya and the 'Ajam; secondly, Sufi-oriented Shi'ism, among Twelver thinkers who openly sympathise with 'genuine' or 'real' Sufism, as presented by Mathieu Terrier. In both cases, the task at hand is to thoroughly analyse the reciprocal predicative relationship between Shi'ism and Sufism, in order to ascertain the extent to which Shi'i Sufism is Shi'i and Sufi-oriented Shi'ism is Sufi, without any concession towards essentialism; but always from the standpoint that Imami Shi'ism and Sufism – whether or not institutionalised – are both social and spiritual historical constructions.

The first part of the volume studies alternative approaches to the so-called 'majority' and 'orthodox' anti-Shi'i Sufi discourse, before and during the Safawid period. In the chapter 'The Defence of Sufism among Twelver Shi'i Scholars of Early Modern and Modern Times: Topics and Arguments', Mathieu Terrier sheds light on an authentic 'tradition of rapprochement between Shi'ism and Sufism', illustrated by four important works of the 9th–11th/15th–17th centuries: *Jāmi' al-asrār* of Ḥaydar Āmulī, *Mujlī mir'āt al-munjī* of Ibn Abī Jumhūr, *Majālis al-mu'minīn* of Nūr Allāh Shūshtarī (d. 1019/1611) and *Maḥbūb al-qulūb* of Quṭb al-Dīn Ashkiwarī (d. *ca* 1090/1679). A threefold argumentation is analysed. Firstly, a pseudo or mytho-historic argumentation, asserting the existential links between the masters and founders of Sufism and the Shi'i Imams; secondly, a conceptual argumentation based on the triad of the revealed law (*sharī'a*), the spiritual path (*ṭarīqa*) and the essential truth (*ḥaqīqa*), symbolising in turn clerical Shi'ism, doctrinal Sufism and gnostic philosophy; finally, a linguistic and analogical argumentation, which compares two language-games, namely the 'theo-imamosophic sermons' of the Shi'i Imams and the 'theopathic locutions' (*shaṭaḥāt*) of the Sufi masters, in order to demonstrate the harmony between these corresponding states of consciousness. This threefold argumentation embraces the three epistemic authorities of the *naql*, i.e. the scriptural tradition, of the *ʿaql*, i.e. the rational intelligence, and of the *kashf*, the intuitive unveiling, favoured respectively by the scripturalists, the rationalists and the Sufis. The article demonstrates both the permanence of these topics and arguments through the centuries, and an evolution of their respective weight from one author to another, in different social, political and religious contexts.

In 'The Limits of "Orthodoxy"? Notes on the Anti-Abū Muslim Polemic of Early 11th/17th-Century Iran', Andrew Newman examines three treatises, all composed in Persian in the early 11th/17th century in Isfahan, the capital of the Safawid kingdom, criticising the popular veneration of Abū Muslim (d. 137/755), the Iranian agent of the Abbasid movement in Khurasan, and taking the defence of Mīr Lawḥī who had been attacked for his own criticism of the veneration of Abū Muslim. These treatises are *Ṣaḥīfat al-rashād*, completed by Muḥammad Jaʿfar Riḍawī (d. 1041/1631), *Iẓhār al-ḥaqq wa miʿyār al-ṣidq*, written by Sayyid Aḥmad al-ʿAlawī (d. between 1054/1644 and 1060/1650) in 1043/1633 and *Khulāṣat al-fawāʾid* of ʿAbd al-Muṭṭalib Ṭāliqānī, composed in the years immediately before 1063/1652. Whilst the earliest works of this anti-Abū Muslim polemic, in the 10th/16th century, were penned in Arabic and addressed to the Twelver clerical class, the use of Persian in these latter essays dating from the early 11th/17th century attests to a concern with the urban-based Tajik (native Persian) elements of society. Yet this anti-Abū Muslim polemic was closely linked to the anti-Sufi polemics of the middle and later years of the century. It thus appears that Sufism and messianism were not only interconnected, but also strong enough, in the second half of the Safawid era, to give rise to such a literature. However, the fact that only these three essays attacking Abū Muslim's popularity have survived, suggests that 'the minority status of the views of such scholars (. . .) on Abū Muslim, if not also – at least implicitly – on a range of other issues', meant that the so-called 'orthodoxy' of Isfahan's scholarship failed to penetrate the whole of Iranian society.

The second part of the volume focuses on the social and intellectual history of the most popular and documented of the three Shiʿi Sufi orders in Iran, that of the Niʿmat Allāhiyya. Four moments in its history, four aspects of its identity, are described and examined in four articles differentiated by distinctive scientific approaches. In 'Between the Spiritual and Material: The Niʿmat Allāhī Order's Institutionalisation and Architectural Patronage in the 9th/15th Century', Peyvand Firouzeh shows how architectural history is relevant to the debate over the Shiʿi or Sunni origins of the order. Her article deals with the development of the order during a period around the first half of the 9th/15th century. She studies the process of construction, enlargement and enrichment of the shrine of Shāh Niʿmat Allāh Walī (d. 834/1431) in Mahan, and of that of the Shāh Walī *khānaqāh* (lodge) in Taft (province of Yazd), as well as the relationship between the two monuments and the activities taking place in them, under the patronage of several such dynasties as the Bahmanids (r. 748–933/1347–1527), whose religious policies were relatively fluctuating. The development of these shrines and their activities and ceremonies was attendant upon the process of institutionalisation which would ensure the survival of the order and its integration in the new social and political system during the following centuries.

Fabrizio Speziale, in 'The *mujaddid* and the *majdhūb*: Shāh ʿAlī Riḍā (d. 1215/1801) and the Different Narratives of the Niʿmat Allāhī Renewal', re-examines the episode, often referred to but little known, of the restoration of the Niʿmat Allāhī order in Iran during the 18th century, after a period of exile and renewal in the Indian Deccan consequent to its persecution under the Safawid regime in Iran. The author pays particular attention to Indian sources rarely exploited until now, giving a portrait of Shāh ʿAlī Riḍā, considered to be the architect of this restoration, quite different from that commonly painted by Iranian sources, with a more contrasted view on the history of the brotherhood, its adoption of Shiʿism and its re-establishment in Iran. These Indian sources also give much more information on Shāh ʿAlī Riḍā's life in the Deccan, where he was both an ecstatic Sufi (*majdhūb*) devoted to his *dargāh*, and an intimate of the Sunni ruler of Hyderabad, Niẓām ʿAlī Khān (r. 1762–1803), who commonly associated the Shiʿa with his government. Whilst Iranian Niʿmat Allāhī sources lay stress on Shāh ʿAlī Riḍā's role as renovator (*mujaddid*) of the order, having sent two of his disciples, Shāh Ṭāhir and Maʿṣūm ʿAlī Shāh (d. *ca* 1211/1797), to Iran for this purpose, Indian sources mention neither the plan for a restoration of the order in Iran, nor the names of these two disciples, something that puts in question the 'official historiography' as recorded in the archives of the order.

Another moment in the Niʿmat Allāhiyya's process of institutionalisation is studied by Denis Hermann and Omid Rezai, in 'The Institutionalisation of Niʿmat Allāhī Sufism during the Pahlavi Era: A Study of the Establishment of the Ḥusayniyya of Amīr Sulaymānī as a *waqf* in Tehran'. The authors examine the social structures of the Niʿmat Allāhī Sulṭān ʿAlī Shāhī order and its mid 20th-century integration within the modern social framework, by means of the establishment of a large *ḥusayniyya* in the centre of Tehran as a *waqf*. The Ḥusayniyya Amīr Sulaymānī may be described as a religious complex having several religious and social functions. The polyvalence of this settlement reflects the different needs of the order in the modern period: to organise the Niʿmat Allāhī community expanding in the capital of Iran, and to protect its autonomy and its activities as far as possible. The study of the legal document, the *waqf-nāmah*, establishing this place as a *waqf*, also reveals some aspects of the cult within the Niʿmat Allāhī Sulṭān ʿAlī Shāhī Sufis, such as the status of martyr (*shahīd*) attributed to certain masters (*quṭb*) of the order, and the centrality of the commemoration of their death. Furthermore, the authors' fieldwork has revealed the existence within the site of numerous cultural and social activities, such as the development of a public library, and the provision of legal support and employment assistance.

Finally, 'Text and Contest: Theories of Secrecy, *taqiyya* and Archiving Practices in 20th- and 21st-Century Niʿmat Allāhī Sufism', by Seema Golestaneh, deals with the current situation of the Nurbakhsh order, a subset of the Niʿmat Allāhī order in Iran, named after the *quṭb*, Javad Nurbakhsh (d. 2008), a Sufi who left Iran around the time of the 1979 revolution. Employing an anthropological approach based on fieldwork conducted in various major cities throughout Iran, the author explores the paradoxical situation of a Sufi order, which in some respects maintains its adherence to a policy of secrecy whilst in others being relatively transparent. After an examination of the culture of dissimulation within both Sufism and Twelver Shiʿism, she shows how the Niʿmat Allāhī order currently combines the divulgation of the 'public archives' on its website and the cultivation of secret 'private archives' by initiated or even uninitiated members. Surprisingly, many of the 'Sufi' or 'mystical' texts treated as secret in these collections, mostly composed by Nurbakhsh himself, are still widely circulated. This fact suggests that the real purpose of these 'private archives' is to 'guarantee the continued existence of a certain practice or epistemology or system of power', which is proper to Sufism and to esoteric Shiʿism as well, in what one may call 'the age of exotericism'.

The third part of the volume examines the relationship between Shiʿism and Sufism within literary traditions different from those of the Shiʿi scholars or *ʿulamāʾ* studied in the first part of the volume, such as from those of the Niʿmat Allāhī order examined in its second part. For being even more marginal than those studied before, these literary traditions are not less interesting. Among the reasons for this marginality, we may mention their being situated in an area of the Shiʿi world far from Iranian and Iraqi centres, their subjection to a Sunni power, or their flourishing within the working classes of society, reasons which may in some cases be combined. For these very reasons, studies of these traditions shed new light on the relationship between Shiʿism and Sufism in the early modern and modern periods.

The first of these literary forms, examined by Michel Boivin in 'Sufism and Shiʿism in South Asia: *Shahādat* and the Evidence of the Sindhi *marthiya*', is the Sindhi form of the *marthiya*, an elegy specially composed for the martyrdom of the third Shiʿi Imam Ḥusayn and sung during the month of Muḥarram. This tradition appeared in Sindh, where Sufism and Shiʿi 'extremist' currents (*ghulāt*) interacted for many years in the 18th century, with the translation of *Rawḍat al-shuhadāʾ*, the Persian martyrology composed by Wāʿiẓ Kāshifī (d. 910/1505). But the first Sindhi author of *marthiya*s is Shāh ʿAbd al-Laṭīf (d. 1165/1752), in his *Shāh jo risālo*, especially in a section devoted to the martyrdom of Imam Ḥusayn, entitled *Sur Keḏāro*. Unlike the *marthiya*s composed in Persian or Urdu, which pertained to a court culture, those penned in Sindhi emerged from a popular and rural milieu and clearly express Sufi-Shiʿi relations. Giving access to a little-known source, Boivin throws new light on the process of integration of Shiʿi topics and tenets in Sufi poetry, whose literary forms are different from those much studied elsewhere within the context of Iranian Sufism and Persian poetry.

Also explored in this section is the Alevi-Bektashi tradition in Turkey, a tradition embacing two separate orders commonly described as 'heterodox', whose creed is clearly pervaded by Twelver Shiʿism. Rıza

Yıldırım introduces it in 'Red Sulphur, Great Remedy, and the Supreme Name: Faith in the Twelve Imams and Shi'i Aspects of Alevi-Bektashi Piety', by paying special attention to sermon literature. He analyses an untapped work in Ottoman Turkish preserved in manuscript copies, The Book of the Sermon of Twelve Imams (*Kitāb-i khuṭba-yi dawāzdah imām*), translated, with substantial additions, from the Arabic by a Ḥurūfī in the 9th/15th century. The original is a eulogy composed by Naṣīr al-Dīn Ṭūsī (d. 672/1274). The text reveres the holy family of the Prophet, the *ahl al-bayt*, in terms and patterns closer to those of the original Imami esotericism, as conserved within the *ghulāt* currents, than to those of rationalised and institutionalised Shi'ism. The analysis suggests that it was probably written in the same milieu where Qizilbash Shi'ism emerged in Anatolia, a fact which brings more evidence of the penetration of Ottoman Sufism by unorthodox Shi'ism in the 9th/15th century, a process which also generated the 'Safawid synthesis'.

The third tradition is that of the Khāksāriyya order. After the above-mentioned pioneering work of Richard Gramlich, recent expansion of our knowledge of this Sufi-Shi'i order is largely due to the efforts of Mihrān Afshārī, the editor of many Khāksār treatises and *futuwwat-nāmah*s (guild treatises) dating from the Qajar period. These texts, he suggests, provide evidence that the Iranian Khāksār dervishes have directly inherited their initiation practices from the ancient *futuwwat* or *jawānmardīhā*, which were at the same time corporations of workers and spiritual brotherhoods, and whose links with 'Alidism were primarily emphasised by Henry Corbin, and from the *qalandarī* tradition, generally considered antinomian and heterodox, among Muslim theologians and heresiographers as well as Western writers and orientalists.

The purpose of the study of Alexandre Papas, 'The Khāksār Shi'i Sufi order: An Updated Introduction', is to review the written production of this order and to summarise the results of recent scholarship in the field. After a survey of the corpus of manuscripts discovered and studied by Mihrān Afshārī, the author proposes a historical sketch of the Sufi-Shi'i order, despite the paucity of reliable information, giving an account of its emergence during the Qajar period from the fusion of two existing *qalandar* groups, namely the Ḥaydariyya and the Jalāliyya, and its subsequent fragmentation into several further groups, among which the Ghulām 'Alī Shāhī sub-branch remains the better identified. Furthermore, Papas describes the stages of the Khāksār initiatory path with its own specific terminology and material culture, such as the internal organisation of the order and the way of life of its dervishes within society at large.

Lloyd Ridgeon, in "Ajam Sufis and Shiʿi Spirituality in 13th/19th-Century Iran', offers a study of both the literary production and the social practices of the ʿAjam sub-order of the Khāksāriyya, particularly active in the principal cities of Iran during the Qajar period. Unlike the Khāksār dervishes, the ʿAjam appeared as a confederation of guild workers and shopkeepers in the Iranian bazaar, claiming their adherence to a strict Twelver Shiʿi orthodoxy. The author illuminates these trends by examining the content of a 19th-century ʿAjam treatise edited by Mihrān Afshārī, the *Wasīlat al-najāt* ('the Tool [or Means] of Salvation'). In the process of this analysis, Ridgeon also describes the institution of the *sukhanwarī*, a poetical competition and public declamation taking place commonly in traditional coffee houses. The strong participation of the ʿAjam in this popular urban event suggests the capacity of a certain Shiʿi Sufism to be widely present in different social strata.

Finally, two Khāksār treatises, edited by M. Afshārī, translated into English for the first time, introduce us to the history, practices and doctrines of the Khāksār order. The first, the *Chahārdah khānawāda* (Fourteen Families), which has been copied many times, translated by Yaser Mirdamadi, is a survey established by the Khāksāriyya to elucidate the origin of the Sufi paths and to define their classification. It is a precious testimony of both the 'mytho-history' and the cultural memory of the Khāksār order. The second epistle, simply entitled *Faqriyya* (Poverty), translated by Mehrdad Arabestani, discusses in the form of question and answer the physical and spiritual entry into the path of Sufi poverty. It is a unique document concerning the spiritual discipline, the ethical values and the material culture of the Khāksār dervishes.

In conclusion, a renewal of both Shiʿi and Sufi studies by rethinking the relations between the two, in terms of doctrine, text, social and political processes, considering their long-time evolution and the interconnected spaces of their manifestations and traditions seems necessary. This can only be done across many different approaches such as philosophy, the religious sciences, anthropology, social and art history, and by promoting the study of oral and literary traditions, even those considered marginal, all of which requires extensive interdisciplinary work. This book is intended as a first step in this direction.

NOTES

1 This is the case in the classical studies of Martin Lings, *What is Sufism?* (London, 1975); and of Arthur J. Arberry, *Sufism. An Account of the Mystics of Islam* (London, 1979). More recently, Alexander Knysch, in *Islamic Mysticism: A Short History* (Leiden, London and New York, 2000), says nothing about the ancient relationship between Shiʿism and Sufism and mentions it only in a chapter entitled 'Sufism in a Shīʿī Context: The Niʿmatullāhiyya', pp. 239–244.

2 On the congruence between the Islamic and the Western academic orthodoxies, see Mathieu Terrier, 'Violences politiques, écritures canoniques et evolutions doctrinales en islam: des approaches traditionnelles à la nouvelle approche critique de Mohammad Ali Amir-Moezzi', *JSAI*, 40 (2013), pp. 402–427.

3 See Mohammad Ali Amir-Moezzi, 'Introduction', in Mohammad Ali Amir-Moezzi et al., ed., *L'Ésotérisme shiʿite, ses racines et ses prolongements/Shiʿi Esotericism, Its Roots and Developments* (Turnhout, 2016), pp. 1–11.

4 Henry Corbin, *En islam iranien* (4 vols., Paris, 1971–1972), index s.v. 'walâyat' and 'walî', esp. vol. 1, p. 48, n.20; vol. 3, p. 10; Ahmet T. Karamustafa, *Sufism: The Formative Period* (Berkeley, CA, 2007), pp. 6–10, 17–18 and index, s.v., 'walāya' and 'walī'; Michael Ebstein, *Mysticism and Philosophy in al-Andalus* (Leiden, 2014), chapter 3, pp. 123–156.

5 Richard Gramlich, 'Pol und Scheich im heutigen Derwischtum der Schia', in Toufic Fahd, ed., *Le Shîʿisme imâmite* (Paris, 1970), pp. 175–182; Oliver Scharbrodt, 'The *quṭb* as Special Representative of the Hidden Imam: The Conflation of Shiʿi and Sufi Vilāyat in the Niʿmatullāhi Order', in Denis Hermann and Sabrina Mervin, ed., *Shiʿi Trends and Dynamics in Modern Times (XVIIIth-XXth centuries) – Courants et dynamiques chiites à l'époque moderne (XVIIIe-XXe siècles)* (Beirut, 2010), pp. 33–49.

6 Ignaz Goldziher, *Le dogme et la loi dans l'Islam*, Fr. tr. F. Arin (Paris, 2000), pp. 111–155.

7 Louis Massignon, *La Passion de Ḥusayn ibn Manṣûr Ḥallâj* (4 vols., Paris, 1975), vol. 2, p. 23.

8 John Spencer Trimingham, *The Sufi Orders in Islam* (Oxford and New York, 1971, 2nd ed. 1998).

9 Trimingham, *The Sufi Orders in Islam*, p. 11.

10 Ibid., p. 14.

11 On Ḥurūfism, see Hellmut Ritter, 'Die Anfange der Hurufisekte', *Oriens*, 7 (1954), pp. 1–54; Kāmil Muṣṭafā al-Shaybī, *al-Ṣila bayna'l-taṣawwuf wa'l-tashayyuʿ* (Beirut and Baghdad, 2011), pp. 155–214; Orkhan Mir-Kasimov, *Words of Power: Ḥurūfī Teachings between Shiʿism and Sufism in Medieval Islam, The Original Doctrine of Faḍl Allāh Astarābādī* (London and New York, 2015). On the links between Ḥurūfism and Shiʿism in the thought of a gnostic scholar such as Rajab Bursī (d. 814/1411), see Todd Lawson, 'The Dawning Places of the Lights of Certainty in the Divine Secrets Connected with the Commander of the Faithful', in Leonard Lewisohn, ed., *The Legacy of Mediaeval Persian Sufism* (London and New York, 1992), pp. 261–276.

12 Henry Corbin, *L'imagination créatrice dans le soufisme d'Ibn 'Arabî* (Paris, 1958); 'Sayyid Haydar Amoli, théologien shîʿite du soufisme', in *Mélange d'orientalisme offert à Henri Massé* (Tehran, 1963), pp. 72–101; Sayyid Ḥaydar Āmulī, *La philosophie shîʿite*. 1.

Somme des doctrines ésotériques (Jāmiʿ al-asrār wa manbaʿ al-anwār) 2. Traité de la connaissance de l'être (Naqd al-nuqūd fī maʿrifat al-wujūd), ed. H. Corbin and O. Yahia (Tehran, 1347 Sh./1968–9); Henry Corbin, *En Islam iranien*, vol. 3; 'Introduction analytique' to Morteza Sarraf ed., *Rasâ'il-e Javânmardân. Traités des compagnons-chevaliers* (Tehran and Paris, 1973), pp. 5–109, which analyses the doctrines and rituals of guilds (*futuwwāt, jawānmardīhā*) as a synthesis between Sufism and Shiʿism.

13 Paul Ballanfat, 'Henry Corbin et le soufisme iranien', in Mohammad Ali Amir-Moezzi, Christian Jambet and Pierre Lory, ed., *Henry Corbin. Philosophies et sagesses des religions du Livre* (Turnhout, 2005), pp. 119–134, see p. 122.

14 Among the former, Seyyed Hossein Nasr, 'Le shîʿisme et le soufisme. Leurs relations principielles et historiques', in Toufic Fahd, ed., *Le shîʿisme imâmite*, pp. 215–233; Stéphane Ruspoli, 'Ibn ʿArabî et la prophétologie shîʿite', in Christian Jambet, ed., *Henry Corbin* (Paris, 1981), pp. 224–239. Recently, Michael Ebstein, 'Spiritual Descendants of the Prophet: al-Ḥakīm al-Tirmidhī, Ibn al-ʿArabī and Ikhwān al-Ṣafāʾ on Ahl al-bayt', in Amir-Moezzi, et al., ed., *L'ésotérisme shiʿite*, pp. 539–571. Among the latter, Michel Chodkiewicz, *Le sceau des saints. Prophétie et sainteté dans la doctrine d'Ibn ʿArabî* (Paris, 1986, repr. 2012), most of which is a response to the work of Corbin; 'Ibn ʿArabī dans l'œuvre de Henry Corbin', in M.A. Amir-Moezzi, Ch. Jambet and P. Lory, ed., *Henry Corbin. Philosophies et sagesses des religions du Livre*, pp. 81–91; Claude Addas, *Ibn ʿArabî et la quête du soufre rouge* (Paris, 1989), p. 281; Roger Deladrière, introduction and notes to Ibn ʿArabî, *La profession de foi*, Fr. tr. R. Deladrière (Paris, 1985).

15 William C. Chittick, *Sufism: A Short Introduction* (Oxford, 2000), p. 19.

16 Ballanfat, 'Henry Corbin et le soufisme iranien', p. 120.

17 Alexandre Popovic and Gilles Veinstein, ed., *Les voies d'Allah. Les ordres mystiques dans le monde musulman des origines à aujourd hui* (Paris, 1996): Thierry Zarcone, 'L'Iran', pp. 309–321; Nathalie Clayer, 'Bektashiyya', pp. 468–474, stresses the fact that the latter venerate the same imams as the Twelver Shiʿis, but prefers to qualify them as syncretic and heterodox.

18 Éric Geoffroy, *Le soufisme. Voie intérieure de l'Islam* (Paris, 2003), pp. 41–47.

19 Goldziher, *Le dogme et la loi dans l'Islam*, p. 131.

20 Knysch, *Islamic Mysticism*, p. 265. On this, see also G. L. Lewis, 'Bayramiyya', *EI2*.

21 Hamid Algar, 'Naqshbandīs and Safavids: A Contribution to the Religious History of Iran and Her Neighbors', in Michel Mazzaoui, ed., *Safavid Iran and Her Neighbors* (Salt Lake City, UT, 2003), pp. 7–48. For a case study of the anti-Shiʿi activism of the Naqshbandiyya, see Sajida Alvi, 'Sunni Ulama's Discourses on Shiʿism in Northern India during the Eighteenth and Nineteenth Centuries: An Overview', in Denis Hermann and Sabrina Mervin, ed., *Shiʿi Trends and Dynamics in Modern Times* (Beirut, 2010), pp. 131–153.

22 Alessandro Bausani, 'Religion under the Mongols', in J.A. Boyle, ed., *The Cambridge History of Iran*, vol. 5., *The Saljuq and Mongol Periods* (Cambridge, 1968), pp. 538–549; Jean Calmard, 'Le chiisme imamite sous les Ilkhans', in Denise Aigle, ed., *L'Iran face à la domination mongole* (Tehran, 1997), pp. 261–292.

23 Marijan Molé, 'Les Kubrawiya entre sunnisme et shiisme aux huitième et neuvième siècles de l'hégire', *Revue des Études Islamiques*, 29 (1961), pp. 61–142. See also Devin DeWeese, 'The Eclipse of the Kubravīyah in Central Asia', *Iranian Studies*, 21, 1–2 (1988), pp. 45–83.

24 See John Masson Smith, *The History of the Sarbadār Dynasty 1336–1381 A. D. and its Sources* (The Hague and Paris, 1970); Hans R. Roemer; 'The Jalayrids, Muzaffirids and Sarbadārs', in Peter Jackson and Laurence Lockhart, ed., *The Cambridge History of Iran*, vol. 6, *The Timurid and Safavid Periods* (Cambridge, 1986), pp. 1–41; Jean Aubin, 'Aux origines d'un mouvement populaire médiéval: le cheykhisme du Bayhaq et du Nichapour', *Studia Iranica*, 5 (1976), pp. 213–224; 'La fin de l'État Sarbadār du Khorassan', *J. Asiat.*, 262 (1974), pp. 95–118.

25 See Jean Calmard, 'Une famille de Sadat dans l'histoire de l'Iran: Les Marʿaši', *Oriente Moderno*, 79 (1999), pp. 413–428; 'Marʿashis', *EI2*, vol. 6, pp. 496–502.

26 Paul Luft, 'Mushaʿshaʿ', *EI2*, vol. 7, pp. 672–675; al-Shaybī, *al-Ṣila bayn al-taṣawwuf wa'l-tashayyuʿ*, vol. 2, pp. 268–291. On the Mushaʿshaʿyān, the Sarbadār and the Marʿashī, see also Denis Hermann, 'Aspectos de la penetración del shiismo en Irán durante los periodos ilkhâní y timurí. El éxito político de los movimientos Sarbedâr, Marashi y Mushaʿshaʿyân', *Estudios de Asia y África*, 29 (2004), pp. 673–709.

27 On this, see Michel M. Mazzaoui, *The Origins of the Safawids (Shiʿism, Sufism and the Ghulât)* (Wiesbaden, 1972).

28 See the pioneer article of Claude Cahen, 'Le problème du shīʿisme dans l'Asie mineure turque préottomane', in T. Fahd, ed., *Le shîʿisme imâmite*, pp. 115–129.

29 See D. Aigle, 'Le soufisme sunnite en Fārs: Šayḫ Amīn al-Dīn Balyānī', in her *L'Iran face à la domination mongole*, pp. 233–261.

30 Bausani, 'Religion under the Mongols', p. 546, talks about an imperceptible transition from Sunnism to Shiʿism. Calmard prefers to say that 'A (Sunni) Sufism tinged with "good Shiʿism", that is to say moderate (*tashayyuʿ-e ḥasan*), remaining the essential characteristic of this period' ('Le chiisme imamite sous les Ilkhans', p. 285).

31 Said Amir Arjomand, *The Shadow of God and the Hidden Imam* (Chicago, 1984); Mohammad Ali Amir-Moezzi and Christian Jambet, *Qu'est-ce que le shîʿisme?* (Paris, 2004). For a critical survey of Imami studies before and after 1979, see Andrew Newman, *Twelver Shiʿism. Unity and Diversity in the Life of Islam, 632 to 1722* (Edinburgh, 2013), pp. 1–15.

32 On this, see among others Jean Calmard, 'Les rituels shiites et le pouvoir. L'imposition du shiisme safavide: eulogies et malédictions canoniques', in J. Calmard, ed., *Études safavides* (Paris and Tehran, 1993), pp. 109–150; Andrew Newman, 'Fayd al-Kashani and the Rejection of the Clergy/State Alliance: Friday Prayer as Politics in the Safavid Period', in Linda Walbridge, ed., *The Most Learned of the Shiʿa* (Oxford, 2000), pp. 34–52; Kathryn Babayan, *Mystics, Monarchs, and Messiahs. Cultural Landscapes of Early Modern Iran* (London, 2002); Rula Jurdi Abisaab, *Converting Persia. Religion and Power in Safavid Empire* (London and New York, 2004).

33 For a survey, see Seyyed Hossein Nasr, 'Spiritual Movements, Philosophy and Theology in the Safavid Period', in P. Jackson and L. Lockhart, ed., *Cambridge History of Iran*, vol. 6, pp. 656–697. On the latter, see Fazlur Rahman, *The Philosophy of Mullā Ṣadrā* (Albany, NY, 1975); Corbin, *En islam iranien*, vol. 4, pp. 54–122; Christian Jambet, *L'acte d'être* (Paris, 2002); *Mort et résurrection en islam* (Paris, 2008); *Le gouvernement divin* (Paris, 2016); *La fin de toute chose* (Paris, 2017); Sajjad H. Rizvi, *Mullā Ṣadrā Shīrāzī. His Life and Works and the Sources for Safavid Philosophy* (Oxford, 2007). On the former, see Toshihiko Izutsu, 'Mīr Dāmād and his Metaphysics', in Mīr Dāmād, *Kitāb al-qabasāt*, ed. M. Muḥaqqiq and T. Izutsu (Tehran, 1395 Sh./2016), pp. 1–15; Corbin, *En islam iranien*, vol. 4, pp. 9–53; Hamid Dabashi, 'Mīr Dāmād and the Founding of the School of Isfahan', in Seyyed Hossein Nasr and Oliver Leaman, ed., *History of Islamic Philosophy* (London, 1996), pp. 597–634; M. Terrier, 'De l'éternité ou de la nouveauté du monde. Parcours d'un problème philosophique d'Athènes à Ispahan', *J. Asiat.*, 299 (2011), pp. 395–420; 'Aspects d'une lecture philosophique du Coran dans l'œuvre de Mīr Dāmād', *Mélanges de l'Université Saint-Joseph*, 64 (2012), pp.101–126; 'Mīr Dāmād (m. 1041/1631), philosophe et *mujtahid*. Autorité spirituelle et autorité juridique en Iran safavide shīʿite', *Stud. Islam.*, 113 (2018), pp. 121–165.

34 Mazzaoui, *The Origins of the Safawids*.

35 K. Babayan, 'Sufis, Derviches and Mullas: The Controversy over Spiritual and Temporal Domination in Seventeenth-Century Iran', in Charles Melville, ed., *Safavid Persia, The History and Politics of an Islamic Society* (London and New York, 1996), pp. 117–138; 'The Safavid Synthesis: From Qizilbash Islam to Imamite Shīʿism', *Iranian Studies*, 27

(1994), pp. 135–161; *Mystics, Monarchs, and Messiahs. Cultural Landscapes of Early Modern Iran* (London, 2002). For a problematisation of this presentation, see Shahzad Bashir, 'The Origins and Rhetorical Evolution of the Term Qizilbāsh in Persianate Literature', *Journal of the Economic and Social History of the Orient*, 57 (2014), pp. 364–391. On Shāh Ismāʿīl's messianic convictions, see Vladimir Minorsky, 'The Poetry of Shāh Ismāʿīl', *BSOAS*, 10, 4 (1942), pp. 1006–1053. Also Irène Melikoff, 'Kizilbas', *Turcica*, 6 (1975), p. 58; Erica Glassen, 'Schah Ismāʿīl und die Theologen seiner Zeit', *Der Islam*, 48 (1971–1972), pp. 254–268; 'Schah Ismāʿīl, ein Mahdi der Anatolischen Turkmenen?', *ZDMG*, 121 (1971), pp. 61–69.

36 See Rasul Jaʿfariyān, 'The Immigrant Manuscripts: A Study of the Migration of Shīʿī Works from Arab Regions to Iran in the Early Safavid Era', in Andrew Newman, ed., *Society and Culture in the Early Modern Middle East: Studies on Iran in the Safavid Period* (Leiden, 2003), pp. 351–370.

37 Devin Stewart, 'Notes on the Migration of ʿAmili Scholars to Safavid Iran', *JNES*, 55 (1996), pp. 81–103.

38 On the evolution of this clerical administration, see S.A. Arjomand, 'The Mujtahid of the Age and the Mullā-Bāshī: An Intermediate Stage in the Institutionalization of Religion in Shiʿite Iran', in S.A. Arjomand, ed., *Authority and Political Culture in Shiʿism* (New York, 1988), pp. 80–97; 'Two Decrees of Shāh Tahmasp concerning Statecraft and the Authority of Shaykh ʿAlī al-Karaki', in *Authority and Political Culture in Shiʿism*, pp. 250–262; 'The Office of Mullā-Bāshī in Shīʿism', *Stud. Islam.*, 57 (1983), pp. 135–146; Devin Stewart, 'The First Shaykh al-Islam of the Safavid Capital Qazvin', *JAOS*, 3 (1996), pp. 387–405.

39 On the fluctuations of this policy, see Andrew Newman, *Safavid Iran: Rebirth of a Persian Empire* (London and New York, 2006).

40 Among the anti-Sufi works of this period, it is worth mentioning Muqaddas Ardabīlī (attributed to), *Ḥadīqat al-Shīʿa*, ed. Ṣ. Ḥasanzādah (Qumm, 1420/1378 Sh./1999–2000); al-Ḥurr al-ʿĀmilī, *al-Risāla al-ithnāʿashariyya fi'l-radd ʿalā'l-ṣūfiyya*, ed. A. al-Jalālī (Qumm, 1432/1390 Sh./2011–2). For analysis of this literature, see Andrew Newman, 'Sufism and anti-Sufism in Safavid Iran', *Iran*, 37 (1999), pp. 95–108; Nasrollah Pourjavady, 'Opposition to Sufism in Twelver Shiism', in Frederick de Jong and Bernd Radtke, ed., *Islamic Mysticism Contested. Thirteen Centuries of controversies and Polemics* (Leiden, 1999), pp. 614–623. Robert Gleave has called into question the general anti-Sufi position of the 'scripturalist' or *akhbārī* thinkers in his 'Scriptural Sufism and Scriptural Anti-Sufism: Theology and Mysticism among the Shīʿī Akhbāriyya', in Ayman Shihadeh, ed., *Sufism and Theology* (Edinburgh, 2007), pp. 158–176.

41 See Denis Hermann, *Le shaykhisme à la période qajare. Histoire sociale et doctrinale d'une École chiite* (Turnhout, 2017).

42 See Arjomand, *The Shadow of God*, pp. 112–119; Babayan, *Mystics, Monarchs, and Messiahs*, pp. 403–437; L. Lewisohn, 'Sufism and the school of Iṣfahān: *Taṣawwuf* and *ʿIrfān* in Late Safavid Iran (ʿAbd al-Razzāq Lāhījī and Fayḍ Kāshānī on the Relation of *Taṣawwuf, Ḥikmat* and *ʿIrfān*)', in Leonard Lewisohn and David Morgan, ed., *The Heritage of Sufism* (Oxford, 1999), vol. 3, pp. 63–134; 'The *Qawā'im al-Anwār* of Rāzi Šīrāzī and Shiʿi Sufism in Qajar Persia', in Denis Hermann and Fabrizio Speziale, ed., *Muslim Cultures in the Indo-Iranian World during the Early-Modern and Modern Periods* (Berlin, 2010), pp. 247–271.

43 On this alternative tradition, Mathieu Terrier, 'Apologie du soufisme par un philosophe shīʿite. Nouvelles remarques sur le *Maḥbūb al-qulūb* d'Ashkevarī', *Stud. Islam.*, 109 (2014), pp. 240–273, and in his chapter in the present volume.

44 On this, see Shahram Pazoukī, 'Fiqh et soufisme à la période qajare: quelques notes sur l'œuvre juridique des maîtres niʿmatullāhī gunabādī', in D. Hermann and S. Mervin, ed., *Shiʿi Trends and Dynamics in Modern Times*, pp. 113–127; Denis Hermann, *Kirmānī Shaykhism and the* ijtihād. *A study of Abū'l-Qāsim Khān Ibrāhīmī's* Ijtihād wa taqlīd (Würzburg, 2015).

45 Newman, *Twelver Shi'ism*, and his article in the present volume.
46 al-Shaybī, *al-Ṣila bayn al-taṣawwuf wa'l-tashayyuʿ*, was first edited in Baghdad in 1963–1964. The second volume was edited separately under the title *al-Fikr al-shīʿī wa'l-nazaʿāt al-ṣūfiyya ḥattā maṭlaʿ al-qarn al-thānī ʿashara al-hijrī* (Baghdad, 1966) and translated into English as *Shiʿism and Sufism* (Surbiton, 1991). This work is referenced in Seyyed Hossein Nasr's pioneering article referred to in the next footnote.
47 Nasr, *Shiʿism and Sufism*, pp. 230–231.
48 Ibid., p. 242.
49 See the two articles mentioned in n. 42 above.
50 On this, see the articles of Alexandre Papas and Lloyd Ridgeon (esp. the introductions) in this volume.
51 Mihrān Afshārī, ed., *Futuwwat-nāmah-hā wa rasā'il-i khāksāriyya* (Tehran, 1382 Sh./2003–4).
52 In Persian: Asad Allāh Khāwarī, *Dhahabiyya. Taṣawwuf-i ʿilmī, āthār-i adabī* (Tehran, 1395 Sh./2016–17); ʿAbd al-Ḥusayn Zarrīnkūb, *Dunbālah-yi justujū dar taṣawwuf-i Īrān* (Tehran, 1389 Sh./2010–11), index, s.v., 'dhahabiyah'; see also Nūr al-Dīn Modarresī Cahārdahī, *Sayrī dar taṣawwuf dar sharḥ-i ḥāl-i mashāyikh wa aqṭāb* (Tehran, 1379 Sh./2000–1), pp. 202–215; Maʿṣūm ʿAlī Shāh, *Ṭarā'iq al-ḥaqā'iq* (Tehran, 1382 Sh./2003–4), index, s.v., 'dhahabiyah'. In English: Hamid Algar, 'Dahabiyyah', *EIR*, vol. 6, pp. 578–581; Leonard Lewisohn, 'An Introduction to Modern Persian Sufism, Part II', *BSOAS*, 62 (1999), pp. 36–59; 'The *Qawā'im al-anwār* of Rāzī Šīrāzī and Shiʿi Sufism in Qajar Persia'; Ata Anzali, 'The Emergence of the Zahabiyya in Safavid Iran', *Journal of Sufi Studies*, 2 (2013), 149–175; *'Mysticism' in Iran: The Safavid Roots of a Modern Concept* (Columbia, SC, 2017).
53 Anzali, 'The Emergence of the Zahabiyya'.
54 Zarrīnkūb, *Dunbālah-yi justujū*, p. 265, see also pp. 183–87, 263–66, 332–36, 347–48, 386.
55 Shaykh Muḥammad ʿAlī Mu'adhdhin Sabzawārī Khurāsānī, *Tuḥfa-yi ʿAbbāsī* (Tehran, 1382 Sh./2003). English translation by Mohammad H. Faghfoory, *Tuḥfa-yi ʿAbbāsī, The Golden Chain of Sufism in Shiʿite Islam* (Lanham, MD, 2008).
56 Zarrīnkūb, *Dunbālah-yi justujū*, p. 333.
57 Gramlich, *Die schiitischen Derwishorden Persiens. I. Die Affiliationen*, pp. 4–26; DeWeese, 'The Eclipse of the Kubraviyah in Central Asia', pp. 45–83; A. Anzali, 'The Emergence of the Zahabiyya', p. 150.

PART ONE

ALTERNATIVES TO ANTI-SUFI DISCOURSE IN PRE-MODERN AND MODERN SHIʿI LITERATURE

1

The Defence of Sufism among Twelver Shiʿi Scholars of Early Modern and Modern Times: Topics and Arguments

Mathieu Terrier

Introduction

From the pre-modern era to the present day, the Twelver Shiʿi or Imami world has been concerned with what one might call the 'Sufi question', a question rife with doctrinal, but also socio-political, issues: should Sufism be accepted as an essential dimension of the 'genuine' Twelver Shiʿi religion, or must it be rejected for being a 'condemnable innovation' (*bidʿa*) and/or an excrescence of Sunni Islam? It is currently said that during the reign of the Safawids in Iran (906–1134/ 1501–1722), the lawyers and theologians hostile to Sufism eventually prevailed and ultimately succeeded in wiping out most of the Sufi brotherhoods from their original birthplace.[1] However what is less known is that during the same period, within the Imami *ʿulamāʾ* community itself, an alternative discourse persevered which was apologist and concordist, promoting rapprochement, or even union, between Sufism and Twelver Shiʿism. This discourse made the reinstatement of Sufism in 18th-century Iran theoretically possible, although it was actually established by an outside decision.[2] A series of interrelated works, from the pre-modern period to the modern era, which established this pro-Shiʿi Sufi discourse as an authentic intellectual and literary tradition, has been transmitted to the present day in certain Sufi circles and is still considered authoritative by certain historians and thinkers.[3]

Without claiming to be exhaustive, the present essay will introduce four great works and their authors as the main milestones of this parallel tradition, which I will refer to as the 'tradition of reconciliation', a tradition revitalised century after century, from the Ilkhanate era to the end of the Safawid dynasty. These four works are *Jāmiʿ al-asrār wa manbaʿ al-anwār* (The Sum of Secrets and the Source of Lights) by Sayyid Ḥaydar Āmulī (d. after 786/1385);[4] *Kitāb al-Mujlī mir'at al-munjī fi'l-kalām wa'l-ḥikmatayn wa'l-taṣawwuf* (Polishing the Mirror of the Saviour: About Theology, the Twin Wisdoms and Sufism) by Ibn Abī Jumhūr al-Aḥsā'ī (d. after 906/1500–1);[5] *Majālis al-mu'minīn* (Sessions of the Believers) by Nūr Allāh Shūshtarī (d. 1019/1610);[6] and *Maḥbūb al-qulūb* (The Beloved of the Hearts) by Quṭb al-Dīn Ashkiwarī (d. between 1088/1677 and 1095/1684).[7] Although other works could have been considered from writers such as Ḥāfiẓ Rajab Bursī (d. 813/1411) or Shams al-Dīn Lāhījī (d. 918/1512), to name but two,[8] which state in an implicit manner such a rapprochement, these four works are particularly noteworthy in that they assume explicitly the ecumenist position, are linked by close intertextual relationships, the most recent substantially plagiarising the preceding ones, and thus lend themselves to the analysis of subtle variations within a unique and single discourse. In order to shed light on both the common purpose of these four works and some distinctive features of each of them, I have chosen to set out the main topics and arguments of these texts rather than give a linear and chronological description.

After a brief presentation of the four authors and their works, a threefold argumentation will thus be analysed: first a (mytho-) historical argumentation, showing the links of the original Sufi masters to the Shiʿi imams; then a conceptual argumentation, systematising the relationships between *sharīʿa* (religious law), *ṭarīqa* (spiritual path) and *ḥaqīqa* (essential reality or truth); finally a linguistic and 'phenomenological' argumentation, showing the analogy between specific locutions pronounced respectively by Shiʿi imams and Sufis.

The Tradition of Reconciliation and its Representatives

Ḥaydar b. ʿAlī b. Ḥusayn al-Ḥusaynī al-Āmulī, known as Sayyid Ḥaydar Āmulī, born in 719/1320,[9] and died after 787/1385,[10] can be considered the founder of this tradition of reconciliation between Shiʿism and Sufism.[11] Coming from a large family of *sayyids* from

Āmul, in the province of Tabaristan, he belonged to a subset of the Iranian population already converted to Twelver Shiʿism before the Safawid era, and he served as minister to Prince Fakhr al-Dawla Ḥasan b. Shāh Kay-Khusraw b. Yazdgird, who was assassinated in 750/1349.[12] According to his short autobiography, which recalls al-Ghazālī's *al-Munqidh min al-ḍalāl* in its apologetic tendency,[13] Ḥaydar Āmulī relinquished his mundane career probably one year before this event, and at the age of thirty, donned the Sufi cloak (*khirqa*), took the road to Mecca in the company of a Sufi master called Nūr al-Dīn Ṭihrānī, and from here returned to the Shiʿi sacred places (*ʿaṭābāt*) of Iraq.[14] During this Iranian period he may have composed his theological treatise *Anwār al-ḥaqīqa wa aṭwār al-ṭarīqa wa asrār al-sharīʿa* (The Lights of Truth, the Stations of the Path and the Mysteries of the Revealed Law), devoted to the conceptual triad studied in the third part of this essay.[15] In Iraq, he was the pupil of Fakhr al-Muḥaqqiqīn al-Ḥillī (d. 771/1370), the son of al-ʿAllāma al-Ḥillī (d. 726/1326), from whom he was granted an *ijāza* (a permission from the teacher to teach books studied with him) in 761/1360–61, something which afforded him considerable legitimacy as a Shiʿi scholar. Apparently under the command of Fakhr al-Muḥaqqiqīn, he wrote in 769/1367–8 a polemic and sectarian epistle entitled *Rafʿ al-munāzaʿa wa'l-khilāf* (The Resolution of Quarrel and Dispute) in order to justify, according to Shiʿi tenets, the passive attitude of Imam ʿAlī during the reigns of the three first caliphs.[16] Ḥaydar Āmulī composed most of his works during his Iraqi period, the most important of which are *Jāmiʿ al-asrār wa manbaʿ al-anwār*, which Henry Corbin dates around 752/1351; his commentary of the Qur'an, or more exactly, his treatise about Qur'anic *tafsīr* and *ta'wīl* (respectively 'exoteric' and 'esoteric' interpretation of the Qur'an), *al-Muḥīṭ al-aʿẓam wa'l-baḥr al-khiḍamm fī ta'wīl kitāb Allāh al-ʿazīz al-muḥkam* (The Vast Ocean and Fathomless Sea: An Esoteric Commentary on the Holy and Firm Book of God), completed in 777/1375–6; and *Naṣṣ al-nuṣūṣ fī sharḥ al-fuṣūṣ* (The Text of Texts: a Commentary on the *Bezels [of Wisdom]*), a commentary on Ibn ʿArabī's *Fuṣūṣ al-ḥikam* (the Bezels of Wisdom) written in 782/1380. Both latter books go together as Ḥaydar Āmulī was considering the Qur'an as revealed to the Prophet Muḥammad (*al-nāzil ʿalayhi*) and the *Fuṣūṣ al-ḥikam* as proceeding from him (*al-ṣādir minhu*).[17] Despite the fact that Ibn ʿArabī was probably not Shiʿi, an issue that remains problematic, Ḥaydar Āmulī strived to incorporate his theosophy into mainstream Twelver Shiʿism, something which can be regarded with Henry Corbin as Āmulī's foremost contribution to Islamic culture.[18] Corbin edited his *Jāmiʿ al-asrār wa manbaʿ al-anwār*, with his *Risālat Naqd al-nuqūd fī maʿrifat al-wujūd* (Criticism of the Criticisms, on the Knowledge of the Being), under the title 'Shiʿi Philosophy.' This title remains somewhat enigmatic because of the minor part of 'philosophy' in the common meaning that it contains, but takes a full meaning in later developments of this line of thought.[19] Actually, the *Jāmiʿ al-asrār* does not deal with philosophy, but with both Twelver Shiʿism and Sufism that the author intends to reconcile.

At the time of Ḥaydar Āmulī, under Ilkhanid rule (656–756/1258–1355) and the post-Ilkhanid/pre-Timurid semi-anarchic interregnum (756–807/1355–1400), Iran was predominantly Sunni. Nevertheless, Shiʿi ideas also permeated throughout the empire, emanating from the residing Sufi brotherhoods which remained at least nominally Sunni. The *Jāmiʿ al-asrār* was thus written during an age when Shiʿis and Sufis were two minority yet powerful groups in a double process of conflicting and coalescing within a state lacking any fixed religious policy.[20] Ḥaydar Āmulī himself states that his book is addressed to Sufis and Twelver Shiʿas with the aim of establishing concord amongst them, and to lead each group to its own truth,[21] respectively the esoteric part (*al-bāṭin*) and the exoteric one (*al-ẓāhir*) of the same superior Truth contained in the teachings of the Imams.[22] In other words, Ḥaydar Āmulī's endeavour is to reunite two opposing groups, in conflict only through ignorance of their fundamental kinship. His most famous and bold theory identifies the 'true Sufis' (*al-ṣūfiyya al-ḥaqqa*) with the 'real' or 'true Shiʿa' (*al-shīʿa al-ḥaqīqiyya*), in other words the 'well-tested believer' (*muʾmin mumtaḥan*) alluded to in a famous *ḥadīth* almost identically expressed by the first, fifth and sixth imams: 'Our Cause is difficult; the only ones able to bear it are a Prophet missioned by God, an angel of Proximity, and a faithful believer whose heart has been tested by God for faith (*muʾmin imtaḥana Allāhu qalbahu liʾl-īmān*)'.[23]

Muḥammad b. ʿAlī b. Abī Jumhūr al-Aḥsāʾī (d. after 904/1499), author of the second work studied here, can be seen as the continuator and propagator of this tradition of reconciliation. His birthdate is not certain,[24] nor the exact location of his homeland al-Aḥsāʾ, a Shiʿi region in the north-east of the Arabian Peninsula or a city in Baḥrayn.[25] However, he certainly inherited a Shiʿi traditional lineage dating back to the eighth imam. Compared to Ḥaydar Āmulī, he seems to have had a more conventional life of Shiʿi medieval scholar. After he completed his scientific and religious formation in the Shiʿi centres of Najaf and Karak Nūḥ in Jabal ʿĀmil, he spent his life between the holy places of Iraq, the city of Tus in Iran, later called Mashhad, where the sanctuary of Imam Riḍā (d. 203/818) is, and his native country.[26] In 896/1490, he completed his *Mujlī mirʾāt al-munjī fīʾl-kalām waʾl-ḥikmatayn waʾl-taṣawwuf*,[27] a super-commentary of a previous theological work.[28] The explicit aim of the book is to integrate with Imami Shiʿism, on the one hand Ashʿari and Muʿtazili *kalām*, and on the other the philosophy of *Ishrāq* and Sufism.[29] Extensively borrowing the most esoteric *ḥadīth*s of the imams from Ḥaydar Āmulī's *Jāmiʿ al-asrār*, he also professed the historical and ontological affiliation of Sufism with the 'True religion' that is Twelver Shiʿism.

It is particularly noteworthy that this work was written only ten years before the shaykh of the Ṣafawiyya, the young Shāh Ismāʿīl, acceded to the throne in Tabriz and established Twelver Shiʿism as the official religion of Iran (906/1501), in other words on the eve of a new era for Shiʿism and Sufism. At the time of the *Mujlī*'s redaction, the foremost holy places and learning centres of Shiʿism, in Iraq and Lebanon, were under Sunni Ottoman rule, and although Iran was still predominantly Sunni, Persian Sufism had to a large extent completed its 'imperceptible transition from Sunnism to Shiʿism.'[30] Thus, Ibn Abī Jumhūr is one of the last witnesses of a time during which the two movements he principally aimed to approach or to re-approach, Sufism and Twelver Shiʿism, were on an equal social and political footing. He was also the last to be able to urge reconciliation without having to defend himself from attacks launched by the Shiʿi or the Sunni orthodox party, therefore without having to 'write between the lines', to quote Leo Strauss. It is unsettling to note that his contemporary ʿAlī al-Karakī (d. 940/1534), who had been a pupil of the same theologian ʿAlī b. Hilāl al-Jazāʾirī in Jabal ʿĀmil, would become the official theologian of the Shiʿi Safawid state and, within this remit, eventually define an orthodoxy which marginalised the mystical and philosophical form of Shiʿism represented by Ibn Abī Jumhūr.[31] The latter's call for a spiritual 'revolution' of Shiʿism, to quote Kāmil Muṣṭafā al-Shaybī, went mostly unheard by the *fuqahā'* of his time.[32] Moreover, the religious policy of the clergy and the Safawids would shatter his hopes for a sacred union between Shiʿism and Sufism. Ibn Abī Jumhūr was criticised for his 'extremist Sufism' by both Muḥammad Bāqir al-Majlisī (d. 1111/1699) and his pupil Mīrzā ʿAbd Allāh al-Iṣbahānī Afandī, author of *Riyāḍ al-ʿulamā'*.[33] His collection of *ḥadīth*s, *ʿAwālī al-la'ālī*, was particularly censured for different motives such as quoting some of its traditions from Sunni sources, comprising traditions of 'mystical flagrance' (*tastashimmu al-maṭālib al-ʿirfāniyya*), and comprising traditions peculiar to 'exaggerating' or 'extremist' Shiʿism (*ghuluww*). This fact attests that Ibn Abī Jumhūr shared with Ḥaydar Āmulī both a radical Shiʿi affiliation and an ambiguous ecumenist trend aiming not only to reconcile Shiʿas and Sufis, but also to bring up the positions of Shiʿas and Sunnis.[34] Although his works were held in esteem during the Safawid era by scholars with mystical leanings, such as Ashkiwarī and Muḥsin Fayḍ Kāshānī (d. 1091/1680), the Shiʿi-Sufi concordist discourse would thereafter continue under persecution, in both Sunni and Shiʿi circles, as the two final actors of this intellectual tradition will show *nolens volens*.

Sayyid Ḍiyā' al-Dīn Nūr Allāh b. al-Sayyid al-Sharīf al-Ḥusaynī al-Marʿashī al-Shūshtarī, known as Nūr Allāh Shūshtarī and famous, among the Shiʿa, by the title of the 'Third Martyr' (*al-shahīd al-thālith*), was born in 956/1549–50 in Shushtar, into a lineage going back to al-ʿAllāma al-Ḥillī. He became a *faqīh* and, following in his grandfather's footsteps, a member of the Nūrbakhsh Sufi fraternity which had converted to Shiʿism after the messianic claim of its eponymous founder.[35] In 992/1584–5, he emigrated from Mashhad to India in order to escape from the troubles in Khurasan, probably also with the aim to diffuse Twelver Shiʿism amongst the scholars of the Mughal court, where he shortly became an intimate of the young sovereign Shāh Akbar (r. 964–1014/1556–1605); thus, his case was different from that of many Sufis among his contemporaries, going incessantly back and forth between India and Iran.[36] He served as *qāḍī* in Lahore, applying *ijtihād* and issuing *fatwā*s according to the four schools of Sunni jurisprudence (*fiqh*). After Shāh Akbar's death, at the beginning of the reign of his son, Jahāngīr (r. 1014–1037/1605–1627), Shūshtarī ceased to conceal his Shiʿi faith (*taqiyya*), or was denounced by his adversaries for having composed, in response to a Sunni refutation, his apology of Shiʿi jurisprudence entitled *Iḥqāq al-ḥaqq*.[37] He is said to have been the first scholar to openly profess Shiʿism in India,[38] for which reason he fell victim to the 'tragic confrontation between the Shiʿi and Sunni *kalām*',[39] and was executed in 1019/1610.[40]

The main work of Shūshtarī, *Majālis al-muʾminīn*, was written in India around 990/1582–3 and could also have played a role in the tragic end of its author.[41] *A priori* it belongs to the *ṭabaqāt* genre, in other words 'categories' or 'generations' of illustrious men. Shūshtarī's intention was to bring together the companions of the Prophet, theologians, philosophers, princes, Sufis, poets, etc., who were secretly or notoriously Shiʿis in the widest sense, as defined by the acknowledgment of the sacred right of ʿAlī b. Abī Ṭālib to succeed the Prophet Muḥammad.[42] The main justification of his large census is that many scholars and rulers of Islam had been forced to practise *taqiyya* or 'sacred concealment of the faith' in order to escape from the persecutions of the Sunni power; however, with the glorious reign of the Safawid Shāhs, the time of concealment was now over.[43] With this goal in mind, he endeavours to show, especially in the sixth *majlis* of the book, that the great spiritual leaders of Sufism were all Shiʿis, although most of them were nominally Sunni.[44] For this reason, Shiʿi authors of prosopographical works consider it unreliable for having 'exaggerated' its inventory, in other words to have classified as Shiʿas men who were not.[45] The aim of the book has also determined its reception by modern scholarship: the text is still used as an historical trustworthy source by certain modern historians like al-Shaybī and Seyyed Hossein Nasr, while being denounced by others like Jean Calmard for its blatant bias.[46]

Quṭb al-Dīn Ashkiwarī, also called Bahāʾ al-Dīn al-Lāhījī or al-Sharīf al-Lāhījī (d. between 1088/1677 and 1095/1684), is the final and least known of our concordist authors. He had been in his youth the student of Mīr Dāmād (d. 1040/1631), then inherited from his father the office of *shaykh al-islām* of the district of Lahijan, in Gilan. This position, although containing important prerogatives in justice and economy, reflects a relatively secondary rank in the Safawid hierocracy, compared to that of the *ṣadrāt* which is progressively established during the Safawid period, especially in

Lahijan where the central authority faced many difficulties in applying its politics. Due to his socio-historical situation, he was a solitary philosopher and a latecomer to the 'philosophical renaissance of Safawid Iran', being active during the reign of Shāh Sulaymān (1077–1105/1666–1694), in which anti-Sufi and anti-philosophical reaction intensified. Aside from Muḥsin Fayḍ Kāshānī, his contemporaries included sworn opponents of philosophy and Sufism like al-Ḥurr al-ʿĀmilī (d. 1104/1693) and Muḥammad Bāqir al-Majlisī.

His foremost work, the *Maḥbūb al-qulūb*, written at the end of his life, takes resolute issue with this reactionary current. In this work appertaining to both universal history and the *ṭabaqāt* genre, he purposes no less than to assemble all the wise men, starting from the first of them, Adam, in three discourses (*maqālāt*): the first covers the sages predating Islam, in particular the Greek philosophers; the second savants (physicians, translators, astronomers) but also philosophers (*falāsifa*) and spiritual masters (*mashā'ikh*) of the Islamic era; and the third the twelve imams and twelve pre-eminent Shiʿi authorities. In the second volume Ashkiwarī dedicates a series of entries to 'unitarian Sufis' (*al-ṣūfiyya al-muwaḥḥida*). Discretely borrowing information as well as a number of allegations from Ḥaydar Āmulī, Ibn Abī Jumhūr and Nūr Allāh Shūshtarī, his aim is clearly to harmonise original Sufism with esoteric Shiʿism, but without explicitly maintaining that all the Sufi masters were Shiʿis. Thus Ashkiwarī reactivated the tradition of reconciliation between Sufism and Shiʿism, but he did so between the lines, and with the concerns of his time: to save what could be of Sufism and philosophy in Safawid Iran. In contrast with Shūshtarī, the all-encompassing category of his encyclopaedia is not that of Shiʿis, but of the sages; Sufis are not defended because they are Shiʿis as such, but because they are wise, as are *a priori* the Greek philosophers and the imams themselves.

These four works transmit a number of rational (*maʿqūl*) and traditional (*manqūl*) arguments defending the idea that primitive Sufism is an essential dimension of the Imami Shiʿi 'True religion'. This marginal yet stubborn discourse resisted the rising tide of anti-Sufism among Shiʿi scholars during the Safawid era, whose exponents included such influential figures as ʿAlī al-Karakī, al-Ḥurr al-ʿĀmilī and Muḥammad Bāqir al-Majlisī.[47] In the following pages, I will examine the principal strategies of argumentation which inform the four works included.

History-Based Argumentation: The Masters of Sufism as Disciples of the Shiʿi Imams

The first strategy is historical in approach, or rather pseudo-historical or even mytho-historical. It purports to show the fundamental identity or harmony that exists between Sufism and Shiʿism through the genealogy of Sufism, and more precisely by showing the affiliation of the founding great masters of Sufism (1st–3rd/7th–9th centuries) to the historical imams. Whereas our four authors are agreed that the first Sufis were disciples of the imams, they do not trace the origins of Sufism, and consequently of Shiʿism, to the same dates or to the same protagonists. As the historical validity of these arguments is generally rather weak, it is more rewarding to study the constants and the evolution of these different rewritings of the origins of Sufism, as of Shiʿism; if these works are not reliable for a history of Shiʿism and Sufism, they are primary materials for a 'history of the history' of both, that is to say a history of the representation of their historical origins and developments.

To Ḥaydar Āmulī 'the particular category of Shiʿa is designated as the initiated or 'well-tested' believers – the term *mu'min* broadly meaning 'Shiʿi' in the general sense – is that of the Sufis.'[48] He argues that if Sufis are commonly thought to be Sunni, it is because, like the Shiʿis, they possess many branches, only one of which is the genuine or 'the true one.'[49] The true Shiʿis, the 'believers' in the exoteric sense (*ẓāhir*) are the Twelvers, which excludes the Ismailis, who are 'exaggerators' (*ghulāt*),[50] and the Zaydis; the true Sufis, who are also the true Shiʿis in the esoteric sense (*bāṭin*), are not those who bear this name among his contemporaries, but men such as Salmān the Persian (presumed to have died in 35/655–6 or 36/657),[51] Uways al-Qaranī (presumed to have died in 37/657 at the battle of Ṣiffīn),[52] and the 'men of the bench' (*aṣḥāb al-ṣuffa*) at the time of the Prophet; then came Abū Dharr al-Ghifārī (d. 32/653), ʿAmmār b. Yāsir (d. 37/658 at the battle of Ṣiffīn) and al-Miqdād b. Aswad (d. 33/654), companions of ʿAlī b. Abī Ṭālib; and 'after them' Kumayl b. Ziyād al-Nakhaʿī (d. 82/701–2?), Abū Yazīd Basṭāmī (d. 234/848 or

261/874) and Junayd al-Baghdādī (d. 298/911), who were 'pupils, disciples and repositaries of the secrets of the Impeccable Imams.'[53] Thus there are three classes or generations of original Sufis and true Shiʿis: first the 'companions' of the Prophet (*al-ṣaḥāba*), followed by the 'successors' (*al-tābiʿūn*), who accompanied the first imam, and finally the contemporaries and disciples of the subsequent imams. The paradox in this picture is that the 'particular Shiʿis', who are the 'true Sufis', predate the 'Shiʿis in the general sense' who are the Twelvers, since they came into being following the occultation of the twelfth imam (260/874 for the lesser one, 329/940–1 for the greater one). It is clear that differentiating between 'Twelver Imamis' and Ismailis, Zaydis or *ghulāt* before the end of the 3rd/9th century is near impossible, and that the boundaries between different Shiʿi groups were porous during these ancient times.[54] It seems that in Āmulī's vision of history, for the Shiʿis in the broadest sense, the true Sufis are not only a spiritual elite, but a genuine avant-garde testifying to the authentic and elemental character of Twelver Shiʿism.

The first Sufi mentioned by Ḥaydar Āmulī is Salmān the Persian, a companion of the Prophet and of Imam ʿAlī, whose social status was modest since he was a non-Arab. He is an emblematic figure of Islamic Persia. Widely recognised as the founder of Sufism, he figures in the initiatory chains of a number of Sunni brotherhoods, where he is placed as a disciple of the first caliph Abū Bakr.[55] According to a prophetic *ḥadīth* currently quoted in the Shiʿi sources, he is considered as a 'member of the Holy family' (*ahl al-bayt*), an adoptive familiar of the Fourteen Impeccables.[56] Moreover, certain traditions accredit him with having received spiritual and secret instruction from ʿAlī, to the extent that he is said to have learned the 'Supreme Name' of God (*al-ism al-aʿẓam*).[57] Following Salmān are Abū Dharr al-Ghifārī, ʿAmmār b. Yāsir and al-Miqdād b. Aswad, who are chiefly known for their physical and political engagement alongside ʿAlī. These four figures are among the first Muslims of humble and non-Qurayshi origin and are associated with each other in numerous Imami traditions dating back to the Prophet.[58] They are celebrated as 'pillars of Shiʿism' (*arkān al-shīʿa*) in Imami circles, for having always fought or resisted alongside Imam ʿAlī, particularly in the critical times following the death of Muḥammad and the event of Saqīfa.[59] Whereas Salmān represents the esoteric face of proto-Shiʿism, the other three characters represent the exoteric, ascetic and especially militant aspect. According to a tradition of al-Kulaynī's *Kāfī* related to the sixth imam:

> One day, someone was mentioning pious dissimulation (*taqiyya*) in the presence of ʿAlī b. al-Ḥusayn [the fourth imam]. He said: 'If Abū Dharr had known what was in Salmān's heart, he would have killed him, although the Messenger of God had established a pact of fraternity between them. So what do you think all the people [would have done]? The knowledge of the [true] knowers (*ʿilm al-ʿulamāʾ*) is difficult and tough. No one can assume it except a Prophet, an angel of Proximity or a faithful believer whose heart has been tested by God for faith. Salmān became one of the knowers because he's a man from us, the People of the Holy Family (*liʾannahu minnā ahl al-bayt*)'.[60]

By identifying these 'pillars of Shiʿism' with the fathers of Sufism, Ḥaydar Āmulī purports to demonstrate the original kinship between these two movements.

In the works of the three succeeding authors, starting with Ibn Abī Jumhūr, the historical reconstructions include the same protagonists, but differ on an important point: the worthy companions of the Prophet, such as Salmān, are initiates, however they are not considered the fathers of Sufism; the particular science of Sufism goes back to certain 'successors' of the Prophet who are reputed to have sworn allegiance to ʿAlī. Thus, according to Ibn Abī Jumhūr: 'Among the successors are Kumayl b. Ziyād al-Nakhaʿī and Ḥasan al-Baṣrī; with these two begins the science of the insiders (*aṣḥāb al-bāṭin*) and that of the Sufis (*ahl al-taṣawwuf*); and similarly Uways al-Qaranī.'[61] These three characters are very different both in historical status and also in their relations, according to the historiography, with Sufism and Shiʿism.

Ḥasan al-Baṣrī (d. 110/728) is well known in both Islamic and Western historiography. Sunni historians recognise that he was a disciple of ʿAlī b. Abī Ṭālib, and as such he is present in the initiation chains of numerous Sufi orders. However, this ascetic and author of sermons was claimed early on by all the emerging theological schools, starting with the *ahl al-sunna waʾl-jamāʿa* and the Muʿtazilis.[62] In early Shiʿi sources, he appears sometimes as a pure supporter of ʿAlī and the *ahl al-bayt*, sometimes as a doctrinal adversary refuted by the fifth imam.[63] Before Ibn Abī Jumhūr, Ḥaydar Āmulī mentioned him as well as a disciple of Imam ʿAlī.[64] Ibn Khaldūn (d. 808/1406), a contemporary of Ḥaydar Āmulī, condemned these latter-day Sufis, influenced by Shiʿi views, who portray Ḥasan al-Baṣrī as a Shiʿi.[65] To be sure, the Sunni positions of Ḥasan al-Baṣrī are solidly established by traditionists and Sunni, or pro-Sunni, historians, and it can be noticed that Shiʿi *ʿulamāʾ* tend to avoid him rather than try to claim him.[66] His presence in Ibn Abī Jumhūr's picture of history is another sign of the ecumenist trend of this thinker. Thus did he gradually disappear from the picture of the origins of Sufism described by our authors: after Ibn Abī Jumhūr, neither Shūshtarī, nor Ashkiwarī mention him in their works.

Unlike Ḥasan al-Baṣrī, Uways al-Qaranī is a semi-legendary figure who pertains more to sacred history than empirical and scientific history. Within the Sufi community, there are rival claims of his affiliation to both Sunnis and Shiʿis. According to prevailing Islamic tradition, the Prophet designated this Yemenite without having ever seen him, like a hidden saint or an intercessor, and urged both ʿUmar and ʿAlī to seek him out in order to implore God's forgiveness. ʿUmar is reputed to have found him during the final year of his caliphate; their conversation is related by Farīd al-Dīn ʿAṭṭār in his *Memorial of Saints* (*Tadhkirat al-awliyāʾ*).[67] We know that, in consequence, many Sufis are named, or name themselves, *Uwaysiyya*, since they do not have a visible and contemporary human guide (*murshid*) but rather receive initiation from the 'spiritual essence' (*rūḥāniyya*) of a deceased saint.[68]

Amongst our philosophers of reconciliation, Ashkiwarī's treatment of Uways al-Qaranī is the most extensive and also the most significant in that he refers to him both as the first Sufi and as the first Shiʿi. He derives his information from the *Majālis al-muʾminīn* of Shūshtarī who, for his part, did not classify Uways as a Sufi but as a believer among the immediate followers of the Prophet (*al-tābiʿūn*).[69] While Shūshtarī was quoting ʿAṭṭār's report as a testimony of Uways's disdain towards ʿUmar,[70] Ashkiwarī, in the chapter dedicated to him, completely disregards the role of ʿUmar, asserting implicitly that Uways was recommended by the Prophet solely to ʿAlī and did not meet any caliph before him. Ashkiwarī's rejection of ʿUmar is thus more radical than that of Shūshtarī; unlike the latter, the former did not have to compromise with a Sunni milieu. The first tradition quoted by Ashkiwarī describes Uways as a famous ascetic, converted to Islam during the Prophet's lifetime, who appeared for the first time at the battle of Ṣiffīn (37/657), dressed in rags and with his head shaven, in order to swear allegiance to ʿAlī and fight until death for him.[71] If the woollen coat (*ṣūf*) is a sign that identifies Sufis, and is probably the origin of the word 'Sufism' (*taṣawwuf*), and if the shaven head is associated with a certain kind of dervish, what defines Uways as the first Sufi ontologically, far more than these exterior signs, is his explicit designation by the Prophet and his complete allegiance to the Imam, until his death.

The third key figure in this reconstruction of the common origins of Sufism and Shiʿism is Kumayl b. Ziyād. His historicity is established, as is his affiliation to the first followers of Imam ʿAlī. He is known to the Shiʿa as the imam's closest companion and confidant, an ardent combatant for his cause and also as one of the first Shiʿi martyrs. Many Sufi brotherhoods, such as the Nūrbakhshiyya, who wielded great influence under the Safawids, regard him as the first link of their initiation chain, following ʿAlī b. Abī Ṭālib.[72] If one asks in what regard Kumayl may be considered to be a Sufi, the reply is that according to several authoritative traditions, he received esoteric instruction from the Imam: it is first of all Shiʿi spirituality that underwrites the historical Sufism of Kumayl. The evidence of this rank amongst the insiders seems to be a dialogue concerning spiritual truth (*al-ḥaqīqa*) between the imam and his disciple, a dialogue that our four authors faithfully reproduce and that is typical of Shiʿi esoterism.[73] 'It is said that [ʿAlī] (...) had taken Kumayl behind him on the camel he was riding. Kumayl said: 'O Prince of believers, what is Truth?' The imam answered: 'What care you about the Truth?' Kumayl said: 'Am I not a companion of your Secret?' 'Yes, [answered the imam], but what spills out from me penetrates into you." There follows a brief series of symbolic and apophatic definitions of the Truth, at the end of which the imam cuts short his discourse and announces: 'Put out your lamp, dawn has come.' This tradition would seem to prefigure two major trends within Shiʿi spirituality: the first part points towards a magical conception of the transmission of the sacred Science through the medium of the humours of the body – here sweat, elsewhere saliva; the latter part develops a philosophising or spiritualistic discourse which culminates in an injunction to mystical silence.[74]

Kumayl b. Ziyād personifies the deep-rooted kinship between Sufism and Shiʿism by virtue of his spiritual initiation on the one hand, but also because he died as a martyr for ʿAlī's cause at the hands of Ḥajjāj b. Yūsuf, the governor of Iraq and a sworn enemy of the Shiʿis. The story, as related by Shūshtarī and Ashkiwarī is astonishing: appearing before him, Kumayl declared he had been forewarned by Imam ʿAlī that his assassin would indeed be Ḥajjāj; in response Ḥajjāj accused Kumayl of having taken part in the murder of ʿUthmān, the third caliph, and ordered his decapitation.[75] The accusation made by Ḥajjāj is not contradicted, either by Kumayl in the text (*matn*) or by the reporter al-Mughīra in his account of the *khabar*.[76] When one is aware that the murder of ʿUthmān was at the origin of the great *fitna*, the rift that tore Islam apart during its early centuries, to let any degree of doubt subsist as to the responsibility of Kumayl is particularly significant: this original and most spiritual form of Shiʿism is revealed to be also the most militant, and it is this Shiʿism, as spiritual as it is political, that is at the root of Sufism.

Following Kumayl, who was the last disciple of the first imam, the next connections between Sufis and imams made by our authors are Abū Yazīd Basṭāmī, affiliated to the sixth imam Jaʿfar al-Ṣādiq (d. 148/765); Shaqīq al-Balkhī (d. 194/809–10) and Bishr al-Ḥāfī (d. 226–227/841), affiliated to the seventh imam Mūsā b. Jaʿfar al-Kāẓim (d. 183/799); Maʿrūf al-Karkhī (d. 200/815), affiliated to the eighth imam ʿAlī b. Mūsā al-Riḍā (d. 203/818). All were individual Sufis who predated the foundation of brotherhoods, but nevertheless belonged to numerous *silsila*s, whose traditions were strictly oral. Before we examine these affiliations more closely, one can already wonder why this initiation of Sufis by imams ceases between the first and the fifth imams, and conversely, why this transmission began again with the sixth, given that the initiation of Kumayl already included all the esoteric secrets? Our authors never answer the first question: everything is described as if Sufism went through an eclipse, a temporary occultation between Kumayl and Abū Yazīd Basṭāmī, even though Shūshtarī attempts to consider the Sufi Ibrāhīm b. Adham (d. 160–1/777) as a disciple of the fifth imam Muḥammad b. ʿAlī al-Bāqir (d. 115 or 119/732 or 737);[77] in modern times, Maʿṣūm ʿAlī Shāh, in his *Ṭarāʾiq* *al-ḥaqāʾiq*, contends even that Ibrāhīm b. Adham is affiliated to the fourth imam ʿAlī b. al-Ḥusayn (d. 92 or 95/711 or 714).[78] To our second question, a more historical answer can be outlined: following the tragedy of Karbala, the Imami doctrine was rebuilt on new foundations by the fifth and especially the sixth imam, Jaʿfar al-Ṣādiq, which would imply, according to the logic of esotericism, a new initiation, all the more so given that Jaʿfar is famous even in Sunni sources for having dispensed a large body of instruction.

Abū Yazīd Basṭāmī died in 234/848 or 261/874, yet he is unanimously presented by our authors as the disciple and the water-supplier (*saqqā*) of Jaʿfar al-Ṣādiq, who died in 148/765. This hiatus is simply never questioned by either Ḥaydar Āmulī or Ibn Abī Jumhūr. Shūshtarī is the first among our thinkers to mention the objections that can be made to this affiliation, but only in order to better refute them. These objections, apparently originally formulated by Shiʿi Sufis, are corroborated by reliable dates: the traditionist Shaykh Nūr al-Dīn Abu'l-Futūḥ deems it possible that Bāyazid Basṭāmī served under the eighth imam, ʿAlī b. Mūsā b. Jaʿfar, and that the scribes might have made a slip of the pen; while Mīr Sayyid Sharīf, author of *Sharḥ al-muwāfaq*, contends that Abū Yazīd received initiation from the 'spiritual essence' (*rūḥāniyya*) of Imam Jaʿfar.[79] Shūshtarī rejects these hypotheses and affirms that Basṭāmī was effectively affiliated to the sixth imam; to resolve the hiatus, he records from the *Muʿjam al-buldān* that there were two Abū Yazīds in Basṭām, 'the old one' (*al-kabīr*) and 'the young one' (*al-ṣaghīr*), the first being the disciple of the imam and the second who lived later and the date of whose death is known.[80] Following in the steps of Shūshtarī, Ashkiwarī makes extensive use of this counter-argument, showing just how important the affiliation of Basṭāmī to Imam Jaʿfar was to him but also that the historical objections to this affiliation were too important for him to ignore. Ultimately this counter-argument was attributed to Basṭāmī himself, as Shūshtarī reports: 'Had I not found my way to our Master al-Ṣādiq, I would have died apostate. He is among the friends of God as Gabriel is among the angels, as though his point of departure was that of arrival for the seekers of Truth (*al-sālikīn*)'.[81] Similarly, Ashkiwarī, refusing to make of Basṭāmī an insider having received initiation by the sole spiritual essence of the Imam, that is to say an Uwaysī, asserts on the authority of al-ʿAllāma al-Ḥillī that: 'The greatest among the shaykhs prided themselves on having served the imams, and Abū Yazīd Basṭāmī prided himself on having served as water-supplier in the house of Jaʿfar al-Ṣādiq (. . .). This account and the others like it leave no room for allegoric interpretation (*ta'bā al-ta'wīl*)', in other words, they are to be taken at face value.[82] I will return later to the significance of Basṭāmī for our authors, which may shed some light on their obstinacy in repeating such a problematical assertion. Regardless of what Ashkiwarī might think, the meaning of this historical allegation might very well be symbolic: the described role of water-supplier suggests once more the need of a concrete, physical and 'humoral' medium for the transmission of the sacred science of the imam.[83]

Two great Sufi masters are then presented by our authors as disciples of the seventh imam Mūsā b. Jaʿfar al-Kāẓim (d. 183/799): Sḥaqīq b. Ibrāhīm al-Balkhī (d. 194/809–10), an important link in the chain of transmission, and who, Shūshtarī argues, died as a martyr for having being accused of Shiʿi heresy (*bih tuhmat-i rafḍ shahīd shud*);[84] and Bishr al-Ḥāfī (d. 227/841–2), who repented and was converted at the hands of the imam. While this latter account of conversion, borrowed from al-ʿAllāma al-Ḥillī's *Minhāj al-karāma*, might possess an element of historical truth, its literary and mythical character makes it somewhat difficult to believe for our rational minds, all the more so since it is neither mentioned in the great historical works, nor in the Sufi *ṭabaqāt*. One day, as the imam was passing by the house of Bishr in Baghdad, he is said to have heard the sound of merriment coming from within and asked the servant: 'The master of this house, is he a free man or a slave (*ḥurr aw ʿabd*)?' – 'A free man, of course' – 'You speak the truth, since had he been a slave [of God], he would have feared his master (*mawlāhu*).' When told about the conversation by his servant, as he was sitting at table and drinking, the master went outside barefoot, from whence his sobriquet (*laqab*): *al-ḥāfī*, which means 'who goes barefoot.'[85]

Maʿrūf al-Karkhī, another important figure in the origins of Sufism, is presented as the gatekeeper of the eighth imam ʿAlī b. Mūsā al-Riḍā. Shūshtarī, followed by Ashkiwarī, reports a popular narrative in which the Sufi master is revealed to be the operator of the imam's theurgic powers, and the imam is revealed to be the source of the Sufi's charisma. A merchant, asking for protection during his travels at sea, was given a talisman by the imam to be invoked in the event of a storm. It read: 'O sea! By the right of Maʿrūf al-Karkhī, gatekeeper of ʿAlī b. Mūsā al-Riḍā, calm yourself!' Later, as a storm was raging, the distraught trader threw the talisman into the sea, and the storm immediately abated.[86] According to another tale quoted from ʿAṭṭār's *Tadhkirat al-awliyāʾ*, Maʿrūf heroically defended the gate of the imam's audience chamber against the 'exaggeration' or 'extremism' (*ghuluww*) of a crowd of Shiʿis, and this was the cause of his death.[87] The symbol behind this anecdote is powerful: the Sufi is seen as the rampart of the esoteric teaching of the imam against the extremism of his partisans claiming his divinity. Ironically, this story would itself be deemed an 'exaggeration' by the Shiʿi *ʿulamāʾ*, who would criticise Shūshtarī for it.

According to the same report, the teachings were transmitted from Maʿrūf al-Karkhī to Sarī al-Saqatī (d. 253/867) and from him to Junayd al-Baghdādī, 'the master of the sect of the Sufis' (*shaykh al-ṭāʾifa*). The latter is included among the direct disciples of the imams, as are the previously mentioned masters, by Ḥaydar Āmulī, followed by Ibn Abī Jumhūr and Shūshtarī.[88] However, Junayd is a contemporary of the final imams, who are not credited with any links with the Sufis, and of the Minor Occultation of the twelfth imam (260–329/874–941). Moreover, he is widely considered to be Sunni, which Nūr Allāh Shūshtarī explains, as can be expected, by the necessary concealment of the faith (*taqiyya*).[89]

Historians of Sufism and Shiʿism have stressed on many occasions that, following al-Riḍā, there is no evidence of contact between Sufis and the Shiʿi imams.[90] This fact is acknowledged but never explained by the four authors here studied. We know that the ninth imam Muḥammad b. ʿAlī al-Jawād or al-Taqī (d. 220/835) died very young and that the following two – ʿAlī b. Muḥammad al-Hādī (d. 254/868) and al-Ḥasan b. ʿAlī al-ʿAskarī (d. 260/874) – lived under house arrest in Samarra. An oral tradition, recorded by al-Shaybī, does exist, according to which Imam Riḍā transmitted the 'spiritual path' (*ṭarīqa*), the esoteric dimension of the religion, to Maʿrūf al-Karkhī and after him to the Sufis, while the letter, as opposed to the spirit, of the revelation (*sharīʿa*) and its exoteric learning remained in the lineage of the imams, starting from al-Jawād.[91] This would imply a first schism between exoteric and esoteric Shiʿism dating back to the time of the historical imams, and holding one of them responsible for it, although none of our authors seem ready to admit this. As for anti-Sufi Shiʿis, they rely on a *ḥadīth* of the tenth imam ʿAlī al-Hādī: 'All Sufis oppose us, their way is contrary to ours, and they are but the Christians or the Mazdeans of this community.'[92] This hostile tradition is never mentioned by our promoters of reconciliation, not even to refute it.

As a conclusion to this first analysis, one could say that the 'historical' arguments of our authors would hardly be considered so in the modern sense of the word: dates are ignored or rejected; the accounts are readily fabulous or hagiographic; moreover, Shūshtarī's paradigmatic use of the notion of *taqiyya* has to be considered as an 'unfalsifiable' argument in the negative sense of the term in Karl Popper's epistemology. It is conceivable that our authors were well aware of this fact and that the significance of these historical allegations resided first and foremost in their symbolism. The chronology of events remains paradoxical nevertheless, as the first 'true' Sufis and 'true' Shiʿis predate not only the brotherhoods, which is undoubtedly intentional, but the emergence of Sufism and Shiʿism in the general sense. Finally, it is notable that this (pseudo-)historical argumentation is not defended with the same zeal by the four authors: the manner in which Ḥaydar Āmulī and Ibn Abī Jumhūr repeat these allegations is dogmatic, and their approach to the reconciliation of Sufism with Shiʿism, or the identification of the one with the other, is essentially conceptual. Shūshtarī argues the historical link with the most fervour, at times deliberately exaggerating the Shiʿi genealogy of the Sufis. Ashkiwarī is more restrained, and refrains from explicitly 'Shiʿitising' a number of Sufi masters to whom he pays tribute, while nevertheless affirming the affiliation of Basṭāmī to Imam Jaʿfar.

The Conceptual Argumentation: The Triad of the Law, the Path and the Truth

Over and above the historical perspective, our four Shiʿi authors share the same underlying theory: the convergence a priori between *sharīʿa*, the 'revealed' Law, i.e. the exoteric part of the religion; *ṭarīqa*, the mystical and spiritual 'Path', term also used for 'brotherhood'; and *ḥaqīqa*, the spiritual 'Reality' or 'Truth', i.e. the object that the gnostic philosophers, sometimes known as the *muḥaqqiqūn*, are searching for. This conjunction is based on, and introduced by, a prophetic *ḥadīth* which seems not to be present in the 'classical' or 'orthodox' collections of *ḥadīth*s, be they Sunni or Shiʿi, but rather to be specific to our heterodox tradition of thought: 'The Law is my speeches (*aqwālī*); the Path is my actions (*afʿālī*); the Truth is my [spiritual] states (*aḥwālī*).'[93]

Ḥaydar Āmulī develops this conceptual triad in his *Anwār al-ḥaqīqa wa aṭwār al-ṭarīqa wa asrār al-sharīʿa* ('The Lights of Truth, the Stations of the Path and the Mysteries of the Revealed Law'). He considers the Law, the Path and the Truth, to be three degrees of the same reality, the highest being the Truth, the medium being the Path and the lowest being the Law. The Law, he says, is true without the Path, but the Path is not true without the Law; just as the Path is true without the Truth, but the Truth is not true without the Path; because each higher level is the perfection of that below. Consequently, the people of the Truth (*ahl al-ḥaqīqa*) are superior to the people of the Path (*ahl al-ṭarīqa*) and the latter are superior to the people of the Law (*ahl al-sharīʿa*).[94] In this early work, composed before Āmulī relinquished his mundane career and donned the Sufi cloak (*khirqa*), he identifies the people of the Law with the jurists (*al-fuqahāʾ*), the people of the Truth with the Gnostics (*al-ʿārifūn*) and, more surprisingly, the people of the Path with the scholars and philosophers (*al-ʿulamāʾ waʾl-ḥukamāʾ*), avoiding open mention of the Sufis. For this he quotes a saying of Imam ʿAlī: 'The Law is a river and the Truth is a sea. The jurists (*al-fuqahāʾ*) are making circumambulations around the river, the wise (*al-ḥukamāʾ*) are plunging into the sea in search of pearls, and the Gnostics (*al-ʿārifūn*) are wandering on the ships of salvation (*sufun al-najāt*)'. From a universal perspective, he identifies the people of the Law with the community of Moses, the people of the Path with that of Jesus, and the people of the Truth with that of Muḥammad.[95]

While emphasising the hierarchy between these three dimensions of the Revelation (*sharʿ*), Ḥaydar Āmulī and Ibn Abī Jumhūr, the latter quoting the former, both stress their harmony and complementarity, with the implicit aim to solve the conflict between jurists, Sufis and gnostic philosophers:

> Know that the exoteric Law (*sharīʿa*), the mystical Path (*ṭarīqa*) and the spiritual Truth (*ḥaqīqa*) are synonymous terms for the single Truth, which is the Truth of the Muḥammadan Revelation (*ḥaqīqat al-sharʿ al-aḥmadī al-muḥammadī*), but viewed from

> different standpoints and at different levels. There is, on examination, no contradiction between these standpoints and these levels. The Revelation (*sharʿ*) is like the complete almond, which contains the shell (*qishr*), the kernel (*lubb*), and the kernel of kernels (*lubb al-lubb*): the shell may be likened to the Law, the kernel to the Path, the kernel of kernels to the esoteric Truth of the Innermost (*al-ḥaqīqa al-bāṭina li'l-bāṭin*), and the almond is the union of all.[96]

The symbolism of the kernel and the shell refers partly to the Qur'an where the word *albāb* (plural of *lubb*) is frequently used for 'spirit' in the expression *ūlū'l-albāb*, and partly to the *Theology* of Pseudo-Aristotle where the shells (*qushūr*) appear as the material clothes of the soul.[97] The dual couple of the kernel and the shell seems to have been attributed first to Empedocles (d. *ca* 424 BC) in *Kitāb al-Milal wa'l-niḥal* of al-Shahrastānī (d. 548/1153) and is defined as follows: '[Empedocles] often expressed the body and the spirit by the shell and the kernel'; it also takes part of the doctrine of the Neoplatonist Proclus (d. 485 AD) in the same source.[98] For what concerns the notion of 'kernel of kernels', it is defined in the *Iṣṭilāḥāt al-ṣūfiyya* (Terminology of the Sufis) of ʿAbd al-Razzāq al-Qāshānī (d. 730/1330), the famous disciple of Ibn ʿArabī, as the matter of the divine sacred Light which assists intellect so that it purifies itself from the shells.[99] To my knowledge, this symbolism is absent in Imami *ḥadīth* and thus must be of philosophical and Sufi-mystical origin.[100]

By taking up this symbolism in its triadic form (*qishr*, *lubb*, *lubb al-lubb*) and not in its dualistic one (*qishr*, *lubb*), Ḥaydar Āmulī, Ibn Abī Jumhūr and Ashkiwarī after them, make it correspond to the triad of Law, Path and Truth, and thus argue that there is an essential harmony between exoteric religion, the initiation of the Sufis, and the gnosis of the philosophers. There is here a subjacent and authentic philosophical theory. This 'pre-established harmony', in Leibniz' terms, between *sharīʿa*, *ṭarīqa* and *ḥaqīqa*, is justified by a conception of reality which comprises varying degrees of depth, from the material to the spiritual and from the apparent to the concealed. This conception, which distinguishes between, and articulates, both an outside and exoteric (*ẓāhir*) and an inside and esoteric (*bāṭin*) aspect in all things, is axial in the teachings of the imams.[101] It is developed in Shiʿi philosophy which accepted and reactivated the strong influence of Neoplatonic ideas, as it had already appeared in the *Theology* of Pseudo-Aristotle.[102] In the triadic scheme defended by our authors, the intelligible Truth (*ḥaqīqa*) functions as the dialectic synthesis of the traditional opposition between the exoteric Law (*sharīʿa*) and the mystical Path (*ṭarīqa*): here the innermost dimension, that of the Truth, contains the outermost, that of the Law, and the outer facet of the innermost, that of the Path.

The Sufis have often made use of this triadic theme for defensive purposes, arguing that the initiatory Sufi Path (*ṭarīqa*) is the necessary link between the religious Law (*sharīʿa*) and the divine Truth (*ḥaqīqa*).[103] However it would appear that the meaning of the terms and the general conception are different in the case of our Shiʿi authors. First of all, they consider the spiritual Truth (*ḥaqīqa*) as the object of a direct contemplation (*mushāhada*) which may coincide with gnosis (*ʿirfān*), something which enables a certain philosophy to become the ultimate science and arbiter between exoteric religion and the different forms of Sufism. For example, Ibn Abī Jumhūr wrote:

> Upon examination (*ʿinda'l-taḥqīq*), Law is the expression of assent to the teaching of the prophets and the messengers and action according to their obligations by conformism and obedience. Path is the expression of realisation of the acts and manners of the prophets and messengers by the way of certitude and ornamentation. Truth is the expression of contemplation of their spiritual states and stations by the way of the faculties of unveiling and tasting, followed by their abiding by the way of the spiritual state and the ecstatic consciousness (*mushāhadat aḥwālihim wa maqāmātihim kashfan wa dhawqan wa'l-qiyām bihā ḥālan wa wijdānan*).[104]

This system of the Law (*sharīʿa*), the Path (*ṭarīqa*) and the Truth (*ḥaqīqa*), is related by analogy to another conceptual triad, the one of the legislative Mission (*risāla*), the Prophecy (*nubuwwa*) and the divine Alliance (*walāya*), the latter being identified by our authors with the exclusive dignity of the imams in a Shiʿi sense. As Ḥaydar Āmulī asserts: 'In reality, the exoteric Law is part of the necessity of the legislative Mission; the mystical Path is part of the necessity of the Prophecy; and the spiritual Truth is part of the necessity of the divine Alliance.'[105] The same thinker criticises those, including al-Shaykh al-Akbar himself, who say that the seal of the saints in the absolute meaning (*khātam al-awliyāʾ muṭlaqan*) is Jesus son of Maryam and that the seal of the saints in the determined meaning (*khātam al-awliyāʾ muqayyadan*) is Ibn ʿArabī, by asserting that the former is no one but ʿAlī b. Abī Ṭālib and that the latter is no one but Muḥammad b. al-Ḥasan, the awaited Mahdi.[106] However, the definition given for the divine Alliance does not exclude its possession by the Gnostic or the Sufi: 'The divine Alliance is the expression for the direct contemplation of His Essence, His attributes and His actions, in the *loci* of manifestation of His perfections (*maẓāhir kamālātihi*), the *loci* of self-disclosure of His pre-eternal and post-eternal definitional characters (*majālī taʿayyunātihi al-azaliyya wa'l-abadiyya*); this is the essence of the Truth.'[107] Ibn Abī Jumhūr infers that no supporter of the Law, the Path or the Truth – meaning no Shiʿi *faqīh*, Sufi or Gnostic – can deny any other without denying the three together and thereby without being impious (*kāfir*).[108]

Concerning the *notion* of *ṭarīqa*, it should be noted that both Ḥaydar Āmulī and Ibn Abī Jumhūr take it in a purely spiritual meaning, that of the inner journey through the different states (*aḥwāl*) or stations (*maqāmāt*), without its social meaning as 'brotherhood', suggesting that the social brotherhood is excluded *a priori* from the spiritual Path. It is this metaphoric use of the notion of *ṭarīqa* that will enable Ashkiwarī to put forward this theory two centuries later, during a time when the Sufi brotherhoods, bearing the same name of *ṭarāʾiq* (sing. *ṭarīqa*), were publicly held in contempt.

According to Ibn Abī Jumhūr's sayings, the reason he recalls this fundamental unity is not only to protect the Sufis from serious accusations made against them, but also to protect these very accusers, the Shiʿi *fuqahāʾ*, against their own guilty ignorance. In the writings of Ashkiwarī, composed during the reign of Shāh Sulaymān when the authority of al-Majlisī was rising, the plea of Ibn Abī Jumhūr, written two centuries earlier, seems all the more topical, something which points to what one may call the historicity of concepts:

> The reason for the accusation of impiety and heresy (*al-kufr wa'l-zandaqa*) aimed at this sect [that of the Sufis who testify to God's uniqueness], from what has been said among our [Shiʿi] doctors, by Ibn Abī Jumhūr in his book *al-Mujlī*, is only a reflection of the ignorance of [Sufi] principles and rules (*bi-uṣūlihim wa qawānīnihim*). Indeed, if [the doctors of the Law] knew the founding principles [of the Sufis], if they realised that the Law, the Path and the Truth are truly synonyms to designate

> a sole reality (*ḥaqīqa wāḥida*), that of the Revelation (*ḥaqīqat al-sharʿ*), they would not use such language, and would leave aside this intolerance (*taʿaṣṣub*), this polemic, this rejection and opposition, they would strip their hearts of these envious and thoughtless words, and would free their souls from the abyss of sophisms and doubt.[109]

Ibn Abī Jumhūr also bestows a symbolic and spiritual meaning on the term *khirqa*, the coarse garment worn by the first ascetics and symbol of the spiritual initiation of the disciple by the master. The transmission of the *khirqa* is mentioned in ancient sources as the earliest form of initiatic lineage, dating back to the prophet Muḥammad, and constituted the 'pedestal for the edification of the Sufi orders' from the 6th/12th century onwards.[110] The theme of the *khirqa* is without doubt one in which the Shiʿis recognise in Sufism their own inheritance, to quote Henry Corbin.[111] S.H. Nasr considers that the wearing and the transmission of the cloak as symbols of the spiritual teachings they have received find their origin in the Shiʿi *ḥadīth* of 'The Five of the Cloak' which relates how Muḥammad covered with his cloak his daughter Fāṭima, his cousin ʿAlī, and their two sons al-Ḥasan and al-Ḥusayn, as well as himself.[112] Ibn Abī Jumhūr maintains that the original cloak, given to the Prophet by the archangel Gabriel during his ascent to heaven (*miʿrāj*), was transmitted to ʿAlī on God's order, and henceforth from imam to imam down to the Mahdi. This archetypal and transcendental cloak gave rise to three others, and three paths of initiation, transmitted from the imams to the Sufis: from Imam Mūsā al-Kāẓim to Shaqīq al-Balkhī; from Imam Jaʿfar al-Ṣādiq to Abū Yazīd Basṭāmī; from Imam ʿAlī al-Riḍā to Maʿrūf al-Karkhī, who initiated Sarī al-Saqatī, who in turn initiated Junayd, 'the Master of the sect of the Sufis.'[113] Following a Neoplatonic schema, Ibn Abī Jumhūr perceives the physical cloak transmitted from Sufi to Sufi as an image pertaining to the archetypal cloak held by the imam.[114] Once more this is a dialectic of integration and overtaking of the social dimension of Sufism within Shiʿi spirituality. This spiritualisation of the notion of *khirqa* was not, however, as successful as the analogous operation on the notion of *ṭarīqa* as seen before: the notion of *khirqa* will remain associated with Sufi brotherhoods, the latter remaining considered as incompatible with Twelver Shiʿism. Thus, this argument is not used by Ashkiwarī within the contemporary context of extreme hostility of the Shiʿi political and theological establishment towards the Sufis.

This argumentation, based on the triad of Law, Path and Truth, stands side by side with a series of antinomies opposing 'true' and 'false' Shiʿis, 'true' and 'false' Sufis, 'true' and 'false' savants. This antonymic schema is characteristic of Shiʿi spirituality, as shown by M.A. Amir-Moezzi and Ch. Jambet.[115] To our four authors, the reconciliation of true Shiʿism and true Sufism necessarily implies dissociation from the forms of Shiʿism and Sufism considered to be false. These false forms of Shiʿism are Ismailism and 'exaggeration' (*ghuluww*), the latter notion including any and all forms of heterodoxy (anti-Sunni positions, messianism, divinisation of the imam, pretension to the vision of God), especially those from whom our authors intend to dissociate themselves. These false forms of Sufism comprise the organisational aspect of the brotherhoods, the *ṭarīqa* as a social and historical institution, and antinomianism (*ibāḥiyya*), in other words the rejection of the obligations of Law (*sharīʿa*) by those who claim having acquired the knowledge of the ultimate Truth (*ḥaqīqa*).[116]

It is well known that Shiʿi scholars have for the major part prevented mystical schools of thought from organising themselves into brotherhoods or congregations: probably, as Corbin affirms, because Imami Shiʿism considers itself the spiritual path;[117] and probably also because the doctors of Shiʿi law, whose organisation was comparable to that of a veritable clergy during the Safawid era, were intent on maintaining total hegemony over Shiʿi society. It is noteworthy that while none of our defenders of reconciliation explicitly condemns the materialisation of the *ṭarīqa* in brotherhoods, they all, with the notable exception of Shūshtarī, denominate as 'true Sufis' – who are by this definition also 'true Shiʿis' – only spiritual masters who predate the foundation of the first brotherhoods. The exclusion is thus implicit.

In contrast, the explicit condemnation of licentious and antinomian Sufis was commonplace, and even a compulsory exercise for the gnostic philosophers of Safawid Iran, the latter always being suspected of deviant sympathies.[118] The formulation of Ashkiwarī is interesting in that it combines philosophical speculation with traditional arguments, from both Shiʿi and Sufi authorities. Thus, he quotes

Junayd in order to assert that the connection with the divine (*wiṣāl*) does not spare one from respecting social and cultural obligations, that knowledge of the Path (*ṭarīqa*) does not exempt anyone from obeying the Law (*sharīʿa*), and that believing otherwise is tantamount to satanic imagination. Then, in his own words, Ashkiwarī develops the idea that the exterior forms (*ṣuwar*) of the cult are the '*loci* of manifestation' (*maẓāhir*) of the 'spiritual realities' (*al-maʿānī*). The dualist schema opposing true to false is here converted into a twofold schema which articulates the apparent with the hidden, the exoteric outermost (*ẓāhir*) with the esoteric innermost (*bāṭin*). Finally, he quotes a *ḥadīth* of Imam Jaʿfar taken from the *Kitāb al-Kāfī* of al-Kulaynī: 'God only approves an action made with knowledge, and only approves knowledge with action. Thus, to him who knows God, knowledge shows the action. He who does not act has no knowledge. However, in faith, the one comes from the other.'[119] The correlation between knowledge and action is also an axial principle of philosophy or wisdom (*ḥikma*) in the sense of the ancient Greeks that Ashkiwarī reactivates in the first part of his *Maḥbūb al-qulūb*.[120] It is the correlation between the apparent and the hidden, the physical action and the spiritual state of being, that appears to Ashkiwarī as the common vocation of Imami Shiʿism, Sufism and philosophy.

This principle of the unity of knowledge and action leads Ashkiwarī to distance himself both from legalist or literalist lawyer-theologians on the one hand and from licentious or passive mystics on the other. Both criticisms echo one another: as he expresses in his notice devoted to Shihāb al-Dīn al-Suhrawardī (d. 587/1191), 'the murdered master' (*al-shaykh al-maqtūl*), just as antinomian dervishes do not deserve the title of Sufi, doctors of the law condemning rational sciences and the spiritual Path usurp the title of *fuqahāʾ*.[121] Expounding an original exegesis of the last verse of the sura *al-Fātiḥa*, Ashkiwarī identifies 'those who earned [God's] anger' (*al-maghḍūb ʿalayhim*) with Sufis discarding exoteric religious law in the name of their knowledge of spiritual truths (*ḥaqāʾiq*), and 'those who went astray' (*al-ḍāllīn*) with the doctors who reject spiritual Truth and esoteric science in the name of the letter of the Law.[122]

To conclude this second analysis, it seems that for our thinkers the transcendental unity between the Law, the Path, and the spiritual

Truth implies the conciliation of Shiʿism and Sufism under the auspices of philosophical gnosis. The more the defence of this thesis appears marginalised and of little account, the more the issue becomes all important, since ultimately the survival of Sufism depends on it, as does the place of philosophy in a Shiʿi state.

The Linguistic Argumentation: The Analogy of Imams' and Sufis' 'language-games'

Our authors employ a further, and noteworthy, mode of argument. It is founded neither on traditional authority, nor indeed on rigorous conceptions, but on the similarities or the analogies between certain types of discourse, Shiʿi or Sufi, which I will refer to, borrowing Ludwig Wittgenstein's expression, as 'language-games.'[123] The strategy is to highlight parallels and consonances between certain particularly esoteric declarations made by the imams and some of the most paradoxical statements of the Sufis. The first language-game pertains to certain sermons during which the imam proclaims his own divinity and goes so far as to verbally identify himself with God, which M.A. Amir-Moezzi technically qualifies as 'theo-imamosophical' sermons.[124] These declarations have played a crucial role within Shiʿism: on the one hand they may well have given rise to the branches of Shiʿism associated with 'extremism' or 'exaggeration' (*ghulāt*) – the exaggeration residing not in *what* is said regarding the divine status of the imam, but in that it *is* said, and hence implies a break with the discipline of the arcane, or *taqiyya* –; and on the other hand, the preservation or the censorship of these sermons distinguishes the Shiʿis who have remained attached to this original tradition from the rationalist Shiʿi scholars. The second language-game is that of the *shaṭaḥāt*, or 'paradoxes of the Sufis', those famous ecstatic utterances in which the Sufi speaks in the name of God, or God speaks through the mouth of the Sufi, and which Louis Massignon translates as 'theopathic locutions.'[125] Basṭāmī and Ḥallāj are two of their most illustrious authors. These phrases have been the object of countless condemnations, emanating from both Sunnis and Shiʿis, and even from certain Sufis such as al-Hujwīrī (d. 465/1071), Ibn ʿArabī or al-Jurjānī (d. 816/1413).[126] Yet, in a bold gesture, Ḥaydar Āmulī identifies the *shaṭaḥāt* with the theo-imamosophical sermons of Imam ʿAlī:

> An individual, when he contemplates True-God (*al-ḥaqq*) in the light of True-God, knows only one station which is the station of his extinction within Him, called 'extinction of the knower in the known', or 'extinction of the contemplator in the contemplated', or 'extinction of the servant in the Lord', etc. This can only proceed from lifting the duality of the simple point of view, the disappearance of creational multiplicity, and the vanishing of egoity which prevent true connection. As one of them [Ḥallāj] declared regarding this spiritual station (*maqām*): 'Between You and I, my I holds me back/ By your grace, remove my I from the interval!' As says another: 'When poverty is perfected, he is God.' As says another [Basṭāmī]: Glory to you, how great is my cause!' As says another [Ḥallāj]: 'I am True-God' (*anā'l-ḥaqq*). As says our Guide and Master, the Pole of the lords of divine unicity, the Prince of the believers, [Imam ʿAlī]: 'I am the face of God, I am the flank of God, I am the hand of God, I am the proof of God, I am the First and the Last, I am the Manifest and the Concealed.'[127]

For Ḥaydar Āmulī, a Shiʿi first and foremost, Sufi masters and imams are doubtless not on an equal footing: the Sufi momentarily attains identity with God at the culmination of the contemplative exercise whereas the imam is the actual manifestation of the Science and of the Power of God.[128] The semantic and phenomenological comparison between the ecstatic verbalisations of the Sufis and the self-glorifying sermons of the imams does not imply that they are ontologically equivalent, but suggests that, through his own effort and then only intermittently, the Sufi can say what the imam says, the latter by virtue of his very essence. The fact remains that the interpretation proffered by Ḥaydar Āmulī with regard to these utterances, and which was subsequently echoed by Ibn Abī Jumhūr and Ashkiwarī, bestow qualities on the Sufi that Imami orthodoxy normally attributes exclusively to imams.

Our thinkers Ḥaydar Āmulī and then Ibn Abī Jumhūr, also record certain mystical *ḥadīth*s of Imam ʿAlī, on the topics of love (*ḥubb*, *ʿishq*), intoxication (*sukr*) and ecstasy (*ṭarab*, *wajd*). For example:

> God has a potation for His friends. When they drink it, they become intoxicated. When they are intoxicated, they go into a trance. When they go into a trance, they better themselves. When they better themselves, they melt. When they melt, they purify

> themselves. When they purify themselves, they seek. When they seek, they find. When they find, they join. When they join, they connect themselves. When they connect themselves, there is no difference between them and their loved one.[129]

Here also, these conceptions are frequently taxed with exaggeration (*ghuluww*) in Shiʿi circles.[130] The analogy which this tradition suggests between esoteric Shiʿism and ecstatic or 'intoxicated' Sufism is probably the reason why it is rejected by most traditionalists – since it does not appear in the authoritative literature –, but it is probably also the reason why it is adopted by Ḥaydar Āmulī, Ibn Abī Jumhūr or even Fayḍ al-Kāshānī. It enables Ibn Abī Jumhūr to justify the ecstatic discourse of the Sufis Basṭāmī and Ḥallāj. His philosophical exegesis is reiterated word for word by Ashkiwarī in his apology of Ḥallāj:

> Ibn Jumhūr (sic), hallowed be his secret, declared, in his book *al-Mujlī*, that the soul, when it is united to certain immaterial lights during certain furtive occasions and is stripped of its body, through the power of intellectual delectations and spiritual elations which adhere to it, through the intensity of the shining auroras, retires from its essence and from the conscience of its essence. The sovereign of the immaterial and intellectual lights takes hold of it and it then disappears from its own essence (*tafnā ʿan dhātihā*). They describe this state as 'unification' (*ittiḥād*). When the traveller towards God reaches this station, that the weaker light is extinguished in that which is more powerful and intense, that [traveller] is drunken from the pleasures of the victorial lights, that these immaterial lights became the *loci* of manifestation where rational minds unite, then this soul is in such a state that it only sees the *locus* of manifestation, and speaks only with the language of this *locus* of manifestation. Till the point where al-Ḥusayn al-Ḥallāj, who had reached this station, prayed to God and said to Him: 'O Lord, my "I" is holding me back, lift hence through your "It is I" my "it is I"!' God granted his prayer and said: 'I am True-God'.[131]

For Ashkiwarī, the defence of Sufi *shaṭaḥāt* in the name of the ascendancy of mystical states of being can justify certain forms of antinomianism. In this state of mystical intoxication, he writes, 'the pilgrim on the path of God leaves the sphere of prescription and the domain of reason (*az dā'ira-yi taklīf wa tūr-i ʿaql bīrūn uftād*); his heart can no longer respect the seemly practices prescribed by the Saint [the Prophet]; however in this state, the abandonment of right behaviour is the right behaviour in itself (*tark-i adab ʿayn-i adab bāshad*).'[132] The apparent antinomianism, on the exoteric level, could mask, on the esoteric level, an inner comprehension and a superior respect of the Law. Ashkiwarī concludes with a call for tolerance with regard to the ecstatic utterings of the Sufis, quoting a verse in Persian of Jalāl al-Dīn Rūmī (d. 672/1273):

> If men, drunk from the pure beverage of union, express themselves, in this drunkenness and this spiritual state, in such a way that, if compared to the learned and lucid people of the schools, they might appear a wrong behaviour (*sū'-i adab*), one must nevertheless not admonish them. In consideration of the place and the state from which they speak, one must be accepting and seek no quarrel.
>
> Forgive him, whom You have intoxicated and then deprived, if he strays due to his drunkenness (*mastī*).[133]

This is without a doubt our Shiʿi authors' boldest defence of Sufism, for this 'intoxicated Sufism' hailed by Ḥallāj was generally abhorred by their lawyer-theologians. This is in all likelihood the reason why all four support, regardless of the overwhelming evidence, the historical affiliation of Abū Yazīd al-Basṭāmī to Imam Jaʿfar, since Basṭāmī is the father of this form of ecstatic Sufism, which reached its climax with Ḥallāj. The two later thinkers of our study, Shūshtarī and Ashkiwarī, are also eager to show that Ḥallāj was Shiʿi. My hypothesis is that the pseudo-'Shiʿitisation' of these historical figures is a tactic which aims to defend ecstatic Sufism and its theopathic locutions, and this defence is itself devised in order to ultimately pave the way for the new experiences and new ecstatic utterances of the Gnostics (*ʿurafā'*) like Ashkiwarī's first master Mīr Dāmād.[134] It is worth noting that the specialist *par excellence* of the Ḥallāj dossier, Louis Massignon, classifies Ashkiwarī as 'pro-Ḥallājian' and isolated in the midst of the rationalist (*uṣūlī*) clergy.[135] This begs the following question: could one be both pro-Ḥallājian and *faqīh uṣūlī*? It seems rather that this defensive stance was emblematic of the resistance of the original, non-rational and esoteric form of Shiʿism, against the rise in power of the rationalist *uṣūlī*, without ever becoming an *akhbārī* discourse.

Conclusion

The works of these four authors thus form a coherent intellectual system, which serves a cause both spiritual and political: the peaceable and fertile coexistence between Twelver Shiʿism, Sufism and gnostic philosophy. Notwithstanding the apparent repetition of the same discourse, the originality of each work in its particular historical context is apparent, both in the differing emphasis placed on particular modes of argumentation and in the development or elision of different elements of information. Whereas the first authors in this tradition of reconciliation were confident of its own true orthodoxy, later authors had progressively to come to terms with its minority status and marginality. Given subsequent history, from a contemporary perspective the reconciliation attempted by our thinkers is between the most esoteric forms of Shiʿism and Sufism, the first frequently accused of exaggeration by the Shiʿis themselves, and the second equally repudiated by a great number of Sufis. In other words, and not least paradoxically, it is a synthesis of heterodoxies which has been elevated here to a veritable intellectual tradition.

NOTES

1 Concerning the 'Sufi question' in Imami Shiʿism, see Nasrollah Pourjavady, 'Opposition to Sufism in Twelver Shiism', in Frederik de Jong and Bernd Radtke, ed., *Islamic Mysticism Contested. Thirteen Centuries of Controversies and Polemics* (Leiden, 1999), pp. 614–623; during the Safawid era specifically, see Said Amir Arjomand, *The Shadow of God and the Hidden Imam* (Chicago and London, 1984), pp. 112–119; ʿAbd al-Ḥusayn Zarrīnkūb, *Dunbālah-yi justujū dar taṣawwuf-i Īrān* (Tehran, 1389 Sh./2010), in particular pp. 223–266; Leonard Lewisohn, 'Sufism and the School of Iṣfahān: *Taṣawwuf* and *'Irfān* in Late Safavid Iran ('Abd al-Razzāq Lāhījī and Fayḍ-i Kāshānī on the Relation of *Taṣawwuf, Ḥikmat* and *'Irfān*)', in Leonard Lewisohn and David Morgan, ed., *The Heritage of Sufism* (Oxford, 1999), vol. 3, pp. 67–77; Kathryn Babayan, *Mystics, Monarchs, and Messiahs, Cultural Landscapes of Early Modern Iran* (London, 2002), pp. 403–437.

2 Concerning the reinstatement of the Niʿmat Allāhī in Iran in the12th/18th century, see Fabrizio Speziale, 'À propos du renouveau *niʿmatullāhī*. Le centre de Hyderabad au cours de la première modernité', *Studia Iranica* 42 (2013), pp. 91–118, and his chapter in this volume.

3 One can find a revivified version of this discourse, with references to the works and authors mentioned in this article, in the historical encyclopaedia of Sufism written by an eminent member of the Niʿmat Allāhī order, Maʿṣūm ʿAlī Shāh (d. 1344/1925–6), *Ṭarā'iq al-ḥaqā'iq* (Tehran, 1387 Sh./2008). This discourse is also recurrent in the works of Seyyed Hossein Nasr; e.g. S.H. Nasr, 'Le shîʿisme et le soufisme. Leurs relations principielles et historiques', in Toufic Fahd, ed., *Le shîʿisme imâmite* (Paris, 1970), pp. 215–233. See also Shahrām Pāzūkī, 'Bāzkāwī-yi tārīkhī-yi nizāʿ-i ṣūfiya wa fuqahā', in his *'Irfān wa hunar dar dawra-yi mudirn* (Tehran, 1393 Sh./2014–15), pp. 216–232.

4 Sayyid Ḥaydar Āmulī, *La philosophie shiʿite*, 1. Somme des doctrines ésotériques (*Jāmiʿ al-asrār*). 2. Traité de la connaissance de l'être (*Fī maʿrifat al-wujūd*), ed. H. Corbin and O. Yahia (Tehran and Paris, 1347 Sh./1968). On this thinker, see Khanjār ʿAlī Ḥamiya, *ʿIrfān-i shīʿī. Pazhūhishī dar bāb-i zindigī wa andīshah-yi Sayyid Ḥaydar-i Āmulī* (Tehran, 1392 Sh./2013); Mathieu Terrier, 'Āmulī, Sayyid Ḥaydar', in Henrik Lagerlund, ed., *Encyclopedia of Medieval Philosophy* (Dordrecht, 2018), online: https://doi.org/10.1007/978-94-024-1151-5_585-1. In this paper, I will also take into account two other works of this thinker: *al-Muḥīṭ al-aʿẓam wa'l-baḥr al-khiḍamm fī ta'wīl kitāb Allāh al-ʿazīz al-muḥkam*, ed. S.M. al-Mūsawī Tabrīzī (Qumm, 1414/1994–5), also ed. unknown (Beirut, 1433/2012); and his *Anwār al-ḥaqīqa wa aṭwār al-ṭarīqa wa asrār al-sharīʿa*, ed. S.M. al-Mūsawī Tabrīzī (Qumm, 1436/1394 Sh./2015–16); also known as *Asrār al-sharīʿa wa aṭwār al-ṭarīqa wa anwār al-ḥaqīqa*, ed. M. Khājawī (Tehran, 1362 Sh./1983). See below for their introduction.

5 Ibn Abī Jumhūr al-Aḥsā'ī, *Mujlī mir'at al-munjī fi'l-kalām wa'l-ḥikmatayn wa'l-taṣawwuf*, ed. R.Y. Fārmad (Beirut, 2013). This is the first critical edition of the book, thanks to a foundation devoted to the diffusion of the works of Ibn Abī Jumhūr, based on three manuscripts in addition to the earlier lithographic edition by Aḥmad al-Shīrāzī, reprinted with an introduction by Sabine Schmidtke (Tehran, 2009), and completed by references to the author's sources. On this thinker, see Mathieu Terrier, 'Ibn Abī Jumhūr al-Aḥsā'ī', *Encyclopedia of Medieval Philosophy*, online: https://doi.org/10.1007/978-94-024-1151-5_588-1. For the appointing of Ibn Abī Jumhūr's death date, see Fārmad's introduction to his edition of the *Mujlī*, p. 67.

6 Qāḍī Nūr Allāh Shūshtarī, *Majālis al-mu'minīn*, ed. I. ʿArabpūr, M. Sitāyish, M.R. Muḥammadyān et al. (7 vols., Mashhad, 1393 Sh./2014). This new edition is the first critical one, based on ten manuscripts, augmented and corrected by references to Shūshtarī's sources. The earlier, confusing edition from Intishārāt Islāmiyya (Tehran, 1335 Sh./1955; re-ed. 1391 Sh./2012) should also be mentioned.

7 Quṭb al-Dīn al-Ashkiwarī, *Maḥbūb al-qulūb, al-maqālat al-ʿūlā*, ed. I. al-Dībājī and H. Ṣidqī (Tehran, 1378 Sh./1999); *Maḥbūb al-qulūb, al-maqālat al-thāniya*, ed. I. al-Dībājī and H. Ṣidqī (Tehran, 1382 Sh./2003). The third part has not been published yet. On this work, see M. Terrier, 'Le *Maḥbūb al-qulūb* de Quṭb al-Dīn Ashkevarī, une œuvre méconnue dans l'histoire de l'histoire de la sagesse en islam', *J. Asiat.*, 298 (2010), pp. 345–387; 'Quṭb al-Dīn Ashkevarî, un philosophe discret de la renaissance safavide', *Studia Iranica*, 40 (2011), pp. 171–210; *Histoire de la sagesse et philosophie shiʿite. « L'Aimé des cœurs » de Quṭb al-Dīn Aškevarī* (Paris, 2016).

8 Ḥāfiẓ Rajab Bursī, *Mashāriq anwār al-yaqīn*, ed. A. al-Māzandarānī (Qumm, 1426/1384 Sh./2005–6); Shams al-Dīn Lāhījī, *Mafātīḥ al-iʿjāz fī sharḥ Gulshān-i rāz*, ed. M.R. Barzigar Khāliqī and I. Karbāsī (Tehran, 1391 Sh./2012–13).

9 In the introduction of his *Naṣṣ al-nuṣūṣ*, ed. H. Corbin and O. Yahia (Tehran and Paris, 1988), and now ed. M. Bīdārfar (Qumm, 1394 Sh./2015), p. 537 (C-Y), 853 (B), Ḥaydar Āmulī writes that he finished it in 782/1380 at the age of sixty-three. See Ḥamiya, *ʿIrfān-i shīʿī*, p. 8.

10 The date of his last work, *Risālat al-ʿulūm al-ʿāliyya*. See Corbin, introduction to Āmulī, *La philosophie shiʿite*, p. 20.

11 Ibid., pp. 5–76; Kāmil Muṣṭafā al-Shaybī, *al-Ṣila bayna'l-taṣawwuf wa'l-tashayyuʿ*, (2nd ed., Beirut, Baghdad and Freiberg, 2011), vol. 2, pp. 104–115. See also Ḥamiya, *ʿIrfān-i shīʿī*, pp. 38–41.

12 Corbin, introduction to Āmulī, *La philosophie shiʿite*, p. 17.

13 Āmulī, *Naṣṣ al-nuṣūṣ*, pp. 535–537 (C-Y), 851–853 (B); Abū Ḥāmid al-Ghazālī, *al-Munqidh min al-ḍalāl* (Deliverance from Error), ed. F. Jabre (Beirut, 1969). In both reports one can find the same claim of a split from the mundane world for a purely spiritual purpose, and the same silence on the possible political-mundane motives of this decision.

14 Corbin, introduction to Āmulī, *La philosophie shiʿite*, pp. 18–23; Corbin, *En Islam iranien* (Paris, 1971–1972), vol. 3, pp. 162–167.
15 See above, n. 4. Its composition was prior to that of the *Jāmiʿ al-asrār* as it mentions the latter, pp. 88 and 367.
16 *Rafʿ al-munāzaʿa waʾl-khilāf*, ed. Ḥ. Kalbāsī Ashtarī (Tehran, 1396 Sh./2017).
17 *Naṣṣ al-nuṣūṣ*, p. 3 and 148 (C-Y), 3 and 216 (B). Ibn ʿArabī says that the *Fuṣūṣ* had been given to him in a dream by the Prophet. See Ibn ʿArabī, *Fuṣūṣ al-ḥikam*, ed. A. ʿAfīfī (Beirut, 1423/2002), pp. 47–48.
18 Corbin, *En Islam iranien*, vol. 3, p. 155; and his *Histoire de la philosophie islamique* (Paris, 1986), *passim*.
19 See Daniel De Smet, 'Introduction to Part VIII: "Philosophy and Intellectual Traditions" ', in Farhad Daftary and Gurdofarid Miskinzoda, ed., *The Study of Shiʿi Islam* (London, 2104), pp. 545–562, and my *Histoire de la sagesse et philosophie shiʿite*, pp. 731–735.
20 See Jean Calmard, 'Le chiisme imamite sous les Ilkhans', in Denise Aigle, ed., *L'Iran face à la domination mongole* (Tehran, 1997), pp. 261–292, esp. p. 282; Monika Gronke, 'La religion populaire en Iran mongol', in *L'Iran face à la domination mongole*, pp. 205–207; Marijan Molé, 'Les Kubrawiya entre sunnisme et shiisme aux huitième et neuvième siècles de l'hégire', *Revue des Études Islamiques* (1961), pp. 61–142; Alessandro Bausani, 'Religion under the Mongols', in John A. Boyle, ed., *The Cambridge History of Iran*, vol. 5, *The Saljuq and Mongol Periods* (Cambridge, 1968), pp. 538–549.
21 Āmulī, *Jāmiʿ al-asrār*, p. 254; Corbin, Introduction, p. 25.
22 Āmulī, *Jāmiʿ al-asrār*, pp. 41 and 222.
23 Ibid., pp. 32–33, 36–37, 39 and 600; Corbin, Introduction, pp. 27–29. On this *ḥadīth*, see Mohammad Ali Amir-Moezzi, *Le guide divin dans le shîʿisme originel* (Paris, 1992–2007), pp. 144, 278 and 328–330.
24 al-Shaybī proposes 838/1435.
25 The first option has the favour of Fārmad in his introduction to Ibn Abī Jumhūr, *Mujlī*, vol. 1, p. 65; the second one has those of al-Shaybī, *al-Ṣila*, vol. 2, p. 312, of Ṣamad Mowaḥḥed, 'Ibn Abī Jumhūr', in Kāẓim Mūsawī Bujnūrdī, ed., *Daʾīrat al-maʿārif-i buzurg-i islāmī*, (Tehran, 1367 Sh./1988), vol. 2, p. 635, and of Todd Lawson, 'Ebn Abī Jomhūr Aḥsāʾī', *EIR*, vol. 7, p. 662.
26 Fārmad, Introduction to *Mujlī*, vol. 1, pp. 65–67.
27 On this work, see Āqā Buzurg al-Ṭihrānī, *al-Dharīʿa ilā taṣānīf al-shīʿa* (25 vols., Tehran and Najaf, 1353–1398/1934–1978), vol. 20, p. 13, n.1726; Wilferd Madelung, 'Ibn Abī Jumhūr al-Aḥsāʾī's Synthesis of Kalām, Philosophy and Sufism', in *La signification du Bas Moyen Âge dans l'histoire et la culture du monde musulman* (Aix-en-Provence, 1978), pp. 147–156; Sabine Schmidtke, *Theologie, Philosophie und Mystik im zwölferschiitischen Islam des 9./15. Jahrhunderts. Die Gedankenwelten des Ibn Abî Ǧumhûr al-Aḥsâʾî (um 838/1434–35 – nach 906/1501)* (Leiden, 2000).
28 Ibn Abī Jumhūr composed a first epistle entitled *Maslak al-afhām fī ʿilm al-kalām* in 886/1482; then in the margins of it, a commentary entitled *al-Nūr al-munjī min al-ẓalām* in 893/1488; and finally a commentary on this commentary, the *Mujlī mirʾāt al-munjī*, achieved in 896/1490. See S. Schmidtke, introduction to the lithographic edition of the *Mujlī*, pp. iv–v, and Fārmad, introduction to Ibn Abī Jumhūr, *Mujlī*, vol. 1, pp. 85–86.
29 Ibn Abī Jumhūr, *Mujlī*, vol. 1, pp. 134–135.
30 Bausani, 'Religion under the Mongols', p. 546.
31 Al-Shaybī, *Ṣila*, vol. 2, p. 313. About the role of al-Karakī, see Arjomand, *Shadow of God*, pp. 133–137 and 140–142; Rula Jurdi Abisaab, *Converting Persia. Religion and Power in Safavid Empire* (London and New York, 2004), pp. 15–20; Andrew J. Newman, *Safavid Iran* (London and New York, 2006), *passim*.
32 Al-Shaybī, *Ṣila*, vol. 2, p. 319.
33 Muḥammad Bāqir al-Majlisī, *Biḥār al-anwār*, ed. J. al-ʿAlawī et al. (111 vols., Tehran, 1376–1405/1957–1985), vol. 10, pp. 183–184; Mīrzā ʿAbd Allāh al-Iṣbahānī Afandī,

Riyāḍ al-ʿulamāʾ, quoted by Muḥsin al-Amīn in *Aʿyān al-Shīʿa* (Beirut, 1406/1986), vol. 9, p. 434; see also al-Ḥurr al-ʿĀmilī, *al-Risāla al-ithnāʿashariyya fi'l-radd ʿalā al-ṣūfiyya*, ed. A. al-Jalālī (Qumm, 1390 Sh./2011), p. 32.

34 *ʿAwālī al-laʾālī* (Qumm, 1404/1983), preface by Ayatollah Shihāb al-Dīn al-Ḥusaynī al-Marʿashī al-Najafī, pp. 4–5; al-Shaybī, *Ṣila*, vol. 1, p. 314; Muwaḥḥid, 'Ibn Abī Jumhūr', pp. 635–636. Even Maʿṣūm ʿAlī Shah, in the laudatory notice he devotes to him, criticises his lack of reliability as a traditionist: see Maʿsūm ʿAlī Shāh, *Ṭarāʾiq al-ḥaqāʾiq*, vol. 1, p. 249.

35 Shūshtarī, *Majālis*, vol. 1, introduction of the editors, pp. 195–198; vol. 3, p. 456 for the account of his grandfather's affiliation; vol. 4, pp. 374–388, for a hyper-eulogistic notice on Muḥammad Nūrbakhsh (d. 869/1464) and his son Shāh Qāsim. See also Zarrīnkūb, *Dunbālah-yi justujū*, p. 186.

36 Maʿṣūm ʿAlī Shāh, *Ṭarāʾiq al-ḥaqāʾiq*, vol. 1, p. 254; Arjomand, *Shadow of God*, p. 115.

37 Shūshtarī, *Majālis*, vol. 1, introduction of the editors, pp. 156–173.

38 al-Amīn, *Aʿyān al-Shīʿa*, vol. 10, pp. 228–229, quoting from al-Ḥurr al-ʿĀmilī, *Amal al-ʿĀmil.*

39 Corbin, *Histoire de la philosophie islamique*, p. 441.

40 On this title, see Maʿṣūm ʿAlī Shāh, *Ṭarāʾiq al-ḥaqāʾiq*, vol. 2, p. 253.

41 Ṭihrānī, *Dharīʿa*, vol. 19, n.1652, pp. 370–371.

42 Shūshtarī, *Majālis*, vol. 1, p. 29; Tehran ed., vol. 1, p. 10.

43 Ibid., vol. 1, pp. 8–9; Tehran ed., vol. 1, pp. 4–5.

44 This includes, among cases less contested, Abū Ḥāmid al-Ghazālī and Muḥyī al-Dīn Ibn ʿArabī. See Shūshtarī, *Majālis*, vol. 4, pp. 480–503; Tehran ed., vol. 2, pp. 191–201, for the former; ibid., vol. 4, pp. 196–212 for the latter; Tehran ed., vol. 2, pp. 61–69.

45 Mīrzā ʿAbd Allāh al-Isbahānī, quoted by al-Amīn, *Aʿyān al-Shīʿa* (Beirut, 1406/1986) vol. 10, p. 229.

46 Al-Shaybī, *Ṣila*, vol. 1, pp. 224–246, on the historical relations between Sufi masters and Shiʿi imams, refers to Maʿṣūm ʿAlī Shāh, *Ṭarāʾiq al-ḥaqāʾiq*, himself quoting Shūshtarī's *Majālis*; Nasr, 'Le shīʿisme et le soufisme', notably p. 226 where the author does not quote his source; Calmard, 'Le chiisme imamite sous les Ilkhans', p. 261, n.1 and *passim*.

47 Among the anti-Sufi treatises from this period: attributed to the chief of the Akhbāriyya, Aḥmad al-Ardabīlī (d. 993/1585), *Ḥadīqat al-shīʿa*, ed. S. Ḥasanzādah (Qumm, 1377 Sh./1998); al-Ḥurr al-ʿĀmilī, *al-Risāla al-ithnā ʿashariyya* (Qumm, 1390 Sh./2011); Muḥammad Ṭāhir b. Muḥammad Ḥusayn Qummī, *Tuḥfat al-akhyār* (Qumm, 1973).

48 Āmulī, *Jāmiʿ al-asrār*, p. 40.

49 Ibid., p. 41.

50 On *ghuluww* and the *ghulāt* ('exaggerators'), see Marshall G.S. Hodgson, 'Ghulāt', *EI2*, vol. 2, pp. 1119–1121; Amir-Moezzi, *Guide divin*, pp. 313–317.

51 See Giorgio Levi Della Vida, 'Salmān al-Fārisī', *EI2*, vol. 12, Supplement, pp. 701–702.

52 See Julian Baldick, 'Uways al-Ḳaranī', *EI2*, French ed., vol. 10, p. 1035.

53 Āmulī, *Jāmiʿ al-asrār*, pp. 614–615.

54 On the technical meaning and the late appearance of the appellation Twelver Shiʿi, see Etan Kohlberg, 'Early attestations of the term "*ithnā ʿashariyya*"', *JSAI* 24 (2000), pp. 343–357; Amir-Moezzi, *Guide divin*, pp. 247–248.

55 Levi Della Vida, 'Salmān al-Fārisī'; al-Shaybī, *Ṣila*, vol. 1, pp. 29–37.

56 Majlisī, *Biḥār al-anwār* (henceforth: Beirut 1403/1983), vol. 10, p. 123; vol. 17, p. 170; vol. 18, p. 19; vol. 22, p. 326. Āmulī, *Jāmiʿ al-asrār*, pp. 25 and 500. On this *ḥadīth*, see Louis Massignon, 'Salman Pak et les prémices spirituelles de l'Islam iranien', in *Opera minora* (Paris 1969), vol. 1, pp. 453–455, esp. 443–483.

57 Amir-Moezzi, *Guide divin*, p. 232, n.478. Bursī, *Mashāriq anwār al-yaqīn* (Qumm, 1384/2005–6), p. 428, records that Salmān was the man with greatest knowledge of God (*aʿraf bi'llāh*) because he was the man with greatest knowledge of ʿAlī.

58 A whole chapter of the *Biḥār al-anwār* is devoted to them: vol. 22, *bāb* 10, pp. 315–355.

59 al-Shaybī, *Ṣila*, vol. 1, pp. 37–50 and 55–57; James Robson, 'Abu Dharr al-Ghifārī', *EI2*, French ed., vol. 1, p. 118; Hermann Reckendorf, "Ammār ibn Yāsir', *EI2*, French ed., vol. 1, p. 461; G.H.A. Juynboll, 'al-Mikdād ibn ʿAmr', *EI2*, French ed., vol. 7, pp. 32–33. Their loyalty to ʿAlī after the death of the Prophet and the '*coup d'état*' of Saqīfa is stressed in *Kitāb Sulaym b. Qays al-Kūfī* or *Kitāb al-saqīfa* (Beirut, n.d.), esp. pp. 75–76, 81 and 128. On this book expressing the genuine Shiʿi perception of history, see Mohammad Ali Amir-Moezzi, *Le Coran silencieux et le Coran parlant* (Paris, 2011), chapter 1, pp. 27–61; see also Maria Massi Dakake, 'Writing and Resistance: The Transmission of Religious Knowledge in Early Shiʿism', in *The Study of Shʿi Islam*, pp. 181–201.

60 Muḥammad b. Yaʿqūb Kulaynī, *Uṣūl al-Kāfī* (Beirut, 1426/2005), *Kitāb al-ḥujja, bāb fī mā jā'a anna ḥadīthanā ṣaʿb mustaṣʿab*, pp. 238–239; Āmulī, *Jāmiʿ al-asrār*, p. 34; Majlisī, *Biḥār al-anwār*, vol. 22, p. 343.

61 Ibn Abī Jumhūr, *Mujlī*, p. 1245.

62 Hellmut Ritter, 'al-Ḥasan al-Baṣrī', *EI2*, French ed., vol. 3, pp. 254–255.

63 E.g. Majlisī, *Biḥār al-anwār*, vol. 35, p. 59; vol. 38, pp. 101–102, quoted from Shaykh Ṣadūq's *Āmālī*, for the first case; ibid., vol. 6, pp. 65 and 91; vol. 24, p. 232, quoted from al-Ṭabarsī's *Iḥtijāj*, for the second.

64 Āmulī, *Jāmiʿ al-asrār*, pp. 4, 223–224.

65 Ibn Khaldūn, *Muqaddima* (Beirut, 1426/2005), pp. 282–283; *Le livre des exemples* (Paris, 2002), p. 671. Al-Shaybī, *Ṣila*, vol. 1, pp. 86–87, and Nasr, 'Le shīʿisme et le soufisme', p. 217, quote this passage as a confirmation of the historical link between Shiʿism and Sufism, something which obviously distorts Ibn Khaldūn's intention.

66 On Ḥasan al-Baṣrī's Sunni positions, see Louis Massignon, *La Passion de Husayn ibn Mansûr Hallâj* (4 vols., Paris, 1975, vol. 1, pp. 195, 376, 520; vol. 3, pp. 172, 203, 223.

67 Farīd al-Dīn ʿAṭṭār, *Tadhkirat al-awliyā'*, ed. R.A. Nicholson (Tehran 1378 Sh./1999), pp. 81–85; 412–413.

68 J. Baldick, 'Uwaysiyya', *EI2*, French ed., vol. 10, pp. 1035–1036; Corbin, *En islam iranien*, vol. 1, p. 264; ibid., vol. 4, pp. 453–454; H. Corbin, *L'imagination créatrice dans le soufisme d'Ibn ʿArabî* (2d ed. Paris, 2006), pp. 32–33. Abū Yazīd Basṭāmī and Farīd al-Dīn ʿAṭṭār may be considered as Uwaysī, according to traditions expressed by ʿAṭṭār.

69 Shūshtarī, *Majālis*, vol. 2, pp. 408–419, Tehran ed., vol. 1, pp. 279–283.

70 Ibid., vol. 2, pp. 412–414; Tehran ed., vol. 1, pp. 280–281. It is notable that Shūshtarī also considered ʿAṭṭār to be a Shiʿa practising *taqiyya* under duress.

71 Ashkiwarī, *Maḥbūb*, vol. 2, pp. 493–494; Shūshtarī, *Majālis*, vol. 2, pp. 417–418; Tehran ed. vol. 1, pp. 282–283.

72 About Kumayl in Shiʿi traditions, see ʿAbbās al-Qummī, *Safīnat al-biḥār* (8 vols., Tehran, 1373 Sh./1994), vol. 7, pp. 538–539, referring to numerous *loci* of the *Biḥār al-anwār*. About the *silsila kumayliyya*, see Maʿṣūm ʿAlī Shāh, *Ṭarā'iq al-ḥaqā'iq*, vol. 2, pp. 83–108. About Kumayl for the Nūrbakhshiyya, see Shūshtarī, *Majālis*, vol. 2, p. 11.

73 Āmulī, *Jāmiʿ al-asrār*, pp. 28–29; see the translation and the commentary on this tradition by Corbin, *En Islam iranien*, vol. 1, pp. 110–112. Ibn Abī Jumhūr, *Mujlī*, pp. 481, a fragment only; Shūshtarī, *Majālis*, vol. 4, pp. 28–30; Tehran ed., vol. 2, pp. 10–11; Ashkiwarī, *Maḥbūb*, vol. 2, pp. 497–498. See also Lāhījī, *Mafātīḥ al-iʿjāz*, pp. 247–248.

74 For a famous modern formulation of the latter idea, see Ludwig Wittgenstein, *Tractatus logico-philosophicus*, French trans. by G-G. Granger (Paris, 1993), prop. 7, p. 112.

75 Shūshtarī, *Majālis*, vol. 4, p. 31; Tehran ed., vol. 2, p. 12; Ashkiwarī, *Maḥbūb*, vol. 2, p. 498.

76 The relater of the *ḥadīth* could be al-Mughīra b. Saʿīd al-Ijlī (d. 119/737), one of the most famous disciples of the fifth imam considered as *ghulāt*. See Abū ʿAmr Muḥammad al-Kashshī, *Rijāl al-Kashshī*, ed. S. Aḥmad al-Ḥusaynī (Beirut, 1430/2009), pp. 164–167.

77 Shūshtarī, *Majālis*, vol. 4, p. 58; Tehran ed., vol. 2, p. 24.
78 Maʿṣūm ʿAlī Shāh, *Ṭarāʾiq al-ḥaqāʾiq*, vol. 2, p. 109; al-Shaybī, *Ṣila*, vol. 2, pp. 472–473. This Sufi master is also said to have been affiliated to the sixth imam Jaʿfar al-Ṣādiq. See Maʿṣūm ʿAlī Shāh, *Ṭarāʾiq*, vol. 2, p. 109; Nasr, 'Le shīʿisme et le soufisme', p. 226.
79 Shūshtarī, *Majālis*, vol. 4, pp. 53–54; Tehran ed., vol. 2, p. 22.
80 Ibid., vol. 4, pp. 55–56; Tehran ed., vol. 2, p. 23.
81 Ibid., vol. 4, p. 50; Tehran ed., vol. 2, p. 21. Shūshtarī quoted it from a mysterious Nūr al-Dīn Jaʿfar al-Badakhshānī's *Kitāb al-aḥbāb*.
82 Ashkiwarī, *Maḥbūb*, vol. 2, pp. 517–518, for all the historical argumentation.
83 Amir-Moezzi, *Guide divin*, pp. 190–195.
84 Shūshtarī, *Majālis*, vol. 4, p. 57; Tehran ed., vol. 2, p. 24. See also al-Shaybī, *Ṣila*, vol. 1, p. 235, quoting al-Yaʿqūbī's *Taʾrīkh*, ed. M.S. Baḥr al-ʿUlūm (Najaf, 1384/1964).
85 Shūshtarī, *Majālis*, vol. 4, pp. 32–33; Tehran ed., vol. 2, p. 12; Ashkiwarī, *Maḥbūb*, vol. 2 p. 511. Al-Shaybī, *Ṣila*, vol. 2, p. 31, expresses his doubts about the authenticity of this event.
86 Shūshtarī, *Majālis*, vol. 4, pp. 65–67; Tehran ed., vol. 2, pp. 27–28; Ashkiwarī, *Maḥbūb*, vol. 2 p. 499; also resumed by Maʿṣūm ʿAlī Shāh, *Ṭarāʾiq*, vol. 2, p. 290.
87 Shūshtarī, *Majālis*, vol. 4, p. 67; Tehran ed., vol. 2, p. 28; ʿAttār, *Tadhkirat al-awliyā*, p. 365.
88 Āmulī, *Jāmiʿ al-asrār*, pp. 225, 431 and 614–615; Ibn Abī Jumhūr, *Mujlī*, pp. 1246 and 1262; Shūshtarī, *Majālis*, vol. 4, pp. 70–71; Tehran ed., vol. 2, p. 30.
89 Shūshtarī, *Majālis*, vol. 4, p. 71; Tehran ed., vol. 2, pp. 30–31.
90 al-Shaybī, *Ṣila*, vol. 1, p. 245; Nasr, 'Le shīʿisme et le soufisme', p. 226.
91 al-Shaybī, *Ṣila*, vol. 1, pp. 244–245.
92 al-Ḥurr al-ʿĀmilī, *Ithnāʿashariyya*, p. 27.
93 This *ḥadīth* is quoted by Āmulī in the opening of his Qurʾanic *Taʾwīl al-Muḥīṭ al-aʿẓam*, I, p. 195 (Qumm, 1414/1994–5), p. 17 (Beirut, 1433/2012); also in his *Anwār al-ḥaqīqa* (Qumm, 1436/1394 Sh./2015–16), pp. 21 and 70, or *Asrār al-sharīʿa* (Tehran, 1362 Sh./1983), pp. 8 and 24; also in *Jāmiʿ al-asrār*, p. 346. It appears in Ibn Abī Jumhūr's controversial collection of *ḥadīth*s, *ʿAwālī al-laʾālī*, 4, pp. 124–125, §212; also in his *Mujlī*, p. 1073. But this is absent from the *Biḥār al-anwār*, something which suggests that it is not related by a Shiʿi imam but rather appeared in a Sufi-Sunni milieu.
94 Āmulī, *Anwār al-ḥaqīqa* (Qumm, 1394 Sh./2015), pp. 99–100; or *Asrār al-sharīʿa* (Tehran, 1362 Sh./1983), pp. 31–32.
95 Āmulī, *Anwār al-ḥaqīqa*, pp. 106–107; or *Asrār al-sharīʿa*, pp. 35–36; the saying of ʿAlī is also quoted in *Jāmiʿ al-asrār*, pp. 358–359.
96 Ibn Abī Jumhūr, *Mujlī*, p. 1072; Āmulī, *Jāmiʿ al-asrār*, pp. 14, 41 and 344; quoted by Ashkiwarī, *Maḥbūb al-qulūb*, vol. 2, p. 486.
97 e.g. Q 2:179, 197 and 269; 3:7 and 190; and *Aflūṭīn ʿind al-ʿarab*, ed. A. Badawī (Cairo, 1955; second ed. Kuwait, 1977), pp. 32, 99–100.
98 al-Imām al-Shahrastānī, *Kitāb al-Milal wa'l-niḥal*, ed. M. Badran (Cairo, 1375/1956), vol. 2, p. 74 for Empedocles, p. 160 for Proclus.
99 ʿAbd al-Razzāq al-Qāshānī, *Iṣṭilāḥāt al-ṣūfiyya*, ed. ʿĀṣim al-Kayālī (Beirut, 2005), p. 68.
100 The couple *qishr, lubb* is at least absent from al-Majlisi's *Biḥār al-anwār*.
101 Mohammad Ali Amir-Moezzi and Christian Jambet, *Qu'est-ce que le shîʿisme?* (Paris, 2004), pp. 31–35.
102 *Aflūṭīn ʿind al-ʿarab*, p. 84.
103 See Ignaz Goldziher, *Le dogme et la loi dans l'islam* (Paris, 1920–2005), p. 146; Corbin, *Histoire de la philosophie islamique*, p. 264; Éric Geoffroy, *Le soufisme. Voie intérieure de l'islam* (Paris, 2003), pp. 95–104.
104 Ibn Abī Jumhūr, *Mujlī*, p. 1078.
105 Āmulī, *Jāmiʿ al-asrār*, p. 346.
106 Ibid., pp. 384–385.

107 Ibid., pp. 346–347.
108 Ibn Abī Jumhūr, *Mujlī*, pp. 1080–1081.
109 Ashkiwarī, *Maḥbūb*, vol. 2, p. 486; Ibn Abī Jumhūr, *Mujlī*, p. 1081.
110 É. Geoffroy, 'L'apparition des voies: les *khirqa* primitives (XIIe siècle – début XIIIe siècle)', in Alexandre Popovic and Gilles Veinstein, ed., *Les Voies d'Allah* (Paris, 1996), p. 45.
111 E.g. *En islam iranien*, vol. 3, pp. 153 and 156.
112 Nasr, 'Le shīʿisme et le soufisme', pp. 220–221.
113 Ibn Abī Jumhūr, *Mujlī*, pp. 1245–1246; this passage is quoted by Maʿṣūm ʿAlī Shāh, *Ṭarāʾiq*, vol. 1, pp. 525–526.
114 Ibn Abī Jumhūr, *Mujlī*, pp. 1257–1258; Nasr, 'Le shīʿisme et le soufisme', pp. 221–222.
115 Amir-Moezzi and Jambet, *Qu'est-ce que le shîʿisme?* pp. 36–40.
116 On this topic, see Hamid Algar, '*Ebāḥīya* (or *Ebāḥatīya*)', *EIR*; Alexandre Papas, 'Antinomianism (*ibāḥa, ibāḥiyya*)', *EI3*.
117 To summarise one of Corbin's arguments in *Histoire de la philosophie islamique*, pp. 55–58; *En islam iranien*, vol. 2, p. 11.
118 E.g. Ashkiwarī, *Maḥbūb*, vol. 2, pp. 489–490, and vol. 1, p. 73, in his autobiography. See M. Terrier, 'Apologie du soufisme par un philosophe shīʿite de l'Iran safavide. Nouvelles remarques sur le *Maḥbūb al-qulūb* d'Aškevarī', *Stud. Islam.*, 109 (2014), pp. 248–252, for the first part; *Histoire de la sagesse et philosophie shiʿite*, pp. 77–78 and 98, for the second part.
119 Ashkiwarī, *Maḥbūb*, vol. 2, p. 490. Kulaynī, *Uṣūl al-Kāfī, Kitāb faḍl al-ʿilm, bāb man ʿamila bi-ghayr ʿilm*, p. 29.
120 See Terrier, *Histoire de la sagesse et philosophie shiʿite*; Pierre Hadot, *Qu'est-ce que la philosophie antique?* (Paris, 1995).
121 Ashkiwarī, *Maḥbūb*, vol. 2, p. 349.
122 Ibid., p. 492. It is worth pointing out that Rajab Bursī interprets the former as the Sunnis and the latter as the *ghulāt*. See Ḥāfiẓ Rajab Bursī, *al-Durr al-thāmin fī khamsamiʾa āya nuzilat fī mawlānā amīr al-muʾminīn*, ed. A. ʿAshūr (Beirut, 1424/2003), pp. 29–30.
123 This notion of language-game refers to the existence of practical rules, not to a lack of seriousness: L. Wittgenstein, *Investigations philosophiques*, French trans., F. Dastur et al. (Paris, 2004). On this, see P. Hadot, *Wittgenstein et les limites du langage* (Paris, 2004).
124 M.A. Amir-Moezzi, 'Aspects de l'imamologie duodécimaine I. Remarques sur la divinité de l'Imâm', *Studia Iranica*, 25 (1996), pp. 193–216, in *La religion discrète* (Paris, 2006), pp. 89–108; (in English) 'Some Remarks on the Divinity of the Imam', in *The Spirituality of Shiʿi Islam* (London, 2011), pp. 103–131, see p. 105.
125 On the *shaṭaḥāt*, see L. Massignon, *Essai sur les origines du lexique technique de la mystique musulmane* (Paris, 1922); *idem*, *Passion*, p. 319, Index, s.v. 'shath', 'shathîyât'; Corbin's introduction to Rūzbihān Baqlī Shīrāzī, *Sharḥ-i shaṭḥiyyāt*, ed. H. Corbin (Paris and Tehran, 1962, 2nd ed. 2004); Paul Nwyia, *Exégèse coranique et langage mystique* (Beirut, 1970); Carl Ernst, *Words of Ecstasy in Sufism* (New York, 1995).
126 Massignon, *Passion*, vol. 1, pp. 431–432; vol. 3, pp. 359–367; see the definition of *shaṭḥ* in ʿAlī b. Muḥammad al-Sharīf al-Jurjānī, *Kitāb al-Taʿrīfāt*, ed. G. Flügel (Leipzig, 1845), p. 132; on Ibn ʿArabī's position, see Pierre Lory, *La science des lettres en islam* (Paris, 2004), pp. 129–131.
127 Āmulī, *Jāmiʿ al-asrār*, pp. 364–365. See also p. 172, where Āmulī traces the parallel between a sermon of Imām ʿAlī addressed to Kumayl and an ecstatic speech by Ḥallāj. Rajab Bursī, *Mashāriq anwār al-yaqīn*, pp. 309–321, records these sermons in extensive versions.
128 Amir-Moezzi, *Guide divin*, p. 314.

129 Āmulī, *Jāmiʿ al-asrār*, pp. 363–364 and 676; *Anwār al-ḥaqīqa* (Qumm, 1436/1394 Sh. /2015–16), pp. 86–87; or *Asrār al-sharīʿa* (Tehran, 1362 Sh./1983), p. 28, where Āmulī brings this tradition together with the *shaṭaḥāt* of the Sufis under the station of 'extinction in the assumption of God's unity' (*al-fanāʾ fi'l-tawḥīd*); Ibn Abī Jumhūr, *Mujlī*, p. 1682. al-Shaybī, *Ṣila*, vol. 1, p. 241, makes an analogy with a passage in al-Ḥallāj's *Kitāb al-Ṭawāsīn*, ed. L. Massignon (Paris, 1913), see pp. 32–33.

130 Fayḍ Kāshānī, *Kalimāt maknūna*, ed. ʿA. al-Ḥ. Ḥājjī Abu'l-Ḥasanī (Tehran, 1390 Sh. /2011), pp. 185–186, quotes these traditions from *al-Mujlī*. In a footnote, the editor denounces the 'corruption' of these *ḥadīth*s and the influence of 'extremist Sufism' on Ibn Abī Jumhūr.

131 Ashkiwarī, *Maḥbūb*, vol. 2, p. 540; Ibn Abī Jumhūr, *Mujlī*, p. 649. This interpretation is resumed from Shams al-Dīn al-Shahrazūrī, *Rasāʾil al-shajara al-ilāhiyya*, ed. N. Ḥabībī (Tehran, 1385 Sh./2006), vol. 3, pp. 474–475.

132 Ashkiwarī, *Maḥbūb*, vol. 2, p. 542. On this notion of 'ascendancy' (*ghalaba*), see Abū Bakr Muḥammad al-Kalābādhī, *al-Taʿarruf li-madhhab ahl al-taṣawwuf*, ed. Y. al-Jayb Ṣādir (Beirut, 1427/2006), p. 82; Kalâbâdhî, *Traité de soufisme*, French trans., R. Deladrière (Paris, 1981), p. 126.

133 Ashkiwarī, *Maḥbūb*, vol. 2, pp. 542–543. Jalāl al-Dīn Mawlawī (Rūmī), *Mathnawī maʿnawī*, ed. R. Nicholson (Tehran, 1390 Sh./2011), p. 194. See also Lāhījī, *Mafātīḥ al-iʿjāz*, p. 252.

134 Those ecstatic reports have been related by Ashkiwarī himself in the last notice of the third volume of the *Maḥbūb*. The text is edited in Mīr Dāmād, *Kitāb al-qabasāt*, ed. T. Izutsu and M. Mohaghegh (Tehran, 1977), pp. 31–53. See a French translation and a commentary in H. Corbin, 'Confessions extatiques de Mîr Dâmâd, maître de théologie à Ispahan (ob. 1041/1631–2)', in H. Massé, ed., *Mélanges offerts à Louis Massignon* (3 vols., Damascus, 1956), vol. 1, pp. 331–378; and in *En Islam iranien*, vol. 4, pp. 9–53.

135 Massignon, *Passion*, vol. 1, p. 87; vol. 2, pp. 23 and 44–45.

2

The Limits of 'Orthodoxy'? Notes on the Anti-Abū Muslim Polemic of Early 11th/17th-Century Iran

Andrew Newman

There has been a fair amount of attention to the anti-Sufi polemics of later 11th/17th-century Safawid Iran in the recent secondary literature.[1] Some, albeit much less, attention has been devoted to the 10th/16th-century attacks on the veneration of Abū Muslim (d. 137/755), the Iranian agent of the Abbasid movement in Khurasan.[2] By contrast, distinctly less attention has been devoted to the anti-Abū Muslim polemic of the first half of the 11th/17th century.

The present essay examines three treatises in the anti-Abū Muslim polemic. These, all composed in Persian, are *Ṣaḥīfat al-rashād*, completed by one Mīr Muḥammad Zamān b. Muḥammad Jaʿfar Riḍawī (d. 1041/1631) before 1041/1631, *Iẓhār al-ḥaqq wa miʿyār al-ṣidq*, written by Sayyid Aḥmad al-ʿAlawī al-ʿĀmilī (d. between 1054/1644 and 1060/1650) in 1043/1633 and *Khulāṣat al-fawāʾid*, of ʿAbd al-Muṭṭalib b. Yaḥyā Ṭāliqānī, whose death date is not known; the latter is as yet undated but, as suggested below, was likely composed in the years immediately prior to 1063/1652. These three are the only essays remaining of some 24 works inveighing against Abū Muslim in the first half of the 11th/17th century. The three have been mentioned in passing in the secondary literature, including in works by the present author, as among those many works penned in defense of one Mīr Lawḥī who had been attacked for his own criticism of popular veneration of Abū Muslim. To date, however, the actual texts have yet to be discussed in any detail, either in their own right or in comparison with each other.

This chapter commences with a review of the earlier anti-Abū Muslim and anti-Sufi polemic of the 10th/16th and the early 11th/17th centuries, arguing that the use of Arabic for the earliest of these essays suggests that this was, as the Arabic-language debates over the legitimacy of Friday prayer in the same years, largely restricted to the Twelver clerical class. The appearance of Persian-language essays attacking the veneration of Abū Muslim in the later 10th/16th and, especially, the early 11th/17th century attests to a rising messianism among the Safawid realm's tribal and, especially, urban-based Tajik (native Persian) elements, in line with growth in the latter. This growth was itself commensurate with, and was a product of, the growth in Iran's urban centres, particularly Isfahan following its designation as the capital by ʿAbbās I (d. 1038/1629). The connection between the city's growth and rising urban millenarianism is further attested by contemporary events and sources.

Careful, detailed examination of the three Persian-language treatises then follows. The essays, *Ṣaḥīfa* in particular, the earliest of the three, suggest Abū Muslim's popularity in these years was limited to Isfahan. They also add considerably to the understanding of the nature of that polemic as well as of the discourse of those for whom Abū Muslim was a popular figure. The essays' growing length and increasing attention to historical detail and the religious texts point to ever-increasing dismay among elements of the scholarly class at the growing feeling for Abū Muslim. Indeed, that only these three of more than twenty anti-Abū Muslim treatises composed in the years from before 1041/1631 and up to 1063/1652 survived and, further, that so few copies of these three are extant today attests to the minority status of the anti-Abū Muslim polemic in the city in these years.

Examination of these essays also reveals clear links between the anti-Abū Muslim polemics of these years and the anti-Sufi polemics of the middle and later years of the century. Thus, references to such activities as songs and singing and claims to *ḥulūl*, the ever-larger number of references to religious texts, especially the imams' *ḥadīth* and the authors' use of Persian – all usually thought of as part and parcel only of the later anti-Sufi polemic – are in fact also features of these earlier essays. Also, even more clearly than hitherto discussed in the secondary sources, the single personality referenced in all these essays and in the later anti-Sufi polemic, and who stands, therefore, as something of a bridge between the two, is one Mīr Lawḥī.

Setting the Stage: The 10th/16th-Century Attacks on Abū Muslim

The attacks on the veneration of Abū Muslim over the 10th/16th century[3] were few in number, composed mainly in Arabic and took place within a socio-religious dynamic different to that of the latter years of the same century and the 11th/17th century.

In the early years of the 10th/16th century one of the first Twelver clerics to decry Abū Muslim's popularity was 'Alī al-Karakī (d. 940/1534), one of the few Twelver scholars who came to Safawid Iran from Arabic-speaking lands during the decades following the 907/1501 capture of Tabriz by Ismā'īl I (d. 930/1524) – this event conventionally cited as marking the commencement of the realm – and the subsequent declaration of Twelver Shi'ism as the realm's official faith. Al-Karakī became an associate of Ismā'īl's court and was attached to that of his son and successor Ṭahmāsp (d. 984/1576) as well. The latter, in a *firmān* dated 939/1532, in the midst of the years of civil war that followed Ismā'īl's death, designated al-Karakī *nā'ib al-imām*, the representative of the Hidden Imam during the latter's absence.[4]

Ismā'īl came to power in the region having identified himself, in his own poetry, for example, with a range of Muslim, Shi'i and Christian figures and even personalities from Tajik literary history. These included Abū Muslim. This heterodox discourse resonated both with the largely rural-based members of the various Turkic tribes that composed Ismā'īl's Qizilbash tribal confederation, and with the largely urban-based Tajik elements. Ismā'īl did move forcefully against contemporary movements, e.g. the Musha'sha' Arabs of southern Iraq and the Nizārī Ismailis, that exhibited similar messianic tendencies, particularly those whose discourse encompassed a distinctly Shi'i millenarianism and, as such, challenged the Safawids' exclusive recourse thereto.

This millenarianism, including praise for Abū Muslim, reappeared at Ismā'īl's death, an event that sparked years of civil war and invasions of Safawid territory by their Uzbeg and Ottoman enemies.[5]

Among his many works, al-Karakī composed *Maṭā'in al-mujrimiyya*. Although this work is lost, later accounts attest to its inclusion of a refutation both of Sufism and of the public veneration of Abū Muslim by *qiṣṣa-khwānān* (storytellers). Al-Karakī also issued a short Arabic-language *fatwā* (legal opinion) in which he approved of the cursing of Abū Muslim.[6] In 972/1564–5 al-Karakī's son al-Ḥasan authored, and dedicated to Ṭahmāsp, the Arabic-language *ʿUmdat al-maqāl fī kufr ahl al-ḍalāl.*[7]

That the language of these interventions was Arabic suggests their intended audience was primarily, as in the case of exchanges on the legitimacy of Friday prayer during the continued absence of the Hidden Imam, members of the same scholarly class.[8] Such of the latter as might have been convinced thereby, or already agreed, could then have utilised the arguments in any public discourse, that was more likely to have been carried out in Persian.

In the later years of the century the growing popularity of militant millenarianism both rural and urban, is increasingly attested.

Clearly reflecting a growing urban-based Tajik interest in Abū Muslim, ʿAlī al-Karakī's student Muḥammad b. Isḥāq al-Ḥamawī (d. after 938/1531) completed a Persian-language work *Anīs al-muʾminīn*, in which he also attacked the veneration of Abū Muslim. Ṭahmāsp himself also banned recitation of stories about Abū Muslim and ordered the tongues cut out of any of those storytellers who refused.[9]

After Ṭahmāsp fell ill in 982/1574, during the years of the second civil war that followed his death two years later in 984/1576 and also following the accession of Ṭahmāsp's grandson Ismāʿīl II (r. 984–985/1576–1577) to the throne, among urban and rural and, especially tribal elements there resurfaced the same messianic egalitarian Shiʿi-style Sufism that had so rallied Qizilbash tribal elements as to allow Ismāʿīl the military wherewithal to carve out his realm. Ṭahmāsp's illness, for example, spurred Nuqṭawī risings in villages near Kashan. Their discourse, centring on the cyclical renewal of prophecy, suggests links to Ḥurūfī, Ismaili and other millenarian discourses. These same years also witnessed the revival of the Abū Muslim traditions – as after the death of Ismāʿīl I.[10]

After Ismāʿīl II's death, Ismailis, that is in reference to Ismāʿīl I, described as *qalandars* (dervishes) unattached to any recognised Sufi order, enjoyed support among Tajik elements in Luristan, Fars, Khuzistan, Hamadan, Gilan and Khurasan; one was based in the

Ardabil area, the spiritual home of the Safawid Sufi order. These also enjoyed support among non-Qizilbash tribal elements, Kurds and Lurs especially.[11]

Following the enthronement of Ṭahmāsp's grandson ʿAbbās I in 996/1587 some Sufis openly questioned him about the identity of their *pīr*, suggesting that ʿAbbās' father, the still-living Muḥammad Khudābandah (d. 1003/1595–6), who had been deposed by ʿAbbās' tribal and Tajik backers, was still viewed as the head of the Safawid Sufi order. ʿAbbās and his tribal supporters executed these as they had, in 1000/1591, the leader of a group of Sufis in Lahijan – whose numbers had provided support for Ismāʿīl I – and who now also questioned the identity of ʿAbbās as the present *pīr*.[12]

After the 962/1555 Amasya treaty with the Ottomans, Ṭahmāsp changed the capital from Tabriz to Qazwin. Around 999/1590 ʿAbbās I designated Isfahan the capital. Around 1000/1591 the Nuqṭawī Darwīsh Khusraw rose up in Qazwin. The dervish, from a family of refuse collectors and well-diggers, had been active and popular there and popular also in Sava, Nain and the cities of Kashan, Isfahan and Shiraz. Although this rising was put down with the shah's personal intervention, such sentiments were visible also in Mashhad and Fars. With the execution of an Ustajlu *amīr* and other Qizilbash tribal elements associated with this rising, it is clear its millenarian dimensions spoke to continued tribal but also a growing urban interest in such discourse.[13]

The Growing Urban Polemic

It was in these very same years that the urban scene itself experienced further expansion. Isfahan in particular, especially following its designation as capital, underwent significant growth in its commercial, political and spiritual infrastructure. As suggested elsewhere, the Safawid centre's support for expansion on such a grand scale spoke to its perception of the existential nature of both the internal and external challenges to the realm following the death of Ṭahmāsp and throughout ʿAbbās I's own reign into those of his successors.[14] To be sure, the centre lavished attention on other conurbations but not to the same degree. Indeed, later in the century the French Huguenot Jean Chardin, who arrived in Iran in the late 1660s, described Isfahan's impressive physical infrastructure and compared the size of its population to that of London.[15]

The growth of urban popular classes in Isfahan at this time, of court-based and also non-court-based commercial and artisanal guilds, is well evidenced.[16]

Contemporary sources also attest that the distinctly urban dimension of messianic tendencies apparent toward the end of the 10th/16th century only continued to expand. In 1016/1607 an unknown author composed the Persian-language *Arbaʿīn ḥadīth fī radd al-ṣūfiyya,* a work of forty *ḥadīth*s attacking Sufism and Sufis with a section citing prominent *ʿālims*' condemnation of Sufism.[17] The use of Persian suggests the urban-based Tajik population as the primary target of such discourse and, thus, as the primary constituency associated with such activities.

In addition, no less a figure than the famous Mullā Ṣadrā, Ṣadr al-Dīn Muḥammad al-Shīrāzī (d. 1050/1640), in his 1027/1618 *Kasr al-aṣnām al-jāhiliyya*, decried the abandonment by artisans and craftsmen, drawn from precisely those classes whose numbers experienced such growth in these years,[18] of their professions to associate with popular Sufi movements.[19]

In these same early years of the 11th/17th century urban Tajik affection for Abū Muslim in particular became a distinct feature of the Safawid spiritual landscape. By contrast with the handful of mainly Arabic-language contributions composed by a few scholars in the previous century, between the 1030s/1620s and 1063/1652, that is over the later years of the reign of ʿAbbās I (997–1038/1588–1629) through the reign of Ṣafī (1038–1052/1629–1642) and into that of ʿAbbās II (1052–1077/1642–1666), some 24 works were composed attacking the veneration of Abū Muslim and, in the process, defending one Mīr Lawḥī, Sayyid Muḥammad b. Muḥammad al-Ḥusaynī (d. after 1083/1672), who was then engaged in Isfahan in attacking that veneration.[20]

Ṣaḥīfat al-rashād (A Page of Good Sense)

Of the score or more essays composed attacking Abū Muslim's veneration in the early years of the 11th/17th century, only the above-named three Persian-language essays remain.

The first of the three considered here is the earliest. It was completed sometime before 1041/1631, the year of the death of its author, Mīr (i.e. sayyid) Muḥammad Zamān b. Muḥammad Jaʿfar al-Riḍawī.

The distinct lack of attention paid to this essay in Western-language literature to date[21] matches the lack of interest in, and/or knowledge of, the author apparent in the contemporary biographical literature.

In his *Amal al-ʿāmil*, completed in 1096/1685, Muḥammad b. al-Ḥasan, al-Ḥurr al-ʿĀmilī (d. 1104/1693),[22] then based in Mashhad, noted only that the author was a *faqīh*, a *ḥākim* and a *mutakallim*, that he composed a commentary on *Qawāʾid al-aḥkām* of Jamāl al-Dīn al-Ḥasan b. Yūsuf, al-ʿAllāma al-Ḥillī (d. 726/1325)[23] and that he taught Shaykh Zayn al-Dīn b. Muḥammad b. al-Ḥasan b. al-Shahīd al-Thānī ('the second martyr') who had praised his teacher. Al-Ḥurr then cites the entry on the author in *Sulāfat al-ʿaṣr*, the biographical dictionary authored by Sayyid ʿAlī al-Madanī (d. 1120/1708–9), completed in 1082/1671, an entry of less than one line, that Riḍawī was an important scholar and that he died in 1041/1631.[24] The entry on Riḍawī in the later *Riyāḍ al-ʿulamāʾ*, the biographical dictionary completed by ʿAbd Allāh Afandī (d. *ca* 1130/1718), a student of Muḥammad Bāqir al-Majlisī (d. 1110/1699), author of the multi-volume *ḥadīth* compilation *Biḥār al-anwār*, simply reprised that of al-Ḥurr al-ʿĀmilī, down to the citation of al-Madanī.[25]

None of these biographers mention the present essay, let alone the author's association with Mīr Lawḥī.[26]

The essay repays detailed attention for the further information it reveals both about the author, about developments in the capital of Isfahan and, if only indirectly, about those in the author's home of Mashhad, some 500 miles directly northeast, or nearly 800 miles by land via the Qumm-Varamin-Simnan-Sabziwar road.

The essay, less than four-and-a-half pages in its printed form,[27] consists of some introductory remarks followed by a single *faṣl* (section).

Riḍawī opens the essay by identifying himself as a resident in Mashhad, and says that when he was younger and studying with his own father, one Sayyid Muḥammad came to the city. The author says he was of the greatest sayyids of Sabziwar.[28] The Sayyid traced his lineage to Ibrāhīm, a son of Imam Mūsā al-Kāẓim (d. 183/799), the seventh imam, from whom the Safawids themselves claimed descent,[29] and Riḍawī's father admired him greatly.

The Sayyid had a son called Mīr Lawḥī who was a particular student of *ḥadīth*. Riḍawī quotes his own father that 'Lawḥī' was a pen name the father got from the father of the woman whom he married when in Isfahan after a visit to Karbala.

Riḍawī says he studied with Sayyid Muḥammad. After the Sayyid and his son left the city for Isfahan, Riḍawī lost track of them until he himself undertook a *ziyāra* (visitation) to the shrine of al-Ḥusayn (d. 61/680–1), the third imam, in Karbala, and stopped in Isfahan on his way home. There he saw that his host was very vexed. Upon asking why, Riḍawī was told that a certain sayyid was trying to instruct the *khalq* (the common people) in 'correct behaviour' at one point forbidding the veneration of Abū Muslim. Because of this, the host said, the Sayyid was in *āzār* (torment) and the host's own heart was in a similar state. This was, Riḍawī explains, the same Mīr Lawḥī who had devoted his life to work with the *ḥadīth* and the *akhbār*. Riḍawī says he then determined to compose an essay on Abū Muslim and to send it to Isfahan to convince the people of the city to apologise to Mīr Lawḥī and forswear veneration of Abū Muslim. This he did, and called the essay *Ṣaḥīfat al-rashād*.

He opens the essay's sole *faṣl* by saying that the *qiṣṣa-khwānān* (storytellers) would have it that Abū Muslim was a friend of *ahl al-bayt* and Imam al-Bāqir, the fifth imam (d. 114/733) and that the latter had given approval for Abū Muslim's *khurūj*, that is his open/public 'coming out' or rising/rebellion.[30]

Riḍawī says this is a lie and then recounts Abū Muslim's life and involvement with the Abbasids to his death according to, he says, *ʿulamāʾ-yi imāmiyya* (the Imami *ʿulamāʾ*).

Abū Muslim, he says, was a Kufan sent by the Abbasids to Khurasan to call the people there to accept the Abbasid claim to the imamate; in the process, he deceived the people.

Naṣr Sayyār, he continues, the *ḥākim* (governor) of Khurasan on behalf on Marwān the *ḥimār* (donkey), fled toward Sham. When he reached Sava he died and went to Jahannam (a Qurʾanic reference to Hell).

Qaḥṭaba b. Shabīb, whose father, says the author, was of the Khawārij imams, at the command of Abū Muslim advanced toward Kufa but, in a battle near Kufa, was drowned.[31] His son al-Ḥasan led the army into Kufa.

Riḍawī writes that news arrived that Marwān had killed Ibrāhīm b. Muḥammad, who had sent Abū Muslim to Khurasan. When the imam's brothers, al-Saffāḥ and Abū Jaʿfar Dawānīqī, heard this news all the family swore *bayʿat* (an oath of allegiance) to al-Saffāḥ. A letter was sent to Abū Muslim informing him of this and he convinced the people of Khurasan to pledge allegiance to al-Saffāḥ. Al-Saffāḥ then sent an uncle of his at the head of an army to attack Marwān. The latter was killed and the *pādishāhī* (kingship) of al-Saffāḥ was proclaimed. Al-Saffāḥ died some four years later of an illness, having designated his brother Abū Jaʿfar as the imam and *khalīfa*.

Between Abū Jaʿfar and Abū Muslim, writes Riḍawī, there had been some *kudūrat* (resentment). After al-Saffāḥ's death this only grew worse until Abū Muslim was killed and went to Jahannam.

Riḍawī then notes that Abū Muslim's many abuses include the fact that he set the Abbasids above the imams and that the Abbasids then went on to murder the next six of the imams as well as several thousand prominent ʿAlids and the Shiʿa of Imam ʿAlī. Another was that he accepted the Abbasids' claim to the imamate. Abū Muslim, he says, also laid claim to *ḥulūl*.[32]

Riḍawī then cites a statement, which he says can be found in a reliable work with *asānīd-i ṣaḥīḥa* ('correct' chains of transmitters), via Aḥmad b. Muḥammad b. ʿĪsā, from Imam ʿAlī al-Riḍā, the eighth imam (d. 203/818), that Abū Muslim's name is on a list of the imams' enemies. The author first cites the imam's statement in Arabic and then gives a Persian translation:

> I was sitting with Abu'l-Ḥasan al-Riḍā, on him be peace, with a group of his companions when Muḥammad b. Abū ʿUmayr drew near, said his greeting and sat down. He then said: O Son of the Prophet of God, may I be your sacrifice, what do you say about Abū Muslim from Marw who rose up against the Umayyads and their followers?
>
> He, on him be peace, said: His name is on *al-ṣaḥīfa* (the page) on which are the names of our enemies the Umayyads and their followers.
>
> He said: There are a group of those who oppose you (pl.) and they say that he [i.e. Abū Muslim] is of your Shiʿa [your followers].
>
> He [the Imam] said: They lie and are debauched, may God curse them. He was fierce in his opposition to us and our Shiʿa.

> Whoever likes him detests us. Whoever accepts him rejects us. Whoever praises him censures us. O Ibn Abū ʿUmayr [from whom the text is narrated], whoever wants to be one of our Shiʿa let them be free of him.[33] Whoever is not free of him is not one of us. We are free of him in this world and the next.[34]

Any true believer, Riḍawī then says, 'must be free of Abū Muslim' and his 'associates and those who praise him'. Those, he continues, who are free of 'that noble sayyid [Mīr Lawḥī] and desire attending the gatherings of the storytellers and show friendship with Abū Muslim have not heard that His Excellency Imam Jaʿfar al-Ṣādiq [the sixth imam (d. 148/765)], on Him be peace, said:

> Whoever sits down with those who forced us into occultation or praises our enemies or joins with he who forsakes us or forsakes one who joins with us or befriends our enemy or is an enemy of our friend then certainly he is a *kāfir* (unbeliever) to that Lord God who sent down *al-sabʿa al-mathānī* (the seven often-repeated) and [sic] the Holy Qur'an.[35]

As in the case of the previously cited text, the author first cites the Arabic text and then offers a Persian translation.

There are, Riḍawī says, many further *ṣaḥīḥ* statements of the imams supporting this statement but, he says, he considers citing these to be sufficient.[36]

Here the essay ends.

That it was composed in Persian and that the two statements of the imams were, after being cited in the original Arabic, then rendered into Persian, reveals something of the author's sense of his immediate audience. Riḍawī's citation of the Arabic texts of the two *ḥadīth* reinforces both the texts' authenticity and his own credentials as a scholar. The subsequent recourse to Persian attests that those venerating Abū Muslim were not conversant in Arabic, and were certainly drawn from the growing urban-based elements, including the artisanal and commercial classes to whom Ṣadrā, for example, had referred in *Kasr*.

Riḍawī makes no reference to Mashhad, his hometown, as affected by the Abū Muslim phenomenon. Indeed, Riḍawī, whose visit to the Iraqi shrine cities attests to his being something of a traveller but also to the vitality of these cities,[37] makes no mention of such discourse either in any other urban or even rural settings on the Iranian plateau, or in such locales off the plateau as the shrine cities.[38] Isfahan, a growing commercial, political and religious centre in these years, would therefore seem to have been at the heart of the pro-Abū Muslim discourse where, earlier in the previous century especially, such messianic sentiments seem to have been a relatively more rural and tribal phenomenon.

The essay also suggests that Mīr Lawḥī had few active supporters in the capital, even among the clerical classes. Indeed, the balance of 'public opinion' seems to have been such that, although Riḍawī's host was in sympathy with Mīr Lawḥī, it was Riḍawī who took up his pen, but that only after he had returned to Khurasan.

The essay also indicates that in these years Isfahan was something of a magnet for scholars, especially those elsewhere on the Iranian plateau. Mīr Lawḥī and his father came to Mashhad, but did not tarry long there before heading for the Safawid capital, where, if that had not already been their home, given family connections, they settled permanently.[39]

Interestingly in this very short essay Riḍawī pays only brief attention to the historical details of events surrounding Abū Muslim. To be sure he does not shy away from the use of some invective: Marwān is referred to as the *ḥimār*[40] and imprecations are showered on Abū Muslim himself. The second Abbasid caliph, al-Manṣūr (d. 158/775), is referred to as Abū Jaʿfar Dawānīqī.[41] The latter attribution, however, is not parsed, and neither these or any of the other historical figures mentioned in the essay are identified in any detail, some not at all. Riḍawī cited no sources for any aspects of this historical discussion.

It may have been that he assumed, or knew, his audience knew these figures. In any case, Riḍawī, writing from quite a distance, clearly felt it more important to lay out the reasons for which he composed the essay and to refer to Abū Muslim's privileging of Abbasid interests over those of the imams, the latter's murder of six of the imams and numerous ʿAlids and their followers, and to Abū Muslim's acceptance of both the Abbasid claim to the imamate, to his own claim to *ḥulūl*, to the statements of Imam Jaʿfar and Imam al-Riḍā condemning Abū Muslim and his followers and to define as an unbeliever any who associated with the imams' opponents respectively. The Abbasids themselves emerge as of somewhat secondary importance.

Just as he cited no sources for his historical accounts, however, Riḍawī did not cite sources for the two narrations from imams al-Riḍā and Jaʿfar. The poetry is also unidentified.

Iẓhār al-ḥaqq wa miʿyār al-ṣidq (The Demonstration of the Correct and the Measure of the Truth)

Riḍawī's essay clearly did not 'win the day'. Indeed, the second of the three surviving essays deploring the veneration of Abū Muslim attests both to the continuation of the latter's popularity and, also, to Isfahan-based clerics taking up the attack.

Iẓhār al-ḥaqq wa miʿyār al-ṣidq was completed by Sayyid Aḥmad b. Zayn al-ʿĀbidīn al-Dīn al-ʿAlawī al-ʿĀmilī in 1043/1633, that is, at least two years after *Ṣaḥīfa*, composed some time before 1041/1631. Like *Ṣaḥīfa*, *Iẓhār* was written in Persian.

Like Riḍawī, it is not immediately clear whether Sayyid Aḥmad (d. between 1054/1644 and 1060/1650) was accorded great status in his own time. Indeed, his fellow ʿĀmilī scholar, al-Ḥurr al-ʿĀmilī, awards him an entry of only three lines, mentioning his having studied with Muḥammad Bāqir b. Muḥammad al-Ḥusayn, known as Mīr Dāmād (d. 1041/1632), well known in the Western sources as a Shiʿi philosopher, from whom he received an *ijāza* praising him, and with Shaykh Bahāʾī. Afandī's later entry is word for word the same as that of al-Ḥurr.[42] The fact that Sayyid Aḥmad was also both first cousin and son-in-law of Mīr Dāmād, is not noted by either of the two contemporary biographers.[43]

By the time he penned *Iẓhār*, however, Sayyid Aḥmad had demonstrated his philosophical and apologetic interests and abilities. One of his earliest works was a gloss on logic completed in 1005/1596, more than a decade before his *ijāza* from Mīr Dāmād and just before the accession of ʿAbbās I. In 1011/1602 he completed, and dedicated to ʿAbbās I, a super-commentary on metaphysics. In 1023/1614 he finished an Arabic-language commentary on a work by Mīr Dāmād. His works on Judaism and Christianity date to early in the next decade: his *Lawāmiʿ-i rabbānī* (The Divine Flashes), in which he engaged with the Old and New Testaments, was completed in 1031/1621–2. The

Sayyid's Persian-language *Miṣqal-i ṣafā'* (The Polisher of Purity) a reply to a work by a Christian missionary, was completed in 1032/1622, some 11 years before *Iẓhār*.[44]

It is for these works that Sayyid Aḥmad has attracted the attention of Western scholars to date.[45]

Iẓhār has been too little studied.[46]

If we take this eight-page essay,[47] consisting of a preface, an introduction (*muqaddima*), three chapters (*fuṣūl*) of *mi'yār* and a conclusion (*khātima*), as a commentary on the general state of anti-Abū Muslim discourse to date, if only as epitomised by and visible in Riḍawī's earlier, shorter, essay, then Sayyid Aḥmad would seem to have been of the view that till then the discourse lacked both historical and 'textual' gravitas. In *Iẓhār* both, especially the historical, loom much larger.

In his opening remarks, noting the date as 1043/1633, the Sayyid says that the *Ikhwān al-ṣafā' wa khullān al-wafā'* (brothers of honesty and intimate friends of fidelity) had asked him whether *sālikān-i masālik-i dīn* (followers of the path of faith) liked Abū Muslim or considered that *tabarrā* (distancing oneself) from him was *wājib* (obligatory).

This essay, he said, was his reply.

The Sayyid's intention to rally history to his cause is signalled from the get-go: he commences his short introduction by noting that he would be citing from the chronicle *Murūj al-dhahab wa ma'ādin al-jawhar* (Meadows of Gold and Mines of Gem[s]) penned by the historian 'Alī b. al-Ḥusayn al-Mas'ūdī (d. 345/956). Seemingly to head off potential challenges to the latter's credentials, or perhaps responding to questions thereon already raised in public discussion, the Sayyid cites the statement of the Shi'i scholar Muḥammad b. Idrīs, (d. 598/1202) in his *al-Sarā'ir*, that al-Mas'ūdī was 'of our *aṣḥāb*'. He then cites the *rijāl* work of al-'Allāma al-Ḥillī in which the latter noted that al-Mas'ūdī had composed works on the imamate and a work on the *ithbāt al-waṣiya* (The Certainty of the Successorship), testifying to the succession and imamate of Imam 'Alī.[48] The Sayyid then lists some others of al-Mas'ūdī's works, including several on the imamate.[49]

Sayyid Aḥmad then explains that the *mi'yār* (measure) on the *ḥāl* (life) of Abū Muslim will be in three *fuṣūl* (sections).

Murūj figures prominently in the first of these, on the *aṣl* (origins) of Abū Muslim. Sayyid Aḥmad quotes al-Mas'ūdī that some said Abū

Muslim was an Arab and others that he was a freed man from a village near Kufa. He continues that Abū Muslim was a *mulāzim* (companion) of Idrīs b. Maʿqil al-ʿIjlī and then Muḥammad b. ʿAlī b. ʿAbd Allāh b. ʿAbbās and then Ibrāhīm b. Muḥammad. The latter, he says, called himself the imam. Ibrāhīm sent Abū Muslim to Khurasan to call the people to pledge allegiance to him. After he had become strong he chose black clothing; his *ʿilm* (knowledge) also was black, says the Sayyid. The first people to wear such clothing were those in Nasa. Thereafter, he says, those in 'many of cities of Khurasan' began to wear black.

Having provided this text in Persian, the Sayyid then provides the Arabic original, verbatim.[50]

In a subsection within this section, Sayyid Aḥmad then cites the Arabic original of a tradition from *Man lā yaḥḍuruhu al-faqīh* of Ibn Bābawayh.[51]

In this text Jibra'īl appears to the Prophet wearing a black *qabā* (tunic) and a belt with a dagger. The Prophet asked about these and the Angel Gabriel replied that this was the manner of the children of his uncle ʿAbbās. The Prophet thereupon went to ʿAbbās saying 'woe will be to my offspring from your offspring!' ʿAbbās then asked if he should kill himself. The Prophet replied that the pen proceeds according to what is in it.

Sayyid Aḥmad then offers a Persian translation of the text.[52]

This text, the Sayyid continues, makes it clear that the Abbasid caliphs were *ẓulm kunandigān* (oppressors) of the family of the Prophet. The truly faithful know, he says, that the oppressors of the imams and those who help them merit both being distant from *raḥmat-i ilāhī* (divine mercy) and *sizāwār-i laʿnat-i nā muntāhī*[53] (endless cursing) in accord with sura 11:113.[54] Similarly, anyone who claimed the imamate but was not an imam was an oppressor,[55] as was anyone who conferred the imamate on those other than the People of the imamate.

Thus, he said, those who love the family of the Prophet's *walāyat* must loathe the Abbasid caliphs and must also loathe any who assist them.

It is clear, the Sayyid continues, that Abū Muslim Marwazī (the latter *nisba* associating him with Marw), was among those who assisted the Abbasids not *ahl al-bayt* and considered the former family as the imams. Believers therefore must exercise *tabarrā* (distancing) from him because affection for him will lead to the Fire. Sayyid Aḥmad then cites sura 17:72.[56]

The Second *faṣl*

The very short second *faṣl* addresses Abū Muslim's *madhhab* (school of faith).

Sayyid Aḥmad notes that those who followed Muḥammad b. al-Ḥanafiyya (d. 81/700–1)[57] were of several groups.

Some maintained that Ibn al-Ḥanafiyya became the imam after Imam al-Ḥasan and Imam al-Ḥusayn. Some held that he was the imam after Imam ʿAlī. These, says the Sayyid, included Abū Muslim Marwazī and his followers.

After the imamate of Muḥammad b. al-Ḥanafiyya they affirmed the imamate of his son Abū Hāshim (d. 98/718).[58] After Abū Hāshim, the Sayyid writes, these maintained that ʿAlī b. ʿAbd Allāh b. ʿAbbās b. al-Muṭṭalib [the Prophet's uncle] was the imam, and after him his son Muḥammad b. ʿAlī and after him, his son Ibrāhīm b. Muḥammad.

Ibrāhīm, the Sayyid continues, sent Abū Muslim to proselytise among the people of Khurasan. At Ibrāhīm's death, this group considered al-Saffāḥ, Ibrāhīm's brother, to be the imam.

These were called the *Jurmāniyūn*, deriving from Jurmān, that is Abū Muslim, ʿAbd al-Raḥmān b. Aḥmad Marwazī. This group believed that Abū Muslim was the imam after al-Saffāḥ.[59]

Thus it is clear, says Sayyd Aḥmad, that Abū Muslim's *ʿaqīda* (doctrine) was *fāsid* (corrupt). From after the Prophet he did uphold the imamate of the Amīr al-Mu'minīn. On this, he says, Abū Muslim was not *thābit* (firm), and he did not accept the imamate of any one of the other imams.

The Third *faṣl*

This, the last section, addresses the fact that Abū Muslim was one of the *muʿānidān* (enemies) of *ahl al-bayt*.

The Sayyid commences by noting that Abū Salama Khallāl, known as Ḥafṣ b. Sulaymān, was in those days the vizier of the Āl Muḥammad and was from Hamadan.

Abū Salama sent a letter to Imam Jaʿfar al-Ṣādiq, the sixth imam, saying that the imam should come from Madina to Kufa so that he could bring the people of Khurasan to pledge allegiance to him. The imam knew that this would not happen, and so he burned Abū Salama's letter and told the messenger that this was his reply.[60]

The Sayyid then notes that the messenger had not yet returned to Kufa when Abū Ḥāmid Ṭūsī Marwazī was told by Sābiq Khwārizmī that Marwān had ordered Ibrāhīm killed but that Ibrāhīm had made his brother al-Saffāḥ *waṣī* (successor) and imam. Ṭūsī with his army swore allegiance to al-Saffāḥ as did Abū Salama.[61]

At this point Abū Salama, having sworn allegiance to al-Saffāḥ, came to Kufa. Abū Muslim's spies had informed Abū Muslim of the letter that Abū Salama had sent to Imam Jaʿfar. Abū Muslim then wrote to al-Saffāḥ advising that Abū Salama be killed.

The Sayyid cites the Arabic text of this brief note to al-Saffāḥ, in which Abū Muslim wrote that Abū Salama had betrayed al-Saffāḥ, as cited by al-Masʿūdī, and then gives a Persian translation.[62]

Sayyid Aḥmad explains that the betrayal lay in Abū Salama's letter to Imam Jaʿfar. The Sayyid then cites al-Saffāḥ's reply as cited by al-Masʿūdī and offers a Persian translation of this text as well. Al-Saffāḥ is quoted as stating that he could not kill someone who was one of his followers and friends, especially someone such as Abū Salama who had organised the *daʿwa* and the pledge of allegiance and had so sacrificed himself and his resources for him and had fought his enemies. Al-Masʿūdī's text continues that both al-Saffāḥ's brother Dawānīqī and his uncle also urged that Abū Salama be killed owing to Abū Muslim's claim to them that Abū Salama had betrayed al-Saffāḥ. Al-Saffāḥ replied to them that he could not set aside all the good he had done and all the trouble he had gone to for a *khaṭra* (notion, in the original Arabic), which Sayyid Aḥmad translates into Persian as *laghzish* (slip, offense) that came from Satan and human *ghafla* (inadvertence).[63]

The *laghzish*, the Sayyid explains, refers to the letter that Abū Salama sent to the imam.

They then replied to al-Saffāḥ that he should be careful and that they did not trust Abū Salama day or night.

When Abū Muslim heard that Abū Salama was not to be killed and that in fact his greatness had increased he became afraid and plotted to have him killed by some trick. 'They say', says the Sayyid, that one night when Abū Salama left al-Saffāḥ and was alone some of Abū Muslim's men killed him. The Sayyid then quotes from al-Masʿūdī the poem composed by Al-Saffāḥ when he heard of the death, and provides a Persian translation thereof.[64]

Any discerning person should see, the Sayyid notes, that Abū Salama's letter to Imam Jaʿfar, Abū Muslim's letter to al-Saffāḥ urging Abū Salama be killed and the letters to Dawānīqī and his uncle also urging Abū Salama be killed all stemmed from Abū Muslim's opposition to Imam Jaʿfar as the rightful imam.

In the essay's very brief conclusion, Sayyid Aḥmad noted that when Abū Muslim called people to swear allegiance to the Abbasids, he would say that as for anyone who does not acknowledge them as Amīr al-Mu'minīn, it is *mubāḥ* (licit) to shed their blood and, Sayyid Aḥmad said, Abū Muslim then held such a person must be killed. Therefore, the Sayyid says, it is clear that Abū Muslim maintains that the shedding of the blood of those who acknowledge the rightly-guided imams is licit.

The Sayyid closes saying that this is clear 'for whoever has a heart or who listens while he is present'.[65]

Riḍawī's approach, in his very brief essay, involving a rather minimal use of both history and two statements of the imams, one condemning Abū Muslim by name and another by implication, relatively underplays the Abbasids' role per se and makes no effort to cite referencing. By contrast, Sayyid Aḥmad is more concerned with legitimising his critique and with ascribing, and documenting, evil both to the Abbasids and to Abū Muslim as their supporter.

He first takes pains to legitimise his recourse to al-Masʿūdī and then cites him either verbatim or indirectly on Abū Muslim. Where Riḍawī offered two texts from the imams, one condemning Abū Muslim by name, Sayyid Aḥmad offers but one. However, he is careful to identify its source – an early, named collection of Twelver texts by a known collector which compilation, along with others of his works, was being rediscovered in these years.[66] Also, where for Riḍawī the Abbasids were arguably somewhat incidental to the narrative, in *Iẓhār* the Sayyid chooses a text that explicitly condemns the Abbasids as oppressors of *ahl al-bayt*. The Sayyid then condemns any who supported them, including Abū Muslim.

Abū Muslim is the subject of the short second *faṣl*. There, albeit absent citations, the Sayyid condemns Abū Muslim's active failure to uphold the imamate of ʿAlī and his progeny.

Sayyid Aḥmad's third section returns to al-Masʿūdī, referencing him on all those occasions on which he offers historical information. Here Sayyid Aḥmad refers to a communication from the Abbasid administration to Imam Jaʿfar, and to the intra-Abbasid feuding that highlighted, he argues, Abū Muslim's failure to accept the imamate of Imam Jaʿfar. He notes, too, Abū Muslim's arguing for the legitimacy of killing any who opposed the Abbasids.

To be sure, Sayyid Aḥmad does identify more, if not all, of the historical personalities who appear, in the first *faṣl*, for example, than did Riḍawī. As with Riḍawī, he may have felt such figures as Ibn al-Ḥanafiyya were well-enough known to his audience. But, in a marked upgrade to Riḍawī, the Sayyid carefully cites his historical and religious sources before he, as Riḍawī did, then offers Arabic originals of both his historical and religious sources and then Persian translations.

Both attest to Sayyid Aḥmad's effort both to further enhance the legitimacy of these sources and, thereby, to highlight his superior skill and, not-so-implicitly therefore, his authority to his non-Arabic speaking audience.

It is noteworthy, however, that nowhere in his essay does Sayyid Aḥmad explicitly refer to Mīr Lawḥī. The Sayyid also does not refer to Abū Muslim making any claims concerning *ḥulūl*.

Khulāṣat al-fawāʾid (Summary of the Useful Lessons)

This essay, considerably longer than the two discussed earlier, has likewise received little detailed attention in the western-language sources to date.[67]

Once again, this parallels the lack of interest in its author, ʿAbd al-Muṭṭalib b. Yaḥyā Ṭāliqānī, in the contemporary biographical sources. In his three-line entry on Ṭāliqānī, Afandī notes that Ṭāliqānī was a student of Mīr Dāmād, as were both Mīr Lawḥī and Sayyid Aḥmad, and that he, Afandī, saw in Mazandaran a large Persian-language work of Ṭāliqānī entitled *Ghaniyyat al-mutaʿabidīn* on *āʿmāl al-sana* (actions during the year) which Afandī says was very good.

None of his other works, including *Khulāṣa*, are mentioned.[68] Al-Ḥurr accords Ṭāliqānī no entry.

Khulāṣa, is, as the title suggests and as is corroborated in the essay itself by the author, a 'summary' of Ṭāliqānī's earlier *Fawā'id al-mu'minīn* (Useful Lessons for the Believers).[69]

The work itself is, as yet, undated.[70]

To be sure, in *al-Dharī'a* al-Ṭihrānī notes that, in notes dated 1063/1652 penned on the back of a copy of Sayyid Aḥmad's *Iẓhār al-ḥaqq* by Sayyid Aḥmad's own son, *Khulāṣa* was mentioned as one of 17 essays on Abū Muslim written to defend Mīr Lawḥī.[71] Ṭāliqānī's own list, in chapter one of *Khulāṣa*, of 18 works written attacking the veneration of Abū Muslim, including several not cited by al-Ṭihrānī as being mentioned in the 1063/1652 document,[72] does not mention *Ḥadīqat al-shī'a*. This text, combining an anti-Abū Muslim with an anti-Sufi diatribe and, as such bridging the two waves of 11th/17th century discourse, dates to between 1058/1648 (15 years after *Iẓhār*) and 1060/1650.[73] Thus, *Khulāṣa* may have been composed as many as five years before the 1063/1652 notes made by Sayyid Aḥmad's son.

As for the text itself, Ṭāliqānī's opening is short. He cites two *ḥadīths*. The first, with no *sanad* or mention of its source, states that the *'ālim* (the scholar) should not *yatakkalim bi hawā' al-nās* (speak based on the whims of the people), and that he would suffer worst of all on the Day of Judgement. A second, whose *sanad* and source also are not given, cites the Prophet as saying that on the Day of Judgement God would consign to the Fire whoever *katama* (suppresses) the knowledge he has.[74] Both are cited only in Arabic; no Persian translation is given.

Ṭāliqānī continues that it was this fear of the Fire that motivated him to write *Fawā'id al-mu'minīn* on Jurmān and that he cited there what he had heard from his *ustād* (teacher) Mīr Dāmād, 'May God have mercy on him' (suggesting his teacher had died), and what he had seen in reliable works of the Imāmī *'ulamā'*. He was then asked to undertake a shorter version of that text and this he did and called it *Khulāṣat al-fawā'id*.

The main body of the essay itself comprises ten *abwāb* (chapters) with no summary/conclusion.[75]

The first of these addresses the reason that contemporary *'ulamā'* had composed so many books and essays on Abū Muslim whom the Shi'i *'ulamā'* called Abū Mujrim or Jurmān. The second discusses the obligatory nature of opposing the enemies of the imams. The remaining chapters, respectively, discuss Abū Muslim's beliefs; his birth and *nasab* (genealogy); the Abbasid *daʿwat*, the *khurūj* of Abū Muslim and of Naṣr Sayyār from Khurasan and the latter's being consigned to *ātesh* (fire, in Persian); the events from the latter's death to the killing of Marwān the *ḥimār*; the events associated with the reign of al-Saffāḥ; the events associated with the beginning of the reign of Abū Jaʿfar Dawānīqī to the killing of Abū Muslim; on why Sunnis and *mulḥidūn* (apostates) approve of Jurmān (Abū Muslim); and, finally, why the *ẓulm* of the Abbasids against the *ʿitra* (the Prophet's progeny) was greater than that of the Umayyads and their followers.

Riḍawī covered the same issues, Abū Muslim's origins and the same historical events to the killing of Abū Muslim, and referenced the imams and alluded to the contemporary scene that caused him to compose his essay. Sayyid Aḥmad also quoted the imams. Sayyid Aḥmad's 'new and original' contribution to the polemic mainly involved the addition of historical detail, based on a named source – al-Masʿūdī's *Murūj* – that he took pains to show was a reliable, Shiʿi-authored account, and via which he did add some additional details to Riḍawī's historical narrative.

As the above 'table of contents' suggests, however, Ṭāliqānī's is a lengthy discussion. Indeed, where *Ṣaḥīfa* was less than four-and-a-half pages in its published form, and *Iẓhār* is about twice that long, in its published form Ṭāliqānī's *Khulāṣa* is 27 pages long.[76] The original *Fawā'id* must, therefore, have been of considerable length.

Perhaps *Khulāṣa*'s most noticeable addition to the extant polemic is a marked upgrade to the historical narrative surrounding Abū Muslim and his rise, and his association with the Abbasids. In so doing Ṭāliqānī also makes use of accounts that are no longer extant or are hard to identify.

As to his references to these sources, Ṭāliqānī's citations from some of the lost treatises attacking Abū Muslim composed in the early 11th/17th century, and other such works, offer the only information on these available to date.

Also, in comparison with the earlier two essays examined above, *Khulāṣa* makes much greater use of and reference both to the *ḥadīth*, of which there are some dozen citations, and to earlier religious texts.

Finally, it is notable that in its use of the latter texts and other references, Ṭāliqānī's *Khulāṣa* offers a much more detailed picture of the contemporary spiritual scene, including information on the involvement of such contemporary figures as Mīr Dāmād, Sayyid Aḥmad's teacher and father-in-law and Ṭāliqānī's teacher, and his associate and fellow confidant of the Safawid court, Shaykh Bahā'ī, than is available in *Ṣaḥīfa* and *Iẓhār* or has been related from other sources to date.

Altogether, *Khulāṣa* clearly represents both a quantitative and qualitative step-up from the discourse of the time, at least as exemplified by *Ṣaḥīfa* and *Iẓhār*. As such the essay suggests the author's understanding that these two as well as the many other essays composed to date had failed to check the widespread contemporary affection for Abū Muslim.

Additions to the Historical Narrative

In the main, as suggested by the above 'table of contents', Ṭāliqānī's essay constitutes an historical discussion of the infidelity of Abū Muslim, of the rise of the Abbasids and the course of Abū Muslim's association with them and of the Abbasids' unparalleled oppression of the ʿAlids, the imams and their followers. This narrative is offered in such detail that Ṭāliqānī must have envisioned his essay as an effort to improve coverage of the material on offer at the time, both in the two essays already discussed above and, implicitly also, on the numerous other contemporary contributions to the polemic against Abū Muslim.

Riḍawī in *Ṣaḥīfa* covered the 'history' in but half a page, within his single *faṣl*.[77] Sayyid Aḥmad covered this material in only his third *faṣl*, of two-and-a-half pages.[78]

In marked contrast, Ṭāliqānī's 'history' chapters – five through eight – covering the very same time frame – the commencement of the Abbasid *daʿwa* (call) and the *khurūj* of Abū Muslim to the killing of Abū Muslim – run to 14 pages in the printed edition.

In the process Ṭāliqānī cites from both older and contemporary works in this genre. Both sets of works include 'lost' items or hard-to-identify works. References thereto allow Ṭāliqānī to add new information, and thus further legitimise, his attack on both Abū Muslim and the Abbasids.

These historical chapters, as others, also contain further detail on the contemporary scene.

The longest of Ṭāliqānī's several 'history' chapters and, indeed, the longest chapter in the essay, chapter eight, of five pages, covers events from the start of the *pādishāhī* (kingship) of Abū Jaʿfar Dawānīqī in 136/754, to the killing of Abū Muslim, some nine months after the caliph's accession, in 137/755.[79] A comparison between coverage of this period as offered in all three essays discussed here well illustrates both the quantitative and qualitative advancement that Ṭāliqānī's essay represented over the previous two.

Riḍawī covered these years in less than three lines, saying – as noted above – that al-Saffāḥ, a brother of Ibrāhīm, ruled for but four years and a few months, became ill and designated his other brother Abū Jaʿfar Dawānīqī as his *waṣī*. Riḍawī then noted that between Abū Jaʿfar and Abū Muslim there had been some *kudūrat* (resentment). After al-Saffāḥ's death this only grew worse until Abū Muslim was killed and went to Jahannam.[80]

Sayyid Aḥmad, in his third *faṣl*, does not, in fact, discuss these years at all.[81]

Ṭāliqānī's very detailed account of the events of these years in chapter eight highlights the general perfidy and specifically anti-Twelver sentiments, and actions, of both Abū Muslim and the Abbasids.[82]

Ṭāliqānī commences the section noting that when news of al-Saffāḥ's death [in 136/753–4] and Abū Jaʿfar's accession reached Shām [Syria] his uncle, one ʿAbd Allāh b. ʿAlī, claimed the caliphate and the Syrians and those Khurasanis who were there swore allegiance to him. Abū Jaʿfar [i.e. the caliph al-Manṣūr] sent Abū Muslim – whose own ambitions to the caliphate, and al-Manṣūr's knowledge of and anger therewith, Ṭāliqānī had detailed in the previous chapter – with an army against him.[83] Abū Muslim routed his opponent and seized much wealth along with the sword of ʿAbbās b. ʿAbd al-Muṭṭalib [the Prophet's paternal uncle]. Abū Jaʿfar sent for a messenger asking for the wealth and the sword. Abū Muslim's response was anger: 'I killed how many thousand for the son of Sallāma [i.e. Abū Jaʿfar] and he wants this money from me?' The messenger returned and reported this to the caliph.[84]

At that time a letter arrived from al-Ḥasan [b.] Qaḥṭaba[85] to Abū Ayyūb, the vizier of Abū Jaʿfar, in which he reported that he saw Abū

Muslim throw the caliph's letter to Mālik b. Haytham[86] and they both laughed.

In those days, Ṭāliqānī continues, the sons of Qaḥṭaba, al-Ḥasan and Ḥumayd, knew that Abū Muslim had laid claim to the imamate and to the caliphate and was obliging the people to swear allegiance to him. Ḥasan wrote to Abū Jaʿfar to say that the *dīv* (bad spirit) that had taken over the brain of ʿAbd Allāh b. ʿAlī had now done the same in the case of Abū Muslim in that he was now claiming the imamate and the caliphate.[87]

Ṭāliqānī then quotes from *Kifāyat al-barāya*, a work authored by one Quṭb al-Dīn Kaydharī Nayshabūrī, a figure variously dated to the 6th/12th and 7th/13th centuries. Ṭāliqānī quotes the work as saying that Abū Muslim had now laid claim to *ḥulūl*, saying that Abū Muslim said that *Khudā* (God) was indwelt in Adam, then in all of the prophets, then in Muḥammad and after that in Abū Muslim himself.[88]

The narrative then resumes with Ṭāliqānī saying that Abū Muslim then turned toward Khurasan without Abū Jaʿfar's permission. Abū Jaʿfar sent several notes calling him but to no avail.[89] The caliph then sent letters to all the *umarā'* (rulers) of Khurasan and especially Abū Dāwūd [Khālid b. Ibrāhīm], who Ṭāliqānī says was Abū Muslim's *ḥākim* in Khurasan,[90] saying that if Abū Dāwūd had recognised him as imam and caliph then he could not be obedient to Abū Muslim and should not give the latter passage in Khurasan.[91]

He sent Abū Ḥumayd Ṭūsī[92] to Abū Muslim requesting that Ṭūsī devise a way to send Abū Muslim to him, and that if he was unsuccessful that he should say to Abū Muslim that the Commander of the Faithful *sugand khurd* (took an oath) that he was not a member of the Āl ʿAbbās [i.e. an Abbasid] if Abū Muslim went to Khurasan without his permission and that he would have him killed. Abū Ḥumayd delivered the message[93] at Rayy, at the same time as Abū Dāwūd's letter and that of most of the rulers of Khurasan reached Abū Muslim, and told him that he should not anger the caliph by going to Khurasan without the caliph's *firmān* (command).[94] Abū Muslim then had 12,000 troops in Rayy with him as well as many *hawādār* (supporters) elsewhere.

Abū Muslim told Abū Ḥumayd that he would come to the caliph but that he feared him and that he would first send Abū Isḥāq[95] to Abū Jaʿfar to get a sense of what the atmosphere was. This is what he did.[96]

Ṭāliqānī then again cites *Kifāya* that this was when Abū Muslim decided to support on the Banū Fāṭima[97] so that the Imami Shiʿa would support him and in this way defeat Abū Jaʿfar and also gradually win the allegiance of the Imāmis for his own caliphate. Abū Muslim sent a letter to Imam Jaʿfar al-Ṣādiq to win his support for his claim to the caliphate. He also sent Abū Isḥāq to Abū Jaʿfar to get a sense of the latter's intentions – as noted above.

When Abū Muslim's messenger came to Imam Jaʿfar in Madina and the imam became aware of what was in the letter he angrily told the messenger to leave. This, says Ṭāliqānī, is the origin of the imam's *ḥadīth* cited by Thiqat al-Islām Muḥammad Kulaynī.[98] He then cites the Arabic text and provides a Persian translation thereof, confirming the event and that the Imam told the messenger to leave. The text also cites the imam as rebuking the narrator's questioning of the imam's expulsion of the messenger and the offer by warning that *Khudā* (God) was not bound by the same *shitāb* (haste).[99]

When Abū Isḥāq reached Abū Jaʿfar the caliph told him that by any means he knew he must get Abū Muslim to wait on him [i.e. the caliph] and that if he did so, he, Abū Isḥāq, could be hopeful of his, the caliph's, *ʿawāṭif* (solicitudes).[100]

When the messenger reached Abū Muslim from Madina and informed him of the situation Abū Muslim knew, says Ṭāliqānī, that Imam Jaʿfar would not be taken in by his *farīb* (deception). Abū Isḥāq returned from seeing the caliph at the same time and employed such *fusūn* (deceit) that Abū Muslim decided to wait on the caliph. As Abū Muslim approached Madāʾin the caliph commanded that he be welcomed. Abū Muslim entered the city and four days later Abū Jaʿfar summoned ʿUthmān b. Nahīk and three others to the room near his *majlis* and ordered that when Abū Muslim was present and he clapped his hands three times then they were to come out and kill him.[101]

When Abū Muslim entered, Abū Jaʿfar said to him, 'do you remember what you did during the time of my brother? I greeted you and you did not reply. And you killed our Shiʿa (followers) and the son of our follower Sulaymān b. Kathīr in my presence.[102] And, when my brother died you wanted the caliphate which was my *ḥaqq* (right, due) to go to my nephew ʿĪsā b. Mūsā [d. 167/783–4][103] and you wanted to marry Amīna the daughter of ʿAlī who is my paternal uncle, which means that you were going to be her husband.'[104]

Abū Muslim replied that it was he 'who brought your *dawlat* (state) into existence'.

Abū Ja'far said: 'O Ibn al-Khabītha (son of an evil one) *Khudā* (God) Almighty wanted my claim, our victory and our state brought into being, and the return of *ḥaqq-i mā* (what is rightfully ours). If a *kanīzak-i siyāhī* (a black slave girl) had been in your place that which you brought into being would have been brought into being. You created a *mulḥaq* (connection) to us so you could claim the imamate and the caliphate. Does not *'ālamiyān* (humankind) know that you are a slave and the son of a slave of the Banū Ma'qil. If you were the son of Salīṭ[105]you would still be the son of a slave of ours.'

Abū Muslim said: 'O Commander of the Faithful, who am I that you have reached this degree of anger with me?'

Abū Ja'far said: 'you are the one who claims *khudā'ī* (divinity).' When the exchange reached this point,[106] says Ṭāliqānī, the caliph clapped his hands and four men[107] with swords drawn came out of that room. Abū Muslim ran forward and threw himself at Abū Ja'far's feet to kiss his feet and wanted to say: 'O Commander of the Faithful' but said 'O Prophet of God, *al-amān* (safety)'. Abū Ja'far replied: 'O Enemy of God, can't you distinguish between the Commander of the Faithful and the Prophet of God' – Ṭāliqānī gives both the Arabic original and the Persian translation of this reply.[108] The men then thrust their swords into him. Abū Muslim begged to be left to fight the caliph's enemies, to which the caliph Ḥasan replied 'who is more my enemy than you?' At this, says Ṭāliqānī, the last word, Abū Muslim died.[109] The caliph then ordered that the body be wrapped in a rug and thrown into a corner.

'Īsā b. Mūsā, the son of the caliph's uncle, then entered and asked where Abū Muslim was. The caliph replied he was there in the rug. 'Īsā said: 'You did this and his troops are still here, all of whom believe he is *Khudā*?' Abū Ja'far then said to those who held that Abū Muslim was the caliph that he was a slave who exceeded his own limits. 'Now you are happy that, while you had been *mulāzim* (attendant) on Abū Muslim, you will attend on me.' At this point, Abū Muslim's head and his gold were thrown from the roof of the palace. When those who believed Abū Muslim to be *Khudā* saw the gold each was robbed of his senses, says Ṭāliqānī. Abū Ja'far decreed that Abū Muslim, wrapped in the rug, should be thrown into the Shaṭṭ (the Tigris river). Some *safīhān* (foolish people) around Nishapur who erected a tomb were killed.[110] Al-Masʿūdī in his *Murūj* and Kaydharī in *Kifāya*, says Ṭāliqānī, named this the tomb of Abū Muslim. This was a *maṭāf* (a place of circumambulation) for the *ʿawwām* (common people).[111]

Ṭāliqānī then refers to a *ḥadīth* that God will impose a penalty (*sallaṭa*) on whomever assists an oppressor (*ẓālim*),[112] and notes Abū Muslim aided the Banū ʿAbbās.

Ṭāliqānī then cites al-Masʿūdī, first in the original Arabic and then in Persian translation, that when the news of Abū Muslim's death reached Khurasan but also elsewhere in the Jibāl area, that is, western Iran, the Khurramiyya became agitated. They were, he says, a group that maintained that Abū Muslim was the imam.[113] Some said he had not died and would never die until he made his *ẓuhūr* (rising, appearance) and filled the earth with justice. Another group held that he had died and believed in the imamate of his daughter, Fāṭima, and these were the Fatimids.[114]

Al-Masʿūdī, says Ṭāliqānī, was one of the greatest of the Imami *ʿulamāʾ* and in his *Iẓhār al-ḥaqq* Mīr Sayyid Aḥmad talked about al-Masʿūdī and the works that he had written about the imamate and other works. Kaydharī, the author of *Kifāyat al-barāyā*, Ṭāliqānī continues, was one of the greatest *mujtahid*s of the Shiʿa, and wrote many works. Among these is the Persian-language *Mabāhij al-muhaj fī manāhij al-ḥujaj* (The Delights of the Souls on the Manners of the Proofs).[115] Ḥasan Shīʿī Sabziwārī has selected some of the miracles of the fourteen immaculates from that book and translated them into Persian and entitled it *Bahjat al-mabāhij* (The Splendour of the Delights).[116]

Mīr Dāmād, says Ṭāliqānī, said that Kaydharī was a great scholar, a *faqīh* and *thiqa* (reliable) and a student of Naṣīr al-Dīn al-Ṭūsī (d. 672/1274) who himself was, says Ṭāliqānī, a contemporary of Ibn Shahr Āshūb (d. 588/1192).[117] He is, continues Ṭāliqānī, often cited as a source in transmissions, he has written three commentaries on *Nahj al-balāgha* and many works in both the *ʿaqlī* (rational) and *naqlī* (transmitted) sciences. It is he whom Shaykh-i Shahīd,[118] in his commentary on al-ʿAllāma al-Ḥillī's *Irshād al-adhhān*,[119] cites on the issue of *mutʿa* (temporary marriage) and in other places as well.

After the killing of Abū Muslim, Ṭāliqānī continues, Sunbād the Majūsī gathered a number together, some of whom maintained that

Abū Muslim was *Khudā* and a group without number who believed in his imamate such that within a matter of days he had more than 100,000 soldiers. Abū Jaʿfar sent an army against him and defeated them. Sunbād, he says, was a *khāʾin kāfir* (unbelieving traitor) to whom Abū Muslim had given an army to kill Muslims as, says Ṭāliqānī, he had discussed in *Fawāʾid al-muʾminīn.*[120] If Abū Muslim had been a Muslim, says Ṭāliqānī, he would not have done this.

The lying storytellers, when they discuss Aḥmad Zamchī, an associate of Qaḥṭaba,[121] say that after Abū Muslim's killing Aḥmad asked for some of Abū Muslim's blood and the *ʿawwām*, who are like *anʿām* (sheep), were ensnared with such *muzakhrafāt* (deceptions).

After the killings of Abū Muslim and Sunbād, Abū Jaʿfar commenced the killing of the descendants of the Prophet. He killed many of them, says Ṭāliqānī, including Imam Jaʿfar, whom he described as a *shahīd* (martyr).[122]

Sources Brought to Light

In his detailed account of the events of those years in chapter eight, Ṭāliqānī relies on sources 'lost', little known or unclear today.

The lost *Kifāya* is a key source cited to substantiate Ṭāliqānī's assertion, probably, given its earlier mention by Riḍawī, widespread at the time, that Abū Muslim claimed *ḥulūl,*[123] and to Abū Muslim's ties to the Banū Fāṭima. Ṭāliqānī also uses it to corroborate the suggested reference by al-Masʿūdī to Abū Muslim's tomb. Other references to his claims, e.g., the face-to-face argument between Abū Muslim and al-Manṣūr, are not sourced.

Kifāya also figures prominently elsewhere in *Khulāṣa.*

The sixth chapter contains three such citations.

One involved letters sent by Abū Salama to Imam Jaʿfar and two other ʿAlids, asking for a meeting between them and the Abbasids. The imam burned his letter, and declared this to be his reply. The other two also rejected Abū Jaʿfar's overtures.[124]

The other two, however, relate to the actions and character of Abū Muslim. In the first, Abū Muslim is said to have arrived in Nishapur on a donkey and that one of the *awbāsh* (oafs) there docked the animal's tail and that it was on this animal that he reached Ibrāhīm b. Muḥammad. When he came to power and his followers took

Khurasan he went to Nishapur and ordered the killing of the people of that quarter, it being mainly an 'Imami Shi'i' quarter.

As to the second, citing the same source, Ṭāliqānī says reliable sources maintained that Abū Muslim killed some two thousand 'Imami Shi'a'. Sunbād, an associate of Abū Muslim,[125] asked what had been their crime. Abū Muslim mentioned the docking and that people had laughed at him. Sunbād asked if the man in question was among those now dead. When Abū Muslim answered that he did not know the latter's identity, Sunbād said it was then strange that he ordered so many killed. Abū Muslim is said to have replied that at least their *jarīma* (crime) was clear. Sunbād asked what was that crime. Abū Muslim replied that they had not recognised the imamate of the family of ʿAbbās instead of that of the descendants of the Ṭālibids.

In chapter seven, Ṭāliqānī cites Kaydharī that when the ʿAlid ʿUbayd Allāh b. al-Ḥusayn al-Aṣghar b. ʿAlī al-Aʿraj reached Abū Muslim in Khurasan the people of Khurasan greatly praised him and sent him much *arzāq* (wealth). This angered Abū Muslim who then wanted to kill 'Ubayd Allāh, along with Sulaymān Kathīr.[126] Sulaymān, whose statement Ṭāliqānī gives in Arabic and then in Persian translation, told the ʿAlid he had erred in pledging his allegiance to someone else. Sulaymān then offered to pledge to the ʿAlid and to canvas the people in support of 'Ubaydallāh. The ʿAlid, suspecting this was a trick devised by Abū Muslim, told the latter of the encounter. Abū Muslim then expelled 'Ubayd Allāh from Khurasan and had Sulaymān killed in Abū Jaʿfar's presence.[127]

Elsewhere, the author's source references are not immediately clear.

Thus, in reference to Aḥmad Zamchī, in chapter six, Ṭāliqānī cites a history of Yazd that some ignorant people erected a stone near one of the gates of the *balad* (city) and named it the *sang-i falākhan* (slingshot stone) of Aḥmad Zamchī, and would perform *ṭawwāf* (circumambulation) and *ziyāra* to it.[128]

In chapter seven Ṭāliqānī cites the otherwise unidentified *Kitāb al-malāḥim* that when the ʿAlid ʿAbd Allāh b. Yaḥyā, Ṭālib al-Ḥaqq (Seeker of Justice) [d. 130/748], arose in Yemen during the reign of al-Saffāḥ,[129] al-Saffāḥ feared for his rule and sent a letter to Abū Muslim asking him to rid him of the *sharr* (evil) of this ʿAlid and Abū Muslim sent an army to Yemen. The Abbasids defeated the army of

'Ubayd Allāh [sic] and brought him to Abū Muslim. Abū Muslim beheaded him and sent the head to al-Saffāḥ. When he returned to Khurasan al-Saffāḥ made Abū Jaʿfar crown prince[130] and sent him to Khurasan to secure the allegiance of the people there to him.[131]

In *Khulāṣa* Ṭāliqānī also makes reference to some of the lost treatises attacking Abū Muslim composed in the early 11th/17th century. As such these constitute the only information on these now available.

Thus, as we have seen, in chapter one, aside from his listing of the 18 essays, he also specifically refers to *Mashā'in* and *Mīzān al-maḥāsin wa'l-masha'īn*, and to passages from both. In chapter three, as further discussed below, Ṭāliqānī refers to the Kaysaniyya sect as being discussed in 'Anīs al-abrār',[132] '*Illat al-iftirāq* (The Disease of Division)',[133] the extant *Iẓhār al-ḥaqq*[134] and *Nuṣrat al-Islām fī 'ilm al-kalām*[135] authored by the grandfather of Mīr Lawḥī. Chapter four cites Shaykh ʿAlī's *Maṭāʿin*, as does chapter nine. 'Anīs' is also referred to in chapter nine, where he says it contains a *fatwā* on cursing Abū Muslim issued by a contemporary of Shakyh ʿAlī al-Karakī. Chapter nine also refers to Shaykh al-Ḥasan's *ʿUmdat al-maqāl*, where Ṭāliqānī cites it as challenging Sunnis for being friendly to Abū Muslim, and to Riḍawī's extant *Ṣaḥīfa*; the latter is also cited in chapter ten. He refers to *Iẓhār* also in chapter four. Of course Ṭāliqānī also refers to his own, earlier *Fawā'id* in several chapters, in chapters one, eight, a 'history' chapter, and nine.

In chapter ten, Ṭāliqānī notes that the caliph al-Mutawakkil (r. 232–247/847–861) ordered that Najaf and Karbala be razed. Al-Mutawakkil was, says Ṭāliqānī, worse than Yazīd b. Muʿāwiya because in his time[136] the people could undertake *ziyāra* to Imam al-Ḥusayn's tomb. By contrast, during the time of al-Mutawakkil *ziyāra* was forbidden and he killed many who performed it. He then says some of the oppressions of the Abbasids are recorded in *Mathālib al-ʿabbāsiyya* (The Disgraces of the Abbasids).[137] He notes that in *Minhāj al-hidāya* (The Programme of Guidance)[138] the *jabābira* (tyrants) of the Banū ʿAbbās are said to have killed 120,000 ʿAlids and innumerable Imamis.

In chapter nine, as will be noted below, Ṭāliqānī refers to two works by Shaykh Bahā'ī attacking Abū Muslim.

A comparison of the two lists of items in the anti-Abū Muslim polemic dated to these years yields a total of 21 items.[139] If the above-mentioned *Minhāj* and these two works by Bahāʾī are added, the total is then 24. At the same time, *Nuṣrat al-islām* can safely be added to the number of items composed in the previous century.

Marshalling the *ḥadīth*

In their, albeit very much shorter, contributions Riḍawī and Sayyid Aḥmad do cite the imams in support of their polemic. The former cited two texts – one condemning Abū Muslim by name and another by implication, but without citing the sources for either. In his longer *Iẓhār al-ḥaqq*, Sayyid Aḥmad cited only one text, condemning the Abbasids as oppressors of *ahl al-bayt*, but did name its source as Ibn Bābawayh's *al-Faqīh*.

As suggested, Ṭāliqānī's main purpose, and most easily perceived contribution to the polemic, was his addition to the historical narrative. He also made greater use of the imams' *ḥadīth*s than did his two predecessors. In the process he used a wider range of sources, and usually referenced them.

Ṭāliqānī's brief opening, as already noted, cited two texts, neither with any *sanad* or source, though the second can be traced. Neither is translated into Persian. In chapter one, as seen below, Ṭāliqānī cites a text, only in Arabic, which is unsourced but which, in fact, is traceable.

The third, short, chapter addresses the fact that Abū Muslim was not of the Imamis, that is, explains Ṭāliqānī, the Twelver Shiʿa and that he opposed them. This he says is clear, based on the *ḥadīth* of the Prophet 'My *umma* will divide into 73 groups, one of which will be saved and others will be consigned to *al-nār*'.[140] Ṭāliqānī cites the Arabic of this text and then offers a Persian translation. In further support of the text, he offers the Arabic only of the well-known text, 'As the people of my House so the ship of Nūḥ: who boards it will be saved, and who turns away from it will drown', without any *sanad*.[141]

In chapter five, the first of the four, successive 'history' chapters, just before he notes that the storeytellers had convinced the *ʿawwām* that Qaḥṭaba b. Shabīd, the latter's sons and Aḥmad Zamchī,[142] one of his associates, were the greatest of *ashrāf* and sayyids, he cited from Ibn Bābawayh's *ʿUyūn akhbār al-Riḍā*, that Ḥumayd b. Qaḥṭaba killed 60 sons of the imams.[143]

In chapter six, Ṭāliqānī in his discussion, based on *Kifāya*, as cited above, of Imam Jaʿfar's receipt of Abū Salama's letter to him refers, but without citing the text verbatim, to the imam's 'reply' as consisting of burning the letter and declaring this to be his reply to the letter.[144]

In chapter eight, as already noted, Ṭāliqānī references *al-Kāfī* by name for a text – given in the original Arabic and then in Persian translation, that, he says, is explained as being the imam's refusal to receive a messenger from Abū Muslim. In the same chapter, also as already noted, Ṭāliqānī refers to the fragment of an unsourced but traceable text, not translated into Persian, that God will impose a penalty (*sallaṭa*) on whosoever assists an oppressor (*ẓālim*).

Four texts are cited in the ninth chapter, to be noted below. Part of the first, a traceable text attributed to Imam ʿAlī, is cited in Arabic but in Persian Ṭāliqānī summarises the main point(s). The second, given only in Persian translation, is cited by name from Ibn Bābawayh's *al-Faqīh*.

In the same chapter, Ṭāliqānī cites a text from Imam Jaʿfar from Ibn Bābawayh's *Iʿtiqādāt* and, he says, other [unnamed] sources.

In chapter nine also, again to be noted below, Ṭāliqānī refers to the text from Imam ʿAlī al-Riḍā, the eighth imam, in which the imam stated that Abū Muslim's name is on a list of the imams' enemies. Ṭāliqānī says that Shaykh ʿAlī al-Karakī noted in his *Maṭāʿin*, that was also cited in *Ṣaḥīfa* and Mīr Dāmād saw it both in the former source and in a named source dating to the late 3rd/early 10th century.

In chapter ten, the essay's final chapter, Ṭāliqānī cites the second of the two texts that Riḍawī had cited in *Ṣaḥīfa*, noting, as Riḍawī had not, its source as Ibn Bābawayh's *al-Amālī*. Like Riḍawī, Ṭāliqānī offers both the Arabic original and a Persian translation.

This is a total of 14 texts, of which the first cannot be traced and that in *Maṭāʾin* also cannot be traced but was apparently vouchsafed by Mīr Dāmād.

Elsewhere, to be sure, Ṭāliqānī refers to other unnamed texts from unnamed sources. In chapter three, having cited two, Ṭāliqānī then refers to many texts that prove that the 'saved sect' refers to the Shiʿa. In chapter nine, he states that by *tawātur* (multiply-attested traditions) it is attested that Abū Muslim empowered the Āl ʿAbbās who were oppressors of the *ahl al-bayt* of the Prophet and brought people to pledge allegiance to them. In support of this, he adds, he cited many traditions in his *Fawāʾid al-muʾminīn*. In the same chapter, he refers to many other texts that censure the Abbasids, after citing one from Ibn Bābawayh's *al-Faqīh*.

New Light on the Contemporary Discourse

Both chapters one and nine in particular repay attention for the new light that *Khulāṣa* sheds on the state of the anti-Abū Muslim polemic of the day, as it had moved on from the years before the composition of *Ṣaḥīfa*, sometime prior to 1041/1631, and for Ṭāliqānī's references to earlier, but now lost, works composed in this genre.

Indeed, Ṭāliqānī opens chapter one by saying that the storytellers were ignorant of the story of Abū Muslim and so publicised him and turned *ʿawwām al-nās* (the common people) to those lies. Most of the *ʿulamāʾ* were themselves unaware of their *ikhtirāʿ* (contrivance) until a sayyid of the residents of Isfahan named Mīr Lawḥī undertook to challenge this. Ṭāliqānī says he heard of all this via Mīr Dāmād.

Some *safīhān* (foolish people) believed the storytellers' lies, did not accept any of what Mīr Lawḥī was saying and spread *buhtān* (lying) and *iftirāʾ* (slander) about him. These, he says, who called themselves *pīr*s and leaders, would say that he [Mīr Lawḥī] cursed all of these our *pīr*s and predecessors. They also turned on the *akābir* (prominent figures) among the Shiʿa and those figures whom Mīr Lawḥī mentioned – the first perhaps referring to prominent contemporary Twelver scholars and the second perhaps a reference to past scholars whom he cited in his arguments.

Ṭāliqānī cites the author of the contemporary *Mashāʾīn* (The Scandalous)[145] as branding their hatred of Mīr Lawḥī as one of the greatest sins of the people of Isfahan even though they counted themselves Shiʿa. Their *bughḍ* (hatred) and *ʿinād* (obstinacy) increased because, citing the *muʿtabar* text 'Man congregates with whoever loves him', he warned them about opposing *Khudā* and being friendly to Abū Muslim; he did not translate into Persian or cite a source for this text.[146]

Ṭāliqānī then cites the author of *Mīzān al-maḥāsin waʾl-mashāʾin* (The Balance of the Goodnesses and the Scandalous)[147] who says that the author of *Mashāʾin* erred in saying that all the people of Isfahan hated Mīr Lawḥī. Those who hated Mīr Lawḥī were not the majority of the people of Isfahan.

Ṭāliqānī himself continues that he has not seen anyone who hated Mīr Lawḥī who was not *maʿyūb* (blemished) with sin. Ṭāliqānī again cites the author of *Mashāʾin* who looked into the character of Mīr Lawḥī's opponents and found these were either known for *ilḥād* (apostasy) or *fasād-i iʿtiqād* (false belief) *or khubs-i ṭīnat* (bad character), being a *rāshī* (receiving bribes), being a *sāriq* (thief), *khāʾin* (treacherous), a liar or a *nammān* (slanderer). They, he continued, 'incline to *surūd* (songs) and *ghinā* (singing)[148] and to *lahw* (playing) and *laʿb* (joking).'

In response, he says, most of the *ʿulamāʾ*, to strengthen the faith and guide the ignorant, composed *fatwa*s, treatises and books containing proofs and evidence on the cursing of Abū Muslim. Ṭāliqānī then lists the 18 works discussed above. Their authors, he says, are upright.

Chapter nine also references the contemporary discourse. Apostates, he says, like Abū Muslim because he claimed *ḥulūl* and *Sunniyān* (the Sunnis) like him because he brought the Abbasids to power. Ṭāliqānī cites an example of the slander marshalled in support of Abū Muslim's veneration, a statement attributed to Imam ʿAlī, at the battle of Ṣiffīn,[149] that the imam, upon inquiring as to the whereabouts of Abū Muslim, was told he was at the end of the lines. Abū Muslim's supporters, Ṭāliqānī says, argue that ʿAlī was not referring to Abū Muslim Khawlānī,[150] but in fact to Abū Muslim Marwazī who, from the eastern side, was coming out with black *rāyāt* (banners) and who was fighting several battles to establish *ḥaqq-i Allāh* (the truth of God).[151] Part of the text is cited in Arabic but in Persian Ṭāliqānī summarises the main point(s).

Ṭāliqānī also cites the Sunnis as claiming ʿAlī stated that the Abbasids were the *khulāfā-yi* [sic] *bar ḥaqq* (the rightful caliphs).

In fact, Ṭāliqānī says, there are many *ḥadīth*s that censure the Abbasids. Thus Ibn Bābawayh, in his *al-Faqīh*, narrates the tradition, of which Ṭāliqānī offers only a Persian translation, that Jibraʾīl came to the Prophet and said 'Woe to your children will be from the children of ʿAbbās'.[152]

Ṭāliqānī notes this same narration was cited by Mīr Sayyid Aḥmad in his *Iẓhār* and by himself in his earlier *Fawāʾid al-muʾminīn*. As already noted, Ṭāliqānī adds that Mīr Dāmād said that this text is in *Kitāb al-Ḍiyāʾ* with a reliable *sanad*.[153] Ṭāliqānī says that by *tawātur* (multi-attested traditions) it is attested that Abū Muslim empowered the Āl ʿĀbbās who were oppressors of the *ahl al-bayt* of the Prophet and brought people to pledge allegiance to them. He says he cited many such traditions in his *Fawāʾid al-Muʾminīn*.

Ṭāliqānī then cites the first part of Qurʾan 11:113 in the original Arabic, and then in a Persian translation.[154] Based on this verse, Ṭāliqānī says, anyone who supports Abū Muslim belongs in Jahannam as there is no greater oppression than taking *ḥaqq-i ʿitra* (what rightfully belongs to the family of the Prophet) and giving it to their enemies.

He refers to Ibn Bābawayh, in his *Iʿtiqādāt* and in other books of *ḥadīth*, citing Imam Jaʿfar as saying: 'He who doubts the *kufr* (infidelity) of our enemies who have wronged us is himself an infidel.'[155] Ṭāliqānī cites the Arabic and then offers the Persian translation. Abū Muslim was an oppressor and, based on these firm pieces of evidence and *tawāṭur* traditions narrated by multiple narrators, his unbelief is certain. Based on Qurʾan 9:23,[156] any who support him are also oppressors and deserve *ātesh* (the fire).

He then notes that Shaykh ʿAlī al-Karakī, in his *Maṭāʿin*, cited a text by his own *isnād* on cursing Abū Muslim and that the author of *Ṣaḥīfa* also cited this text with a *ḥadhf* (shortened) *isnād*. Ṭāliqānī himself then cites it, 'with a view to brevity' minus the *sanad*, both in the original Arabic text and then in Persian translation, as had Riḍawī. It was in this rather long text that, as cited and translated above in the discussion on *Ṣaḥīfa*, Imam ʿAlī al-Riḍā, the eighth imam, stated that Abū Muslim's name is on a list of the imams' enemies.

Ṭāliqānī says he showed this tradition in *Maṭāʿin* to Mīr Dāmād.[157] The latter, Ṭāliqānī continues, said that he had heard the tradition from his *khāl* (maternal uncle), the son of Shaykh ʿAlī, who narrated the text from his father by the aforementioned *sanad* from Imam al-Riḍā. Mīr Dāmād also heard from Shaykh al-Ḥusayn b. ʿAbd al-Ṣamad, the father of Shaykh Bahāʾī, that he also narrated the text from his grandfather by this *sanad* from the imam. Mīr Dāmād said he had also seen the text in *Kitāb al-Ḍiyāʾ*, of Saʿd b. ʿAbd Allāh Ashʿarī Qummī, cited with 'correct' *asānīd*.[158]

Ṭāliqānī says that during the time of Shaykh ʿAlī, a *wāʿiẓ* (preacher) cursed Abū Muslim. The people asked him for *fatwās*. The preacher issued such a ruling and the author of 'Anīs al-abrār'[159] cited one of these at the end of his book and Ṭāliqānī says he also cited it in his

Fawā'id.[160] Ṭāliqānī writes that Mīr Dāmād repeatedly said that listening to the story of Abū Muslim was not permitted because it is a *maḥḍ* (pure) lie and complete slander, and Abū Muslim is corrupt, debauched and cursed. And, there are a great many seekers of *'ilm* (knowledge) and others who heard from Shaykh Bahā'ī that he cursed Abū Muslim. He then refers to two writings by the aforementioned Shaykh [Baha'i] on the cursing of Abū Muslim.

Ṭāliqānī then notes that, as he mentioned in his own *Fawā'id*, Shaykh al-Ḥasan, 'Alī al-Karakī's son, in his *'Umdat al-maqāl fī kufr ahl al-ḍalāl* (The Support of the Proposition, on the Unbelief of the People of Error) challenged the Sunnis for being friendly to Abū Muslim.

Chapters two, three and four also cast some light on the contemporary scene. All quite short, these address respectively, the necessity of showing enmity for the opponents of the imams, the *madhhab* of Abū Muslim and his genealogy and birth.

In chapter two, Ṭāliqānī argues that such *dushmanī* (enmity) towards and *tabarrā* of those who oppose the infallible imams is among the *wājibāt* (obligations) and the most *aḥubb* (loved) of the *'ibādāt*. God curses the *ẓālim*, such that the oppressor is kept far from God's mercy. The meaning of *ẓālim* is that cited in the Qur'an, he says.[161] So, it is permissible to curse anyone who commits a *kabīra* (major sin) and someone who, although he praises Shi'ism, does not curse those non-Muslims who oppress the *'itra* of the Prophet or impedes cursing them.

In the third chapter Ṭāliqānī argues that Abū Muslim was not an Imami, by which, he says, he means the Twelver Shi'a, and that he opposed them. Ṭāliqānī cites the *ḥadīth* – again, first in Arabic and then in Persian translation – of the Prophet 'My *umma* will divide into 73 groups, one of which will be saved and others will be consigned to the Fire', but without any *sanad.*[162] In support of this text, he then also cites the Arabic of the text only: 'As the people of my House so the ship of Nūḥ: who boards it will be saved, and who turns away from it will drown', again without any *sanad.*[163] Ṭāliqānī notes that there are many other such texts proving that the 'saved sect' refers to the Twelver Shi'a and the others are in the Fire.

One of the latter groups, he says, is the Kaysaniyya and they also are divided into subgroups as the author of the book *Anīs al-abrār*[164] and the author of *ʿIllat al-iftirāq*[165] have said. Sayyid Aḥmad who, Ṭāliqānī notes, was the son-in-law of Mīr Dāmād, mentioned the group in his *Iẓhār al-ḥaqq*.[166] Amīr Sayyid Muḥammad al-Muṣṭafā al-Ḥusaynī al-Mūsāwī al-Sabziwārī, the grandfather of the Sayyid [Mīr Lawḥī], in his book *Nuṣrat al-islām fī ʿilm al-kalām* (The Assistance of Islam in the Science of Kalām) also mentioned some of the subgroups of the Kaysaniyya and other deviant groups. Ṭāliqānī says he saw one volume of this latter work, and showed it to Mīr Dāmād, who explained that the entire work was in seven volumes and that it was a great work.[167]

Of the Kaysaniyya, Ṭāliqānī continues, there was one group that maintained that Muḥammad b. al-Ḥanafiyya was the imam after ʿAlī, to be succeeded by his son Abū Hāshim, then ʿAlī b. ʿAbd Allāh b. ʿAbbās, then his son Muḥammad and then the latter's son Ibrāhīm. It was, he explains, Ibrāhīm who sent Abū Muslim to call the people of Khurasan. After Ibrāhīm al-Saffāḥ was the imam.[168]

Abū Muslim, he says, initially held this position but then changed his belief, to say that ʿAbbās [the uncle of the Prophet] was the imam after the Prophet and then after him his descendants and that anyone who did not accept the Abbasids as such was a *kāfir*. Then he laid claim to the imamate and to *ḥulūl*.

So, Ṭāliqānī concludes, Abū Muslim was not an Imami and, based on the *ḥadīth*, he is condemned to Jahannam.

In the fourth chapter, Ṭāliqānī commences by noting that historians disagree on Abū Muslim's genealogy, his name and his father's name.[169] According to the Imami *ʿulamā*ʾ, Ṭāliqānī says, Abū Muslim was born in the environs of Kufa, and his name was ʿAbd al-Raḥmān and his father's name was Aḥmad. The storytellers say his father's name was Asad b. Junayd.[170] It is not clear, he says, what sort of a person he was or what was his faith.

Ṭāliqānī notes that Sayyid Aḥmad in *Iẓhār* cited al-Masʿūdī, whom Ṭāliqānī says was one of the great Shiʿi figures during the lesser occultation of the Hidden Imam, that Abū Muslim was from Kufa and was an associate of Idrīs b. Maʿqil al-ʿIjlī.[171] Ṭāliqānī notes that Shaykh ʿAlī in his *Maṭāʿin* said that he was from Kufa and most non-Shiʿi *ʿulamā*ʾ agree with our *ʿulamā*ʾ on this.

They have said that his mother was of the ʿIjlī with a Maʿqil connection and that she gave him the name Muslim. The Banū Maʿqil said he was their *bandah* (slave) and claimed he was freed: when in Khurasan he became stronger he claimed he was of the children of Salīṭ b. ʿAbd Allāh b. ʿAbbās.[172] This says Ṭāliqānī, will be discussed further in the eighth chapter. But, he adds, some say that Abū Muslim was the product of an adulterous liaison.

Pace the reference to Aḥmad Zamchī cited in chapter nine, he had been mentioned in chapter five. There Ṭāliqānī also sheds light on contemporary practice by noting that the storytellers have caused the *ʿawwām* (common people) to accept that Qaḥṭaba and his sons and Aḥmad were the greatest of *ashrāf* and sayyids and to reject the *faḍl* (virtue) and the *sharaf* (honour) of the Banū Hāshim and the pious ones of the family of Abu'l-Qāsim.[173] These, Ṭāliqānī says, even venerate Yazīd who martyred Imam al-Ḥusayn. The common people side with what is *bāṭil* (falsehood). Even Luqmān[174] advised his son against the common people, he says.

In chapter eight are references, noted above, to alleged, contemporary practices, for example, storytellers' references to the request of Aḥmad Zamchī for some of Abū Muslim's blood.

In the ninth chapter, as discussed, Ṭāliqānī cites Shaykh al-Ḥasan's *ʿUmdat al-maqāl* as challenging Sunnis for being friendly to Abū Muslim, and refers to his own discussion of this in his 'Fawāʾid'. He adds that 'our *ʿulamā*ʾ' have challenged those who profess the Shiʿi faith but nevertheless attend to the 'lying storytellers'.

Ṭāliqānī's final chapter, ten, also says much about the contemporary scene. Here, Ṭāliqānī argues that Abbasid oppression of the Prophet's family was greater than that of the Umayyads and their followers, suggesting that the opposite was a contemporary view among those venerating Abū Muslim.

The Umayyads, says Ṭāliqānī, were 14 in number, ruled for 91 years and *shahīd kardan* (martyred) four of the infallible imams. The Abbasids were 37 in number, killed six of the infallible imams[175] and ruled for 524 years. In this period they so oppressed the children of the Prophet that in the world there was nothing nor any sign of them.

Abū Jaʿfar Dawānīqī, the second [Abbasid] caliph, killed a large number of the descendants of the Prophet and imprisoned others in houses made of salt such that when water was poured on them the houses collapsed on them. Others were buried alive in mud. Others had their hands and feet bound inside hollowed columns made of chalk and brick the tops of which were then finished with chalk and brick. Others were kept hungry and thirsty. His successors after him did the same. Ḥumayd b. Qaḥṭaba, whom the storytellers count as one of the noble sayyids, was one of the followers of the Abbasids who, on one night, killed 60 ʿAlid sayyids.[176]

He then notes, as already mentioned, that the Abbasid caliph al-Mutawakkil ordered that Najaf and Karbala be razed. Al-Mutawakkil was, says Ṭāliqānī, worse than Yazīd b. Muʿāwiya during whose time *ziyāra* to Imam al-Ḥusayn's tomb could be performed. During al-Mutawakkil's reign *ziyāra* was forbidden and he killed many who performed it. Ṭāliqānī refers to the oppressions of the Abbasids as recorded in the book *Mathālib al-ʿAbbāsiyya*[177] and that in *Minhāj al-hidāya*[178] the Abbasids killed 120,000 ʿAlids and innumerable Imamis.

Some, says Ṭāliqānī, hold ʿUmar al-Khaṭṭāb[179] as equivalent to Abū Muslim, again suggesting this was a contemporary argument, in that he was the cause of the victory of the Banū Umayya as Abū Muslim was of the Banū ʿAbbās. ʿUmar claimed the imamate and the caliphate as did Abū Muslim. ʿUmar won the allegiance of the people for Abū Bakr as Abū Muslim did for al-Saffāḥ. ʿUmar was an enemy of the Amīr al-Muʾminīn just as Abū Muslim was an enemy of Imam Jaʿfar. But Abū Muslim laid claim to *ḥulūl* which ʿUmar never did.

Ṭāliqānī ends his essay saying that being with the lying storytellers and listening to their *muzakhrafāt* is opposition to *Khudā*. This is because God said: O you who have believed, fear God and be with those who are true.[180] These oppose God and abandon the speech of the *ʿulamāʾ* and the virtuous and gatherings of *mufassirūn* (those who explicate the Qurʾan) and *muḥaddithūn* (those who narrate the traditions).[181]

Summary and Conclusions

Scholars have discussed the essays of the anti-Sufi polemic of the later years of the 11th/17th century and also have addressed the anti-Abū Muslim discourse of the 10th/16th century. The anti-Abū Muslim polemic of the first half of the 11th/17th century has received relatively less attention.

In addition to identifying one further work in this genre dateable to the previous century, this paper has identified some 24 works as having been composed in the years from before 1041/1631 through 1063/1652 attacking the veneration of Abū Muslim.

This paper has examined in detail the three essays remaining from those 24. Scholars, including the present author, have referred to these three and their having been written in defence of Mīr Lawḥī who had been attacking popular affection for Abū Muslim. But, to date, these essays have yet to be examined in any detailed, comparative manner in their own right.

Unlike the mainly Arabic-language works of the 10th/16th century these Persian-language essays suggest a rising millenarian tendency among an urban-based, Persian-speaking artisanal and craft population whose numbers were growing, especially in Isfahan in the early 11th/17th century. This growth was commensurate with the expansion of the city's commercial, political and spiritual infrastructure following its designation as the Safawid capital late in the previous century.

Written across the reigns of three Safawid rulers, the growing length of the three essays reflects the authors' increasingly detailed references and citations from both historical and religious, text-based sources. As such, they reflect the increasing frustration of their authors with the growing popularity of the Abū Muslim tradition and their inability to check it.

Careful, cautious examination of the three, taken together, also reveals something of the nature of the veneration of Abū Muslim in these years, if not as much information as may be desired.

Abū Muslim's popularity seems mainly to be an Isfahan-based phenomenon. His veneration is not mentioned in this period in connection with other sites on the Iranian plateau or in Iraq.[182]

These essays suggest that this veneration included, for example, Abū Muslim being understood to have been a friend of *ahl al-bayt* and the Imam al-Bāqir, the fifth imam, as having approved of Abū Muslim's *khurūj*. Abū Muslim is thought of as having been an incarnation of the Divine. Suggesting the continued presence of a Sunni population in the city, Sunnis and 'apostates', that is those Shiʿa whom the authors were attacking, are said to have approved of Abū Muslim's role in bringing the Abbasids to power and to be citing Imam ʿAlī as to the legitimacy of the Abbasids. There are also suggestions of favourable views of Abū Muslim's genealogy, of Qaḥṭaba and his sons, of the caliph Yazīd and Abū Muslim's associate Aḥmad Zamchī/Zamjī. Abbasid behaviour toward the imams and the faithful was understood to have been better than that of the Umayyads. Kaysānī views, in support of the legitimacy of Ibn al-Ḥanafiyya, seem also to be extant.

There are also references to the practice of such activities as songs and singing, and claims to *ḥulūl*, attacks thereon previously having been thought, including by the present author, based mainly on an examination of polemics of the later years of the century, to be a feature of the later spiritual scene and the later anti-Sufi polemic in particular.

In all this, the presence of 'storytellers' and their role in spreading pro-Abū Muslim sentiments is repeatedly referenced.[183]

The essays also suggest that such well-known figures in the Western-language literature on the period as Shaykh Bahāʾī and Mīr Dāmād were actively involved in attacking the veneration of Abū Muslim. Via those denunciations and through their student Mīr Lawḥī, and their overt support for him, both can be linked also to the later anti-Sufi discourse, if indirectly.

It is clear from these essays that the reaction against Mīr Lawḥī's effort to check Abū Muslim's popularity in Isfahan in these years was considerable, even if the author of one essay suggests not everyone in the city hated him, as it was against the otherwise unidentified, contemporary *akābir* of the faith.

On balance, many aspects of Twelver 'orthodoxy' as defined by clerics well known in the Western-language scholarship to date, such as Bahāʾī and Mīr Dāmād would seem to have made quite limited inroads in Isfahan, if not also the larger realm, by mid-century.[184]

That such scholars as these were on the defensive is further attested by the fact that Riḍawī only felt confident in penning his essay once he had left Isfahan to return home to Mashhad. Other contributors to both the anti-Abū Muslim, and the later anti-Sufi polemic, chose to hide their identities: the 1016/1607 Persian-language essay 'Arbaʿīn Ḥadīth' was authored anonymously. The authors of *Ḥadīqat al-shīʿa* and the 1060/1650 *Salwat al-shīʿa* did not own up to their contributions.[185] Even Sayyid Aḥmad refrained from explicitly referring to Mīr Lawḥī and did not refer to, and thereby avoided an opportunity to criticise, Abū Muslim's claims to *ḥulūl*.

What points to the minority status of the views of such scholars as Bahā'ī, Mīr Dāmād, Mīr Lawḥī, Riḍawī, Sayyid Aḥmad and Ṭāliqāni on Abū Muslim, if not also, at least implicitly, on a range of other issues, is the fact that only these three essays of the 24 items suggested as having been composed in these years attacking Abū Muslim's popularity have survived. Also, very little information is to be found in the bibliographical sources on Riḍawī, Sayyid Aḥmad and Ṭāliqānī and even then these same sources pay scant attention to their participation in the anti-Abū Muslim discourse. Indeed, the in-depth consideration of Sayyid Aḥmad's legacy to date nearly ignores his involvement in this polemic. It may well be that contemporary biographers did not want to be seen to pay attention to these scholars and, especially, their participation in the polemic.

At the same time, that so few copies of the three extant essays survive suggests that even these texts were in very limited circulation. Such other works in this discourse as al-Karakī's *Maṭā'in* and *Nuṣrat al-'ilm*, did not survive into the early 11th/17th century.[186]

Altogether, it would certainly seem that such works and such discourse in general were not popular in their own time let alone in the later years of the century.

To the extent that the limited legacy of this written record of this polemic reflects the state of the discourse on Abū Muslim 'on the street', then such 'orthodox' scholars as those named above together with the authors of the many 'lost' essays, must have felt beleaguered and isolated at times over these years, even before the already-known reports of such attacks in later years.[187]

To be sure, with the mention of songs, singing and *ḥulūl* as well as the use of Persian and the pivotal role of Mīr Lawḥī between both sets of polemics, the stage was set for the evolution of aspects of anti-Abū Muslim polemic into later anti-Sufi discourse and then that which centred on the condemnation of certain 'Sufi' practices as singing; these also involved Persian-language exchanges, as has been mentioned in the secondary sources discussed at the outset of this paper.

The use of Persian also featured in contemporary debates over the legitimacy of Friday prayer during the continued absence of the Imam.[188]

In both cases, the use of Persian may be indicative of an effort to engage directly with the populace over the heads of some clerical elements, underlining further the suggestion that some proportion of the scholarly class was, understandably, somewhat reticent to challenge majority opinion on such issues or to encourage lower ranks of clerics to do so. It is perhaps no wonder that as they evolved over the century these discourses, featured ever greater reference to earlier religious and other texts, and the imams' *ḥādīth*s in particular. In the process, these polemics both contributed to and benefitted from the more general 'rediscovery' of earlier resources that marked the later years of the second Safawid century.

Such discourses, however much they attest to discord and disagreement, together with the marked expansion of the realm's religious, distinctly Twelver, material infrastructure over the same time frame, were nevertheless instrumental in the final 'establishment' of the Twelver faith in Iran.[189]

NOTES

1 Among the first to discuss this literature was Kathryn Babayan in her 'The Waning of the Qizilbash: The Spiritual and the Temporal in Seventeenth Century Iran' (PhD dissertation, Princeton University, June 1993). See also her 'The Safavid Synthesis: From Qizilbash Islam to Imamite Shiʿism', *Iranian Studies*, 27 (1994), pp. 135–161; 'Sufis, Dervishes and Mullas: The Controversy over the Spiritual and Temporal Dominion in Seventeenth-Century Iran', in Charles Melville, ed., *Safavid Persia, The History and Politics of an Islamic Society* (London and New York, 1996), pp. 117–138. See also the relevant portions of her *Mystics, Monarchs, and Messiahs: Cultural Landscapes of Early Modern Iran* (Cambridge, MA, 2002), as cited below. Contributions by the present author include: 'Clerical Perceptions of Sufi Practices in Late Seventeenth-Century Persia: Arguments Over the Permissibility of Singing *(Ghinā)*', in Leonard Lewisohn and David Morgan, ed., *The Heritage of Sufism, vol. 3: Late Classical Persianate Sufism: The Safavid and Mughal Period (1501–1750)* (Oxford, 1999), pp. 135–164; 'Sufism and Anti-Sufism in Safavid Iran: The Authorship of the "Ḥadīqat al-Shīʿa" Revisited', *Iran*, 37 (1999), pp. 95–108; the later chapters of *Safavid Iran: Rebirth of a Persian Empire* (London, 2006); 'Clerical Perceptions of Sufi Practices in Late 17th-Century Persia, II: al-Ḥurr al-Āmilī (d. 1693) and the Debate on the Permissibility of *Ghinā*', in Yasir Suleiman, ed., *Living Islamic History: Studies in Honour of Professor Carole Hillenbrand* (Edinburgh, 2010), pp. 192–207. More recently, see also Ata Anzali, *Mysticism in Iran: The Safawid Roots of a Modern Concept* (Columbia, SC, 2017).

2 See, for example, Babayan, 'The Waning', part 4, esp. section 1 and portions of section 3; *Mystics*, pp. 142, 145–147, 159 n.74, 281 n.1, 409 n.42, with her defining of the second 'wave' as 1626–1649, and also 250f, 265, 283 n.21; Newman, as cited above; Anzali, *Mysticism*, pp. 31–37, 43, 60, 101, 108. See also Anzali, 'The Emergence of the Ẓahabiyya in Safavid Iran', *Journal of Sufi Studies*, 2 (2013), p. 161f.

3 On earlier veneration of Abū Muslim, see Irène Melikoff, *Abū Muslim, le "porte-hache" du Khorasan dans la tradition épique turcoiranienne* (Paris, 1962).

4 On al-Karakī, see our 'The Myth of the Clerical Migration to Safawid Iran: Arab Shīʿite Opposition to ʿAlī al-Karakī and Safawid Shīʿism', *Die Welt des Islams*, 33 (1993), pp. 66–112; *Safavid Iran*, s.v.; *Twelver Shiism. Unity and Diversity in the Life of Islam*,

632–1722 (Edinburgh, 2013), esp. pp. 155f. As suggested in these discussions, the *firmān* may well have been composed by al-Karakī himself.

5 See Newman, *Safavid Iran*, pp. 14–15 n.6, 20, 31–32. See also Babayan, *Mystics*, pp. 145f; Jean Calmard, 'Popular Literature Under the Safavids', in A. J. Newman, ed., *Society and Culture in the Early Modern Middle East: Studies on Iran in the Safavid Period* (Leiden, 2003), pp. 318–321, 336–337.

6 The text of al-Karakī's *fatwā*, in Arabic, as cited in *Anīs al-Mu'minīn*, the Persian-language work of al-Karakī's student al-Ḥamawī, can be found in Rasūl Ja'fariyān, *Ṣafawiyya dar 'arṣa-yi dīn, farhang, wa siyāsat* (3 vols., Qumm, 1379 Sh./2000), vol. 2, p. 868. For an English translation, see Babayan, *Mystics*, p. 121. On al-Ḥamawī, see also further below.

On *Maṭā'in* see Aqā Buzurg al-Ṭihrānī, *al-Dharī'a ilā taṣānīf al-Shī'a* (Tehran and Najaf, 1353–1398), 21, p. 138; Ja'fariyān, *Ṣafawiyya*, vol. 2, pp. 521, 860f. Babayan (*Mystics*, p. 430 n.9) says this work was 'probably' composed in 932/1526 but offers no supporting evidence. Anzali (*Mysticism*, p. 37 n.39) refers to the work as lost but offers no date.

See our *Twelver Shiism* for an extensive discussion of Twelver works nearly or completely lost across Twelver history.

On the storytellers, see Babayan, *Mystics*, pp. 121f; Ja'fariyān, *Ṣafawiyya*, vol. 2, pp. 851–879.

7 On this work, see al-Ṭihrānī, *al-Dharī'a*, 15, p. 241; Ja'fariyān, *Ṣafawiyya*, vol. 2, pp. 521–522; Babayan, *Mystics*, p. 430 n.9; Anzali, *Mysticism*, p. 35, nn.37,39, where he says it is lost.

8 On the Friday prayer essays composed in this century, see our *Twelver Shiism*, pp. 184f.

9 On al-Ḥamawī, see Babayan, *Mystics*, pp. 145f, 250–251, 282–289; Ja'fariyān, *Ṣafawiyya*, vol. 2, pp. 862f; Anzali, *Mysticism*, pp. 34–35. See also Babayan, 'Sufis', in *Safavid Persia, The History and Politics of an Islamic Society*, ed. Ch. Melville, pp. 124–125; 'The Safavid Synthesis', pp. 143–147; Calmard, pp. 318–321.

10 Newman, *Safavid Iran*, pp. 31, s.v. See also p. 51 for further discussion of the tribal dimension. On the Nuqṭawis, see also Abbas Amanat, 'The Nuqṭawī movement of Maḥmūd Pisīkhānī and his Persian cycle of mystical-materialism' in Farhad Daftary, ed., *Mediaeval Isma'ili History and Thought* (Cambridge, 1996), pp. 281–297; I. Ishraqi, '"Noqtaviyya" à l'époque Safavides', in Newman, *Society and Culture*, pp. 341–349.

11 Roger Savory, 'A Curious Episode of Safavid History', in Clifford Edmond Bosworth, ed., *Iran and Islam* (Edinburgh, 1971), pp. 461–473. On the *qalandar*s more generally, see Lloyd Ridgeon, *Morals and Mysticism in Persian Sufism: A history of Sufi-futuwwat in Iran* (Oxford and New York, 2010), pp. 132f.

12 Newman, *Safavid Iran*, p. 51.

13 Ibid., p. 51 n.10. See also Babayan, *Mystics*, pp. 148, 351. On the date of Isfahan's designation as perhaps as early *ca* 999/1590, rather than the oft-cited 1006/1597–8, see Newman, *Safavid Iran*, pp. 28, 55–56; Stephen P. Blake, *Half the World: The Social Architecture of Safavid Isfahan, 1590–1722* (Costa Mesa, CA, 1999), pp. 15–27.

14 On the internal and external challenges facing the realm in these years and the expansion of the capital in these years, see Newman, *Safavid Iran*, pp. 50f, 55f.

15 Ibid., p. 103; see p. 6 n.12 on the dates of Chardin's residence in Iran. On 'Abbās' attention to other cities, see, for example, ibid., p. 58. On the growth of Isfahan over the entire period see, for example, Blake, *Half the World*.

16 See ibid.; Mehdi Keyvani, *Artisans and Guild Life in the later Safavid Period* (Berlin, 1992).

17 On this essay, see Babayan, *Mystics*, p. 430 n.11. This work does not appear to be listed by al-Ṭihrānī nor is it mentioned by Anzali in his *Mysticism*.

18 Rula Jurdi Abisaab, *Converting Persia, Religion and Power in the Safavid Empire* (London, 2004), pp. 82–85, notes the anger of Luṭf Allāh al-Maysī (d. 1032/1622–3), recipient of 'Abbās I's patronage, to challenges to his authority from precisely these same, clearly well-organised, elements in the city. She sees 'racial overtones' (i.e. Arab v. non-Arab) to this mutual hostility (p. 84). But, it seems more likely the opposition of the 'artisans

and guildsmen' (p. 85) and their clear disdain for the *mujtahid* class generally that she says al-Maysī ascribed to these elements was more rooted in the socio-religious than she suggests. This anti-clerical sentiment could only fuel the rise of a desire for a more immanent spiritual experience—unmediated by court-based clerical elites, Arab or not—that was at the heart of these classes' interest in millenarian discourse.

19 Ṣadr al-Dīn Muḥammad Shīrāzī, *Kasr al-Aṣnām al-Jāhiliyya*, ed. M.T. Dānishpazhūh (Tehran, 1340 Sh./1962), p. 3. See also Ṣadr al-Dīn Shīrāzī (Mullā Ṣadrā), *Breaking the Idols of Ignorance*, tr. M. Dasht Buzurgi and F. Asadi Amjad, ed. S.K. Toussi (London, 2008), p. 4. Anzali's discussion of the text (*Mysticism*, pp. 60–62, 66) misses the vocational dimension.

See also Babayan, *Mystics*, pp. 165f, 176f, 213f, on the historical links between guilds and Sufi ʿAlid movements, focusing especially on *Futuwwat-nāmah-yi ṣulṭānī*, the undated work of Ḥusayn Kāshifī (d. 910/1505), which has been translated by J.R. Crook as *The Royal Book of Spiritual Chivalry* (Chicago, 2000). See also Ridgeon, pp. 125f; G.H. Yousofi, 'Kāshifī', *EI2*.

20 Anzali (*Mysticism*, p. 34) criticises Babayan's reference (citing 'The Waning', p. 204) to the early 11th/17th-century anti-Abū Muslim essays as the second wave thereof because the 10th/16th century essays were not 'coordinated' and so did not constitute a 'first' wave. On Mīr Lawḥī, see further below.

21 The essay is mentioned in passing by Babayan in her *Mystics*, pp. 158 n.73, 159 n.77, 430 n.15, 453–454. She suggests (p. 431 n.17) that the work was completed between 1035/1626 and 1038/1629, but offers no evidence to support this. Anzali's brief reference to the text (*Mysticism*, pp. 35–36) contains no mention of its composition in Persian nor offers any date of composition.

22 On this work and its author, see our 'Clerical Perceptions of Sufi Practices in Late 17th-Century Persia, II: al-Ḥurr al-Āmilī (d. 1693) and the Debate on the Permissibility of Ghinā'', in *Living Islamic History: Studies in Honour of Professor Carole Hillenbrand*, pp. 192–207.

23 On al-ʿAllāma, see our *Twelver Shiism*, pp. 122f.

24 Muḥammad b. al-Ḥasan, al-Ḥurr al-ʿĀmilī, *Kitāb ʿAmal al-ʿāmil* (Baghdad, 1385/1965–6), vol. 2, p. 273; Sayyid ʿAlī al-Madanī [aka Ibn Maʿṣūm], *Kitāb Sulāfat al-ʿaṣr* (Cairo, 1324/1906–7), p. 499.

Shaykh Zayn al-Dīn was a student of Bahā' al-Dīn Muḥammad (d. 1030/1621), known as Shaykh Bahā'ī, al-Ḥurr's father, and of Muḥammad Amīn al-Astarābādī (d. 1036/1626–7). The latter is often designated as the founder of the Akhbārī school in Twelver Shiʿism. On Shaykh Zayn al-Dīn, who died in Mecca and the various dates given for his death, see al-Ḥurr, 1, pp. 92f, esp. 93 n.3; 1062/1652 and 1064/1654 are noted as dates given for his death. See also al-Mīrzā ʿAbd Allāh al-Isbahānī Afandī, *Riyāḍ al-ʿulamā'* (Qumm, 1401/1980–1), vol. 2, pp. 387f, giving 1063/1653 and 1064/1654. On al-Shahīd al-Thānī, see our *Twelver Shiism*, pp. 162–164. On Bahā'ī and his associate Mīr Dāmād, a descendant of ʿAlī al-Karakī, see further below.

25 Afandī, *Riyāḍ al-ʿulamā'*, 5, pp. 104–105.

26 Aghā Buzurg al-Ṭihrānī's entry on Riḍawī in his *Ṭabaqāt aʿlām al-shīʿa*, 5 (Qumm, n.d.), p. 234, references these and later sources. Riḍawī was, himself, descended from Imam Muḥammad al-Jawād (d. 220/835), the ninth imam. See *Ṭabaqāt*, 5, p. 114.

27 Mīr Muḥammad Zamān b. Muḥammad Jaʿfar al-Riḍawī, *Ṣaḥīfat al-Rashād* in *Mīrāth-i islāmī-yi Īrān*, R. Jaʿfariyān, ed., 2 (Qumm, 1374 Sh./1995–6), pp. 268–272. On this essay see al-Ṭihrānī, *al-Dharīʿa*, 15, p. 17.

28 Their arrival in Mashhad predated 1025/1616 as al-Ṭihrānī (*Ṭabaqāt*, 5, p. 114) notes that as the year Riḍawī's father died. See also *al-Dharīʿa* (9/4, pp. 1220–21), where al-Ṭihrānī, citing *Ṣaḥīfa*, refers to Mīr Lawḥī and his father as 'returning' to Isfahan—though the text itself says *bih Iṣfāhān raftand* (they went to Isfahan). Mīr Lawḥī is said to have been born in Isfahan *ca* 1000/1591, to a woman his father married on his way

back from a visit to Iraq. It would seem the two, at least, had been on a sojourn of unknown duration in Sabziwar. On Mīr Lawḥī see *al-Ṭabaqāt*, 5, pp. 479–481, where he is identified as a Ḥusaynī, and further below.

29 On this identification, see our *Safavid Iran*, pp. 30, 67, 92, 178 n.20, 229 n.66, 240 n.56. See also 14, 14 n.5. Note that in his *Ṭabaqāt* entry on him al-Ṭihrānī, see below, identifies Mīr Lawḥī as a Ḥusaynī but acknowledges the Musawid claim.

30 Babayan ('The Waning', n.528) notes that in his *Anīs* al-Ḥamawī mentioned such a claim being advanced.

31 In a personal communication, Dr Hannah-Lena Hagemann, an ERC Research Associate, Asien-Afrika-Institut, Universität Hamburg, has suggested the author may have been confusing this Shabīb with Shabīb b. Yazīd, a Kharijite rebel of the Banū Shaybān who, after his 1st/7th-century rising was, also, said to have drowned fleeing from the troops of al-Ḥajjāj. See her 'History and Memory: Khārijism in Early Islamic Historiography' (PhD dissertation, University of Edinburgh, 2014), pp. 22f, 189f, and the sources cited therein. See also Karl Vilhem Zettersteen and Chase F. Robinson, 'Shabīb b. Yazīd', *EI2*.

32 A reference to the 'infusion', indwelling or incarnation of God in a creature. See Louis Massignon [Georges C. Anawati], 'Ḥulūl', *EI2*.

33 Using the fifth form of the Arabic *bari'a*, in Persian *tabarrā*, meaning 'to free oneself from', or 'be free of', that is to distance oneself from.

34 Here the editor (*Mirath-i islāmī-yi Īrān*, 2, p. 271 n.2) notes that, according to Ṭāliqānī in his later *Khulāṣat al-fawā'id*, this text was cited by al-Karakī in his *Maṭā'in* but that he, the editor, could not locate it in any collections of the imams' *ḥadīths*. On Ṭāliqānī's having seen it in a work by Sa'd b. 'Abd Allāh al-Ash'arī al-Qummī (d. 299–301/911–914), see also below. On Sa'd, see our *The Formative Period of Twelver Shi'ism*, pp. 14, 42. Al-Ṣaffār al-Qummī, Muḥammad b. al-Ḥasan (d. 290/902–3), in his *Baṣā'ir al-darajāt*, ed. M. Kūchah-bāghī (Tabriz, 1381/1961; Qumm, 1404/1983–4), pp. 190f, includes traditions in which the imams stated they possessed *al-Ṣaḥīfa* on which was written a list of those in heaven and *al-nār* (another Qur'anic reference to Hell). A challenge by Hasan Ansari to *Baṣā'ir* as a work of al-Ṣaffār has been rejected by M. A. Amir-Moezzi. See the latter's 'The Silent Qur'an and the Speaking Qur'an: History and Scriptures through the Study of Some Ancient Texts', *Stud. Islam.*, 108 (2013), p. 159 n.37.

35 The editor (2, p. 272 n.1) refers to this text as found in Muḥammad Bāqir al-Majlisī's (d. 1111/1699) *Biḥār al-anwār* (Beirut, 1404/1983–4), 27, p. 52, but adds that it is corrupted. However, the text also can be found in the much earlier *Amāli* of Ibn Bābawayh, Muḥammad b. 'Alī, al-Shaykh al-Ṣadūq (d. 381/991) (n.p., 1362/1943), p. 56.

The 'seven often-repeated', in Q 15: 87, refers to the seven verses of the first sura of the Qur'an.

36 Prior to this last statement, and clearly intending to follow on from the citation of the text by Imam Ja'far, Riḍawī cites the following Persian poetry:

Dūstī bā dushmanān vā dushmanī bā dūstān
Mīkunī āngāh lāf dūstdārī mīzanī

The present writer has not been able to identify this poetry. R. Ja'fariyān, in a private communication, noted its affinity with the poetry of Dastghayb Shīrāzī, the Safawid period poet.

37 This in contrast to accounts portraying the shrines as in relative ruin in these years. See our *Twelver Shiism*, pp. 165, 190–91. See also nn. 39, 40.

38 The shrines were lost to the Ottomans in 941/1534, during the first civil war. 'Abbās I retook the area in 1033/1623–4. But, as noted in our *Twelver Shiism* (pp. 190–191), the shifting boundaries did not impede scholars' movements between the two realms.

39 Western scholarly attention has focused on the supposedly large numbers of Arab Shiʿi scholars who came to Iran after Ismāʿīl I proclaimed Twelver Shiʿism to be the official faith of the realm. See n.4 and Abisaab as cited above. Much less attention has been paid to the travel patterns of local, in this case, Iran-based scholars in the Safawid period. The example of Mīr Lawḥī and his father only further suggests Isfahan's star was on the rise. See the latter chapters of our *Twelver Shiism* and, especially, Appendix I.

On Mīr Lawḥī's birth in Isfahan *ca* 1000/1591, to a woman his father married in the city on his way back from Iraq, see above. It might have been that the family moved back to Sabziwar sometime after Mīr Lawḥī's birth, or that father and son had ventured there for a visit to the former's family. In any case, the capital clearly represented was a more attractive choice as a permanent abode than either his father's home town Sabziwar or, for that matter, Mashhad.

40 Gerald Hawting, in his *EI2* article on 'Marwān II', notes that the appellation can be understood as either positive—for bravery—or for his fondness for a particular flower, as insulting.

41 On this appellation, see further below.

42 al-Ḥurr, *Kitāb Amal al-āmil*, 1, p. 33; Afandī, *Riyāḍ al-ʿulamā'* 1, p. 39. In his 'Aḥmad ʿAlawī', *EIR*, Henry Corbin cites two *ijāzāt* from Mīr Dāmād, dated 1017/1608 and 1019/1610, and one from Shaykh Bahā'ī dated 1018/1609. In his *al-Dharīʿa* (1, p. 237), al-Ṭihrānī refers to an *ijāza* from Shaykh Bahā'ī dated 1012/1603. Mīr Lawḥī and even his opponent Muḥammad Taqī al-Majlisī (d. 1070/1659), father of Bāqir al-Majlisī, both seem to have studied with Bahā'ī and Mīr Dāmād. To be sure Afandī (2, p. 118f), does not list Mīr Dāmād as a teacher of Taqī al-Majlisī although al-Ḥusayn b. Muḥammad al-Nurī (d. 1320/1902), in his *Mustadrak al-wasā'il* (Qumm, 1409/1989), vol. 3, p. 416f, does. As for Mīr Lawḥī's association with both, this is based on his own later claims. On Mīr Lawḥī, see also Abdul-Hadi Hairi, 'Mīr Lawḥī', *EI2*. On Taqī al-Majlisī, see Rainer Brunner, 'Majlesi, Moḥammad Taqi', *EIR*. See also Jaʿfariyān, *Ṣafawiyya*, 2, p. 870.

43 See also n.46 below. On both Shaykh Bahā'ī and Mīr Dāmād, their associations with the court and their expansionist views of the authority of the senior clergy over the interpretation of doctrine and the implementation of practice during the absence of the Hidden Imam, see our *Safavid Iran*, s.v.

44 In his 'Aḥmad ʿAlawī', Corbin gives a good listing and description of his key works and a good summary of *Miṣqal*. See also the 2010 essay of Denis Halft cited below, which article includes a discussion of the many extant manuscript copies of *Lawāmiʿ-i rabbānī*. Halft's 'Hebrew Bible Quotations', also cited below, discusses the extant copies of both works. *Miṣqal*, edited by Ḥ.N. Iṣfahānī, was published in Qumm in 1373/1994.

45 See Corbin, 'Aḥmad ʿAlawī'; See also ʿAbdul-Hadi Hairi, 'Reflections on the Shiʿi Responses to Missionary Thought and Activities in the Safavid Period', in Jean Calmard, ed., *Études Safavides* (Paris and Tehran, 1993), pp. 155f; Francis Richard, 'L'apport des missionnaires européens à la connaissance de l'Iran en Europe et de l'Europe en Iran', in ibid., pp. 260f; Abisaab, *Converting Persia*, pp. 79–81. More recently, see also D. Halft, 'Schiitische Polemik gegen das Christentum im safawidischen Iran des 11./17. Jhdts. Sayyid Aḥmad ʿAlawī's *Lawāmiʿ-i rabbānī dar radd-i shubha-yi naṣrānī*', in Camilla Adang and Sabine Schmidtke, ed., *Contacts and Controversies between Muslims, Jews and Christians in the Ottoman Empire and Pre-Modern Iran* (Istanbuler Texte und Studien 21) (Würzburg, 2010), pp. 273–334; 'Hebrew Bible Quotations in Arabic Transcription in Safavid Iran of the 11th/17th Century: Sayyed Aḥmad ʿAlavī's Persian Refutations of Christianity', *Intellectual History of the Islamicate World*, 1 (2013), pp. 235–252.

46 See Babayan, *Mystics*, pp. 248–249, 159 nn. 77–78, 412, 431 n.17, 480 n.99; on Sayyid Aḥmad himself, see p. 431 n.20. In his brief mention of the essay (*Mysticism*, p. 60), as in the case of *Ṣaḥīfa*, Anzali does not note that *Iẓhār* was composed in Persian, nor does he note Sayyid Aḥmad's familial connection(s) to Mīr Dāmād.

47 Sayyid Aḥmad al-ʿAlawī al-ʿĀmilī, *Iẓhār al-ḥaqq va miʿyār al-ṣidq*, in *Mīrath-i islāmī-yi Īrān*, ed. R. Jaʿfariyān, 2 (Qumm, 1374 Sh./1995–6), pp. 260–267. On this essay see al-Ṭihrānī, 11, p. 91.

48 Charles Pellat, who wrote 'al-Masʿūdī', *EI2*, agrees with the idea of al-Masʿūdī's 'active sympathy for the [sic] 'Ahl al-Bayt and Twelver Imāmī Shīʿism'. Pellat queries the attribution of the book on *waṣiya*, and cites his 'Masʿūdī et l'imāmisme' in Toufic Fahd, ed. *Le Shīʿisme imāmite*, (Paris, 1970), pp. 69–80. Michael Cooperson, the author of 'Masʿūdī', *EIR*, concludes that he was a Shiʿi of the rationalist (Muʿtazilī) persuasion.

For the Sayyid's references, see Muḥammad b. Ibn Idrīs, *al-Sarāʾir* (Qumm, 1410–12/1990), 1, p. 161; al-ʿAllāma al-Ḥillī, *Khulāṣat al-rijāl*, ed. J. al-Quyyūmī (Qumm, 1417/1996), p. 186. On these two figures, see our *Twelver Shiism*, pp. 109f, 122f.

49 See also his works as cited in the secondary sources cited above.

50 Al-Masʿūdī, *Murūj al-dhahab*, ed. M.M. ʿAbd al-Ḥamīd (Beirut, 1403/1982), 3, p. 254. The editor cites a different edition of this text.

51 *Al-Faqīh* was the third of the 'four books', the four compilations of the imams' traditions assembled between the disappearance of the twelfth imam in the 250s/870s and the arrival of the Saljūqs in Baghdad in 447/1055. On the four, see our *Twelver Shiism*, sv.

52 The editor (*Mīrāth-i islāmī-yi Īrān*, p. 263 n.1) cites the text as from Ibn Bābawayh, *Man lā yaḥḍuruhu al-faqīh* (Qumm, 1413/1992–3), 1, p. 252/769. See also, however, the latter's *ʿIlal al-sharāʾiʿ* (Qumm, n.d.), pp. 348–347, with an *isnād*.

53 The word is *mutanāhī* in the text (*Mīrāth-i islāmī-yi Īrān*, 2, p. 263).

54 'And incline not toward those who do wrong, lest the Fire should touch you. . .'

55 This is the position of the same Ibn Bābawayh in his *al-Iʿtiqādāt*. See our *Twelver Shiism*, p. 68.

56 'And whoever is blind in this [life] will be blind in the Hereafter and more astray from the Path.' He follows this with a *bayt* of Arabic-language poetry to the effect that many start out but few arrive at a destination. A version of this *bayt* is cited by Qāḍī Nūr Allāh al-Shūshtarī (d. 1019/1610) in his *al-Ṣawārim* (n.p., 1367/1947–8), p. 269.

57 This was the half-brother of imams al-Ḥasan and al-Ḥusayn whom al-Mukhtār (d. 67/687) proclaimed imam and *mahdī*. See our *Twelver Shiism*, pp. 20–21.

58 Ibid., pp. 21–22. On the connection between these and the Kaysaniyya, *pace* Ṭāliqānī, see below.

59 The editor says (*Mīrāth-i islāmī-yi Īrān*, 2, p. 264 n.2) that he could not find any mention of this group.

60 al-Masʿūdī, 3, p. 269. On this text, see further below.

61 Ibid., pp. 269–270.

62 Ibid., p. 284.

63 Ibid., p. 284.

64 'To hell let him go! What is there, in his likes, which if we miss we should regret?' al-Masʿūdī, 3, p. 285.

65 Q 50:37.

66 See our *Twelver Shiism*, pp. 177f.

67 Babayan's references to the author are mainly made in passing (*Mystics*, pp. 153 n.37, 155 n.50, 159 n.76, 159 n.78, 251–252, 265, 283–284 nn.16, 17, 24–6, 287–8 nn. 48, 58. More recently, Anzali (*Mysticism*, p.60), as with his references to the first two essays examined herein, did not note *Khulāṣa* was composed in Persian. As to 'Iẓhār', see *Mysticism*, p. 38n, 41n, 60.

68 Afandī, 3, p. 268. On *Ghaniyya*, see al-Ṭihrānī, *al-Dharīʿa*, 18, p. 174. The same al-Ṭihrānī, in his multi-volume bio-bibliography of Shiʿi scholars over the centuries, notes that in 1029/1620 Ṭāliqānī copied a work produced the previous year by his teacher Mīr Dāmād on *al-raḍāʿ* (wet-nursing). See al-Ṭihrānī, *Ṭabaqāt*, 5, p. 356. Wet-nursing was a major topic of contention in the previous century between Mīr Dāmād's ancestor ʿAlī al-Karakī and Ibrāhīm al-Qaṭīfī. On their exchanges, including those on

this issue, see our 'The Myth of the Clerical Migration to Safawid Iran: Arab Shīʿite Opposition to ʿAlī al-Karakī and Safawid Shīʿism', *Die Welt des Islams*, 33 (1993), pp. 83–89. Also on Ṭāliqānī, see Jaʿfariyān, *Ṣafawiyya*, 2, pp. 869f.

69 On *Fawāʾid*, see al-Ṭihrānī, *al-Dharīʿa*, 16, p. 361. On *Khulāṣa*, see al-Ṭihrānī, 7, p. 231. That, as noted below, in the essay's first *faṣl* Ṭāliqānī says he heard about Mīr Lawḥī attacking Abū Muslim from his teacher Mīr Dāmād, suggests he was not a native of the capital and was, at best, a recent arrival to the city. *Khulāṣa* was, as suggested, composed after Mīr Dāmād's death (see below), but the composition date of the original *Fawāʾid* is not clear.

70 In *Mystics* (p. 159 n.76) Babayan says the essay was 'probably' done 'in the third decade of the seventeenth century' but, as with her dating of *Ṣaḥīfa* above, cites no supporting evidence.

71 See al-Ṭihrānī, *al-Dharīʿa*, 4, pp. 150f.

72 A cross check of the 18 essays listed here in *Khulāṣa* (2, p. 277) and the 17 listed by al-Ṭihrānī (4, p. 151), as 1063/1652, reveals one essay in the latter (number 8 which is, in fact, *Khulāṣa* itself) as not listed in the former, and, similarly, four listed by Ṭāliqānī (14, pp. 16–18) that do not appear in al-Ṭihrānī, 4, pp. 151–152 (cf. Babayan, *Mystics*, p. 159 n.78, who notes only three). Items 4 to 6 in al-Ṭihrānī are cited as a single essay, *Anīs al-Abrār*, by Ṭāliqānī as the first item in his list.

Ṭāliqānī's listing of 18 items (p. 277) includes his own, earlier, *Fawāʾid al Muʾminīn* (which is number 13 in both lists) but he does not cite such later works as *Tawḍīḥ al-Mushribīn* (on which see al-Ṭihrānī, 4, pp. 495f).

Based on both of these lists, as many as 21 items seem to have been composed attacking the veneration of Abū Muslim and in defence of Mīr Lawḥī. To be sure, given that, as noted above, Mīr Lawḥī is not referred to by Sayyid Aḥmad in his *Iẓhār*, it may well also be the case that others of these essays were also 'indirect' defences. In any case, as discussed below, adding to these 21 other works of the same genre cited by Ṭāliqānī elsewhere in *Khulāṣa*, as discussed below, as many as 24 such items may have been composed in these early years. In addition, as noted below, a further work, *Nuṣrat al-ʿilm*, can also be identified as having been composed in the previous century.

Ṭāliqānī's reference, cited below, to his teacher Mīr Dāmād as dead also means the present work was completed after 1041/1631–2.

73 On *Ḥadīqa* as a bridge between both polemics, see our 'Sufism and Anti-Sufism'. On the work itself see also al-Ṭihrānī, *al-Dharīʿa*, 6, p. 386.

The 1060/1652 notes on the back of *Iẓhār* also do not mention *Ḥadīqa*. In our 'Sufism and Anti-Sufism' (pp. 98–99) we noted that the 1060/1650 (not 1050 as erroneously cited in the article at p. 98 but correctly as 1060 on p. 99) Persian-language 'Salwat al-shīʿa'—itself not cited in either of the above two lists—seems to be the first work to refer to *Ḥadīqa*.

74 ʿAbd al-Muṭṭalib b. Yaḥyā Ṭāliqānī, *Khulāṣat al-fawāʾid*, in *Mīrāth-i islāmī-yi Īrān*, ed. R. Jaʿfariyān (Qumm, 1374 Sh./1995–6), vol. 2, p. 273. Neither the editor nor the present writer could trace the first. He traced a version of the second, with an *isnād* to al-Majlisī's *Biḥār* (57, p. 301). The exact text, still minus a full *sanad*, may be found in Warrām b. Abū Farās al-Ḥillī (d. 605/1208), *Majmaʿa warrām* (Qumm, n.d.), 2, p. 7. Al-ʿAllāma al-Ḥillī also cited the text in his *Nahj al-ḥaqq* (Qumm, 1407), p. 37.

75 As noted below, the editor notes (*Mīrāth-i islāmī-yi Īrān*, 2, p. 300 n.2) that the end is incomplete but speculates that no more than a page is missing.

76 ʿAbd al-Muṭṭalib b. Yaḥyā Ṭāliqānī, *Khulāṣat al Fawāʾid*, in *Mīrāth-i islāmī-yi Īrān*, vol. 2, pp. 273–300.

77 Riḍawī, *Mīrāth-i islāmī-yi Īrān*, 2, p. 270.

78 Aḥmad al-ʿAlawī, *Mīrāth-i islāmī-yi Īrān*, 2, pp. 265–267.

79 Ṭāliqānī, in *Mīrāth-i islāmī-yi Īrān*, 2, pp. 280–294. This is Abū Jaʿfar ʿAbd Allāh b. Muḥammad, known as al-Manṣūr (d. 158/775), the second Abbasid caliph.

'Dawānīqī', meaning 'master of dinars'—an appellation widely used of him by Shiʿi scholars though not noted as such in the articles 'al-Manṣūr' by K.V. Zetterstéen in *EI1* and 'al-Manṣūr' by Hugh Kennedy in *EI2*—refers to his miserliness, as noted by Meir M. Bar-Asher in his *Scripture and Exegesis* (Leiden, 1999), p. 110 n.94. On these dates, see H. Kennedy, 'al-Manṣūr', *EI2*.

80 Riḍawī, '*Ṣaḥīfa*', *Mīrāth-i islāmī-yi Īrān*, 2, pp. 265–267.

81 Aḥmad al-ʿAlawī, '*Iẓhār al-ḥaqq*', *Mīrāth-i islāmī-yi Īrān*, 2, pp. 265–267.

82 To better chart this process, Ṭāliqānī's coverage will be compared to that on offer in the history of Aḥmad b. Abū Yaʿqūb, al-Yaʿqūbī (d. after 292/905), *Ta'rīkh al-Yaʿqūbī*, ed. M.S. Baḥr al-ʿUlūm, 3 (Najaf, 1384/1964), that of Muḥammad b. Jarīr al-Ṭabarī (d. 310/923) and the excellent discussion of the early years of the Abbasids by Saleh Said Agha, *The Revolution Which Toppled the Umayyads* (Leiden, 2003), to which Dr. A. Marsham kindly directed me. On al-Yaʿqūbī's death date, see Muhammad Qasim Zaman, 'al-Yaʿkubī', *EI2*.

83 Cf. al-Ṭabarī, *The History of al-Ṭabarī*, tr. J.D. McAuliffe (Albany, NY, 1995), 28, pp. 4f, esp. 10f. Abū Jaʿfar is said to have been wary of his uncle from the start (4).

84 Al-Ṭabarī (28, p. 22) mentions the wealth seized and letters back and forth, but there is no reference to this sword or, in the letters, to a demand for the wealth. During his later face-to-face confrontation with Abū Muslim (28, p. 36) Abū Jaʿfar does refers to 'two blades', otherwise unremarked, that Abū Muslim seized when he defeated ʿAbd Allāh b. ʿAlī and one of which Abū Muslim surrendered on the spot.

85 Qaḥṭaba b. Shabīb, an Abbasid general, mentioned briefly by both Riḍawī and Sayyid Aḥmad, was killed at or drowned during the Abbasid battle for Kufa in 132/749. His son al-Ḥasan then assumed command and took the city. See Moshe Sharon, 'Kaḥṭaba', *EI2*.

86 Mālik was one of the 12 Abbasid *naqībs* and a confidant of Abū Muslim. See Agha, *The Revolution* s.v., esp. pp. 264 n.4, 359. On Abū Muslim's treatment of the caliph's letter, see al-Ṭabarī, 4, pp. 22f.

87 This is not recorded by al-Ṭabarī.

88 On this work by Kaydharī, see al-Ṭihrānī, 18, p. 89, on the text itself, as *Kitāb al-barāya fī maʿrifat al-anbiyā' wa'l-awliyā'* and saying the author was alive in 526/1131 when he completed the work. See also al-Ṭihrānī, 25, p. 16. In 7, pp. 214–215, see also al-Ṭihrānī's references to his being alive in 610/1213. Muḥsin al-Amīn, in his *Aʿyān al-shīʿa* (Beirut, 1406/1986), 9, pp. 250f, also cited the 610/1213 date. Al-Ḥurr (2, p. 220) mentions him only as *faqīh*. Afandī (4, p. 401) is not sure of his name.

The editor of *Khulāṣa* said (*Mīrāth-i islāmī-yi Īrān*, 2, p. 259) he could not find a copy of Kaydharī's text.

For more on Kaydharī, see also below.

89 On efforts by Abū Jaʿfar, though not letters he sent directly to Abū Muslim, see al-Ṭabarī, 4, pp. 27–28. See also further below on Abū Ḥumayd's conversation with Abū Muslim.

90 One of the original Abbasid *naqībs* (Agha, p. 356). Elsewhere, it seems he became governor of Khurasan after Abū Muslim's death; al-Ṭabarī describes him as Abū Muslim's deputy in the province. See also al-Ṭabarī, 28, pp. 11, 11n62, 29.

91 al-Ṭabarī (28, p. 29) refers to such a letter from Abū Jaʿfar to Abū Dāwūd but only that in it Abū Jaʿfar stated Khurasan was his 'for as long as [i.e. Abū Dāwūd] should live'. Al-Ṭabarī also refers to Abū Muslim's decision not to come to the caliph but to rise against him.

92 A close associate of Abū Muslim (Agha, p. 362). See also al-Ṭabarī, 28, p. 11 n.61 that he served under ʿAbd Allāh b ʿAlī.

93 See al-Ṭabarī, 28, p. 28, on the dialogue mission and the dialogue between Abū Ḥumayd and Abū Muslim.

94 This letter is mentioned in al-Ṭabarī, 28, p. 29.

95 A close associate of Abū Muslim. See Agha, pp. 356–357; al-Ṭabarī, 28, p. 11 n60.

96 al-Ṭabarī refers (28, pp. 29–31) to such a mission by Abū Isḥāq, to the caliph's promise to him that he would be governor of Khurasan if he could change Abū Muslim's mind, to Abū Isḥāq's return to Abū Muslim, to the latter's decision to come to the caliph and apologise, to Abū Muslim's letter to the caliph, but to a subsequent decision by both Abū Muslim and al-Manṣūr each to kill the other.

97 On Fatimid associations see also below.

98 The editor cites the text from Muḥammad b. Yaʿqūb al-Kulaynī, *al-Kāfī*, ed. A.A. al-Ghaffārī (8 vols., Tehran, 1377–1379/1957–1960), vol. 8, p. 274–412.

99 al-Ṭabarī does not here refer to any communication between Abū Muslim and the imam.

100 al-Ṭabarī, 28, p. 30.

101 This account tallies with that in al-Ṭabarī, 28, pp. 32f, though other accounts cite other numbers.

102 This was mentioned by Ṭāliqānī in his previous chapter, chapter 7 (*Mīrāth-i islāmī-yi Īrān*, 2, p. 286), on Abū Muslim's activities during the time of al-Saffāḥ. In that chapter Ṭāliqānī had noted that at al-Saffāḥ's death Abū Muslim had sent a letter to Abū Jaʿfar but did not acknowledge his succession and had backed ʿĪsā. This is discussed further below. On the killing of Sulaymān himself, as another example of material cited from the work of Kaydharī, see further below.

103 On him, see al-Ṭabarī, 28, pp. 201, 201 n.973, and s.v. See also Dominique Sourdel, "ʿĪsā b. Mūsā', *EI2*.

104 These two points feature in one account of the exchange between the two men in al-Ṭabarī (28, p. 38). But, for the marriage issue, see also 28, p. 39. On Amina, the daughter of the caliph's paternal aunt, see al-Ṭabarī, 28, p. 38 n.169. The marriage would have helped solidify Abū Muslim's claim to being a member of Āl ʿAbbās. See also the following note.

105 In chapter seven of 'Fawā'id' Ṭāliqānī had also referred to Abū Muslim trying to construct familial links to Salīṭ b ʿAbd Allāh b. al-ʿAbbās to make him an Abbasid, and so protect himself from Abū Jaʿfar, with whose accession Abū Muslim had been angry—feeling that he should have been made caliph—and with whom he had then began to act badly such that Abū Jaʿfar began to slander him. Agha (53, p. 70) explains that this would have further cemented Abū Muslim's own claim to be an Abbasid. See also al-Ṭabarī, 28, pp. 38–39, 38 n.169, the previous note and al-Ṭabarī, 28, pp. 3–4 where al-Ṭabarī notes Abū Muslim's pledge of allegiance to Abū Jaʿfar at the latter's accession.

106 This exchange is not cited by al-Ṭabarī, though the reference to a slave girl is included in the same account above (28, p. 39) as that which refers to the marriage with Amina. See above on the issue of two swords that Abū Muslim had taken from ʿAbd Allāh b. ʿAlī, one of which he surrendered to the caliph during this face-to-face confrontation.

107 On other numbers for the group, see al-Ṭabarī, 28, pp. 36–38.

108 This is not in al-Ṭabarī who, twice (28, p. 40), cites Abū Muslim as referring to Abū Jaʿfar as 'Commander of the Faithful'.

109 The exchange about Abū Muslim being an enemy is included in one account cited by al-Ṭabarī (28, p. 40).

At this Abū Jaʿfar recited a poem. The editor of *Khulāṣa* points out (2, p. 292 n.1) that al-Ṭabarī (28, p. 39), al-Masʿūdī (3, p. 304) and al-Yaʿqūbī (3, p. 107) all cite different versions of the first two *bayt* of the entire poem. In fact, they each cite only parts thereof.

110 On ʿĪsa's entrance, but absent the reference to the claim to *ḥulūl*, the reply about Abū Muslim's army and the subsequent detail, see al-Ṭabarī, 28, p. 40.

111 Not, apparently, in al-Masʿūdī. Babayan (*Mystics*, p. 146) cites al-Ḥamawī in his *Anīs* that Ismāʿīl I destroyed this site but notes this is unnoticed in the 'official chronicles'. Interestingly, Ṭāliqānī does not refer to such an action by Ismāʿīl I.

112 The editor (*Mīrāth-i islāmī-yi Īrān*, 2. p. 293, n.1) cites this text from al-Majlisī, *Biḥār*, 92, p. 172, but it is also found in Quṭb al-Dīn al-Rawāndī's (d. 573/1177) *al-Kharā'ij wa'l-jarā'iḥ* (Qumm, 1409/1988–9), 3, p. 1058.

113 That the text is from al-Masʿūdī, 3, p. 305 is unnoticed by the editor.

For a general introduction to the Khurramiyya, and their pre-Islamic roots in Iran, see Wilferd Madelung's article in *EI2* and his chapter thereon in his *Religious Trends in Early Islamic Iran* (Albany, NY, 1988), pp. 1f. See also below on al-Ṭabarī and Khurramiyya.

114 al-Masʿūdī (3, p. 305) also refers to both these groups and the latter as the Fatimids, and describes their beliefs as such. But, see Marius Canard, 'Fāṭimids', *EI2*.

115 The editor of '*Khulāṣa*' (p. 293, n.2) notes the work is discussed by al-Ṭihrānī, *al-Dharīʿa* 3, pp. 163–164. The main entry, not cited by the editor, is 19, p. 46. On Kaydharī, see both above and below.

For others of Kaydharī's works see also al-Ṭihrānī, ibid., 2, p. 431; 3, p. 80, 6; 381; 6, p. 285 (where his name is given as al-Kundarī); 6, p. 381; 8, p. 116; 12, p. 223 (this with the title of *Salwat al-shīʿa*, the same title as an anti-Sufi work of the 11th/17th century on which see al-Ṭihrānī, 12, pp. 223–224; 14, p. 146; 18, p. 89 (on the *Kifāya*); 18, p. 282; 23, p. 245.

116 The editor cites al-Ṭihrānī, 19, p. 46 on this work. This refers only to the title. The main entry on the work is in al-Ṭihrānī, 3, p. 163, where the work is dated to the 8th/14th century.

117 On Muḥammad b. ʿAlī, Ibn Shahr Āshūb, see our *Twelver Shiism*, pp. 113–115, 121, 132. Al-Ṭihrānī (2, p. 487) also says that Kaydharī was a student of al-Ṭūsī.

118 This is the first Twelver Shiʿi martyr, Shaykh Muḥammad b. Makkī (d. 786/1384), Ibn Makkī, on whom see our *Twelver Shiism*, pp. 140f. On this commentary, entitled *Ghāyat al-murād*, see al-Ṭihrānī, 6, p. 17.

119 On al-ʿAllāma, see above.

120 al-Ṭabarī, 28, p. 39 notes a figure of 600,000 as being alluded to in the poetry that Abū Jaʿfar cited when Abū Muslim was slain.

On the rising of Sunbād, a Zoroastrian follower of Abū Muslim said to have reverted to his original faith after Abū Muslim's death, see al-Ṭabarī, 28, pp. 44–46. Al-Ṭabarī makes no reference to belief in Abū Muslim's divinity. See also al-Masʿūdī (3, p. 306, calling him Sunfād) and al-Yaʿqūbī (2, pp. 107–108) calling him Sunbādh. Wilferd Madelung, in his 'Sunbādh', *EI2*, also notes he was called Sunfādh. See also Babayan, *Mystics*, pp. 265–266.

al-Ṭabarī's editor (28, p. 44 n.188) notes the conflation of these with the above-mentioned Khurramiyya and other *ghālī* (extreme) elements. The editor also refers to al-Masʿūdī's reference to the Khurramiyya, cited above.

121 On Zamchī, see further below.

122 Ibn Bābawayh maintained the later imams were killed while his student Muḥammad b. Muḥammad b. Nuʿmān, al-Shaykh al-Mufīd (d. 413/1022) disputed this. See our *Twelver Shiism*, pp. 68, 81.

123 Babayan (*Mystics*, pp. 121, 422–423) discusses earlier attributions of *ḥulūl* to Abū Muslim and others.

124 The second recipient, Ashraf, is otherwise known as ʿUmar al-Ashraf b. Zayn al-ʿĀbidīn, whom Agha says some sources name as a third recipient. Al-Masʿūdī (3, p. 268) and al-Yaʿqūbī (3, p. 89) agree on two, Imam Jaʿfar and ʿAbd Allāh b. al-Ḥasan b. al-Ḥasan [whom al-Masʿūdī calls al-Ḥusayn] b. ʿAlī. Cf. Agha, pp. 121–124, using a variety of sources and citing an argument between Imam Jaʿfar and ʿAbd Allāh and ʿAbd Allāh's interest. But, as agreed by the Kaydharī account, by that time al-Saffāḥ had already been proclaimed caliph.

The text containing the imam's reply is given only in Persian and the editor (2, p. 284, n.1) cites it from al-Majlisī, *Biḥār*, 47, p. 133. It also can be found in Ibn Shahr Āshūb's *al-Manāqib* (Qumm, 1379), 4, pp. 228f.

125 On Sunbād, see above.

126 Sulaymān b. Kathīr, a Yemeni Arab, was one of the original 12 Abbasid *naqībs*. See Patricia Crone, 'Sulaymān b. Kathīr', *EI2*. See also Agha, s.v., esp. pp. 74–75, 188, 297, 309, 372. Crone and Agha imply ethnic and political matters underlaid his killing by Abū Muslim. But see also the following note. See also al-Ṭabarī, 28, p. 38 n.170.

127 al-Ṭabarī, 27, pp. 184–185; 28, p. 157. Al-Ṭabarī (27, p. 184), in 132/749–50, i.e. during al-Saffāḥ's caliphate, quotes Sulaymān b. Kathīr as implicitly acknowledging 'Ubayd Allāh and offering the latter his own support. The 'Alid, suspicious, reported this to Abū Muslim, fearful that if he did not report this Abū Muslim would seek his own death. Abū Muslim then confronted Sulaymān and had him killed. In the aftermath Abū Ja'far later reported to al-Saffāḥ that Abū Muslim 'does just what he pleases' and he was no caliph if he did not order Abū Muslim killed. Al-Ṭabarī records no mention of the 'Alid's expulsion from the province.

On Sulaymān see also the preceding note. On his son having been killed by Abū Muslim, according to Ṭāliqānī, see above.

128 The exact source is not clear. However, Ja'far b. Muḥammad b. Ḥasan Ja'farī's *Tārīkh-i Yazd* dates to the 9th/15th century. In his edition of the work (Tehran, 1338 Sh./1959–60), I. Afshar refers to a manuscript copy dated to 1037/1627. In the two-page discussion of Yazd in the Abbasid period (pp. 17–18), the author mentions Aḥmad Zamjī [sic], the looting of the city and its wealth being dispatched to al-Saffāḥ in Kufa. The author thereupon turns to the Saffarid period. The Saffarids ruled in eastern Iran from 247/861 to 393/1003; see Clifford Edmund Bosworth, 'Saffarids', *EIR*. On Aḥmad see also below.

129 The revolt appears to have had Ibāḍī Shi'i connections. See al-Ṭabarī, 27, pp. 53 n.122, 90, 118–120, 120 n.312. Al-Ṭabarī records 'Abd Allāh as killed in 130/748, placing the revolt prior to the rise of the Abbasids, let alone the reign of al-Saffāḥ (132–136/749–754). See also 'al-Ibāḍīya', *EI1*.

130 al-Ṭabarī (27, p. 212; 28, p. 1) dates this designation to 136/753–4, and notes that Abū Muslim took the oath of allegiance to him (28, pp. 3–4)

131 The source here is unclear. The genre of *malḥama/malāḥim* literature often refers to predictions or apocalyptic prophecies, Sunni and Shi'i. See Toufic Fahd, 'Malḥama', 'Djafr', *EI2*. See also, Etan Kohlberg, *A Medieval Muslim Scholar at Work. Ibn Ṭāwūs and His Library* (Leiden, 1992), pp. 142–143, 245–246; al-Ṭihrānī, 22, pp. 187–190.

There is also, however, a genre of literature on *fitan wa malāḥim*, i.e. battles. 'Alī b. Mūsā, Ibn Ṭāwūs (d. 664/1266), for example, authored a work entitled *al-Malāḥim wa'l-fitan* (Najaf, 1948; Qumm, 1398/1999). Kohlberg (pp. 42, 60–61) cites the work (and other published editions) but with a different title. He notes that it includes selections from earlier works on the subject. See al-Ṭihrānī (4, pp. 189–90; 16, pp. 113–114; 22, p. 189). The present writer has not had access to this work to determine if Ṭāliqānī's citation is drawn from this volume. Even if not, Ṭāliqānī might have been referring to portions of these earlier works not cited by Ibn Ṭāwūs, let alone other works in this genre.

132 al-Ṭihrānī lists three titles for this work, a small, medium and large version, as it were, as numbers four, five and six, in his list where, as noted above, this is a single, and the first, item in Ṭāliqānī's list.

133 This is the 12th work cited in al-Ṭihrānī, 4, pp. 150f, and the third of those listed by Ṭāliqānī in the present essay's first chapter.

134 Discussed above, this was the third essay in al-Ṭihrānī's list and the fourth in Ṭāliqānī's list. As noted below, Sayyid Aḥmad's reference to the Kaysaniyya there is indirect.

135 This essay, clearly written before the attacks on Mīr Lawḥī but nevertheless attacking the veneration of Abū Muslim according to Ṭāliqānī is not cited in Ṭāliqānī's earlier list or, as such, by al-Ṭihrānī in *al-Dharī'a*. See further below.

136 Yazīd was the second Umayyad caliph, reigning from 60/680 to 64/683. Yazīd's governor in Iraq led the forces that killed Imam al-Ḥusayn at Karbala in 61/680.

137 This is the 14th of the 17 works listed by al-Ṭihrānī (4, p. 151) and the second in Ṭāliqānī's list. See also al-Ṭihrānī, 19, p. 75.

138 al-Ṭihrānī (23, pp. 179–181) lists only three works with this title; none of these is an obvious candidate for being the reference cited herein. Given its being listed immediately following the otherwise contemporary *Mathālib*, it would seem *Minhāj* also was a contemporary work.

139 The figures include counting 'Anīs al-Abrār' as three items, following al-Ṭihrānī (4, pp. 150f), for a total of 17 and notes that items 14, 16, 17 and 18 in Ṭāliqānī's list in 'Khulāṣa' are not mentioned in al-Ṭihrānī.

140 The editor (*Mīrāth-i islāmī-yi Īrān*, 2, p. 278 n.1) cites the text as in al-Majlisī, *Biḥār*, 28, p. 30 and 36, p. 336, but a version from the Prophet can be found in Ibn Bābawayh's *Maʿānī al-akhbār* (Qumm, 1361/1942–3), p. 323. See also Abu'l-Fatḥ Muḥammad b. ʿAlī al-Karājakī (d. 449/1057), *Kanz al-fawā'id* (Qumm, 1410/1989–90), 209. See also al-Kulaynī, *al-Kāfī*, 8: 224 for a variation of the text narrated from Imam Jaʿfar. Imam ʿAlī is cited as making this statement in *Kitāb Sulaym b. Qays* (Qumm, 1419/1998–9), p. 605. See also ibid., pp. 803, 913. On this text, see Robert Gleave, 'Early Shiite Hermeneutics and the Dating of *Kitāb Sulaym ibn Qays*', *BSOAS*, 78 (2015), pp. 83–103.

141 The editor gives no references, but, among the earliest sources, see *Kitāb Sulaym b. Qays*, p. 724; al-Ṣaffār, *Baṣā'ir al-darajāt*, p. 297, citing the Prophet; Ibn Bābawayh, *al-Āmālī* (n.p., 1362/1943), p. 269, with a *sanad.*

142 He is not mentioned by Agha or in the relevant volumes of al-Ṭabarī. See Marina Gaillard, 'Un asocial singulier: Aḥmad-e Zamji «le fou»', *Journal Asiatique*, 300/1 (2012), 139–69, where he is known as Zamjī and it is noted that he is mentioned by storytellers as a supporter of Abū Muslim. See above.

143 On Qaḥṭaba, see above. On the text about Ḥumayd, the editor of this essay cites (2, p. 80 n.1) al-Majlisī, *Biḥār*, 48, p. 322 with this statement and that this killing of '60 sayyids of the family of the Prophet' was on the order of the caliph Hārūn al-Rashīd (d. 193/809), 'as in *al-ʿUyūn*'. That text may be found in Ibn Bābawayh, *ʿUyūn akhbār al-Riḍā* (n.p., 1378/1958–9), 1, p. 108.

144 See above on this text.

145 This is the 17th essay cited by Ṭāliqānī in his list of 18 treatises. It is not cited in the list referenced in al-Ṭihrānī.

146 Although he cites no source for the text, a version thereof, cited from the Prophet, can be found in *Tafsīr Imām al-ʿAskarī* (Qumm, 1409/1988–9), pp. 370–371. The reference is to *yawm al-ḥashr*, the day on which humankind will be resurrected and judged. Among the earliest sources in which similar statements can be found, see also al-Kulaynī, *al-Kafī*, 3, p. 185; Ibn Bābawayh, *al-Faqīh*, 1, p. 168.

147 This is the 18th and last essay cited by Ṭāliqānī in his list of essays. It is not cited in al-Ṭihrānī's list.

148 On these terms, see our 'Clerical Perceptions'.

149 In 37/657, between Muʿāwiya and ʿAlī, fought near what is now Raqqa, in Syria. See Michael Lecker, 'Ṣiffīn', *EI2*.

150 A Yemeni (d. 62/682), who was, it seems, critical of Muʿāwiya but offered the latter his service to ameliorate Muʿāwiya's feelings toward ʿAlī. See G.H.A. Juynboll, 'al-Khawlānī', *EI2*.

151 Here (p. 295 n.1) the editor cites this text as appearing in *Biḥār*, 41, p. 310. In fact, however, it can also be found in the earlier *Manāqib āl Abī Ṭālib* (Qumm, 1379), 2, p. 262, by the same Ibn Shahr Āshūb.

152 As noted above, this text can be found in Ibn Bābawayh, *al-Faqīh*, 1, p. 252/769; idem, *ʿIlal*, 2, p. 348.

153 Here (2, p. 295 n.3) the editor notes this was a work by Saʿd b. ʿAbd Allāh al-ʿAshʿarī, on whom see above. He cites al-Ṭihrānī (15, p. 121) that in his *fihrist* Aḥmad b. ʿAlī al-Najāshī (d. 450/1058) [*Rijāl al-Najāshī*, Qumm, 1407/1986–7, p. 177] mentions it but notes that al-Ṭihrānī himself does not mention a copy of it, and concludes that Mīr Dāmād saw this book. Thus, as with other books such as Ibn Bābawayh's *Madīnat*

al-ʿilm and several volumes of *Nuṣrat al-ʿilm*, to be discussed below, this work disappeared sometime in the Safawid period. On the former, see our *Twelver Shiism*, pp. 75 n.31, 197 n.8, 200 n.44. On *al-Ḍiyāʾ* see also further below.

154 'And do not incline toward those who do wrong, lest you be touched by the Fire.' On the issue of Persian translations of the Qur'an, see our *Twelver Shiism* (pp. 105, 105 n.13, citing Travis Zadeh's *The Vernacular Qur'an. Translation and the Rise of Persian Exegesis* (Oxford, 2012).

155 The editor (2, p. 296 n.1) cites only al-Majlisī, *Biḥār*, 8, p. 366, which does not refer to Ibn Bābawayh. However, al-Ḥurr in his *Wasāʾil al-shīʿa* (Qumm, 1409/1988–9), 28, p. 345, cites the text from that source. In translation the text may be found in *Iʿtiqādāt*, Asaf A.A. Fyzee, ed and tr. *A Shiite Creed* (Tehran, 1420/1999), pp. 94–95. Note that in none of these sources is a *sanad* for the text cited.

156 'O you who have believed, do not take your fathers or your brothers as allies if they have preferred disbelief over belief. And whoever does so among you — then it is those who are the wrongdoers.'

157 Mīr Dāmād's name is not given as such here (2, p. 297) but the editor has previously identified '*sayyid al-mujtahidīn*' as such. The references following corroborate this.

158 It will be remembered that neither the editor nor the present author could locate this text, although al-Ṣaffār, in *Baṣāʾir*, cited similar texts. On *al-Ḍiyāʾ*, see above.

159 This is the first of the pro-Mīr Lawḥī essays cited by Ṭāliqānī in his list (2, p. 277), and cited also by al-Ṭihrānī as three items, four through six.

160 The editor notes that indeed the text is in the edition of al-Ḥamawī's *Anīs al Muʾminīn*, and that he himself cited it in his introductory remarks to these three essays (2, p. 253).

The text is as follows: 'The most lying of the storytellers who are the people nearest to *ʿiqāb* (punishment) and *ʿaḍāb* (pain) are those who slandered Imam Bāqir and his ancestors and cite a narrative on Abū Muslim who was corrupt and cursed and was not a Shiʿa of the imams and did not acknowledge their *ḥaqq*. The most lying storytellers are those who *wārūnah* (turn upside down) his life and his actions and induce the ignorant to an affection for him.'

161 Though Ṭāliqānī himself cites no text, the editor (*Mīrāth-i Islāmī-yi Īrān*, 2, p. 277 nn.1, 2) cites 35, p. 32 and also 24, pp. 6, 7.

162 See above.

163 See above.

164 al-Ṭihrānī (4, pp. 150f), as noted above, lists three titles for this work, a small, medium and large version, as it were, as numbers four, five and six, in his list where, as noted above, this is a single, and the first, item in Ṭāliqānī's list.

165 This is the 12th work cited in al-Ṭihrānī (4, pp. 150f), and the third of those listed by Ṭāliqānī in the present essay's first chapter.

166 Sayyid Aḥmad did not mention the Kaysaniyya by name but, as noted above, did refer to those who maintained that Ibn al-Ḥanafiyya was the rightful imam. On the connection between these and the Kaysaniyya, see further below.

167 This essay, clearly written before the attacks on Mīr Lawḥī but nevertheless, according to Ṭāliqānī, attacking the veneration of Abū Muslim, is not cited in Ṭāliqānī's earlier list or by al-Ṭihrānī in his *al-Dharīʿa*.

168 Sean W. Anthony's 'Kaysānīya', *EIR*, confirms this connection to the Abbasids via the partisans of Abū Hāshim. See also W. Madelung, 'Kaysāniyya', in *EI2*.

169 Agha (pp. 53–57) discusses the issue, and the primary and secondary sources, extensively.

170 As Babayan notes (*Mystics*, pp. 139–141), this Junayd was said to be a descendant of ʿAlī himself, but Junayd was also the name of Ismāʿīl I's grandfather. The latter Junayd (d. 864/1460) was said to have been that Safawid figure associated with the turn to radical messianic, Sufi egalitarian discourse taken by the Safawid order concomitant with an influx of Turkic tribes into the movement. See also Newman, *Safavid Iran*, pp. 10–11, 13.

171 An apothecary (*'aṭṭār*) in Kufa and of the Banū 'Ijl. Idrīs 'made' the family fortune and Agha (pp. 48, 59–61, 330) suggests the means in doing so were 'not above suspicion'.
172 On Salīṭ, see above.
173 A reference to the Prophet.
174 A pre-Islamic period wise man for whom was named the thirty-first sura of the Qur'an but who was, however, also a popular figure in Persian literature, referred to by Rūmī and Sa'dī. Thus, Ṭāliqānī's reference to him, in an essay clearly written with a Persian-speaking audience in mind, cannot have been random. See Bernard Heller [Norman A. Stillman], et al., 'Lukmān', *EI2*.
175 On Ibn Bābawayh's maintaining that the Abbasids murdered these imams and his student al-Mufīd's view to the contrary, see above.
176 See the reference to Ibn Bābawayh's *'Uyūn akhbār al-Riḍā* above.
177 As noted, this is the 14th of the 17 works listed by al-Ṭihrānī (4, p. 151) and the second in Ṭāliqānī's list. See also al-Ṭihrānī, 19, p. 75.
178 An unknown work but, as suggested above, its being listed immediately following the otherwise contemporary *Mathālib* suggests *Minhāj* was a contemporary work.
179 The second Umayyad caliph who was killed in 23/644.
180 Q 9:119, for which Ṭāliqānī also provides a Persian translation.
181 The text ends here, notes the editor. He notes that the essay has ten *bāb* and this is the tenth and that this is the end of the tenth but that it is probable that some lines are missing.
182 At the end of the century a prominent member of the Dhahabī Sufi order left Isfahan for Shiraz and found the 'environment more hospitable' (Anzali, 'The Emergence', p. 168).
183 On 'Abbās I's concern with the capital's storytellers, if not details on their activities, and his efforts and those of clerics of the day to check their discourse, see our *Safavid Iran*, p. 69.
184 As discussed in our *Twelver Shiism*, pp. 155f.
185 See our 'Sufism and anti-Sufism'. The author of *Salwat* is Muḥammad b. Miqdādī, usually said to have been Mīr Lawḥī himself. See also Ja'fariyān's introduction to the three essays (2, pp. 247f) on the authorship of this and other 'anonymous' works of the time. On 'Salwat' see also above.
186 Based on a comparative examination of the multi-volume M. Dirāyatī, et al., ed., *Fihristvāri-yi Dastnivishtihā-yi Irān* (Mashhad, n.d.), the notes of the editor of these three essays (2, pp. 253f) and reference to <www.aghabozorg.ir>, of *Ṣaḥīfa* there is but the one copy (*Fihristvāri*, 7, p. 59). Of *Iẓhar* four copies have survived (ibid, 1, p. 1148) and there is but one copy of *Khulāṣa* (ibid 4, p. 960). As in the case of such analysis (see our *Twelver Shiism*, p. 11) such figures cannot be taken as absolute but rather are indicative of a relative lack of availability.
187 See our *Safavid Iran*, p. 77, on Mīr Lawḥī's claims, in his own *Arba'ūn* (completed in 1083/1672, sometime after which he died) that he was assaulted in the street. On these dates see al-Ṭihrānī, 9/4, p. 1220. See also *Safavid Iran*, p. 215 n.33 and references to Mīr Lawḥī above.
188 See our *Twelver Shiism*, p. 184f.
189 On the loss of such texts over the centuries following the 447/1055 Saljuq conquest of Baghdad and their recovery in this period, see our *Twelver Shiism*.

PART TWO

THE SOCIAL HISTORY OF A SHIʿI SUFI BROTHERHOOD: THE NIʿMAT ALLĀHIYYA

3

Between the Spiritual and Material: The Niʿmat Allāhī Order's Institutionalisation and Architectural Patronage in the 9th/15th Century

Peyvand Firouzeh

The poet and Sufi, Shāh Niʿmat Allāh Walī (d. 834/1431), is the eponym of a Sufi order which became influential in Iran, and flourished in Deccan India in the 9th/15th century. The Niʿmat Allāhī Sufi order has enjoyed great scholarly interest in past decades. Aubin's collection of the hagiographies of Shāh Niʿmat Allāh in *Matériaux pour la biographie de Shāh Niʿmatullāh Walī Kirmāni* was an important moment for the study of the order.[1] Much of the previous scholarship has focused on the biographical and historiographical aspects of the order, or a sectarian approach, in which the debates on the Shiʿi or Sunni origins of the order play an important role. The emphasis on Shiʿi-Sunni debates originates from the order's political and marital ties with the Safawids (r. 907–1135/1501–1722) who established Twelver Shiʿism as the empire's official religion. The order's close connections with the Bahmanid dynasty (r. 748–933/1347–1527) of the Deccan have also contributed to further discussions. Yet the Bahmanids' commitment to Shiʿism is itself a matter of debate. Amidst these biographical and confessional ambiguities, there are several reasons for architectural historians to get involved in the discussion, not only because there exist examples of the order's monuments, including fully or partially extant shrines and *khānaqāhs* in Iran and India whose artistic and stylistic quality calls for close analysis, but also because existing biographical and historiographical scholarship on the order is not appropriately connected to the history of architecture and its patronage.

While each of the most significant monuments of the order – the Shāh Walī *khānaqāh* in Taft (Iran), the shrine of Shāh Niʿmat Allāh Walī in Mahan (Iran), and the mausoleum of Shāh Khalīl Allāh (d. *ca* 850/1445–6),[2] Shāh Niʿmat Allāh's son, in Bidar (India) – deserves a detailed study of its own, such analyses fall outside the scope and aim of this chapter.[3] Instead, the current study is an attempt to bridge the previous scholarship on the biographical research, doctrinal arguments and history of the order with the social history of their shrines and *khānaqāh*s and their patronage in both historical and geographical contexts of Iran and India in the 9th/15th century. A particular emphasis will be laid on the role played by the son of the founder of the order, Shāh Khalīl Allāh, in the institutionalisation and shaping of the social history of these buildings.

But what do we mean when we refer to the institutionalisation of Sufi orders and what happens during such a process, especially in terms of their architecture? The institutionalisation of a Sufi order consists of the process of embedding the order within a social and political system as a whole, the process during which the order moves towards the regulation of its internal and external affairs and/or has to abide by certain financial, political, and doctrinal rules of the society within which they are functioning.

This is when the order might start to establish ties with the political rulers of the society. Perhaps the first unavoidable prompt for such involvement comes with the management of the order's *awqāf* (endowments), as soon as they start to accumulate landed property and the like, whether it comes from patrons within the governing body or not. The particularities of the process depend on questions such as the following: are these properties exempt from taxation or not, and if they are, is the tax exemption granted to the order as a gift or sought by members of the order? The answers to these questions are of course intertwined with those about the patronage of the order, as state patronage could largely depend on how the order's doctrine and political involvement related to the ruling powers.

From an architectural point of view, this could potentially be the moment of transition from modest buildings to the usually state-sponsored monumental *khānaqāh*s and shrines that functioned as regulated public and charitable institutions. The splendour of the buildings, the patrons who supported such structures, and the sources of money to be used for building purposes all depended directly on the decisions that were made at these transitional moments.[4]

In his dissertation *The Niʿmatullāhī Sayyids of Taft*, Connell distinguished the indicative factors of the gradual institutionalisation of the Niʿmat Allāhī order as follows: the crystallisation of a distinct Niʿmat Allāhī *silsila*, the expansion of their network of followers and their integration into the Niʿmat Allāhī biographical tradition, the development of distinctive Niʿmat Allāhī beliefs and practices, and the patronage of a wide range of diverse institutions by the *shaykh*s of the *ṭarīqa* including *khānaqāh*s and shrine complexes, as well as educational, charitable, and commercial interests.[5] The critical role of this period in the formation and development of new and existing architecture associated with the Niʿmat Allāhī order is the reason that this time frame and the order's emerging leader, namely Shāh Khalīl Allāh, the only son and successor of the founder, are the foci of this article for the study of architecture.

The institutionalisation process of the Niʿmat Allāhī Sufi order involved the erection of multiple buildings and complexes from after 814/1411 to sometime after 850/1445–6 in different geographies and with different purposes. The time frame of this paper is set around the period that starts with the construction of the *khānaqāh* in Taft in 814/1411 under the patronage of Iskandar Mīrzā (r. 812–817/1409–1415), the Timurid governor of Fārs, and ends with the building of Shāh Khalīl Allāh's mausoleum in Bidar (also known as Muḥammadābād) probably after 850/1445–6 by the Bahmanids (fig. 3.1). Although the shrine at Mahan is the architectural focus of this article, this time frame enables us to think about the shrine's intertwined history with other buildings of the order.

What complicates the task of understanding buildings constructed during this phase of the order's history is how the interrelation between them has sometimes resulted in new and altered functions. In particular the function and evolution of the shrine of Shāh Niʿmat Allāh Walī in Mahan, whose developments, at least compared to their other centres before the Safawid period, did not meet the expectation one would have of the most venerated centre of an order, were influenced by this multiplicity of Niʿmat Allāhī shrines and *khānaqāh*s.

Figure 3.1. Shāh Walī mosque (right) and Khalīl Allah II's mausoleum (left) in Taft, view towards the north-east. This and all photographs in this chapter are the author's own.

During the course of studying Shāh Khalīl Allāh's role in the institutionalisation of the Niʿmat Allāhī order, the challenges that they faced along the way and what they meant for their architecture will be taken into account. By shifting the biographical focus from Shāh Niʿmat Allāh Walī as the key figure of the order in previous scholarship to his son, the one who managed financial and political matters on behalf of the order, I will address understudied issues around the patronage of the order's architecture, especially in terms of the relationship between the Shāh Walī *khānaqāh* in Taft and the shrine at Mahan and the functions taking place within them.[6]

Shrines and *khānaqāhs* of the Niʿmat Allāhī Order under the Patronage of the Timurids and Bahmanids

We know from textual references that a *khānaqāh* existed in Mahan, about forty kilometres south-east of Kirman, before Shāh Niʿmat Allāh's death.[7] We do not know exactly what it looked like but from textual sources, it appears to have been a modest structure. Nor do we know what financial sources were used to build this *khānaqāh*, but we know that Shāh Niʿmat Allāh Walī had landed property, among which were gardens of Khayrābād in Mahan where his *khānaqāh* was located.[8] Most probably, these projects did not involve any state patronage. In this light, while the chronology of the two *khānaqāhs* in Mahan and Taft before the death of the founder are obscure, the Shāh Walī *khānaqāh* in Taft should be counted as the first complex built under state patronage.[9]

Almost nothing remains of the first phase of the *khānaqāh* in Taft built in the first half of the 9th/15th century, except for the highly restored *buqʿa* (mausoleum), known as *buqʿa-yi Shāh Khalīl Allāh-i thānī* (Khalīl Allāh II, d. 925/1519–20), a descendant of Shāh Niʿmat Allāh Walī who was buried in the building in the early Safawid period about a century after its construction. Although many elements of the *khānaqāh* complex are lost, textual descriptions offer us a picture of what was happening in it. In *Jāmiʿ-i Mufīdī* (written by Muḥammad Mufīd Mustawfī in the 11th/17th century), there is the description of a heaven-like *khānaqāh* in Taft with an excellent lofty *kūshk* (pavilion) in the middle, around which houses and *ḥujras* (cells) were built for the poor and *shaykhs*, and a good kitchen where food was prepared daily for the poor and the rich.[10] In addition, it is noted in *Tārīkh-i jadīd-i Yazd* (written by Aḥmad b. Ḥusayn Kātib Yazdī in 862/1457–8) that there was also a bath and a holy mausoleum in the complex. The date of completion of the *khānaqāh* is reported to be 817/1415, which falls within Shāh Niʿmat Allāh Walī's lifetime.[11] Therefore, before he passed away, the centre in Taft was a working *khānaqāh*.

The occasion of Shāh Niʿmat Allāh Walī's death in Kirman in 834/1431 and his burial in Mahan made necessary the building of a tomb for the founder of the order. This is when the first phase of his shrine complex started at Mahan. The shrine today is a combination of four open courtyards that are arranged in a linear fashion along an east-west axis (figs 3.2, 3.3). The only part of the complex that was built within the time frame of this study is the mausoleum of Shāh Niʿmat Allāh Walī, originally a single-domed chamber (figs 3.4, 3.5).[12] In *Jāmiʿ-i mufīdī*, it is mentioned that after Shāh Niʿmat Allāh Walī's death and the performance of prayers for him at the Friday mosque (*masjid-i jāmiʿ*) in Kirman, his body was carried to Mahan and buried near his *khānaqāh*, in the middle of his own garden, Khayrābād, in Mahan.[13]

The main entrance of the square-shaped domed chamber that was built over the tomb of Shāh Niʿmat Allāh lay on the west, which today is situated inside the later-added *Riwāq-i Shāh ʿAbbāsī* (fig. 3.6). A

Figure 3.2. The shrine at Mahan, view from the western court (Ṣaḥn-i Muḥammad Shāhī) eastward.

Figure 3.3. The shrine at Mahan, view from the south to the dome chamber. Minarets of the current entrance to the mausoleum can be seen to the right.

Figure 3.4. The dome of the mausoleum surrounded by octagonal skylights of the *Riwāq-i Shāh ʿAbbāsī.*

Figure 3.5. Interior of the dome chamber and its zone of transition.

foundation inscription in *thuluth* script, bearing the name of the patrons, Aḥmad Shāh Bahmanī (r. 825–839/1422–1436) and his son, ʿAlāʾ al-Dīn Aḥmad Shāh Bahmanī (r. 839–862/1436–1458), is located above this entrance. The inscription states that Aḥmad Shāh Abu'l-Maghāzī ('father of conquests') ordered the construction of this stable dome and lofty well-founded structure, which was finished at the time of his beloved son Sulṭān ʿAlāʾ al-Dawla wa'l-Dīn wa'l-Dunyā Aḥmad Shāh. The inscription was written in the year 840/1436 (figs 3.7, 3.8, 3.9).

While a group of the Niʿmat Allāhīs was received at the court of the Bahmanids at Bidar, and buildings were erected for the order under their royal patronage in the 9th/15th century, the dome chamber at Mahan remained unchanged until the Safawid period. This is when a gallery, known as *Riwāq-i ʿAbbāsī* or *Dār al-ḥuffāẓ*, was added to the western side of the mausoleum in 998/1590 under the patronage of Bektāsh Khān, the governor of Kirman and Baluchistan during the reign of Shāh ʿAbbās (r. 996–1038/1588–1629) (figs 3.10, 3.11).

So let us imagine the shrine at Mahan, the way it was after the first phase (the mausoleum) was completed in 840/1436, and before its

Figure 3.6. The original entrance of the mausoleum now located inside the *Riwāq-i Shāh ʿAbbāsī.*

Figure 3.7. Inscription on the original entrance to the dome chamber with the beginning of Aḥmad Shāh Bahmanī's titles.

Figure 3.8. Inscription with the names of Aḥmad Shāh Bahmanī, as the patron of the mausoleum, and his son 'Alā' al-Dawla Bahmanī, whose donations were used for the completion of the mausoleum.

Figure 3.9. Inscription dated Muḥarram 840/July 1436.

Figure 3.10. *Riwāq-i Shāh 'Abbāsī*. The original (western) entrance to the mausoleum with its *muqarnas* can be seen to the right.

Figure 3.11. Inscription above the entrance to the Ṣaḥn-i Shāh ʿAbbāsī from *Riwāq-i ʿAbbāsī* dated 998/1590.

first addition (the *Riwāq-i Shāh ʿAbbāsī*) was built in 998/1590. What was happening during these 154 years of architectural inactivity in terms of the patronage of the order? And what was happening in the shrine at Mahan as the most venerated site of the order in Iran? These are the questions to which I shall come back later in this study.

Sometime before the completion of the mausoleum in Mahan, Shāh Khalīl Allāh travelled to the Deccan. Around the time of his death (*ca* 850/1445-6) and most probably during the reign of ʿAlāʾ al-Dīn Aḥmad Shāh Bahmanī II, a mausoleum was built to commemorate his grave as the spiritual leader of the order in the Deccan (figs 3.12, 3.13). The mausoleum is locally known as the Chaukhandi,[14] and is located a short distance to the west of the Ashtūr tomb complex of the

Figure 3.12. The mausoleum of Shāh Khalīl Allāh outside Bidar, India, view from the road leading to the Bahmanid necropolis.

Figure 3.13. The mausoleum of Shah Khalīl Allāh outside Bidar, India, view from the south.

Bahmanid rulers, including that of Aḥmad Shāh Bahmanī the first Bahmanid patron of the Niʿmat Allāhīs. To my knowledge, the only mention of Khalīl Allāh's mausoleum in the Deccani primary sources, written in the two centuries that followed its erection, is limited to the Kirmani keeper of the mausoleum in *Tārīkh-i Firishtah* (written *ca* 1009/1600).[15]

Closing this brief introduction to the architecture built for the Niʿmat Allāhī order in the time frame under study, I will now turn to the question of the patronage of the order. The following part in particular, will consist of an overview of the challenges, especially those concerning the *khānaqāh*s, that the leaders of the order faced during the 9th/15th century and the way they reacted to them.

Institutionalisation of the Niʿmat Allāhī Sufi Order: Challenges

Except for a few additions to properties that were transferred to the order, for instance in Yazd, the monumental architecture of the Niʿmat Allāhī order was promoted by influential patrons of the order from different dynasties such as the Timurids (771–912/1370–1507) and the Bahmanids (748–933/1347–1527) of the Deccan.[16] The architectural patronage of the order ranged from indirect patronage, i.e. money, gifts and donations given for non-specific purposes, for instance some of the gifts from Aḥmad Shāh Bahmanī; direct patronage, i.e. money given for a special purpose or project, such as the lands given to the family by Iskandar Mīrzā in Taft; and finally tax exemption on *waqf* lands, buildings, gifts and donations, such as the ones granted by Shāhrukh (r. 807–850/1405–1447), Tīmūr's son and successor, at times. All this, however, did not come to the order at no expense.

Much has been said about the cold relationship between Tīmūr and Shāh Niʿmat Allāh Walī, reflected in Shāh Niʿmat Allāh Walī's banishment from Samarqand by Tīmūr after he ascended the throne.[17] Neither was the Niʿmat Allāhī order alone in receiving such treatment from the Timurids,[18] nor did it matter much, as long as the rebellious Timurid Prince Iskandar Mīrzā, later known as Iskandar Sulṭān, granted not only land and tax relief to Shāh Niʿmat Allāh Walī in Taft, but also allocated the revenue of Taft and its dependencies for four years to the building of a *khānaqāh* in Taft,[19] some four hundred kilometres from the base of the order in the final years of Shāh Niʿmat Allāh's life in Mahan. This is the first time we know of the Niʿmat Allāhīs receiving direct patronage by any ruler.

Shāhrukh's attitude was not much different from his father's. Neither he, nor any of his officials, ever patronised buildings for the order, in contrast to Shāhrukh's and Gawharshād's image as patrons who embarked on grand scale projects such as expanding the shrine of Imam Riḍā (d. *ca* 203/818) in Mashhad, developing the shrine of Bāyazīd-i Basṭāmī (d. 234/848 or 261/875) in Bastam (Iran), and building a shrine at the tomb of Khwājah ʿAbd Allāh Anṣārī (d. 481/1089) in 829/1425 in Gazurgah, near Herat, to name a few.

The real challenge came after the reign of Iskandar and the death of Shāh Niʿmat Allāh Walī. We sense the critical situation of the order in the movements of Shāh Khalīl Allāh, amidst his meeting with Shāhrukh, in which the continuation of tax exemption on the landed property of the order was discussed, and in his journey to the Deccan, before the construction of his father's tomb in Mahan was finished in 840/1436. This challenging time, however, coincided with the privilege of patronage offered to the order from the Deccan-based Aḥmad Shāh Bahmanī and his descendants.

This opportunity, which the Niʿmat Allāhī leaders took and fully enjoyed, is what differentiated the order from its contemporaries. Unlike some orders that only began to emigrate following the arrival of the Safawids, the Niʿmat Allāhīs started their emigration in the Timurid period and were already settled in their second home in Bidar by the mid-9th/15th century. Although settling in this second home had some influence on the evolution of the order and the development and patronage of its architecture in Iran, it did not foreclose the maintenance of their bases in Mahan and Taft. In other words, the order existed in parallel geographies, occupying different homes at the same time.

References to patronage from the Bahmanids differ in number and details in textual sources. In *Burhān-i maʾāthir* (written by ʿAlī Ṭabāṭabā in 1592–94 or 1595), there is only one reference to gifts and donations from Aḥmad Shāh Bahmanī; in *Jāmiʿ-i Mufīdī* it is mentioned at least twice before Shāh Niʿmat Allāh Walī's death; and in *Tārīkh-i Firishtah* three times. The value of these gifts was apparently so high that the Timurid court faced the dilemma of whether to tax the gifts or not.[20] According to Firishtah, in the first instance, one of the disciples of Shāh Niʿmat Allāh Walī from the Deccan arrived in Kirman with such donations.[21] In response, Mullā Quṭb al-Dīn Kirmānī, a disciple of Shāh Niʿmat Allāh in Kirman, returned with the Deccan-based disciple to Bidar taking along a green devotional hat and a letter addressing Aḥmad Shāh Bahmanī by the title *walī*.[22]

In the same year, two other envoys, Khwājah ʿImād al-Dīn Simnānī and Sayf Allāh Ḥasanābādī were sent to Kirman to ask Shāh Niʿmat Allāh Walī to send one of his sons to the Bahmanid court. This time, there is no mention of any gifts, but one imagines that envoys coming to visit with such a request would not travel without generous offerings. This is when Shāh Niʿmat Allāh Walī sent his grandson, Mīr Nūr Allāh b. Khalīl Allāh (d. 834/1430–1), to the Deccan, where, according to Firishtah, he was received warmly and his arrival was celebrated by the building of mosques and other buildings in the village of Niʿmatābād near Bidar.[23] The last mention of gifts from Aḥmad Shāh I occurs in 834/1430–1, when he heard about Shāh Niʿmat Allāh Walī's death.[24]

Making sense of the question of patronage will reveal the complicated character of the institutionalisation of the Niʿmat Allāhī order as reflected in their architecture. While the standard process of architectural institutionalisation comes with the death of the order's founder (or one of its important leaders) and the building of his tomb, in the case of the Niʿmat Allāhīs things are not so straightforward. The construction of the founder's mausoleum in Mahan was paralleled by other equally important architectural activities, a result of the multiple geographies in which the order was functioning.

As discussed earlier, Shāh Niʿmat Allāh Walī died in Kirman in 834/1431 and was buried in Mahan. By a comparison of dates, the mausoleum at Mahan was erected while the complex in Taft was already functioning and being developed. This leaves us with the question of the priority of the two centres. While traditionally, priority would be given to the venerated tomb of the deceased Sufi, what came after the completion of the building at Mahan was to some extent surprising. Until 998/1590 when the *Riwāq-i ʿAbbāsī* was built, nothing was added to the mausoleum at Mahan, while we know that the complex at Taft was being developed into a fully-functional funerary, economic and – as I will argue – teaching centre. In fact, if we accept the date of the addition or refurbishment of the mosque to the *khānaqāh* in Taft before 1564 as it is attributed to Khānish Begum, sister of Shāh Ṭahmāsp (r. 930–984/1524–1576), then it occurred before the Safawid addition to the mausoleum in Mahan.[25] What could have caused this preference for the expansion of Taft over the venerated tomb of the founder of the order? Juxtaposing this observation with the textual references to Shāh Khalīl Allāh's negotiations at the court of Shāhrukh for tax exemption and his move to the Deccan before the completion of the tomb at Mahan, one can sense the urgency caused by the financial and political complications the order was facing.

Negotiations: The Role of Shāh Khalīl Allāh

Burhān al-Dīn Khalīl Allāh, the only child of Shāh Niʿmat Allāh, was born in Kuhbunan, about 175 kilometres to the north-west of Kirman. His date of birth has been a matter of debate, two different dates, 775/1373–4 and 800/1397–8, have been suggested.[26] What of Khalīl Allāh's role in the institutionalisation of the order? It is arguable that Shāh Niʿmat Allāh Walī's approach towards financial matters and relations with rulers determined the inevitability of the institutionalisation of the order and that Shāh Khalīl Allāh, who was appointed as his successor, consolidated this process.

Similar to what Andrew Peacock has shown in the case of the relations of the Sufi order of Jalāl al-Dīn Rūmī, with the Saljuqs of Anatolia,[27] the Niʿmat Allāhīs not only relied on rulers for financial support and tax exemption, but also explicitly sought this sponsorship through negotiations that are recorded in their letters to the Timurid elites.[28] Yet, the Niʿmat Allāhīs' relationships with two separate courts, the Timurids and the Bahmanids, allowed for more manoeuvring. In an important account of gifts arriving from India (that corresponds to the second appeal from the Deccan among the narratives mentioned in the previous section) it is recorded:

> The Sultans of India sent more valuable gifts to Mahan which the bearer left in the middle of the river in front of the *khānaqāh*. Because Shāh Niʿmat Allāh was on a retreat, no one had the courage to [interrupt and] inform him. After three days when he finished the retreat, he noticed the gifts and asked about them. They told him the truth of the matter and mentioned the value of the gifts which was as much as the tax value of the region. He ordered that they divide the gifts into three shares, all equal, and said: 'one should go to Mirzā Shāhrukh, whose army is large in numbers; one should go to Khalīl Allāh, for he likes a fortune

(*jāh*), and the third share should be spent on the expenses of the *āstāna* (holy tomb, lit. threshold) at Mahan'.[29]

Whether reconstructed retrospectively or not, the above account is extremely interesting for several reasons. Firstly, it highlights the paths of development Shāh Niʿmat Allāh Walī, or his retrospective character, was opening before the order: the equal importance of enhancing political ties with the ruling powers, empowering his heir financially, and promoting the architecture of the order and its maintenance. By donating money to the army of Shāhrukh, Shāh Niʿmat Allāh Walī gave a sarcastic twist to the traditional image of Sufi–Sultan relations and exerted his power over the ruler. The Sufi in this image, not only avoids depending on the ruler, but enjoys such a financial privilege as to lend a hand - probably in a patronising gesture - to the ruler, who will soon become ungenerous enough to tax the previously-exempt landed properties of the order in the region.[30] It is equally possible that gifting money to Shāhrukh was a preventive measure to avoid taxation from the government.

After mentioning the division of donations, the account ends as follows: 'And there was a piece (*zar'*) of linen on the baggage. [Shāh Niʿmat Allāh] picked it up and said: 'so that the dervishes (referring to himself), too, can wipe their sweat.' In this way, it is emphasised how his only share of the gifts as an individual was the piece of linen. However, one cannot ignore the fact that he had indeed accepted and was using the gifts to empower the order. He was actively making decisions about financial and political affairs in this narrative, decisions that were blended with sarcasm and future plans, most importantly, promoting his son as someone who would directly deal with money matters.

Perhaps the most important point to emphasise in this account is the image of Shāh Khalīl Allāh who was someone not detached from worldly matters, but interested in, and perhaps in charge of financial matters. This division of responsibilities is witnessed among later descendants of Shāh Niʿmat Allāh too; the *quṭb* of the order would keep a distance from financial matters, while other members of the family dealt with them and managed the maintenance of the order.

In an important letter from Amīr Ẓahīr b. Nūr Allāh (a grandson of Shāh Khalīl Allāh) to a Timurid elite on the issue of tax exemption, he informed the addressee that his father (Amīr Nūr Allāh) who was in the Deccan at the time, had sent one of his sons and two dervishes with special letters to Herat to acquire approval on tax terms. The father made it clear that this was an important and indeed very urgent issue (with a specific deadline) and emphasised that it was necessary that the issue be resolved, since, if the tax exemption were withheld, it could appear as if this were the reason for his upcoming visit to Herat, while he preferred that his journey be free from the 'impurities of the material world.'[31] These accounts clearly illustrate the constant tensions and negotiations that the order faced in maintaining a balance between its material and spiritual image.

Shāh Khalīl Allāh's boldest move was probably his decision to emigrate to India. The fact that Shāh Niʿmat Allāh Walī was not willing to send him to the Deccan during his lifetime hints at the possibility that he wanted his son to be in charge of the order in Iran. It is worth noting in what context Shāh Khalīl Allāh's decision was made. We know from the sources, as mentioned before, that one of Shāh Khalīl Allāh's sons, Mīr Nūr Allāh, was already in the Deccan before Shāh Niʿmat Allāh's death. However, Nūr Allāh died in 1430 or 1431, shortly after emigrating. A tombstone with an inscription in *naskh* script published in *Epigraphia Indica* provides us with information about his death date. Yazdani found the inscription on a loose slab lying under a tree, on a platform to the south of Shāh Khalīl Allāh's shrine.[32] According to the inscription, the tomb of Shāh Nūr Allāh Ḥusaynī fell into ruin (was broken) during the time of the Barīdī kings (who ruled Bidar in the 10th/16th century).[33] The chronogram, *Jannat al-firdaws*, gives the date 834/1430–1 as the date of the demise of Shāh Nūr Allāh. Given the early death of his son, Shāh Khalīl Allāh was to decide between leading the order in Iran or India. So what might have motivated Shāh Khalīl Allāh in choosing the Deccan over ʿIrāq-i ʿAjam? It is clear that the willingness of a wealthy patron was encouraging enough, but the court at Khurasan, too, played a role in this decision, or at least the textual sources offer such a picture.

Shāh Khalīl Allāh visited Herat following Shāhrukh's request soon after the death of Shāh Niʿmat Allāh.[34] Most likely after his visit to Herat, he appointed his son Shāh Shams al-Dīn Muḥammad as head of the *āstāna* at Mahan, and left for the Deccan, with his other two sons, Shāh Muḥibb al-Dīn Ḥabīb Allāh, and Shāh Ḥabīb al-Dīn Muḥibb Allāh.[35]

It is recorded in an account in *Jāmiʿi-i Mufīdī* that when Khalīl Allāh visited the court of Shāhrukh, Amīr Fīrūz Shāh, one of the great emirs of Shāhrukh, confronted Khalīl Allāh for not paying the *kharāj* (agricultural tax) on their properties to the government.[36] The fact that the case was taken to Herat hints at either the considerable amount of money that must have been involved, or the souring of the relationship between the order and the court. Could the encounter between Shāh Khalīl Allāh and Shāhrukh have motivated the former to make a firm decision about emigrating to Bidar? There is no doubt that we should approach this account with some degree of caution. Being a victim of the government would not hurt the public image of the Sufi orders, and what better time for being treated unkindly by rulers at home when other powerful and wealthy patrons from far away were willing to support them.

Khalīl Allāh responded to this confrontation by comparing the situation to the conflict between Ḥusayn b. ʿAlī b. Abī Ṭālib (d. 61/680), the Prophet's grandson, and the Umayyad caliph, Yazīd (r. 60–64/680–683), that resulted in the massacre of Ḥusayn and most of the members of his family in Karbala on 10 Muḥarram 61/October 680. In response, Shāhrukh took Khalīl Allāh's side by reprimanding the great *amīr* and lifting the taxes.[37] One cannot help but notice the symbolic weight of the confrontation between Shāh Khalīl Allāh and Shāhrukh due to the analogy with the conflict between Ḥusayn and Yazīd. By such an analogy Shāh Khalīl Allāh was on the right side of a confrontation between good and evil, whereas Shāhrukh's side was bound to fail.[38]

The use of such an analogy, alongside other similar accounts, leads us to the ongoing debate about the Shiʿi origins of the order and its role in patronage. The question is, how significantly Shiʿi was the Ḥusayn-Yazīd dichotomy at the time? This and other Sunni-Shiʿi tropes will be briefly addressed in the following part before returning to the analysis of the patronage offered to the order in Mahan, Taft and Bidar.

Shāh Niʿmat Allāh and the Sunni-Shiʿi Dichotomy

The argument over the Sunni-Shiʿi origins of the Niʿmat Allāhī order is divided into two groups: first, those who argue that the order had Shiʿi inclinations from the beginning, and second, those who believe that the Niʿmat Allāhīs started as a Sunni order and later, by the arrival of the Safawids, turned into a Shiʿi order.

From the first group, for example, Pāzūkī believes that the Niʿmat Allāhīs were Shiʿi in origin. He points to the Shiʿi beliefs of Maʿrūfiyya, the *ṭarīqa* with which Shāh Niʿmat Allāh was affiliated. He also rejects the idea that their Shiʿi inclinations could be due to the order's *taqiyya* (pious dissimulation) and refers to the role of the Niʿmat Allāhīs in converting people to Shiʿism in the Deccan,[39] an idea also briefly discussed by H. K. Sherwani.[40] The basis of Pāzūkī's argument was that at a time when many Sufi orders defined their *silsila* as reaching back to Imām ʿAlī, this was a sign of their Shiʿi inclination.[41] Similarly, while in *Taḥqīq dar aḥwāl wa naqd-i āthār wa afkār-i Shāh Niʿmatullāh Walī*, Ḥamīd Farzām pointed to the strong Sunni beliefs in the works of Shāh Niʿmat Allāh,[42] he also wrote of a 'Shiʿi tendency' in the works of the founder of the order based on his veneration of ʿAlī.[43]

This idea has been debated by Lawrence G. Potter, Beatrice Forbes Manz, and Denise Aigle among others. Potter argued that the incorporation of ideas associated with Shiʿism into some orders, such as the veneration of ʿAlī and the expectation of the Mahdi, was an important phenomenon of the 14th and 15th centuries, but not necessarily a sign of belonging to Shiʿism.[44] Potter believes that 'the Niʿmatullāhīs evidently changed allegiance after the accession of Shāh Ismāʿīl in the early 16th century.'[45] Connell, too, argued that Shāh Niʿmat Allāh was a Sunni, affiliated with the Shāfiʿī and Ḥanafī juridical schools, but then during the Safawid period the order adopted the state religion of Shiʿism. In his opinion that is the reason for a period of close relationships between the Safawids and the order.[46]

The reasoning of both sides of the argument is varied as implied by the examples above. The most common reasons are affiliations to Imam ʿAlī (by the first group) and Shāh Niʿmat Allāh Walī's educational background with Sunni Sufis (for the second group), both challenged in previous scholarship. Accounts of patronage of the order have been the object of such debate as well. Among them are the accounts of the relationship between Tīmūr and Shāh Niʿmat Allāh Walī. Scholars who are in favour of grounding the clash between the two in Shiʿi-Sunni relations consider the order Shiʿi at birth and find it unsurprising that Tīmūr, who was allegedly affiliated with the Naqshbandīs, would not welcome Shāh Niʿmat Allāh Walī's growing popularity. In that regard, Aubin reminds us that the pro-Shiʿi sources 'portray the pre-Naqshbandi Khwājagān saint Sayyid Amīr Kulal (d. 772/1370) as warning Tīmūr that Niʿmat Allāh's influence could be used to stir up revolt and hence urging that he be expelled.'[47] Those who take the opposite stance argue that the reason Tīmūr asked Shāh Niʿmat Allāh Walī to leave the region was merely his growing popularity and the rivalry between him and *shaykh*s of the Naqshbandī order, such as Amīr Kulal, who had an influence on Tīmūr.[48] The bottom line, however, is that Tīmūr's reaction did not go beyond asking Shāh Niʿmat Allāh Walī to leave the region.

Patronage of the Bahmanids of the Deccan has been treated similarly: the patronage offered by the supposedly Shiʿi leader of Bidar, Aḥmad Shāh Bahmanī, is considered a sign that the order was Shiʿi too. Inherent in this argument is the idea that the Bahmanids were Shiʿi at the time, a possibility too uncertain to depend on: the only basis of such an argument is either retrospective historical accounts, such as that of the twelve-segmented green hat of discipleship sent to Aḥmad Shāh Bahmanī by Shāh Niʿmat Allāh Walī (in later histories such as the 11th/17th-century *Tārīkh-i Firishtah*), or interminable matters of a debate, such as the use of the title *walī*, given by the latter to the former and used by the ruler with enthusiasm. The pro-Shiʿi arguments take the latter as a Shiʿi sign whereas the pro-Sunni arguments could invoke the common rejection of the Shiʿi implications of the word *walī* by way of its etymology (meaning helper, friend, friend of God). In the absence of sufficient textual and material evidence however, these arguments remain speculative.

Nevertheless, Sunni-Shiʿi inclinations cannot explain the reasons for patronage of the order or the lack thereof. Manz's approach would perfectly explain the context within which the relationships between the Niʿmat Allāhīs and their patrons took place. In *Power, Politics and Religion in Timurid Iran* she drew our attention to 'the widespread veneration for the descendants of the prophet, which brought conspicuous respect to the memory of ʿAlī and the other Shiʿi imams'. She argued that in earlier scholarship, this tendency was sometimes taken as evidence of Shiʿism, thus, some dissent movements, earlier ascribed to Shiʿi belief, now demand reconsideration.[49]

It is in light of such ambiguity and complexity that one should look at the veneration of the Prophet's family, ʿAlī, and the Shiʿi imams (for instance the inscriptions under the dome of Aḥmad Shāh Bahmanī's tomb in Bidar), and accounts such as the Ḥusayn-versus-Yazīd analogy for the confrontation between Shāh Khalīl Allāh and Shāhrukh.[50]

Architectural Institutionalisation and the Financial and Educational Agenda of the Order

How did the process of institutionalisation of the Niʿmat Allāhī order – by nature a political and social process – influence the architecture made for the order? This, firstly, calls for more investigation into the consequences of Shāh Khalīl Allāh's decision to take a considerable part of the high-status human resources of the order to the Deccan. As Connell argued, until the last decades of Shāh Niʿmat Allāh Walī's life, which paralleled his move to Mahan, the order had remained relatively local. However, during the last decades, it began to attract disciples from other regions, including northern Iran (Tabriz, Gilan, and Mazandaran), Khurasan, and India.[51] At first glance, this resulted in an architectural expansion. Mīrzā Iskandar's donation of land and tax relief in Taft meant the establishment of a centre there. Buildings were built for the order in the Deccan and Shāh Niʿmat Allāh Walī's own grave was adorned with a mausoleum. Yet, the evolution and functions of their architecture in Iran were affected as well.

In 1978, Eaton wrote about an important aspect of the architectural development of the Chishtī Sufi order in the Deccan:

> . . . a vibrant tradition of Sufi teaching frequently terminated with the construction of a great mausoleum over a Sufi's grave. For it was roughly at this point that the institutions of the Sufis became replaced by the institutions of the *dargāh*. . . . As the tomb became the focal point of popular devotionalism in the Deccan the descendants of Gisu Daraz . . . became too occupied administrating the affairs of the *dargāh* as well as the vast estates bestowed upon their illustrious ancestor to turn their attention to teaching Chishtī doctrine.[52]

In generalised terms, what the building of a *dargāh* could potentially impose on the performance of a Sufi order was to undermine the mobility of a non-institutionalised order in favour of a venerable permanent home on the one hand, and letting administrative affairs eat into teaching time on the other. While Eaton wrote about one side of the relationship between architecture and teaching agendas, the other side of the relationship also played an important role in the case of the Niʿmat Allāhī order, i.e. how the financial and the educational agenda of the order affected the development of the shrine at Mahan.

Although we do not have much information on the teaching activities of Shāh Khalīl Allāh and his sons upon their arrival in the Deccan, we can imagine how the emigration of their most significant leader to the Deccan left the order in Iran – as Graham has stated – 'headless'.[53] It is true that Shāh Khalīl Allāh's son was taking care of their affairs in Mahan, and Taft was being developed as another important centre of the Niʿmat Allāhīs, but his rank was inferior to that of Shāh Khalīl Allāh. This could potentially have led to a decline in the teaching programmes of the order in Iran and might have been one of the reasons why for a long time the venerated site of the order in Mahan, unlike its counterparts within contemporary Sufi orders, did not develop as a teaching centre.

As discussed earlier, and as Connell has pointed out, the order's financial dependency, at least in Mahan, on agricultural lands and incomes, as well as the dispute over the region, namely Iskandar's and Pīr Muḥammad's invasion of Kirman in 812/1409 and those after Shāhrukh's death (in 851/1447) could be the reason for their financial vulnerability in Mahan. This was coupled by reducing the fiscal advantages of the Niʿmat Allāhīs and other religious figures in the region, as Aubin has pointed out.[54] These factors played an important role in Mahan's loss of its significance as a teaching centre despite its spiritual importance.

That Mahan was left untouched and rather neglected in terms of patronage was also directly related to what was going on in Taft. One has to take into account the need for charismatic spiritual leaders and financial managers who could handle the affairs of the order in at least three centres, Taft, Bidar and Mahan. There is evidence that the order was indeed struggling over training such leaders for its multiple locations. Connell writes about three of Khalīl Allāh's grandchildren, sons of the future *quṭb* of the *ṭarīqa*, Ḥabīb al-Dīn Muḥibb Allāh, all born and raised in the Deccan, who left the Deccan for Taft rather than Mahan to join their cousins towards the middle of the 9th/15th century.[55] Moreover, we should take into account that based on descriptions from primary sources, the complex in Taft was already established with enough space for teaching activities. Perhaps the order's income at the time was not sufficient to build similar spaces in Mahan.

The *waqf-nāmah*s

To explore the possibility of the existence of teaching spaces in Mahan or lack thereof, one should also look at the *waqf-nāmah*s (endowment documents) of the shrine at Mahan.[56] To my knowledge, the oldest *waqf-nāmah* of the shrine at Mahan was the 9th/15th-century *waqf-nāmah* of Niʿmat Allāh-i Thānī Ḥusaynī, who endowed the revenue of *darb-i āb qanāt*[57] and *qanāt-i Ṭāhirābād* in Mahan to the mausoleum (*buqʿa*).[58] The patron must have been the great great-grandson of Shāh Niʿmat Allāh Walī, also known as Shāh Naʿīm al-Dīn Niʿmat Allāh II, who died after 906/1500–1. The *waqf-nāmah* is dated 884/1479–80 and is supposedly kept at the provincial *awqāf* office of Kirman. However, despite several attempts, I have not been able to see this specific document to this date. Between this *waqf-nāmah* and the Qajar documents (the earliest of which is dated 1255/1839), which have been analysed for this study there is a long gap of about 350 years.[59]

Among the later documents, some can shed light on possible earlier documents: for instance, lists of endowments found in the National Archives of Tehran. Dated 1942, the two most important lists are those of the 'endowments known as the old endowments' (*mawqūfāt-i maʿrūf bih qadīm*) that 'do not have a *waqf-nāmah*' and the list of 'endowments with a *waqf-nāmah* whose purposes are specified'. The earliest endowment in this latter list is that of Muḥammad Shāh Qājār in 1255/1839. Therefore, we can assume that the 'old endowments' include those that belong to an earlier date than 1255/1839. Furthermore, another document in the National Archives of Tehran, a letter dated 1334 Sh./1975–6, reveals what the term 'old endowment' meant. The letter is about the share of the revenue from the old endowments that should go to the Niʿmat Allāhī family via the *mutawallī* (superintendent). The term 'old' is explained in brackets as Safawid, but a handwritten note added above this reads 'and that of Shāh Niʿmat

Allāh Thānī', the 9th/15th-century *waqf-nāmah* of the shrine mentioned earlier.[60] Given the common tradition of making frequent copies of *waqf-nāmahs* and the fact that the text refers to the five-hundred-year continued tradition of financial benefits from these properties received by the Niʿmat Allāhī family, it is possible that the 'old documents' consist of merely one Timurid endowment – that is the endowment of the *qanāt* by Niʿmat Allāh-i Thānī Ḥusaynī – and the later untitled Safawid endowments (in the lists mentioned above). This still leaves us with a curious gap during the Timurid period. How then was the shrine at Mahan maintained? It could not have depended merely on the water rights mentioned above and the donations of pilgrims to the shrine.

This is where the Indian documents play a role. There exist two *farmāns* (decrees) of the Bahmanid period that give us some hints about how, in addition to the sources of funding mentioned above, the shrine at Mahan was managed. These are two similar *farmāns*, dated 870/1465 and 894/1489, the earlier of which is from the reign of Muḥammad Shāh Bahmanī (r. 867–887/1463–1482) and bears the seal of Khwājah Maḥmūd Gāwān (d. 886/1481), the influential Iranian figure at the Bahmanid court, the vizier of Aḥmad Shāh and his sons, the patron of the grand *madrasa* in Bidar who gathered scholars from Iran and beyond, and who was known to be a disciple of the Niʿmat Allāhī family. The decrees specify that a sum of the revenue of lands in the suburbs of Muḥammadābād (Bidar), should be handed to Āmīrzā Muḥibb Allāh (d. *ca* 911/1505–6),[61] the *mutawallī* of the mausoleum of Shāh Niʿmat Allāh Walī.[62] The money could be spent by the *mutawallī* in whatever capacity he found appropriate.

But what can one make of these documents for this study? In none of the *farmāns* and *waqf-nāmahs* related to the old, as well as new, endowments of the shrine at Mahan is there any mention of teaching taking place. Instead, the endowments to the shrine at Mahan were to be used for the salary of the *mutawallī* and the attendants (*mustakhdima*), building and renovation activities, the poor or dervishes (*fuqarāʾ*), purchase of dishes, clothes for the poor or dervishes, mourning for Imām Ḥusayn and passion plays (*taʿziya*), the lighting of the shrine, and the coffee-house of the *āstāna*.

In the absence of any evidence of teaching activities and expenses related to them in the *waqf-nāmahs* and of any space allocated in the shrine at Mahan to such activities before the Safawid period, one possibility is that no large-scale teaching was taking place in Mahan at the time. On the other hand, in light of the textual references to such spaces in the *khānaqāh* in Taft, as attested by the reference to 'houses and *ḥujra*s built for the poor and shaykhs', I suggest that it was actually in Taft that such functions were taking place.[63] The *ḥujras* for the *shaykhs* were most probably used for new initiates, as there were no pilgrims coming to visit a tomb in the *khānaqāh* in Taft because, although a mausoleum was built at the complex, no one was buried there at least until 848/1444-5.[64] It is possible, too, that these lodges were used by travellers and merchants who were passing by, which also provided a chance for the order to spread its teachings.

In a complicated way, the decline of the order's teaching agenda in Mahan after Shāh Niʿmat Allāh's demise was perhaps a consequence of the multiplicity of geographies in which the order was flourishing, which itself was the result of the pragmatic approach of the order to financial and political issues. This meant that they opted for parallel and overlapping solutions, which guaranteed their eventual survival, even if this came at the price of organisational challenges and separation within the order.

Final Remarks: The Heterogeneous Processes of Institutionalisation and the Function of the Shrine at Mahan

To use Nile Green's terms to describe the Niʿmat Allāhīs, one could say that they embodied the character of both the 'wandering' Sufis and the 'sedentary' Sufis,[65] and in this way they tried to establish themselves in multiple centres: central and south Iran, the Deccan, and later at the Mughal court. They started settling in the Deccan, following the invitation of the Bahmanid court, at the time they were struggling to secure financial support from the Timurid court and long before the arrival of the Safawids.

Above I considered whether the Shiʿi-Sunni affiliation can explain the reasons for patronage offered to or withheld from the Niʿmat Allāhī order. The short answer is no. Apart from the ambiguity of available sources on the religious affiliations of the Niʿmat Allāhīs, the Timurids, and the Bahmanids, and the retrospective nature of the post-Safawid sources, on which many of the arguments rely, the time frame of this study coincides with an uncertain religious atmosphere, and a transitional moment for the Sufi orders, undergoing the process of institutionalisation. This is not an appropriate time to expect any degree of certainty regarding the Sunni-Shiʿi dichotomy.

Shāh Niʿmat Allāh welcomed patronage from the Deccan and supported the idea of emigration; he referred to his grandson Mīr Nūr Allāh b. Khalīl Allāh as the spiritual leader of India from a young age and encouraged family and disciples to move to India. It was his son, Shāh Khalīl Allāh, however, who lent the emigration firmer status when he himself moved to the Deccan after his father's death. Given the financial limitations of the order due to the policies of the Timurid court, they decided to play it safe at the price of branching off geographically. In general, the Niʿmat Allāhīs would opt for a pragmatic approach in a variety of situations. The orders' later intermarriages with the royal families in the Deccan and Safawid Iran could also be seen in the same light.[66]

The process of institutionalising of the order was a complicated process that involved establishing relations with local and dynastic rulers of the time, accumulating wealth, formulating a teaching agenda and engaging in architectural development. While during this process the patronage they received and the practical decisions made by Shāh Niʿmat Allāh and Shāh Khalīl Allāh shaped their financial and teaching agenda between Iran and India, the effect of financial matters and their teaching agenda on their architecture was not negligible. The distribution of their spiritual leaders between Iran and India perhaps meant that they could not afford two teaching centres in central Iran, namely in Mahan and Taft. Moreover, the existence of spaces that were built under Iskandar's patronage in Taft for this very purpose resulted in the preference for Taft by the next generation of the Niʿmat Allāhīs in Iran as the working centre of the order, and the development of Mahan as a venerated pilgrimage destination.

The relationship between Shāh Khalīl Allāh's decision to emigrate to the Deccan and the development of the shrine at Mahan might seem a far-fetched connection at first glance. Yet, based on the analysis of the social, political and financial contexts in which the Niʿmat Allāhī Sufi order was functioning, textual sources on the *khānaqāh* in Taft, and the *waqf-nāmahs* of the shrine at Mahan, I suggested that the reason why the shrine at Mahan was not developed before the Safawid period is that the teaching, and in fact, financial, heart of the order in Iran had shifted to Taft after (if not already before) Shāh Niʿmat Allāh's death. It is hard to look at the shrine complex at Mahan today and imagine a time when this magnificent and venerated site of the Niʿmat Allāhī order, which has evolved and expanded so harmoniously through time, was not the working centre of the order. The fact that the spaces in Taft that took over from the shrine at Mahan before the Safawid period are lost makes this image harder to develop. Yet, when we put architectural and textual evidence together, Taft's dominance over Mahan is apparent. By analysing the social history of the buildings in question, I have engaged with questions regarding the 'function' of two of the important examples of the order's architecture, perhaps in a way that would not have been possible from a reading of the architecture itself. In this light, the shrine at Mahan (in its periods of construction, development, or lack thereof) becomes a site of negotiation between the 'material' and the 'spiritual' for the order; concretising their acceptance, management and allocation of financial resources, and thereby, their self-image as a growing Sufi order.

NOTES

1 Jean Aubin, *Matériaux pour la biographie de Shāh Niʿmatūllah Wali Kermani: Textes persans* (Tehran, 1956). Several conferences on Shāh Niʿmat Allāh Walī in Europe and the United States in the past two decades have enhanced the ongoing discussion: St Jose 2002, Leiden 2003, Seville 2004, and Sofia 2005. Michael Paul Connell's 2004 dissertation has extensive sections dealing with biographical information on Shāh Niʿmat Allāh Walī and his descendants: M.P. Connell, *The Niʿmatullāhi Sayyids of Taft: A Study of the Evolution of a Late Medieval Iranian Sufi Tariqah* (PhD dissertation, Harvard University, 2004), pp. 12–22.

2 There is some discrepancy in accounts of Shāh Khalīl Allāh's death date in written sources. According to the chronology of events during the reign of ʿAlāʾ al-Dīn Aḥmad Shāh Bahmanī (r. 839–862/1436–1458) in *Burhān-i maʾāthir*, the death date of Shāh Khalīl Allāh should be about 841–2/1437–9. See ʿAlī ʿAzīz Allāh Ṭabāṭabā, *Burhān-i maʾāthir* (Delhi, 1936), pp. 78–81. But in *Maṭlaʿ al-saʿdayn*, Shāh Khalīl Allāh is reported to have been seen in Kirman in 845/1441–2: ʿAbd al-Razzāq Kamāl al-Dīn b. Isḥāq Samarqandī, *Maṭlaʿ al-saʿdayn wa majmaʿ al-baḥrayn*, ed. ʿAbd al-Ḥusayn Nawāʾī (2nd ed., Tehran, 2004), vol. 2, p. 513. On the other hand, we know that he must have been dead by 858/1454 when *Tuḥfat al-muḥibbin* (a calligraphic treatise written in the middle of the 9th/15th century by Sirāj al-Shīrāzī in Bidar) was finished and dedicated to Shāh Muḥibb Allāh (his son) the *quṭb* of the order in the Deccan. See Carl W. Ernst, 'Sufism and the Aesthetics of Penmanship in Sirāj Al-Shīrāzī's "Tuḥfat Al-Muḥibbīn" (1454)', *JAOS*, 129 (2009), pp. 431–433.

3 In previous scholarship there are no detailed monographs on the most significant surviving examples of the shrines and *khānaqāh*s of the order in Mahan, Taft, and Bidar.

My PhD dissertation was dedicated to the study of these buildings in the context of Iran-Deccan connections: Peyvand Firouzeh, *Architecture, Sanctity, and Power; Niʿmatullahi shrines and khanaqahs in fifteenth-century Iran and India* (PhD dissertation, University of Cambridge, 2016). Apart from Mahan's appearance in Lisa Golombek and Donald Newton Wilber, *The Timurid Architecture of Iran and Turan* (Princeton, NJ, 1988); Robert Hillenbrand, *Studies in Medieval Islamic Architecture* (London, 2006); and Bernard O'Kane, *The Appearance of Persian on Islamic Art* (New York, 2009), in which he studies some of the inscriptions of the mausoleum, there is an article on the shrine, by Mehrdad Qayyumi Bidhendi; a conference paper published as M. Qayyumi Bidhendi, 'Majmūʿa mazār-i Shāh Niʿmatullāh Walī', in Shahrām Pāzūkī, ed, *Majmūʿa maqālāt darbāra-yi Shāh Niʿmatullāh Walī* (Tehran, 1383 Sh./2004–5), pp. 173–195. Recently, a thesis by Negin ʿIsazadeh focused on the shrine at Mahan throughout its history: Negin ʿIsazadeh, *Tak-nigārī-yi majmūʿa-yi Shāh Niʿmatullāh Walī dar Māhān* (MA dissertation, Shahid Beheshti University, 2010).

The Shāh Walī *khānaqāh* in Taft has been treated in the same way, being discussed in the catalogue of Golombek and Wilber and more recently in an article: Karim Mardomi, Mohammadreza Noghsanmohammadi, and Mohsen Dehghani Tafti, 'An Inquiry in Historical Evolution and Retrieval of the Process of Formation and Transformation of Shah Wali complex, Taft, Iran', *International Journal of Architectural Engineering and Urban Planning*, 23 (2013), pp. 92–102.

The mausoleum of Ḥaḍrat Khalīl Allāh (son of Shāh Niʿmat Allāh Walī) in Bidar has been the subject of architectural analysis (among other monuments of Bidar) in Ghulam Yazdani, *Bidar, its History and Monuments* (London, 1947), and was discussed briefly in George Michell and Mark Zebrowski, *Architecture and Art of the Deccan Sultanates, The New Cambridge History of India* (Cambridge, 1999), pp. 73–77. See also Helen Philon, 'The Chaukhandi at Ashtur, Outside Bidar: A Bahamani Period Saintly Funerary Complex', in Seyed Ayub Ali, ed., *Studies in Medieval Deccan History (14th-17th century): Dr. M.A. Nayeem Festschrift* (Deccan History Society, 2015), pp. 51–56.

4 In her book, Zeynep Yürekli discusses the role of authoring hagiographies on the life of the *shaykhs* (in the case of the Bektashi order) in seeking architectural patronage. See Z. Yürekli, *Architecture and Hagiography in the Ottoman Empire: The Politics of Bektashi Shrines in the Classical Age* (Farnham and Burlington, VT, 2012), p. 79.

5 Connell, *The Niʿmatullāhi Sayyids of Taft*, pp. 106–107.

6 Exceptions to this include works such as Terry Graham, 'The Niʿmatullahi Order under Safavid Suppression and in Indian Exile', in Leonard Lewisohn and David Morgan, ed., *The Heritage of Sufism (Vol. III): Late Classical Persianate Sufism* (Oxford, 1999), pp. 165–200; Connell, *The Niʿmatullāhī Sayyids of Taft*. Although these works do engage with matters of patronage of the order, they do not approach the subject from an architectural point of view.

7 See for instance Aubin, *Matériaux*, pp. 200–201.

8 Ibid., p.179.

9 Graham suggested that Taft became an alternative base for the order as opposed to Kirman and Mahan, to avoid the raids from the Baluchi tribesmen. See: Graham, 'The Niʿmatullahi Order', pp. 166–167. However, biographies of Shāh Niʿmat Allāh Walī give a different picture at times, one that implies Taft was a base for the order even before Shāh Niʿmat Allāh Walī went to Kirman and Mahan. For instance, see: Aubin, *Matériaux*, pp. 49–52.

10 Muḥammad Mufīd, *Jāmiʿ-i Mufīdī*, ed. I. Afshar (Tehran, 1340 Sh./1961), vol. 3, pp. 685–687.

11 Aubin, *Matériaux*, p. 48.

12 The Safawid additions will be briefly discussed later in the chapter. Post-Safawid additions include: *Ṣaḥn-i Muḥammad Shāhī*, also known as *Ḥusayniyya*, built during

the reign of Muḥammad Shāh Qājār (r. 1250–1264/1834–1848) when the order was already Shiʿi, whether the transition happened during the Safawid period or earlier; the eastern *riwāq*, known as *Riwāq-i wakīl al-mulkī*, together with *Ṣaḥn-i wakīl al-mulkī* after Muḥammad Ismāʿīl Khān Wakīl al-Mulk (r. 1274–1283/1858–1866) who was one of the governors of Kirman during the rule of Nāṣir al-Dīn Shāh Qājār (r. 1264–1341/1848–1869); and finally, the newest and most eastern court, known as *Ṣaḥn-i Atābakī* after Mīrzā ʿAlī Aṣghar Khān Atābak (d. 1325/1907) who served as the *ṣadr-i aʿẓam* (prime minister) at different times under Nāṣir al-Dīn Shāh Qājār, Muẓaffar al-Dīn Shāh Qājār and Muḥammad ʿAlī Shāh Qājār.

13 Aubin, *Matériaux*, p. 193.

14 *chau* (چو) means four and *khand* (کهنڈ) could mean portion, piece, division, section, and storey among others. Yazdani interprets the latter as storey and argues that the term Chaukhandi is referring to the mausoleum as a four-storeyed building taking into account the two major flights of steps that lead to the two-storeyed mausoleum. See Yazdani, *Bidar, Its History and Monuments*, p. 141. The etymology and history of usage of the word *Chaukhandi* is an ambiguous one and there are more possibilities for the interpretation of the mausoleum as a *Chaukhandi*. It could mean a square-shaped mausoleum, an enclosure of uncovered walls around a venerated grave, or simply a mausoleum.

15 Muḥammad Qāsim Hindū Shāh Astarābādī Firishtah, *Tārīkh-i Firishtah* (Bombay, 1831), pp. 669–670. During Sulṭān Maḥmūd Khalajī's blockade of Bidar, he engaged in a conversation with Mawlānā Shams al-Dīn Ḥaq-Gūy-i Kirmānī who was at the mausoleum of Khalīl Allāh. The tone and content of the sentence suggests that he was based at the mausoleum and was perhaps its keeper.

16 Examples include additions to Bāgh-i Aharistān and ʿImārat-i ʿAbbāsiyya in Yazd.

17 Aubin, *Matériaux*, pp. 13–14.

18 Examples include Sayyid ʿAlī Hamadānī (d. 786/1385), the Kubrawi Sufi master who was asked to leave the region by Tīmūr, as well as ʿAlī Ibn Muḥammad Sayyid Sharīf Jurjāni (d. 816/1413), exiled from Shiraz to Samarqand by Tīmūr.

19 Aubin, *Matériaux*, p. 48.

20 Considering the number of gifts arriving, Amīr Ghanā (Ghunā) Shīrīn, ruler of Kirmān, ordered the tax value to be calculated; it was seventy thousand *tūmāns*. He was dubious whether to tax Shāh Niʿmat Allāh's gifts or not. In the end, he wrote to Shāhrukh's court in Herat to seek advice. Shāhrukh consulted his wife Gawharshād. She believed that if he taxed the gifts, historians would write in chronicles that the king of Hindustan sent so many gifts to the Sayyid that Shāhrukh, king of Iran, could not exempt him from tax: he therefore wrote to Ghanā Shīrīn and ordered him to avoid the taxation: Aubin, *Matériaux*, pp. 189–190.

21 Shaykh Ḥabīb Junaydī accompanied by Mīr Shams al-Dīn Qummī: Firishtah, *Tārīkh-i Firishtah*, pp. 633–635.

22 Ibid.

23 Firishtah, *Tārīkh-i Firishtah*, pp. 633–635.

24 Ibid.

25 Muḥammad Mufīd, *Jāmiʿ-i Mufīdī*, p. 687. For a discussion of the dating of the mosque see Firouzeh, *Architecture, Sanctity, and Power*, pp. 30–33.

26 In sources such as works of Wāʾiẓī, Abarqūyī and Kirmānī it is recorded as 775/1373–4 when Shāh Niʿmat Allāh Walī would be roughly 45 years old: Aubin, *Matériaux*, pp. 47, 287. Connell argues that this is a mistake based on, for instance, a *ghazal* repeated in Ṣunʿ Allāh's biography indicating that Khalīl Allāh, as Shāh Niʿmat Allāh Walī puts it in verse, was born when he was seventy (ibid., p. 172). Connell therefore suggests a date around 800/1397–8: Connell, *The Niʿmatullāhī Sayyids of Taft*, pp. 35–36.

27 Andrew Peacock, 'Sufis and the Seljuk Court in Mongol Anatolia: Politics and Patronage in the Works of Jalāl Al-Dīn Rūmī and Sulṭān Walad', in Sara Nur Yildiz and

Andrew Peacock, ed., *The Seljuks of Anatolia: Court and Society in the Medieval Middle East* (London and New York, 2013), pp. 206–226.

28 Sharaf al-Dīn ʿAlī Yazdī, *Munsha'āt*, ed. Īraj Afshār and Muḥammad Riḍā Abū'ī Mihrīzī (Tehran, 1388 Sh./2010), pp. 149–155. For a brief general discussion of these letters see: Graham, 'The Niʿmatullahi Order', p. 179, n.36.

29 Aubin, *Matériaux*, p. 190.

«و همچنین بعد از این سلاطین هند دیگر بار تحفه‌ئی از سابق لایق‌تر و بی‌شمارتر بخدمت آنحضرت فرستادند. آورنده آن را در میان رودخانه ماهان برابر خانقاه گذاشت. چون حضرت شاه در خلوت بود احدی را یارای آن نبود که بعرض رساند. بعد از سه روز آنحضرت از خلوت بیرون آمده نظرش بر آنها افتاده احوال پرسید. حقیقت عرض کردند و قیمت تحفها و ارمغان، که خراج اقلیمی میشد، مذکور ساختند. حضرت ولایت منزلت فرمود تا آنها را سه حصّه کردند موافق، و گفت: «یک حصّه بحضرت خاقانی میرزا شاهرخ دهید که لشکر او بسیار است؛ صرف لشکر نماید. و حصّه دیگر به خلیل الله دهید، که او جاه دوست میدارد. و حصّه سیوم صرف اخراجات آستانه ماهان نمائید.»

Connell interprets '*ikhrājat-i āstāna-yi Mahan*'—the third division of the gifts—as to be spent for the needy in Mahan. Connell, *The Niʿmatullāhī Sayyids of Taft*, p. 64. However, these were not limited to the needy and could include expenses for disciples, as well as the upkeep of whatever buildings existed on the site, and activities such as recitation of Qur'an as reflected in the later *waqf-nāmah*s of the shrine at Mahan.

30 Also see Connell's discussion on this, how the biographies of Shāh Niʿmatullāh Walī 'go to great length to contrast Shāh Niʿmat Allāh Walī's detachment from material affairs with Shāhrukh's greed.' (ibid.)

31 Sharaf al-Dīn ʿAlī Yazdī, *Munsha'āt*, pp. 154–155.

32 G. Yazdani, ed., *Epigraphia Indica* (New Delhi, 1927), p. 19.

33 Ibid. With a minor correction on Yazdani's reading, the inscription reads as follows:

مقبره شا[ه] نورالله حسینی تیار بود در زمان بریدیان شکستند بعده اسدالله خان نبیره شاه مذکور از سر نو در عمل محمدشاه بادشاه در سنه ۱۱۹۵ باتمام رسانید.

34 Aubin, *Matériaux*, p. 199.

35 2–203. Ṣunʿ Allāh stated here that Shāh Khalil Allāh left for the Deccan, where his other son Shāh Nūr Allāh had already been based since Shāh Niʿmat Allāh's time. According to the epigraphic information mentioned earlier in this article, and the chronology of the events implied from Ṭabāṭabā's accounts of the time, Shāh Nūr Allāh must have died after his father arrived in the Deccan in the same year. See: Ṭabāṭabā, *Burhān-i ma'āthir*, p. 65.

36 Aubin, *Matériaux*, pp. 199–201.

37 Ibid., pp. 200–201.

38 A contemporary use of the same analogy is found in the *Maqāmāt-i Ṭāhir al-Dīn Muḥammad wa Shams al-Dīn Ibrāhīm*, the latter a contemporary of Shāh Niʿmat Allāh Walī in Bam. At the time the governor of Bam, Shaykh ʿAbd Allāh, was holding the fort in siege against Sulṭān Pīr Budāq, Shaykh ʿAbd Allāh and Sayyid Ṭāhir al-Dīn were not on good terms. Shaykh ʿAbd Allāh summoned the author of *Maqāmāt* and asked him if he had heard that the Sayyid referred to him as Yazīd. Then he commanded the author to take a message to the Shaykh: 'Go tell him that if you are willing to become Ḥusayn Ibn-i ʿAlī, then I am Yazīd'. See Saʿīd Nafīsī, ed., 'Maqāmāt-i Ṭāhir al-Dīn Muḥammad wa Shams al-Dīn Ibrāhīm', *Farhang-i Īrān-zamīn*, 2 (1333 Sh./1954–5), p. 130.

39 Shahrām Pāzūkī, 'Naqdī bar mukātibāt: kand wa kāwī dar tashayyuʿ-i Shāh Niʿmat Allāh Walī wa Mawlawī', *Haft Āsimān*, 14 (1381 Sh./2002–3), p. 153.

40 H.K. Sherwani and P.M. Joshi, ed., *History of Medieval Deccan* (Hyderabad, 1973), vol. 1, p. 166.

41 Pāzūkī, 'Naqdī bar mukātibāt', p. 147.

42 Similar to his earlier works such as: Ḥ. Farzām, 'Ikhtilāf-i jāmī bā Shāh Walī', *Dānishkādah adabiyyāt wa ʿulūm-i insānī-yi dānishgāh-i Iṣfahān* (Isfahan, 1343 Sh./1964–5), vol. 1, pp. 48–57.

43 Ḥamīd Farzām, *Taḥqīq dar aḥwāl wa naqd-i āthār wa afkār-i Shāh Niʿmatullāh Walī* (Tehran, 1391 Sh./2012–13), pp. 587–603. It should be noted that Richard Gramlich, in his monography *Die schiitischen Derwischorden Persiens* (Wiesbaden, 1965–1981), starts from the 19th century, when the order is indeed Shiʿi, and goes backwards. He does not necessarily discuss the reasons for categorising the order as Shiʿi during the 15th century.

44 Similarly, Denise Aigle argues that veneration of ʿAlī during the Ilkhanid period, although a reminiscent of Shiʿi tendencies, is not formally considered a sign of Shiʿism. See: Aigle, 'La Religion Populaire en Iran Mongol', in D. Aigle, ed., *L'Iran face à la domination mongole* (Tehran, 1997), p. 206.

45 Lawrence G. Potter, 'Sufis and Sultans in post-Mongol Iran', *Iranian Studies*, 27 (1994), p. 80. See also Hamid Algar, 'The Naqshbandī Order: A Preliminary Survey of Its History and Significance', *Stud. Islam.*, 44 (1976), p. 126.

46 Connell, *The Niʿmatullāhī Sayyids of Taft*, p. 5.

47 Aubin, *Matériaux*, pp. 13–14.

48 T. Graham, 'Shāh Niʿmatullāh Walī: Founder of the Niʿmatullāhī Sufi Order', in L. Lewisohn and D. Morgan, ed., *The Heritage of Sufism (Vol. II): The Legacy of Mediæval Persian Sufism*, p. 182.

49 Beatrice Forbes Manz, *Power, Politics and Religion in Timurid Iran* (Cambridge, 2007), p. 209. As examples of such earlier scholarship see: Biancamaria Scarcia Amoretti, 'Religion in the Timurid and Safavid Periods', in P. Jackson, ed., *The Cambridge History of Iran*, vol. 6, *The Timurid and Safavid Periods* (Cambridge, 1986), pp. 610–616; and Jean Aubin, 'De Kûhbanân à Bidar : La famille Niʿmatullahī', *Studia Iranica*, 20, 2 (1991), pp. 242–244.

50 For a sectarian interpretation of the inscriptions at the tomb in Bidar see: Sara Mondini, 'Vague Traits: Strategy and Ambiguities in the Decorative Program of the Aḥmad Šāh I Bahmanī Mausoleum', in Stefano Pellò, ed., *Borders: Itineraries on the Edges of Iran, Eurasiatica*, 5 (Venice, 2016), pp. 155–180.

51 Connell, *The Niʿmatullāhī Sayyids of Taft*, p. 41.

52 Richard Maxwell Eaton, *Sufis of Bijapur, 1300–1700: Social Roles of Sufis in Medieval India* (Princeton, NJ, 1978), p. 55. Gīsū Darāz was the Sufi *shaykh* who brought the Chishtī teachings to the Deccan under the Bahmanids' patronage.

53 Graham, 'The Niʿmatullahi Order', p. 167.

54 Aubin, *Matériaux*, pp. 69–70.

55 Connell, *The Niʿmatullāhī Sayyids of Taft*, p. 119; Aubin, *Matériaux*, p. 207.

56 The endowments are managed under the supervision of Islamic Endowments and Charitable Affairs Organization.

57 A network of wells and gently sloping canals to channel water.

58 Catalogued in Umīd Riḍāʾī, *Fihrist-i asnād-i mawqūfāt-i Īrān: asnād-i mawjūd dar sāzmān-i awqāf wa umūr-i khayriyya* (Tehran, 1382 Sh./2003–4), vol. 2, p. 267.

59 The *waqf-nāmah* of Muḥammad Shāh (dated 1295/1878) indicates that lands in the villages of Farmītan and Bābā Ḥusayn (villages near Mahan) were endowed to the shrine at Mahan. Nāṣir al-Dīn Shāh later re-affirmed this *farmān* (decree). The letter is published in an article by Bāstānī Pārīzī in Sh. Pāzūkī, ed., *Majmūʿa-yi maqālāt darbārah-yi Shāh Niʿmatullāh Walī* (Tehran, 1383 Sh./2004–5), pp. 143–171.

60 The line reads:

> . . . جمعیت سادات اولاد حضرت سید نورالدین شاه نعمت اله ولی نوراله مضجعه طبق احکام دادگستری و استمداد پانصد ساله مستحق دریافت یک ثلث عواید موقوفات قدیم (صفویه (و شاه نعمت الله ثانی)) آستانه مقدسه ماهان بوده.اند . . . .

61 Nurbakhsh and Graham mention the year 1508 as his death date: Javad Nurbakhsh, *Masters of the Path: A History of the Masters of the Nimatullahi Sufi Order* (New York, 1980), pp. 70–71; and Graham, 'The Niʿmatullahi Order', p. 185. I have not come across any date in any of the primary sources I have consulted so far. In Sunʿ Allāh's biography

of Shāh Niʿmat Allāh, there is a note that Muḥibb Allāh lived for 78 years and 2 months and 12 days (Aubin, *Matériaux*, p. 206). We know from biographies of Shāh Niʿmat Allāh that Muḥibb Allāh was born when Shāh Niʿmat Allāh was still alive and after the order's Indian connection was established; Shāh Niʿmat Allāh predicted that he will be the Shāh (here meaning spiritual leader) of India. This means Muḥibb Allāh was probably born between *ca* 832/1428–9 and 834/1430–1, therefore his death date could be between 910/1504–5 and 912/1506–7. Thus, a date about 911/1505–6 is a safe guess.

62 Published in Yusuf Husain Khan, *Farmans and sanads of the Deccan sultans* (Hyderabad, 1963), pp. 3–4.

63 Muḥammad Mufid, *Jāmiʿ-i Mufidī*, pp. 685–687.

64 For the reference to the earliest tombstone in the mausoleum at Taft see Īraj Afshār, *Yādgārhā-yi Yazd: muʿarrifi-i abnīyah tārīkhī wa āthār-i bāstānī* (Tehran, 1348 Sh./1969–70), pp. 413–417.

65 Nile Green, 'Migrant Sufis and Sacred Space in South Asian Islam', *Contemporary South Asia*, 12 (2003), p. 493.

66 Graham, 'The Niʿmatullahi Order', p. 185; Andrew Newman, *Safavid Iran: Rebirth of a Persian Empire* (London, 2008), p. 54. For a chart of the order's intermarriages with the Safawids see, Firouzeh, *Architecture, Sanctity, and Power*, p. 195.

4

The *mujaddid* and the *majdhūb*: Shāh ʿAlī Riḍā (d. 1215/1801) and the Different Narratives of the Niʿmat Allāhī Renewal

Fabrizio Speziale

This chapter looks at the history of the Niʿmat Allāhī order in the Deccan region of India and of the Niʿmat Allāhī centre which was established in Hyderabad in the second half of the 11th/17th century. The development of this branch and its new line of masters can be regarded as the main element of renewal of the order in the Deccan during the early modern period. The first part of the chapter outlines the features and the phases of the Niʿmat Allāhī presence in the Deccan. It looks at the events that led to the Shiʿitisation of the Niʿmat Allāhī branch of Hyderabad and at how this Shiʿi group of Sufis integrated themselves in the local environment. The second part looks in particular at one master of this lineage of Sufis, Shāh ʿAlī Riḍā Dakanī (d. 1215/1801) who is considered the architect of the plan to restore the order in Iran by sending a group of disciples among whom was Maʿṣūm ʿAlī Shāh Dakanī (d. *ca* 1211/1797). This narrative is based on the biographical accounts written in Iran after the migration of ʿAlī Riḍā's disciples to this country and is closely related to the construction of another narrative, the one presenting Maʿṣūm ʿAlī Shāh Dakanī as the only successor of Shāh ʿAlī Riḍā. In this study I investigate the different image of the latter's mystical career which emerges from the biographies of the Sufis written in the Deccan. The Indian sources reveal several elements which were omitted in the account of their master made by the Niʿmat Allāhī who migrated to Iran, especially the issue of the controversy between Shāh ʿAlī Riḍā and his brother for leadership of the order's headquarters in Hyderabad.

The Niʿmat Allāhīs in the Deccan Environment

Shortly after the foundation of the order in Iran by Shāh Niʿmat Allāh Walī (d. 834/1431, Mahan), the Indian region of Deccan occupies a central role in the history of the Niʿmat Allāhī order for about four centuries. The significance of this is not related to the spread and influence of the order in the Deccan or elsewhere in India, but mainly to the fact that it was here that during the early modern period the main lineage of the Niʿmat Allāhī masters, still recognised by the Iranian Niʿmat Allāhīs, was active. If the Safawid (906–1134/1501–1722) attitude towards Sufism, which was most often adverse, did not determine the disappearance of the order in Iran, however, it did lead to its adaptation to the new political and social context and to the redefinition of the religious and spiritual authority of the masters' order in Iran.[1] The role of the Indian branch was closely related to the fact that at the beginning, and seemingly until mid 11th/17th century, the masters of the Deccani line were direct descendants of Shāh Khalīl Allāh (d. 860/1455–6, Bidar), the only son of Shāh Niʿmat Allāh Walī. However, although it was the direct descendants of the founder that established the order in the Deccan, they did not play any active role in the renewal and return of the order to Iran, which occurred in the second half of the 18th century.

The history of the Niʿmat Allāhiyya in the Deccan can be divided into two main periods. During the first, the order is based in the city of Bidar, where the descendants of Niʿmat Allāh Walī arrived in the first half of the 9th/15th century, shortly after which the city became the capital of the Bahmanī sultanate (748–934/1347–1528), the first independent sultanate of the Deccan. During the second period, from the second half of the 17th century up to the return to Iran, the centre of the order moved to a hill on the western outskirts of Hyderabad. By this time, the descendants of the founder had already given over leadership of the order to a new line of masters issuing from Mīr Maḥmūd (d. 1100/1689), a Shiʿi of Iraqi origin who was initiated at Bidar before settling at Hyderabad. This chapter deals with this second period, which precedes the revival of the order operated in Iran by Maʿṣūm ʿAlī Shāh Dakanī.

As far as the Bidar centre is concerned, the history of the first Niʿmat Allāhī masters of the Bahmanid age has been studied by a number of scholars.[2] On the contrary, almost nothing is known of the later Niʿmat Allāhī masters of Bidar, when the city fell under the control of the Barīd Shāh (r. *ca* 897–1028/1492–1619) at the end of the 9th/15th century, and then of the ʿĀdil Shāh of Bijapur,[3] who annexed Bidar in 1028/1619. Moreover, the *tadhkirat* and other historical accounts describing both the first masters of Bidar and those of Hyderabad, do not include entries on the later Niʿmat Allāhī masters of Bidar. The research on new sources regarding the later masters of Bidar must then be held to be of primary importance for future studies aiming to present a first comprehensive view of the history of the order in India.

The main sources about the Niʿmat Allāhīs of Hyderabad are the regional *tadhkirāt* (biographies) written in Persian and Urdu. We do not know of any monographic *tadhkirāt* specifically devoted to the masters of the Hyderabad line. Moreover, no text on Sufism or other topics is ascribed to the Niʿmat Allāhī masters of Hyderabad.[4] Biographical entries on them do appear in some biographical and historical works written in Hyderabad in the 19th and early 20th century.[5] Two works written in Persian are the *Mishkāt al-nubuwwat*, a biography of the Sufis composed in 1219/1804–5 by Ghulām ʿAlī Qādirī (d. 1258/1842),[6] and the *Gulzār-i āṣafiyya*, a historical work with a chapter on the biographies of the Sufis, by Ghulām Ḥusayn Khān (b. 1199/1784–5) a court physician of the third Niẓām of Hyderabad Sikandar Jāh (r. 1218–1244/1803–1829).[7] Both authors were Sunni Sufis and contemporaries of Shāh ʿAlī Riḍā and his son Shāh Mīrān (d. 1230/1814), the last masters of the Hyderabadi branch. Another important work is the *Maḥbūb-i dhī al-minan: Tadhkira-yi awliyāʾ-i Dakan*, a biographical dictionary of the Sufis of the Deccan written in Urdu by ʿAbd al-Jabbār Khān Malkāpūrī at the beginning of the 20th century.[8] It constitutes the third volume of the author's historical-biographical work entitled *Maḥbūb al-tawārīkh.* A more recent work is the *Tadhkira-yi awliyāʾ-i Ḥaydarābād* by Murād ʿAlī Ṭāliʿ which was published in the 1970s and is mainly based on the works of Ghulām ʿAlī Qādirī, Ghulām Ḥusayn Khān and ʿAbd al-Jabbār Malkāpūrī, in the chapters concerning the Niʿmat Allāhīs.

The Hyderabadi branch was established by ʿImād al-Dīn Maḥmūd al-Ḥusaynī (d. 1100/1689), known as Mīr Maḥmūd. According to Ghulām Ḥusayn Khān and to Malkāpūrī, he was a *sayyid* descended from the eighth Twelver imam ʿAlī al-Riḍā (*sādāt-i riḍāwiyya*).[9]

However, Ghulām ʿAlī Qādirī never defines Mīr Maḥmūd and his successors as *sayyids*. Mīr Maḥmūd stayed at Bidar for three years before receiving the Niʿmat Allāhī *khilāfa* from Shams al-Dīn Ḥusaynī, the master of the Bidar centre. Once in Hyderabad, Mīr Maḥmūd settled on a hill located about six kilometres away from the city. According to one account, when he first arrived on this hill he fell into a state of mystical intoxication (*mastānah*) and when he woke up a couple of days later, he decided to build his *dargāh* there.[10] The *dargāh* became the centre of the order and it is there that the master and his descendants were buried. The place became known as Kūh-i Mīr Maḥmūd (the hill of Mīr Maḥmūd) and stands nowadays on the western side of the Mīr ʿĀlam Tank, an artificial reservoir created at the beginning of the 19th century (fig. 4.1).

It is not known with certainty why Mīr Maḥmūd left Bidar. It should be considered, however, that Bidar had become a provincial town by then, while Hyderabad hosted an important Shiʿi community and was the opulent capital of the Quṭb Shāh sultans (924–1098/1518–1687), who had long generously patronised Shiʿi scholars at their court. Moreover, according to a well-known account, the founder of the dynasty, Sulṭān Qulī Quṭb al-Mulk (d. 950/1543), had received the spiritual blessing of Nūr al-Dīn Niʿmat Allāh II (d. after 906/1500),

Figure 4.1. The *dargāh* of Mīr Maḥmūd seen from Mīr ʿĀlam Tank, after Campbell, *Glimpses of the Nizam's Dominions*, 1898, p. 228.

a Yazd-based master, in Iran before travelling to India.[11] However, when Mīr Maḥmūd arrived at Hyderabad things had changed considerably. Abu'l-Ḥasan Tānā Shāh (r. 1083–1098/1672–1687), the last Quṭb Shāh sultan, was no longer a Shiʿi, but a Sunni disciple of a Chishtī master, and he did not extend any patronage to Mīr Maḥmūd. Moreover, a dispute arose between Mīr Maḥmūd and Shāh Rājū (d. 1092/1681–2), the Chishtī master of the sultan and according to one account, the sultan even tried to prevent Mīr Maḥmūd from building his *dargāh*.[12] Mīr Maḥmūd died in 1100/1689 and was succeeded by his son, Shams al-Dīn, who spent most of his life in spiritual isolation at the *dargāh*, where he died in 1161/1748. Shams al-Dīn was succeeded by his elder son Shāh ʿAlī Riḍā whose authority was contested by Shams al-Dīn's second son Muḥammad ʿAlī, although Shāh ʿAlī Riḍā was finally able to transmit the directing of the centre to his son, Shāh Mīrān (fig. 4.2).

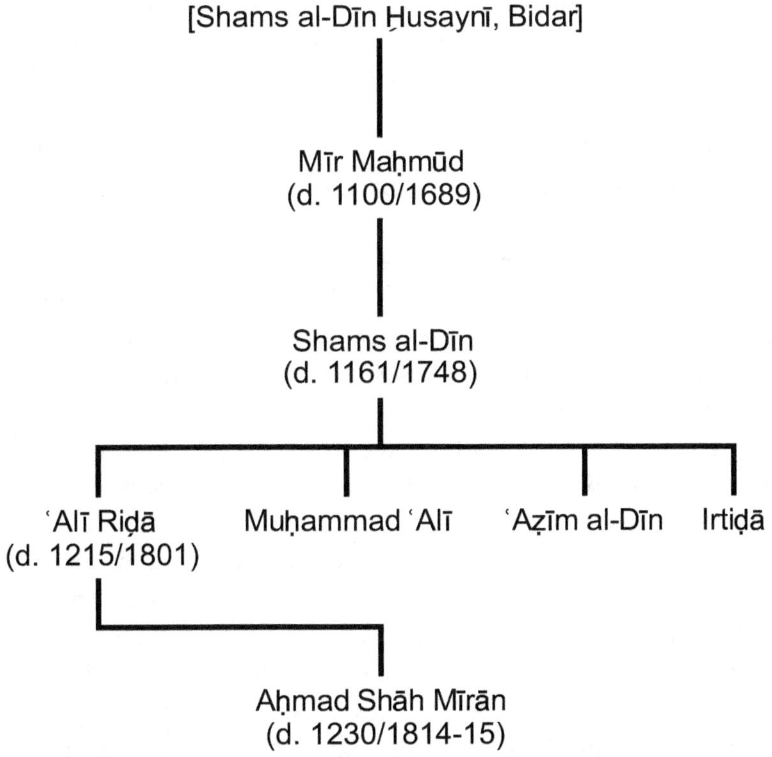

Figure 4.2. The Niʿmat Allāhī family of Hyderabad.

According to the classification of the Indian Sufi orders proposed by Marc Gaborieau, the Niʿmat Allāhīs of the Deccan can be considered a 'noble' order, connected to the noble (*ashrāf*) elite, and a 'minor' order, that is to say an order of regional proportions and reach.[13] The available sources make no reference to other Niʿmat Allāhī centres in the Deccan or in other regions of India besides those of Bidar and Hyderabad, although we cannot rule out the existence of smaller groups at some period in nearby towns even if they are not mentioned in the sources. As for the Niʿmat Allāhīs of Hyderabad, the sources do not mention any other *khalīfa* (successor) of these masters, except for the sons who succeeded them. Although the Indian sources clearly say that Mīr Maḥmūd and his heirs had many disciples and enjoyed a popular devotion stretching beyond the Shiʿi community, it is nonetheless likely that many of the disciples initiated to the order came from the Shiʿi community of the city.

The Niʿmat Allāhīs of Hyderabad, operating in a Sunni majority society, did not enjoy a popularity in any way comparable to that attained later on by the order in Iran. Moreover, the masters of Hyderabad did not receive royal patronage comparable to that granted by the Bahmanī sultans of Bidar, who were Sunni, to the descendants of Niʿmat Allāh Walī. Nevertheless, although the Niʿmat Allāhīs of Hyderabad remained a group of elite Sufis, they were able to integrate themselves in the local context at different levels. Shāh ʿAlī Riḍā and his son gained the favour of the second and the third Niẓāms, the rulers of the princely state of Hyderabad. The *ḥaydarābādī* masters started to celebrate the *ʿurs*, the ceremony on the occasion of the death of a saint during which *ṣandal*, a sandal paste, is taken in procession.[14] As witnessed by an astonished Iranian Niʿmat Allāhī who visited Hyderabad in 1881, during the days of the *ʿurs* people from different sects and religions, Hindus, Muslims and others would visit the *dargāh*.[15]

Notwithstanding the limits of the order's influence at the local level, it is worth outlining certain features of the specific place occupied by the Niʿmat Allāhī centre of Hyderabad in the history of Indian Sufism. At a transnational level, the circulation of Sufis between India and the rest of the Muslim world was mainly characterised by the migration toward South Asia of Sufi lineages originating from the western lands of the Muslim world. The reverse process was less frequent and in very few cases led to a success comparable to that obtained by the Niʿmat Allāhīs in Iran.[16] As for the South Asian context, the Niʿmat Allāhī masters of Hyderabad established one of the few Shiʿi centres of Indian Sufism, which is dominated by Sunni orders.[17]

A central question about the Indian Niʿmat Allāhīs concerns the process of Shiitisation of the order. When and why did the order become Shiʿi in the Deccan? It certainly was not Shiʿi when it arrived in India in the 9th/15th century, but it was already so by the time Maʿṣūm ʿAlī Shāh was sent to revamp the order in Iran. About the Bidar period, we should agree with what has been noted by Jean Aubin in his article on the Niʿmat Allāhī family: there is no evidence that the descendants of Niʿmat Allāh Walī who settled in Bidar were Shiʿa.[18] It is impossible to formulate any hypothesis about the later Niʿmat Allāhī masters of Bidar who lived during the post-Bahmanide period and seem to disappear from the major biographical works on the Sufis of the Deccan.

The masters of Hyderabad are the first masters of the order to be openly mentioned by the Sunni biographers of the Deccan for their connection with Shiʿism. Mīr Maḥmūd, the founder of the *ḥaydarābādī* branch, was born into a family of *mutawalli*s of the shrine of ʿAlī b. Abī Ṭālib in Najaf.[19] Ghulām ʿAlī Qādirī writes about Mīr Maḥmūd's son, Shams al-Dīn, that 'Many of his disciples are Iranians. These people affirm that he [Shams al-Dīn] is one of them', while according to the opinion of Ghulām ʿAlī 'he observes the *madhhab* of the Sufis.'[20] However, at the end of the biographical note on Shams al-Dīn, Ghulām ʿAlī openly remarks upon the excess (*ghuluww*) of his affection (*maḥabbat*) for the *ahl al-bayt*.[21] Another element which clearly testifies to the Shiʿi faith of these Sufis is the *ʿāshūr-khānah* that is part of the *dargāh* of Mīr Maḥmūd. In the Deccan, the *ʿāshūr-khānah*s are places devoted to the Shiʿi cult where the *ʿalam*s, the standards of the martyrs of Karbala carried during the procession of *muḥarram*, are preserved.

Therefore, the Shiitisation of the order in Hyderabad occurred for reasons very different from those that led the Niʿmat Allāhīs to convert to Shiʿism in Safawid Iran. Though Shiʿism had been the official religion of the Quṭb Shāh sultanate, when Mīr Maḥmūd arrived in Hyderabad anti-Sunni tendencies comparable to those of Safawid Iran no longer existed in the town.[22] In the Deccan, the Shiitisation of the order occurred basically because the spiritual authority was transmitted within a Shiʿi family, that of Mīr Maḥmūd. Afterwards, in the milieu of the Shiʿi disciples of Hyderabad who congregated around these masters, emerged Maʿṣūm ʿAlī Shāh who connected the Indian branch to the Shiʿi culture of Iran. That the Shiitisation of the order in India took place at a later period and that it was a partial process, seems to be confirmed by the fact that nowadays the descendants of the Niʿmat Allāhīs in the Deccan include both Sunni and Shiʿi families.[23]

The transmission of Niʿmat Allāhī leadership in the Deccan context remains mostly based on family inheritance. Shams al-Dīn Ḥusaynī, the master of Bidar who initiated Mīr Maḥmūd, is mentioned as one of the descendants (*awlād*) of Shāh Khalīl Allāh.[24] Therefore, it is likely that until the 17th century the leadership of the Bidar branch remained within the family of the founder of the order. Afterwards, the leadership of the order at Hyderabad remained within Mīr Maḥmūd's family. It is therefore important to remark that the two fundamental events marking the renewal of the order in the early modern period – the foundation of the *ḥaydarābādī* branch by Mīr Maḥmūd and the return of the order to Iran through Maʿṣūm ʿAlī Shāh – also constitute fundamental breaks to this rule of family-based succession.

Shāh ʿAlī Riḍā and the Niʿmat Allāhī Revival

Shams al-Dīn had four sons: ʿAlī Riḍā Ḥusaynī (d. 1215/1801),[25] Muḥammad ʿAlī, ʿAẓīm al-Dīn and Irtiḍā. The Indian biographers offer no details about the last two. The first two, ʿAlī Riḍā and Muḥammad ʿAlī, competed for the leadership of the *dargāh* until the Niẓām of Hyderabad was eventually called to settle the dispute and to restore the right of the eldest son. Considering that Shāh ʿAlī Riḍā lived about seventy years, it can be inferred that he was born around 1145/1732–3, and that he was still young, around sixteen, when he succeeded to the directing of the *dargāh* upon his father's death.

Shāh ʿAlī Riḍā remained around one year as the head of the *dargāh* instructing disciples. Then he was driven by a powerful divine 'attraction' (*jadhb*) and became a *majdhūb*.[26] At this point, his younger brother Muḥammad ʿAlī put forward a letter, allegedly written by his father, Shams al-Dīn, attesting that Shāh ʿAlī Riḍā had gone mad and was dangerous and that his will was that Muḥammad ʿAlī become his regent (*nāʾib*) until Shāh ʿAlī Riḍā's recovery. Muḥammad ʿAlī arranged to have the letter signed by all the Sufi masters of the city, managing to take over the directing of the *dargāh* as the *sajjāda-nishīn.*[27] Moreover, he confined his brother to a room of the *dargāh* where, according to one version, water and food were given him through a hole. After around twelve years, Aḥmad, the young son of Shāh ʿAlī Riḍā, asked ʿAlī Khān (r. 1175–1218/1761–1803), the second Niẓām of Hyderabad, to set his father free. Shāh ʿAlī Riḍā was thus freed by the order of the Niẓām and also thanks to the intervention of Iḥtishām-i Jang Ẓafar al-Dawla, who later became the governor of Berar province and was buried in the *dargāh* of Shāh Khalīl Allāh at Bidar.[28]

The Indian biographers such as Ghulām Ḥusayn Khān and Malkāpūrī do not specify in which year Shāh ʿAlī Riḍā regained his position. However, considering that he was confined for twelve years one can infer that he must have been around 29 years old when his son asked for the intervention of the Niẓām. Shāh ʿAlī Riḍā then headed the *dargāh* for a long period of about forty years. He started to teach again and had a number of disciples. He remained nonetheless a Sufi of ecstatic temperament, who wore red clothes and loved perfumes, music and dance.[29] From time to time he would go with his mare to the centre of Hyderabad for the Friday prayer at the Mecca mosque. He remained in the courtyard of the mosque, under a banyan tree, where a large crowd of people came to meet him. He then went to the *ʿāshūr-khānah* of Ḥusaynī ʿAlam where he used to spend the night before returning to the *dargāh* the next day.[30] Dhu'l-Faqār ʿAlī Shāh, the *khādim* (attendant) of the *ʿāshūr-khānah* of Ḥusaynī ʿAlam, was his disciple and other followers came to meet him there. On this occasion, the Niẓām used to send 25 trays of food.[31]

At that time, the relationship between the Niʿmat Allāhī masters and the aristocracy of the city had changed considerably from the epoch of Mīr Maḥmūd's arrival and rivalry with the local Chishtī master of the Quṭb Shāh sultan. Despite their being Sunni, the Niẓām continued the Mughal policy of employing Shiʿi scholars at their court and in the administration of the State. Some Shiʿi figures come to occupy prominent positions, such as in the case of Māh Laqā Bāī (d. 1240/1824),[32] an influential courtesan contemporary of Shāh ʿAlī Riḍā and his son, and the powerful Sālār Jang family in the 19th century. The Indian biographers say that Niẓām ʿAlī Khān held Shāh ʿAlī Riḍā in the highest honour and that the Sufi supported the Niẓām with his prayers (*duʿā*) and spiritual influence (*tawajjuh*). This was the case during the battle of Khardla, which took place in Shaʿbān 1209/March 1795, when the Niẓām was defeated by the Marathas. According to one account, ʿAlī Riḍā was at the *dargāh* when he felt that the Niẓām was in danger. Falling into an ecstatic state (*mastī*) which lasted the entire day, he engaged in a spiritual fight at the side of the Niẓām, chopping at the trees of the garden of the *dargāh* with his sword in the process.[33]

However, according to an account given by the historian Qādir Khān Munshī in the *Tārīkh-i Āṣaf-jāhī*, written in 1266/1849–50, a few years after the battle of Khardla, ʿAlī Riḍā was no longer disposed to give his spiritual protection to the Niẓām. After the defeat against the Marathas and the death of his son, the Niẓām fell into depression and spent his days listening to music. The night of 13 Shaʿbān 1211/11 February 1797, he suffered an attack of hemiplegia that physicians were unable to treat. He called for the spiritual intercession of the Sufis, but in vain. The Niẓām sent presents consisting of gold coins and jewellery to Shāh ʿAlī Riḍā through Mama Barun and Mama Champa,[34] asking him to distribute them among the poor. Shāh ʿAlī Riḍā however did not accept the present of the Niẓām.[35] But according to the version of Ghulām Ḥusayn Khān, ʿAlī Riḍā accepts the *nadhr* (donation) brought by Mama Barun and Mama Champa and is willing to pray for the Niẓām.[36] According to the works of the Iranian Niʿmat Allāhīs,[37] ʿAlī Riḍā also enjoyed the favour of the prime minister (*dīwān*) of Hyderabad state, Arisṭū Jāh (d. 1219/1804), who had Iranian ancestry and after the battle of Khardla was sent for two years as hostage to the Marathas.

Among the Indian masters of the order, Shāh ʿAlī Riḍā occupies a very important place for the Iranian Niʿmat Allāhīs. He is considered the first reformer (*mujaddid*) of the order, first and foremost for having sent, in 1190/1776–7, his disciple Maʿṣūm ʿAlī Shāh to Iran with the aim of restoring the order in its primeval homeland.[38] During the Mughal period (932–1274/1526–1857) and the 18th century, Indian Sufism was indeed characterised by multifaceted trends of renewal which concerned the doctrinal thought of the orders but also the genres of Sufi writings, as well as the spread of new orders and sub-orders. ʿAlī Riḍā was a contemporary of such figures as Shāh Walī Allāh (d. 1176/1762) and Mīrzā Maẓhar Jān-i Jānān (d. 1195/1781), two prominent Naqshbandī masters of Delhi. The Sufi scene of

Hyderabad under the Niẓāms was receptive to the renewal trends arriving from Northern India, thanks in particular to the migration of many Sufis, such as Shāh Yūsuf al-Dīn and Shāh Sharīf al-Dīn, two *khulafāʾ* (successors) of Shāh Kalīm Allāh (d. 1142/1729) of Delhi, one of the leading authors of the Chishtī renewal of the Mughal period.

However, in the biographical works on the Deccan Sufis we do not find any trace of some of the fundamental events of the narrative told by the Iranian sources. The sources written in the Deccan do not say a word about the role of Shāh ʿAlī Riḍā as a *mujaddid* and as the architect of the plan aiming to restore the order in Iran. Moreover, the Indian sources completely ignore Maʿṣūm ʿAlī Shāh as well as Shāh Ṭāhir, who according to the *Ṭarāʾiq al-ḥaqāʾiq*, was the first disciple sent to Iran by Shāh ʿAlī Riḍā. Indian sources are also completely silent about the six other disciples to whom Shāh ʿAlī Riḍā gave permission to initiate disciples as well as about Sayyid Muḥammad, the Iranian disciple of Shāh Ṭāhir who was sent to Hyderabad, where he stayed for seven years to complete his spiritual training under the guidance of Shāh ʿAlī Riḍā.[39] Indian sources never mention Maʿṣūm ʿAlī Shāh as a *khalīfa* of Shāh ʿAlī Riḍā, nor do they make any reference to the famous dream in which Shāh ʿAlī Riḍā saw the eighth Twelver imam ʿAlī Riḍā who ordered him to send his disciples to Iran.[40] In addition, the works written in Deccan make no reference to some of the Shiʿi stances and practices mentioned by some of the Iranian sources, such as the fact that ʿAlī Riḍā would curse (*laʿn*) the first three caliphs when he came out of his ecstatic raptures.[41]

On the other hand, the sources written in Iran, such as the *Ḥadāʾiq al-siyāḥa* by Mast ʿAlī Shāh (d. 1253/1837–8), the *Riyāḍ al-ʿārifīn* by Riḍā Qulī Khān Hidāyat (d. 1288/1871) and the *Ṭarāʾiq al-ḥaqāʾiq* by Maʿṣūm ʿAlī Shāh Shīrāzī (d. 1344/1926), make no reference to the dispute between the two brothers and to the period when Shāh ʿAlī Riḍā was segregated by Muḥammad ʿAlī. However, it is certain that Maʿṣūm ʿAlī Shāh was aware of these events as he left Hyderabad in 1190/1776–7 several years after his master had been released. Another divergent narrative of major importance concerns the succession at the head of the order in Hyderabad. The main aim of the Iranian narrative on this matter is apparently to legitimise the status of Maʿṣūm ʿAlī Shāh as the only successor of ʿAlī Riḍā. According to the *Ṭarāʾiq al-ḥaqāʾiq*, after bestowing the *khirqa*[42] on Maʿṣūm ʿAlī Shah, ʿAlī Riḍā ceased teaching the mystical path to other disciples and did not appoint other *shaykhs*.[43]

However, we know that the *ḥaydarābādī* line survived the master of Maʿṣūm ʿAlī Shāh for at least one generation. On the death of Shāh ʿAlī Riḍā in 1801, his son Aḥmad, known as Shāh Mīrān, succeeded him at the head of the *dargāh*. Shāh Mīrān (d. 1230/1814–15) is described as a charismatic master who had many disciples. Like his ancestors he led a life of isolation, he lived at the *dargāh* and rarely went to Hyderabad. Shāh Mīrān continued to maintain good relations with the aristocracy of Hyderabad. The third Niẓām of Hyderabad met with him and sent him a donation (*nadhr*) of 500 rupees.[44] According to Ṭāliʿ, the Shiʿi Mīr ʿĀlam (d. 1809), who succeeded Arisṭū Jāh as prime minister of Hyderabad, also had faith in him.[45] Abu'l-Qāsim Mīr ʿĀlam Bahādur was the son of Sayyid Riḍā Shūshtarī (d. 1780), a Shiʿi scholar from Shūshtar who emigrated to India and settled in Hyderabad, where he received the support of the first Niẓām.[46] In 1804, Mīr ʿĀlam commissioned the reservoir which was named after him, the Mīr ʿĀlam Tank, which is located at the foot of the hill where the Niʿmat Allāhī *dargah* stands. Shāh Mīrān died in 1230/1814–15, therefore heading the local branch of the order for a period of about fifteen years.

After Shāh Mīrān the information about the *sajjāda-nishīn* of the *dargāh* becomes very fragmentary and it seems that the spiritual authority of the *ḥaydarābādī* line declined soon after his death. Ghulām Ḥusayn Khān, who wrote his book about thirty years after ʿAlī Riḍā's death, says that in those days 'one may go to the *dargāh* only to perform the *ziyāra* (pilgrimage) to the graves of the dead masters: although there is a *sajjāda-nishīn*, there's no point in meeting him (*qābil-i mulāqāt nīstand*).'[47] A similar account is given by Maʿṣūm ʿAlī Shāh Shīrāzī, the author of the *Ṭarāʾiq al-ḥaqāʾiq*, who travelled in the Deccan and visited the *dargāh* between November 1880 and January 1881. Shīrāzī deplores the state of ruin (*inhidām*) into which the *dargah* had fallen and openly blames the *sajjāda-nishīn* Aḥmad ʿAlī for ignoring the teachings of the order and using the revenues (*madākhil*) of the *dargāh* to finance his personal expenses.[48] In the early 20th century, Malkāpūrī writes that there was still a *sajjāda* who received a salary (*waẓāʾif*) from Hyderabad state, as well as an annual donation (*sālānah*) for the *ʿurs* and a daily one (*yawmiyya*) to buy incense and flowers.[49] A few decades later, Bilgrāmī reported however that the *dargāh* received no government subsidy but only a contribution for the *ʿurs* of Mīr Maḥmūd which was offered by the Pāygāh Khurshīd Jāhī, an aristocratic family of Hyderabad that traced its origins to Farīd al-Dīn Ganj-i Shakar, a prominent Chishtī master who lived in the 7th/13th century in northern India.[50]

Concluding Remarks

This chapter has looked at the later period of Niʿmat Allāhī history in India, when the spiritual leadership of the order passed from the old line of Bidar to the new branch of Hyderabad. The formation of this branch and its new line of masters, which are no longer direct descendants of Shāh Khalīl Allāh, constitutes the most important element of renewal in the structure and the ramification of the Niʿmat Allāhīs in the early modern Deccan and is most likely the fundamental event which led to the Shiitisation of the order in India. The Iranian sources on the masters of the Niʿmat Allāhī order offer very few descriptions of the *ḥaydarābādī* masters before Shāh ʿAlī Riḍā, whereas the biographical notes included in the Indian sources allow for a better understanding of some of the main events and features of the development of the order in post-Bahmanid Deccan.

The Indian sources in particular make it possible to discern and contextualise the various stages of the mystical career of Shāh ʿAlī Riḍā and to shed new light on certain events which did find their place in the key narrative about the return of the order to Iran written and transmitted by the Iranian scholars. The narrative depicting Shāh ʿAlī Riḍā as a *majdhūb* is ignored by the Iranian writers. This delicate account about the ecstatic Sufi who is segregated by his brother and freed thanks to the efforts of his son and direct heir, is lost during the migration and it is replaced by the narrative of the *mujaddid* which on the other hand is unknown to the biographers of the Deccan. How should this discrepancy be read? Should these accounts be considered as incompatible versions which exclude each other or as complementary and interrelated narratives to be placed in a chronological order where the early stage of the *majdhūb* is followed by the phase of the *mujaddid*? The two spiritual experiences at the core of these narratives seem to be separated by several years. Shāh ʿAlī Riḍā was most likely enraptured by the divine *jadhb* when he was around sixteen or seventeen years old, while the dream in which he saw the imam ʿAlī al-Riḍā instructing him to send his disciples to Iran may have occurred some time before he dispatched Maʿṣūm ʿAlī Shāh, an event that we know took place when Shāh ʿAlī Riḍā was forty-five years old.

The two narratives ignore each other, the two groups of writers are not aware of what the other says. However, the two narratives do not deny or exclude what the other says. Shāh ʿAlī Riḍā's ambitious plan to revive the order in Iran could have been known by his disciples but remained unnoticed to the biographers of the Sufis in the Deccan, considering also that Shāh ʿAlī Riḍā did not leave any writing about his thought. Moreover, this plan proved to be a difficult task while Shāh ʿAlī Riḍā was alive. Maʿṣūm ʿAlī Shāh and the disciples that gathered around him after he arrived in Iran had to face the hostility of the Shiʿi clerics opposed to Sufism and finally Maʿṣūm ʿAlī Shāh was arrested and executed in Kirmanshah after having been accused of 'licentiousness and immorality' (*fisq wa fujūr*).[51]

The discrepancy actually shows the differences between the perspectives from which narratives were written and read. The narrative told by the local chroniclers describes events that certainly became well known in the city and within its religious milieu and which raised different reactions, considering that Muḥammad ʿAlī's appointment as the head of the *dargāh* was approved by the other Sufi masters of Hyderabad while later on this decision was revoked by the Niẓām. On the other hand, the narrative of the *mujaddid*, formulated and transmitted by, and for, the Niʿmat Allāhīs in Iran, provided a powerful account for the foundation of the new Iranian branch. The second narrative involves a selective rewriting of the master's biography and mystical path. Its specific features, the imam's order bestowed in a dream that highlights the association with the Twelver faith and the removal of the unorthodox image of the ecstatic Sufi, can be seen as components of a discourse that aimed to accommodate the identity of the group to the Iranian environment and to shape an image of the master's order that could better defend its authority against the anti-Sufi discourse of the Shiʿi clergy.

Nonetheless, the limits of the descriptions included in the Indian sources do not allow us to clarify better some important points. The Indian *tadhkirāt* do not say anything about the doctrines and the methods that were taught and practised by the Niʿmat Allāhī masters of

Hyderabad. Moreover, there is a lack of more precise information on how the Niʿmat Allāhī *khilāfa* was transmitted outside the family and the right of the elder son. Most likely, Shams al-Dīn did not even transmit the Niʿmat Allāhī *khilāfa* to his younger sons. The account of the dispute between Shāh ʿAlī Riḍā and Muḥammad ʿAlī shows quite clearly that the latter was not a *khalīfa* of his father, and he only managed to become for a while the regent (*nā'ib-i khilāfa*) of his brother.[52] We can therefore pose the question whether one of the elements of the reformist strategy effected by Shāh ʿAlī Riḍā was precisely to transmit the *khilāfa* and the authorisation to initiate other disciples outside the family circle. Iranian sources, which do not mention Shāh ʿAlī Riḍā's son, speak on the contrary of eight Sufis to whom ʿAlī Riḍā gave permission to initiate other disciples. Two of them, Maʿṣūm ʿAlī Shāh and Shāh Ṭāhir, were certainly sent to Iran. What happened to the other six, such as Asad ʿAlī Shāh Dihlawī, Aḥmad ʿAlī Shāh Hindūstānī, Ḥaydar ʿAlī Shāh Hindī and Maḥmūd ʿAlī Shāh Dakanī,[53] who apparently did not migrate to Iran? Did they remain in India? Unfortunately, the biographies of the Sufis of Deccan do not seem to offer any answer.

Mīr Maḥmūd and his successors were Shiʿi as were many of their disciples in Hyderabad, and the Niʿmat Allāhiyya remained the only Shiʿi Sufi order of the city. Paradoxically, the first Niʿmat Allāhī master of Hyderabad did not receive support from the Quṭb Shāh sultans, in spite of the connection of its founder with the Iranian Niʿmat Allāhīs. But later on his heirs enjoyed the favour of several local noblemen when the city was ruled by the Sunni dynasty of the Niẓāms. It is at this moment, when the Niʿmat Allāhī masters gained major influence among the local elite, that the order returned to Iran thanks precisely to the efforts of a Shiʿi from a local aristocratic family, Maʿṣūm ʿAlī Shāh Dakanī. The transmission of spiritual authority in the Hyderabad branch lasted only one generation after Shāh ʿAlī Riḍā. After the death of Shāh Mīrān in the early 19th century, the centre of Hyderabad became a *dargāh* without masters, directed by a hereditary line of *sajjāda-nishīn* without any spiritual authority and where the only important rituals became those, such as the *ʿurs*, related to the cult of the dead saints.

NOTES

1 On the Niʿmat Allāhīs in Safawid Iran, see Terry Graham, 'The Niʿmatu'llāhī Order Under Safavid Suppression and in Indian Exile', in Leonard Lewisohn and David

Morgan, ed., *The Heritage of Sufism*, vol. 3: *Late Classical Persianate Sufism (1501–1750)* (Oxford, 1999), pp. 165–200; Sholeh A. Quinn, 'Rewriting Niʿmatu'llāhī History in Safavid Chronicles', in ibid., pp. 201–222.

2 Muhammad Suleman Siddiqi, *The Bahmani Sufi* (Delhi, 1989), pp. 78–85, 155–162; Haroon Khan Sherwani, *The Bahmanis of the Deccan* (Delhi, 1985), pp. 133–134; Jean Aubin, 'De Kûhbanân à Bidar: La famille niʿmatullahī', *Studia Iranica*, 20 (1991), pp. 233–261, esp. pp. 239–246, 252–254; Athar Abbas Rizvi, *A History of Sufism in India* (Delhi, 1992), pp. 55–57; Hamid Algar, 'Niʿmat-allāhiyya', *EI2*, VIII, 1995, pp. 44–48, at p. 46; Graham, 'The Niʿmatu'llāhī Order', pp. 173–178.

3 The ʿĀdil Shāh adopted Shiʿism as the state religion for a period.

4 A few lines of poetry ascribed to ʿAlī Riḍā are mentioned by R.Q. Hidāyat, in *Riyāḍ al-ʿārifīn* (Tehran, 1316 Sh./1937–8), p. 451, and Maʿṣūm ʿAlī Shāh Shīrāzī, *Ṭarāʾiq al-ḥaqāʾiq* (3 vols., Tehran, n.d.), vol. 3, p. 168.

5 See also Fabrizio Speziale, 'À propos du renouveau *niʿmatullāhī*. Le centre de Hyderabad au cours de la première modernité', *Studia Iranica*, 42 (2013), pp. 95–97.

6 Ghulām ʿA. Qādirī, *Mishkāt al-nubuwwat* (Hyderabad, 1982–1985).

7 Ghulām Ḥusayn Khān, *Tārīkh-i gulzār-i āṣafiyya* (Bombay, 1308/1891).

8 ʿAbd al-Jabbār Malkāpūrī, *Maḥbūb-i dhī al-minan: Tadhkira-yi awliyāʾ-i Dakan* (2 vols., Hyderabad, 1332/1913–14).

9 Malkāpūrī, *Maḥbūb-i dhī al-minan*, vol. 2, p. 767; Khān, *Tārīkh-i gulzār-i āṣafiyya*, p. 341.

10 Malkāpūrī, *Maḥbūb-i dhī al-minan*, vol. 2, pp. 767–768.

11 *Tārīkh-i Muḥammad Quṭb Shāhī*, MS 174. Paris, Bibliothèque Nationale, supplément persan.

12 See F. Speziale, 'À propos du renouveau *niʿmatullāhī*', pp. 104–106.

13 Marc Gaborieau, 'Les ordres mystiques dans le sous-continent indien, un point de vue ethnologique', in Alexandre Popovic and Gilles Veinstein, ed., *Les ordres mystiques dans l'Islam. Cheminement et situation actuelle* (Paris, 1986), pp. 106–107.

14 Khān, *Tārīkh-i gulzār-i Āṣafiyya*, p. 344; ʿAlī Sayyid Murād Ṭāliʿ, *Tadhkira-yi awliyāʾ-i Ḥaydarābād* (4 vols., Hyderabad, 1984) vol. 1, p. 136. On the use of *ṣandal* in Muslim rituals in India, see Jaʿfar Sharīf and Gerhard Andreas Herklots, *Islam in India or the Qānūn-i Īslām* (Delhi, 1999), pp. 150, 188, 193, 210, 216, 309; Fabrizio Speziale, *Soufisme, religion et médecine en Islam indien* (Paris, 2010), pp. 156–158.

15 Maʿṣūm ʿAlī Shāh Shīrāzī, *Ṭarāʾiq al-ḥaqāʾiq*, vol. 3, p. 170.

16 One of the other major events of this kind in the history of Indian Sufism takes place shortly after the migration of the Niʿmat Allāhī of Hyderabad to Iran. Around ten years after the death of ʿAlī Riḍā in Hyderabad, the Kurdish Sufi Mawlānā Khālid (d. 1242/1827) was initiated in Delhi by Shāh Ghulām ʿAlī (d. 1240/1824) and then spread the Naqshbandī-Mujaddidī order in the Ottoman world. See Arthur Buehler, 'Mawlânâ Khâlid and Shâh Ghulâm ʿAlî in India', in B. Abu-Manneh, ed., *The Naqshbandiyya-Khâlidiyya Sufi Order, JHS*, 5 (2007), pp. 199–213; Cyrille Chodkiewicz, 'Mawlânâ Khâlid', in *ʿAyn al-ḥayât. Quaderno di Studi della Tarîqa Naqshbandiyya*, 3 (1997), pp. 75–96, esp. at pp. 81–83.

17 Another case is that of the Nūrbakhshiyya, a messianic movement with Sufi and Shiʿi tendencies that was introduced in Kashmir by Shams al-Dīn ʿIrāqī (d. 932/1526) towards the end of the 15th century. On the introduction and development of the Nūrbakhshiyya in Kashmir and in the regions of Baltistan and Ladakh, see the work of Shahzad Bashir, *Messianic Hopes and Mystical Visions: The Nūrbakhshīya between Medieval and Modern Islam* (Columbia, SC, 2003), pp. 198–282.

18 Aubin, 'De Kûhbanân à Bidar', pp. 241–242.

19 Qādirī, *Mishkāt al-nubuwwat*, vol. 6, p. 246; Malkāpūrī, *Maḥbūb-i dhī al-minan*, vol. 2, p. 767; Ṭāliʿ, *Tadhkira-yi awliyāʾ-i Ḥaydarābād*, vol. 1, p. 125.

20 Qādirī, *Mishkāt al-nubuwwat*, vol. 7, p. 86.

21 Ibid.

22 The first part of the Quṭb Shāh epoch on the contrary had been marked by a religious policy that did not welcome the establishment of Sunni Sufi masters and orders. Very few Sufis settled near the walls of Golconda, the first capital of the Quṭb Shāh sultanate, see Speziale, *Soufisme, religion et médecine en Islam indien*, pp. 87–88.

23 Graham, 'The Niʿmatu'llāhī Order', p. 174, n.23.

24 Khān, *Tārīkh-i gulzār-i Āṣafiyya*, p. 341; Malkāpūrī, *Maḥbūb-i dhī al-minan*, vol. 2, p. 767.

25 According to Malkāpūrī he died on 8 Ramaḍān 1215/23 January 1801, when he was around 70 years old; according to Ghulām Ḥusayn Khān he died on 20 Ramaḍān 1215/4 February 1801 (Malkāpūrī, *Maḥbūb-i dhī al-minan*, vol. 1, p. 560; Khān, *Tārīkh-i gulzār-i Āṣafiyya*, p. 345). According to the Iranian sources he would have lived more than 100 years, see Mast ʿAlī Shāh, *Ḥadā'iq al-siyāḥa* (n.p., n.d.), p. 348; Hidāyat, *Riyāḍ al-ʿārifīn*, p. 451; Maʿṣūm ʿAlī Shāh Shīrāzī, *Ṭarā'iq al-ḥaqā'iq*, vol. 3, p. 167.

26 The *majdhūb* (lit. 'attracted') is the ecstatic Sufi who experiences the state of *jadhb*.

27 Literally, the one who sits on the prayer carpet (*sajjāda*), i.e. the head of a *dargāh*.

28 Khān, *Tārīkh-i gulzār-i āṣafiyya*, p. 343; Malkāpūrī, *Maḥbūb-i dhī al-minan*, vol. 1, pp. 558–559. On Iḥtishām-i Jang Ẓafar al-Dawla see Muḥammad Qādir Khān Munshī, *Tārīkh-i Āṣaf-jāhī* (Hyderabad, 1994), p. 71 and also Muḥammad Qādir Khān Munshī, *Sayr al-Hind* (Hyderabad, 1994), pp. 143–147.

29 Malkāpūrī, *Maḥbūb-i dhī al-minan*, vol. 1, p. 560.

30 This *ʿāshūr-khānah* was established during the Quṭb Shāh epoch. Here was kept a sword said to be owned by the sixth imam Jaʿfar al-Ṣādiq (d. 148/765) which was brought from Arabia to Golconda the reign of Sultan Muḥammad Qulī (r. 988–1020/1580–1612), the founder of Hyderabad, see Sadiq Naqvi, *Muslim Religious Institutions and their role under the Qutb Shahs* (Hyderabad, 1993), pp. 182–183.

31 Khān, *Tārīkh-i gulzār-i āṣafiyya*, p. 344; Ṭāliʿ, *Tadhkira-yi awliyā'-i Ḥaydarābād*, vol. 3, p. 31.

32 She was an expert in music and dance and was one of the first woman poets to write a full *dīwān* of *ghazals* in Urdu, see Scott Kugle, 'Courting ʿAlī: Urdu Poetry, Shiʿi Piety and Courtesan Power in Hyderabad', in Denis Hermann and Fabrizio Speziale, ed., *Muslim Cultures in the Indo-Iranian World during the Early-Modern and Modern Periods* (Berlin, 2010), pp. 125–166.

33 Malkāpūrī, *Maḥbūb-i dhī al-minan*, vol. 1, pp. 559–560; see also Khān, *Tārīkh-i gulzār-i āṣafiyya*, p. 345.

34 Two nurses and advisers of the second Niẓām who led the female regiment at the Battle of Khardla, see William Dalrymple, *White Mughals* (London, 2002), p. xxiii.

35 Munshī, *Tārīkh-i Āṣaf-jāhī*, pp. 68–69. According to the historian of medicine Rahbar Fārūqī, Niẓām ʿAlī Khān suffered from the attack of hemiplegia (*falij*) in Shaʿbān 1212/19 January 1798/16 February 1798 [Muʿīn al-Dīn Rahbar Fārūqī, *Islāmī ṭibb Shahānah sar-parastiyūn min* (Hyderabad, 1420/1999), p. 158]. On alms used to seek the intercession of Sufi saints in case of illness, see Speziale, *Soufisme, religion et médecine en Islam indien*, pp. 112–113.

36 Khān, *Tārīkh-i gulzār-i Āṣafiyya*, p. 344.

37 Maʿṣūm ʿAlī Shāh Shīrāzī, *Ṭarā'iq al-ḥaqā'iq*, vol. 3, p. 167; Mast ʿAlī Shāh, *Ḥadā'iq al-siyāḥa*, p. 349.

38 Maʿṣūm ʿAlī Shāh Shīrāzī, *Ṭarā'iq al-ḥaqā'iq*, vol. 3, pp. 167, 171.

39 See Maʿṣūm ʿAlī Shāh Shīrāzī, *Ṭarā'iq al-ḥaqā'iq*, vol. 2, p. 332, vol. 3, pp. 167–168; Mast ʿAlī Shāh, *Ḥadā'iq al-siyāḥa*, p. 348; see also William Ronald Royce, 'Mīr Maʿṣūm ʿAlī Shāh and the Niʿmat Allāhī Revival 1776–77 to 1796–97: A Study of Sufism and its Opponents in Late Eighteenth-Century Iran' (PhD dissertation, Princeton University, 1979), pp. 83–85.

40 See Nasrollah Pourjavady and Peter Lamborn Wilson, *Kings of Love: The History and Poetry of the Niʿmatullāhī Sufi Order of Iran* (Tehran, 1978), pp. 93–94; Richard Gramlich,

Die schiitischen Derwischorden Persiens. 1: Die Affiliationen (Wiesbaden, 1965), p. 30f.; Royce, 'Mīr Maʿṣūm ʿAlī Shāh', p. 90; H. Algar, 'Dakanī, Sayyed Mīr ʿAbd al-Ḥamīd Maʿṣūm ʿAlīšāh', *EIR*, 1993.

41 Riḍā Qulī Hidāyat, *Riyāḍ al-ʿārifīn* (Tehran, 1316 Sh./1937–8), p. 451; Mast ʿAlī Shāh, *Ḥadāʾiq al-siyāḥa*, p. 348.

42 The *khirqa* is the cloak given by a Sufi master to his *khalīfa* and symbolises the transmission of the spiritual authority.

43 Maʿṣūm ʿAlī Shāh Shīrāzī, *Ṭarāʾiq al-ḥaqāʾiq*, vol. 3, p. 170; see also Algar 'Dakanī'. Pourjavady and Wilson write in their study that after the death of ʿAlī Riḍā—who died after his disciple Maʿṣūm ʿAlī Shāh—the directing of the order including the Indian branch passed into the hands of the Iranian master Ḥusayn ʿAlī Shāh Iṣfahānī (d. 1234/1818) (*Kings of Love*, pp. 143–144). Nurbakhsh also writes that after ʿAlī Riḍā's death the '*qoṭb* of the order in India was Ḥosayn-ʿAlīšāh' (Javad Nurbakhsh, 'Dakanī, Reżā ʿAlīšāh', *EIR*, 1993).

44 Khān, *Tārīkh-i gulzār-i Āṣafiyya*, pp. 345–346; Ṭāliʿ, *Tadhkira-yi awliyāʾ-i Ḥaydarābād*, vol. 3, pp. 48–49.

45 Ṭāliʿ, *Tadhkira-yi awliyāʾ-i Ḥaydarābād*, III, p. 48.

46 Mīr ʿĀlam was the cousin of Mīr ʿAbd al-Laṭīf Khān Shūshtarī (d. 1220/1806) who however in his travelogue *Tuḥfat al-ʿālam* makes no reference to the Niʿmat Allāhī masters of Hyderabad. On Mīr ʿĀlam, see Khān, *Tārīkh-i gulzār-i Āṣafiyya*, pp. 305–315; Munshī, *Tārīkh-i Āṣaf-jāhī*, pp. 82–90.

47 Khān, *Tārīkh-i gulzār-i Āṣafiyya*, p. 346.

48 Aḥmad ʿAlī lived three generations after ʿAlī Riḍā, Maʿṣūm ʿAlī Shāh Shīrāzī, *Ṭarāʾiq al-ḥaqāʾiq*, vol. 3, p. 169.

49 Malkāpūrī, *Maḥbūb-i dhī al-minan*, vol. 1, p. 417, vol. 2, p. 770.

50 S.A.A. Bilgrāmī, *Maʾāthir-i Dakan* (Hyderabad, 1924), p. 93. Ṭāliʿ reports that the last *sajjāda-nishīn* of his time was Shāh ʿAlī Riḍā Ḥusaynī II who died around the early 1940s. He had no sons and therefore his place was taken by his daughter Fayḍ al-Nisāʾ Begum. Ṭāliʿ also gives a short description of the ʿ*urs* of Mīr Maḥmūd which included the procession of the *ṣandal*, Ṭāliʿ, *Tadhkira-yi awliyāʾ-i Ḥaydarābād*, vol. 1, p. 136, vol. 3, p. 49. For a group of Niʿmat Allāhī who gathered in Hyderabad in the early 1980s, see David Pinault, *The Shiites: Ritual and Popular Piety in a Muslim Community* (New York, 1993), p. 61.

51 See Algar, 'Dakanī'.

52 Khān, *Tārīkh-i gulzār-i āṣafiyya*, p. 343.

53 Maʿṣūm ʿAlī Shāh Shīrāzī, *Ṭarāʾiq al-ḥaqāʾiq*, vol. 2, p. 332.

5

The Institutionalisation of Niʿmat Allāhī Sufism during the Pahlavi Era: A Study of the Establishment of the Ḥusayniyya Amīr Sulaymānī as a *waqf* in Tehran[1]

Denis Hermann and *Omid Rezai*

The popularity of the Niʿmat Allāhiyya during the early days of 19th-century Iran lasted throughout the rule of the Pahlavi dynasty despite the profound changes that took place in the country. The sources enabling us to study Iranian Sufism of the Qajar and Pahlavi periods are many, and in particular feature those concerned with the Niʿmat Allāhī order. The *waqf-nāmah*s (the legal documents allowing the establishment of a *waqf*, an inalienable endowment in Islamic law), as we have already indicated elsewhere, are key primary sources, and are of great value in the study of the religious history of Iran during the Qajar and Pahlavi eras.[2]

The purpose of this chapter is to contribute to the writing of social and doctrinal history of the Sulṭān ʿAlī Shāhī branch of the Niʿmat Allāhī during the Pahlavi era, by studying a *waqf-nāmah* which in 1947 enabled the construction of the Ḥusayniyya Amīr Sulaymānī,[3] a major religious centre in Tehran. This document highlights little-known facets of the beliefs, the rituals and, furthermore, the hierarchical structure of the Niʿmat Allāhī Sulṭān ʿAlī Shāhī. Finally, and more generally, it exemplifies the strategic use made of the *waqf* by minority Shiʿi currents during the Pahlavi era to secure their financing and hence their continued existence. In this respect, the establishment of this *waqf*, and the key role it was to play, demonstrate the profound determination of the Niʿmat Allāhī, and indeed of all the other religious currents of modern Iran, to establish stable institutions essential to the organisation, development and visibility of their respective communities.

Despite the legal restrictions Riḍā Shāh Pahlavī (d. 1944) imposed during his reign, which aimed at limiting both the influence of, and recourse to, the *waqf*, their number continually grew,[4] largely as a consequence of the rapid increase in population occurring at the same time. These new laws also forced the *wāqif* (the founder of the *waqf*) to be more precise when writing the *waqf-nāmah* than during the previous Qajar era, in order to prevent potential litigious situations which could open the way to government confiscation. Tehran, having always attracted the highest number of migrant populations from the provinces, certainly saw the highest expansion of *waqf* establishments. Many Sufi brotherhoods made use of the latter during the Pahlavi era in order to create *ḥusayniyyas*[5] or lodges (*khānaqāhs*) throughout the whole country.[6] These centres played a crucial role in the popularity of Sufism under the Pahlavis. Particularly noteworthy is the transformation, in 1326 Sh./1947–8, of an extensive property in Tehran into the second largest religious centre of the Niʿmat Allāhī Sulṭān ʿAlī Shāhī after Baydukht.

Introduction to the Social and Doctrinal History of the Niʿmat Allāhī Sulṭān ʿAlī Shāhī

The emigration during the 1770s from the Indian Deccan to Iraq and Iran of several Niʿmat Allāhī Sufi masters, such as Maʿṣūm ʿAlī Shāh (d. 1209/1795) and Shāh Ṭāhir Dakanī, generated widespread popularity of the order amongst both the aristocracy and the working classes.[7] The repression they were subjected to, by both the government and part of the clergy, during the reign of Fatḥ ʿAlī Shāh (r. 1211–1250/1797–1834), does not seem to have noticeably checked this momentum.[8] The Niʿmat Allāhī possessed indubitably the highest number of disciples of all the brotherhoods during the Qajar era. We know from hagiographical sources that the successor of Maʿṣūm ʿAlī Shāh, Nūr ʿAlī Shāh Iṣfahānī (d. 1211/1797), had tens of thousands of disciples.[9] The probable affiliation to the Niʿmat Allāhī order of Muḥammad Shāh (r. 1250–1264/1834–1848) offered them protection and they became less liable to attacks from the clergy, even though the assassination of their masters continued throughout the Qajar era. The prime minister of Muḥammad Shāh, Ḥājj Mīrzā Āqāsī (d. 1265/1849) was himself a Niʿmat Allāhī *pīr* (master) and it seems likely the Shāh himself had been one of his direct disciples.[10] Henceforth, the brotherhood greatly benefitted from Qajar patronage, even though its extent varied from one region to the next. Even though Nāṣir al-Dīn Shāh (r. 1264–1313/1848–1896) did not personally share his father's interest in Sufism, he never questioned his religious policy, and it was certainly during his reign that the success of the Iranian Shiʿi Sufi brotherhoods reached its peak. The number of disciples was considerable and their literary output major. Certain Iranian witnesses attest to the success of Sufism at the end of the 19th century: 'One fifth of the Qajar Persian population were Darwīsh or disciples of a Darwīsh group.'[11] Although they do not give precise figures western travellers were also impressed by the popularity of Sufi orders in Qajar society.[12]

The right to lead the Niʿmat Allāhī was claimed by a multitude of masters during the 19th century, which led to its division into three principal branches following the death of Raḥmat ʿAlī Shāh in 1278/1861.[13] Munawwar ʿAlī Shāh (d. 1301/1884) founded the Munawwar ʿAlī Shāhī branch, also called Mūnis ʿAlī Shāhī and Dhuʾr-Riyāsatayn.[14] Ṣafī ʿAlī Shāh (d. 1316/1899) gave his name to the Ṣafī ʿAlī Shāhī, which subdivided again into several groups after his death.[15] Finally, Saʿādat ʿAlī Shāh (d. 1293/1876) founded the branch which we will examine below.[16] It is known under four main names: Sulṭān ʿAlī Shāhī, Gunābādī, Mūllā Sulṭānī and Ṭāwūsiyya. Even though the second is most commonly used today, we will refer to it as the Niʿmat Allāhī Sulṭān ʿAlī Shāhī, as this is the name under which they most often signed the treatises written during the Pahlavi era, as in the *waqf-nāmah* studied here. For a short while they were also known as the Ṭāwūsiyya, since their founder bore the honorary title (*laqab*) Ṭawūs al-ʿUrafā (The Peacock of the Mystics). The successor of Saʿādat ʿAlī Shāh, Sulṭān ʿAlī Shāh (d. 1327/1909), first studied in Bīland, then in Mashhad and subsequently in Sabziwar, where he was able to study the teachings of the philosopher Ḥājj Mullā Hādī Sabzawārī (d. 1290/1873).[17] He continued his instruction in the *ʿAtabāt* (the holy Shiʿi towns of Iraq) under Shaykh Murtaḍā Anṣārī (d. 1276/1860).[18] Upon his return from Iraq, Sulṭān ʿAlī Shāh settled in Tehran, where he taught for a time, before returning to Sabziwar.[19] There he met Saʿādat ʿAlī Shāh and entered the service of the master of the Niʿmat Allāhī, eventually succeeding him as *quṭb* (pole).[20] He remained in Baydukht, a few kilometres east of Gunābād, in southern Khurasan, until his death.[21] For this reason this brotherhood is also known under the name Gunābādī. As well as attracting many disciples through his religious teaching, Sulṭān ʿAlī Shāh also succeeded in transforming the brotherhood into an economically prosperous order within the region, notably thanks to the use of agriculture.[22] Sulṭān ʿAlī Shāh is also famous for having redefined the statute of *quṭb*.[23] He was assassinated in 1327/1909 during the Constitutional Movement of 1906–1911.[24] Despite the good relations he had maintained with Nayyir al-Dawla, one of the governors of Khurasan, it seems that his order did not benefit from the same level of patronage as the Ṣafī ʿAlī Shāhī.[25] The son of Sulṭān ʿAlī Shāh became the next *quṭb*, and his son after him. To this day the succession is strictly hereditary.[26] The son of Sulṭān ʿAlī Shāh, Nūr ʿAlī Shāh Thānī (d. 1337/1918), did not appreciate Sufism in his youth, however. He spent seven years exploring other regions of the Muslim world before becoming reconciled to his father at the end of the 19th century, and succeeding him only a few years later.[27] He was poisoned at Kashan,[28] but not before making Baydukht the foremost centre of the Niʿmat Allāhī Sulṭān ʿAlī Shāhī in Iran, by erecting a mausoleum for his father, and thus establishing a funerary mosque (*mashhad*)[29] which was to become the destination of many pilgrims. Nūr ʿAlī Shāh Thānī greatly contributed to the increase in popularity of the order in Khurasan.[30] The brotherhood thereafter continued to prosper economically under the direction of the grandson of Sulṭān ʿAlī Shāh, Ṣāliḥ ʿAlī Shāh (d. 1386/1966). Like his father, Ṣāliḥ ʿAlī Shāh travelled extensively before assuming the role of *quṭb* in 1918. His religious writings are nevertheless modest in scope. He is mostly known for his *Pand-i Ṣāliḥ* (Ṣāliḥ's Advice) which is a treatise on Islamic moral values.[31] He is also buried in the mausoleum at Baydukht.

The Principal Characteristics of the Niʿmat Allāhī Sulṭān ʿAlī Shāhī

Until the mid-Pahlavi era, the Sulṭān ʿAlī Shāhī conserved a provincial, rather than national, character, unlike other branches of the Niʿmat Allāhī. Its population was concentrated mainly in Khurasan, and specifically in the towns of Baydukht and Gunabad.[32] The tomb of Sulṭān ʿAlī Shāh became the heart of a funerary mosque, around which esplanades, two *ḥusayniyyas* and a library were built.[33] The site has been regularly expanded and reorganised, notably following the violent earthquake of 1388/1968–9.[34] A caravansary, additional land and a number of *qanāt* were also designated as *waqf*, in order to finance this religious centre.[35] The initial, and most important, *waqf* was established in Dhū'l-Qa'da 1331/October 1913 by Nūr 'Alī Shāh Thānī.[36] Its administration (*tawliyat*) was entrusted to the *quṭb* of the order. The master lived in Baydukht until 1979, and until then the place acted as a religious school welcoming many students in the hundred and ten cells (*ḥujra*) provided for this purpose.[37] Solidly implanted in Khurasan, the Ni'mat Allāhī Sulṭān 'Alī Shāhī also financed building projects elsewhere in the region, notably in Gunabad.[38]

The Ni'mat Allāhī Sulṭān 'Alī Shāhī were not very politically minded and had little appetite for the political and religious reforms more willingly undertaken by the other branches of the order, and by the Ṣafī 'Alī Shāhī in particular. Eminent members of the latter branch actively participated in the constitutional movement, whereas the Sulṭān 'Alī Shāhī were accused of being conservative, and partisans of autocracy.[39]

Finally, and this is particularly relevant to the present article, most of the masters of the Ni'mat Allāhī Sulṭān 'Alī Shāhī were also Muslim lawyers (*fuqahā'*) who recognised the use of *ijtihād*. In fact, they studied law (*fiqh*) under the most respected *marja'-i taqlīd*s of the time. Sulṭān 'Alī Shāh studied under Shaykh Murtaḍā Anṣārī and Mīrzā Muḥammad Ḥasan Shīrāzī (d. 1312/1895). As for Ṣāliḥ 'Alī Shāh, he studied in the religious school at Isfahan.[40] It is therefore natural that the Ni'mat Allāhī Sulṭān 'Alī Shāhī enjoyed good relationships with certain parts of the *uṣūlī* clergy, i.e. those who were not openly hostile to Sufism. Ṣāliḥ 'Alī Shāh regularly visited the *marja'-i taqlīds*,[41] for example. The Ayat Allāh 'Abd Allāh Ḥā'irī Māzandarānī (d. 1356/1938) happened to be one of his *shaykh*s,[42] and this was no isolated case.[43] This privileged relationship lasted throughout the reign of Muḥammad Riḍā Shāh (d. 1980), and continued even under the revolutionary regime. Ḥājj Sulṭān Ḥusayn Tābandā (d. 1992), the successor of Ṣāliḥ 'Alī Shāh, widely criticised the Pahlavis, and spoke in support of Ayat Allāh Khomeini (d. 1989) in the early 1980s.[44] He received his most prestigious *ijāza-yi ijtihād* (the authorisation to exercise *ijtihād*) from Ayat Allāh Muḥammad Ḥusayn Āl-i Kāshif al-Ghiṭā (d. 1373/1954).[45] Thus, the Niʿmat Allāhī Ṣafī ʿAlī Shāhī were more regularly the victims of attacks emanating from a section of the clergy during the late 19th century and the 20th century. They were often accused of having links with freemasonry and Baha'ism.[46] The Munawwar ʿAlī Shāhī for their part have been mainly accused of being partisan to secularism.

Study of the Amīr Sulaymānī *waqf* in Tehran

The *waqf* was certainly the most effective means for religious groups in Iran to fend off potential attacks from the political establishment as it provided long-lasting protection for their activities. The *waqf* here studied was established in 1326 Sh./1947. This date marked the end of a seven-year period of widespread religious revival. Following the exile of Riḍā Shāh to Mauritius in 1941 and the real exercise of power of Muḥammad ʿAlī Furūghī (d. 1321 Sh./1942), the different religious currents felt less inhibited and were thus more active.

During the months of Mihr 1326/September-October 1947, Amīr Muṣṭafā Amīr Sulaymānī, a reputed member of the Niʿmat Allāhī Sulṭān ʿAlī Shāhī, established as *waqf* an estate which included two houses with their adjoining courtyards, and partial use of two *qanāt*s. Amīr Sulaymānī bore the prestigious title of 'Mushīr al-Salṭana Sābiq.'[47] His grandfather, Mūsā Khān, belonged to the Quwānlū clan of the Qajar family, and was the maternal uncle (*dā'ī*) of the future Nāṣir al-Dīn Shāh. His father, ʿAlī Riḍā Khān ʿAḍud al-Mulk, had served Nāṣir al-Dīn Shāh since childhood as *ghulām-bachah*.[48] In 1271/1854–5, ʿAlī Riḍā Khān ʿAḍud al-Mulk became head of this group of children who served at the court (*ghulām-bachah bāshī*) before becoming a personal servant of the Shāh (*pīshkhidmat-i Shāh*). At the end of his political career, in 1327/1909–10, he was *niyābat-i salṭanat* (royal guardian) of Aḥmad Shāh (d. 1348/1930) – the latter was then eleven or twelve years old.[49] The *laqab* bestowed upon ʿAlī Riḍā Khān, "Aḍud al-Mulk', was rare and prestigious.[50] Amīr Sulaymānī rallied the Niʿmat Allāhī Sulṭān ʿAlī Shāhī brotherhood through the influence of one of his *shaykh*s, Shaykh Ismāʿīl Dizfūlī (d. 1320/1941), who was responsible for the royal library of the Qajar court. His father, ʿAlī Riḍā Khān ʿAḍud al-Mulk, made the same choice a few years later.[51]

The estate dedicated as *waqf* was in the popular district of Sangilaj, north-east of the bazaar. The first *qanāt* crossed its whole area and was called ʿAlī Ḥamāmī. The second, Gul-Afshān, was situated outside the property. Amīr Sulaymānī transformed the property into the most important religious centre for the Niʿmat Allāhī Sulṭān ʿAlī Shāhī community after Baydukht. The property had survived the destruction of the district of Sangilaj, which had been completed by 1309 Sh./1930–1.[52] Amīr Sulaymānī then combined several estates in the south of Tehran and around Rayy to establish another *waqf* in 1340 Sh./1961–2, and founded there a theological school in Mashhad, the Amīr Sulaymānī Khān Qājār Madrasa, with the grandson of Ākhūnd Muḥammad Kāẓim Khurāsānī (d. 1330/1912) at its head.[53] He also played a part in financing the embellishment of the Baydukht mausoleum.[54]

Before this *waqf* was created, ʿAlī Riḍā Khān ʿAḍud al-Mulk was already organising *ʿāshūrā* ceremonies at the residence. Amīr Sulaymānī thus rationalised and perpetuated this activity thanks to the *waqf* system. The house was built in 1280/1863–4 and was also a *ḥusayniyya* from 1283/1866–7 onwards.[55] Amīr Sulaymānī was the self-designated *mutawallī* (administrator) there, until his death. The administration was then to be handed over to the *quṭb* of the brotherhood. But as the law of December 1934 required, no *nāẓir* (administrator) would thereafter be designated since the ministry of the *waqf* automatically exercises this responsibility. The primary purpose of this *waqf* was to officially organise the mourning ceremonies (*ʿazādārī*) for Imām Ḥusayn (d. 61/680) during the months of Muḥarram and Ṣafar. However, the programme of religious commemorations is far more detailed and varied, and contains over one hundred and twenty days of congregation a year at the property. The *waqf-nāmah-yi rasmī* (official) was clearly drafted.[56] It contains a variety of information pertinent to the organisation, rituals and hierarchy of the Niʿmat Allāhī Sulṭān ʿAlī Shāhī.

Translated excerpts of this document:[57]

> [Eulogical formulas]
>
> (. . .) Amīr Muṣṭafā Amīr Sulaymānī, celebrated under the name Mushīr al-Salṭana Sābiq, (. . .) son of ʿAlī Riḍā Khān ʿAḍud al-Mulk Nāyib al-Salṭana, who resides in Khayyām Street, situated in the fourth district of Tehran, is grateful to God for

having established a great house (*ḥayāṭ*) with a metal roof as an eternal (*mu'abbad*) *waqf*.[58] Since the time of Nāyib al-Sulṭāna, commemorations have been held each year for His Holiness ʿAbd Allāh al-Ḥusayn [Imām Ḥusayn] – peace be upon him – and for this reason the site has become a famous *ḥusayniyya*.

The *wāqif* still acts as *rawḍa khwān*.[59] To this site, he [the *wāqif*] appends an outer house (*ḥayāṭ-i bīrūnī*) and an inner house (*ḥayāṭ-i andarūnī*).[60] They are adjacent and are located to the west of the *ḥusayniyya*. They are part of the fourth district [of Tehran], called Sangilaj, and are situated on Khayyām Street.

(. . .). This place is to become the residence of the *quṭb* of the Niʿmat Allāhī Sulṭān ʿAlī Shāhī brotherhood each time he visits Tehran and if he so wishes. However, when he is not present in Tehran, one of his authorised *shaykh* (*mashāyikh-i ma'dhūnīn*) will be allowed to reside there. If none of the authorised *shaykh* are in Tehran and the house remains empty, one of the disciples of the brotherhood (*fuqarā'-yi silsila*)[61] will be allowed to live there for a maximum of three days. The latter must be a native of the province, must not possess a place of residence in Tehran and must have been granted permission by the *mutawallī* or by his representative.

These different residents will each year participate in the ceremonies given so that my soul may be blessed [in the next world]. They will assemble during the months of Muḥarram and Ṣafar for seven consecutive days at least.[62] They will organise public meetings (sing. *majlis*) during which they will celebrate the names of the 'great men of the religion' (*buzurgān-i dīn*)[63] and will commemorate the mourning (*ʿazādārī*) of his Holiness Abī ʿAbd Allāh al-Ḥusayn [Imām Ḥusayn] – peace be upon him. They will also assemble during the sacred month of Ramaḍān for seven consecutive nights starting with the 17th.[64]

The collective prayer (*iqāma-yi jamāʿat*) must be led by the *mutawallī*.[65] The Qur'an must be read and the memory of the 'great men of the religion' preserved. The ceremony must end with the commemoration of the name *ḥaḍrat-i mawlā* [Imām ʿAlī]. The disciples of the brotherhood will be served food and drink. On the Sunday and the Thursday evenings,[66] assemblies will be organised in the meeting house of the members of the brotherhood, during which the collective prayer will be led by the *quṭb* of the order or by an authorised *shaykh*. This must be followed by the *dhikr-i khudā* and by readings from the Qur'an, from the *akhbār*, and finally from the works of the 'great men of the religion.' Each year on the anniversaries of the deceased Āqā Ḥājj Mūllā Sulṭān Muḥammad Sulṭān ʿAlī Shāh Gunābādī and Āqā Ḥājj Āqā Mūllā ʿAlī Nūr ʿAlī Shāh Thānī, which correspond to nights 26 and 15 of Rabīʿ al-awwal, there will be a reading of the Qurʾan and a ceremony in their memory (*tarḥīm*). One must also recall the virtues of the members of the order, of 'People of the House of Impeccability' (*ahl-i bayt-i ʿiṣmat*) and of the other 'great men of the religion', and of the trials they underwent (*maṣāʾib*).

Food and drink will be served to the members of the brotherhood. Furthermore, it will be necessary to employ a person (*mustakhdim*) approved by the *quṭb* or an authorised *shaykh* (*majāzī*) in Tehran. He must maintain the site, keep it clean, clear the snow, water the plants in the courtyard and carry out such other tasks as may be needful.[67] Since it is essential to finance these four programmes, I have established as a *waqf* the partial letting of two *qanāt*s, that of ʿAlī Ḥamāmī at Rustam Ābād Ikhtāriyya[68] and Gul-Afshān, which is its source, located in Salṭanat Ābād. This letting corresponds to 24 hours of 93.[69]

Once the cost of necessary maintenance to the *qanāt* has been met and the salary of the caretaker attributed,[70] the remaining profits will be divided into five equal parts. The first will be attributed to the ceremonies of the month of Ramaḍān, the second to the months of Muḥarram and Ṣafar, the third to the meetings of Sunday and Thursday evenings, the fourth to the assemblies of 15th and 26th Rabīʿ al-awwal and the last part is to cover the salary of the employee.

If the building is in need of maintenance or renovation, the caretaker will deduct what is necessary from the budget attributed to the month of Ramaḍān. If this is not sufficient, he will thereafter take from the budget of the months of Muḥarram and Ṣafar. If money is still lacking, the caretaker may use the budgets of the third and fourth programmes. However, as long as it is possible, he will refrain from reducing the finance of both the Thursday and Sunday weekly meetings, as well as the commemorations on the 15th and 26th Rabīʿ al-awwal.

The *wāqif* will be solely responsible for the two *qanāt*s until his demise. Their supervision will thereafter be attributed to the venerable scholar Āqā Sulṭān Ḥusayn Tābandā, the son of His Excellency (*ḥaḍrat*) Āqā Ḥājj Shaykh Muḥammad Ḥasan Ṣāliḥ

> ʿAlī Shāh Gunābādī. Upon the demise of Sulṭān Ḥusayn Tābandā, supervision will be transferred to the *quṭb* of the august brotherhood (*quṭb-i silsila-yi ʿilahiyya*) Niʿmat Allāhī Sulṭān ʿAlī Shāhī. All these reunions must be led by the *mutawallī* or by someone specifically designated by him for this occasion. If the *mutawallī* wishes to modify certain aspects of the programme or of this *waqf*, permission from the *quṭb* of the brotherhood is necessary. (. . .). Since this *waqf* is private (*khāṣṣ*),[71] no official (*rasmī*)[72] or non-official (*ghayr-i rasmī*) can become integrated within it.[73]
>
> Mihr 1326/September-October 1947.
> Signature: Amīr Muṣṭafā Amīr Sulaymānī.

Though this residence dedicated as *waqf* has remained famous to this day under the name Ḥusayniyya Amīr Sulaymānī, it is evident that the *wāqif* made it into far more than a 'mere' *ḥusayniyya*. A more adequate term might be 'religious centre', as better reflecting the complexity of the place and its different functions. Moreover, the brotherhood had already owned a *ḥusayniyya* in Tehran since 1315/1897–8, the Ḥusayniyya Ḥāʾirī.[74] The Ḥusayniyya Amīr Sulaymānī, however, is far more extensive. It consists of two structures separated by a courtyard. The first, and very large, building functions essentially as both a mosque and a *ḥusayniyya*, whereas the second is strictly speaking a *khānaqāh*. This place is primarily devoted to the service of the *quṭb* of the brotherhood, who can reside there if so desired, however its doors also remain open to the *shaykhs* and the *fuqarāʾ* of the order. We know, however, that until 1979 the successive masters preferred to live in Baydukht. Ṣāliḥ ʿAlī Shāh and his successor taught the *Bayān al-saʿāda fī maqāmāt al-ʿibādāt* there every afternoon.[75] The *quṭb* at the time would only visit Tehran three or four times a year. The bulk of the religious ceremonies were thus conducted by the *shaykhs* who more often made use of this *khānaqāh*. The regular presence of the *shaykhs* and disciples in this second building have made of this place a teaching centre for the Niʿmat Allāhī Sulṭān ʿAlī Shāhī, frequently visited by those most advanced initiates of the mystical path of the order. However, when the *quṭb* moved to Tehran in 1979, he did not make this *khānaqāh* his place of residence, even though the *waqf* entitled him to do so.[76] The intense religious programme offered by Amīr Sulaymānī goes well beyond the *ʿāshūrā* commemorations.

These elements all show that the site was more a vast religious centre than a simple *ḥusayniyya*. In fact, in this document Amīr Sulaymānī initially describes the use of the *khānaqāh* before giving details of the actual religious programme as such. The Ḥusayniyya Amīr Sulaymānī became the most important centre for Niʿmat Allāhī Sulṭān ʿAlī Shāhī in Iran after Baydukht, at a time when Tehran was undergoing profound changes.[77] However, no *quṭb*s or *shaykh*s have been buried in this place, which never became a funerary mosque. We must note here that the use of this *waqf* did not extend to supporting the publications of the order, or to financing the acquisition of mystical and religious works, particularly those pertaining to Islamic mysticism.[78]

Concerning the Rituals of the Niʿmat Allāhī Sulṭān ʿAlī Shāhī

The esoteric dimension of Sufism and its practices naturally favour a cult of secrecy which extends to its rituals, of which little is disclosed in the works of the masters. The study of this *waqf-nāmah* is particularly useful in this regard since it describes with precision the organisation of the ceremonies that are to be held at the Ḥusayniyya Amīr Sulaymānī. The crucial importance of this programme for the Niʿmat Allāhī Sulṭān ʿAlī Shāhī community, makes it probable that Amīr Sulaymānī consulted the *quṭb* of the order before drafting this *waqf-nāmah*. It is composed of four parts, each falling into one of two separate categories. The first concerns the calendar of those ceremonies which are common to the Shiʿa at large and which are held during the months of Muḥarram, Ṣafar and Ramaḍān. The second category concerns the ceremonies specific to the order. Even though the *wāqif* clearly and repeatedly stated on the document that the entire programme was destined exclusively for members of the order, in actual fact access has been granted to all.[79] The Ḥusayniyya Amīr Sulaymānī has been a famous *ḥusayniyya* since the early 19th century and has always been frequented by inhabitants of the neighbourhood of Sangilaj, particularly for the *majlis* during the months of Muḥarram, Ṣafar and Ramaḍān. Food is shared between all the participants regardless of their affiliation to the order. We know that the religious commemorations most amply financed by the *waqf* in Iran since the Qajar era are precisely those of Muḥarram, since *ʿāshūrā* is the focal point of the Shiʿi calendar.[80] It is natural therefore that the *wāqif* should begin by describing this ceremony in detail.

> The first part of the programme specific to the Niʿmat Allāhī Sulṭān ʿAlī Shāhī is the most important. Of particular note are two extended meetings scheduled weekly by the *wāqif* on Thursday and Sunday evenings. These reunions have become the bedrock of the community in Tehran. The *quṭb* begins with the recitation of a *dhikr* before intoning the canonical prayer with the whole congregation. A second *dhikr*, *dhikr-i khudā*, is then followed by readings from the Qurʾan, the recitation of the 'traditions' (*akhbār*) of the Prophet and the Imams, and finally come readings from the 'great men of the religion' (*buzurgān-i dīn*). The second part of the programme is the commemoration of the martyrdom of Sulṭān ʿAlī Shāh and Nūr ʿAlī Shāh Thānī. This begins with readings from the Qurʾan, and is followed by a reminder of their life and work, the *dhikr-i khayr*. A sermon on the Fourteen Impeccables of Shiʿism and the 'great men of the religion' is then given.

The document confirms that this ritual, central and specific to the Niʿmat Allāhī Sulṭān ʿAlī Shāhī, consists in the repeated practice of the *dhikr* conducted by the *quṭb* or one of his *shaykhs*. It is certainly the form of devotion most fundamental to Sufism, whether Sunni or Shiʿi. One could literally translate this term as 'rememoration.' It consists of an invocation performed by repeating a formula or a sacred word. One can distinguish between two principal types: the first is silent (*khafī*) and concentrates on the heart (*qalbī*). The second is verbal or outspoken (*jalī*) and stems from the language (*lisānī*).[81] We know that the Niʿmat Allāhī Sulṭān ʿAlī Shāhī practise only the silent *dhikr*.[82] Only the *quṭb* or a *shaykh* is allowed to teach the *dhikr* to disciples of the brotherhood, depending on their respective spiritual capacities and their progress along the mystical path of the order.[83] The most important *dhikr* are attributed to the founder of the brotherhood. Amīr Sulaymānī evokes different types: *dhikr*, *dhikr-i khudā*, *dhikr-i khayr*. This document formally confirms that it was customary among Sufi orders to precede the canonical prayer with the *dhikr*.[84] The central role played by this spiritual practice throughout the programme of ceremonies shows once more that the latter were intended for members of the brotherhood, even though individuals outside the order could be present. However, without proper initiation to the ritual, the latter could only be contemplative.

The initiation to the *dhikr* completes the process by which a new *faqīr* (pl. *fuqarā'*) will be formally received into the brotherhood. This is a very rigorous process for the Niʿmat Allāhī Sulṭān ʿAlī Shāhī. The first step is a 'pact of initiation' (*bayʿat*), which to the brotherhood is a mystical initiation on to the esoteric path. The *bayʿat*, conducted by the *quṭb* or a *shaykh*, is where the 'Imam of Time' approves the aspiration of the postulant to join the order. For Shiʿi Sufis, in this *bayʿat* the postulant declares his faith in and his love (*wilāyat*) of the Imam of Time. The Sufis attribute the origin of this practice to Adam and consider that the prophets that have succeeded him have made it compulsory to their initiates.[85] As such, it is a key concept developed by a majority of the masters of the order. In order to carry out this *bayʿat* the disciple must accomplish five major ablutions (*ghusl*).[86] Each of them must be performed with a different intention (*niyya*). The first symbolises repentance (*tawba*), the second consists in expressing the need for spiritual salvation (*najāt*), the third is an allegory of the religious pilgrimages (*ziyārat*), the fourth a reaffirmation of faith in Islam (*islām*) and the fifth corresponds to the *ghusl* recommended (*mustaḥabb*) for Friday mornings.[87] The disciple must thereafter give five presents to the *quṭb* or the *shaykh*, who in turn offers them to the disciples of the order. The first is a walnut, half filled with water, which symbolises the absolution of all sins committed prior to the initiation; the second is a ring; he then offers a coin; a piece of sugar or a cake that represents all the delectable things to which he will be initiated within the brotherhood; finally he brings a white robe. The new disciple is then officially enthroned by the *quṭb* who demands of him obedience and never to reveal the secrets of the order. He then typically will offer a meal to the other disciples known as *dīgjūsh* (boiled lamb).[88] This whole process of enthronement is akin to rebirth, or even a 'reconversion' to Islam. It is only at the end of this series of formal acts and engagements that the first *dhikr* is taught to the new member of the order.[89]

In addition to the *bayʿat*, the new disciple commits to serving the others (*khidmat bih khalq-i Allāh*), in particular during the twelve years following his enthronement.[90] His time and his competencies must be offered voluntarily, and financial donations can in no way be a substitute for this personal investment. For the Niʿmat Allāhī Sulṭān ʿAlī Shāhī, this service is compulsory, as is the *zakāt* or the *khums*. Thus, at the Ḥusayniyya Amīr Sulaymānī there are different departments (*madadkārī*) dedicated to supporting distinct populations: medical help, food aid, legal support, housing support, employment assistance, etc. Thus the *ḥusayniyya* provides the ideal conditions for the new disciple to carry out the services to which he is committed. The other important Sulṭān ʿAlī Shāhī *ḥusayniyya* of Tehran, the Ḥusayniyya Ḥāʾirī, hosts a comprehensive academic support programme for schoolchildren. This programme is all the more significant in that it is located at the East of the Bazaar, one of the most underprivileged neighbourhoods of the capital. The *ḥusayniyya*, which also houses a library, now occupies over three thousand square metres and is regularly extended. The *waqf* is administered by the *quṭb* of the order.

Concerning the Hierarchy of the Niʿmat Allāhī Sulṭān ʿAlī Shāhī

This document is also revealing of the spiritual hierarchy that prevails within the order. To the members of the brotherhood, this hierarchy personifies the spiritual elite of the world at large, given its proximity to the Imām of Time and God. Under the authority of the *quṭb* and of the *shaykh* of the *shaykh*s, are placed the 'simple' *shaykh*s described by Amīr Sulaymānī in the *waqf-nāmah* as 'authorised' *shaykh*s (*shaykh-i maʾdhūnīn* or *shaykh-i majāzī*), that is to say formally designated by the *quṭb*. He is the only person empowered to designate the *shaykh*s, whatever their rank.[91] Of course there exists a hierarchy among the latter. Their status depends first of all on the date on which they were designated. However, depending on their spiritual progression they can thereafter rise quickly among the ranks or conversely stagnate. If their development is swift, the *quṭb* will delegate more responsibilities to them. For example, a given *shaykh* may be appointed more frequently to receive the 'pact of initiation' (*bayʿat*) of new disciples. Following the same model, the rank of the *faqīr* also depends initially on the date on which their *bayʿat* was performed, but thereafter on their respective progress along the mystical path of the order. There exists another intermediate stature between *shaykh* and *faqīr*, which is not mentioned in this *waqf-nāmah*. *Ma'dhūnīn-i namāz* is the rank that authorises a disciple to lead the collective prayer.

By attributing privileged access to the *khānaqāh* first to the *quṭb*, then the *shaykh*s and finally the *fuqarā'*, this document fully reveals the importance of the hierarchy within the Niʿmat Allāhī Sulṭān ʿAlī Shāhī. The disciples from outside the city are not allowed to reside there for more than three days at a time. Moreover they require permission from the *quṭb*, or from one of the *shaykh*s, which implies that disciples are not granted access on an equal basis. Those of higher rank are thus given privileged access to the building. The positioning of the *shaykh*s during the religious ceremonies is also indicative of hierarchy since the *quṭb* faces the *qibla* and his disciples, whereas next to him stand the *shaykh*s of highest rank.

Recent Developments of the Ḥusayniyya Amīr Sulaymānī

As the Ḥusayniyya Amīr Sulaymānī was no longer able to welcome the thousands of the faithful wishing to attend on Thursday and Sunday evenings, the son of Amīr Sulaymānī tried during the 1960s and 1970s to establish as *waqf* the house of his father which adjoins the eastern wall of the *ḥusayniyya*, but the *waqf-nāmah* was never validated.[92] The site remained active for years until recently when new tensions emerged with anti-Sufi factions. Before that the main building was completely destroyed following an act of criminal arson on the night of *ʿāshūrā* in 1400/30 November 1979.[93] It has since been rebuilt. Thus, on the first floor of the *ḥusayniyya*, a library, the administrators of which are also responsible for editing the publications of the brotherhood, was inaugurated under the name *Kitābkhāna-yi Ṣāliḥ* in November 1982.[94] Sulṭān Ḥusayn Tābandā thereafter opened a clinic in 1984. One of its two buildings is attached to the western part of the *ḥusayniyya* and the other is to the north.[95] Since the establishment of the *quṭb* in Tehran in 1979, and his regular presence at the meetings organised there, the Ḥusayniyya Amīr Sulaymānī has gained even more importance in the eyes of the disciples of the brotherhood. New ceremonies were added to the already impressive schedule. Persian poems were recited every Friday morning following the ritual reading of the lineage of the order. The *ḥusayniyya* was also open every day to visitors wishing to use the library. A *ma'dhūnīn-i namāz* then conducted the evening prayer (*maghrib*).

Conclusion

Even though there exist many works by masters of the Niʿmat Allāhī Sulṭān ʿAlī Shāhī on the history of their order, its organisation and its cult, and more so than any other Sufi community in Iran, the information contained in this *waqf-nāmah* remains a valuable tool in the study of its contemporary history. As we have seen, it gives us considerable insight into their rituals as well as a detailed description of the internal hierarchy.

NOTES

1 We wish to thank Shahrām Pāzūkī for the information he kindly gave us regarding the evolution of the inner workings of the Ḥusayniyya Amīr Sulaymanī in post-revolutionary times. Interview of 4 June 2007. We wish also to thank the journal *Iran* for its kind permission to publish here a revised and translated version of an article published in 2008: Denis Hermann and Omid Rezai, 'Constitution en *vaqf* d'une 'mosquée sanctuaire' niʿmatullāhī à Téhéran à l'époque pahlavī', *Iran*, 46 (2008), pp. 87–131.

2 Denis Hermann and Omid Rezai, 'Le rôle du *vaqf* dans la formation de la communauté *shaykhī kermānī* à l'époque qājār (1259–1324/1843–1906)', *Studia Iranica*, 36 (2007), pp. 87–131.

3 The *ḥusayniyya* and the mosque have two distinct legal statuses in Shiʿi law. Declaring this place a *ḥusayniyya* rather than a mosque had many practical advantages. For women, notably, access to a *ḥusayniyya* is possible during menstruation, which is not the case for a mosque.

4 The primary objective of Riḍā Shāh was to bring the *waqf* under direct government control. In February-March 1931, the sovereign decided that income from the *waqf* should be entirely donated to the state, and be used for the creation of schools. However, this project partly failed, due to firm opposition from the clergy. Later, in December 1934, the parliament voted a general law pertaining to the *waqf* (*qānūn-i awqāf*), which profoundly modified its administration, and subjected it entirely to state authority.

5 A congregation hall for Shiʿi commemoration ceremonies, and in particular during the month of Muḥarram.

6 For the history of the *khānaqāh* in Iran, consult M. Kiyānī, *Tārīkh-i khānaqāh dar Īrān* (Tehran, 1369 Sh./1990–1).

7 Maʿṣūm ʿAlī Shāh was sent to Iraq and Iran by the master of the order, Riḍā ʿAlī Shāh Dakanī (d. 1215/1800–1). The Niʿmat Allāhī order had been forced into exile in the Indian Deccan during the second century of the Safawid era. On this subject, see Terry Graham, 'The Niʿmatullahi Order under Safavid Suppression and in Indian Exile', in Leonard Lewisohn ed., *The Heritage of Sufism, Volume 3: Late Classical Persianate Sufism* (1501–1750), (Oxford, 1999), pp. 165–200; Jean Aubin, 'De Kûhbanân à Bidar. La famille ni'matullahī', *Studia Iranica*, 20 (1991), pp. 233–255. For Riḍā ʿAlī Shāh Dakanī,

see Muḥammad Bāqir Sulṭānī Gunābādī, *Rahbarān-i ṭarīqat wa ʿirfān* (Tehran, 1383 Sh./2004–5), pp. 203–205.

8 For the popularity of Sufism in the early 19th century, regardless of repression, see Leonard Lewisohn, 'An Introduction to the History of Modern Persian Sufism, Part I: the Niʿmatullāhī Order: Persecution, Revival and Schism', *BSOAS*, 61 (1998), pp. 437–464, see pp. 440–446; William R. Royce, 'Mir Maʿsum ʿAlī Shāh and the Niʿmat Allāhī Revival 1776–77 to 1796–97: A Study of Sufism in Late Eighteenth-Century Iran' (PhD dissertation, Princeton University, 1979), p. 173; Many Sufi masters, such as Maʿṣūm ʿAlī Shāh, Nūr ʿAlī Shāh, Mushtāq ʿAlī Shāh (d. 1206/1792) or Muẓaffar ʿAlī Shāh (d. 1214/1800) were assassinated and thus became martyrs (*shahīd*) in the eyes of their followers. An important member of the clergy, Āqā Muḥammad ʿAlī Bihbahānī (d. 1216/1801), ordered many assassinations and even earned the nickname *Ṣūfī-kush* (killer of Sufis).

9 Matthijs van den Bos, *Mystic Regimes. Sufism and the State in Iran, from the Late Qajar Era to the Islamic Republic* (Leiden, 2002), p. 60.

10 For the relationship between Ḥājj Mīrzā Āqāsī and Muḥammad Shāh see the comments of Hamid Algar in *Religion and State in Iran, 1785–1906: The Role of the Ulama in the Qajar Period* (Berkeley, CA, Los Angeles, 1969), pp. 103–120.

11 J. Shahrī, *Ṭihrān-i qadīm* (Tehran, 1371 Sh./1992–3) and quoted by van den Bos, *Mystic Regimes*, pp. 65–66.

12 Le Comte de Gobineau, *Trois ans en Asie* (Paris, 1859), vol. 2, pp. 51–118; Sir John Malcom, *History of Persia* (London, 1829), vol. 2, p. 292.

13 Richard Gramlich, *Die Schiitischen Derwischorden Persiens* (3 vols., Wiesbaden, 1965–1981), vol. 1, pp. 53–58. Prior to Raḥmat ʿAlī Shāh the order had already given birth to two new branches named Kawthariyya and Shamsiyya (ibid., vol. 1, pp. 43–50).

14 Ibid., vol. 1, pp. 58–59.

15 On this subject, see ʿAṭā Karīm Barq, *Justujū dar aḥwāl wa āthār-i Ṣafī ʿAlī Shāh* (Tehran, 1352 Sh./1973–4); Nile Green, 'A Persian Sufi in British India: The Travels of Mīrzā Ḥasan Ṣafī ʿAlī Shāh (1251/1835–1316/1899)', *Iran*, 42 (2004), pp. 201–218; 'Mīrzā Ḥasan Ṣafī ʿAlī Shāh: A Persian Sufi in the Age of Printing', in Lloyd Ridgeon, ed., *Religion and Politics in Iran: A Reader* (London, 2005), pp. 99–112.

16 Saʿādat ʿAlī Shāh was the representative of Raḥmat ʿAlī Shāh in Isfahan. See Gramlich, *Die schiitischen*, vol. 1, p. 64.

17 On Ḥājj Mullā Hādī Sabzawārī see Sajjad Rizvi, '*Ḥikma mutaʿāliya* in Qajar Iran: Ḥājj Mullā Hādī Sabzavārī and the School of Mullā Ṣadrā', in Denis Hermann and Sabrina Mervin, ed., *Shiʿi Trends and Dynamics in Modern Times (XVIIIth–XXth centuries). Courants et dynamiques chiites à l'époque moderne (XVIIIe-XXe siècles)* (Beirut, 2010), pp. 51–70.

18 Shaykh Murtaḍā Anṣārī is generally considered the founder of the *marjaʿiyyat* and the first *marjaʿ-i taqlīd* in the history of Shiʿism. According to the doctrine of the dominant *uṣūlī*-rationalist trend, the non-*mujtahids* are *muqallids* (imitators) compelled to observe their *taqlīd* (imitation) following a living *mujtahid* who is, therefore, capable of carrying out *ijtihād*, the independent effort to interpret the law. *Marjaʿ-i taqlīd* literally means 'source to imitate' and is a label provided to the highest level Shiʿi authority within the living *mujtahids*.

19 Gramlich, *Die schiitischen*, vol. 1, p. 65.

20 The term *quṭb* designating the master of the brotherhood is commonly used throughout the different Shiʿi Sufi orders established in Iran during the modern period. The concept can be translated as 'pole', but also 'mystical axis' and came to designate the imam in Twelver Shiʿism. In modern Shiʿi Sufism it has also come to mean the supreme representative embodiment of the twelfth imam. For more informations on this concept see Alessandro Cancian, 'Translation, Authority and Exegesis in Modern Iranian

Sufism: Two Iranian Sufi Masters in Dialogue', *Journal of Persianate Studies*, 7 (2014), pp. 88–106, see p. 89.

21 On Gunābād see M. Yusuf-Nežad, 'Gonābād', *EIR*, 11 (2003), pp. 121–122.

22 See van den Bos, *Mystic Regimes*, pp. 77–78. The principal works of Sulṭān ʿAlī Shāh are certainly *Majmaʿ al-saʿādāt* (2nd ed., n.p., 1394/1974–5); *Wilāyat-nāmah* (Tehran, 1385/1965–6); and *Bayān al-saʿāda fī maqāmāt al-ʿibāda* (Beirut, 1988). He has also written two commentaries on the works of Bābā Ṭāhir (d. *ca* first half of the 11th century), *Tuḍīḥ* and *Īḍāḥ*.

23 For thoughts pertaining to the technical term *quṭb* throughout the different branches of the Niʿmat Allāhī see Oliver Scharbrodt, 'The *Quṭb* as Special Representative of the Hidden Imam: The Conflation of Shiʿi and Sufi *Vilāyat* in the Niʿmatullāhī Order', in D. Hermann and S. Mervin, ed., *Shiʿi Trends and Dynamics*, pp. 33–49. Several researchers have concluded that statements attributing to Sulṭān ʿAlī Shāh the highest rank, akin to that of the Messiah or the Prophet, were largely self-proclaimed. See Gramlich, *Die schiitischen*, vol. 1, p. 66; Algar, 'Gonābādī Order', *EIR*, 11, pp. 122–126, at p. 123; Basil Nikitine, 'Ṭāwūsiyya', *EI2*, 10, p. 426; William M. Miller, 'Shiʿah Mysticism (The Sufis of Gunābād)', *The Muslim World*, 13 (1923), pp. 343–363.

24 Thenceforth, the Niʿmat Allāhī Sulṭān ʿAlī Shāhī elevated their master to the state of martyr (*shahīd*). See Sulṭān Ḥusayn Tābandā, *Nābigha-yi ʿilm wa ʿirfān dar qarn-i chahārdahum* (Tehran, 1384 Sh./2005–6), pp. 163–186.

25 van den Bos, *Mystic Regimes*, pp. 78, 131.

26 Lewisohn, 'An Introduction to the History of Modern Persian Sufism, Part 1', p. 451.

27 He visited Turkestan, Iraq, Egypt, Syria, India, Afghanistan and the Arabian Peninsula. See Gramlich, *Die schiitischen*, vol. 1, pp. 67–68; van den Bos, *Mystic Regimes*, p. 81; *idem* 'A Modern Iranian Shiite Friend of God—Nūr ʿAlī Shāh II (1867–1918)', *Persica*, 18 (2002), pp. 1–15. His most famous treatises are without doubt *Dhū'l-faqār* (n.p., n.d.) and *Rujūm al-shayāṭīn* (Tehran, 1315/1898–9) whose subject is the life of Sulṭān ʿAlī Shāh.

28 Violent confrontations had already taken place with Sulṭān ʿAlī Shāhī in Kashan in 1311/1893–4. See Sulṭān Ḥusayn Tābandā, *Nābigha-yi ʿilm*, pp. 394–395.

29 On the concept of the funerary mosque see J. Pedersen, 'Masdjid', *EI2*, vol. 6, pp. 636–639.

30 Miller, 'Shiʿah Mysticism', p. 345.

31 Certain passages also refer to *sharīʿa*. Ṣāliḥ ʿAlī Shāh, *Pand-i Ṣāliḥ/Ṣāliḥ's Advice* [Persian and English text] (Tehran, 1372 Sh./1993–4).

32 An American traveller who visited Khurasan in the 1920s affirmed that all the inhabitants of Gunābād were without exception members of the brotherhood. See Miller, 'Shiʿah Mysticism', p. 346. During the first half of the 19th century Isfahan was certainly the second most important centre.

33 Publication of the Ṣāliḥ library, *Yādnāmah-yi Ṣāliḥ* (Tehran, 1380 Sh./2001–2), pp. 647–649. Photos of the funerary mosque are reproduced in the same work pp. 31, 650–651. For a description of the ceremonies held in the Baydukht sanctuary, and more generally on the religious life which prevailed in the region, see M. Madanī, *Dar khānaqāh-i Baydukht chi mī guzarad?* (Tehran, 1376 Sh./1997–8).

34 Maḥbūb ʿAlī Shāh, *Khurshīd-i Tābandā* (Tehran, 1377 Sh./1998–9), pp. 245–250; Sulṭān Ḥusayn Tābandā, *Nābigha-yi ʿilm wa ʿirfān dar qarn-i chahārdahum* (Tehran, 1384 Sh./2005–6), pp. 629–643.

35 A *qanāt* is a gently sloping tunnel which permits the supply of water over long distances.

36 See the publication of the Ṣāliḥ library, *Yādnāmah-yi Ṣāliḥ*, p. 648. The text of the first *waqf-nāmah* has been inserted at the end of the work.

37 Each cell would generally house two students.

38 Maḥbūb ʿAlī Shāh, *Khurshīd-i Tābandā*, pp. 251–252.

39 On the role of the Niʿmat Allāhī Ṣafī ʿAlī Shāhī in the constitutional movement, see Lloyd Ridgeon, 'Revolution and a High-Ranking Sufi: Zahir al-Dowleh's Contribution

to the Constitutional Movement', in Houchang E. Chehabi and Vanessa Martin, ed., *Iran's Constitutional Revolution. Popular Politics, Cultural Transformations and Transnational Connections* (London, 2010), pp. 143–162.

40 Publication of the Ṣāliḥ library, *Yādnāmah-yi Ṣāliḥ*, pp. 74–75. For more information on the role as jurists of the Sulṭān ʿAlī Shāhī masters, see Shahram Pazouki, '*Fiqh* et soufisme à la période qajare: quelques notes sur l'œuvre juridique des maîtres Niʿmatullāhī gunābādī', in Denis Hermann and Sabrina Mervin, ed., *Shiʿi Trends and Dynamics*, pp. 113–127.

41 van den Bos, *Mystic Regimes*, p. 132.

42 By the term *shaykh* Sulṭān ʿAlī Shāhī means representatives of the *quṭb*. On Shaykh ʿAbd Allāh Ḥā'irī Māzandarānī see the redaction of *ʿIrfān-i Īrān*, 'Sharḥ-i aḥwāl-i marḥūm-i Ḥājj Shaykh ʿAbd Allāh Ḥā'irī Raḥmat ʿAlī Shāh', *ʿIrfān-i Īrān*, 11 (1380 Sh./2001–2), pp. 67–78.

43 For a detailed list, see Pazouki, '*Fiqh* et soufisme'.

44 For a critical account of the Pahlavi regime and the westernisation of the country by Ḥājj Sulṭān Ḥusayn Tābandā see *Naẓar-i madhhabī bi iʿlāmiyya-yi ḥuqūq-i bashar. Nigārish-i Sulṭān Ḥusayn Tābandā Gunābādī* (Tehran, 1354 Sh./1975–6) [translated into English under the title *A Muslim Commentary on the Universal Declaration of Human Rights* (London, 1970)]; and van den Bos, *Mystic Regimes*, pp. 135–141.

45 van den Bos, *Mystic Regimes*, p. 133.

46 Ibid., p. 91. And see Lewisohn, 'An Introduction to the History of Modern Persian Sufism, Part 1', p. 455.

47 The Pahlavis prohibited this kind of title, hence the appellation 'Sābiq' (ancient).

48 This term designates the child 'servants' or 'slaves' of the court.

49 Mahdī Bāmdād, *Sharḥ-i ḥal-i rijāl-i Īrān dar qarn-i 12, 13, 14 hijrī* (Tehran, 1347–1353 Sh./1968–1975), vol. 1, p. 96 and vol. 2, pp. 435–442; E. al-Salṭana, *al-Mā'athir wa'l-athār (tārīkh-i chihil sālah-yi Īrān)* (Tehran, 1363 Sh./1984–5), p. 316.

50 On the use of titles during the Qajar era, see K. Sulaymānī, *Alqāb-i rijāl-i dawra-yi qājār* (Tehran, 1379 Sh./2000–1), pp. 109–110.

51 Publication of the Ṣāliḥ library, *Yādnāmah-yi Ṣāliḥ*, pp. 185–187.

52 B. Hourcade, 'Tihrān (c). La ville depuis l'avènement des Pahlavī', *EI2*, vol. 10, pp. 529–531.

53 *Sāzmān-i awqāf wa umūr-i khayriyya*, File 1583, Tehran.

54 Publication of the Ṣāliḥ library, *Yādnāmah-yi Ṣāliḥ*, p. 190.

55 Maḥbūb ʿAlī Shāh, *Khurshīd-i Tābandā*, p. 265.

56 Since 1307 Sh./1928–9, the government of Riḍā Shāh has required that documents such as the *waqf* must be officially inventoried. The *ʿulamā'* possess for this purpose recognised offices (*daftar*). One then refers to official documents (*sanād-i rasmī*). These offices are classified according to three different categories. Those in the first category (*daraja-yi yik*) can record all types of legal documents. The offices pertaining to the second and third categories (*daraja-yi du* and *daraja-yi sih*) have more limited prerogatives. See A. Mahdawī Dāmghānī, 'Daftar-i asnād-i rasmī', *EIR*, 6, pp. 563–564.

57 *Sāzimān-i awqāf wa umūr-i khayriyya*, File 1583, Tehran.

58 The *wāqif* specifically indicates his address since his house adjoins the two buildings he is establishing as *waqf* and shares the same address. Amīr Sulaymānī wishes to make clear which part remains his private property and which is established as *waqf*.

59 The *rawḍa khwān* is the person who is charged, during the ceremonies of mourning, with recounting the history of the martyrs to the assembly.

60 This term generally designates the interior of a house and the area reserved primarily for women and children.

61 *Fuqarā'*, which literally means 'the poor', is here synonymous with *darwīsh* or Sufi. It designates the simple disciples of the order.

62 Today, the Ḥusayniyya Amīr Sulaymānī hosts 17 *majālis* in memory of the martyrdom of Imām Ḥusayn during the months of Muḥarram and Ṣafar.

63 The 'great men of the religion' here refers to the mystics (*ʿurafā'*) who were always celebrated, regardless of whether they had been members of the Niʿmat Allāhī brotherhood or not. It is the task of the *quṭb* present, or a *shaykh*, to choose which books will be read during the assembly. The *dīwān* of Jalāl al-Dīn Rūmī (d. 672/1273), Ḥāfiẓ (d. *ca* 793/1390), Shāh Niʿmat Allāhī Walī (d. 834/1431) and Bābā Ṭāhir are certainly the most frequently recited of them all.

64 Three of these seven nights are central to the Shiʿi calendar. The night of the 19th of Ramaḍān corresponds to the day upon which Imām ʿAlī was struck in the face by a poisoned sword and the night of the 23rd to his death. For the Shiʿa, the night of destiny (*shab-i qadr*) is not known with certainty. Nocturnal wakes take place on the 19th, 22nd and 23rd of the month of Ramaḍān.

65 This implies that the *mutawallī* must be present in Tehran during these seven nights of the month of Ramaḍān. However, a clause inserted at the end of the document enables him to appoint a representative or make changes to the organisation.

66 This second night is central to the Shiʿi calendar. It corresponds to the reading of *duʿā kumayl*. During the course of the first night, the Shiʿis are invited to read the supererogatory prayers (sing. *duʿā*) for Imām ʿAlī and Fāṭima. Both these nights follow the weekly fasting days most recommended (*mustaḥabb*) in the *ḥadīth*.

67 Today, dozens of volunteers welcome the faithful during the *majlis*, but the religious centre still has only one regular employee who looks after the place and resides there during the week.

68 This district is situated in north-east Tehran.

69 At the time the *waqf* was established, almost all the population of Tehran made use of the *qanāt* for their personal consumption. However, in the past 50 years almost all the *qanāt* of Tehran have been destroyed or fallen out of use. In 1356 Sh./1977–8, less than 10 per cent of the 280 surviving *qanāts* were still in use. In 1375 Sh./1996–7, there were 100 remaining, only a handful of which were in use. On this subject, see A. Mālikī, 'Guzārish az qanawāt-i Tihrān', *Majmūʿa-yi maqalāt-i qanāt*, 2 (1379 Sh./2000–1), pp. 585–601. To remedy this problem, wealthy disciples make regular donations in order to finance these ceremonies, whilst others designate other types of assets as *waqf* for the same purpose. For the most part, these goods are essentially real estate.

70 No indication of his salary is given. Normally in this case, custom (*ʿurf*) demands that 10% of the total revenue be attributed to him. For an example of this, see Omid Rezai, *Panjāh-wa yik ʿarīḍa wa ḥukm-i sharʿī az ʿulamā'-yi dawra-yi qājār darbāra-yi umūr-i jārī-yi mawqūfāt (1253–1346)* (Tehran, 1384 Sh./2005–6), pp. 154–155.

71 Since the beginning of the Pahlavi era this type of *waqf* has been considered as a public utility (*ʿāmm*). Only strictly familial *waqf* can be established as private (*khāṣṣ*). It is probable that Amīr Sulaymānī shared this traditional approach to the *waqf*. He also hopes that it will provide an additional argument with which to resist any 'possible' future contestation of the *waqf*.

72 By 'officials' (*rasmī*), the *wāqif* here is referring to civil servants working for the government, and more specifically to the ministry of the *waqf* and the tax office.

73 The phrase with which the *wāqif* concludes was commonly used during the Timurid (*ca* 771–912/1370–1506) and especially Safawiḍ (907–1135/1501–1722) eras. On this subject see Omid Rezai, 'Barrasī-yi taṭbīqī-yi chand ʿibārat dar waqfiyya-yi Qāḍī Rukn al-Dīn ʿAmīd al-Mulk', *Mīrāth-i jāwīdān*, 59 (1386 Sh./2007–8), pp. 66–101.

74 The Ḥā'irī Ḥusayniyya was established as a *waqf* later on, in 1351 Sh./1972–3. It is situated in the historic neighbourhood of ʿŪdlājān (Imām-zāda Yaḥya) at the east of the bazaar of Tehran. The disciples congregate there mainly on Friday mornings. Today, it has the role of a religious centre with a variety of activities. It is equipped with a library in which instruction takes place. The favoured themes revolve around religion, for

obvious reasons. One can follow lectures on the Qur'an, mystical poetry or the history of Sufism, but one can also prepare for the university entrance examination. The *waqf-nāmah* can be consulted at the *Sāzmān-i awqāf wa umūr-i khayriyya*, File 1876, Tehran. For more information on the Ḥusayniyya Ḥā'irī, see Maḥbūb 'Alī Shāh, *Khurshīd-i Tābandā*, pp. 264–265.

75 See Ṣāliḥ 'Alī Shāh, *Pand-i Ṣāliḥ*, pp. 7, 11.

76 The ground floor of this two-storey house is today a library in which the works of the brotherhood are sold. On the first floor resides the guardian of the *ḥusayniyya*.

77 See M. Habibi, 'Réza Chah et le développement de Téhéran (1925–1941)', in Charhyar Adle and Bernard Hourcade, ed., *Téhéran. Capitale bicentenaire* (Paris and Tehran, 1992), pp. 199–206.

78 A member of the Ni'mat Allāhī Munawwar 'Alī Shāhī branch, Muḥammad 'Alī Niẓām Māfī, however, established in 1337 Sh./1958–9 an important *waqf* in Tehran, the purpose of which was to finance the purchase of works devoted to mysticism for the library of the *khānaqāh* of the order, situated in the south of Tehran [Omid Rezai ed., *Fihrist-i asnād-i mawqūfāt-i Īrān*, vol. 4, *Ustān-i Tihrān* (Qumm, 1386 Sh./2007–8)].

79 One finds the following quotation in the *waqf-nāmah*: 'for those who have lodged [in the *khānaqāh*];' 'for the members of the brotherhood;' 'food and drink for the members of the brotherhood', etc.

80 For the central role of *'āshūrā* in Shi'i Islam, see Mahmoud Ayoub, *Redemptive Suffering in Islam: A Study of Devotional Aspects of 'Ashura' in Twelver Shi'ism* (The Hague, 1978); Khalid Sindawi, 'The dreams of *Ḥusayn Ibn 'Alī* and his family in Shī'īte Maqātil literature', *Ancient Near Eastern Studies*, 39 (2002), pp. 182–200; E. H. Waugh, 'Muḥarram rites: community death and rebirth', in F. E. Reynolds and Earle H. Waugh, ed., *Religious encounters with death* (Philadelphia, PA, 1977), pp. 200–213.

81 Louis Gardet, 'Dhikr', *EI2*, vol. 2, pp. 230–233.

82 The Ni'mat Allāhī Sulṭān 'Alī Shāhī *quṭb*s and *shaykh*s have fully justified this preference in several works, of which *Abḥāth-i 'ashara* by Muḥammad Khān Qarāguzlū.

83 Ṣāliḥ 'Alī Shāh, *Pand-i Ṣāliḥ*, pp. 29–31.

84 van den Bos, *Mystic Regimes*, p. 227.

85 Sulṭān 'Alī Shāh, *Wilāyat-nāmah*, pp. 38–42.

86 Ibid., p. 39.

87 Gramlich, *Die schiitischen*, vol. 3, pp. 75–77.

88 This last meal was also a ritual among the *ahl-i ḥaqq* and the Khāksār.

89 Gramlich, *Die schiitischen*, vol. 3, pp. 75–77.

90 For this service on the subject of God's creatures (*khidmat-i bih khalq-i Allāh*), see Ṣāliḥ 'Alī Shāh, *Pand-i Ṣāliḥ*.

91 The Ni'mat Allāhī Sulṭān 'Alī Shāhī maintain that there was only one exception in the history of the order, due to the return to Iran at the end of the Zand era. Riḍā 'Alī Shāh Dakanī authorised Ma'ṣūm 'Alī Shāh, whom he had sent to Iran as *shaykh* of the *shaykh*s, to appoint *shaykh*s, because of the geographical distance between himself and Iran.

92 During the early 1980s this house was requisitioned by the army.

93 Maḥbūb 'Alī Shāh, *Khurshīd-i Tābandā*, pp. 266–267.

94 The library today comprises over 16,000 works covering varied and wide-reaching domains and including subjects other than religion. It is particularly rich in Persian literature. See Maḥbūb 'Alī Shāh, *Khurshīd-i Tābandā*, pp. 267–270. The publishing house itself is named Ḥaqīqat.

95 Like the library, it is named *Ṣāliḥ*. See Maḥbūb 'Alī Shāh, *Khurshīd-i Tābandā*, pp. 270–272.

6

Text and Contest: Theories of Secrecy, *taqiyya* and Archiving Practices in 20th- and 21st-Century Niʿmat Allāhī Sufism

Seema Golestaneh

He did not wish to speak about mysticism, but wanted to show me some texts he had in his possession instead. These would tell me what I needed to know, he assured me.

I had not met Iraj in person, but was referred to him by a mutual friend. I spoke to him over the phone, and while my primary goal had been to initiate a real conversation in person, he demurred at my attempts until I agreed to pick up these textual materials as a sort of ethnographic consolation prize. He did not explain to me what kind of texts they were but only made very clear that I must take great care not to misplace these materials and they must absolutely be returned to him. In our two phone conversations he made me promise multiple times that I would treat these texts with the utmost caution and respect. So adamant was he in his imploring me to safeguard and return his materials, that I initially assumed he must have something extremely valuable in his possession: perhaps some handwritten manuscript, handed down through generations, or perhaps some transcriptions of a sermon delivered long ago. I assured him that they would be treated with great care.

*Imagine my surprise then, when picking up the materials from his wife at his house, as he himself was out, that they were nothing more than two books, one hardcover and one paperback, by the Sufi master (*quṭb*) Javad Nurbakhsh (d. 2008), which I had come across numerous times before and which were even available online for purchase. Was this some kind of gentle joke at the expense of an overeager researcher? Or perhaps this self-identified dervish was really just a kind of poseur or charlatan? But no, I went over our conversations in my mind and decided that he had in fact been sincere in his proclamations of worry over their potential displacement.*

After my initial disappointment faded, however, what remained in its wake was the sharp contrast between the presumed lack of value of the materials and Iraj's treatment of them as precisely the opposite. Here were texts that might be found in a good number of bookstores in Iran being treated as the rarest of manuscripts, as if a common library book was suddenly worth its weight in gold. Moreover, as I found out throughout the course of my fieldwork, this apparent dissonance between something with a presumed low value – in terms of rarity, scarcity, in some cases authenticity – and the regard with which its owners viewed it was not a rare occurrence but something I encountered again and again. Small stashes and modest collections preserved carefully, presented either eagerly or with deliberation, as if revealing a secret.

Since its inception, the Niʿmat Allāhī Shiʿi Sufi order of Iran has adhered to a policy of secrecy in regard to the dissemination of its ideas, largely to protect against the 'misunderstanding' or 'misappropriation' of mystical concepts by the uninitiated. This policy is made evident in the contemporary era through such practices as closed meetings, lengthy initiation practices, the circulation of weekly 'secret words', and the safeguarding of any written work from non-members. Regarding the latter, such careful maintenance and preservation of textual materials by individual members – materials including hagiographies and other stories of prominent members of the order's chain of succession (*silsila*), medieval poetry collections, personal notes taken during sermons, handwritten advice from shaykhs, and more – has led to the development of what I am calling here a 'personal' or 'private' archive.

This adherence to secrecy has grown more complicated, however, as in the last few years the Sufis have published on their own website a digital archive of sermons, exegetical works, and electronic versions of foundational texts. In other words, many of these very texts and sermons which delineate the necessity and virtue of the maintenance of secrecy within the order now exist in digital form on an unprotected website, and hence are now potentially accessible to all electronic passersby.

Despite this significant move on the part of the Sufi authorities to leave these texts more exposed to those outside of mystical circles, as well as similar shifts to disclosure within the broader socio-theological and socio-political sphere of Iran, however, individual Sufis curiously continue to insist on the secret or private nature of their home collections, taking pains to keep them hidden and insisting that the materials only be entrusted to a select few. The question then arises: what is the purpose of this continued maintenance of careful safeguarding of these personal textual materials, where similar if not identical documents are accessible to all elsewhere?

This chapter will explore mystical practices of secrecy through the cultivation of private archives, the growing trend towards various forms and practices of transparency in Iran as seen through both Twelver Shiʿism as well as Shiʿi Sufism, the persistence of the concealment of these personal archives despite the increased accessibility of Sufi texts, and the broader implications for the question of the archive contained therein.

To provide some background, this essay draws from my research conducted during the years 2009 to 2012 in various major cities throughout Iran. My interlocutors are primarily Sufis who might be categorised as 'unranked', meaning not holding any recognised rank of spiritual authority such as the position of shaykh, and the question of the order to which they belong will be addressed shortly. As is often the case with fieldwork, I had not intended to study the practice of keeping a personal collection of materials, nor was I even aware that such accumulating or curating habits even existed. Indeed, I only became aware of these personal archives while conducting interviews in individuals' homes, where I noticed that people often kept what might be called designated 'Sufi materials' within their homes. For example, when asked about reading habits, people often brought down certain items from a bookshelf or drawer unprompted. These materials were sometimes displayed casually, but oftentimes with great care. Indeed, while discussing their experiences with mysticism, I found that people were often eager to show me either textual materials or any relics or photographs they might have as a central part of their personal experience.

The individuals with whom I worked adhered to the teachings of the *quṭb*s and shaykhs of the Niʿmat Allāhī Shiʿi order, meaning that they trace their lineage (*silsila*) back to the founding shaykh of the order, Shāh Niʿmat Allāhī Walī (d. 834/1431). I am not delving into further detail concerning the order due to reasons of the scope of this chapter as well as to further obfuscate the identities of my interlocutors. My decision to focus on this group is simply based on the fact that these were the individuals to whom I had access. I will note, however, that I am categorising these individuals as following the teachings within the Niʿmat Allāhī canon rather than being formal—meaning initiated—members, because not all the individuals with whom I worked were, in fact, initiated members. Indeed, the individuals with whom I spoke fall within the following categories:

1) initiated members,
2) uninitiated members who attended meetings at a *khānaqāh* or *mahdawiyya*,
3) those who attended meetings sparingly or almost not at all but claimed to adhere to the writings and teachings of the shaykhs of a certain order.

This final category was determined through my conversations with them.

I utilise what might be considered more 'loose' criteria very intentionally. First, although they don't advertise or seek out new members, the Niʿmat Allāhī orders currently active in Iran do hold open meetings. Hence, a person without any prior training or affiliation might be able to listen to a sermon and thus be exposed and possibly inclined to follow that teaching. As a result, there are people who might be interested but in a much more casual capacity than those who are active in the order, meaning those who are initiated or help organise events or the day-to-day activities.

Finally, I should note my inclusion of the works of Dr Javad Nurbakhsh (d. 2008). During my fieldwork, I was surprised to find that many of the texts of Nurbakhsh, a Sufi who began his own order in the mid-20th century and left Iran around the time of the 1979 revolution, were still in heavy circulation. While once boasting a small but devoted following, the Nurbakhsh order, no longer operates within Iran, nor do any of my interlocutors identify as part of the Nurbakhshiyya. Nevertheless, given how ubiquitous his writings were, for the purposes of this article, I categorise those people who are currently utilising Nurbakhsh's writings, using them as an ethical guide and engaging with the arguments, as part of the Niʿmat Allāhī order, as he too claims lineage to the chain of succession (*silsila*) of Shāh Niʿmat Allāhī Wali.

Ultimately, then, my interlocutors in this article are those individuals who identified as either 'Sufi' or 'dervish' and possessed the texts which I will discuss shortly. They may or may not be initiated members of any order. During my research, I also spoke with others who either self-identified as 'Sufi' or 'dervish' but, as they did not follow the teachings of either order, are not included within the analysis for this article.

Theories of Secrecy in Niʿmat Allāhī Sufism

To begin, the mystics' policy of secrecy operates at a number of levels, and it is of note to briefly outline these different forms and manifestations within Iranian Sufism. To aid in our explorations, I turn to two texts commonly used and widely circulated by mystics today: *Pand-i Ṣāliḥ*, or *Ṣāliḥ's Advice*, written by Ḥājj Shaykh Muḥammad Ḥasan Ṣāliḥ ʿAlī Shāh Baydukhtī (d. 1386/1966), a prominent 20th-century spiritual leader (*quṭb*) of the Niʿmat Allāhī sub-set Sulṭān ʿAlī Shāhī order, in 1993, and *The Path: Sufi Practices*, a collection of the writings of Javad Nurbakhsh, the spiritual leader and independent publisher of the Niʿmat Allāhī sub-set Nurbakhsh order, dating back to works from the 1960s through the 1990s. It is the works of both spiritual leaders that are found most frequently in the homes of self-described Niʿmat Allāhī Sufis.

Before venturing further, however, one might inquire as to *what* exactly is being so closely withheld, and why must it be guarded at all costs? For our purposes here, it is beneficial to simply understand these unspoken enigmas as any and all of the basic tenets, beliefs, and practices which comprise Sufi epistemologies; those ideas that either appear in canonical texts or are directly relayed by the master or teacher (*pīr*) to the student (*murīd*) as well as all the experiences which accompany such revelations. As Nurbakhsh writes in his text: 'These secrets consist of the remembrance and contemplation he or she is given, as well as all discoveries and revelations witnessed in the world of Unity.'[1] In other words, that which is taught, remembered, meditated over, witnessed: these are the categories which must remain hidden.[2] Rather than explore the content, debates and discourse surrounding these concepts and experiences themselves, however, what is put to question here is the logic of safeguarding, rather than what is being protected.

The first and perhaps most important use of the policy of secrecy would be the guarantee that the communication of Sufi ideals does not fall upon the ears of those outside the proper circles, namely the uninitiated and the untrained. Understood to be complex and abstract concepts, their transmission occurs in only the most specific and proscribed of contexts – that of the presence of the master – as they are thought to be easily misunderstood or misappropriated. The dangers here are hence twofold: (1) The transmission of mystical ideas to those who have not been approved to hear them, and (2) The inevitable misrepresentation and/or distortion of the ideas as relayed by a student. For these reasons, these 'remembrances' must remain unspoken. The following passages give further nuance to the claim:

> Such secrets should be spoken of to no one but the master. In this way, the secret will not fall into the hands of one unable to keep it. At the beginning of travelling on the Path (*sulūk*), the Sufi makes a commitment not to reveal to anyone the secrets he or she is told—regardless of whether that person is a stranger, friend or fellow dervish.[3]
>
> The secrets of religion should be kept hidden, particularly that which has been ordered to be concealed and which he has taken upon himself. And he should not give utterance to whatever is inspired in his heart, be it a spiritual state (*ḥāla*) or a belief, since he should, follow the *pīr*, pass and step beyond it.[4]

As evidenced above, Nurbakhsh not only stresses that one must guard against the secret falling into the hands of one 'unable to keep it', but that the very commitment to embarking on the path of mysticism is contingent upon the maintenance of the secret. Moreover, he remarks this withholding of the discussion of ideas can extend even to communications with fellow Sufis (*darwīsh*), a thought which is later elaborated upon as especially those not as 'advanced on the path', or as advanced in their study. The Ṣāliḥ ʿAlī Shāh quote perhaps goes even further, remarking that one should not even verbalise, 'give utterance' to, those thoughts and feelings provoked by Sufi ideals, if only because it might prevent one from moving forward on the path. In this case, this form of withholding of information is used more as a tactic for keeping oneself on the proper path and not being distracted, even by 'inspiration', such that one is caught up at a particular state (*ḥāla*) but instead continues to follow the *pīr*, or master, in addition to guarding information from others.

Another common theme supported by the practice of secrecy and only implied thus far is the affirmation afforded to the supreme importance of the Sufi teacher or master *(pīr)*. Beyond protecting the ideas from falling into the wrong hands, the silence surrounding the communication and debate of mystical ideals gives weight to the belief that there is only one audience appropriate for such discussion: that when one is before the *pīr*. In this way, secrecy is used to further cement one of the fundamentals of Sufism: the master-disciple (*pīr-murīd*) relationship, and the relaying of ideas from teacher to student.[5] To limit any verbalisation of ideas to exist purely within the confines of this relationship is undoubtedly to place a great significance upon it. As Ṣāliḥ ʿAlī Shāh remarks: 'And he should have respect for the orders of the Saints. He should refrain from revealing his secrets to others.'[6] Thus, the act of the concealment of the divine mysteries which comprise Sufism is seen in part as an act of respect towards the saints; not only one's own *pīr* but the chain of succession (*silsila*) that came before him, affirming the belief that it is only the masters who are capable of engaging with such potent ideas.

And it is indeed the question of the very potency of these epistemologies to which we might turn our attention now. For not only does the adherence to secrecy affirm the highest respect for the saints (sing. *walī*) and *pīr*s as the only individuals able to transmit and communicate these ideas, as well as protect against the exposure of the ideas to those outside the circle, but the fact that Sufi tenets much be so closely guarded infers the understanding of the almost dangerous nature of the very ideals as themselves. These are ideas which must be hidden at all costs, lest they be used for ill purposes. Forms of knowledge so powerful that they may supersede or overpower those who possess them, to throw them down a wrong path if they are not yet ready, or these ideas could be manipulated into something else, something that will be undeniably potent. Such epistemologies are what must be kept hidden at all costs. Thus, for the Sufis, this secrecy is absolutely tantamount to the resolute belief in the potency of their epistemologies as well as the intellectual might of their shaykhs. In other words, it is only because they are so formidable that they must be guarded so closely.

Understanding *taqiyya*: Theories of Secrecy in Twelver Shiʿism

In our discussion of these Sufi beliefs and practices of secrecy, it is imperative to remember that these groups are also resolutely Shiʿi. In considering this, then, one might reflect upon those aspects of Shiʿism which also involve elements of secrecy, other practices and beliefs which entertain some iteration of a concealing or preserving. Most notably, there are those scholars who have championed either the 'esoteric' nature of Shiʿism as a whole, meaning the obscure or hidden, or the esoteric nature of the knowledge of the imamate.[7] For our purposes, it might be most helpful to limit our discussion and remain focused on the practice of *taqiyya*, or dissimulation as a means of self-preservation, as a means of comparison, for in both instances of Sufi *rāz-pūshī* and *taqiyya* information is purposefully withheld by the believer, rather than merely existing as an unattainable form of divinely inspired knowledge.

Also translated as concealment, precaution, or keeping of secrets, under the invocation of *taqiyya* a person is allowed to keep their identity as a Shiʿi hidden to themselves, either by voluntarily not disclosing such information or even verbalising a lack of connection with Shiʿism. The two most oft-quoted pieces of evidence to support the concept are the following Qurʾanic passages:

> 3:28 Believers should not accept as protecting friends unbelievers rather than believers... unless [it is done] as a precaution in order to guard yourselves from them [or, out of fear of them].
> 16:106 Whoever expresses disbelief in God after once believing [will suffer greatly], unless that person is under compulsion while yet remaining at peace in belief in the heart.

As the prominent 20th-century Iranian thinker ʿAllāma Sayyid Muḥammad Ṭabāṭabāʾī (d. 1981) has written: 'As is clear from this sacred verse, God, the Most Exalted, forbids with the utmost emphasis *walāya* (meaning in this case friendship and amity to the extent that it affects one's life) with unbelievers and orders man to be wary and have fear in such a situation.'[8]

While these two verses are almost always cited in research concerning *taqiyya*, this is a concept with a deep and varied history.

In his article 'Some Imami Shiʿi Views on *taqiyya*', Etan Kohlberg has meticulously laid out many of the differing interpretations of *taqiyya* by Imami Shiʿis, as well as the various contexts and situations that have been attributed to invocations of the concept. This has included everything from explaining Imam ʿAlī's behaviour after the death of Muḥammad, specifically his hesitance in assuming a position of political power, to the administration of *ḥadd* punishment, to those instances when *taqiyya* was specifically forbidden. He notes too that *taqiyya* was invoked not only in those instances as a means of self-preservation against a hostile force, but 'was sometimes applied to those relationships among the Shiʿis themselves'. Amir-Moezzi takes this point further, observing that scholars have overemphasised the instances where *taqiyya* was used in response to the political climate of the times, rather than those instances when it was used to contain the teachings of the imams within the realm of the Shiʿa. He argues too that it is in fact this second usage which should be viewed as the more essential version as it primarily involves the initiated rather than the first usage which also involves hostile actors, and I would certainly agree. In consideration of this, if here I appear to over-emphasise the interpretation of *taqiyya* involving external dangers, it is only because the Sufi literatures utilised here emphasise such a viewpoint on the matter, while their understanding of secrecy (*rāz-pūshī*) aligns more closely to the version of *taqiyya* as primarily preserving the secret of the occult teachings of the imams. This curious distinction is certainly worthy of more discussion than space allows here.

The concept was first made prominent by the fifth and sixth Shiʿi imams, Muḥammad al-Bāqir (d. *ca* 114/732) and Jaʿfar al-Ṣādiq (d. 148/765), during a time of great persecution of the Shiʿa under Sunni Abbasid rule.[9] It was noted as necessary for pure survival, when one's life, body, or property was in jeopardy were one to reveal their Shiʿi faith. After Shiʿis were accused of practising *taqiyya* as a means of lying or exhibiting cowardice, later *mujtahid*s offered more specific guidelines and restrictions as to its use. More specifically, Ṭabāṭabāʾī has written: 'In our view, the practice of *taqiyya* is permitted if there is a definite danger facing one's own life or the life of one's family, or the possibility of the loss of the honour and virtue of one's wife or of other female members of the family, or the danger of the loss of one's material belongings to such an extent as to cause complete destitution and prevent a man from being able to continue to support himself and his family.'[10] By outlining specific parameters under which *taqiyya* may be evoked, these later jurists (*mujtahids*), including Ṭabāṭabāʾī, have attempted to curtail any such abuses and accusations of unconditional use of the concept.

Upon reflection, however, the intentional concealment of one's faith in order to avoid bodily harm suggests a paradoxical note within Shiʿism, a faith which heavily draws upon the paradigm of the battle of Karbala as well as the martyrdom of the second and third Shiʿi imams, al-Ḥasan (d. 49/669) and al-Ḥusayn (d. 61/680), at the hands of the proto-Sunni opposition.[11] Ayat Allāh Subḥānī has mentioned such a seeming paradox in his writings, noting that most of the impeccable ones (sing. *maʿṣūm*) were in fact martyred. Despite this, he still makes the case for *taqiyya*, remarking that it must be utilised only under certain conditions; there are times when it is 'necessary' and times when it is 'forbidden', but ultimately giving further support to Ṭabāṭabāʾī's claim that when one's life, property, or honour is in danger, preservation of life is superior to outward expression of belief. Going further he clarifies that 'In truth, dissimulation is a weapon in the hands of the weak in the face of merciless tyrants. It is obvious that in the absence of any danger a person will not need to hide his beliefs, nor act in opposition to his beliefs.'[12] In other words, it is only an immediate threat which prompts *taqiyya*, and not any other form of motivation. Moreover, it exists at the level of the personal and, alluding to the intense persecution of the Shiʿi minority at the hands of the Abbasids. What is at stake is not the entire system of belief as was at the battle of Karbala, but the life and livelihood of one individual. He writes that *taqiyya* may be evoked when: 'No positive advantage is derived from their being killed.' This dissimulation of faith by the believer is thus in essence an act of preservation through disappearance. It is the construction of a recognition, a recognition which affirms the boundary between one's inner self and the outer world. When one's own well-being is at stake and no one else's is in question, the cloak of *taqiyya* is used to re-assert that 'belief in the heart' supersedes the external declaration of allegiance.

In consideration of this, an inevitable question arises: how might one understand the relationship between practices of *taqiyya* and secrecy, these dual modes of dissimulation? Certainly, the interpretations of both concepts vary wildly and this is by no means meant to be a wholly conclusive discussion of the matter. By utilising the delineations heretofore mentioned, however, we may be able to view the contours and colours of each as they exist in comparison to one another under these particular guidelines.

In doing so, it must first be noted that the Sulṭān ʿAlī Shāhī Sufis understood *taqiyya* as a category separate from secrecy, as they recognise it as a concept and endorse it as a means of self-preservation when faced with a dangerous situation. Indeed, secrecy is referred to as *rāz-ḥāfiẓ*, *rāz-pūshī* or *sirr*, and *taqiyya* is utilised much more sparingly. In looking through the English translation of the text too, *rāz-ḥāfiẓ*, *rāz-pūshī* and *sirr* are translated as 'the keeping of secrets', 'secrecy', or 'mystery' respectively, while *taqiyya* goes entirely untranslated or, if not, as 'dissimulation'. While this language usage and translation decisions might then suggest two or three wholly distinct terms, the formal definition of *taqiyya* reveals the situation to be a bit more complicated. More specifically, it is defined in *Pand-i Ṣāliḥ's* glossary as the following: '*Taqiyya*, dissimulation. It is the dissimulation of one's religion and the hiding of particular religious practices from the opponents in case of danger. It is also the hiding of words which are not advisable to be said to others.'[13] In other words, Sufi *taqiyya* denotes two uses: (1) concealment when confronted with a threat, and (2) purposeful concealment of words and information from those who should not hear it. Thus, the first usage suggests something similar to that of more mainstream Shiʿi opinion, while the second usage aligns itself more closely with other mystical ideals concerning secrecy as a means to maintain exclusivity amongst the initiated.

With this in mind, the two distinct evocations of Sufi *taqiyya* highlight the disparate uses of secrecy within the orders. When invoked as a protection from bodily harm, with the usual caveats that there are no innocent victims or threat to the greater religion as a whole, *taqiyya* is used as a means of self-preservation within the *physical realm*; here the stakes are immediately corporeal, tangible, and often responding to a larger socio-theological context, especially as one must judge the consequences of undertaking such a concealment. When *taqiyya* is used as a form of *rāz-pūshī*, the safeguarding of mystical knowledge, it is evoked when a Sufi is not facing any adversaries or threat, and speaks more directly to the spiritual-epistemological realm. In other words, this form of secrecy is evoked not as a response to a threat, but as a precautionary measure to prevent the inappropriate spreading and manipulation of mystical ideals. Indeed, it is also significant to remember that this preservation of knowledge does merely apply to the world beyond the Sufis, meaning the uninitiated and those outside such Sufi circles, as a means to prevent some form of persecution. But, as mentioned earlier, as even fellow Sufis (*darwīsh*) must be guarded from knowledge for which they are not ready, one must assume that it is the possession of the knowledge itself which makes one vulnerable, rather than any external threat to one's person. These ideals are dangerous, and may cause damage and lead someone down the wrong spiritual path if they are ill-prepared for them, if the revelations they contain are too strong. In this way, the keeping secret of mystical ideals gestures to a realm at least in part beyond the socio-political realm, one that could be called the realm of the existential or spiritual, a realm which, for the Sufis, possesses the highest stakes. In a sense, this form of concealment is interested less in protecting he who possesses the knowledge and more in protecting the one who does *not*. The potency and ontology of the beliefs are never in doubt, nor even is the one who disseminates them necessarily in the line of danger, but rather it is the fate of one who may come into contact with them that is put into question.

Essentially then, while Niʿmat Allāhī Sufis interpret the concept of *taqiyya* much in the same way as Twelver Shiʿis in one sense, their use of the concept extends further. While overlapping in the first definition where concealment in the face of danger is advocated, they diverge over the second, Sufi definition which blurs the boundaries between *taqiyya* and other forms and practices of the careful disclosure of mystical ideals.

Tactics for the Maintenance of Secrecy

With this basic understanding of the logic of safeguarding, we might now turn our attention to the specific strategies that were employed to maintain exclusivity amongst the order within the 20th and 21st centuries. Namely, specific practices that were utilised to both maintain privacy and act as identifying markers for other Sufis, some of which continue today. For example, secret handshakes are still used amongst Sufis of the Niʿmat Allāhī Sulṭān ʿAlī Shāhī order, in a small series of movements including the bowing of the head and the clasping of another's hands. This is usually used as a greeting only within the confines of a Sufi meeting-place (*khānaqāh*) or within the home of a dervish. A simple gesture, certainly, but the knowledge of which demonstrates clear membership within an order.

Earlier in the century, meetings were also closed to non-members, or at least those who had not made themselves known either to the shaykh, his students, or those *darwīsh* who ran the *khānaqāh*, such that to enter a Sufi meeting-place was to enter an exclusive locale of a predetermined few. Today, however, meetings are open to any and all, and the significance of this change will be discussed in the latter portion of this chapter.

Another engagement with secrecy emerged amongst certain chapters in the Iranian cities of Simnan, Ahwaz, and Kirman that previously entertained the intriguing custom of weekly 'secret words', where each week the shaykh would designate either a word or phrase that was said to have the same effect as a prayer.[14] One could either repeat the word or phrase to oneself, or say a prayer if the word was spoken in passing. Central to this activity, however, was the idea that only the Sufis would possess the knowledge of the 'secret word' of the week and must not speak it loudly for fear of revealing the information to non-Sufis. Here then, not only do we again see the power of the shaykhs, able to imbue even the mundane with the mysteries of the divine, but yet another practice where the possession of mystical knowledge is contingent upon its concealment.

Finally, there were also stories circulated that spoke to the presentation of a whole nutmeg (*juz*), as a means of initiation into the order, as supported by the following Nurbakhsh quotation:

> *Juz* represents the head of the traveller. In presenting *juz* to the master, the traveller consents to never reveal the Divine secrets that are confided in him or her. That is, even if threatened with decapitation, one should not reveal such secrets. In other words,

> the traveller's head is symbolically presented to the master here as a hostage for God's secrets.[15]

From the moment of initiation, the primacy of concealment is made apparent, one's life symbolically offered in exchange for the secrets of the divine.

The Cultivation of Private Archives

From here, we might turn our attention to the last practice in cultivating secrecy to be discussed in this essay: the private collections of texts and other materials by individual Sufis which I am calling 'private archives'. Before discussing their contents, however, it is important to note how such practices of collecting documents are framed within Sufism as a whole. Namely, that due to their adherence to maintain exclusivity, many of their activities are conducted without a written record of their having occurred. This includes descriptions of meeting practices, dates and contents of gatherings, names of initiates, dialogues between *darwīsh* and *pīr*s, to name a few. In some instances, I was told of records of names and addresses of members taken earlier in the 20th century, but these were either destroyed, or perhaps never taken in the first place as there was disagreement as to what exactly had transpired. There was of course 'official' documentation that existed and continues to exist today, with official documentation being defined here as any records that involved the state, the most significant of these which would be *waqf* documentation, or religious endowment land deeds.[16] My intention here is not to discredit or devalue the significance of these transactions and records, far from it, but rather to note the absence of documents which recorded the internal activities, debates, and names of members Sufi orders; ultimately, recordings which went unwritten due to adherence to a general policy of secrecy. What has persisted, however, are these personal collections. Collections which demonstrated not only the thoughts and concerns of the unranked Sufis, but those debates and discourses that shaped the Niʿmat Allāhī order as well.

To begin, it is significant to note what these personal archives ultimately contained. They almost always contained a variety of items, the most common of which were books. Now, these books ranged from collections of poetry to published texts about mysticism, the most common of which were the writings of Javad Nurbakhsh and works from his publishing house the Khānaqāh Niʿmat Allāhī. Although his publishing house was shuttered after the revolution alongside his departure from Iran, the books were subsequently published through a different press and as a result remained in circulation.[17] Today, Khānaqāh Niʿmat Allāhī Publications operates as a non-profit in the United States managed by the descendants of Javad Nurbakhsh. The texts are usually produced in Farsi within Iran and in English in the West, and those which I found were mainly published prior to the Islamic Revolution, although there were a small number from after as well. These texts cover materials ranging from 'General Principles of Sufism', an introduction of sorts, to in-depth discussions of a single concept such as 'annihilation of the self' (*fanā'*) to remembrance (*dhikr*), to hagiographies of past saints of the order. Prior to fieldwork I did not know such texts existed within Iran at all, and as these books are no longer being published nor readily in circulation in Iran, they were at times treated as valuable materials. This was also particularly odd, however, as these books are actually quite easily accessed via any university library in the US or even via online retailers like Amazon as the Nurbakhsh order has moved its operations, so to speak, to the US and UK, they were simply not readily available within Iran. Still, as my interlocutors shared these texts only with my solemn guarantee that I would return the materials, I found myself making photocopies of these books, books I could purchase online immediately, as if they were some irreplaceable medieval dictionary or hagiography.

The other type of text I found most frequently were poetry books, especially the collections (*dīwāns*) of the major figures of the Persian canon, not unlike any other poetry books you would find in any home in Iran. No notable trend with any specific publisher was found here either. Again then, the only thing that would distinguish these books as being of significance is that they were presented to me as 'Sufi' or 'mystical' materials. In other words, they were understood to be operated and exist within a certain context, in this case the context of contemporary Sufi practice, and so I actively made note of their presence as ethnographic materials.

On a few occasions, people had saved handwritten notes, items or relics that had come from the highest spiritual leader of the order (*quṭb*) or spiritual leader (*shaykh*). These included advice that they had written down in response to a query they had submitted or presented before a spiritual authority, then guarded for safe-keeping or, advice written by the shaykh or *quṭb* themselves. Beyond this written advice, a handful had kept items like a napkin, tissue, a date seed and even a pillow that had all come into physical contact with a *quṭb*. This is something that is not done by all mystics, and indeed some of them found such pilfering of items to be in poor taste, but others certainly adhered to the idea that mere touch of the *quṭb* upon an item was enough to imbue it with certain qualities. I myself witnessed such activity on a number of occasions where, after speaking and rising from his chair, people would reach out to touch the seat, the tea-cup, and take the tissue that the *quṭb* had used as a napkin. As these personal collections make evident then, in certain instances these items were then held onto, transformed into relics.

In addition to the written advice, other common items were people's notes taken during sermons, advice sessions, or poetry groups. These were both their own recordings of spoken advice as well notes which encompassed their own thoughts about the Qur'an, *ḥadīth*, or poetry works. A handful of women, only women, kept a record of their dreams, one of whom wrote down dreams of loved ones who had passed on, as she said these were most dear to her (this also speaks to a popular Iranian idiom that if a deceased family member makes mention of something in a dream, you should recreate that in real life, i.e. if you dream of someone eating a particular kind of soup, you should make that soup in real life).

Finally, there were those who held photos or illustrations, often postcard size, of past *quṭb*s or saints. One claimed to have a portrait taken of the Imam Mahdi, the twelfth and last of the Shiʿi imams who is believed never to have died, but to have gone into occultation. Oftentimes people had paintings of the twelve imams in their homes, a practice common throughout Iran, but I made note of only those which were presented to me as part of their collection of mystical goods.

With this presentation of 'archival' materials in place, everything from very common poetry books to handwritten notes from *shaykh*s, the question one might ask now is: what evidence what might be garnered from these materials? What forms of knowledge were afforded to me from these private stashes, carefully hidden away and stored, in some cases for years? There is first the obvious evidence of trends and patterns that immediately come to mind: (1) what texts were popular, as was briefly touched upon in the instances of the Nurbakhsh texts; (2) what forms of information were being disseminated, transmitted, discussed, what topics were popular to ask shaykhs, everything ranging from questions in regards to passages of poetry to advice about *afsurdigī* (depression – a modern affliction) to asking about praying for someone's child to be admitted to university and in what formulations they were being answered; in other words, a whole host of topics; (3) the importance of relics and photographs. Moreover, the fact that such treasure troves existed at all demonstrates the importance of the construction of a personal library, and the long-term study, and home-based study, that mysticism often requires if not demands. Materials to return to, again and again, as bottomless sources of knowledge and emulation, open to interminable debate and interpretation as the poetry collections, or reassuring confirmations or assertions from a beloved and trusted *pīr*, teachers whose words are slightly less obtuse than the writings from the medieval canon, to also turn to again and again, in times of doubt.

The primary difference between the contents of the personal archives of the two orders was that the Nurbakhsh group tended to have only textual materials, with an occasional photograph or decorative item like the beggar's bowl (*kashkūl*), while the Sulṭān 'Alī Shāhī group had relics as well as textual materials. I would not go so far as to say that the exclusion of relics is necessarily indicative of the Nūrbakhshiyya's attitude toward shaykhs and what is often called 'saint worship' as a whole however. Indeed, my research revealed that within members of both groups the question of the potency of an item which has come into contact with a *quṭb* or spiritual authority figure – items like a tissue, a scrap of paper, a tea cup – was highly controversial. Some Sufis fervently believed in what might be called the miraculous capabilities of the *quṭb*; that they are able to fly for instance, declaring that they had seen such occurrences of flight with their own eyes or, that they were able to cure the sick, allowing the blind to see and the infertile to conceive. In contrast, other members of the same order would with equal passion deny the existence of such occurrences, declaring that these 'superstitions' (*khurāfāt*) had no place in Islam. Again, as this debate was something that was carried out by both groups, I would only venture that the greater quantity of relics within the possession of the Sulṭān ʿAlī Shāhī members was simply due to the fact that their *quṭb* remains within Iran and still adheres to a fairly active sermon schedule and hence there was the opportunity for a greater proliferation of objects that had come in contact with him.[18]

And at this point, I must clarify what I mean when I consider these personal collections as individual archives, as I have been categorising them thus far, thereby bestowing upon them the authority that often accompanies such a title. For beyond the fact that these documents have not been amassed with the direct input of any formal governing body, problems arise: these are largely unverified documents, as well as the fact that many are unoriginal and hence many of the materials would not even constitute what is commonly understood as a primary source.

Certainly, examinations of the role of the archive and its study from an anthropological standpoint have been undertaken by many in the field, most prominently John and Jean Comaroff, Ann Stoler, and Nicholas Dirks, to name a few.[19] And it is by drawing upon these sources that I am able to make the unoriginal conjecture that, in regards to the potential shortcomings of these documents, what an archive ultimately contains are the records that are or were necessary for the functioning of a world. In other words, an archive is defined less by the absolute certainty of the factual accuracy of its documents, and more by the fact that it contains documents which guarantee the continued existence of a certain practice or epistemology or system of power. And, following this logic, these forms of materials I have described thus far – divans of poetry, religious texts, exegesis, direct communications with a spiritual guide – are exactly constitutive of the kind of currency and practices by which the mystics operate. As Ann Stoler has written, the task of the student of the archive 'is less to distinguish fiction from fact than to track the production and consumption of those facilities themselves.'[20] In this way, we see how the production of these 'facilities', in this case people's homes, as well as the consumption of such materials are tied directly to Sufi epistemologies such that there is no central holding place for such documents, but rather individuated study conducted under the watchful eye of the master.

The Emergence of the Digital Archive

Moving onward, we might now shift our focus to consider Sufi practices of secrecy and the cultivation of personal archives within the broader contemporary socio-theological context. Namely, we might then ask how such practices of secrecy and record-keeping have changed in the late 20th century with the advent of the Islamic Republic. Now that the governing body has assumed a Shiʿi mantle before all other modes of authority, are such protective modes necessary as certain esoteric ideas and ways have entered the larger public imagination? Or, perhaps, as was largely the case for the Sufis during the age of the Safawids, the first Shiʿi governing body in proto-Iran, is it necessary to be more clandestine than ever? And would that be the reason for the cultivation of these personal collections of assorted materials?

As it turns out, both such conjectures prove inaccurate. For after all this discussion of concealment and dissimulation, of furtive actions and whispered messages, it must be acknowledged that contemporary Shiʿi Sufism in Iran has entered into an age of relative transparency. By transparency I mean a willingness to engage in activities which render themselves and their epistemologies more readily accessible to those outside of their immediate circles; in other words, a move towards the potential for exposure. For while the maintenance of certain practices of concealment persist, such as the archives and secret handshakes, what has marked the most significant shift in recent years is the fact that Sufis have begun to publish their sermons online. Indeed, as evidenced by the website «Sufism.ir», the Niʿmat Allāhī order has made public on the internet a treasure trove of sermons, some in audio WAV files as well as downloadable PDF files, as well as electronic versions of sacred texts, including *Pand-i Ṣāliḥ* which was referenced here. The site is not password protected in any way so that anyone who chances upon it might have access to these materials. Previously, while these sermons and some texts had existed digitally in the form of physical CDs that were available at bookstores within Sufi meeting-places (sing. *khānaqāh*), and certainly were disseminated in that fashion, I would argue that never has such a large amount of material been so readily available and so publicly available in one place.

Such a public archive might seem, after this long discussion of the care taken in the maintenance of these private archives, like an exposure of the most shocking kind. Indeed, these very passages quoted in this essay – both the writings of Ṣāliḥ ʿAlī Shāh and Nurbakhsh – which advocate the restriction of Sufi knowledge to the most specific of audiences, now suddenly exist online, unprotected and available to all. The possibilities of the technological, it would seem, has overridden the threat to the spiritual.

When questioned as to why such a decision was made, the Sufis had several reasons. The first was that the materials presented on the site were largely 'public' sermons, meaning those lectures which were delivered at the meeting-place (*khānaqāh*) on Friday mornings, rather than before any private or pre-determined group of listeners, and hence were never intended for a large audience. Indeed, this claim is given further weight in consideration of the fact that sermons occur during open meetings – meaning anyone from the street is able to enter the meeting-place and hear the words of the *shaykh*. From this, we are able to deduce that the mystical knowledge revealed by the *shaykh* or *quṭb* during these weekly sermons is specifically tailored for a 'general' audience,[21] meaning appropriate even for those who are uninitiated and not members of the order. Furthermore, the texts which are made available on these online archives were deemed 'introductory materials', or works which outlined the basic tenets of mysticism, and so did not possess anything that might overwhelm a novice on the path. Several of my interlocutors remarked however, that there was a certain danger involved in making the texts public without a teacher, but generally felt that given they were introductory texts, they could not 'cause great distress', as one Sufi put it. I can confirm too, that the first materials given to me when I first asked to learn about mysticism was in fact *Pand-i Ṣaliḥ* which, along with many others, is available at the bookstore in the Ḥusayniyya Amīr Sulaymānī in Tehran; in other words, available to anyone who decides to enter the meeting-place.

This last point, that it is available to those who have decided to enter a *khānaqāh*, rather than chance upon it, is also of significance. Indeed, the bookstore is located well inside the meeting-place complex, which is already situated away from the main road. Thus, their observation that the texts are available to those who have made the decision to come into the space, to have quite literally crossed the threshold into a designated 'Sufi space', also speaks to their next argument regarding the online availability of materials: that, although the nature of an internet archive makes it undoubtedly public, the sermons and texts were simply amassed in this way to make it as accessible as possible for the Sufis themselves. The contents of the website are intended for the Sufis, who in no way advertise the site or use it as a sort of promotional or evangelical tool; it is not linked to any other site, nor are there are offshoots anywhere. Rather, their intention was to make an online library for their members, especially those who do not live in Tehran and are unable to see the *quṭb*, so that they might have past sermons and declarations at their disposal whenever they might need them. In doing so, they give further credence to the belief and practice of individuated study within mysticism, where students and other Sufis are encouraged to read, meditate (*fikr*), and remember on their own. In this way, the mystics view the online archive as something intended exclusively for their own members, a means of delivering the words of the *pīrs* in an organised and readily accessible manner, even if the nature of the vehicle in which it is delivered possesses a capacity to open it to a much wider market.

The final reason the Sufis gave for the creation of this online archive, however, speaks directly to the fact of the public nature of the entire enterprise. Namely, that by having such a public record, the Sufis were able to clear their name, so to speak, by distinguishing themselves from any other Iranian mystical groups, particularly those who may have socio-political leanings.[22] In other words, they are able to refute any accusations made against them, particularly those saying that they to do not swear obedience to the state, by simply referring to the text which addresses them. More specifically, this is evidenced by the availability of sermons and declarations of the order that state their allegiance to Ayat Allāh Khomeini (d. 1989), their firm disinterest in politics, and their adherence to the laws of the Islamic Republic. Also published on the site are texts and sermons which address popular rumours surrounding mystics; in particular, that they utilise drugs, the use of which was banned at the turn of the century, and that they purposefully do not work but beg instead, another practice which was banned by the founding spiritual leader (*quṭb*) of the Sulṭān ʿAlī Shāhī order in the modern era. Thus, when considering this justification for online records, the archive affords the opportunity for the mystics to make public, here meaning unguarded, those accusations which have caused them the most consternation in the past.

Persistent Archives

To conclude then, we must return to the question of our initial topic of inquiry, the private archives of individual members, for the narrative of a general move towards transparency just described does not fit the continued cultivation of such collections, much less the careful way in which they are guarded. Ultimately, the question remains: why do certain mystics insist on treating their collections as secret when in fact the ideas they contain have already been revealed to an audience the scale of which they on the individual level could never even reach? Why keep such careful watch on texts which now exist within a digital format?

I would posit that the answer is twofold: first, as 'lay Sufis' or rather unranked dervishes, these are individuals who are still wary of disseminating ideas, as such a responsibility is relegated to the role of the masters (*pīr*s) as previously discussed in this chapter. As the distribution of notes, communiqués, and even texts which exist online might be seen as analogous to the distributing of ideas, they hence refrain from such activities in order to err on the side of caution.

And it is to this point that the second part of the answer speaks: that what makes such modes of guarding and concealment unusual is that through these acts of safekeeping they are protecting not only themselves, but those *outside* of mystical circles as well. As previously discussed, in the canonical literatures, the ideas must be kept secret because of their sheer potency, and the potential harm which may befall those who are not ready for such powerful mystical epistemologies. Moreover, the possibility for the inappropriate dissemination of ideas is much more likely when the concepts are being conveyed by a lay mystic, one who has not achieved the role of teacher, or master. Thus, those who have been entrusted with these mystical epistemologies yet who do not possess the capacity to teach others about 'the path', must be especially diligent.[23] And while it is true that the integrity of the group as a whole may also be at risk from the larger corruption of the ideas via their inappropriate distribution, at least in part the precautionary actions exist to shield others who may not be 'ready' for them.

Ultimately, then, perhaps what constitutes these scattered collections of written texts, photos and relics as an archive is their insistence on fulfilling the now almost classical understanding of the role of the archive: a device for exclusion, exclusion enacted here in part to preserve the sanctity of the group at the risk of the corruption of their ideas, and in part to protect those 'not ready' for mystical epistemologies. What dangers to an individual are entailed by exposure to Sufi concepts – whether it be simple confusion, the cryptic sounding 'misdirections of the soul' on the 'wrong path', or even pure madness – certainly demands more analysis than afforded here. Essentially, what must be considered is that the danger to the uninitiated, to the non-Sufi, is understood to be very real. These documents and objects became an archive when the creators of these collections decided that they must be guarded from those on the outside.

And while this last statement may contain familiar echoes of previous discussions of archival practice, it is essential to remember that the situation is further complicated in that the Sufis of Iran possess neither great influence nor great power over the 'non-Sufi world' by any standard – be it financial, theological, or political. What this fervent commitment to the safeguarding of ideas and the exclusionary measures to contain them is based upon then, is not in the potency of the group itself, but rather the perceived potency of their own epistemologies. In other words, the discourses of power that typically accompany the question of the archive persist, but here we see an instance where the act of archiving is secondary to *what* is being amassed, organised, and contained; it is both the trace *and* the thing itself or perhaps,[24] the trace that misleads. While the archival process is indeed essential here, revealing those materials deemed worthy of record and posterity as well as the mystics' need for individuated study, what the careful safeguarding of the materials ultimately reveals is the Sufis' belief in the potency contained within the ideas themselves. As seemingly dangerous and reactive as precious metals, these are ideas which contain within them the potential for the greatest and gravest consequences for Sufis: that of the fate of the immortal soul. Thus, those who house the texts which reveal the secrets for such alchemical processes, especially those not yet fully in command of them, must remain ever vigilant.

NOTES

1 Javad Nurbakhsh, *The Path: Sufi Practices* (New York, 2003).

2 There is one concept of which mention should be made here: that of *sirr*, literally the secret, or the idea that there exist forms of mystical knowledge that are contained within oneself, yet are secret from oneself. A simple definition certainly, but even this basic understanding problematises the separation of content and practice that it appears I am suggesting here. Rather than propose such a distinction, however, I only wish to focus on the latter here, due to restrictions of scope.

3 Nurbakhsh, *The Path: Sufi Practices*, p. 45.

4 Ṣāliḥ ʿAlī Shāh, *Pand-i Ṣāliḥ* (Tehran, 1372 Sh./1993), section 9.

5 For more on the significance of this relationship as related to the development and practices of Islamic mysticism, see: Michael A. Sells, *Early Islamic Mysticism* (Mahwah, NJ, 1995); J. Nurbakhsh, *Masters of the Path: A History of the Masters of the Niʿmatullāhī Sufi Order* (New York, 1980); *Sufism: Meaning, Knowledge, Unity* (New York, 1981), among others; Alexander Knysh, *Islamic Mysticism* (Leiden, 2000); Annemarie Schimmel, *Mystical Dimensions of Islam* (Chapel Hill, NC, 1975); Carl Ernst, *The Shambhala Guide to Sufism* (Boston, 1997).

6 Ṣāliḥ ʿAlī Shāh, *Pand-i Ṣāliḥ*, section 9.

7 See Seyyed Hossein Nasr, *Sufi Essays* (Chicago, 1970–1999); Henry Corbin, *En Islam Iranien. Aspects spirituels et philosophiques*, vol. 1, *Le Shiʿisme duodécimain* (Paris, 1971); Mohammad Ali Amir-Moezzi, *The Divine Guide in Early Shiʿism: The Sources of Esotericism in Islam* (Albany, NY, 1994); as well as the theological writings of the Safawid Shiʿi thinker Mullā Ṣadrā: *The Elixir of the Gnostics*, tr. W. Chittick (Provo, UT, 2002); *The Three Principles of Mulla Sadra: Divine Gnosis, Self-Realisation and the Dangers of Pseudo-Knowledge in Islam*, tr. C. Turner (Abingdon, 2016).

8 ʿAllāma Sayyid Muḥammad Ṭabāṭabāʾī, *Shiʿite Islam*, tr. S. H. Nasr (Albany, NY, 1977), p. 223.

9 For a discussion on the use of dissimulation within the writings of Imam Jaʿfar al-Ṣādiq, see Diane Steigerwald, 'La dissimulation (*taqiyya*) de la foi dans le Shiʿisme ismaélien', *Studies in Religion*, 27 (1998), pp. 38–59; M. A. Amir-Moezzi, *The Divine Guide*; 'Dissimulation', *EQ*; 'Dissimulation tactique (*taqiyya*) et scellement de la prophétie (*khatm al-nubuwwa*)', *J. Asiat.*, 302 (2014), pp. 411–438; Etan Kohlberg, 'Some Imami-Shiʿi Views on *Taqiyya*', *JAOS*, 95, 3 (1975), pp. 395–402.

10 Ṭabāṭabāʾī, *Shiʿite Islam*, p. 225.

11 The importance of the Karbala paradigm cannot be underestimated. For a discussion of its importance within contemporary Iran alone, see Kamran Scot Aghaie, *The Martyrs of Karbala: Shiʿi Symbols and Rituals in Modern Iran* (Seattle, WA, 2004); Hamid Dabashi, *Islamic Liberation Theology: Resisting the Empire* (New York, 2008).

12 Ṭabāṭabāʾī, *Shiʿite Islam*, p. 151.

13 Ṣāliḥ ʿAlī Shāh, *Pand-i Ṣāliḥ*.

14 There may have been other chapters carrying out this practice as well, but these were the locations related to me by my interlocutors. I was unable to find any shaykh or spiritual leader who could confirm or further explain the practice, only seniors who had either partaken of the practice or knew of others who had. The distances between the locations of those places reported to those who have carried out these activities are particularly curious as well, and certainly demanding of further investigation.

15 Nurbakhsh, *The Path: Sufi Practices*, p. 135.

16 For a discussion of the history of the religious endowment (*waqf*) documents of the Ḥusayniyya Amīr Sulaymānī in Tehran, see chapter five above.

17 Copyright laws in Iran are famously lax to the point of being non-existent, and such co-opting of textual materials is not unusual.

18 For more on the role of the supernatural in contemporary Iran, I would refer to Alireza Doostdar, 'Fantasies of Reason: Science, Superstition, and the Supernatural in Iran' (PhD dissertation, Harvard University, 2013).

19 See John L. Comaroff and Jean Comaroff, *Ethnography and the Historical Imagination* (Boulder, CO, 1992); Jean Comaroff, *Body of Power, Spirit of Resistance: The Culture and History of a South African People* (Chicago, 1985); Ann Stoler, *Along the Archival Grain: Epistemic Anxieties and Colonial Common Sense* (Princeton, NJ, 2010); and Nicholas Dirks, *Castes of Mind: Colonialism and the Making of Modern India* (Princeton, NJ, 2001).

20 A. Stoler, 'Colonial Archives and the Arts of Governance', in *Archival Science*, 2 (2002), pp. 87–109.

21 This is further evidenced by the common language used by the shaykh, characterised by a conversational rather than scholarly tone, peppered only lightly with Arabic words and concepts and more with anecdotes and allegories. Certainly, however, this decision to utilise colloquial language by the shaykhs requires more discussion than allowed here.

22 In particular, the website «MajzoobanNur.org» (now called «Majzooban.org») had previously contained various discussions of human rights (*ḥuqūq-i bashar*) debates on its pages alongside sermons from the Sulṭān ʿAlī Shāhī order, which had existed on CD and hence uploadable form. Information about the group running the website, including their numbers and meeting practices, remains unclear.

23 The question might inquire into whether there have been shaykhs who have imparted improper or incorrect teaching to their students. So far as my readings have shown, there have been none, an unsurprising fact as *pīr*s and saints are often considered infallible. Accounts and warnings of 'false Sufis' or pretenders, those who profess to be a shaykh or learned elder but are merely charlatans, however, are extremely commonplace.

24 Jacques Derrida, 'Archive Fever: A Freudian Impression', *Diacritics*, 25, 2 (1995), pp. 9–63.

PART THREE

RELATIONS BETWEEN SHIʿISM AND SUFISM IN OTHER SUFI LITERARY TRADITIONS

7

Sufism and Shiʿism in South Asia: *shahādat* and the Evidence of the Sindhi *marthiya*

Michel Boivin

In one of the first Sindhi-English dictionaries published in 1879, the word *marśiyo*[1] is translated as follows: 'An elegy or dirge, particularly one sung during the Muhorrum'.[2] The *marthiya*, in the Arabic form used henceforth, is an elegy composed to lament the passing of a beloved person and to celebrate his merits. When did the word enter the Sindhi language? Unfortunately, it is not possible to answer but the spread of the *marthiya* in Sindhi literature didn't start before the 18th century. This paper addresses a double issue. On the one hand, it wishes to introduce the *marthiyas* from the countryside. What does that mean? In South Asia, the *marthiya* is associated with the court culture of the main states that have flourished in the ruins of the Mughal empire. The leading school of *marthiyas* developed in Lucknow, then the capital of the state of Awadh in North India. As a matter of fact, the *marthiyas* composed by poets such as Mīr Babar ʿAlī Ānīs (Mir Anīs) (1216–1290/1802–1874) were considered as the ultimate reference for the writing of these elegies in the whole Indian subcontinent.

Another centre for the production of *marthiya* literature was the State of Hyderabad, in Deccan. The *marthiyas* schools of Hyderabad and Awadh both used Urdu, which was then becoming the *lingua franca* of the majority of Muslims in colonial India. The Urdu *marthiyas* have long attracted the interest of scholars,[3] but the focus they put on urban and Urdu *marthiyas* gave a distorted image of the art of *marthiyas*. For the *marthiya* genre was also cultivated in peripheral regions where vernacular languages were used for literature, as was introduced as early as 1978 by Christopher Shackle.[4] In studying the

Sindhi *marthiya*, this chapter wishes to address the issue of the relation between the court culture from the imperial cities and the vernacular expression of the *marthiyas*. I draw on the common cleavage used in Muslim South Asia between vehicular languages or lingua franca such as Persian and Urdu, and vernacular languages such as Punjabi, Bengali, Gujarati, Sindhi and so on.

On the other hand, it intends to address the issue of the relationship between Shiʿism and Sufism, an issue which has already been addressed in depth mainly in the context of Iran.[5] The hypothesis is that the Sindhi *marthiya* is a promising venue for such a study. It allows scrutinising the transformation of the issue of martyrdom in Sufi poetry and finally its role as a motif in Sindhi literature. Finally, the chapter wishes to shed some light on the complex process through which Shiʿi topics have nurtured the Sufi culture of Sindh, especially through the incorporation of the Shiʿi motif of martyrdom in Sufi poetry. But first, it is necessary to provide some historical context regarding both Shiʿism and Sufism in Sindh.

Historical Context

The province of Sindh, which is the southern part of the Indus Valley, was conquered by Muḥammad b. Qāsim, an Umayyad general, in 92/711.Thus, the connection of Sindh with both Sufism and Shiʿism is ancient, and one point in particular is intriguing: Sindh, located at an edge of the Muslim Empire, was very soon a privileged place for hosting *ghulāt* groups.[6] Sindh is an early land where these Shiʿis had found refuge, for example Muḥammad Nafs al-Zakiyya's son known in Sindh as ʿAbd Allāh Shāh Ghāzī (d. 156/773). Nafs al-Zakiyya was a great grandson of Ḥasan, ʿAlī's son and the grandson of Muḥammad. He claimed the imamate and rose in rebellion against the Abbasid caliph al-Manṣūr (r. 136–158/754–775) but he was killed in 145/762. After his death, his followers known as the Muḥammadiyya pretended that he was in concealment and would return to fill the earth with justice. A number among them reached Sindh and ʿAbd Allāh Shāh Ghāzī, whose shrine is in Karachi, is supposed to be his son. ʿAbd Allāh Shāh Ghāzī's *dargāh* is currently the most popular *dargāh* in Karachi.[7]

Nevertheless, the booklets in Urdu which can be found all around the shrine do not introduce Nafs al-Zakiyya as a Shiʿi leader, but as a descendant of the Prophet Muḥammad. Neither is ʿAbd Allāh Shāh Ghāzī introduced as a Sufi. It is said that he was a military commander who died fighting the infidels. It is to be noticed that his sanctity thus does not result from a Sufi affiliation, or from ascetic behaviour, but rather from sacrifice, since he died while expanding the *dār al-islām*. Furthermore, no source is quoted about his career in Sindh. However, it is interesting to observe that the interaction between a Sufi figure and the issue of martyrdom is already addressed through ʿAbd Allāh Shāh Ghāzī's veneration. Nonetheless, the cult is probably recent and the narratives framing his story may be contradictory. It implies that the figure presently accepted comes from a late reconstruction rather than from attested historical facts.

Another character related to the *ghulāt* in Sindh is Muḥammad b. al-Ḥanafiyya (d. 81/700). Muḥammad b. al-Ḥanafiyya was the third son of ʿAlī, but not with Fāṭima. He was thus not a descendant of Muḥammad. Nonetheless, after Ḥusayn's death in 680, some partisans acknowledged him as the head of the ʿAlid family. His followers, known as the Kaysanites, headed by al-Mukhtār (d. 67/687), claimed that Muḥammad b. al-Ḥanafiyya was the Mahdī, 'the rightly-guided one', although the word did not yet have eschatological connections since his return was expected imminently and not at the end of time. They also introduced into Islam the themes of occultation (*ghayba*), and return to life *(rajʿa)*.

Masʿūdī (d. 345/956) wrote that a number of Muḥammad b. al-Ḥanafiyya's descendants were settled in Sindh. One of them was the head of a dissident branch of Shiʿism and he was executed in Multan at the beginning of the 4th/9th century.[8] According to the Arab historian Ibn Khallikān (d. 681/1282), Muḥammad b. al-Ḥanafiyya's mother was a Sindhi. Furthermore, Muḥammad b. al-Ḥanafiyya was the hero of the *maqtal-nāmah*s, narratives in which he headed raids in revenge against the authors of the tragedy of Karbala. According to local traditions in interior Sindh, the Amīr Pīr *dargāh* which is run by the Ismailis is actually the tomb of Muḥammad b. al-Ḥanafiyya.

In the 19th century, the eldest son of the first Aga Khan, ʿAlī Shāh (d. 1302/1885), transformed an obscure saint into a well-known character among the early Shiʿi leaders. In the surroundings of the shrine located in interior Sindh, an inscription gives the date of 1852, without any date in the Muslim calendar. In this period, the first Aga Khan,

Ḥasan ʿAlī Shāh, was living in Bombay, but his son and heir, ʿAlī Shāh, was fond of hunting in deltaic Sindh. The reason why ʿAlī Shāh decided to dedicate the place to Muḥammad b. al-Ḥanafiyya and not to another Shiʿi leader of the early centuries of Islam is unknown. Was he already trying to separate his followers, known as the Khojas, from the Twelver Shiʿis? As a matter of fact, since Muḥammad b. al-Ḥanafiyya was not acknowledged by the Twelver Shiʿis, it left room for non-Twelver Shiʿis to construct their own distinct genealogy and consequently, tradition. Furthermore, it is well known that in the second half of the 19th century, the Aga Khans were elaborating a new tradition whose main focus was the rejection of Twelver Shiʿi references.[9]

According to Derryl Mclean, between the middle of the 2nd/8th and the beginning of the 6th/12th centuries, the balance between the Sufis and the Shiʿa was in favour of the Shiʿa, although it is not known to what extent such categories are relevant. However, it is probable that fewer than one Muslim out of five was Shiʿi. In the 4th/10th century, the Ismailis spread in Sindh and the province became an Ismaili state under Fatimid suzerainty. After its destruction by Maḥmūd of Ghaznī (r. 387–420/998–1030) at the beginning of the 5th/11th century, another wave of Ismaili proselytism reached Sindh from the 6th/12th or 7th/13th centuries onwards. Although it is not really attested by local sources, oral tradition states that the Sindhi dynasty of the Sumrās, who ruled Sindh until 751/1350, was Ismaili. In any case, it is quite probable that after the fall of Alamut (654/1256) seized by the Mongols, which occurred two years before the fall of Baghdad (656/1258), the Ismaili imams could have reactivated their oriental network.

Coincidently, in the 7th/13th century, the Ismailiyya were challenged by the Suhrawardiyya settled in Multan and Uch. Bahāʾ al-Dīn b. Zakariyyāʾ (d. 661/1262), the head of the Suhrawardīs, sent a number of his family members to Sindh to build a network which is still very active. In the Indus Valley, the Ismailis and the Suhrawardīs used similar strategies of proselytism to win new followers for their respective spiritual leaders. Briefly put, they used to settle in a place inhabited by non-Muslims, most of the time by Hindus often belonging to the lower castes. They learnt the local language and traditions, and started to compose devotional songs with the local patterns, melodies as well as narratives. They recentred the motifs on the Ismaili or the Suhrawardī spiritual leaders. For example, a song which was devoted to the Devī, one of the figures of the Hindu Goddess, was thus devoted to the imam or to the *pīr*. In addition, with the narration of the many miracles they had performed, part of the local community were gradually becoming followers. Furthermore, the imbrication of the Ismailiyya and the Suhrawardiyya is obvious in a number of polymorphous figures, like that of Pīr Shams, whose shrine is in Multan. Another relevant case is that of Laʿl Shahbāz Qalandar (d. 673/1274), who is given a double genealogy, Shiʿi and Sufi.

The interrelation between the Sufis and the Shiʿa, especially with those termed *ghulāt* by the Muslim heresiographers, dates back to the coming of the Muslims to Sindh, in the early 2nd/8th century. Despite the lack of sources, it can be assumed that such a situation is a main frame for the understanding of the special relation between Sufism and Shiʿism. On the other hand, the Ismaili Shiʿa and the Suhrawardīs faced each other as soon as in the 7th/13th century. Although their historical relations are not well documented, the Suhrawardīs probably borrowed parts of their esoteric doctrine from the Ismailis.[10]

The *Rawḍat al-shuhadāʾ* and the Issue of Martyrdom in 18th-Century Sindhi Literature

However, there is very little data regarding the spread of Twelver Shiʿism into the Indus valley and the issue has not yet merited academic attention. An explanation could be the migration from Khurasan of a number of Iranian Shiʿi lineages of sayyids to the Indus valley, such as for example the Sabzawārīs.[11] However, it is not until the 18th century that a new and strong connection appears in Sindh between Sufism and Shiʿism: Shiʿi devotional literature. This said, some questions are to be addressed: when did Shiʿi devotional literature spread into Sindh? And what was its origin, meaning was it a vernacular production from the starting point, or was it a 'translation' from another literature?

In 1970, Ghulām Rasūl Balūch published the first study devoted to the Sindhi *marthiyas*.[12] He started by introducing the Arabian tradition of *marthiyas*, followed by the Persian tradition. He understood the *marthiyas* as a recollection of great figures, turning to the Arabic root of the word. In the same work, he also quoted Persian poets such as Rūdakī (d. 329/941–2), Firdawsī (d. *ca* 410/1020) and others. For him, the first to have written a *marthiya* understood as an elegy devoted to the martyrdom of the imams at Karbala is Muḥtasham Kāshānī (d. 996/1588), better known in Sindh as Kāshī. As a matter of fact, Kāshānī integrated the pre-Islamic Arabic tradition of *marthiya*s into the context of the Muḥarram ceremonies that had received a new impetus under the Shiʿi dispensation of the Safawid state (906–1134/1501–1722). More interestingly, the poem reached the peak of its popularity during the Qajar period, from 1786 onwards.

The next chapter focused on the Urdu tradition, highlighting the role played by Mīr Ānīs, the leading author of what the author named 'urban *marthiyas*'.[13] It is true that Balūch's work did not follow academic requirements, and he started with the Urdu *marthiya*s probably because for him they were the pinnacle of the genre. Nonetheless, the most amazing point is that in the chapter devoted to the Persian *marthiya*s, Balūch did not mention a main work whose impact on Muslim South Asia is well known, the *Rawḍat al-shuhadā'*.[14]

Yet, a survey of the manuscript catalogues of the British Library collections shows that the Persian treatise played a leading role in the fabric of Shiʿi devotional production in Sindhi.[15] The *Rawḍat al-shuhadā'*, the 'Garden of the Martyrs', is a Persian martyrology of ʿAlī and his family, particularly of Imam Ḥusayn, authored by Ḥusayn Wāʿiẓ Kāshifī (d. 910/1505). But here again, a number of questions are to be raised: when did it reach Sindh? Was it really a starting point for the writing of *marthiya*s? No evidence can be found before the early part of the 18th century, knowing that Kāshifī should have written his work at the beginning of the 10th/16th century, maybe in 907/1502. There is thus a gap of more than two centuries (see fig. 7.1 over).

It could not be the same as the one on which Memon wrote a few lines in his *Sindh jī ādabī tārīkh* (History of Sindhi Literature). According to him, it would be the first Sindhi translation of the *Rawḍat al-shuhadā'*, by Maulvī Aḥmad Marḥūm in 1212/1798,[16] knowing that the first Urdu translation was implemented around 1163/1750 by Faḍal ʿAlī Faḍlī.[17] Another manuscript of the 18th century is a metrical account of the martyrdom of imams al-Ḥasan and al-Ḥusayn, by one Muḥammad Hāshim, probably a loose Sindhi translation in verses of the *Rawḍat al-shuhadā'*.[18] On his side, after he had introduced the Arab tradition and the Persian tradition of *marthiya*, Balūch divided

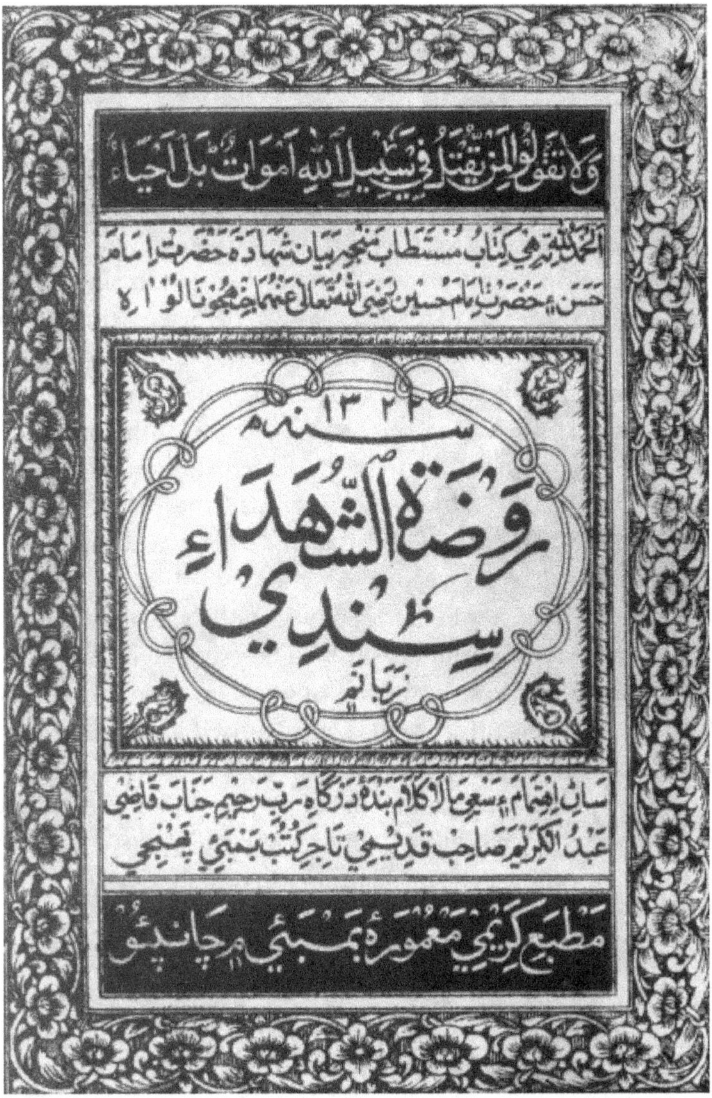

Figure 7.1. Lithograph of the *Rawḍat al-shuhadāʾ sindhī*, Bombay, 1904 (Balūch, 1992, p. 102).

the Sindhi *marthiya*s into two parts: ancient (*qadīm*) and modern (*jadīd*). He stated that the first Sindhi author of *marthiya*s is Shāh ʿAbd al-Laṭīf (d. 1165/1752), to whom I shall return.[19] The most striking point is that Balūch referred to the *Rawḍat al-shuhadāʾ* in the chapter devoted to the Sindhi *marthiya*s: he wrote a few lines on the translation in 'Sindhī *ḏohīṛans*'[20] of the *Rawḍat al-shuhadā'*, adding it was published by Jamnādās Bhagwāndās, who belonged to the Hindu literati.[21]

Of course, this does not mean that Kāshifī's work was not known before in the original Persian version but it is not known whether excerpts of it were read before the singing of the *marthiya*s, as it was performed with the Urdu version in Lucknow. However, it is obvious that the motif of martyrdom was spreading in Sindh since the early 18th century, while it was so to say unknown before, as a literary motif. Among the manuscripts of the British Museum, presently kept in the British Library, there are several versions of the death of ʿAlī Akbar, Imam al-Ḥusayn's son. One of them, from the 18th century, is an anonymous account of the death of the same ʿAlī Akbar.[22]

Amazingly, the first authors of *marthiyas* lived during the period when the Sindhi version of *Rawḍat al-shuhadā'* was completed: was there an influence of the second on the first? It is not possible to answer, but it would hardly be a coincidence. Nonetheless, the first *marthiya*s were written simultaneously in Persian and in Sindhi, but by different authors. In Persian, the *marthiya*s were introduced in Sindh by Muḥammad Muḥsin (d. 1163/1750). Himself a Shiʿi, he authored, among other works, *Tirāz-i Dānish* (The Royal Robe of Knowledge), a *mathnawī* commemorating the birth of Imam Mahdi. He was following the *tarjī'-band*[23] in his *marthiyas*.[24] But Makhdūm Tharo (d. 1160/1748) had already authored Persian quatrains in which he paid tribute to *Asad Allāh*, the Lion of God, the *laqab* of Imam ʿAlī, as well as to the memories of the martyrs of Karbala.

The spread of *marthiya* literature in Persian, Urdu and in Sindhi occurred when, after the death of Aurangzeb in 1707, the Indian subcontinent was going through turmoil. The Mughal empire was on the verge of decline. The internecine quarrels between his successors and the growing threat from the Marathas and the Sikhs opened India to new invasions. Nādir Shāh (r. 1148–1160/1736–1747) was to invade the Mughal empire in 1739, followed by the Afghan ruler Aḥmad Shāh Durrānī (r. 1159–1185/1747–1772) in the 1750s. It is tempting to see the development of laments and dirges in the local literature as mirroring the many wars in which the Subcontinent, including the Indus Valley, had suffered in the main part of the 18th century.

Furthermore, the Urdu *marthiya* blossomed at the same time at the beginning of the 18th century, for example with Muḥammad Rafīʿ Sawdā (d. 1195/1781), who was patronised by the kings of Awadh. The first ruler of Awadh, Burhān al-Mulk (d. 1143/1731), was himself of Iranian descent, and he worked hard for the spread of ʿAlid cults in his kingdom. But contrary to the *marthiya* in Urdu, the Sindhi *marthiya* was not born in a Shiʿi state, it occurred in the ʿĀdil Shāh sultans of Bijapur (894–1097/1489–1686) and the Quṭb Shāhs of Golkonda (924–1098/1518–1687),[25] who were patrons of poetry, and sometimes poets themselves. In Sindh the rulers known as the Kalhorās (r. 1112–1196/1701–1782) were Sunni, and simultaneously affiliated to a local branch of the Suhrawardiyya.[26] There is no evidence that they patronised Shiʿi rituals or literature.

In other regions like the Deccan, numerous poets composed *marthiya* from the 16th century onwards, and some even specialised in it.[27] Like other Urdu poetical forms, the *marthiya* was at first court poetry, and Haywood claims that because of its religious nature it was taken by princes to the people, to form a corporate religio-literary and social activity. It probably played an important part in the development of the *mushāʿiras* (public poetical recital or competition) which became – and still remains – a phenomenon of Indo-Pakistani literary and social life (fig. 7.2).

Sur Keḏāro as the Matrix of the Sindhi *marthiya*

The lives of the first poets of Sindh who authored *marthiyas* in Sindhi as well as in Persian are not well documented. They could have been court poets, and when they were granted royal patronage, it was not only as authors of *marthiyas*. However, the birth of the Sindhi *marthiya* occurred in the countryside. Notwithstanding, a piece of poetry will work as the matrix of the *marthiya* when inserted in a Sufi work, such as the *Shāh jo risālo* by Shāh ʿAbd al-Laṭīf. He was from a Sayyid family settled in Bulri, a small village where his great grandfather, Shāh ʿAbd al-Karīm (d. 1032/1623), was buried. After years of peregrination, Shāh ʿAbd al-Laṭīf went to settle in a remote part of the interior of Sindh where there was no village. His verses praise the simple life of the peasant.

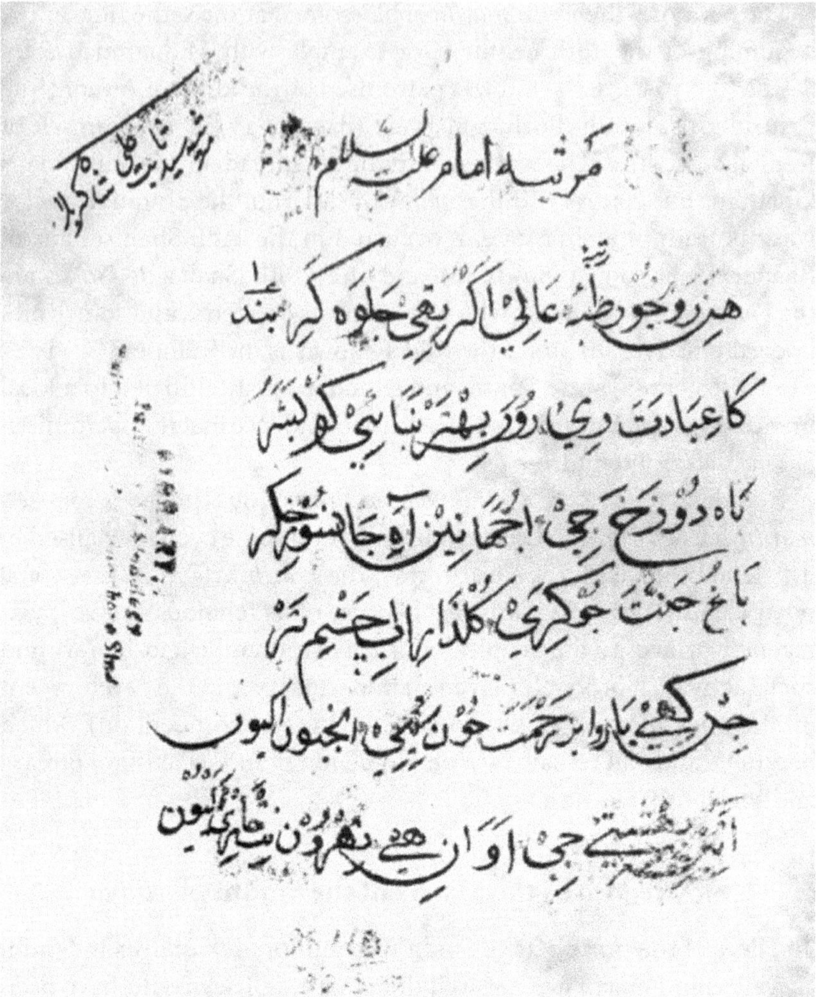

Figure 7.2. *Marthiya imām 'alayhi al-salām*, end of 18th century (Balūch, 1992, p. 88).

As Shāh 'Abd al-Laṭīf is the first to devote a full chapter to Karbala, it is necessary to examine it in detail. My contention here is to decipher the Shi'i elements. It is an easy task since the Sindhi Sufi poets who preceded Shāh 'Abd al-Laṭīf did not use any Shi'i referent, be it in the lexicon or as a literary motif.[28] Before starting, it is interesting to mention that it is not known if Shāh 'Abd al-Laṭīf was Sunni or Shi'i. It is said that some follower asked him the question. He answered: 'I am between both'. The follower said again: 'But master, there is nothing between?' Shāh ʿAbd al-Laṭīf stated: 'So I'm nothing . . .'. Despite the naivety of the story, it highlights a fundamental principle of Sufism in Sindh: Sufism is located beyond religious or confessional, or sectarian, affiliation and belonging.

The *Shāh jo risālo* is a significant sample of the *marthiya* from the countryside. It reflects the vernacularised religious culture that flourished in peripheral regions of the Indian subcontinent.[29] This is a poetry which comes from the very land (*desī*). More than to master the apex of sophistication in aesthetics as in the courtly culture of North India, the poet wishes to move the simple man of Sindh, a province where a large majority of the inhabitants were landless peasants. Also, the poet speaks directly in his poetry to the groups of local society most discriminated against, such as the dyers (*kapṛā*).[30] But since he refers to folk narratives and heroes shared by all creeds and traditions, all Sindhis felt involved in Shāh ʿAbd al-Laṭīf's poetry.

The *Shāh jo risālo* consists of 30 chapters, each centering around one topic and traditional tales which are mystically interpreted and sung in a specific melody, a *sur*. The Sindhi word *sur* is more or less the equivalent of *rāga*, namely a musical mode which is to express a given feeling, and/or to be played at a given moment of the day. In the *Shāh jo Risālo*, there is a *sur* which is of special interest, *Sur Keḏāro*. In Sindhi, the word *keḏaro* means war. It comes from a Sanskrit term with the same meaning of war. In classical Indian music, the *rāga* Keḏār is said to be associated with the god Shiva and is to be sung at mid-day. Furthermore, it is also a contemplative *rāga* and it is represented as an ascetic who is deeply absorbed in meditation. In the 17th century, the *rāga* Keḏār was one of the main *rāga*s performed at the Mughal court.[31]

In the *Shāh jo risālo*, *Sur Keḏāro* is thus the chapter on war. The whole chapter is devoted to the martyrdom (*shahādat*) of the third Shiʿi imam, Ḥusayn, who died in 61/680 at Karbala with many of his family members. A thorough study has yet to be made on the reasons for which Shāh ʿAbd al-Laṭīf introduced a Shiʿi topic in his poetry. However, this is something which distinguishes him from his predecessors in classic Sindhi Sufi poetry. One might think that it could be due to influence from Iran where the *marthiya* genre, the dirge devoted to the martyrdom of Ḥusayn and his family, was booming. The narrative of the Karbala tragedy did not, however, strictly follow the shape of the Persian *marthiya*.

The main argument of *Sur Keḏāro* is that the experience of martyrdom is the experience of meeting God. Subsequently, a sacrifice, regardless of its shape, is necessary to reach God. *Sur Keḏāro* is divided into six parts addressing four main issues. First is the coming of Muḥarram, the month of mourning of martyrdom of Ḥusayn b. ʿAlī, a trial of their love. Second is the apparent helpless state of the imams. The third part is about their bravery in fighting and the fourth part deals with their union with God after death. As in other poetry, Shāh ʿAbd al-Laṭīf involves the natural elements in the grief resulting from the martyrdom of Ḥusayn, when it is said for example that on the last day, the 10th of Muḥarram, the sky darkened. Animals can also play a leading role. For example, a bird (*pakī*) carried the message of the martyrdom to the Prophet's mausoleum in Madina. It could be a reminiscence of the *Rawḍat al-shuhadā'* where it is a pigeon that is the messenger.

Shāh ʿAbd al-Laṭīf's depictions of the different episodes of the battle are made very vivid with precise details. In the first part, he starts by giving a detailed description of the weapons. The poet also points out the bravery of the Imam's party, as well as of the women, especially when he explains how they faced the death of their husbands. In the fifth part the most heartbreaking passage is the depiction of Imam Ḥusayn's end. The red colour, which dominates the narratives through different nuances, has invaded the battlefield and the desert. Even the hoofs of Duldul, the name given to Ḥusayn's horse,[32] are all red. Finally the Imam himself is turning red:

> With blood his beard became crimson red;
> His teeth appeared red like a rose, as they profusely bled.
> Like the full moon on the fourteenth night,
> His majestic turban shone, clear and bright.[33]

The concept of martyrdom is a key concept which links Shiʿism and Sufism. Ḥusayn's martyrdom is the matrix from which the martyrdom of Sufis will be depicted, like Manṣūr al-Ḥallāj (d. 309/922) or Shāh ʿInāyat (d. 1130/1718), to whom I will return. After providing the dramatic feeling of Karbala, Shāh ʿAbd al-Laṭīf reaches his central statement when he sings:

The hardship of martyrdom (*shahādat*), Listen!
Is the day of wedding (*shādī*)

This statement which assimilates *shahādat* with *shādī* is reminiscent of death symbolised as the merging of the Sufi in God: the *ʿurs*, which also means wedding. In another verse, Shāh ʿAbd al-Laṭīf claims: 'The *rend* understands the secret (*rāz*) of Karbala'. It reinforces the identification of the Sufi, with Ḥusayn, and thus the link between Sufism and Shiʿism. It is interesting to note that Shāh ʿAbd al-Laṭīf uses the word *rend*, and not *faqīr* or any other. It refers to Sufis who are embedded in a *ṭarīqa*, limited by a specific *ādāb*. The *rend*, or the *qalandar*, is the one whose desire is only one, to be merged with God. Simultaneously, the *rend* is therefore the only one who can understand properly what occurred at Karbala. The use of this terminology is rare in Shāh ʿAbd al-Laṭīf's lexicon. Maybe it is a kind of reminiscence of a powerful Sufi saint of Sindh, Laʿl Shahbāz Qalandar, since he himself uses the word *rend* in his Persian poetry.[34]

In another verse, Shāh ʿAbd al-Laṭīf says: 'The Friend (*dust*) kills the beloved, the lovers are slain'. Here again, the Karbala tragedy is depicted with Sufi terminology. In the last part of *Sur Keḏāro*, Ḥusayn is described as the bridegroom (*ghoṭ*), a *topos* of Sindhi Sufi poetry which is most of the time attributed to Muḥammad: 'With flower-embroidered dress, O man, be prepared for the wedding'. The bridegroom has decorated his horse, as in Sindhi custom, and he rides for his fatal battle. The issue of the *ghoṭ* is also addressed in regard to Qāsim, who was to be married before he died. A passage of the *sur* pictured him with his uncle Ḥusayn. The latter asks him to rescue his companions and he comes in his beautiful bridegroom garments. In another passage, the word *ghoṭ* (pl. *ghoṭan*) is given to all the companions who, besides Ḥusayn, are to die as martyrs. There is a beautiful and tremendous description of the final part of the battle, when the *ghoṭ*s and their horses (*ghoṭan ghoṛan*) are all intermingled in the savagery of the battlefield.

The metaphor of the wedding is therefore crucial for the integration of Shiʿi elements in Shāh ʿAbd al-Laṭīf's Sufi poetry. The chapter ends with a meaningful verse in which the integration is achieved:

> 'They have become annihilated in God, with Him they have become He'.

Shāh ʿAbd al-Laṭīf employs the Arabic expression *fanāʾ fiʾllāh* which is, interestingly, coupled with, and thus reinforcing, the Sindhi version of *fānī thiya*. The poet carries his argument through associations since he started by associating *shahādat* with *shādī*, and he ends the *sur* in associating *shahādat* with *fanāʾ*. In concluding *Sur Kedāro*, Shāh ʿAbd al-Laṭīf exhorts God to provide him the vision of the martyrs, in a typical Sufi mood. It is noteworthy that here, he doesn't use the Persian word *dīdār*, although one can find it in other *surs*, but the very Sindhi verb *dekhāraṇ*. In referring to this main Sufi achievement, Shāh ʿAbd al-Laṭīf definitively embodies Shiʿi elements into Sufi poetry.

Briefly put, Shāh ʿAbd al-Laṭīf expresses Ḥusayn's martyrdom (*shahādat*) with the Sufi lexicon and main trope. In this respect, it is relevant to see it as the Sufi poet's attempt to capture the emotion of Karbala, as if reaching *fanāʾ fiʾllāh* was only possible by performing a self-sacrifice. Ḥusayn's *shahādat* thus works as a metaphor whose aim is to prove that *fanāʾ fiʾllāh* cannot be realised without the sacrifice of the self. Along the way, he merged Ḥusayn's *shahādat* with that of a number of Sufis who sacrificed their lives in different circumstances.

Devotional literature in Sindhi gives evidence of how Shiʿism and Sufism are interwoven there. It appears that Shāh ʿAbd al-Laṭīf uses Sufi terminology to describe the tragedy of Karbala. Furthermore, the main achievement of his verses is the identification of Ḥusayn with Sufi figures, martyrs and others. It is possible that the identification process of Husayn with a Sufi figure has been reinforced by historical circumstances, both regional and South Asian at large.

The *marthiya* as a Genre of Sindhi Poetry

Regarding regional history, a major event occurred in 1197/1783: a Baluch clan, the Ṭalpūrs, seized power and interestingly, founded a state which was divided into three distinct territories, each of them ruled by a king (*mīr*) established in a separate capital, at Hyderabad in Sindh, Khairpur and Mirpur, presently known as Mirpur Khas. Almost all the Ṭalpūr princes of Sindh were Twelver Shiʿis. Not only did they patronise Shiʿi rituals as well as Shiʿi buildings such as the *imāmbārās*,[35] but a number of them wrote *marthiyas* and other poetry.

The first author who specialised in writing *marthiyas* in Sindhi is Thābit ʿAlī Shāh (d. 1224/1810). He was twelve years old when Shāh

ʿAbd al-Laṭīf passed away. Thābit ʿAlī Shāh was born in Multan, but settled in the holy city of Sehwan Sharif with his father Madar ʿAlī Shāh. He was a sayyid who wrote poetry in Persian, Urdu and Sindhi. He was patronised by the Ṭalpūrs and lived at the court of Hyderabad. It was at the expense of the king that he was able to make a pilgrimage to Karbala and the shrines of all the imams. In 1805, he was sent by the *mīr* of Hyderabad as an ambassador to the king of Iran, Fatḥ ʿAlī Shāh Qājār (r. 1211–1250/1797–1834).

His *marthiya*s are usually filled with Persian and Arabic expressions and terms but he also produced pure Sindhi poetry. They are still sung during the procession of Muḥarram in the main cities of Sindh. Furthermore, Thābit ʿAlī Shāh is also the author of a *maddāḥ*, praise to a saintly figure, devoted to Laʿl Shahbāz Qalandar, which is sung for Imam ʿAlī's birthday inside his shrine. His *marthiya*s move both Muslims and non-Muslims to tears. Although he composed some verses on the martyrdom of the imams in Persian, he was nicknamed the 'Ānīs of Sindh' for his Sindhi *marthiya*s. In his verses which follow generally the form aaabb, Thābit ʿAlī Shāh uses all the references of the genre, naming Ṣaḥab Duldul, ʿAlī's horse, and focusing mainly on the fate of ʿAlī Akbar, one of Ḥusayn's sons. He praises the sacrifice (*qurbān*) they have performed and often quotes the famous *Lā fatā illā ʿAlī lā sayf illā dhū'l-faqār*, 'there is no hero except ʿAlī, there is no sword except *dhū'l-faqār*'.[36]

From the time of Thābit ʿAlī Shāh, the *marthiya* was a genre of Sindhi poetry. Richard Burton is probably the first to mention it as one of the four genres with *maddāḥ*, *munājāt* and *lānat* which are 'common to all the Moslem world', to which he added five others 'more original'.[37] After the fall of the Ṭalpūrs in 1258/1843, other leading Shiʿi families patronised the authors of *marthiya*s, or sometimes they themselves authored *marthiya*s, without these always being published. A good example is that of Makhdūm Muḥammad Zamān Ṭālib al-Mawlā (d. 1993), a scion of the powerful *khāndān* of the Makhdūms of Hala.[38]

The spread of a vernacular form of the *marthiya*s did not prevent the existence of a courtly *marthiya* expressed in Persian. It does not seem that the Persian *marthiya*s were very common in Sindh before the 19th century. After the Ṭalpūrs were defeated by the British in 1843, the states of Hyderabad and Mirpur Khas were suppressed; the

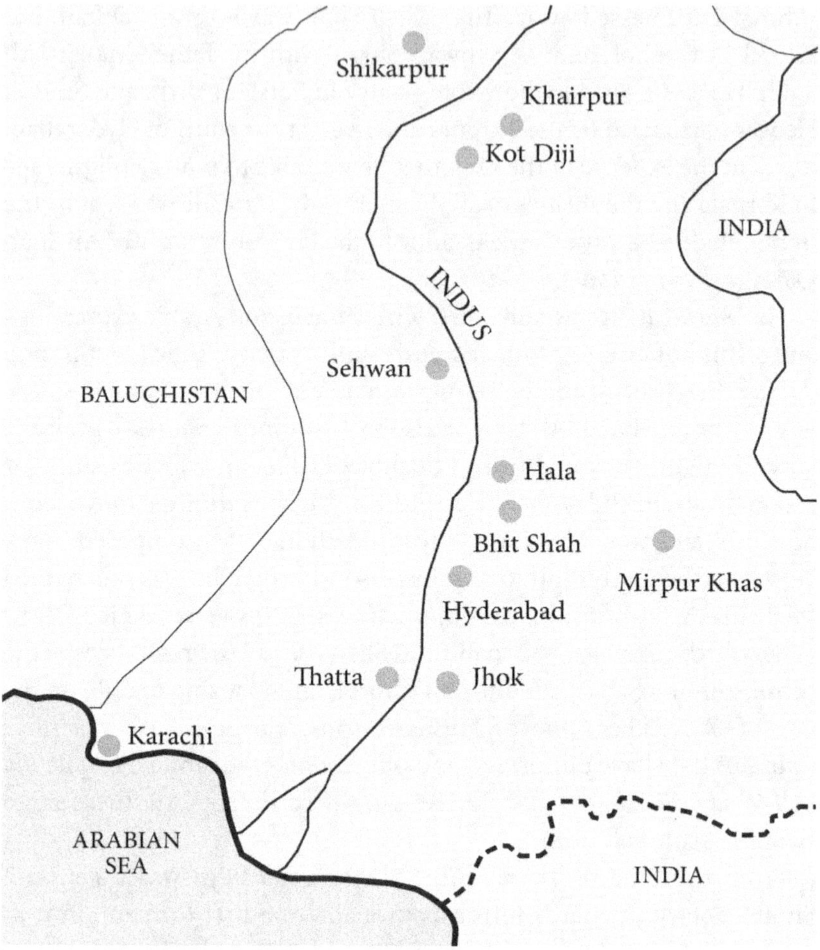

Figure 7.3. Map of Sindh showing the main places mentioned.

state of Khairpur was thus the sole princely state of Sindh ruled by a Shiʿi Ṭalpūr up to 1955, when it was incorporated into Pakistan. During British colonisation, Khairpur became a hotbed of Shiʿism in Sindh. In the last decades of the 19th century, especially during the long reign of Mīr ʿAlī Murād (r. 1257–1311/1842–1894) and that of his successor, Mīr Fayḍ Muḥammad (r. 1311–1326/1894–1909), magnificent palaces were built, such as the Faizi Mahal, as well as beautiful *imāmbārās* and *taʿziyyas*,[39] mainly in the capital, Khairpur, and in Kot Diji, another main residence of the *mīrs* (fig. 7.3).[40]

As Sadarangani pointed out, since the Shiʿi Ṭalpūrs broadly patronised poetry, many Sunni poets wrote in praise of Imam ʿAlī and the martyred imams: 'In the circumstances it becomes difficult for the reader to determine from the works of a poet of the Ṭalpūr Age whether he was a Sunni or a Shiʿi (. . .)'.[41] Mīr Nāṣir Khān Ṭalpūr (d. 1260/1845), a son of Mīr Murād ʿAlī Khān the *mīr* of Hyderabad, was nonetheless himself a Shiʿi who wrote with the pen name of Jaʿfarī. After the British conquest, he was exiled like all the Ṭalpūr princes. He stayed in Calcutta and longed to be buried in Karbala instead of Bengal. In his verse, Jaʿfarī still echoes the assimilation of martyrdom with the wedding with God: 'The blood of the self-sacrificing lover is henna for the beloved's hands!' (fig. 7.4)

Figure 7.4. A *taʿziya* kept by the Ṭalpūrs in Kot Diji, late 18th or early 19th century (©Michel Boivin, 2014).

Despite the dwindling of patronage after the British took control of Sindh, the Ṭalpūr school of Persian poetry did not end. However, there was no special literary form used for the lament. In this context, the use of the word *marthiya* comes from the overall topic rather than from a literary genre. Also, one can find hardly any works that are devoted totally to martyrdom. The best example of this trend is Mīr Sābir ʿAlī (d. 1264/1868) who praised ʿAlī in his verses, figured as *Shāh-i mardān*, to reach self-realisation. One could say it was thus the most common trope of Persian poetry of Sindh in general.

Sachal Sarmast and the Junction of Ḥusayn's *shahādat* with the Sufi Figure of the Martyr

During the last days of Mughal domination in Sindh a Sufi, Shāh ʿInāyat, rose to prominence. He travelled around India, and was initiated into the Qādiriyya and the Suhrawardiyya in Bijapur or Burhanpur. He settled into a life of devotion to God in the village of Jhok, not far from Thatta but on the eastern bank of the Indus River. His reputation of being a high-level mystic spread all around Sindh and in Jhok he provided free land to the peasants who quickly flocked to the place. The bonded farmers of many of the local landlords reached Jhok.

In 1126/1715, the sayyids of the neighbouring villages were given permission by the Mughal governor of Thatta to attack Jhok. Many of the dervishes sacrified their life for their master, Shāh ʿInāyat. In 1127/1716, a new Mughal governor was posted in Thatta after which the Kalhoṛas took northern Sindh under their control. Yār Muḥammad Kalhoṛo was keen to expand his control throughout Sindh. In the summer of 1128/1717, he started a campaign against Jhok, probably with the consent of the Mughal governor. In January 1129/1718, Shāh ʿInāyat decided to surrender to spare the life of his dervishes. He was executed and his head was sent to Delhi.[42]

Shāh ʿInāyat's martyrdom gave birth to many legends in Sindh. The Suhrawardī Sayyid Mīr Jān Muḥammad (d. 1167/1754) from Rohri clearly alluded to Shāh ʿInāyat's martyrdom.[43] He was present at Jhok when it was decided to put him to death. Many other Sufi poets will echo the tragic event in the late 18th and early 19th centuries. Of course, it is not possible to claim it can explain the spread of Kāshifī's work on the martyrdom of Karbala. It is nonetheless undeniable that his martyrdom paved the way for the incorporation of *marthiyas* into Sufi poetry.

Another Sufi poet was a follower of Jhok Sharif. Dalpat Ṣūfī (d. 1842) was a Hindu from Sehwan Sharif. He belonged to the Merāṇī family who used to perform the *mendī* ritual[44] for the death anniversary of Laʿl Shahbāz Qalandar. Dalpat regularly visited Jhok Sharif but he spent the last years of his life as a recluse in Hyderabad. His Sindhi poetry is still much acclaimed in Pakistan and in India. In Persian, he wrote a *mathnawī* entitled *Jang-nāmah* where he deals with the martyrdom of Shāh ʿInāyat as well as with the different phases of the struggle for the eradication of the *nafs-i ʿammāra*, the lower or carnal soul, otherwise known as *jihād-i akbar*, the biggest fight.[45] To some extent, one can surmise Dalpat gave a renewed version of the *Sur Keḏāro* where Shāh ʿInāyat seizes the figure of Imam Ḥusayn, knowing the main issue is to introduce martyrdom as the *fanā' fi'llāh*. However, Shāh ʿAbd al-Laṭīf's language is far more sophisticated that Dalpat's. The latter wrote in simple and very clear Sindhi and he thus contributed to the massification of the issue of *shahādat* among the Sindhis.

Throughout the decades, many hints show that Kāshifī's work was still a main reference regarding the issue of martyrdom in Sindhi poetry. Still in 1278/1862, the *Rawḍat al-shuhadā'* was translated into Sindhi as found in a manuscript kept by the Khojas, the followers of Aga Khan I, Ḥasan ʿAlī Shāh (d. 1298/1881).[46] The Khojki[47] collection of Harvard University provides many samples with *marthiyas* devoted to the imams or their family members, such as Qāsim, Ḥasan's son who was to marry Ḥusayn's daughter. Others are devoted to ʿAlī Aṣghar or ʿAlī Akbar, and even to female figures such as Bībī Khānūm or Sakīna.[48] Other *marthiyas* deal with the martyrdom of some direct ancestors of the Aga Khans. For example, there is a *marthiya* on Shāh Khalīl Allāh, Aga Khan I's father, who was assassinated in Iran in 1232/1817.

Interestingly, there are also devotional pieces known as *vāvīlās*, the Sindhi word for lament, which are attributed to Aga Khan I. In the beginning of the 19th century, the Khojas were among the specialists of *marthiyas* in Sindh. According to Richard Burton: 'They are fond of the Marsiya, or elegiac poetry on the subject of Hasan and Hosayn's martyrdom; such compositions are common among them (. . .)'.[49] In this case, it is interesting to see that although Kāshifī still works as a model, simultaneously, the *marthiyas* were re-oriented to assist the Aga Khan's approach to leading the Khoja caste.[50]

In parallel with Shāh ʿInayāt's *shahādat*, another Sufi martyr was framed into a pattern. According to local historians, a famous martyr paid a visit to Sindh in the early 10th century: Manṣūr al-Ḥallāj (d. 309/922), who died on the gallows in Baghdad because he said publicly that he was God: *anā al-ḥaqq* (lit. 'I am the Truth') in Arabic. Officially, he was accused of being a heretic but the mystics as well as the common people in Sindh claim that it was because he had reached the divine stage. According to Schimmel, Ḥallāj's importance was highlighted first in the lines of the Qādirī mystics,[51] but in Sindh, the motif could have known a new dynamic with the *shahādat* of Shāh ʿInayāt. Ḥallāj was probably a popular figure but nonetheless, it is with Sachal Sarmast (d. 1241/1826), himself a Qādirī, that he was transformed into a trope of Sufi poetry.[52] Although he did not die on the gallows, Sachal Sarmast was known in Sindh as 'Manṣūr Thānī', the second Manṣūr.

Sachal is considered by Balūch to be an author of *marthiyas* belonging to the old school.[53] In his verses, Sachal highlighted the bravery of Ḥusayn and his companions and relatives. He also praises Qāsim's wedding as a prelude to the marriage of the martyr with God. All these references can be seen as reformulations of Shāh ʿAbd al-Laṭīf poetry. Nonetheless the innovation he brought concerns the assimilation of Ḥallāj's death with Ḥusayn's martyrdom. The most striking point is that the focus is put on the martyrdom itself, as if it was a new shape of Ḥusayn's *shahādat*. Sachal Sarmast associates the state reached by Ḥallāj with a triumph. It is thus clear that divinity is the finality of the Sufi path. He also pointed out that sacrifice is but a *sine qua non* condition to reach the state of divinity:

> My head I am ready to sacrifice
> Like this will suffice.[54]

Sachal was only the first of many Sufi poets who referred to Ḥallāj's martyrdom, such as Faqīr Qādir Baksh (d. 1288/1872), a Qādirī Sufi from northern Sindh, better known as Bedil, his son Bekās (d. 1299/1882) or Rakhiyyal Shāh (d. 1358/1940). Once again, martyrdom is a trope of Sufi poetry in the 19th century and other Sufi poets also tried to associate the martyrdom of Ḥallāj with that of Ḥusayn. The construction of Ḥallāj as a trope attracted the interest of a Hindu from Sehwan who published a biography in 1915.[55]

In the mid-19th century, Bedil wrote a pastiche in Persian of the famous *Rawḍat al-shuhadāʾ*. Bedil composed poetry in Sindhi, Siraiki, Urdu and Persian. He also wrote Sindhi *marthiyas*, and consequently he is well represented in Balūch's anthology. His verses are very simple such as:

> When Shāh as a guest (*mihmān*), appeared at the battleground of Karbala,
> The wave of grief (*dard*) and agony (*gham*) highly prevailed there![56]

In his verse, Bedil reproduces the associations operated by Shāh ʿAbd al-Laṭīf whose aim is to implement a fusion between both figures, the Shiʿi imam and the Sufi. He even reinforces the mystical interpretation of Karbala in diminishing the very real depiction of the battle, the wounds, the bleeding of the fighters etc. He proceeds in putting together opposite couples of feelings, such as sadness (*soz*) and love (*piyār*), or pain (*dard*) and love (*dil*).[57] The goal is to show Karbala's lesson that pain and sadness are but a step on the way of divine love.

Mīrzā Qalīch Beg and the Final Bridging of Shiʿism and Sufism

While the trope of *shahādat* was incorporated with Sufi poetry, the spread of the *marthiyas* as a distinct literary genre did not end. A Ṭalpūr *mīr*, Ḥasan ʿAlī Khān (d. 1324/1907), was an author of fine *marthiyas* where he mostly focused on *shāhīdan jo gham*, the word *gham* referring to the last part of the *majlis*, when the narrative gives the more striking details of the martyrdom, inducing tears of grief in the audience.[58] Another Ṭalpūr, Mīr ʿAbd al-Ḥusayn Sangī (d. 1342/1924) also composed *marthiyas* although his work is composed mostly of *ghazals*. He was the grandson of the last *mīr* of Hyderabad, Mīr Nāṣir Khān Ṭalpūr, who was defeated by General Napier at the battle of Miani in 1258/1843. The final incorporation of Shiʿi *shahādat* as a trope of Sindhi poetry is obvious with the work of a Hindu poet, Parsrām Ḍiyāʾ (d. 1377/1958), where one can find reference to Imam Ḥusayn's martyrdom.

At the beginning of the 20th century, the *mīrs* of Khairpur were among the leading figures of the Indian Shiʿi community. In 1928, Mīr ʿAlī Nawāz Khān Ṭalpūr, whole ruled Khairpur from 1921 to his death in 1935, was the president of the All India Shiʿa Conference held in Calcutta, and as such, he was asked to deliver the presidential address (fig. 7.5). Since the late 19th century, the *mīrs* of Khairpur had patronised the building of *imāmbārās*, following the mainstream process centred on Lucknow, tagged by Justin Jones as the building of a 'Shiʿi *qawm*', namely a distinct Shiʿi community. Some of the Shiʿis went so far as to publicly oppose what they saw as the Sunni-run Muslim League.[59]

Mīrzā Qalīch Beg (d. 1929), was a leading intellectual of Sindh, and was very close to the *mīr*, both being Shiʿa. He was a member of the Anjuman Shiʿa Conference, a local branch of the All India Shiʿa Conference, and Mīr ʿAlī Nawāz Khān invited him several times to be his *wazīr* or prime minister but he politely declined the offer. Mīrzā Qalīch Beg was probably the first scholar to take an interest in Shiʿi devotional literature in Sindhi. Knowing the involvement of both Mīr ʿAlī Nawāz Khān and Mīrzā Qalīch Beg, through their membership of the *anjumans*, one can surmise that their concern was to locate the Shiʿism of Sindh in the wake of this Shiʿi reappraisal.

As a matter of fact, in 1925 Mīrzā Qalīch Beg was the first editor of Thābit ʿAlī Shāh's work (*dīwān*), mostly comprised of *marthiyas*.[60] The title was simply *Marthiya Thābit ʿAlī Shāh jā*, or *The Marthiya of Thābit ʿAlī Shāh*.[61] The process of shifting such a poetry genre from the oral corpus, unless manuscripts had been copied, to a published corpus, obviously has a manifold meaning. It occurred more than half a century after the first Sindhi poetry was published, the famous *Shāh jo risālo*, in 1866. Being Shiʿi was thus not an issue in Sindh prior to the 20th century. The main impact of publishing Thābit ʿAlī Shāh's *marthiyas* was both to represent him as the Ānīs of Sindh, and to anchor the Shiʿi community into a unique devotional corpus with which they can be identified. This construction didn't prevent the process of incorporating Shiʿi elements in Sufi poetry in which Mīrzā Qalīch Beg played a leading role. Apart of the *marthiyas* he had himself written,[62] Mīrzā Qalīch Beg published in 1929 a compilation of Sindhi *salāms* and *nuḥās* titled *Tuḥfa-yi imāmiyya, The Gift of the Imāmis*.[63] Consequently, after he had edited Thābit ʿAlī Shāh's *marthiyas*, he felt the need to focus on a

Figure 7.5. Mīr ʿAlī Nawāz Khān Ṭalpūr (d. 1935), *mīr* of Khairpur from 1921 to 1935.

more popular type of Shiʿi literature, which referred to the *majlis* itself, which is the commemorative assembly.[64] The *salāms* are the salutations or benedictions, used especially in the context of the *majlis* as an identity marker of the nascent Shiʿi *qawm* to refer to the opening part. The *nuḥās* are elegies commemorat-ing one of the martyrs of Karbala, mainly chanted during the *mātm*, when the devotees beat their chests. This title is the one given in the British Library catalogue, while the title of the copy kept by the Institute of Sindhology, University of Sindh, Jamshoro, does not include *salām ʿayn nuḥā*. However, there is no place and the date as stated in the introduction is 1919, instead of 1929 as it is put in the British Library copy.

However, the copy kept by the Institute of Sindhology does not include any *salām* or *nuḥā*. The book is mostly a compilation of *marthiyas*, almost 80 percent of the whole, dedicated to the main characters of the Karbala tragedy, including Ḥusayn, ʿAbbās, ʿAlī Akbar, ʿAlī Aṣghar and others. There are other poetic genres, such as *rubāʿiyyāt*, *naʿt*, or *manāqib*. The book ends with different *khuṭbas*, including one for *ʿīd ghadīr*, and finally the *duʿā* of the Twelver Shiʿis in Sindhi.

Mīrzā Qalīch Beg's publications on Shiʿism in Sindhi were a new building-block in the development of the Shiʿi *qawm* of Sindh. Beyond his interest into Shiʿi devotional poetry, Mīrzā Qalīch Beg played a fundamental role in the ongoing process of integrating Shiʿi tropes in Sufism. He could thus not depart from what was the main characteristic of Shiʿism of Sindh, its entanglement with Sufi poetry. In his *Lughat Laṭīfī*, he gave the most important words and expressions of the *Sur Keḏāro* with a Sindhi explanation. It shows a picture of the Shiʿi tropes in Sufi poetry at the beginning of the 20th century. The Shiʿi tropes he pointed out can be classified in three parts. He starts with the military vocabulary. Many words are used for introducing Karbala as a war; first of all is *jang*, but many other Sindhi words are also used.

For example, there is the interesting word *piṛu* for Karbala which is explained as *jang jo maydān*.[65] The name of *piṛu* was also given to the place where the artefacts to be paraded for Muḥarram were kept, also known as *imāmbārā*. Beside this, another trope is that of the Prophet's offspring. Beg gives many words related to the Prophet Muḥammad's daughter and grandchildren. Fāṭima is referred to as a protective figure, she is *bībī*, the princess, or *jannat khātūn*, the Queen of Paradise. Another topic highlighted by Beg is that of *shām*. For him, Karbala is *shām walāyat*.[66] The word *shām* means evening, and also 'historical' Syria, present day Lebanon and Palestine. In Shiʿi context, the mention of the word predicts the terrible suffering that Ḥusayn's little daughter will have to undergo upon reaching Yazīd's capital in that land.[67] But in Sindhi, the word *shām* is also used in a metaphorical way to express the idea of a place of refuge. It is obviously this last meaning Beg was referring to: Karbala as *shām walāyat* means that Karbala was the place where both Ḥusayn and through him the institution of the imamate took refuge, before being slaughtered by their enemies.

After partition, a new thread was added to the tapestry of Shiʿism in Sindh. A number of Muslims who migrated from India in 1947, known as Muhājirs, were Shiʿis, especially those coming from the northern cities including the Shiʿi centres of Lucknow and Amroha, but also from Hyderabad in Deccan. There is thus an interesting connection in relation to the encounter between the Sindhi Shiʿis and the Muhājir Shiʿis. Muhājir Shiʿism was an offspring of the courtly Shiʿi culture expressed in Urdu. In Sindh, although the Persian school was centred in the Khairpur courtly culture, Shiʿism was mainly interwoven with Sufi poetry.

Regarding the encounter between the two Shiʿisms, a key figure was ʿAllāma Rāshid Turābī (d. 1392/1973). According to Hyder, Turābī was probably the best *dhākir* of the Indian subcontinent.[68] He was born in Hyderabad (Deccan), and graduated from the Shiʿa College of Lucknow. He migrated to Pakistan in 1949 and was much acclaimed for the thousands of *dhikr*s he delivered in many countries, and was acknowledged by the main Shiʿi clerics from Iran and Iraq. Although, he was fond of Mīr Ānīs and Mīr Taqī Mīr (d. 1224/1810), Turābī was not a specialist of *marthiya*s but nevertheless, through his many *dhikr*s, he was acclaimed as a main specialist on the issue of martyrdom. His fame attracted the interest of the rulers of the Khairpur State, who invited him to deliver *dhikr*s. Finally, the last *mīr* of Khairpur, Mīr George ʿAlī Murād Khān Ṭalpūr, married one of ʿAllāma Rāshid Turābī's daughters.

A recent publication by a Sindhi scholar, Khādim Ḥusayn Sūmro, still gives the *Sur Keḏāro* as the source of Sindhi *marthiya*s. More than half of the book is devoted to the Sindhi text of *Shāh jo risalo* with an Urdu translation.[69] The second part proposes almost 70 authors of Sindhi *marthiya*s, with a very short biographical notice and the quotation of a few verses. Of course, Sūmro gives excerpts from Thābit, Sachal, Bedil or Beg. Although they are the most popular poets of Sindh, Sūmro treats them like the less known *marthiya* authors.

His main wish obviously is to give access to Sindhi *marthiya*s to the Urdu-speaking inhabitants of Sindh. In the second part, Sūmro introduces the *marthiyas*' authors, and gives an Urdu translation of excerpts of their works. The book can be seen as an attempt to bridge

Shiʿism expressed in Sindhi and Shiʿism expressed in Urdu from northern India and the Deccan. Nonetheless, the Muhājirs still sing Mīr Ānīs's *marthiyas* in Urdu, in Karachi, Hyderabad, and in all other cities of Sindh where they settled after partition.

Conclusion

The *marthiya* appears simultaneously in the literature of Sindh both in Persian and in Sindhi. There is evidence of the role played by Kāshifī's *Rawḍat al-shuhadāʾ*. It was translated into Sindhi in the 18th century and one can find Sindhi versions in different collections. In Shāh ʿAbd al-Laṭīf's *Shāh jo risālo*, the chapter *Sur Kedāro* definitively incorporated the motif of Ḥusayn's martyrdom in Sufi poetry. This is obviously a watershed in Sindhi Sufi poetry and also in Sindhi literature. Furthermore, in giving a detailed description in Sindhi, Shāh ʿAbd al-Laṭīf claims that martyrdom, or sacrifice in general, paved the way for union with God, known as *fanāʾ fī'llāh* in Sufi parlance. One can say that martyrdom thus became a trope. But beyond the issue of literature, two events can also explain the spread of the *marthiya*.

First is the decline of the Mughal empire after Aurangzeb's death. The following invasions largely contributed to the spread of insecurity into Sindh. Second, in the late 18th century, a Baluch clan, the Ṭalpūrs, who were Twelver Shiʿis, seized power and ruled Sindh. As soon as they seized power, they started to patronise Shiʿi poets and Shiʿi ceremonies. A number of the Ṭalpūr dynasty members were themselves poets and the main specialist of *marthiyas* in Sindhi flourished thanks to the liberality of the Ṭalpūr rulers of Hyderabad. Thābit ʿAlī Shāh rose to fame and still today, his *marthiyas* form the bulk of the mourning songs performed for Muḥarram. After the British conquest of 1258/1843, the Princely State of Khairpur became the last territory of Sindh where the Shiʿi poets were patronised.

In this context, the word *marthiya* was used for any work of literature devoted to the martyrdom of Imam Ḥusayn and his family at Karbala. Sometimes, the vernacular Sindhi word *wāwīlā* was also used. In the wake of Shāh ʿInāyat's martyrdom, one can probably observe a shift where the figure of martyrdom is a Sufi, but whose martyrdom is framed on the pattern of Imam Ḥusayn at Karbala. It started with

Dalpat Sufi's *Jang-nāmah* centred on Shāh ʿInāyat, and it was more fully articulated with Sachal Sarmast focusing on Manṣūr al-Ḥallāj's martyrdom.

In the early 20th century, there was an attempt to build a Shiʿi *qawm* in Sindh through the publication of *marthiyas* and *nuḥās*, and the involvement of the leading Shiʿa of Sindh in a wider process spreading all over colonial India. Later, despite the coming of North-Indian Shiʿa after 1947, who were Urdu speaking, the main characteristic of Sindhi *marthiya* is still its embodiment of Sufi poetry, although one cannot deny the parallel development of a distinct tradition, enhanced by some powerful Shiʿi families from interior Sindh. The latter is today only expressed in Sindhi since the use of Persian has totally vanished.

NOTES

1 Although the right word in Sindhi is the masculine *marśiyo*, the Persian and Urdu form *marśiya* (Arabic, *marthiya*) is increasingly predominant even in Sindhi literature. The vernacular words are quoted according to the Sindhi language and transliterated according to Ali S. Asani, *The Harvard Collection of Ismāʿīlī Literature in Indic Languages: A Descriptive Catalog and Finding Aid* (Boston, 1992).

2 G. Shirt, U. Thavurdas and S. F. Mirza, *Sindhi-English Dicitionary* [sic] (Karachi, 1879), p. 773.

3 For a synthesis, see J.A. Haywood, 'Marthiya. 4. In Urdu Literature', *EI2*, vol. 6, pp. 610–612; and Syed Akbar Hyder, *Reliving Karbala. Martyrdom in South Asian Memory* (Oxford, 2006). Also Andreas D'Souza, 'The Influence of the *Rawḍa-ḫwānī* on the development of *Naḥwa* in the Deccan', in Denis Hermann and Fabrizio Speziale, ed., *Muslim Cultures in the Indo-Iranian World during the Early-Modern and Modern Periods* (Berlin, 2010), pp. 167–180.

4 In 1978, Christopher Shackle published a paper on Multani *marśiya*, and in 2003 a small book on Siraiki *marthiya*. His work was obviously one of the earliest dealing with the *marthiyas* out of the scope of Urdu culture. See Christopher Shackle, 'Multani marsiya', *Der Islam*, 55, (1978), pp. 281–311; *Siraiki marsiya* (Multan, 2003). Regarding the Sindhi language, a short article was recently published on the depiction of the *Imām Mahdī* in Sindhi poetry, mostly based on the works completed by members of the Kalhora lineage who ruled Sindh in the late 18th century; Zulfiqar Ali Kalhoro, 'The depiction of Imam Mahdi in Sindhi Poetry of Sindh (Pakistan)', *Rupkatha Journal*, 9, 3 (2015), pp. 162–171.

5 Among the copious literature devoted to this issue, see Henry Corbin, *En islam iranien. Aspects spirituels et philosophiques. Tome III. Les fidèles d'amour. Shî'isme et soufisme* (Paris, 1972), pp. 149–375.

6 The *ghulāt* (plural of *ghālī*), 'extremists' or 'exaggerators', is the name given by the Shiʿi imams and the Muslim heresiographers after them to the Shiʿa who divinised Imam ʿAlī. See Marshall G. S. Hodgson, 'Ghulāt', *EI2*.

7 Michel Boivin, *Historical Dictionary of the Sufi Culture of Sindh in Pakistan and in India* (Karachi, 2015), p. 73.

8 Derryl McLean, *Religion and Society in Arab Sind* (Leiden, 1989), p. 130.

9 I have discussed this topic in detail in my book. See M. Boivin, *Les âghâ khans et les Khojah: Islam chiite et dynamiques sociales dans le sous-continent indien contemporain* (Paris, 2013), pp. 73–76.

10 Regarding this, see the pioneering work by Hasan Alī Khan, drawing mainly on architecture, *Constructing Islam on the Indus. The Material History of the Suhrawardi Sufi Order, 1200–1500 A.D.* (London, 2016).

11 Rubīnah Tarīn, *Shāh Shams Sabzawārī sawānah ḥayāt awr āthār* (Multan, 2007), pp. 33–43.

12 Ghulām Rasūl Balūch, *Sindhī marṡiya nivesī* (Hyderabad, 1970).

13 Ibid., p. 21.

14 For example, Hyder claims that the impact of the *Rawḍat al-shuhadāʾ* on the Urdu *marthiyas* is due to the focus put on the wedding of Qāsim with Ḥusayn's daughter, Sakīna, knowing that weddings were a very popular topic of Indian culture. See Hyder, *Reliving Karbala*, p. 28. On the issue of the wedding, see also Karen G. Ruffle, 'Karbala in the Indo-Persian Imaginaire: The Indianizing of the Wedding of Qāsim an Fāṭima Kubrā', in D. Hermann and F. Speziale, ed., *Muslim Cultures in the Indo-Iranian World*, pp. 181–200.

15 James Blumhardt, *Catalogue of the Marathi, Gujarati, Bengali, Assamese, Orya, Pushtu and Sindhi Manuscripts in the Library of the British Museum* (London, 1905).

16 Muḥammad Ṣādiq Memon, *Sindh jī ādabī tārīkh* (Shikarpur, 2005), p. 201.

17 The Urdu translation was titled *Karbal kathā* (The Narrative of Karbala). According to Hyder, it is one of the first prose works of North Indian Urdu. See Hyder, *Reliving Karbala*, p. 29.

18 J. Blumhardt, *Catalogue of the Marathi, Gujarati, Bengali, Assamese, Orya, Pushtu and Sindhi Manuscripts in the Library of the British Museum*, p. 38. While Kalhoro acknowledges Muḥammad Hāshim as one of the earliest Sindhi authors of *marthiyas*, he did not pay attention to the role played by the *Rawḍat al-shuhadāʾ*; Zulfiqar Ali Kalhoro, 'The Depiction of Imam Mahdi in Sindhi Poetry of Sindh (Pakistan)', p. 165.

19 His theory would be supported some years later by Annemarie Schimmel, who wrote a short paper on the Sindhi *marthiyas*: See A. Schimmel, 'The Marsiya in Sindhi Poetry', in Peter Chelkowski, ed., *Taʾzieh: Ritual and Drama in Iran* (New York, 1979), pp. 210–221.

20 The *d̠ohīṛo* or *dohā* is a kind of Sindhi verse, whose shape varies greatly.

21 Balūch, *Sindhī marṡiya niwīsī*, p. 37.

22 Blumhardt, *Catalogue*, p. 39.

23 *Tarjīʾ-band* is a form similar to that of the *ghazal* and the *qaṣīda*, in that the first half of the opening line rhymes with the second half, but the first halves of the following lines are free from this constraint.

24 H.I. Sadarangani, *Persian Poets of Sind* (Jamshoro and Hyderabad, 1987), p. 100.

25 For a general introduction to the cultural life in the Deccan sultanates, see R.M. Eaton, *Sufis of Bijapur, 1300–1700: Social Roles of Sufis in Medieval India* (Princeton, NJ, 1978); Shrīrām Sharmā and Mubāraj al-Dīn Rafat, *ʿAlī ʿĀdil Shāh kā kāwy-sāgrah* (Agra, 1958).

26 Boivin, *Historical Dictionary*, pp. 220–221.

27 Haywood, 'Marthiya. 4. In Urdu Literature', p. 610.

28 Qāẓī Qāẓan, Shāh ʿAbd al-Karīm and others. See Memon, *Sindh jī ādabī tārīkh.*

29 For a more elaborate discussion on the issue of vernacularised religious culture, see Boivin, *Historical Dictionary*, pp. 12–17.

30 In 18th-century Sindh, social organisation was very much influenced by the caste system. Groups such as the dyers belonged to the untouchables, who were considered impure.

31 *The Raga Guide*, 1999, p. 5.

32 Amazingly, Duldul is the name given here to Ḥusayn's horse at Karbala, although usually it is the name of ʿAlī's horse. Nowadays, as least in the processions of Muḥarram, Ḥusayn's horse is called *Dhu'l-janāḥ*.

33 Ghulām ʿAlī Allānā, *Four Classical Poets of Sind* (Jamshoro, 1983), p. 70.
34 Laʿl Shahbāz Qalandar (d. 673/1274) is said to be the descendant of Ismāʿīl, the sixth imam Jaʿfar al-Ṣādiq's son who was acknowledged as imam by his followers thus known as Ismailis. He was himself a *qalandar* and as such, he travelled in the heartland of the Islamic world, before reaching the Indus Valley soon after the Mongol invasion. He finally settled in Sehwan Sharif, in Sindh, and his mausoleum is one of the most popular in Pakistan. A number of artefacts which are currently revered on different occasions relate him with Shiʿi sacred figures, as for example the fourth imam Zayn al-ʿĀbidīn. See Michel Boivin, *Artefacts of Devotion. A Sufi Repertoire of the Qalandariyya in Sehwan Sharif, Sindh (Pakistan)* (Karachi, 2011), pp. 94–95.
35 In Sindh, the *imāmbārā* is the building where sermons are delivered during the first ten days of Muḥarram, and where the different artefacts which are paraded are kept.
36 Balūch, *Sindhī marthiya niwīsī*, p. 53. The word *dhū'l-faqār* is the name of ʿAlī's sword. Regarding the word *fatā* or *javānmard* in Persian, see Mohsen Zakeri, 'Javānmardi', *EIR*, vol. 14, pp. 594–601.
37 Richard Burton, *Sindh and the Races that Inhabit the Valley of the Indus* (Karachi, 1851), pp. 78–79. Interestingly, Nabī Bakhsh Balūch classified *marthiya* among the devotional songs with *maddāḥ, munājāt mawlūd*, but he didn't publish any of them, contrary to the other three categories: Boivin, *Historical Dictionary*, p. 95–96.
38 Makhdūm, no date. The Makhdūms of Hala are the descendants of Makhdūm Nūḥ, a Suhrawardī Sufi who played a leading role in 16th-century Sindh, working as a scholar of Islam, and also as a mediator with political power. See M. Boivin, *Historical Dictionary of the Sufi Culture of Sindh*, pp. 206–208.
39 In South Asia, *taʿziyya* is the name given to the replica of the tomb of Imam Ḥusayn carried in procession during Muḥarram.
40 Interestingly, the craftsmen belonged to Hindu castes from Jodhpur, in neighbouring Rajputana (nowadays Rajasthan), and Bahawalpur. Regarding architecture, it is said the Ṭalpūrs were influenced by their northern neighbours, the Sikhs of Punjab, particularly the famous architect Bhai Rām Singh.
41 Sadarangani, *Persian Poets of Sind*, p. 152.
42 See a detailed description of Shāh ʿInāyat's martyrdom in Schimmel's pioneering work: Annemarie Schimmel, *Pearls of the Indus. Studies in Sindhi Culture* (Jamshoro, and Hyderabad, 1985), pp. 156–165.
43 Sadarangani, *Persian Poets of Sind*, pp. 102–103.
44 The Sindhi word for henna, a main symbol of a wedding in South Asian culture. As noted above, a saint's death is represented as his wedding with God.
45 Sadarangani, *Persian Poets of Sind*, p. 204.
46 Asani, *The Harvard Collection*, p. 80.
47 Khojki is the name given to the script used by the Khojas. It belongs to the Laṇḍāor 'clipped' scripts used by merchant communities in Sindh and in Punjab.
48 Asani, *The Harvard Collection*, p. 164–166.
49 Burton, *Sindh and the Races*, p. 250.
50 Boivin, *Les âghâ khans et les Khojah*.
51 See the paper Schimmel has devoted to the issue: Schimmel, *Pearls of the Indus*, pp. 87–149.
52 Sachal Sarmast authored poetry in a number of languages such as Persian, Hindustani, Siraiki and Sindhi. I use here his work in Sindhi: Sachal Sarmast, *Risālo Sachal Sarmast (Sindhī kalām)*, ed. ʿUmān ʿAlī Ānṣārī (Kandiyaro, 1997).
53 Balūch, *Sindhī marthiya niwīsī*, pp. 43–44.
54 Allana, *Four Classical Poets of Sind*, p. 105.
55 Deumal Arumal Sehwānī, *Manṣūr jī ḥayātī* (Hyderabad, 1915).
56 Balūch, *Sindhī marthiya niwīsī*, p. 64.
57 Ibid., p. 68.

58 Ibid., p. 74.
59 On the construction of a 'Shiʿi *qawm*' in North India, see the detailed analysis in Justin Jones, *Shiʿa Islam in Colonial India: Religion, Community and Sectarianism* (Cambridge, 2011). Regarding the representation of the Shiʿa in the Muslim League, a number of them were among the founders of the organisation in 1906, such as Sulṭān Muḥammad Shāh, the third Aga Khan. Later on, their number decreased but this issue is still to be investigated. On the early years of the Muslim League, see Francis Robinson, *Separatism among Indian Muslims, 1860–1923* (Cambridge, 1974).
60 Memon, *Sindh jīādabī tārīkh*, p. 162.
61 Balūch, *Sindhī marthiya niwīsī*, p. 102. Nothing more is known about it, and needless to say I was not able to see a single copy.
62 Ibid., pp. 94–96.
63 Mīrzā Qalīch Beg, *Tuḥfa-yi imāmiyya: salām ʿain nuḥā* (Shikārpūr, 1929).
64 The *majlis* is a commemorative assembly held in honour of the martyred members of the Prophet's family.
65 Mīrzā Qalīch Beg, *Lughat laṭīfī* (Hyderabad, 1913), p. 133.
66 Ibid. p. 137.
67 Hyder, *Reliving Karbala*, p. 27.
68 See for example Hyder's detailed analysis of Turābī's *dhikr*: Hyder, *Reliving Karbala*, pp. 40–42. He also claims that Turābī's fame was so powerful that he was represented as a member of the *ahl al-bayt*.
69 Khādim Ḥusayn Sūmro, *Sur Keḏāro awr Sindhī marśiya kī mukhtaṣar ijmālī tārīkh* (Sehwan Sharif, 2000), p. 15–110.

8

Red Sulphur, the Great Remedy and the Supreme Name: Faith in the Twelve Imams and Shiʿi Aspects of Alevi-Bektashi Piety

Rıza Yıldırım

Introduction

The Alevi-Bektashi[1] community forms the largest religious minority in modern Turkey. They are known for their latitudinarian interpretation of Islam which is marked by an indifferent attitude towards the prescribed rules of Islamic law. In that sense the Alevi-Bektashi creed is usually labelled as 'heterodox'. Concerning their sectarian position, common wisdom deems Alevi-Bektashi tradition to lie within the fold of Shiʿi Islam. Given the central place of Imam ʿAlī, the *ahl al-bayt* (People of the House or the Household of the Prophet), the twelve imams, and the offspring of the Prophet in their theology and religious praxis, a strong pro-ʿAlid colouring is obvious. In particular, the dominance of the twelve imams in their faith and rituals forms the hallmark of Alevi-Bektashi tradition. However, one should not confuse their tradition with Twelver Shiʿism, for they have certain differences both in terms of creed and socio-religious structure. Close scrutiny reveals that though a convergence towards a Shiʿi mode of theology is apparent, a recognisably distinct flavour shows through in Alevi-Bektashi theology and religiosity.

Alevi-Bektashi sources put special stress on the primordial essence and divine nature of the Prophetic family and the twelve imams. One may safely argue that both the Alevi creed and their socio-religious stratification are built on the concept of *ahl al-bayt*. A careful study of literary and oral sources shows that the omnipotent image of the imams shaped in a mythological, esoteric and supernatural aura dominates Alevi-Bektashi theology in its entirety. In that respect, Alevi-Bektashi tradition bears familial resemblances with other Shiʿi traditions. It is important to note, however, that the imam as perceived by the Alevi-Bektashi faith has significant differences from the theory of the imamate established by institutionalised Twelver Shiʿism.

Though a general sense of difference is known to modern scholarship, the details of similarities and differences between the Alevi-Bektashi tradition and Twelver Shiʿism have not been studied on the basis of literary sources.[2] Alevis and Bektashis are rather considered under the generic title 'extremist' or *ghulāt* Shiʿism, a medieval Islamic term which is no longer useful for understanding the true nature of these pro-ʿAlid religious traditions in the Islamic world. This study attempts to explore the place and role of the Prophetic family and progeny in the Alevi-Bektashi faith in the early modern period, relying mainly on literary sources produced by these communities. Within this framework it also addresses the question of the relationship between Alevi-Bektashi tradition and the greater Shiʿi world.

Sources

There are many unstudied manuscripts in private and public libraries that deal with the Alevi-Bektashi faith and its rituals. Among them, a special treatise, albeit in multiple versions, is of particular importance for the sake of this study. Usually titled *Kitāb-i khuṭba-yi dawāzdah imām* (*The Book of the Sermon of the Twelve Imams*), these treatises are devoted to explaining the sacred nature of the Prophetic genealogy and its central place in the faith. I have used four copies of this work for this study, none of which has been published or studied before. We have every reason to believe that there are many more manuscript copies in private possession waiting to be explored. The contents of the four copies I consulted show trivial variations that can safely be ignored here. It should also be noted that the bound volumes that include *The Book of the Sermon of the Twelve Imams*, which indeed combine several treatises, also show familial resemblance. In each compilation (in manuscript form) *The Book of the Sermon of the Twelve Imams* is bound just before *Manāqib-i Shaykh Ṣafī* commonly known as the Qizilbash *Buyruq*.[3] The dates of copying of these four manuscripts vary from the early 17th century to the mid-19th century.[4]

The text itself suggests that it was written in the mid-15th century by the famous Ḥurūfī author ʿAbd al-Majīd b. Firishtah (d. 864/1459–60). The author identifies himself as follows,

> I am the poor and humble ʿAbd al-Majīd, son of Firishtah; I translated this *Sermon of the Twelve Imams* (*Khuṭba-yi dawāzdah imām*) from Arabic to Turkish. O dear ones! Know that the age is not permanent; you should make effort to attach yourselves to the shirt-tail of the Prophet so that you can achieve your wishes. One is with his beloved.[5]

ʿAbd al-Majīd b. Firishtah is a well-known prolific Ḥurūfī author. His *ʿIshq-nāmah*, partially a Turkish translation of Faḍl Allāh Astarābādī's (d. 796/1394) *Jāwidān-nāmah*, and other works such as *Ākhirat-nāmah* and *Hidāyat-nāmah* became famous among Ottoman Ḥurūfīs.[6] The above record makes it clear that the original Arabic text constituting the core of our source was written well before the mid-15th century. Unfortunately, ʿAbd al-Majīd b. Firishtah gives no information about his source except to say that it was in Arabic.

Āqā Buzurg al-Ṭihrānī (d. 1389/1970), a prominent Twelver bibliographer and biographer, gives some valuable information in his voluminous *al-Dharīʿa ʿalā taṣānif al-shīʿa*, a comprehensive bibliography of Shiʿi works, that might help us to identify ʿAbd al-Majīd's source. In the entry '*dawāzdah imām*', Ṭihrānī states that '*Khuṭba al-ithnā ʿashariyya*' is a generic title for treatises of entreaty that include invocations and eulogies of the twelve Shiʿi imams. The number of such treatises mushroomed during the early period of Safawid rule (907–1135/1501–1722). In *al-Dharīʿa*, Ṭihrānī lists eleven different treatises titled '*dawāzdah imām*', nine of which were written during the Safawid era by several authors such as Muḥsin al-Fayḍ al-Kāshānī (d. 1090/1679), Mīrzā Qawām al-Sayfī, and Mawlā Muḥsin Kirmānshāhī. One of the two treatises that antedate the Safawid epoch is attributed to Shaykh Muḥyī al-Dīn Ibn ʿArabī (d. 638/1240), which seems barely relevant to our source. The other one, however, deserves particular attention. This is a treatise of prayer and eulogy attributed to Khwājah Naṣīr al-Dīn Ṭūsī (d. 672/1274). Ṭihrānī reports from an unidentified source that Aḥmad Sawijī once asked his master Mullā

Aḥmad Ardabīlī (d. 993/1585) about the best way of beseeching God. Ardabīlī responded to his pupil that the best prayer is the *Khuṭba-yi dawāzdah imām* of Khwājah Naṣīr al-Dīn Ṭūsī, which is reported to have been taught him by Imam ʿAlī in his dream. Ṭihrānī also mentions a commentary of this work that was written by Sayyid Abū ʿAlī b. Sayyid Muḥammad Bāqir.[7]

Elsewhere in the same voluminous work Ṭihrānī says that he saw in the private library of a certain Sayyid Āqā al-Tustarī in Najaf, a manuscript called *Khuṭba-yi dawāzdah imām* from the 10th/16th or 11th/17th century. The text includes eulogies and salutations to the Prophet and the other thirteen impeccable ones (Fāṭima and the twelve imams), as well as a short biography of each one. Apart from the fourteen impeccable ones, this work also includes statements of good wishes for Ḥamza b. ʿAbd al-Muṭṭalib (d. 4/625), Jaʿfar b. Abī Ṭālib, and the sultan (ruler) of the time. As Ṭihrānī cites, the author is recorded as ʿAlī b. Hammād in the text. After summarising his personal eyewitness account, Ṭihrānī goes on to state that when Shāh Ismāʿīl ascended to the throne in Tabriz in 907/1501, he ordered that the first *khuṭba* be read in the name of the twelve imams, a practice that had no precedent in Islamic history.[8] He adds on the authority of ʿAbd al-Aḥad b. Burhān al-Dīn b. ʿAlī al-Sīrjānī (10th/16th century), who presented his exegesis of the sura of Rūm to Shāh Ṭahmāsb (r. 930–984/1524–1576), that *al-Khuṭba al-ithnā ʿashariyya* had been widespread since the early years of Safawid rule. Despite Nāṣīr al-Dīn Ṭūsī's alleged treatise, Ṭihrānī concludes that the early Safawid period must be accepted as *terminus post quem* for the appearance of eulogy-prayer texts under the generic title '*Khuṭbat al-ithnā ʿashariyya*' or '*Khuṭba-yi dawāzdah imām*.'[9]

The testimony of *The Book of the Sermon of the Twelve Imams* does not corroborate Ṭihrānī's conclusion, for it was written sometime in the mid-15th century as a translation of an earlier Arabic text. Hence, it seems reasonable to take the beginning of the tradition rather earlier, at least back to Naṣīr al-Dīn Ṭūsī's treatise. Indeed we have extant manuscripts titled *Duʿā-yi dawāzdah imām* that are allegedly copies of Ṭūsī's treatise.[10] In line with Ṭihrānī's description, the *Duʿā-yi dawāzdah imām* of Ṭūsī consists of eulogies of the twelve imams, including neither biographical information nor mythological stories about the imams.[11] Therefore, the mythological accounts that are recorded by ʿAbd al-Majīd have no counterparts in Ṭūsī's entreaty-eulogy treatise, whereas the Arabic eulogy part at the end looks as though it was extracted from the latter. Taking into account all currently available evidence, then, it seems reasonable to assume that the original Arabic text, which formed the core of 'Abd al-Majīd's treatise, might have been a work built upon the tradition of Ṭūsī's treatise, if not the treatise of Ṭūsī itself. More concrete conclusions on the issue, however, require further research into contemporary sources as well as the discovery of new source materials.

The second problem with *The Book of the Sermon of the Twelve Imams*, no less perplexing than the former, is the question of translation. It is less than clear to what extent the extant text is a translation of the original Arabic work. A close examination suggests that the 17-page text is by no means a literal word-to-word translation. One may further argue that the text is not even a liberal translation in its entirety, but includes substantial additions to the original tradition. It is only towards the middle of the treatise that 'Abd al-Majīd b. Firishtah mentions his name and states that he translated *The Sermon of the Twelve Imams*. Up until this point, he explains that the Prophet and his progeny (the twelve imams) are the reason for the creation of existence, that love for them is obligatory upon true believers, that they have such an exalted status in God's eyes that their intercession between men and God will never be rejected, and that their high status was envied even by great prophets such as Moses. He concludes this first part of the treatise by stating, 'These twelve names constitute *The Sermon of the Twelve Imams* (*Khuṭba-yi dawāzdah imām*). Whoever reads it in the morning, twelve thousand angels watch him until nightfall; whoever reads it in the evening shall be saved by angels from all accidents and troubles.'[12] He also adds that reading *The Sermon of the Twelve Imams* as a request for intercession after prayers or at any other time, leads to the acceptance of requests by God and the forgiveness of sins. It is only after that he says 'I translated this *Sermon of the Twelve Imams* from Arabic into Turkish.' So the general structure of the narrative creates an impression that the six pages before this statement constitute an introduction to the *Khuṭba*, which is presented in the following pages, and hence, the introduction must have been authored by 'Abd al-Majīd himself through compilation from other, unidentified sources.

Furthermore, careful scrutiny of the rest of the text still casts doubts on its fidelity to the original Arabic version. Even the possibility that ʿAbd al-Majīd presented his own work as a translation of a fictive Arabic text, simply to enhance the authority of the text, cannot be omitted entirely. All in all, the most credible assumption regarding the root source of ʿAbd al-Majīd is to trace it back to Ṭūsī's *Khuṭba-yi dawāzdah imām*. In the meantime, ʿAbd al-Majīd's work had presumably benefitted from other veins of tradition regarding the virtues of the twelve imams. For example, a passage referring to the famous Shaykh Najm al-Dīn Kubrā (d. 617/1220–1) not only proves the availability of other sources to ʿAbd al-Majīd, be it oral or written, but is also helpful for determining the *terminus ante quem* for *The Sermon of the Twelve Imams* to be known in the form of eulogy and prayer. The text relates on the authority of Shaykh Najm al-Dīn Kubrā that if a person reads *The Sermon of the Twelve Imams* after praying five times and bestows its spiritual reward (*thawāb*) to the spirits of the Imams, his wishes regarding either this world or the next will be accomplished by God.[13]

Ṭihrānī makes no mention of Najm al-Dīn Kubrā in summarising the contents of *Khuṭba-yi dawāzdah imām* that he examined and catalogued. In the same vein, Naṣīr al-Dīn Ṭūsī's known entreaty-eulogy treatise does not include that information. This can be taken as proof that ʿAbd al-Majīd used various sources other than the central treatise he translated, some of which might well have been oral transmission. Indeed, throughout the text, there are other additional indications supporting this presumption. As said above, *Khuṭba-yi dawāzdah imām* of Ṭūsī is composed of eulogies, invocations and praises of the Prophet and the imams. Our treatise, in contrast, mentions the names of the twelve imams only in the short Arabic prayer-eulogy or blessing (*ṣalawāt*) at the end of the text. The main body of the Turkish text relates three mythological stories all dealing with the sacred history of the human being, none of which appears in Ṭūsī's treatise. The central theme of all these stories is the ontological superiority of the fourteen personages (i.e. Muḥammad, Fāṭima and the twelve imams) as a group, or more precisely speaking as a single entity in essence, over all other creatures, including prophets. Intimately linked to this idea, they are also presented as intercessors in God's affairs on earth and in the heavens. These mythologies shrouded around the primordial essence of the fourteen impeccable ones have no antecedent in the earlier treatise of Ṭūsī. Likewise, the *Khuṭba-yi dawāzdah imām* treatises written under Safawid rule show no verbatim similarity to our treatise, even though a common core is maintained.

Nevertheless, as will be demonstrated below, the mythological stories recorded in the Alevi *khuṭba* have close resemblances to older Shiʿi traditions recorded in classical sources of Imami Shiʿism. This brings us to the conclusion that ʿAbd al-Majīd borrowed certain materials from Ṭūsī's tradition, which seems to have constituted particularly the last eulogy part, and developed his treatise around this core. Nevertheless, he extended his work with further materials derived from other traditions, oral or written, that was current amongst ʿAlid milieus of the time, rejuvenated especially among some Sufi circles. It was presumably the same ʿAlid milieu that cast the grassroots of the Qizilbash movement which emerged during the same period. As a matter of fact, this treatise would later become one of the cornerstones of Qizilbash religious literature.

It should be added as a last point that one comes across sporadic short biographical notes on the imams' historical lives in various Alevi-Bektashi compilations kept as manuscripts. These notes, however, never go beyond a very short summary of the known information about the imams' births and deaths, which are usually oriented to highlight that they were all martyred in one way or another.[14] These summary reports add little to our knowledge regarding the perception of the imams in the Alevi-Bektashi tradition, especially on their supra-human aspects.

A Brief Historical Framework: The Rise of the Faith in the Twelve Imams in the Ottoman Realm

The question when, how, and through which channels did Shiʿi ideals penetrate into lands under Ottoman dominion has yet to be elucidated. Nor is the present study, which limits its aims to analysing the content of *The Book of the Sermon of the Twelve Imams* in comparison with common Shiʿi wisdom literature, framed to address this thorny question. In the meantime, a brief historical framework is required to contextualise my principal source material and the knowledge it provides us with.

The infusion of ʿAlid sentiments and ideals into Anatolian Islamic piety was a long, gradual and multifaceted process. The earliest ʿAlid elements can be detected in sources from the 14th century, if not earlier.[15] Although the scarcity of sources from medieval Anatolia inhibits historians from reaching concrete conclusions, it seems safe enough to argue that a recognisable ʿAlid tinge existed in several forms of Islamic religiosity.[16] One may even postulate that popular Islamic piety in medieval Anatolia was prevalently marked with ʿAlid sentiments. The important point must be made, however, that this piety fell outside both well-defined Shiʿi and Sunni templates of theology and doctrine.

The ʿAlid-dominated piety of Anatolia in the Middle Ages was distinguished by (a) a very strong sentimental memory of Karbala and related revenge narratives (in the form of epics) such as the *Abū Muslim-nāmah*, (b) an entrenched love for the family of the Prophet or *ahl al-bayt*, and (c) a special emphasis on the arch-saint and arch-warrior image of ʿAlī b. Abī Ṭālib. One should note, however, that despite sporadic mention in a few sources from that period, belief in the twelve imams and even the concept of 'Imam' are far from being central elements of Islamic piety at the time. It is only by the mid-15th century that we see an upsurge of twelve imams belief in contemporary sources, a process innately linked to the rise of Shiʿi colouring, particularly amongst Sufi milieus. Elsewhere, I have discussed how the 15th century marked a watershed for the Shiʿitisation process of the *futuwwa* tradition.[17] It is in a *futuwwat-nāmah* written in the mid-15th century that we see, for the first time in *futuwwa* literature, the mention of the twelve imams as exalted spiritual guides and sources of sacred religious knowledge.[18]

Likewise, the earliest reference to the twelve imams in Bektashi literature also appeared synchronously in a poetry compendium presumably written in the second half of the 15th century.[19] Ṣādik Abdāl, a self-declared Bektashi dervish educated and initiated under the auspices of famous Bektashi shaykh Sayyid ʿAlī Sulṭān, provides us with the earliest eulogies of the twelve imams known in Turkish poetry.[20] As will be explained below, this type of poem would soon turn into a genre called '*duwaz-imām*' (Turkish deteriorated pronunciation of Persian '*dawāzdah imām*') in the spiritual-didactic poetry of Shāh Khatāʾī (Shāh Ismāʿīl) and become fundamental prayers of Qizilbash rituals and religiosity.

It is very interesting to note that early Bektashi sources such as the hagiographies of eminent masters and the *Maqālāt* attributed to Ḥājī Bektāsh (d. 669/1270–1), which were all produced prior to the mid-15th century, do not include even the slightest reference to the twelve imams. We know, however, that belief in the twelve imams became a pillar of the Bektashi creed in the course of the 16th century.[21] In this context, the poems of Ṣādik Abdāl stand as an important witness to the all-encompassing process of Shiʿitisation taking place on the ground amongst the 'peripherised' or 'heterodox' Sufi milieus in the Ottoman realm.[22] We have records showing that this current penetrated even into Sufi traditions accredited by the Ottoman Sunni regime.[23] *The Book of the Sermon of the Twelve Imams* should be treated in this conjuncture. From that point of view, it constitutes another cornerstone shedding light upon the process of Shiʿitisation of certain Sufi milieus in the 15th-century Ottoman empire.

Ahl al-bayt and Twelve Imams as the Core of Faith

At the centre of the Alevi-Bektashi faith lies belief in the divine nature of the family of the Prophet (*ahl al-bayt*). When going through sources one immediately notices the double-layered meaning of the term in the Alevi-Bektashi tradition. The core meaning comprises five personages, called *panjāh-yi āl-i abā'*, 'the five people of the cloak.' Derived from the famous Prophetic tradition to be cited below, these personages are Muḥammad, ʿAlī, Fāṭima, Ḥasan, and Ḥusayn. In the second layer, the twelve imams are also considered as part of *ahl al-bayt.*[24] In many cases, even the whole progeny of the Prophet is considered an integral part of *ahl al-bayt.* Scrutiny of Alevi-Bektashi sources reveals that the perception of the members of *ahl al-bayt* goes far beyond historical figures who lived in a particular time period. They are rather believed in as extensions of the divine. They metaphysically exist all the time and constitute the hidden pillars of the worldly order.

The status of the twelve imams is exalted to such a level that their names became the primary constituent of Alevi-Bektashi sacred utterances called *duwaz-imām.* A *duwaz-imām* is in essence a poem which mentions and praises the twelve imams. The term is adopted from Persian '*dawāzdah imām*', meaning the twelve Imams, into

Turkish pronunciation. Although the prayer of *duwaz-imām* constitutes the backbone of all Alevi worship, we do not yet know when and how this specific prayer developed. What is certain is that the overwhelming majority of *duwaz-imāms* in circulation among the Alevi community bear the name of Khatāʾī, the penname of Shāh Ismāʿīl, who is also the earliest amongst *duwaz-imām* authors. Alevi individuals read *duwaz-imām* in critical moments of their daily life as a way to interact with divinity, usually for the purpose of securing divine grace or protection. For example, at the beginning of the day, in the evening, just before going to sleep, and in any time of trouble, they read *duwaz-imām*. Abundantly clear is that by doing so they seek the grace and intercession of the twelve imams in their temporal and spiritual affairs. One should also note that *duwaz-imām* constitutes one of the basic pillars of the *djem* ritual,[25] without which any *djem* cannot possibly be realised.

As discussed above, besides variations from Ṭūsī's work and other *Khuṭba-yi dawāzdah imāms* written during the Safawid period, a concrete common lore – which consists of blessing (*ṣalawāt*), eulogy and invocations of the Prophet and the twelve imams in Arabic – seems to have lingered in the Alevi-Bektashi tradition. I have already postulated that ʿAbd al-Majīd developed his treatise around this shared core knowledge. It must be this core that has been taken as a collection of sacred utterances and adopted into Qizilbash/Alevi rituals as the principal constituent of the prayer. However, those Arabic phrases were not easy to memorise and even pronounce for the Turkoman populace, who formed the social basis of the Qizilbash movement. This problem seems to have been solved by composing Turkish poems which mention and praise the Twelve Imams. These poems came to be known under the generic title *duwaz-imām* or *duwāzdah imām*.

Ahl al-bayt as the Cause and Primordial Essence of Existence

The opening sentences of *The Book of the Sermon of the Twelve Imams* read:

> Know that God says '[O Muḥammad!] Had you not been, I would not have created the heavens and earth', . . . meaning 'O Muḥammad! You are my ultimate beloved in both worlds; I

> created you for Me and the Eighteen Thousand Realms for you! Had you not been, I would not have created the earth, the heavens, and those in between!' It is because of this fact that we are obliged to love him [Muḥammad] from deep in our hearts. By the same token, it is incumbent upon us to love his family and progeny, for they are the ultimate reason behind the creation of the universe.[26]

As is clear enough from this passage, Muḥammad and his family are considered as the ultimate reason for God's creation of existence, which consequently makes their love incumbent upon all believers. We know that it is among pillars of the formalised Shiʿi creed to believe that Muḥammad and the imams are the reason for the creation of everything else, as well as the most excellent beings ever created. Likewise, they are the most beloved in the eyes of God. The famous Shiʿi scholar and *ḥadīth* collector Ibn Bābawayh (d. 381/991), known as al-Shaykh al-Ṣadūq, explains this belief as follows:

> We believe that God, Blessed and Exalted be He above all, created the whole of creation for him [the Prophet] and for the People of his House, and that but for them, God, Glory be to Him, would not have created the heavens or the earth, Paradise or Hell, Adam or Eve, the angels or (any) created thing (*shay'*) – the Blessings of God upon them all. And our belief is that after His Prophet, the Blessings of God upon him, the proofs of God for the people are the Twelve Imams, the first of them being the Prince of Believers ʿAlī b. Abī Ṭālib, then al-Ḥasan, then al-Ḥusayn, ..., then Muḥammad b. al-Ḥasan the Proof (*al-ḥujja*).[27]

Another important point to be stressed here is that the Alevi-Bektashi tradition attributes utmost prominence to the love of *ahl al-bayt*. Indeed, almost all sects of Islam consider love for the members of the Prophet's family in positive terms. In the Shiʿi traditions, however, this love is elevated to the rank of being doctrinally constituent. As is well known, Shiʿi theology regards 'love for the Family and enmity against their enemies' a prerequisite for sound belief. Equally, Alevi-Bektashi tradition holds the idea that without the love for the family of the Prophet, a man cannot attain true faith; hence cannot find the path to salvation. As indicated in the very beginning of The Book of the Sermon of Twelve Imams, all creatures are indeed indebted to the *ahl al-bayt* for God created all existence for their sake.

Shiʿi literature, too, is full of traditions underlying the significance of love for the Family and the imams as part of true belief.[28] For instance, the Prophet is reported to have said, 'He who loves Ḥasan and Ḥusayn, I love him; he whom I love, God loves also; and he whom God loves enters Paradise. But he who hates them, I hate; and he whom I hate, God hates; and he whom God hates enters into the fire.'[29] In a similar vein, Ibn Bābawayh declares, 'And we believe that love for them is true belief (*īmān*) and that hatred for them is unbelief (*kufr*).'[30]

In many respects Muḥammad and his four immediate relatives constitute the formative personages of the Alevi creed. No doubt the origin of such a perception is traced back to the famous Prophetic tradition *ḥadīth-i kisā'* (the tradition of the cloak), which says, upon receiving the verse about *ahl al-bayt* of the Prophet,[31] Muḥammad called Fāṭima, ʿAlī, Ḥasan, and Ḥusayn and placed a cloak over them in such a manner that it covered all five personages. He then said 'O my Lord! These are my *ahl al-bayt*, keep them clean from sin!'[32] This tradition is connected to the Qur'anic verse about the cleansing of the *ahl al-bayt* (33:33).

A closer examination of Alevi sources reveals that they are indeed seen as primordial beings somehow constituted from the essence of existence. Before everything else, God created their souls from his own essence. These souls are manifested as the primordial light, called the Light of Muḥammad. In fact, the concept of the Light of Muḥammad is widely known in Sufi tradition. The significant difference here, which might be considered as a common feature of Shiʿi traditions, is the inclusion of ʿAlī, Fāṭima, Ḥasan, Ḥusayn and the twelve imams in this light. An account in *The Book of the Sermon of the Twelve Imams* clearly shows how primordial and exalted the spirits of these people are:

> It is related that when Adam was wandering in Paradise, he saw an emerald vault made of green light. Damsels and *ghilmans* [male correspondents of damsels] were all taking light from this vault. Adam approached the vault in amazement to find an entrance, an effort to no avail. Not being able to find a gate leading to the interior, he asked God what it was and where the entrance was. He heard a voice from God's side saying, 'O Adam!

> This vault has five floors, each having a gate and an inscription on the gate. You need to read those inscriptions on gates in order to be able to enter and see inside.' Upon hearing that, Adam opened his eyes and saw a gate on which Muḥammad's name was inscribed. When he read the inscription, the gate opened and he entered and there he saw another gate on which 'Alī's name was engraved. He read it and the gate opened. In the same manner, he saw three more gates bearing the names of Ḥasan, Ḥusayn, and Fāṭima consecutively. When the fifth gate, which had twelve apertures on it, opened, Adam entered a room in the middle of which there stood a throne. On the throne was a magnificent Sultan sitting with a light sash girded around her waist, an ornamented hat (*tāj*) on her head, and two light earrings on her two ears. She was so splendid and shining that eyes could not bear to look upon her. The room was full of light.
>
> When he saw this luminous woman, Adam headed towards her and greeted her. The woman in return stood up and greeted Adam, saying, 'Welcome o my father! Did you recognise me?' While Adam was sunk in bewilderment the woman continued, 'I am the daughter of your son Muḥammad Muṣṭafā, the prophet of the last epoch. The ornamented hat on my head is Muḥammad Muṣṭafā [for whom God said] "Had you not been, I would not have created the universe." These twelve apertures whose light radiates through the Heavens and illuminates damsels and *ghilman*s are my sons the twelve imams, for whose sake all the universe was created. Know that through these twelve imams our descendants will endure until doomsday without interruption. Their spiritual auspices will help many sinful people.' The Prophet Muḥammad said, 'Every progeny is doomed to be interrupted except mine.' Again he said, 'The Mahdi will come from Fāṭima's progeny (*'itra*).' O my father! My son Muḥammad Mahdī will appear close to doomsday; he shall extirpate unbelievers and heretics from all over the world and repair the ruins of this world through justice. There is no doubt about this! If a person who gets in trouble or has anguish invokes the names of the twelve imams and implores God through their intercession, for the sake of those names God will send His remedy whatever the difficulty would be.[33]

This long quotation shows that the Alevi faith holds the view that the souls of *ahl al-bayt* were created long before those of other creatures, including Adam. Indeed, their essence, which also constituted the seed of all being, was nothing but a prelude to the creation of everything else. This primordial creative substance of *ahl al-bayt* is depicted as divine light.

According to Shiʿi belief the primordial luminous reflections of the *ahl al-bayt*'s corporeal bodies, silhouettes of light or corporeal silhouettes called *ashbāḥ* or *ashbāḥ nūr*, were created before Adam and even before the angels.[34] The souls of the Shiʿa were created from the clay of these *ashbāḥ*. The traditionist and theologian Muḥammad Bāqir al-Majlisī (d. 1111/1699) records that when, by the command of God, celestial veils were raised, Adam saw five *ashbāḥ* – those of Muḥammad, ʿAlī, Fāṭima, Ḥasan, and Ḥusayn – before God's throne.[35] The spirits of Muḥammad, ʿAlī, and his family were created two thousand years prior to their bodies. These spirits illuminated heaven and earth. God announced their merits and that of their followers throughout the universe. When they entered into paradise, Adam and Eve saw the names of Muḥammad, ʿAlī, Fāṭima and the imams inscribed on the leg of the throne with God's light.[36] According to another tradition, God created the lights of Muḥammad, Fāṭima, and the imams (amounting to 14 in total) fourteen thousand years before the creation of the world.[37] Imam Ḥusayn is alleged to have said: '[Prior to Adam] we were *ashbāḥ* of light, encircling the throne of the Merciful, teaching the angels how to praise God and to laud Him.'[38] It was those *ashbāḥ* who taught angels the words for praising God when they were finally created.[39]

Another tradition says that Adam and Eve saw the image (*ṣūra*) of Fāṭima as a body of light with a crown on her head, which stood for Imam ʿAlī, and two earrings symbolising Ḥasan and Ḥusayn.[40] It is interesting to note that this creed is still alive in the contemporary Alevi community's collective memory, which is by and large substantiated by oral transmission. I have recorded the same tradition of Adam and Fāṭima from more than forty unconnected Alevi *dedes* (spiritual leaders), who are illiterate or semi-literate and have no access to *The Book of the Sermon of the Twelve Imams*, not to mention Shiʿi sources.[41]

According to Shiʿi sources, when Adam was created, God infused these *ashbāḥ* into his loins. Once deposited in Adam's loins, the *ashbāḥ* illustrated horizons, celestial veils, paradise, and the throne. It is a common Shiʿi word of wisdom that the light of *ahl al-bayt* was the only reason for the prostration of the angels to Adam.[42] Ibn Bābawayh states that 'their [the angels] prostration to Adam was out of respect for the prophets and imams whom He [God] had placed in his loins.'[43]

We know that Shiʿi writers used the concept of light extensively in explaining the divine nature of the imams. According to orthodox Shiʿi creed, Muḥammad's family (*ahl al-bayt*) belongs to an eternal line of chosen persons whom God created from His own light.[44] A tradition says, 'When God created paradise, He created it from the light of His face. Then He took the light and dispersed it. One third hit Muḥammad, one third hit Fāṭima, and another third hit ʿAlī. All people whom this light reached found the right path of loyalty to Muḥammad's family; those who missed it went astray.'[45] According to another tradition, when Adam and Eve were wandering in the garden of paradise, they saw names of these five personages inscribed on the leg of the throne with the light of the Almighty. At that moment, God told them that had it not been for their (*ahl al-bayt*) sake, He would not have created them; they were the treasurers of His knowledge and trustees of his great secrets.[46] Shiʿi exegetes commonly interpret the verse of Light (24:35) as an allegory referring to *ahl al-bayt*, i.e. ʿAlī, Fāṭima, Ḥasan, Ḥusayn, and the rest of the imams. Many other verses are interpreted in a similar manner.[47]

According to this view, the original substance of the imams fundamentally differs from that of other human beings, which was dust of the earth.[48] They are believed to be the pillars of the earth and even of the heavens. As the perfect man (*al-insān al-kāmil*), the imam's mere existence is necessary for the subsistence of the world. Imam Jaʿfar (d. 148/765) is reported to have said, as al-Kulaynī (d. 329/940–1) records, if the earth was to be void of the imam, it would melt away with all its inhabitants.[49] Common Shiʿi wisdom also holds the idea that the imams are, or rather the *walāya* they possess is, the primordial covenant between God and the world, as well as His charge (*amāna*) which He offered to the Heavens and the earth (Qurʾan 33:72).[50] As holders of the *walāya*, which means both nearness to God and authority over men, they are entrusted to human beings.[51]

The Twelve Names as Intercessors

According to the Alevi-Bektashi tradition, in addition to being the ultimate cause of creation, the *ahl al-bayt* functioned as intercessors with God to forgive Adam's sin, because of which he descended from Paradise and his body's colour turned from white to black. When Adam saw Fāṭima and witnessed the exalted status of *ahl al-bayt*, says *The Book of the Sermon of the Twelve Imams*, he was overwhelmed by bewilderment. At this moment Gabriel uttered, 'O Adam! Would you like your body to become pure white [i.e. your sin to be forgiven]?' Gabriel then added that for this purpose he had to fast on the thirteenth, fourteenth, and fifteenth days of each month and to recite the names of the twelve imams, so that he would attain their intercession (*shafāʿa*). Adam followed Gabriel's instruction, which led to his catharsis from sin. As a result, his body turned white. Our source underlines that God forgave his sins for the sake of these twelve names.[52]

A Sunni view holds that Adam's repentance was accepted by God when he prayed for the intercession of Muḥammad whose name he saw on the leg of the throne near God's name.[53] The Shiʿi view includes the other four names (ʿAlī, Fāṭima, Ḥasan, Ḥusayn) among the intercessors. According to Shiʿi faith, when he was sent down from the paradise, Adam repented for a while. God wished to forgive his sin and sent Gabriel for this purpose. Gabriel approached Adam and counseled him to entreat through the intercession of the names he had seen on the leg of the throne (i.e. Muḥammad, ʿAlī, Fāṭima, Ḥasan, Ḥusayn). After doing so, Adam and Eve were forgiven for the sake of these names.[54] Indeed, Shiʿis interpret Qur'anic verse 2:37[55] as a divine reference to this fact.[56]

Arguably the most prevalent theme dominating the whole narrative of *The Book of the Sermon of the Twelve Imams* is the belief that attributes to the twelve imams the capacity of mediating with God for the salvation of the human being or acting as intercessor (*shāfiʿ*). The very beginning of the text reads, 'God uttered, "O Muḥammad! For the sake of my glory, majesty, and magnificence, I shall forgive those who love you and your offspring (*awlād*) even if their sins fill the space between the earth and the Heavens. And those who do not love you and your progeny will dwell in Hell forever even if their worship fills the space between the earth and the Heavens".'[57] Elsewhere, the text runs,

> Then God said: 'O my Beloved! I shall reward those people who beseech Me through intercession of your twelve sons as if they

> beseeched Me by My twelve thousand names and I shall bestow upon them My blessing (*thawāb*) as much as the spiritual reward of the angels that filled the earth and the Heavens. O Muḥammad! Any person amongst your people who entreats Me through intercession (*shafāʿa*) of your progeny shall attain his/her goal, be it in this world or in the next! For the sake of your progeny, I will reward them with the bliss of Paradise.' . . . God said, 'O Muḥammad! Whoever reads this *Sermon of theTwelve Imams* for your sake and your progeny's sake or implores Me through their intercession, I will bestow upon them my blessing which amounts to the deeds of the twelve thousand great prophets. Likewise, I shall bestow upon them the reward of twelve thousand accepted pilgrimages. Those who mention you and these twelve names shall attain rewards as if they prayed to Me with twelve thousand names; he/she shall be the most accepted person to Me.'[58]

As we have seen above, *ahl al-bayt* are believed to be the intercessors for the first sin of humankind. When his body turned white, i.e. cleansed from sin, Adam realised the miraculous potency of these twelve names. *The Book of the Sermon of the Twelve Imams* also postulates a prophetic chain of transmission for these thaumaturgic names. Towards the end of his life, Adam instructed his son Seth to recite these names with utmost reverence and to resort to their intercession whenever he beseeched God. Adam also stressed that he could find no remedy for his sins but the intercession of these names. Seth followed his father's instructions and in turn advised Enoch to do the same. After Enoch, Noah invoked these names and was saved from the Deluge.[59] When Nimrod ordered him to be thrown into the fire, Abraham remembered these twelve names and beseeched God through their intercession. Consequently, God ordered the fire to become cool and safe for Abraham. When his brothers threw him into the well, Joseph remembered these twelve names; through their intercession God saved him from the well and made his wishes come true. When chased by Pharaoh to the edge of the Red Sea, Moses resorted to the intercession of these names and God divided the sea so that Moses and his people were saved, while Pharaoh and his people were drowned. By the auspices of these names iron became malleable in David's hands. These names were inscribed on the Solomon's seal, and because of that he gained suzerainty over demons, fairies, and *jinns*, as well as human beings, and his throne was carried by wind. When he was crucified by the Jews, Jesus invoked these names. By the order of God, angels saved him from the cross and took him to the fourth heaven. He will descend to the earth again when Muḥammad al-Mahdī reappears at the end of the time.[60]

The Book of the Sermon of the Twelve Imams ends this narrative of prophetic transmission with Muḥammad and ʿAlī. It states that this knowledge was transmitted through the prophetic line down to ʿAbd al-Muṭṭalib, ʿAbd Allāh, Muḥammad, ʿAlī, and Fāṭima. Finally the twelve imams came to this world in their proper times to call human beings into the light of knowledge from the darkness of illiteracy. At the end of time, Muḥammad al-Mahdī will come back and re-establish the government of the Prophet Muḥammad.[61]

This transmission narrative has many counterparts in Shiʿi literature. Shiʿi conventional wisdom maintains that even before Adam's creation, God created the primordial substance of Muḥammad and the imams from his own light. Then He said to Adam, 'Take this light together with my covenant and contract so that you will deposit the light only within the pure wombs!'[62] Adam in turn asked Seth, 'My son! God ordered me to impose on you a covenant and a compact for the sake of the light on your face, to the effect that you shall deposit it only within the purest women of all mankind. Let it be known to you that God has put upon me a rigid covenant concerning it'.[63] Seth, in due course, passed this testament (*waṣiyya*) to Enoch; in this manner, the light and covenant were passed on through the prophets down to Muḥammad himself. Indeed, God revealed to Adam that this light and accompanied primordial substance was the reason for his own creation, as well as the creation of earth, heaven, paradise and hell.[64]

The following tradition reported by Ibn Bābawayh, and repeated in later sources, shows even closer similarity to the above quoted Alevi-Bektashi narrative. According to this tradition, the Prophet said, "Alī and I were created from the same light ... When Adam reached Paradise, we were in him [literally: 'in his loins'] ... When Noah boarded the Ark, we were in him; when Abraham was thrown into the fire, we were in him ... God never ceased transmitting us from pure loins to pure wombs to the moment we arrived at ʿAbd al-Muṭṭalib; therein he divided our light in two ...'[65]

In spite of the close resemblance in terms of narrative structure, however, the nature and content of the transmitted text shows recognisable variation. In the Alevi-Bektashi case, the entity that had been passed on from prophet to prophet was simply the knowledge of the twelve names. This knowledge was something apart from those prophets, who were not carriers of this entity but its benefiters. It was this knowledge, which operated as intercessor to make their wishes accepted by God, that vested the prophets with the potency to perform great miracles. On the other hand, Shiʿi tradition regards the transmitted entity as a trust to be carried throughout history until it reached its final destination, i.e. Muḥammad and ʿAlī.

The Book of the Sermon of the Twelve Imams presents the knowledge of the names of the twelve imams as the essence of the faith. After summarising human history in the above-mentioned manner, the text adds, 'it is for certain that God bestowed endless extraordinary deeds (*karāmāt-i bī-nahāya*) to the Prophet Muḥammad's offspring. May those who drink from this pool of Kawthar dwell in Paradise! Read, have others read, and understand these words so that your reason shall be saturated and your heart shall be joyful.'[66]

The capacity of the twelve imams to intercede (*shafāʿa*) sometimes goes as far as interfering with affairs between God and humans to the end that people are protected from bad things happening. It is said that whoever invokes the names of the twelve imams, God solves his/her problem for their sake. The text defines these names as 'red sulphur' (*kibrīt-i aḥmar*), 'great remedy' (*tiryāq-i akbar*), and 'the supreme name' (*ism-i aʿẓam*). As the twelve imams are the most beloved of God, they possess the privilege of acting as the means (*sabab-i wasīla*) of attaining every wish and goal from God.[67]

> Whoever reads these names [i.e. *Khuṭba-yi dawāzdah imām*] in the morning, twelve thousand angels watch him/her until the nightfall; whoever reads it in the evening he/she shall be saved from all accidents and troubles by the angels. Even if the whole world becomes his/her enemy and attempts to harm him/her, by the protection of God, they cannot touch his/her hair. Whoever reads this *Sermon of the Twelve Imams* five times a day, he/she shall not fail in any effort. God says for the person who utters the names of these twelve imams aloud or remembers in silence that

> 'for the sake of My being God, I shall comply with his/her every single wish.'[68]

Shiʿi sources unanimously assert that the imams possess sacred powers that are principally derived from their initiatory knowledge. The primary element of the imams' sacred power is the Supreme Name of God (*al-ism al-aʿẓam*). It is believed that this name is composed of 73 letters, one of which is known to God alone. Previous prophets were given some of those letters. But it was only Muḥammad who was taught 72 letters of this name. After the Prophet, these 72 letters of the Supreme Name, with its thaumaturgic powers, were transmitted through the chain of imams until it reached al-Mahdī.[69] On this particular matter, the Alevi-Bektashi source perfectly concurs with the broader Shiʿi tradition. To buttress the claim that the twelve imams have the potency to make wishes accepted by God, *The Book of the Sermon of the Twelve Imams* relates an interesting story. Shaykh Najm al-Dīn Kubrā is reported to have said:

> I personally experienced it several times; it never failed. One should make ablution on Thursday or Friday night, put clean clothes on, have a good fragrance. Then he should perform two *rakʿāt* of prayer (*hācet namazı*). In his entreaty after the prayer he should read *The Sermon of the Twelve Imams*. And then he should bestow the spiritual rewards of this prayer to Imam ʿAlī. In the same manner, he should perform twelve prayers followed by his earnest entreaty and reading *The Sermon of the Twelve Imams*, bestowing their spiritual rewards to the twelve imams accordingly. Once he has completed this ritual and implored God, his wishes, either regarding this world or the other, will be accomplished. If it does not happen, let his curses be upon me, Shaykh Najm al-Dīn Kubrā.[70]

One may easily observe here again that as for the redemptive aptitude of imams, the Alevi-Bektashi creed shows significant convergence with Shiʿi patterns of belief. Early Imami texts mention the idea that the deceased imams were not indeed deceased but were transported to a supersensible celestial abode, where every Thursday evening acts of the faithful are exposed to them.[71] According to the traditions transmitted by Ibn Bābawayh, the faithful can benefit from al-Mahdi's *walāya* during his occultation just as one benefits from the sun even if it is covered by clouds.[72]

Numerous accounts in classical Shiʿi sources claim that the guiding and saving capacity of the divine light has been deposited in the imams. The imams are believed to be intermediaries of communication between God and creatures. Muḥammad Bāqir al-Majlisī relates, for example, 'The divine light of the imams emanates to their followers, whose hearts were purified by God. This very light shines in their hearts more intensely than the sun. God will save them on the day of resurrection, because of their love and loyalty for the imams.'[73] Another tradition in the same compilation says, "Alī had a light in heaven and light on earth; whoever got hold of that light would enter paradise, and whoever missed it would enter hell.'[74] Imam Jaʿfar is alleged to have related that God made the imams intercessors for the sinners of His male and female servants.[75] It is also reported from him that 'through our worship can God be truly worshipped, and without us God would have never been worshipped.'[76]

The Superiority of the Imams over the Prophets

The Book of the Sermon of the Twelve Imams elevates the members of the *ahl al-bayt* to an ontological status which is superior to that of the prophets. It says, for example, that when he stared at his coffin, the Prophet Moses saw the spirits of the prophets and that of the Prophet Muḥammad's progeny. He also saw the spirits of the people (*umma*) of Muḥammad and requested them from God for himself. He heard a voice from God saying that they belonged to His beloved Muḥammad, hence could not be given to anyone else. In the same manner, he requested the month of Ramaḍān, Friday and the night of Qadr, but all his requests were rejected because they were reserved for Muḥammad. Moses finally requested the twelve imams. God, by His glory and beneficence, said, 'O Moses! You cannot be the jeweler of these jewels; they are corals of utmost worth; they are offspring of My beloved Muḥammad. They are ultimately close to Me and dear to Me. Each of them possesses the glory of great prophets . . . They are not to give to you.'[77]

Moses was amazed thinking how high was the value of these personages. At this moment, the spirit of Imam Jaʿfar appeared and showed Moses an endless ocean, asking him to drink it. Moses asked how he could possibly drink such an endless amount of water. Imam Jaʿfar then said, 'Then why do you demand the Maḥmūdiyya post of

Muḥammad? I am a humble member of this family; look at what I do.'[78] He then drank the entire ocean like a drop. When he saw this, Moses lost his mind for a while. In a second, God's words reached his ears: 'O Moses! In the human body, there are four hundred and forty-four bonds, seven hundred and seventy-seven nerves, three hundred and sixty-six veins, and three hundred and twelve thousand hairs. If one of these parts of the body gazes with bad intentions upon one of the descendants of my Beloved [Muḥammad], for the sake of My glory and magnificence, I will place that person in Hell even if he is registered amongst the People of Abraham.'[79] Upon hearing this divine voice, Moses went into prostration imploring 'O God! Register me amongst the people (*umma*) of Muḥammad!' God brought to the attention of Muḥammad all these conversations with Moses to show him the high value of his progeny. When he learned this, Muḥammad was overwhelmed with joy and presented his gratitude to God. God too loved Muḥammad and his offspring.[80]

Another story related on the authority of certain *Asrār al-ʿarifīn* (The Secrets of the Gnostics) explains the reason for the immortality of the Prophet Elias. According to *The Book of the Sermon of the Twelve Imams*, the very reason that God bequeathed Elias immortal life was nothing but his desire to serve the twelve imams. When Azrael arrived to take his soul, the prophet Elias cried. God rebuked him if he did not wish to return to God. Elias answered: 'O my Lord! My crying is not to avoid returning to You. It is because I saw the glory of the twelve imams, the offspring of Muḥammad Muṣṭafā, for the sake of whom you forgave all prophets and saints. My humble request is to live until their times so that I can see their beauty, talk to them, put my face on the soil of their feet, and serve in their entourage!' God accepted Elias's plea and gave him extended life until doomsday. In addition to serving Muḥammad Muṣṭafā and the twelve imams, God ordered Elias to help sincere followers of Muḥammad who love his progeny. God then uttered, 'Let the people know that the status of Muḥammad, his progeny, his genuine followers, and lovers of the Prophetic offspring is the highest in my eyes.'[81]

Superiority of the Prophetic Descent

Besides conspicuous similarity in the occultist perception of the twelve imams, a substantial dissimilarity between the Qizilbash/Alevi tradition and orthodox Shiʿi wisdom becomes apparent in their regard for the kinsfolk of the Prophet Muḥammad. As is well known, Shiʿi theology makes a clear-cut separation between the imams and other ʿAlids. According to the Twelver view, it is the twelve imams alone who are privileged to hold a special exalted status, which is based on inherited special knowledge and divine appointment (*naṣṣ*) along with the Prophet's blood. For Ismailis, the sacred line of imams is uninterrupted to the present time. Yet all the privileges of *imāma* are accumulated in one single person. Those descendants of the Prophet who did not receive the *imāma* are regarded as barely privileged amongst believers. It is true that, as offspring of the Prophet, they command high esteem in the eyes of faithful as well as love in their hearts. Nevertheless, this psychological prestige never imbues them with ontological superiority over the rest of humanity.

In this respect, Shiʿi traditions transmitted by Ibn Bābawayh are illustrative: 'Our belief concerning the ʿAlids (*ʿAlawiyya*) is that they are the progeny of the Messenger of God, and that devotion to them is obligatory, because it is the requital of his apostleship. Says God, exalted is He: 'Say (O Muḥammad, unto mankind): I ask of you no requital therefore, save loving-kindness of (my) kinsfolk' (42–23).'[82] Considered members of the extended prophetic family, they are banned from accepting *ṣadaqa* and *zakāt*, while entitled to receive *khums*. As far as religious responsibilities are concerned, however, Ibn Bābawayh considers no privileged status for ʿAlids. He emphasises that those who act sinfully will be punished doubly, just as their good acts will be rewarded doubly. He records several traditions from ʿAlī b. Abī Ṭālib, Jaʿfar al-Ṣādiq, and others stressing that being the Prophet's kinsfolk does not save a person unless he observes the rules of God.[83]

In regard to the religious status of the Prophetic lineage, Shiʿi and Sunni views converge recognisably. Just like the Shiʿis, Sunni communities pay special tribute to *sayyid*s and *sharīf*s as the kinsfolk of the Prophet. Apart from social and religious prestige, which is usually marked by distinctive dress and occupation, they customarily enjoy tax exemptions.[84] We have evidence revealing that, as members of the extended *ahl al-bayt*, they might even be regarded as the embodiment of divine guidance that believers must follow. In a recent article, for example, Kazuo Morimoto showed how the Mamluk scholar al-Samhūdī (d. 911/1506) depicted kinsfolk of the Prophet as possessors of esoteric authority, which was granted to them by God in spite of the exoteric authority that Ḥasan renounced in the year 40/661. According to al-Samhūdī, it was thanks to this esoteric authority that scholars of *sayyids* and *sharīfs* combine knowledge and blessing, a combination that makes them a model par excellence for saintly scholars; and it was these saintly scholars who guide the *umma*.[85]

The Bektashi position regarding the religious status of the Prophetic progeny remains more or less the same as the general approach widespread in the Islamic world. In the Qizilbash/Alevi tradition, however, the perception of the Prophetic lineage shows substantial difference.[86] Besides allotting exalted superhuman status to the twelve imams alone, the Qizilbash/Alevi creed by no means considers the Prophetic substance of knowledge to be exclusively limited to the imams. Rather, a portion of this substance has been disseminated through all branches of Ḥusaynid descent. This belief in the sacred nature of the prophetic lineage creates an ontological line of separation within the Alevi community. Those who have inherited the sacred substance through genealogy are the sole group of people entitled to hold the privilege of spiritual guidance (*dede*s), while the rest of the community is set into an ontological category of discipleship called *talip*.

In other words, the Qizilbash/Alevi community is divided into two religious classes: *dede*s (also called *ocak-zāde*s) and *talip*s. The first group holds the privilege of harboring sacred knowledge and has religious superiority by birth. They have the sole authority to preside over ritual, including accepting pledges of allegiance and repentance. It is believed that they inherit a sort of sacred knowledge. The second class, which constitutes the majority of the community, on the other hand, forms a religiously dependent group. In order to be able to fulfill their religious responsibilities, they must attach themselves to *ocak-zāde*s, which is indeed a pre-requisite to all other religious activities.[87]

The Alevi faith attributes sacral superiority to Prophetic-ʿAlid blood. It is believed that the ultimate secret knowledge that guides human beings to salvation can only be harboured and transmitted through the Prophetic-ʿAlid lineage. And within this lineage, only the offspring of Ḥusayn are eligible to hold this post. A closer examination reveals that the roots of the *ocak-zāde–ṭalib* relationship lies in the classical Sufi concept of the shaykh–disciple relationship with the substantial difference that the Qizilbash/Alevi tradition gives the privilege of shaykhdom exclusively to a specific branch of the prophetic genealogy: descendants of Ḥusayn.[88]

According to *The Book of the Sermon of the Twelve Imams*, the descendants of the twelve imams, i.e. *sayyids*, are all in a state of honour and glory. Reverence for them is like reverence for Muḥammad, because it is said 'the son is the secret of his father.'[89] The Prophet is reported to have said, 'A man who pledges his allegiance to a shaykh who is not *sayyid* makes himself the disciple of Satan.'[90] The *Buyruq*, the principal canonical texts of the Qizilbash-Alevi faith, also strictly forbid non-*sayyids* from assuming spiritual mastership. It is recorded in a *Buyruq* copy that 'if a person attaches himself to someone whose genealogy does not go back to Muḥammad – ʿAlī, his shaykh is no one but Satan. On the day of resurrection he will be kept away from the people of salvation. The Prophet is reported to have said, 'Whoever attains as a shaykh someone other than my descendants, his shaykh is none but Satan.'[91] Elsewhere, when relating the event of Ghadīr Khumm, the *Buyruq* records the prophetic tradition which reads, 'After me my people will divide into seventy-two parties. Among them only one party will pursue the right track. They are the ones who attach themselves to my progeny; and they are called The People of Salvation.'[92]

Conclusion

Examination of *The Book of the Sermon of the Twelve Imams* has shown that the Alevi-Bektashi belief in the twelve imams bears traits of greater Shiʿi traditions. At the same time, a recognisable dissimilarity from the doctrinal templates of the Twelver Shiʿi sect is maintained. The Alevi-Bektashi faith pictures the imams as loci of creative powers and thaumaturgic potencies, which are indeed attached to their essence and their names. This book highlights the names of the twelve imams much more than their historical personalities, which are indeed totally absent from the text. It is on the utterance of these names of magical potency that the faithful needs to fix their temporal and spiritual life. Such a thaumaturgic capacity is derived from the imams' primordial essence, which also bequeathed them a privileged position in the sacred history of human beings. Another axial idea which characterises the Alevi-Bektashi image of the imams is to consider them as repositories of intercessory capacity between humans and God. Indeed, it is this belief that makes these twelve names an essential part of Alevi-Bektashi piety. A believer should resort to their intercession through reciting these names, particularly in moments of trouble.

The Book of the Sermon of the Twelve Imams makes no mention of the historical lives and the roles of the imams in their temporal lifetimes. The Imam as pictured here is not a leader of a religious community, but an extension of the divine essence, transcendental across temporal and spatial lines. The central tenet of Twelver Shiʿism that regards the imams as the authority (*ūlū'l-amr*) over the faithful, both in temporal and spiritual terms, is simply absent in this text. As a result, the obligation of obedience to the Imams is silenced vis-à-vis remembering and uttering their names. In a similar vein, the Imam's foremost role as infallible teacher, urging the faithful to lawful acts and prohibiting them from unlawful deeds, is never mentioned. Neither the idea of the Imam as the *ḥujja* against unbelievers and *dalīl* for believers is stated in the whole text.[93]

One would conclude, then, that the Alevi-Bektashi belief in the twelve imams can hardly be accommodated within the fold of orthodox Twelver Shiʿi creed. In the meantime, the whole narrative has a great deal in common, both in terms of content and form, with early Shiʿi traditions about the imams. Our study even suggests that the collective memory of the 15th-century ʿAlid milieu, as reflected in our treatise, drew its constitutive elements largely from these deep-rooted Shiʿi strands of tradition traceable back to earlier sources. Given these two seemingly contradictory facts, we may now come back to the question of the relationship between the Alevi-Bektashi faith and Shiʿism.

Moojen Momen argues that the doctrine upheld by the majority of Shiʿi communities during the first two centuries of Islam was almost diametrically opposed to the final, canonical doctrinal position of Twelver Shiʿism. He also argues that this great change in doctrine should be understood in connection with the change in the political fortunes of Shiʿism.[94] From a different point of view, Mohammad Ali Amir-Moezzi argues that the distinction between early extreme Shiʿism and later moderate orthodox Shiʿism, which was constructed from very early times, was indeed artificial.[95] Many ideas attributed to extremists, such as the esoteric interpretation of the Qur'an, metempsychosis (*tanāsukh*), and attributing divinity to the imams are all seen in early Imami sources in one way or another, at least in analogous if not identical forms of thought.[96] Given this observation, staunch curses by imams of some of their disciples who were considered extremist must have occurred because they revealed the secret but not because of what they said.[97]

Hence, the rise of rational Twelver Shiʿism as a juridical sect does not necessarily mean the wane of esoteric-mystic strands of Shiʿi thought and sentiment. Once developed upon a model of a juridical sect, the theological-rational Shiʿism by no means assimilated all mystical, supra-rational currents of earlier Shiʿism. It is plausible to argue that the cognitive patterns, emotional templates, thought and belief structures, and principal mythological narratives of non-rationalised Shiʿism (which modern scholarship usually calls ʿextremist Shiʿism') survived against a backdrop of orthodox Twelver Shiʿism, especially on a popular level and amongst socially and politically marginalised masses. One may even regard this occultist, esoteric and mystical climate as the grassroots background of all sub-branches of Shiʿism, including Ismailis and Zaydis, who had also fashioned their own mainstream interpretations in time.

One should keep in mind that institutionalised Shiʿism, as a kind of orthodoxy characterised by theological-juridical-rational doctrine, addressed an urban-based and well-structured community, which had enough access to learning processes and had possession of an adequate written culture. Direct and indirect contact with political authority also had a share in the formation of the institutionalised Shiʿi sect. It is no coincidence that the great doctors who transformed esoteric and non-rational Shiʿism into Twelver Shiʿism lived under Buyid rule in Baghdad (334–447/945–1055).[98] From this perspective, it is plausible to postulate that the rationalisation process of the early lore of Shiʿi knowledge and sentiments advanced hand-in-hand with the process of building an urban setting for a structured Shiʿi community within the encapsulating Sunni realm, a process interwoven with the dynamics of political formations.

As stated above, however, the whole span of the Shiʿi spectrum did not become subject to such a rationalisation process. Rather, forms of initiatory, esoteric, mystical and occultist doctrine lingered, appealing to the hearts of the masses, who had little relationship with the centralised political powers and orthodox structures of Islam. Furthermore, some elements of this Shiʿism infiltrated Sufi milieus. It must be this corpus of occultist Shiʿi knowledge and sentiments that fed ʿAlid-tinged Sufi movements which escalated in the course of the 15th century all over the Islamic world. Our examination has demonstrated that the reception of twelve imams in the ʿAlid Sufi milieu of the 15th-century Ottoman Empire, as well as in the later Alevi-Bektashi tradition, shows a close resemblance to reports of early Shiʿi sources.

The crucial point is that Alevi-Bektashi belief in the twelve imams shares much more with earlier esoteric-mystical Shiʿism than with later established juridical-rational Twelver Shiʿism. Amir-Moezzi's approach to early Shiʿism proves helpful for understanding the dynamics of the relationship between the Alevi-Bektashi tradition and Shiʿism. Confining Shiʿism to the rationalised Twelver Shiʿi sect and condemning other strands, which had obviously been alive since the early days of Islamic history, as extremism, with the pejorative connotation of heresy, hampers understanding the true nature of Shiʿi-tinged Sufi traditions such as the Alevi-Bektashi tradition. Instead of a clear-cut division between moderate and extremist Shiʿism, we need to conceptualise an extended spectrum of Shiʿism, saturated with green tones. Such a conceptualisation may also help with solving another perennial problem, namely recognising the lines of distinction between Sunni and Shiʿi spaces, which become baffling particularly in the study of Sufi traditions.

NOTES

1 The term 'Alevi-Bektashi' is somewhat confusing and became the subject of criticism by several scholars including the present author. That it presupposes a kind of identification between Alevi and Bektashi is misleading, for both socio-religious communities have their own distinct traits and peculiarities as well as separate, albeit occasionally interdependent, historical trajectories. Nonetheless, we know almost for certain that at least by the mid-17th century, the theologies and dogmas of these two strands show little difference. In particular, the source materials used in this study have been equally adopted and reproduced by both Bektashi and Qizilbash/Alevi communities. Hence they reflect theological stands of both groups. It is because of that, that the present study uses the term 'Alevi-Bektashi' simply in the sense that it reflects a common framework of theology. For a detailed discussion of Bektashi identity and its relationship with the Qizilbash/Alevi groups, see R. Yıldırım, 'Bektaşi Kime Derler?: 'Bektaşi' Kavramının

Kapsamı ve Sınırları Üzerine Tarihsel bir Analiz Denemesi', *Türk Kültürü ve Hacı Bektaş Veli Araştırma Dergisi* 55 (2010), pp. 23–58.

2 Scholarship on the Alevis and Bektashis generally assumes that the penetration of Twelver Shiʿi beliefs into these communities occurred as a result of Safawid propaganda in the 16th century. This paper and some of my earlier publications, to be cited below, challenge this assertion, arguing some earlier date for the Shiʿitisation of these mystical traditions. For a summary of the common wisdom on Bektashis, see Thierry Zarcone, 'Bektaşiyye', *EI3*. For Alevis, see Markus Dressler, 'Alevīs', *EI3*.

3 A thorough study of the *Buyruq* (the order) has yet to be done. A *Buyruq* text principally deals with the religious teachings of the Qizilbash/Alevi tradition. There are various manuscripts that can be categorised under the generic title *Buyruq*. For an introductory reading, see Doğan Kaplan, *Yazılı Kaynaklarına Göre Alevilik* (Ankara, 2010), pp. 42–160; R. Yıldırım, 'Inventing a Sufi Tradition: The Use of the Futuwwa Ritual Gathering as Model for the Qizilbash *djem*', in John J. Curry and Eric S. Ohlander, ed., *Sufism and Society: Arrangements of the Mystical in the Muslim World, 1200–1800* (London and New York, 2012), p. 178, endnote 5.

4 These four copies are as follows:

a. Mehmet Yaman Private Library: This copy is dated 1241/1845 and held in the private library of Mehmet Yaman, an Alevi spiritual leader or *dede* (henceforth 'Yaman'). The pagination of this manuscript is arranged according to modern style. The volume is a compilation of at least six different treatises. *Kitāb-i Khuṭba-yi dawāzdah imām* is located on pages 1–17. The other treatises are *Manāqib-i Shaykh Ṣafī*, 18–138; *The Letter of ʿAbd al-Bāqī*, 139–171; *Naṣīḥat-nāmah* and some poems, 172–194; *Kitāb-i Futuwwat-nāmah*, 195–227; *Dār Duʿāsı*, 228–235. It is important to note that all of these epistles are regarded as highly-esteemed religious treatises of the Alevi-Bektashi community. An amateur and slightly distorted publication of the *Manāqib* part of this manuscript was made by Mehmet Yaman. See Mehmet Yaman, *Buyruk* (Mannheim, 2002). Since this copy contains the most comprehensive text, references throughout the present study will be made to this manuscript.

b. MS 181. Konya Mevlana Müzesi Abdülbâki Gölpınarlı Kütüphanesi, fols 1a-6b: As we learn from Gölpınarlı, the oldest among these four manuscripts is this one, which was copied in 1017/1608–9. However, the original manuscript is not accessible to us. Gölpınarlı says that he saw it in the private library of Seyyit Muhtar and made a copy for himself. Abdülbâki Gölpınarlı, 'İslâm ve Türk İllerinde Fütüvvet Teşkilâtı ve Kaynakları', *İstanbul Universitesi İktisat Fakültesi Mecmuası*, 11 (1949–1950), p. 68. Fortunately, we have a copy of this original manuscript produced by Gölpınarlı himself, preserved in Konya Mevlana Müzesi Abdülbâki Gölpınarlı Kütüphanesi.

c. MS 198. Konya Mevlana Müzesi Abdülbâki Gölpınarlı Kütüphanesi, fols 1a-12b: This copy is not dated. The handwriting suggests that it must have been copied in the 18th century or earlier.

d. MS Or. Quart 2134. Berlin Staatsbibliothek, fols 1b-21b: This manuscript was copied in 1273/1857. It contains the full text of *Kitāb-i Khuṭba-yi dawāzdah imām* except the last part, the short Arabic salutation or *ṣalawāt* to imams.

5 Yaman, p. 6.

6 Fatih Usluer, *Hurufilik: İlk Elden Kaynaklarla Doğuşundan İtibaren* (Istanbul, 2009), pp. 87–90.

7 Āqā Buzurg al-Ṭihrānī, *al-Dharīʿa ilā taṣānīf al-shīʿa* (25 vols., Tehran, 1950), vol. 8, pp. 268–269.

8 That Shāh Ismāʿīl ordered that the *khuṭba* be read in the name of the twelve imams is attested by early Safawid chronicles. See, for example, Abdüllatif Kazvinī, *Safevi tarihi*, tr. Hamidreza Mohammednejad (Ankara, 2011), p. 34. (This is a Turkish translation of the fourth part of ʿAbd al-Laṭīf Qazwīnī's *Lubb al-tawārīkh*.)

9 al-Ṭihrānī, *al-Dharīʿa*, vol. 7, pp. 194–196.
10 See *Duʿā-yi iʿtiṣām dawāzdah imām*, MS 653. Tehran University Library.
11 For a non-scholarly publication of this treatise aimed at popular consumption, see Khwājah Naṣīr al-Dīn Ṭūsī, *Duʿā-yi dawāzdah imām*, ed. Ḥājī Shaykh ʿAbbās Miṣbāḥzādah (Tehran, 1344 Sh./1965–6). See also Mohammad Ali Amir-Moezzi, *The Spirituality of Shiʿi Islam* (London, 2011), chapter 11.
12 Yaman, p. 6.
13 Ibid., p. 7.
14 See, for example, *Dar bayān-i ahl al-nabī wa awlād-i Āl wa a'imma-yi ithnā ʿashar*, MS 199. Konya, Mevlana Müzesi Abdülbâki Gölpınarlı Kütüphanesi, fols. 26b-31b.
15 For an analysis of the ʿAlid content of some of these sources, see Rıza Yıldırım, 'Beylikler Dünyasında Kerbela Kültürü ve Ehl-i Beyt Sevgisi: 1362 Yılında Kastamonu'da Yazılan Bir Maktelin Düşündürdükleri', in H. Çetin, ed., *Kuzey Anadolu'da Beylikler Dönemi Sempozyumu Bildiriler, Çobanoğulları, Candaroğulları, Pervaneoğulları, 3–8 Ekim 2011 Katamonu-Sinop-Çankırı* (Çankırı, 2012), pp. 344–372.
16 For a summary of scholarly literature on the subject and a general discussion of the question, see R. Yıldırım, 'Anadoluda İslâmiyet: Gâziler Çağında (XII.-XIV. Asırlar) Türkmen İslam Yorumunun Sünni-Alevi Niteliği Üzerine Bazı Değerlendirmeler', *Osmanlı Araştırmaları/ The Journal of Ottoman Studies*, 43 (2014), pp. 93–124.
17 R. Yıldırım, 'Shiʿitization of the *Futuwwa* Tradition in the Fifteenth Century', *BJMES*, 40 (2013), pp. 53–70.
18 A. Gölpınarlı. 'Seyyid Gaybî oğlu Seyyid Hüseyin'in Fütüvvetnâmesi', *İstanbul Üniversitesi İktisat Fakültesi Mecmuası* 17/1–4 (1955–6), pp. 88–90. One should not confuse my argument here with mention of the names of some individual imams in earlier *futuwwat-nāmahs*. True, traditions from imams such as Imam Jaʿfar al-Ṣādiq (d. 148/765) are recited sporadically in some earlier *futuwwa* texts, nevertheless, they do not have any mention of twelve imams as a formulaic phrase for certain forms of religious understanding.
19 For discussion of this literary work as a source for history, see R. Yıldırım, 'Muhabbetten Tarikata: Bektaşî Tarikatı'nın Oluşum Sürecinde Kızıldeli'nin Rolü', *Türk Kültürü ve Hacı Bektaş Veli Araştırma Dergisi* 53 (2010), pp. 155–159.
20 *Sâdık Abdâl Dîvânı*, haz. Dursun Gümüşoğlu (Istanbul, 2009), pp. 120–122.
21 The question of the Shiʿitisation of the Bektashi Order has not been thoroughly addressed yet. For some preliminary remarks, see R. Yıldırım, 'Rum'da Öksöğüyü Tutan Kimdi? *Saltukname* ve *Hacı Bektaş Veli Velayetnamesi'nde* Yer Alan Bir 'Menkıbe'ye Göre Rum Erenleri', in Osman Eğri, Mehmet Evkuran, Muammer Cengil and Adem Korukçu, ed., *Hitit Üniversitesi Hacı Bektaş Veli Araştırma ve Uygulama Merkezi I. Uluslararası Hacı Bektaş Veli Sempozyumu Bildirileri (07–09 Mayıs 2010, Çorum)*, cilt II (Ankara, 2011), pp. 595–633.
22 A thorough examination of this process is yet to be done. For my own examination of *futuwwa* tradition, see Yıldırım, 'Shiʿitization of the *Futuwwa* Tradition'.
23 For example, Seyyid Sahīh Ahmed Dede's (d. 1813) *Majmūʿa'tu't-tevārihu'l-mevleviyye*, which is a compendium of short biographies of saintly personages as received in Mawlawī tradition, includes a full list of the twelve imams referring to them as 'imam' and giving the duration each held the office of imamate. See Seyyid Sahīh Ahmed Dede, *Majmūʿa'tu't-tevārihu'l-mevleviyye*, MS 5446. Mevlāna Müzesi Yazmalar Kütüphanesi, fols 3a-31b. The following phrases from this source show very well how the lines between Shiʿism and Sunnism become vague in certain branches of Sufism: 'Imām Ḥasan al-Askarī died a martyr in 260 AH when he was 28 years old. His imamate as the eleventh imam lasted seven and a half years. His son, Muḥammad Mahdī, who became the twelfth imam, moved to permanent life at five years of age [went into occultation] and left no children.' Sahīh Ahmed Dede, *Majmūʿa*, f. 31b.

24 On this specific issue, the similarity between Twelver Imami Shiʿism and Alevi-Bektashi tradition is more than a resemblance for Imami doctrine too is entirely dominated by these fourteen people called the fourteen impeccables. See, for example, M.A. Amir-Moezzi, *The Divine Guide in Early Shiʿism: The Sources of Esotericism in Islam* (New York, 1994), p. 29.

25 For Alevi *djem*, see R. Yıldırım, 'Ritual as a Microcosm of Society: The '*Ayn-i Cem* of the Kızılbaş-Alevis", in Johannes Zimmerman, Janina Karolewski and Robert Langer, ed., *Transmission Process of Religious Knowledge and Ritual Practice in Alevism between Innovation and Reconstruction* (Berlin, Brussels, New York, 2018), pp. 9–26.

26 Yaman, p. 2.

27 Ibn Bābawayh al-Qummī, *A Shiʿite Creed: A Translation of Iʿtiqādātu'l-Imāmiyyah* (The Beliefs of the Imāmiyyah) *of Abū Jaʿfar Muḥammad ibn ʿAlī ibn al-Husayn Ibn Bābawayh al-Qummī known as ash-Shaykh aṣ-Ṣaduq (306/919–381/991)*, ed. and tr. Asaf A.A. Fyzee (Tehran, 1982), p. 84.

28 For some examples, see Mahmoud Ayoub, *Redemptive Suffering in Islām: A Study of the Devotional Aspects of ʿĀshūrā' in Twelver Shiʿism* (Paris and New York, 1978), pp. 74–92.

29 Muḥammad b. Muḥammad al-Nuʿmān al-Mufīd, *al-Irshād*, ed. al-Sayyid Kāẓim al-Miyāmāwī (Tehran, 1377/1957–8), p. 181. Cited and quoted in Ayoub, *Redemptive Suffering*, p. 79.

30 Ibn Bābawayh, *A Shiʿite Creed*, p. 85.

31 This verse is Q 33:33: 'O people of the household! God intends to purify you from impurity [of sins].'

32 Several versions of this tradition are recorded in Sunni and Shiʿi sources. See, for example, Tirmidhī, *Manāqib*, 3870; Bukhārī, *Faḍā'il al-ṣaḥāba* 61, 2424; Sayyid Hāshim Baḥrānī, *Ghāyat al-marām* (Tehran, 1272/1856), pp. 287ff. (the latter is cited in S.H. Nasr, 'Shiʿism and Sufism: Their Relationship in Essence and in History', in his *Sufi Essays* (Albany, NY, 1991), p. 109.)

33 Yaman, pp. 9–10.

34 Amir-Moezzi, *The Divine Guide*, pp. 32–33. A similar approach considers the imams as luminous entities and primordial ideas in God's mind which found temporal manifestation in corporeal persons occupying a position midway between human and divine beings. See Ayoub, *Redemptive Suffering*, p. 54.

35 Muḥammad Bāqir al-Majlisī, *Biḥār al-anwār*, new edition (110 vols., Tehran, 1376–1394/1956–1974), vol. 11, p. 175.

36 al-Majlisī, *Biḥār*, vol. 11, p. 172–174. Also see al-ʿAmilī, *al-Jawāhir al-sanniya fī al-aḥādīth al-qudsiyya* (Baghdad, 1960), p. 252, cited in Rubin, 'Pre-existence and Light: Aspects of the Concept of Nūr Muḥammad', *Israel Oriental Studies*, 5 (1975), pp. 62–119, esp. p. 107.

37 al-Majlisī, *Biḥār*, vol. 15, p. 23.

38 Cited by Rubin from Ibn Bābawayh's *ʿIlal al-sharā'iʿ* ('Pre-existence and Light', p. 99).

39 al-Majlisī, *Biḥār*, vol. 15, p. 8–9. Also see Amir-Moezzi, *The Divine Guide*, p. 35.

40 al-Suyūṭī, *al-Laʿālī al-Maṣnūʿa fī'l-aḥādīth al-mawḍūʿa*, I (Cairo, 1352 H.), pp. 395–396; al-Dhahabī, *Mīzān al-iʿtidāl*, II, ed. al-Bijāwī (Cairo, 1963), pp. 495–496; al-ʿAsqalānī, *Lisān al-mīzān*, III (Beirut, 1971), p. 346, all cited in Rubin, 'Pre-existence and Light', p. 99.

41 These recordings from oral tradition were made in the years 2013–2015 as part of a greater project. This project, which was supported by TUBITAK, The Scientific and Technological Research Council of Turkey, aimed to determine commonly accepted religious references of the Alevi Tradition—both written and oral—through extensive fieldwork in approximately one thousand Alevi villages of the provinces of Amasya, Tokat, Çorum and Sivas. For a discussion of oral traditions collected during these field

studies, see R. Yildirim, *Geleneksel Alevilik: İnanç, İbadet, Kurumlar, Toplumsal Yapı, Kolektif Bellek / Traditional Alevism: Beliefs, Rituals, Institutions, Social Structure, Collective Memory* (Istanbul, 2018).

42 See, for example, al-Majlisī, *Biḥār*, vol. 11, p. 192.

43 Shaykh al-Ṣadūq then relates a tradition of the Prophet Muḥammad saying, 'I am superior to Gabriel and Michael and Isrāfīl and to all the angels who are nearer [to God], and I am the best of mankind and the leader (*sayyid*) of the sons of Adam.' Ibn Bābawayh, *A Shiʿite Creed*, p. 82.

44 Some traditions interpret even the names Muḥammad, ʿAlī, Fāṭima, Ḥasan and Ḥusayn as derivatives of divine names *al-Maḥmūd*, *al-ʿAlī al-Aʿlā*, *al-Fāṭir*, *al-Muḥsin*, and *Dhū'l-iḥsān*. Amir-Moezzi, *The Divine Guide*, p. 30.

45 al-Majlisī, *Biḥār*, vol. 23, pp. 308–309; Ibn Shahr Āshūb, *Manāqib Āl Abī Ṭālib*, 3 (al-Najaf, 1956), p. 106, cited and quoted in Rubin, 'Pre-existence and Light', pp. 65–66. A similar tradition is reported by Muḥammad b. ʿAlī b. al-Ḥusayn al-Ḥurr al-ʿĀmilī (in his *al-Jawāhir al-saniyya fi'l-aḥādīth al-qudsiyya* [Baghdad, 1964]) on the authority of Imam Jaʿfar al-Ṣādiq. (Cited in Ayoub, *Redemptive Suffering*, p. 56.) Also consider Amir-Moezzi, *The Divine Guide*, pp. 29–30.

46 Ibn Bābawayh, *Kitāb Maʿānī al-akhbār* (Tehran, 1937), p. 109.

47 Rubin, 'Pre-existence and Light', p. 65. Al-Kulaynī writes in his *Kitāb al-uṣūl min al-kāfī* that when asked by one of his disciples, Imam Jaʿfar is reported to have explained the meaning of this verse as follows: 'God is the light of the heavens and the earth; the likeness of His light is as a niche (Fāṭima) wherein is a lamp (Ḥasan), the lamp in a glass (Ḥusayn), the glass as it were a glittering star (Fāṭima is like the radiant star among the women of the world), kindled from a Blessed Tree (Abraham), an olive that is neither of the East nor of the West (neither Jewish nor Christian) whose oil well-nigh would shine (knowledge is about to burst out from it), even if no fire touched it; Light upon Light (an imam proceeding from it after another imam); God guides to His Light whom He will (God guides through the Imams whom He will).' Cited and quoted in Ayoub, *Redemptive Suffering*, p. 57.

48 For some traditions famous among Shiʿi circles, see Mahmoud Ayoub, *Redemptive Suffering*, pp. 54–55.

49 From *Kitāb al-Uṣūl min al-kāfī* cited in Ayoub, *Redemptive Suffering*, p. 55. According to Ibn Bābawayh, the fifth imam Muḥammad al-Bāqir is reported to have said, 'By God! God has not left the earth, since the death of Adam, without there being on it an imam guiding (the people) to God. He is the Proof of God to His servants and the earth will not remain without the Proof of God to His servants.' Cited and quoted in Moojan Momen, *An Introduction to Shiʿi Islam: The History and Doctrines of Twelver Shiʿism* (New Haven and London, 1985), pp. 147–148.

50 Momen, *An Introduction to Shiʿi Islam*, p. 151.

51 Imam Jaʿfar's exegesis of the verse of charge (*amāna*) is reported in a tradition as follows: 'God (blessed and exalted be He) created the spirits (of men) two thousand years before their bodies. He made the spirits of Muḥammad, ʿAlī, Fāṭima, Ḥasan and Ḥusayn and of the other imams the highest and noblest of all. God then manifested them (i.e. the spirits of the Holy Family) to the heavens, earth and mountains and their light dazzled them. He then said to the heavens, earth and mountains, 'These are my beloved ones, my friends (*awliyā*), and my proofs (*ḥujaj*) over my creation and the imams of my human creatures . . . For those who love them I created my paradise, and for them that oppose them and show enmity towards them I created my fire . . . I shall make them intercessors for the sinners of my men and women servants. Their *walāya* (i.e. the imams') is the charge (*amāna*) I laid upon my creation.' Ibn Bābawayh, *Maʿānī*, pp. 108–109, quoted in Ayoub, *Redemptive Suffering*, p. 58. Another tradition recorded in several Shiʿi sources shows more clearly how Shiʿi perception includes the Fourteen Impeccables into the content of this pre-temporal Pact of God with the human being: 'Then God made the prophets take

an oath, saying to them: "Am I not your Lord? Is Muḥammad here not My messenger, and is ʿAlī not the prince of believers?" The prophets answered, "Yes"'. God then says to the prophets that He is their Lord, Muḥammad is the messenger; that ʿAlī the prince of believers; and that his heirs (other Imams) are the responsible directors of His Order and the guardians of His Knowledge. See Amir-Moezzi, *The Divine Guide*, p. 34.

52 Yaman, p. 11.

53 Rubin, 'Pre-existence and Light', pp. 105–106.

54 From Ibn Bābawayh's *Maʿānī*, cited in Ayoub, *Redemptive Suffering*, pp. 59–60.

55 The verse reads: '. . . then Adam received from his Lord [some] words, and He accepted his repentance.'

56 Imam Jaʿfar's exegesis of this verse is reported as, '. . . He [God] created five creatures from the light of His Glory (*nūr ʿaẓamatihi*) and He assigned to each of them a name derived from His own Names. . . . then He placed these names to the right side of His throne. . . . these were the five names that Adam received from his Lord.' Amir-Moezzi, *The Divine Guide*, p. 31. Also see al-Majlisī, *Biḥār*, XI, pp. 176–177. For other sources, see Rubin, 'Pre-existence and Light', p. 107.

57 Yaman, p. 2.

58 Ibid., pp. 5–6.

59 Ibid., p. 11.

60 Ibid., pp. 13–14.

61 Ibid., p. 14.

62 Cited and quoted by Uri Rubin from al-Masʿūdī's *Ithbāt al-waṣiya li'l-imām ʿAlī b. Abī Ṭālib* in his 'Pre-existence and Light', p. 93.

63 Ibid., p. 93.

64 Ibid., p. 95.

65 Cited and quoted in Amir-Moezzi, *The Divine Guide*, p. 41.

66 Yaman, p. 14.

67 Ibid., p. 10.

68 Ibid., p. 6.

69 Amir-Moezzi, *The Divine Guide*, p. 92. Also see Rubin, 'Prophets and Progenitors in the Early Shiʿa Tradition', *JSAI*, 1 (1979), p. 47; Ayoub, *Redemptive Suffering*, p. 62. It is reported from Imam ʿAlī that, 'Our Lord has given us knowledge of the Greatest Name, through which, were we to want to, we would rend asunder the heavens and the earth and paradise and hell; through it we ascend to heaven and descend to earth and we travel to the east and to the west until we reach the Throne (of God) and sit upon it before God and He gives us all things, even the heavens, the earth, the sun, moon and stars, the mountains, the trees, the paths, the seas, heaven and hell.' Quoted in Momen, *An Introduction to Shi'i Islam*, p. 150. Apart from the Supreme Name, imams were also possessors of certain sacred objects usually believed to have come from paradise. Among them are Adam's cloak, Solomon's seal, Moses' staff (*ʿaṣā*), the Ark of covenant (*tābūt*) and the weapon of Muḥammad. The last one is nothing but the *Dhū'l-faqār*, the famous double-edged sabre brought from heaven by the angel Gabriel. (Amir-Moezzi, *The Divine Guide*, p. 93.) Another tradition says, it was made of the leaves of the myrtle of Paradise and brought down to earth by Adam. After Adam, it was transmitted from prophet to prophet until it was given to ʿAlī by Muḥammad. Following ʿAlī, the sword had been kept by imams till Muḥammad al-Mahdī inherited it. Taking it into occultation with him, al-Mahdī would hold *Dhū'l-faqār* when he returns to fill the world with justice. See Rubin, 'Prophets and Progenitors', p. 47. Rubin calls attention to the similarity of tradition regarding Moses's staff, which is also said to have been made of the myrtle of Paradise, brought down by Adam, and transmitted through prophetic channels till it reached Moses.

70 Yaman, p. 7.

71 Amir-Moezzi, *The Divine Guide*, p. 99.

72 Cited in Amir-Moezzi, *The Divine Guide*, p. 116. Indeed, Shiʿi belief makes recognition of the Hidden Imam's *walāya* incumbent upon the faithful for it is a universally established belief that, 'He who dies without knowing his Imam dies the death of ignorant pagans.' This axiom is recorded in works of al-Kulaynī, al-Nuʿmānī, Ibn Bābawayh and many others. See Amir-Moezzi, *The Divine Guide*, p. 123.
73 al-Majlisī, 23, p. 308.
74 Ibid., 23, pp. 319–320.
75 Ayoub cites from Ibn Bābawayh's *Maʿānī*. (*Redemptive Suffering*, p. 58.)
76 Cited and quoted in Ayoub, *Redemptive Suffering*, p. 61. For some other traditions in the same meaning, see M.A. Amir-Moezzi, 'Aspects de l'imâmologie duodécimaine I: remarques sur la divinité de l'imām', *Studia Iranica*, 25, 2 (1996), pp. 201, 204–205; idem, 'Some Remarks on the Divinity of the Imam', in *The Spirituality of Shiʿi Islam* (London, 2011), pp. 103–131.
77 Yaman, p. 3.
78 Ibid., p. 4.
79 Ibid., p. 4.
80 Ibid., p. 5.
81 Ibid., p. 15.
82 Ibn Bābawayh, *A Shiʿite Creed*, p. 99.
83 Ibid., p. 99–102.
84 For their status in Ottoman society, see Rüya Kılıç, 'The Reflection of Islamic Tradition on Ottoman Social Structure: the *sayyids* and *sharifs*', in Kazuo Morimoto, ed., *Sayyids and Sharifs in Muslim Societies: The Living Links to the Prophet* (London and New York, 2012), pp. 123–138.
85 Kazuo Morimoto, 'The Prophet's Family as the Perennial Source of Saintly Scholars: al-Samhūdī on *ʿilm* and *nasab*', in Catherine Mayeur-Jaouen and Alexandre Papas, ed., *Family Portraits with Saints: Hagiographies, Sanctity, and Family in the Muslim World* (Berlin, 2013), pp. 106–124.
86 We should underline here that this differentiation marks the chief doctrinal divergence between the Qizilbash/Alevi tradition and the Bekashi Sufi order.
87 The history of the Alevi *ocak* system is yet to be elucidated. For an introductory study of *ocaks* and *dedes* in contemporary Alevi community, see Ali Yaman, *Alevilik'te Dedelik ve Ocaklar* (Istanbul, 2004); Hamza Aksüt, *Aleviler: Türkiye-İran-Irak-Suriye-Bulgaristan* (Ankara, 2009), pp. 31–316. The reader should be warned that both studies bear methodological shortcomings and need to be treated carefully.
88 It is because of this fact that in the Alevi tradition *ijāzat-nāmah* (diploma of qualification) serves as a proof for possession of Husaynid genealogy rather than qualification of certain merits as is the case in all Sufi orders. For a brief analysis of Alevi *ijāzat-nāmahs* in that perspective, see R. Yıldırım, 'Bektaşi Kime Derler? 'Bektaşi' Kavramının Kapsamı ve Sınırları Üzerine Tarihsel bir Analiz Denemesi', *Türk Kültürü ve Hacı Bektaş Veli Araştırma Dergisi*, 55 (2010), pp. 38–41.
89 Yaman, p. 12.
90 Ibid., p. 3.
91 *Kitāb-i maqām-i manāqib-i quṭb al-ʿārifīn haḍrat-i Shaykh Sayyid Ṣafī*, MS 199. Konya Mevlana Müzesi Abdülbâki Gölpınarlı Kütüphanesi, fols 62a-62b.
92 *Kitāb-i maqām-i manāqib-i quṭb al-ʿārifīn*, f. 76a.
93 To quote from Ibn Bābawayh would be useful to show the remarkable variation in form and content between two perceptions of the imams: 'Our belief regarding them is that they are in authority (*ūlū'l-amr*). It is to them that God has ordained obedience, they are the witness for the people and they are the gates of God (*abwāb*) and the road (*sabīl*) to Him and the guides (*dalīl*, pl. *adilla*) thereto, and the repositories of His knowledge and the interpreters of His revelations and the pillars of His unity (*tawḥīd*). They are immune from sin (*khaṭaʿ*) and error (*ḍalāl*); they are those from whom 'God has

removed all impurity and made them absolutely pure' (33:33); they are possessed of (the power of) miracles (*muʿjizāt*) and of (irrefutable) arguments (*dalāʾil*); and they are for the protection of the people of this earth just as the stars are for the inhabitants of the heavens. They may be linked, in this community, to the Ark of Noah; he who boards it obtains salvation or reaches the Gate of Repentance.' Ibn Bābawayh, *A Shiʿite Creed*, p. 84.

94 According to Momen, this change occurred in two stages: 1) rejecting *ghuluww* doctrines and 2) building the Shiʿi theology upon Muʿtazilī *kalām*. The first step was more or less accomplished by Ibn Bābawayh, a large portion of whose works is devoted to refuting anthropomorphism, while the credit for adoption of Muʿtazilī *kalām*, hence highlighting the role of reason, is given to Shaykh al-Mufīd (d. 413/1022) and his eminent students Sharīf al-Murtaḍā (d. 436/1044) and Muḥammad al-Ṭūsī (d. 460/1067). Momen, *An Introduction to Shi'i Islam*, pp. 76–79.

95 Amir-Moezzi, 'Aspects de l'imâmologie duodécimaine I', pp. 196, 206.

96 As Momen rightly observes, 'The majority [of early Shiʿis] subscribed to such doctrines as anthropomorphism, transmigration of souls, descent of the divine spirit into man, occultation and return, alteration of the Divine will, etc. . . . Most of these doctrines are of course held to be heretical by the final fully-developed Twelver theology.' Momen, *An Introduction to Shi'i Islam*, pp. 70–71. Also see Amir-Moezzi, *The Divine Guide*, p. 130; Amir-Moezzi, 'Aspects de l'imâmologie', pp. 200–201.

97 Amir-Moezzi, *The Divine Guide*, p. 130.

98 It is generally accepted that by the time the great Shiʿi scholar al-Ṭūsī died (460/1067), the legal foundation of Twelver Shiʿism was firmly laid. See, for example, Abdulaziz Abdulhussein Sachedina, *Islamic Messianism: The Idea of Mahdi in Twelver Shiʿism* (Albany, NY, 1981), p. 38.

9

The Khāksār Shiʿi Sufi Order: An Updated Introduction

Alexandre Papas

The Khāksār spiritual path or Khāksāriyya is a recent but prominent Shiʿi Sufi order in Iran. Still an enigma in many respects, the movement itself maintained secrecy and has only lately been the subject of extensive investigation, led chiefly by my colleagues Mihrān Afshārī and Shahrokh Raei. Following the German Islamologist Richard Gramlich (d. 2006) and his pioneering *Die schiitischen Derwischorden Persiens*, previous scholars were inclined to give up the reconstruction of the history of the Khāksāriyya because of the lack of sources, especially of writings produced by the order's members themselves.[1] It is wrong, however, to state that the Khāksār masters (*pīrs*) were indifferent to texts and relied strictly on oral means of transmission. In the present volume, the chapter authored by Lloyd Ridgeon and the two epistles translated from the Persian, respectively by Mehrdad Arabestani and Yaser Mirdamadi, offer significant examples of their written production.[2] My brief essay aims both to review this production and to summarise the results of recent scholarship.

The Manuscript Corpus

According to the discoveries of Mihrān Afshārī, the Khāksār manuscript corpus consists mainly of treatises (*risālas*) of various lengths, all written in Persian. Librarians often classified these works as *futuwwat-nāmahs* (guild treatises) although, strictly speaking, they belong to another spiritual tradition.[3] Besides, we should bear in mind that a part of the Khāksār written patrimony is preserved in private archives and has not been studied yet.

A brief survey of available material includes the following references: originally a manuscript preserved at the Library of Frankfurt University, Microfilm 7104 of the Central Library of Tehran University contains a collection of short treatises. The first one, simply titled *Faqīriyya* (Poverty), discusses in the form of questions and answers the physical and spiritual entry into the path of Sufi poverty. Mehrad Arabestani provides an English version of this epistle for the present volume. A second text of the manuscript is entitled *Tāj nāmah-yi pīrān* (On the Headgear of Masters) although a second title is cited inside the text, *Irshād-i kiswa* (Direction [symbol] of the Garment), whose mythical authorship is attributed to the fifth imām Muḥammad Bāqir (d. *ca* 114/732). It deals with the prophetic and imami origins of Sufi headgear. In the same manuscript but also present partly in *futuwwat-nāmahs*, the *Āyat-hā-yi tarāsh* (Verses of Shaving) reviews the Qurʾanic verses to be recited during the ritual shaving of the dervish (hair, beard, moustache, eyebrows). A last treatise taken from the Frankfurt manuscript, entitled *Suʿālāt-i waṣla wa khirqa* (Questions on Rags and Cloak), articulates in the form of short questions and answers the esoteric meaning of the Sufi cloak.[4]

Numbered among the brief manuscripts is MS 860 of the Library of the Islamic Theology Faculty at Mashhad University. Under the title *Bayān-i arkān* (Exposition of the Pillars), the pamphlet summarises the beliefs of the Khāksārs. Within the same manuscript, the *Hasht maqām-i qaṭārkish* (Eight Stages of the Lining-up) lists the various types of Sufis with their corresponding tutelary prophet. MS 7566 of the Central Library of Tehran University contains two texts: *Risāla dar ṭarīqat* which explains the spiritual path through questions and answers and also enigmas and riddles; and a piece on professional guilds (*aṣnāf*) and their respective patron saints; MS 11510 of the Parliament Library in Tehran includes an untitled, unfinished treatise dealing with the principles of the Khāksāriyya. Several topics are common in two other works, the above-mentioned *Hasht maqām-i qaṭārkish* and the *Risāla-yi ṭarīqat-i Sayyid Jalāl al-Dīn Ḥaydar* to which we shall return.

Among the longer manuscripts of the Khāksār tradition, the *Chahārdah khānawādah* (Fourteen Families), which has been copied many times, is a survey established by the Khāksārs to elucidate the origin of the Sufi paths and to define their classification. Yaser Mirdamadi has translated it into English in the present book. Another source is the *Risāla-yi ṭarīqat-i Sayyid Jalāl al-Dīn Ḥaydar* which exists in at least three copies: MS 860 of the Library of the Islamic Theology Faculty at Mashhad University; MS 57 and MS 1151 of the Parliament Library in Tehran. Falsely attributed to the famous Sufi master Abu'l-Ḥasan Kharaqānī (d. 425/1033), the anonymous treatise is composed of nine chapters: 1. expressing [one's] will [to become a dervish] (*irādat āwurdan*); 2. making [the novice] repent (*tawba dādan*); 3. using the scissors [to cut hair] (*dar miqrāḍ rāndan*); 4. wearing the [dervish] hat (*kulāh pūshīdan*); 5. wearing the cloak (*khirqa pūshīdan*); 6. girding the belt (*miyān bastan*); 7. sitting on the chair [as a sign of spiritual achievement and authority] (*takht nishastan*); 8. sweeping, swinging the beggar's bowl and saying 'God is great' [for mendicancy] (*jārūb zadan wa kashkūl gardānīdan wa takbīr guftan*); 9. the forty-four words [or precepts that the dervish must actualise] (*chihil ū chāhar kalām*). Finally, MS 4419/6 of the Central Library of Tehran University composed in prose and verse by a certain Mīrzā Muḥammad ʿAlī Sharīf Yazdī Shāhrūdī, himself a Khāksār, between 1315–1317/1897–1899. Many topics are covered, among which we find several sequences, such as the twelve or five stations (*manzil*), the four ablutions (*ghusl*) and blows (*ḍarb*), the forty-four stages (*maqām*), the fourteen words of the master (*kalām-i pīr-i dalīl*), the sixteen foursomes of masters (*shānzdah chahār pīr*) and so forth. The manuscript also contains a second piece, much shorter, on two series of seventeen professional guilds and their mythical founders.

Regarding the ʿAjam sub-branch of the Khāksāriyya, MS 4362 of the Central Library of the University of Tehran is a rich collection of Persian poetry copied in 1336/1918. These simple but elegant verses were recited during public declamations (*sukhanwarī*) by ʿAjam dervishes, a practice reminiscent of late medieval 'people of speech' (*ahl-i sukhan*), i.e. panegyrists, poetry reciters and storytellers. A second ʿAjam text describing the rules of the Sufi order, entitled *Wasīlat al-najāt* (Tool of Salvation) and studied by Lloyd Ridgeon in this book (with a table of contents in an appendix), has been edited from MS 9200 of the Parliament Library in Tehran.

Origins and Practices

While reliable information remains fragmentary despite this rich corpus, it is nevertheless possible to shed light on the origins of the

Shiʿi Sufi order.[5] The Khāksāriyya appeared during the Qajar period from the merging of two existing Qalandar groups, namely the Ḥaydariyya and the Jalāliyya. A member of the Indian Jalāliyya, Ghulām ʿAlī Shāh Hindī, moved from India to Iran at an unknown date and bound his lineage to a group of the Iranian Shiʿi Ḥaydariyya,[6] which existed since the Safawid period and should not be confused with the probably Sunni Ḥaydariyya derived from Quṭb al-Dīn Ḥaydar Zāwiʾī (d. 618/1221). According to the *Tuḥfa-yi darwīsh*,[7] written by the Khāksār *pīr* ʿAbd al-Karīm Mudarrisī (b. 1926), Ghulām ʿAlī Shāh was born in Qandahar (in southern Afghanistan) and was buried there; he seems to have spread the Khāksāriyya in Iran from 1300/1882 onwards.[8] In Maʿṣūm ʿAlī Shāh's *Ṭarāʾiq al-ḥaqāʾiq*, a famous Niʿmat Allāhī biographical compendium dated 1333/1915, an explanation of the name *khāksār* (lit. 'dust-like') is given: the movement would find its origin in Hindu sects whose ascetic followers sat on the ground (*khāk*) and covered their bodies with dust.[9] The hypothesis is tempting, for it recalls antinomian Sufi groups in India who were confused with Tantric sects,[10] but lacks historical evidence. The Khāksāriyya treatises provide more solid information: one of the tales of the corpus, apparently written in India between the 11th/17th and the 12th/18th centuries, relates that some *qalandar*s wore ash-coloured (*khākistarī*) garments and rubbed their face with ashes (*khākistar*). This specific practice was called *khāksārī*. Since Khāksārs were influenced by the Indian Jalālī Qalandars, their name might come from this practice. In any case, the word denoting a lowly and humble person can be read as a metaphor of the material and spiritual poverty which characterised the order.[11]

Present-day Khāksārs describe their spiritual chain of transmission (*silsila*) as Khāksār-i Jalālī-yi Abū Turābī, hence establishing a mythical connection between the name of their own *silsila* and the name of Imām ʿAlī (Abū Turāb) with a possible allusion to the word *turāb* meaning dust. More important perhaps, and similar to the Ḥaydariyya, the Khāksāriyya gives as the first link of the chain (*sar-silsila*) the name of Sayyid Jalāl al-Dīn Ḥaydar who had allegedly expounded the beliefs and the rules of the path. Who was he? Contrary to what is sometimes asserted in most scholarship as well as in Khāksār modern writings, this figure should not be identified with Sayyid Jalāl al-Dīn Bukhārī (d. 785/1384), a Sufi scholar of the Suhrawardī order in India and head of the Jalāliyya.[12] Sayyid Jalāl al-Dīn Ḥaydar actually corresponds to Quṭb al-Dīn Ḥaydar Tūnī (d. *ca* 830/1426), a Shiʿi wandering *qalandar* who lived in Azerbaijan and established a Shiʿi Ḥaydariyya order, which spread in the Caucasus and Iran. He was born in Baku and was buried in Tabriz.[13] On the other hand, the hypothesis according to which Khāksārs formed a sub-lineage of the Indian Jalāliyya which joined the Iranian Ḥaydariyya is confirmed by the fact that the Khāksār written traditions mention figures such as Laʿl Shahbāz Qalandar (d. 673/1274) and Fakhr al-Dīn Ganj-i Shakar (d. 664/1265), both well-known Sufis of India, and that their genealogies include Indian names such as Miyākhākī and Nūr Nahāl. Furthermore, like many Indian Sufi orders, Khāksārs rely on the paradigm of the Fourteen families (*chahārdah khānawādah*). On the model of Hujwīrī (d. *ca* 465/1071) who classified spiritual paths into twelve in the *Kashf al-maḥjūb*, Indian hagiographers categorised Sufi orders as dispersed through fourteen families, among whom the Chishtiyya was usually considered the ninth and the Qalandariyya the twelfth.[14]

Besides, remarkable are the similarities with the Ahl-i Ḥaqq movement of Iran. They probably come from the interactions between both spiritual milieus throughout history, although the Khāksārs have always lain explicitly within the strict framework of Islam. At present, their relations are still close in Tehran and Kirmanshah whereas they decreased greatly in Shiraz and Isfahan during the last decade.[15]

Several common traits or evidence of proximity can be highlighted. Although the meeting-place of the Khāksārs is now called a *khānaqāh*, or *takiyya* (lodge), we also find in sources the term *jamkhānah*, which is found in Ahl-i Ḥaqq literature and denotes the place where the mystics get together and perform their rituals. Concerning the latter, Khāksārs have a ceremony known as *jamʿ-i ḥaqīqat* (gathering of truth) which is limited to the members of highest ranks. It is a ceremonial meal accompanied by music, which takes place at the beginning of each month and season. The three-day fast ('fasting of truth', *rūza-yi ḥaqīqat*) undertaken at the beginning of this ceremony is also practised by the Ahl-i Ḥaqq. Regarding rites and habits again, some men of both traditions wear the 'sealed' (*muhr*) moustache, which is never cut, throughout their life. More important, the rite of the 'gate' (*qāpī*) symbolises the passage from one step to the next for the dervish engaged in spiritual progression. There are four gates (i.e. gnosis, law, path, truth) and each of them belongs to a saintly king and his disciples, whose names figure in the Ahl-i Ḥaqq hagiology.[16] Both movements also share the same 'code names', such as Shāh Ayāzī for ʿAlī and Shāh Ibrāhīmī for Ḥasan, to surname the twelve imams in certain rituals and ceremonies. Intriguing too is the use of the long-necked lute (*tanbūr*) in both groups. Among their common beliefs, we find the 'seven holy figures' (*haft tanān*) and 'forty holy figures' (*chihil-tanān*), which are angelic entities. Like the Ahl-i Ḥaqq, the Khāksāriyya *silsila* is related to Salmān al-Fārsī (d. 35/655–6 or 36/656–7) named Sulṭān Maḥmūd Pātīlī or Pāṭilī, who had been initiated to secret doctrines by the Prophet, according to Khāksār mythology. This esoteric descent is also present in the *futuwwat* tradition.[17] A last sign of proximity between Khāksārs and Ahl-i Ḥaqq regards the stages of the initiation.[18]

Initiation to the Khāksārī path

The Khāksārī initiatory path consists of seven stages (*haft-marḥala, haft-maqām*), which mark the spiritual progression of the dervish. The master acknowledges each stage and allows or disallows access to the next step. One should keep in mind that some *pīr*s use a five-level mode of initiation, and that the position and definition of the highest levels do not seem uniform.[19] The seven stages can be described as follows:

1. The 'tongue' (*lisān*): This first step takes place when someone expresses his interest in the Sufi path. At this stage, one of the masters makes the disciple renounce sin, the disciple performs ablutions and the master plucks hairs from his head, eyebrows, moustache and beard—a resumption of the 'four blows' (*chahār-ḍarb*) ritual of the Qalandariyya. Then the disciple commits to observing the rules of the path. This ritual recalls the 'giving of one's word' or 'word of honour' (*jawānmardān-i qawlī*) in the *futuwwat*.
2. The 'goblet' (*piyālah*): This is the stage during which the novice becomes a dervish. He is given by the *pīr* a surname (the 'poverty name', *ism-i faqrī*) followed by the title ʿAlī Shāh. Several dervishes get in line and gird each other with a cloth worn around the waist

called 'lungi of the forty [holy figures]' (*lung-i chihil*); then they drink one after the other a syrup prepared by the master. This also exists in the *futuwwat*. During the ritual, a long poem is read. The majority of Khāksārs remain at this level.

3. The 'garment' (*kiswa*): The master puts a heated coin on the upper arm of the disciple to make a mark on it. Apparently limited to a handful of disciples in the Qajar period, this ritual is said to be no longer performed nowadays, or perhaps in secret. This mark is considered as a 'seal of prophecy' (*muhr-i nubuwwat*), a sort of physical manifestation of the esoteric concept of *khatm al-nubuwwa* derived from Qur'an 33:40.
4. The 'depositing of flower' (*gul sipurdan*): The dervish is now required to submit entirely to God through his master. Probably following the preceding marking ritual, a few days after the disciple shows his wound to the master. The flower refers to the piece of skin that has to be removed from the burn.
5. The 'breaking of the nutmeg' (*jawz shikastan*) or 'entrusting the head' (*sar sipārī*): Only a limited number of members reach this point. The dervish goes to subordinate himself to the Ahl-i Ḥaqq master (*sayyid-i waqt*, 'the master of time') who breaks with a knife a perfumed walnut, a symbolic item which was also used by Niʿmat Allāhīs to signify that the disciple placed himself in the master's hands.[20]
6. The taking of light (*chirāghī giriftan*): the advanced disciple is promoted to the rank of master. Concretely, he takes from the master a light made of several candles. The ritual symbolises mystical illumination, the transmission of esoteric knowledge, and the capacity to enlighten others.
7. The direction (*irshād*): at this stage, the disciple receives from the master a lungi (*lungī-yi irshād*, 'lungi of direction'), which ensures the transmission role of the Sufi cloak and exhibits the legitimacy of the accomplished mystic. The garment is sometimes compared with the 'trousers of the guilds' (*sarwāl-i futuwwat*; *shalwār-i futuwwat*) but one may speculate that it was actually a pagne or a sarong, in reference to the Indian origins of the Khāksāriyya.

Traditionally, the initiation of women was forbidden and even their presence at the weekly *dhikr* sessions was not accepted. However, attitudes changed with modernity and some masters accepted to initiate women to the Khāksārī path.[21] Ḥajj Muṭahhar ʿAlī Shāh (d. 1983) was probably the first to do so. Several women were admitted as disciples, including a classmate of French origin, someone from Mashhad, a few Bakhtyārīs. Most of them remained at the first stage of initiation, the *lisān*. The master of the lodge in Isfahan, Nuṣrat ʿAlī Shāh went a step further by initiating about fifty to sixty women to the first stage and about ten to twenty to the second, the *piyālah*. A few other cases occurred later on. Nevertheless, contrary to the Niʿmat Allāhiyya, this openness to women never developed among Khāksārs and remains controversial today.

In the Qajar period, Khāksār bands used to go to lodges and mosques and ask for money to write prayers or death eulogies, and they used to go begging in the streets and bazaars with their beggar's bowls (*kashkūl*) in their hands. These Khāksārs chanted poetry praising ʿAlī and in exchange received food or money from the passers-by and the traders. They presented their earnings to their masters. Sometimes, they sat in devotion in a corner of the mosque or in Shiʿi shrines (*imāmzādah*) and at sunrise and sunset sang praises to ʿAlī – a practice called 'sitting in quest' (*ṭalab nishastan*). At the end of each year and towards the Iranian New Year, they pitched a tent outside the houses of the nobles and stayed there several days, chanting poetry and making prayers until the owner of the house gave money. On the days of ʿĀshūrāʾ and Tāsūʿāʾ they sang orations.

In principle, each dervish of the order received from his master a written document, which stipulated his mission. The supreme chief (*quṭb*) of the Khāksāriyya assigned a deputy (*naqīb*) in each city who had the authorisation to require that document. If the dervish did not show it or gave wrong answers to questions, the deputy took back his garment. These writings were basically collections of poetry and narratives written either in verse or prose on various topics, such as the stages of the spiritual path, the cooking of food for the poor, the specific cloth and paraphernalia, i.e. cloak, hat, beggar's bowl, belt, shroud, skin cover, staff, axe and pendant stone.[22] All of this material culture, charged with symbolic meaning, represents an important – albeit ghostlike today – aspect of the Khāksār tradition. Old photographs such as the ones published at the end of this article (figs 9.1 and 9.2) give an idea of the physical appearance of dervishes. Symbolic objects now survive as representations in the iconography of jewels, posters, written works, gravestones and buildings' walls. The order's coat of arms resembles that of the Niʿmat Allāhī and consists of two dervish axes (*tabarzīn*), which intersect each other, a *kashkūl* and a rosary (*tasbīḥ*); a horn (*nafīr*) or a staff (*mantashā*) is sometimes added.[23] The current politico-religious situation in Iran as well as friction within the community forced the Khāksārs to remove some of these symbols from the public sphere.

The Khāksār Groups

Historically there were three main groups: the Ghulām ʿAlī Shāhī, the Maʿṣūm ʿAlī Shāhī and the Nūrāʾī, about whom there is no information so far. Another type of Khāksār which existed since the Qajar period was that of the dervishes without *silsila*, known as ʿAjam. They joined the Khāksāriyya after having completed their initiation into their own spiritual path. Under Riḍā Shāh (r. 1925–1941), both the anti-Sufi policy of the state and the reforms introduced by the supreme master Ḥajj Muṭahhar ʿAlī Shāh affected the Khāksāriyya. Over the past years, followers joined other Sufi groups, especially the Niʿmat Allāhiyya, and the Khāksāriyya itself have undergone the influence of other Sufi traditions. Yet, several cities in Iran still shelter either individual members or entire communities of Khāksārs.

Until very recently, there were three groups: the Maʿṣūm ʿAlī Shāhī, the Ghulām ʿAlī Shāhī, and the ʿAjamī. The first group appeared in the Qajar period and included masters such as Shams ʿAlī Shāh and Mīr Kawthar Shīrāzī, both buried in Shiraz.[24] A few Maʿṣūm ʿAlī Shāhīs still existed in Tehran, Mashhad, Kirmanshah and Ahwaz. The last important figures included Sarmast ʿAlī Shāh Ṭurughī and Raḥmat ʿAlī Shāh Dihkurdī. It seems that the last followers joined the Ghulām ʿAlī Shāhīs, even though regularly such or such a master claims to be descended from Maʿṣūm ʿAlī Shāh. Such is the case of Khandān ʿAlī Shāh in Shiraz.[25]

The ʿAjamī sub-branch (perhaps linked to the Nuqṭawīs, surnamed ʿAjam) gradually disappeared despite a rich past and a strong identity. For instance, the *Wasīlat al-najāt* treatise suggests that the ʿAjamīs had discrepancies with the main order and considered themselves as an independent movement. They described themselves as encompassing seventeen professions. ʿAjamīs were experts in the art of acting and, in the evenings of Ramaḍān, they performed poetry recitation, called *sukhanwarī*, in lodges or in coffeehouses according to precise rules. In connection with this ceremony, the practice of water-carrying (*saqqāʾī*) consisted in quenching the thirst of participants during Muḥarram mourning sessions.[26] The reception ritual of the disciple was called *lisān dādan* ('giving his word'), then at each step on the spiritual path the dervish obtained from his master either a permission (*parwānah*) or a licence document (*ijāzat-nāmah*) that they called *mujallā* in addition to special objects and clothes. Like the Ḥaydarīs of the Safawid time, the ʿAjam masters were named *bābā*.[27]

The most important and better identified group is the Ghulām ʿAlī Shāhī. At the end of the Qajar period and the beginning of the Pahlavis, their *quṭb* was Bahār ʿAlī Shāh Yazdī (d. 1936) who succeeded Qaṭār ʿAlī Shāh (d. 1308/1890). Bahār ʿAlī Shāh lived in Najaf and had numerous disciples in Iraq and Iran. A respected scholar and a high social figure, he had close relations with local authorities but also with Sufi leaders as far away as Kurdistan. Bahār ʿAlī Shāh was succeeded by Ḥajj Muṭahhar who lived for more a hundred years according to his disciples. He reformed the Sufi order and established main lodges in Kufa and Mashhad while the centre was located in Tehran. There at Dawlat City Gate, he built a lodge, which still exists today. According to his will, Ḥajj Muṭahhar was buried near the grave of the famous shaykh Zāhid Gīlānī (d. 700/1301) in the garden belonging to the Khāksāriyya.[28] Tensions and conflicts erupted within the order during the *pīr*'s lifetime and after his death. For unclear reasons, one of his devotees, Mīr Ṭāhir (d. 2002), was excluded. He had previously established a competing community located in a lodge in Kirmanshah (near the old cemetery), a city where some Khāksārs were already present. Mīr Ṭāhir reactivated relations with the Jalālīs in Pakistan. His sub-group split again into two branches, each directed by a son of Mīr Ṭāhir. After Ḥajj Muṭahhar's death in 1983, the supervision of the Muṭahhariyya lodge in Tehran was given to Mīr Jalāl al-Dīn Miṣbāḥ Muṭahharī (d. 2008) but his nomination was disputed and other *pīr*s appointed their own representatives. The current master of the Tehran lodge is Baḥr ʿAlī Shāh Thānī, a Shiʿi cleric.[29] Interestingly, Mīr Kawthar (d. 2015), a son of Mīr Ṭāhir, planned to reopen the lodge of

Kufa, which had been shut down several decades ago, and travelled there with followers in 2011 for a religious festival.

Despite this disunity within the Khāksāriyya, a quite frequent phenomenon in the history of Islamic mysticism, the Shiʿi Sufi order through the Ghulām ʿAlī Shāhī group continues to be fairly active not only on the internet, thanks to blogs or websites, but also in the everyday life of Iranians.

Figure 9.1. Khāksār dervish holding an engraved axe (*tabarzīn*), Iran, 1880–1930 (Myron Bement Smith Collection: Antoin Sevruguin Photographs. Freer Gallery of Art and Arthur M. Sackler Gallery Archives. Smithsonian Institution, Washington D.C. Gift of Katherine Dennis Smith, 1973–1985, FSA A.4 2.12. GN.28.07).

Figure 9.2. Khāksār dervish carrying a *kashkūl,* with a 12-sided pendant and a sawfish saw, Iran, 1880–1930 (Myron Bement Smith Collection: Antoin Sevruguin Photographs. Freer Gallery of Art and Arthur M. Sackler Gallery Archives. Smithsonian Institution, Washington D.C. Gift of Katherine Dennis Smith, 1973–1985, FSA A.4 2.12.Up.63).

NOTES

1 Richard Gramlich, *Die schiitischen Derwischorden Persiens* (3 vols., Wiesbaden, 1965–1981), vol. 1, pp. 82–86.

2 Worth mentioning too is the fact that Khāksār authors started to write on the history of their brotherhood—one may cite Hosayn Monajjemi—and that the Jalālī Khāksār lodge (*takiyya*) in Kirmanshah ran a publishing house specialising in the editing of Persianate mystical poetry. Publications include: *Dīwān-i Sayyid Sharaf al-Dīn Bū ʿAlī Qalandar. Bi inḍimām-i Panj ganj-i Khusrawī,* ed. M. Ṭāhir, 1360 Sh./1981; Muḥyī al-Dīn Mīr Khandān, *Sūz-hā wa sāz-hā: majmūʿa-yi ashʿār-i ʿārifāna,* 1361 Sh./1982; *Dīwān-i ʿĀrif-i Hamadānī Mawlānā Shams Maghribī,* ed. M. Ṭāhir and Ṣ. ʿAlī, 1362/1983.

3 Mihrān Afshārī and Abū Ṭālib Mīr ʿĀbidīnī, *Āyīn-i qalandarī: mushtamil bar chahār risāla dar bāb-i qalandarī, khāksārī, firqa-yi ʿajam wa sukhanwarī* (Tehran, 1374 Sh./ 1995); Mihrān Afshārī ed., *Futuwwat-nāmah-hā wa rasāʾil-i Khāksāriyya (sī risāla)* (Tehran, 1394 Sh./2015).

4 It might be of interest to mention on the same subject the *Risāla-yi ādāb-i darwīshī wa qalandarī* (MS 3478, Central Library of Tehran University), on which see M. Afshārī ed., *Futuwwat-nāmah-hā*, p. 286.

5 A first outline was authored by Mihrān Afshārī, 'Khāksāriyya', *Dānishnāmah-yi jahān-i Islām*, online: http://rch.ac.ir/article/Details?id=8315

6 ʿAbd al-Ḥusayn Zarrīnkūb, *Justujū dar taṣawwuf-i Īrān* (Tehran, 1363 Sh./1984), pp. 375–376.

7 ʿAbd al-Karīm Mudarrisī, *Tibyān al-ḥaqq-i āyāt-i wilāyat: bi-inḍimām-i Kitāb-i Safarnāmah yā jild-i awwal-i Tuḥfa-yi darwīsh mamlū az taṣwīr-i ʿurafāʾ wa buzurgān-i silsila-yi jalīla-yi Khāksār wa Kitāb-i Mūnis al-Shīʿa* (Tehran, 1337 Sh./1958), p. 114. There are other interesting aspects in this source that I plan to study in the near future.

8 A remark: the supposedly earliest mention of the Khāksārs, which is in *Riyāḍ al-siyāḥa* (ed. A.Ḥ. Rabbānī, Tehran, 1339 Sh./1960, p. 131), by Zayn al-ʿĀbidīn Shīrwānī (d. 1253/1837) who met them in 1225/1810, in what is now Pakistan, does not in fact correspond to the Khāksār dervishes.

9 Maʿṣūm ʿAlī Shāh, *Ṭarāʾiq al-ḥaqāʾiq* (3 vols., Tehran, 1339 Sh./1960), vol. 3, p. 533; Mihrān Afshārī, 'Yāddāsht-hā-yi darbārah-yi taṣawwuf, futuwwat wa qalandarī', in M. Afshārī, *Nuktāhā-yi nāguftah* (Tehran, 1393 Sh./2014), pp. 19–50 esp. 28–29.

10 Alexandre Papas, 'Antinomianism (*ibāḥa, ibāḥiyya*)', *EI3*.

11 Zahra Taheri, 'Ḵāksār', *EIR*.

12 The most extensive study on this figure is Amina M. Steinfels, *Knowledge before Action. Islamic Learning and Sufi Practice in the Life of Sayyid Jalāl al-Dīn Bukhārī Makhdūm-i Jahāniyān* (Columbia, SC, 2012).

13 On this shaykh, see the important clarification of Mihrān Afshārī, 'Quṭb al-Dīn Ḥaydar-e Tūnī and his Connection to the Ḥaydariyya and Khāksāriyya', in Shahrokh Raei ed., *Islamic Alternatives. Non-Mainstream Religion in Persianate Societies* (Wiesbaden, 2017), pp. 161–165.

14 On this paradigm, see Carl W. Ernst and Bruce B. Lawrence, *Sufi Martyrs of Love: Chishti Sufism in South Asia and Beyond* (New York, 2002), pp. 24, 58, 63; Alexandre Papas, 'When the Dervish Starts Publishing: A Note on Renunciation and Literary Production in the Indian Qalandariyya', in Rachida Chih, Denis Gril, Catherine Mayeur-Jaouen and Rüdiger Seesemann, ed., *Sufism, Literary Production and Printing in the Nineteenth Century* (Wurzburg, 2015), p. 133.

15 Shahrokh Raei, 'Der Zusammenhang zwischen den religiösen Traditionen der Khaksar und denen der Ahl-e Haqq: Eine Perspektive zum historischen Verständnis der Khaksar-Derwische', in Christine Allison, Anke Joisten-Pruschke and Antje Wendtland, ed., *From Daēnā to Dîn. Religion, Kultur und Sprache in der iranischen Welt* (Wiesbaden, 2009), pp. 349–355.

16 Mojan Membrado, 'Qalandars and Ahl-e Haqq', in Michel Boivin and Rémy Delage, ed., *Devotional Islam in Contemporary South Asia. Shrines, Journeys and Wanderers* (London, 2016), pp. 42–43.

17 M. Afshārī and A.Ṭ. Mīr ʿĀbidīnī, *Āyīn-i qalandarī*, pp. 278, 289, 300, 304, 314; M. Afshārī ed., *Futuwwat-nāmah-hā wa rasāʾil-i khāksāriyya*, pp. 180–188, 334.

18 Shahrokh Raei, 'Some Recent Issues and Challenges in the Khāksār Order', in Sh. Raei, ed., *Islamic Alternatives. Non-Mainstream Religion in Persianate Societies* (Wiesbaden, 2017), pp. 175–177.

19 Richard Gramlich, *Die schiitischen Derwischorden Persiens*, vol. 3, pp. 80–117 (with mostly quotations of the Persian poems recited by the master during the rituals); M. Afshārī, 'Khāksāriyya', *Dānishnāmah-yi jahān-i Islām*, online; Ḥusayn Munajjimī,

Mabānī-yi sulūk dar silsila-yi khāksār-i jalālī wa taṣawwuf (Tehran, 1379 Sh./2000), pp. 128–157; Shahrokh Raei, 'Khāksār Order in Kurdistan', in Khanna Omarkhali, ed., *Religious Minorities in Kurdistan: Beyond the Mainstream* (Wiesbaden, 2014), pp. 238–241.

20 R. Gramlich, *Die schiitischen Derwischorden Persiens*, vol. 3, pp. 75–76.

21 Sh. Raei, 'Some Recent Issues and Challenges in the Khāksār Order', pp. 171–175.

22 Ḥ. Munajjimī, *Mabānī-yi sulūk*, pp. 158–186.

23 Shahrokh Raei, 'Somes notes on the Khâksâr coat of arms', *JHS*, 6 (2014), pp. 129–138.

24 Nūr al-Dīn Mudarrisī Chahārdahī, *Khāksār wa Ahl-i Ḥaqq* (Tehran, 1368 Sh./1989), p. 132.

25 Interview with the master and his disciples on 12 October, 2017.

26 Mojtaba Zarvani and Mohammad Mashhadi, 'The Rites of the Water-Carrier: From the Circles of Sufis of the Rituals of Muharram', *JSIS*, 4, 1 (2011), pp. 35–38.

27 Mihrān Afshārī, 'Firqa-yi ʿAjam wa sukhanwarī', in M. Afshārī, *Tāzah bih tāzah, naw bih naw* (Tehran, 1387 Sh./2008), pp. 111–125.

28 Ḥ. Munajjimī, *Mabānī-yi sulūk*, pp. 42–51.

29 Sh. Raei, 'Khāksār Order in Kurdistan', pp. 244–246; Sh. Raei, 'Some Recent Issues and Challenges in the Khāksār Order', pp. 168–171.

10

ʿAjam Sufis and Shiʿi Spirituality in 19th-Century Iran

Lloyd Ridgeon

Introduction

Scholarly attention on Sufism during the 19th century in Iran has in the main focused on the Niʿmat Allāhī revival and its response to opposition from the clerical ranks between 1800–1850,[1] its subsequent growth and development under celebrated masters such as Ṣafī ʿAlī Shāh (d. 1316/1899),[2] and then its splintering into several streams, all vying for the hearts and minds of Sufi sympathisers.[3] A lesser degree of academic interest has been paid to other Sufi orders, such as the Dhahabī,[4] and perhaps the order that has received the least attention is the Khāksār. This may be explained by the literary endeavours of the orders mentioned above; the masters of the Niʿmat Allāhī order composed a number of works in which they elaborated upon various concerns of a Sufi nature, and this stands in complete contrast to Khāksār Sufis who have left a relatively small number of texts.[5] The lack of a sophisticated literature from the Khāksār Sufis is perhaps attributable to a range of factors, including the unease of these Sufis with the written word, as one of their leading masters of the mid-19th century reportedly stated, 'We live as dervishes in practice, not with forms and books'.[6] Another reason for the lack of written sources is related to the social standing of the order, as many of the dervishes were among the working and impoverished classes who most likely did not have access to any formal education.[7]

In this chapter I shall be focusing upon a sub-order of the Khāksār, namely the ʿAjam. I shall commence by investigating the relationship the ʿAjam had with Shiʿism by assessing the extent to which the ʿAjam embraced an 'orthodox' form of Twelver Shiʿism, how they presented themselves, through their own creation of their past, and the kinds of specific ritual activity that reflected the kind of attachment these Sufis had with Twelver Shiʿism. Subsequently I will discuss the distinctive Sufi features of the ʿAjam, and then the social context of these Sufis, in particular, the connection of the ʿAjam with the bazaar, and their participation and leading role in public poetic competitions (*sukhanwarī*) that made the Sufis of this order well known in 19th-century Iran.

Very little has been written about the ʿAjam. Even the *Encyclopaedia Iranica* does not contain a specific entry for this order, instead they are briefly mentioned in an article devoted to the Khāksār written by Zahra Taheri. In Persian, the ʿAjam fare a little better, and of note is the work of Muḥammad Jaʿfar Maḥjūb who composed a series of articles in the journal *Sukhan* which dealt with *sukhanwarī* (poetic compositions) and the ʿAjam.[8] But the scant attention devoted to the ʿAjam is reflected in Zarrīnkūb's chapter on the Khāksār in *Justujū dar taṣawwuf-i Īrān*, which contains only a single mention.[9] Recently interest has been focused upon the ʿAjam in the works of Mihrān Afshārī, who edited an important ʿAjam treatise called *Wasīlat al-najāt* (which can be rendered as the 'Tool [or means] of Salvation').[10] This is a relatively short text of some thirty-nine pages. The text was composed in 1266/1887–8,[11] in the middle of the reign of Nāṣir al-Dīn Shāh (r. 1264–1341/1848–1896), during a period in which the influence of Western thought and science increased, and the military and economic weaknesses of Iran were becoming all too apparent. There is next to nothing known about the author except that his name was Mashhadī Muḥammad Mahdī Tabrīzī, who was an affiliate of the ʿAjam. The text is significant because it supplies scholars with written evidence of the Shiʿi nature of the ʿAjam order, offers a tantalising possibility that such Sufi discourse contained aspects of Iranian nationalism, highlights the feuding and rivalry among the Sufis of late 19th-century Iran (a problem that continued into the early 20th century and arguably contributed to the decline and weakening of the tradition), and illustrates the close connection of this Sufi order with the bazaar. Afshārī's attention to the ʿAjam is also evident in his collection of four edited treatises, under the title of *Āʾīn-i Qalandarī*, one of which is a *sukhanwarī* 'poem'.[12] Afshārī's introduction to the text includes a brief section on the ʿAjam.[13] He has also published a short piece on the ʿAjam and *sukhanwarī* in a collection of his essays, but this does add significantly to his previously published work.[14]

Shiʿism: The ʿAjam and Twelver Shiʿism

The Persian text of *Wasīlat al-najāt* was composed largely in prose. However, the first section of the first chapter (*maqṣad-i awwal*) is in rhyming couplets in which there is an explicit commitment to Twelver Shiʿism. The six introductory sections are (1) an untitled section [27 couplets], (2) divine unity (*tawḥīd*) [21 couplets], (3) justice (*ʿadl*) [23 couplets], (4) prophecy [18 couplets], (5) imamate [72 couplets], (6) the return (*maʿād*) which is a discussion of an eschatological nature [32 couplets]. The length of the section on imamate offers a clear indication of the message the author sought to convey. The couplets do not yield any original content, but simply list the names of the imams in chronological order, sometimes using nicknames (*laqab*), and referring to events in their lives.[15] The couplets are not completely devoid of merit, as there are puns to help the listener memorise the text, for example:

> *After [ʿAlī] [is] Ḥasan, nicknamed 'Mujtabā';*
> *[After him is] Ḥusayn, the king of grief and affliction* (karb wa balā).

The pun is on the words grief and affliction (*karb wa balā*), and it is the Persian words which all too readily would remind the reader/listener of the slaying of Ḥusayn at Karbala. As such, these sections probably served as teaching materials and to reinforce standard Twelver doctrine. Moreover, the 'orthodoxy' of the Sufism is evident in the author's discussion of the superiority of the prophets over the imams. This most likely was to refute any accusation of *ghuluww* (or excessive Shiʿi belief) or even the possibility of identifying the imams as 'friends of God' who in some epochs of Sufi history have been understood as superior to the prophets.[16] The author remarks, 'Whoever says friendship (*walāya*) is greater than prophecy is an unbeliever (*kāfir*).'[17] The use of *kāfir* and *kufr* occurs regularly, which may have been directed at the Sunnis: 'If a person says that there was no imam after Muṣṭafā – know that these words are *kufr*.'[18] The didactic nature of this section continues with reasons for the existence of imamate, and the author lists these as the charge (or testament) (*waṣiyat*) of Muḥammad and refers to the famous *ḥadīth* of Ghadīr Khumm: 'Of whomsoever I had been Master, ʿAlī here is to be his Master.'[19] Other reasons for belief in the imams include their miracles (sing. *muʿjiza*, pl. *muʿjizāt*) and that they possess more virtue than other individuals.

After the introductory couplets, the rest of the first chapter is subdivided into sections that reflect the fundamentals of belief: purity (*ṭahārat*), prayer (*ṣalāt*), fasting (*ṣawm*), almsgiving (*zakāt*), paying the *khums* tax, pilgrimage (*ḥajj*), commanding the good and forbidding the evil (*al-amr bi'l-maʿrūf wa nahy ʿan al-munkar*); the inner and outer struggle (*jihād*), and buying and selling (*bayʿ*).[20] The author carefully observes the dues that have traditionally been associated with the formal Shiʿi functions of the clergy when discussing alms-tax and the *khums*. For example, he states that half of the *khums* must be given to a *mujtahid* or his representative or someone who has his permission, and the other half should go to the poor and orphans.[21] With regard to the *zakāt*, the author does not say who is responsible for the collection, management and distribution of the tax, he merely lists the kinds of worthy recipients, such as the poor and homeless, or says that the *zakāt* may be used to free slaves.[22] 'Orthodox' Twelver doctrine is observed too when the author states that '*jihād* against the unbelievers (*kuffār*) is a duty only at the permission of the [twelfth] Imam.'[23]

The opening chapter of the text locates this form of Sufism within 'orthodox' Shiʿism, and is careful to pay respect to its leading proponents, the *mujtahids*. This may have been an attempt to place ʿAjam Sufis squarely within Qajar society without the kind of trepidation experienced by Sufis under the Safawids (907–1135/1501–1722).[24] This amalgamation of Sufism and Shiʿism is continued later on in the text, in particular with the myths relating to the origins of the ʿAjam.

Origin of the ʿAjam and its Shiʿi Orientation

The origins of the Khāksār are not completely clear, as Taheri has observed, the way that they have reported their history: 'is replete with fanciful tales and mythologies, conveyed in oral narratives, the origins of which are thus difficult to trace.'[25] Zarrīnkūb argued that the origin of the Khāksār rested in an offshoot of Jalālī Sufism at the beginning of the Qajar period, which had strong Shiʿi tendencies.[26] The history of the ʿAjam, likewise, is difficult to reconstruct, but the author of *Wasīlat al-najāt* offers an interesting take on its origins. The opening of the fifth chapter (which is composed of twenty-five questions and answers) asks about the origins of the ʿAjam dervishes, and the author tells the story of a certain 'Ḥabīb Barqānī[27] of Qazwīn' who was a lover or devotee of Imam ʿAlī. Ḥabīb read his poetry in which he described his economic difficulties in ʿAjam (or Persia). ʿAlī told Ḥabīb to recite his panegyric poetry in every city (*shahr*) and land (*bilād*) to which he travelled. Although the historicity of the account is highly dubious,[28] this brief history has three significant elements: first, it connects the ʿAjam with Shiʿism, second it includes an association with the practice of *sukhanwarī* (which was one of the distinguishing features of this order of Sufis, see below), and third there is a link between the ʿAjam Sufis and the country of Iran (which becomes clearer later in the text).

The connection with Shiʿism is further highlighted in the very second question of the fifth chapter, which asks about the seventeen affiliated guilds (*hifdah-silsilah*)[29] and which will be discussed below.[30] The story begins with Āzād Khān (d. 1195/1781); it is assumed that the audience would have been familiar with this Sunni commander who emerged in Iran after the death of Nādir Shāh (r. 1148–1160/1736–1747). Āzād Khān the Afghān is ritually cursed by the author of the text, and we learn that he captured and occupied Isfahan. He ordered that the name of ʿAlī be painted on horses' hooves, so that it would be trod underfoot. All of the Shiʿa in the city observed dissimulation (*taqiyya*) and wore Afghan clothes and they did not have the courage to mention ʿAlī's name. At this point, a dervish (who was 'one of the descendants [*awlād*] of Ḥabīb-i ʿAjam') called Waḥshī came to Isfahan with the aim of calling out the name of ʿAlī in the streets and bazaar. Sixteen other Shiʿi dervishes were told of his plan, each one coming from a different guild (*ṣinf*), and they all took an oath to carry out Waḥshī's plan. The next morning they all set off together, each one in a white shroud and hat (*tāj*), carrying a small axe (*tabarzīn*), and each one poured earth over his head (*khāk bar sar-i khud*) symbolising the preparedness to face death. Each one praised the virtues of ʿAlī, chanting out loud 'Yā ʿAlī!' Āzād Khān ordered their capture, but the seventeen informed other dervishes who were also prepared to sacrifice themselves and they all spilled into the streets, captured and killed Āzād Khān[31] and put Ismāʿīl Shāh[32] on the throne.

This passage attempts to set ʿAjam Sufis securely within a normative Twelver tradition, and one that actively positions the faith against the Sunni tradition. Yet the author does not wish to depict a simple Shiʿi insurrection. These seventeen individuals are dervishes, and they wear identifiable Sufi hats and carry distinctive Sufi tools. Moreover, the seventeen guilds provide evidence of the close connections the ʿAjam enjoyed with the bazaar.

ʿAjam and Shiʿi Pilgrimage

Whereas many Sufi orders trace their descent back to a founder and perform pilgrimages to the tomb of the individual associated with the creation of the *silsila*, the vague origins of the ʿAjam meant that the dervishes of this order were unable to engage in visitations to a 'Sufi' tomb that was specific to them. As we have seen, the ʿAjam highlighted the significance of both Ḥabīb ʿAjamī who is known to have settled in Basra (and most likely died there) and a dervish by the name of Waḥshī who does not appear in books on *tadhkira* Sufi literature, and is most likely a mythical figure. In other words, the ʿAjam had nothing comparable to the Niʿmat Allāhīs.[33] Visitation to tombs was important because it promoted not only the specific ritual activity of the order, but also the formation of identity and the sense of cohesion within the order by establishing an 'orthodox' belief and practice. Guidance and education were frequently provided at the tombs of leading Sufis, and those that were 'adopted' by the ʿAjam Sufis served this purpose. These sites were usually, though not in all cases, the location of the tombs of important individuals who were more commonly identified within the Twelver Shiʿi tradition. *Wasīlat al-najāt* lists seven sacred sites where advanced ʿAjam Sufis (those dervishes of choice or volition, known as *Ikhtiyārī*) must be taught. The author says, '[One] must guide the *Ikhtiyārī* in the seven cities of Iran which have been under the control of Iran, not by the rulers of other countries.'[34] The first of these is the city of Mashhad in which is the tomb of the eighth imam, ʿAlī b. Mūsā Riḍā (d. 203/818). The second is Tabriz, because it will be the location of the arrival of the Qāʾim (*qadamgāh-i qāʾim-i āl-i muḥammad*) (i.e. the twelfth imam). Third is Shiraz because it was the court of Shāh

Chirāgh, the elder brother of the eighth imam. Fourth is Ardabil because it was the court of Shaykh Ṣafī (d. 735/1334) to whom the origin of the Safawid order is traced.[35] Fifth is Isfahan because it was the capital of the Safawid monarchs. Unfortunately the text does not elaborate further on this. Sixth is Qazwin, because it was the court of Imāmzāda Ḥusayn (the son of the eighth imam) but again the text does not specify any visit to the Imāmzāda Ḥusayn.[36] Seventh is Tehran because it is the capital of the monarchs who are the 'possessors of splendour' (*pādshāhān-i ṣāḥib-i sikka*). Again, the text does not mention specific tombs as locations of pilgrimage such as Shāh ʿAbd al-ʿAẓīm in Rayy.

The list above is worthy of reflection because it bears the imprint of only one individual whose tomb is recognised as being of largely Sufi veneration (that of Shaykh Ṣafī). While the tomb of Shāh Chirāgh in Shiraz is often considered a Sufi sacred site, the author makes a specific connection to its Shiʿi heritage. Perhaps the most intriguing site is Tehran: the term *ṣāḥib-i sikka* is awkward to translate, as *sikka* is more commonly understood as a coin. It reflects, perhaps, a nod by the ʿAjam to the secular Qajar rulers. The list is specifically Persian and Iranian. Persian in respect that the main language spoken in Iran is Persian (although Azeri is the native language in the north-west), a point that becomes significant in the light of the oratory competitions in which the ʿAjam were engaged. Visits to locations outside of Iran where Arabic or Turkish was spoken might have belittled the importance of Persian, and thus weakened the ʿAjam ritual of *sukhanwarī*. The list of sacred sites is Iranian in the sense that all of them are within the jurisdiction of the Shiʿi Qajar rulers. The tombs of other revered individuals, such as the tombs of Imam ʿAlī or Imam Ḥusayn were located in Ottoman territories where Arabic was the lingua franca which, given the often fraught relationship between the Ottoman and Qajar dynasties during the 19th century, might have been difficult to reach.

The Sufi Nature of *Wasīlat al-najāt*

A recurring feature in *Wasīlat al-najāt* is the insistence on observing the regulations of the *sharīʿa* (i.e. the legal aspect of religion). A typical example is when the author states at the beginning of chapter three that the wayfarer (*sālik*), a term denoting a Sufi devotee, must not refute the *sharīʿa* of Muḥammad, and must learn and put into practice its duties and religion, and then he may 'step on to the [Sufi] path (*ṭarīqat*); without the *sharīʿa* the *ṭarīqat* is *ḥarām* (or forbidden) for him.'[37] Such a perspective is in fact quite usual within Sufi thinking, as many Persian Sufi masters have advocated such a view, and indeed, it may even be said to reflect the vast majority of Sufi perspectives. That the author felt the need to state such an accepted position suggests that the comment was directed at ignorant, aspiring dervishes or else the order's detractors. Having established this basic rule for novices, the author then proceeds to discuss the absolute requirement for a guide (*murshid*), and cites in Arabic a sentence he attributes to Muḥammad, 'If not for my guide I would not know my Lord.'[38] Again this is a standard Sufi perspective, and many of the manuals and authoritative texts from the classical period testify to this view.

One of the points of interest in the text is the absence of any theoretical discussion about 'mystical' states, or gnosis.[39] The concepts of passing away or annihilation (*fanāʾ*) and subsistence (*baqāʾ*) are not considered, nor is there any extended examination of unity (*waḥdat*, *ittiṣāl*, or similar terms) as might be expected of Sufis interested in the school of the Unity of Being that is associated with Ibn ʿArabī (d. 638/1240). *Wasīlat al-najāt* offers a mere hint of speculative mysticism when the author speaks of the twelve stations of the *Ikhtiyārī* dervish. The first of these includes firstly the knowledge of the secrets in the stage of singularity and solitude (*tafrīd wa tajrīd*) and secondly the belief in unity (*tawḥīd*), and thirdly the remembrance of 'There is no god but God.' Unfortunately, how these technical terms and concepts were understood is not explained: whether God's unity was understood in a *wujūdī* fashion,[40] or whether it preserved and foregrounded an ontological difference between Creator and created cannot be established. In any case, the purpose of the text appears to have been the propagation of ʿAjam doctrines as they relate to origins, its internal hierarchical structure, and its position within the Shiʿi tradition. However, the absence of speculative gnosis may also be due to the kind of people who were associated with the ʿAjam, namely the working classes and those who were occupied in the bazaar. These kinds of people probably did not have much formal education and were unfamiliar with the intricacies of theological and speculative disputation. Despite this, it is likely that there were some affiliates of the ʿAjam who had a reasonable degree of literary ability, as the text includes Arabic quotations from the Qur'an.[41] Moreover, those who engaged in *sukhanwarī* were obliged to recite, and perhaps even compose difficult kinds of poetry.

That there is very little of 'mystical' interest in the text may be associated with the origins and appeal of the ʿAjam, which as mentioned before lies with the working classes. An indication of this is given in a 'Khāksār' treatise from the Qajar period which discusses the seventeen guilds that trace their origins back to the girding of Imam ʿAlī.[42] The ninth person that was girded was Ḥasan-i Baṣrī (d. 110/728–9) and the author states that the ʿAjam dervishes and the ruffians (*lūṭī-hā*) trace themselves back to him.[43] The nature of this connection with the ruffians may be suggestive of the kinds of individuals that were associated with the ʿAjam. The other sixteen of the seventeen guilds mentioned in this Khāksār treatise are the barbers, the water-bearers, the surgeons, the worshippers (*ʿābidān*), the rope-makers, the shoemakers, the merchants and traders, the quilt-makers, tent-sewers, the recitors of *dhikr* and ascetics, the generous (*karīmān*), the artisans (*ahl-i ṣanʿat*), the knowledgeable (*ʿilm-dārān*), the Qur'an memorisers (*ḥāfiẓān-i qur'ān*), and bowl and dish makers.[44] The collection of groups assembled in this treatise are a little more distinguished than the seventeen trades mentioned in *Wasīlat al-najāt*; these were the water-bearers, grocers, chefs, directors of traditional exercises (*kuhnah sawār*), cobblers, masters of the bath, caravan leaders, Qur'an recitors, butchers, smiths, bakers, wrestlers, saddlers, barbers, callers to prayer and the lamentation recitors, and the *naqībs*. But the common element does seem to suggest a lower or working-class support base, which the ʿAjam shared in common with the Khāksār. All of this reveals the intimate connections that these Sufis had with the bazaar, and it is noteworthy that the author remarks that all of the ʿAjam dervishes are drawn from the seventeen families (*hifdah silsilah*).[45] Moreover, on initiation into the order, the representatives of the seventeen 'families' (as listed above) were present.[46]

Despite the close relationship between the ʿAjam and the Khāksār,[47] *Wasīlat al-najāt* includes some intriguing passages that reveal that the ties between the two were not always cordial. The third question and answer of the fifth chapter in *Wasīlat al-najāt* distances the ʿAjam from the Khāksār, and another group that the author, Mashhadī Muḥammad Mahdī Tabrīzī, calls *Sālik*. The Khāksār are said to derive their origin from Shāh Niʿmat Allāh Walī (d. 834/1431), who is lauded by Tabrīzī (as he is accorded the salutation 'may God raise his station'), while the *Sāliks* are said to find their origins in Jalāl al-Dīn Harātī.[48] Tabrīzī finds the *Sāliks* deficient to the extent that they should not teach other Sufis, nor should they preach in public. They should be reclusive and perform their litanies.[49] But it is the Khāksār who receive the strongest criticism:

> The Khāksār is a *ṭarīqa* that has gone wrong (*bāṭil*) because [the members] are innovators and they deny the *sharīʿa* of Muḥammad Muṣṭafā. [They] are not on the straight path of the religious school (*madhhab*) of Imam Jaʿfar al-Ṣādiq and they do not assert the prophetic *sharīʿa*, rather they deny it and say, 'We are followers of the *ṭarīqa*; the *sharīʿa* is cut away (*sāqiṭ*) from us.' They do not pray and they do not fast. They do not marry . . . they do not greet [others with] 'Salām'. They say, 'With the help of ʿAlī (*yā ʿAlī madad*)', instead of 'Salām'. When it is time to eat they do not say, 'In the name of God', and when they have finished eating they do not give thanks to God. So they are not followers of the *sharīʿa* and they have taken and walk along the wrong path. They are masters of innovation (*ṣāḥib-i bidʿat*).[50]

The author reiterates his opposition to the Khāksārs in his answer to the question of whether a Khāksār can become an ʿAjam dervish. He answers that if the dervish in question does not realise he is acting in opposition to the prophetic *sharīʿa* then there is no fault in admitting him into the order. He is admitted in the usual way: his head is shaved, he is taken to the bath where he performs ablutions for joining the order (*ghusl-i ṭarīqat*). If such a dervish wishes to become an ʿAjam Sufi and realises he is denying the prophetic *sharīʿa* then he cannot be admitted.

There is no indication of the reason behind this dispute between the ʿAjam and the Khāksār; it is possible that it was a local rivalry, or a dispute about doctrine, or perhaps a conflict of leadership in the group, similar to that which beset the Niʿmat Allāhīs in the first half of the 20th century. Whatever the case, it is an example of a tendency among Sufi orders to splinter and develop offshoots which carry the possibility of creating new identities that are responsive to changing contexts.

As mentioned above much of Tabrīzī's *Wasīlat al-najāt* is concerned with explicating the hierarchy of the order, in which there are specific terms for the ranks of spiritual attainment. These begin with the novices, or the *kūdak-i abdāl* (child devotees) who carry out the orders of the other dervishes.[51] The hierarchy develops with masters of tongue, or novices who wish to make a pledge of the tongue (*ṣāḥib-i lisān*) to the ʿAjam master. These are of two kinds: the 'tongue of flight' (*lisān-i parwāzī*) and the 'tongue of service' (*lisān-i khidmat*).[52] The difference between the two is that the *lisān-i parwāzī* is able to engage in his profession or trade after giving his oath to the spiritual master. The *lisān-i khidmat* occupies himself in serving the spiritual master after giving his oath. It appears that the term of service for the *lisān-i khidmat* was three years and three days.[53] The ranks of the ʿAjam are provided in a short but clear passage in the text: 'The *lisān-i khidmat* is the deputy (*nāʾib*) of the soldier or warrior (*qazāwat*) and the *qazāwat* is the deputy of the solitary one (*mufrid*), and the *mufrid* is the deputy of the dervish of free choice (*ikhtiyār*).[54] The *ikhtiyār* is the deputy of the Superintendent (*sarkār naqīb*).'[55] Each of these have specific spiritual stations, and they are given specific Sufi implements, so that for example, the tools (*wasīla*) of the *mufrid* are the hat (*tāj*), tablecloth (*sufra*), small axe (*tabarzīn*), begging bowl (*kashkūl*), shroud (*iḥrām*), staff (*ʿaṣā*), the rope of forty threads to tie around the headgear (*chihiltār*) and the coloured shawl (*rashm-i katība*).[56]

Of particular interest within the Sufism of 19th-century Iran was the institutionalisation of the tradition which mirrored the practice of the Shiʿi *ʿulamāʾ* in issuing certificates which legitimised and authenticated the learning beneath a cleric. This certificate was known as an *ijāza* (meaning 'permission', that is, the recipient was allowed to transmit a text that had been memorised, and even teach law and issue legal opinions).[57] By the 19th century the practice of authenticating the learning and ability of Sufis through issuing certificates, known as *majallā* became widespread among ʿAjam and Khāksār Sufis. Afshārī notes that these took the form of handwritten documents that the dervishes would carry with them whenever they went to a new location. Among the Khāksār was a high-ranking Sufi called a *naqīb*, who had the authority to inspect the *majallā* and ask the dervishes about the secrets of the path. The *naqīb* would remove the cloak from any dervish whose *majallā* was defective or who could not answer his questions.[58] In effect this was a form of self-regulation. It meant that the ʿAjam dervishes were knowledgeable of their tradition, and that they conformed to a form of Sufism that was located within Twelver Shiʿism. *Wasīlat al-najāt* includes sections that discuss the granting of such certificates to ʿAjam dervishes.

The Sufi nature of *Wasīlat al-najāt* is beyond doubt. While the technical term Sufi does not appear, other idiomatic Sufi words occur frequently, including *dervīsh* and *ṭarīqa*, and distinctive Sufi implements are discussed, such as the *kashkūl* (the begging bowl) and *tabarzīn* (small axe). Although the daily activities that the ʿAjam should perform are not mentioned, the ritual initiation and progression through the hierarchical ranks of the order are discussed, which gives some indication of the kinds of ritual activities that were performed by the Sufis of this order. There is mention of begging in the bazaar (*parsah-yi bāzār*), which as Afshārī notes was performed by Khāksār dervishes in the bazaar on Friday evenings.[59] ʿAjam dervishes also engaged in a kind of public recitation and praising of the imams, known as *guzar khwānī*,[60] and helped with some kind of public performance (*pīshkār-i maraka*), probably related to the propagation and praise of Twelver Shiʿism.[61] Also of note are forms of rituals known as *kharman* (literally, harvest or reaped corn) which Afshārī explains is probably a form of begging, which had its origins in rural areas.[62] There is also mention of the more general forms of accepted 'Sufi' manners, most notably the right behaviour towards God's creation and abandoning all kinds of blameworthy actions.[63] Such mental attitudes are not explained further, but there are indications that these would have been somewhat demanding, as the author mentions forty-four stations (*maqām*) which would have entailed the requisite spiritual qualities and virtues. But there is no mention of formal *dhikr* sessions or *samāʿ* performances, nor is there discussion of any of the more 'outlandish' kinds of acts that are sometimes associated with Sufism.

The ʿAjam and *sukhanwarī*

Tabrīzī's *Wasīlat al-najāt* does not give any information about the *sukhanwarī*, a practice that has been highlighted by Maḥjūb and mentioned briefly in passing by several other scholars. The most notable are the works of Bayḍāʾī, who links the Khāksār with the practice of water carrying[64] and *sukhanwarī*,[65] and Afshārī, whose works have already been referenced. So for the sake of providing a degree of comprehensive coverage on the ʿAjam, this section will summarise and describe Maḥjūb's work.

The apogee of these competitions was during the 19th century, and they were held in coffee-houses (Maḥjūb mentions fifty in Tehran alone)[66] which were popular among the working classes and guild workers in the latter half of the reign of Nāṣir al-Dīn Shāh. It was during the month of Ramaḍān, from nightfall until morning prayers, when these competitions occurred. At other times of the year, the participants would have been busy in their occupation, and they would have spent their free moments memorising the poetry that was necessary for success in *sukhanwarī*. Those engaged in the competition were the ʿAjam dervishes, and around twenty recitors of poetry would have gathered at any coffee-house. Their aim was not commercial, as they did not collect or expect payment; the aim was most probably religious in nature, although an element of showmanship and entertainment cannot be discounted from these performances. The oratory competition sometimes took the form of engagements between the groups of recitors that were affiliated to different coffee-houses. This was all performed with appropriate respect and as mentioned above, during Ramaḍān, when sentiments of spirituality were heightened.

The competitive nature of the poetic recitations featured around the knowledge of the 'seventeen guilds'. Each of the guilds had a distinctive symbol or implement which was used in the profession, and these were used in the decoration of the coffee-house (along with particular animal skins) which were fastened to the walls and ceilings of the coffee-house during Ramaḍān. The competition revolved around a series of questions and answers (to be rendered in poetry) between the recitors which largely focused upon the mythical histories, 'secrets' and implements of these seventeen guilds.[67] Each guild had its own mythic history, its 'patron-saint' with specific association to the guild, and particular secrets pertaining to the trade.[68] The knowledge that an oratory-recitor required therefore was vast. Moreover, it should not be assumed that the recitors were simpletons, as the recitations frequently involved complex compositions, such as the recitation of ghazals before the competition proper commenced, that were made up of letters without dots, or without the alif.[69] There were other forms of wordplay within the poetry of *sukhanwarī*, including forms of acrostic poetry.[70] Not all questions asked were related to the seventeen families, as Maḥjūb has claimed that it was religion in general that was the subject of many such questions that were posed in poetic form. He gives the example of a recitor asking how many creatures were created without a mother or father. The answer is Adam, Eve, a she-camel produced by God for the prophet Ṣāliḥ (Q 7:73), the ram sent by God to Abraham as a substitute sacrifice for his son, and Moses' staff that was transformed into a snake.[71]

Perhaps the significance of this activity of the ʿAjam dervishes is how *sukhanwarī* demonstrated the integration of Sufism within society, in particular within the bazaar. Sufism has always had strong connections with the marketplace, and to view the tradition as 'navel-gazing' and divorced from social realities would be to misrepresent a long-standing engagement of groups such as *futuwwat*,[72] orders including the Mevleviyya among others, whose masters have promoted participation of tradesmen and workers. The strong links with the bazaar may also have persuaded the ʿAjam dervishes (if any encouragement was needed) of the respect and deference to Twelver Shiʿism, as the connections between the bazaar and Shiʿi clerics have often been noted.[73]

The nature of *sukhanwarī* changed in the 20th century. There were more questions of a scientific nature, such as those on astronomy. Moreover, some of the poetic competitions became infused with foreign words, to the extent that one recitor spoke of 'seventeen languages' and included Indian, Ethiopian, Russian, French and English. There were, of course, other challenges that *sukhanwarī* faced, including the strong competition from new forms of entertainment that became popular in Iran as a result of increasing contact with the West. These included new sports (which had arguably had a detrimental impact on the traditional forms of 'martial' engagement in the *zūrkhānah* – and it is worthy of note that one of the seventeen 'guild' members was the *kuhna sawar*, who led the group exercises in this institution),[74] and the emergence of the cinema and radio.[75] Moreover the impact of 'rationalising' Westernising thought may also be associated with the numerical decline of Sufis, and the changing nature of modes of economic activity also must have been detrimental to the ʿAjam order and its associations with the workers in the bazaar.

Conclusion

The ʿAjam offer an insight into Shiʿi spirituality in late 19th-century Iran, a period in which all manner of transformations were taking place within society due to increasing education, advances in technology, and better mobility among a host of other changes. The challenges to Sufism at this juncture of history were considerable, and may have contributed to the ʿAjam Sufis locating their devotional activities and beliefs within 'normative' Twelver doctrines. The absence of mystical themes in the text of *Wasīlat al-najāt* may also reflect this, but it is also possible that the contents of this ʿAjam text, being oriented towards affiliates who came from the less well educated, did not facilitate gnostic themes. Of greater concern were ethical and ritual considerations, along with a care to establish correct ʿAjam history along with the strict hierarchy among its members. It is surprising that the text makes no reference to *sukhanwarī*; perhaps the author expected his readers to automatically make an association with the tradition and had nothing new to write on the topic. The inclusion of the ʿAjam and Khāksār dervishes is imperative if Iranian spirituality in the 19th century is to be fully appreciated. The focus on Niʿmat Allāhī Sufism, while worthy and necessary, has overshadowed the other forms of Sufism in Iran in this period, and it is fortunate that texts such as *Wasīlat al-najāt* have survived to provide modern observers with a wider perspective. It provides an excellent illustration of how Sufism was manifested within some parts of the lower classes of society, and as such, offers an interesting contrast to the aristocratic varieties of Sufism in Iran during the late 19th and early 20th centuries, typified by the likes of Ẓahīr al-Dawla (d. 1924) and the Society of Brotherhood (*anjuman-i ukhuwwat*).[76]

Appendix: Contents of *Wasīlat al-najāt*

1 First Chapter/Aim (*maqṣad-i awwal*): The Courtesies of the Principles of Religion (*ādāb-i uṣūl-i dīn*)

> first section: (*bāb-i awwal*); second section: Unity (*bāb-i duwwum: tawḥīd*); third section: Justice (*bāb-i siwwum: ʿadl*); fourth section: Prophecy (*bāb-i chahārum: nubuwwat*); fifth section: Imāmate (*bāb-i panjum: imāmat*); sixth section: Return (*bāb-i shīshum: maʿād*).

2 Second Chapter/Aim (*maqṣad-i duwwum*): The Rules of Prayer (*aḥkām-i namāz*)

first section: Purity (*bāb-i awwal: ṭahārat*); second section: Prayer (*bāb-i duwwum: ṣalāt*); third section: Fasting (*bāb-i siwwum: ṣawm*); fourth section: Alms-tax (*bāb-i chahārum: zakāt*); fifth section: Religious tax (*bāb-i panjum: khums*) (Customs); sixth section: Pilgrimage (*bāb-i shīshum: ḥajj*); seventh section: Commanding the good (*bāb-i haftum: amr bih maʿrūf*); eighth section: Effort (*bāb-i hashtum: jihād*); often associated with the Qur'anic term 'struggle in the way of God' and can denote physical or non-physical struggle; ninth section: Buying and selling (*bāb-i nuhum: bayʿ*).

3 Third Chapter/Aim (*maqṣad-i siwwum*): Rules of the Way (*aḥkām-i ṭarīqat*)

first section: Promise of the novice to the guide (*bāb-i awwal: lisān dādan-i murīd bih murshīd*); second section: Courtesies of guidance (*bāb-i duwwum: ādāb-i irshād*);

4 Fourth Chapter/Aim (*maqṣad-i chahārum*): Rules of the Certificates (*aḥkām-i majallā*)

first section: Certificate of rules for the *ikhtiyārī* (*bāb-i awwal: majallā-yi aḥkām-i ikhtiyārī*); second section: Rules for the certificate of the *mufrad-abdālī* (*bāb-i duwwum: aḥkām-i majallā-yi mufrad-abdālī*); third section: Customs of the certificate for *ghazāwat* (*bāb-i siwwum: ādāb-i majallā-yi ghazāvat*); fourth section: Customs of the promise to enter the order, *lisān nāmchah* (*bāb-i chahārum: ādāb-i lisān nāmchah*); fifth section: Note on the first dervish's service (*bāb-i panjum: iqrār-nāmchah-yi khidmat*).

5 Fifth Chapter/Aim (*maqṣad-i panjum*): Rules concerning the Questions for the Seeker about the Way and [their] Answers (*aḥkām-i su'āl namūdan-i ṭālib az rāh-i ṭarīqat wa jawāb farmūdan*)

first section: Courtesies of the ʿAjam genealogy (*bāb-i awwal: ādāb-i kursī-yi ʿAjam*).

NOTES

1 In European languages the most accessible sources on the Niʿmat Allāhīs are (in English) Leonard Lewisohn, 'An Introduction to Modern Persian Sufism, Part I', *BSOAS*, 61, 3 (1998), pp. 437–464; (in German) Richard Gramlich's three-volume study should be

consulted: *Die schiitischen Derwischorden Persiens* 1–3 (Wiesbaden, 1965–1981). 1. *Affiliationen* (1965); 2. *Glaube und Lehre* (1976); 3. *Brauchtum und Riten* (1981). In Persian the literature on the Niʿmat Allāhī order is considerable, partially as a result of many of their leaders having composed treatises. This literature has been investigated in two PhD dissertations: W. Ronald Royce, 'Mīr Maʿsūm ʿAlī Shāh and the Niʿmat Allāhī Revival 1776–77 to 1796–97: A Study of Sufism and its Opponents in Late Eighteenth-Century Iran' (Princeton University, 1979); R. Tabandeh, 'The Rise of Niʿmatullahi Shiʿite Sufism in Nineteenth-Century Qājār Persia' (Exeter University, 2014). In Persian see M. Humayūnī, *Tāʾrīkh-i silsilahā-yi ṭarīqa-yi Niʿmatullāhī dar Īrān* (London, 1992).

2 For Ṣafī ʿAlī Shāh, see Nile Green, 'A Persian Sufi in the Age of Printing: Mirza Hasan Safi ʿAlī Shāh (1835–99)', in Lloyd Ridgeon, ed., *Religion and Politics in Modern Iran* (London, 2005), pp. 99–112. For Ẓahīr al-Dawla (Ṣafī ʿAlī Shāh's successor, and leader of the Society of Brotherhood) see L. Ridgeon, 'Revolution and a High-Ranking Sufi: Zahir al-Dawleh's Contribution to the Constitutional Movement', in Houshang Chehabi and Vanessa Martin, ed., *Iran's Constitutional Revolution: Popular Politics, Cultural Transformation and Transnational Connections* (London, 2010), pp. 143–162; ʿAṭa Karīm Barq, *Justujū dar aḥwāl wa āthār-i Ṣafī ʿAlī Shāh* (Tehran, 1352 Sh./1973–4).

3 For a general survey into late 19th-century Sufism in Iran, see Lloyd Ridgeon, *Sufi Castigator: Ahmad Kasravi and the Iranian Mystical Tradition* (London, 2006), chapter one. See also Matthijs van den Bos, *Mystic Regimes: Sufism and the State in Iran, from the Late Qajar Era to the Islamic Republic* (Leiden, 2002).

4 Leonard Lewisohn, 'An Introduction to Modern Persian Sufism, Part II', *BSOAS*, 62, 1 (1999), pp. 36–59; Lewisohn, 'The *Qawāʾim al-anwār* of Rāz-ī Šīrāzī and Shiʿi Sufism in Qajar Persia', in Denis Hermann and Fabrizio Speziale, ed., *Muslim Cultures in the Indo-Iranian World during the Early Modern and Modern Periods* (Berlin, 2010), pp. 247–271. In Persian see R. Khāwarī, *Dhahabiyya: Taṣawwuf-i ʿilmī, āthār-i adabī* (Tehran, 1362 Sh./1983–4).

5 For a Khāksār text that focuses on its rituals, and the various implements that make up the material culture of the Khāksār dervish, and which also reveals the nature of the author's Shiʿi belief and spirituality, and typical Khāksār stylistics in prose and poetry see the third chapter of Mīr ʿAbidī and Mihrān Afshārī, ed., *Āyīn-i Qalandarī* (Tehran, 1374 Sh./1995–6), pp. 247–332.

6 Z. Taheri, 'Ḳāksār', *EIR*, 15 (2010), pp. 356–359.

7 See Willem Floor, 'Luṭi', *EIR*, online (2010).

8 M.J. Maḥjūb, '*Sukhanwarī*', was first published in three parts within *Sukhan* (9) 1337 Sh./1958, pp. 530–535, 631–637, and 779–786. The three sections were published as one continuous article in Ḥasan Dhū al-Faqārī, ed., *Adabiyāt-i ʿammiyāna-yi Īrān* (Tehran, 1382 Sh./2003–4), pp. 1053–1078.

9 ʿAbd al-Ḥusayn Zarrīnkūb, 'Qalandar wa Khāksār', in his *Justujū dar taṣawwuf-i Īrān* (Tehran, 1369 Sh./1990–1), pp. 359–379.

10 The text is in Mihrān Afshārī, ed., *Futuwwat-nāmah-hā wa Rasāʾil-i Khāksāriyya* (Tehran, 1382 Sh./2003), pp. 233–294.

11 See above, *Wasīlat al-najāt*, p. 294, henceforth cited as W.N.

12 ʿAbidī and Afshārī, ed., *Āyīn-i Qalandarī*, pp. 348–450.

13 Ibid. pp. 336–338.

14 M. Afshārī, *Tāzah bih tāzah, naw bih naw* (Tehran, 1385 Sh./2006–7), pp. 111–125.

15 W.N. p. 239.

16 See the discussion in Jawid Mojaddedi, *Beyond Dogma* (Oxford, 2012), pp. 28–62.

17 W.N. p. 241.

18 Ibid., p. 240.

19 This tradition is affirmed by a number of Sunni scholars including Ibn Ḥanbal (d. 241/855) in his *Musnad* (Cairo, 1313/1896), vol. 4, p. 281.

20 W.N. pp. 244–255.

21 Ibid., p. 251.
22 Ibid., p. 250.
23 Ibid., p. 252.
24 Said Amir Arjomand, 'Religious extremism (*Ghuluww*), Sufism and Sunnism in Safavid Iran: 1501–1722', *Journal of Asian History*, 15, 1 (1981), pp. 1–35; Andrew Newman, 'Sufism and Anti-Sufism in Safavid Iran', *Iran*, 37 (1999), pp. 95–108; Lloyd Ridgeon, *Morals and Mysticism in Persian Sufism* (London, 2010), pp. 123–165.
25 Taheri, 'Ḳāksār', *EIR* vol. xv, fasc. 4 (2010).
26 ʿA. Zarrīnkūb, *Justajū dar taṣawwuf-i Irān* (third edition: Tehran, 1367 Sh./1988–9), p. 376.
27 M. Afshārī suggests that the text should read Baraghānī, as Baraghānī is a mountainous region between Karaj and Qazwin (W.N. p. 280, n.3).
28 For classical Sufi understandings of Ḥabīb ʿAjamī see ʿAṭṭār, *Memorial of God's Friends*, trans. by P. Losensky (New York, 2009), pp. 90–96. For Hujwīrī on Ḥabīb ʿAjamī see *Kashf al-Maḥjūb of Al-Hujwiri: The Oldest Persian Treatise on Sufism*, tr. R.A. Nicholson (London, 1911), pp. 88–89.
29 On the symbolism of seventeen among Sufi Persian groups, see Lloyd Ridgeon, *Morals and Mysticism*, pp. 137, 139, and 144.
30 W.N. p. 280.
31 In his *EIR* entry, 'Āzād Khan Afḡān' (vol. 3, fasc. 2, pp. 173–174), J. R. Perry states, '[Āzād Khān Afḡān] ended his days comfortably in Shiraz as an honoured pensioner of the generous Zand ruler, and on his death in 1195/1781 was taken to Kabul to be buried in accordance with his will', which contradicts the 'history' of the author of *Wasīlat al-najāt*. The intended identity of Ismāʿīl Shāh in the story is probably the infant Shāh Ismāʿīl III, the grandson of the last Safawid king who was put on the throne in 1757 by Karīm Khān Zand (r. 1173–1193/1760–1779).
32 The identity of Shāh Ismāʿīl in this story is unclear. The narrative mentions the historical figure of Āzād Khān who died in 1195/1781, and according to the story this took place before the aforementioned Shāh Ismāʿīl came to power. The only Safavid monarch who was known as Shāh Ismāʿīl died in 930/1524. It is to be wondered whether the narrator of the story was unfamiliar with Iranian history, and simply employed a name (Ismāʿīl) that most people knew, or associated with the Safavid monarchs.
33 The Niʿmat Allāhīs in Mahan are famous for the tomb of Shāh Niʿmat Allāh Walī. See Bāstānī Pārīzī, 'Ḥaram-i Shāh Walī chigūnah idāra mīshūd?', in Shahrām Pāzūkī, ed. *Majmūʿa-yi Maqālāt darbārah-yi Shāh Niʿmatullāh Walī* (Tehran, 1382 Sh./2003).
34 W.N. p. 284.
35 For the shrine at Ardabīl see A.H. Morton, 'The Ardabīl Shrine in the Reign of Shāh Ṭahmāsp', *Iran*, 12 (1974), pp. 31–64, and *Iran*, 13 (1975), pp. 39–58.
36 Qazwin is the location of the so-called 'Imāmzāda-yi Ḥusayn' which was constructed in the 16th century and renovated in the Qajar period. A contemporary image is contained in Eugène Flandin, *Voyage en Perse*, Gide et Baudry, ed. (Paris, 1851).
37 W.N. p. 255.
38 Ibid., p. 256 which is repeated on pp. 267 and 274.
39 The ʿAjam certainly had doctrines of a mystical nature. See Mohammad Ali Amir-Moezzi, *The Spirituality of Shiʿi Islam: Belief and Practices* (London, 2011), pp. 364–365. Amir-Moezzi discusses the works of Sayyid Aḥmad Dehkordī (d. 1339/1920), in which there is a sevenfold hierarchy of mystical attainment.
40 That is to say, in a fashion that was influenced by the school of Ibn ʿArabī, that is commonly associated with *waḥdat al-wujūd*.
41 W.N. p. 268.
42 Although the treatise does not specifically identify itself as a Khāksār work, it is a common feature of Khāksār works that such issues are discussed.
43 'Risāla dar bayān-i aṣnāf', in M. Afshārī, ed., *Futuwwat-nāmah-hā*, p. 221. *Lūṭīs* became associated with *futuwwat* most probably because of the inclusion of strongmen and

wrestling heroes like Pūryā-yi Walī (d. 722/1322) who is a household name in Iran. Pūryā-yi Walī was also the author of poetry addressing Sufi themes (Angelo Piemontese, 'La leggenda del santo-lottatore Pahlavan Mahmud Xvarezmi "Purya-ye Vali" (m. 722/1322)', *Annali dell'Istituto Universitario Orientale di Napoli*, NS 15 [1965], pp. 167–213). For the poetry of Purya-yi Walī see Ḥamīd Ḥamīd, *Zindagī wa rūzgār wa andīshah-yi Pūriyā-yi Walī, Pahlawān Maḥmūd Khwārazmī, bā matn-i intiqādī-i Kanz al-ḥaqa'iq* (Tehran, 1342 Sh./1963–1964). In short, the ideal lūṭī, like the *pahlawān* (or wrestling champion), used force and violence in an appropriate fashion and did not resort to acts of extortion, bribery and thuggery. It is likely for this reason that such individuals were included in such treatises.

44 W.N. pp. 221–222.

45 Ibid., p. 290.

46 Ibid., p. 258.

47 Nūr al-Dīn Mudarrasī Chahārdahī, *Khāksār wa Ahl-i ḥaqq* (Tehran, 1358 Sh./1979–80). See his discussion on the ʿAjam, from page 49–106. Afshārī claims that the ʿAjam dervishes were described as the servants of the Khāksār, and carried out the orders and wishes of Khāksār masters. Moreover, the courtesies and customs of the ʿAjam were similar to those of the Khāksār (Afshārī, ed., *Futuwwat-nāmah-hā*, pp. 282–283, n.6). There are many cases of similarities between the ʿAjam and Khāksār. While the ʿAjam of *Wasīlat al-najāt* pay special attention to Ḥabīb ʿAjamī, the Khāksār regard him as the deputy (*khalīfa*) of al-Ḥasan al-Baṣrī, whom they consider as one of their 'four *pīrs*', see W.N. p. 209.

48 The identity of this individual is uncertain. Zarrīnkūb has made a connection between the Khāksār and one Ghulām ʿAlī Shāh Hindī who lived at the end of the Zand period or beginning of the Qajar era. Very little is known about him. See Zarrīnkūb, *Justujū dar taṣawwuf-i Īrān*, pp. 375–376.

49 W.N. p. 290.

50 Ibid., p. 282. See also the comments on p. 288, where the repentance of the Khāksār is not accepted if he wishes to become an ʿAjam Sufi.

51 Maḥjūb, '*Sukhanwarī*', in Ḥ. Dhū al-Faqārī, ed., *Adabiyyāt-i ʿammiyāna-yi Īrān*, p. 1072. See Afshārī's comments, W.N., p. 257, n.4.

52 W.N. pp. 256–257.

53 Ibid., p. 277.

54 Maḥjūb, '*Sukhanwarī*', p. 1072. The *ikhtiyār* is able to train an aspiring *darvīsh*.

55 W.N. p. 273. Maḥjūb says that there was a sevenfold hierarchical structure: *abdāl, mufrid, qaṣṣāb, darwīsh-i ikhtiyār, ʿilm-dār, dast-i naqīb*, and *naqīb*.

56 W.N. p. 285.

57 See Devin J. Stewart, 'Ejāza', *EIR* (2011), vol. 8, fasc. 3, pp. 273–275.

58 Afshārī's comments, W.N. p. 256, n.5.

59 W.N. p. 272, also see pp. 272–273, n.9.

60 Ibid., p. 272.

61 W.N. p. 275.

62 Ibid., p. 272, also see pp. 272–273, n.8. Although not a public ritual activity, but certainly a ritual that contributed to Sufi identity was tattooing known as *gul-gīrī* (literally, picking flowers) [W.N., p. 272.]. It appears that dervishes had tattoos made on their arms by branding them with hot coins.

63 W.N. p. 269.

64 See Mojtaba Zarvani and Mohammad Mashhadi, 'The Rite of the Water-Carrier: From the circles of Sufis to the Rituals of Muharram', *JSIS* 4, 1 (2011), pp. 23–46.

65 Ḥusayn Partaw Bayḍā'ī, *Tārīkh-i Warzish-i Bāstānī* (Tehran, 1382 Sh./2003–4), pp. 45–46.

66 Maḥjūb, '*Sukhanwarī*', p. 1056. On coffee-houses, see ʿAlī Bulūkbāshī, *Qahwa-khānah-hā-yi Īrān* (Tehran, 1375 Sh./1996–7). This work does not elaborate on *sukhanwarī*.

67 Maḥjūb, '*Sukhanwarī*', p. 1060, has listed these seventeen guilds as: (1) dervish; (2) lamentation-recitor (*rawḍa-khwān*); (3) caravan leader; (4) water-bearer; (5) usher

(*nishān kursī bābā*); (6) traditional sports champion (*pahlawān*); (7) grain-sifter (*būjār*): (8) *shāṭir*—there were different kinds of occupations that went by this name. There were *shāṭir* who placed bread in ovens, those who were messengers, those who were spies and worked for the government (9) night-watch (*shab-ruw*); (10) escorts for retinues (*shāṭir-i jilaw-dār*); (11) smith; (12) muleteer; (13) butcher; (14) tent-maker; (15) washer of the dead; (16) barber; (17) coffee-maker.

68 The patron-saints, histories and their secrets are contained in '*futuwwat-nāmah*' (or guild-treatises) which date from around the beginning of the Safawid period until the 19th century. A number of these have been edited and published by M. Afshārī in his edited work *Futuwwat-nāmah-hā*.

69 Maḥjūb, '*Sukhanwarī*', p. 1063.

70 Ibid., p. 1065.

71 Ibid., p. 1075.

72 For the tradition of *futuwwat* (or *jawānmardī*) in Iran see Ridgeon, *Morals and Mysticism*.

73 An interesting example in this respect, and not too far in time from when *Wasīlat al-najāt* was written, is the dispute over the Tobacco Concession in 1891. On this, see Nikki Keddie, *Religion and Rebellion in Iran: The Tobacco Protest of 1891–92* (London, 1966).

74 On the *zūrkhānah* in the modern period see Lloyd Ridgeon, 'The Zūrkhāna Between Tradition and Change', *Iran*, 45 (2007), pp. 243–266; see also H. Chehabi, 'Zūr-ḵāna', *EI2*, online (2006); Philippe Rochard, 'The Identities of the Iranian Zūrkhāna', *Iranian Studies*, 35, 4 (2002), pp. 313–340.

75 For the cinema in Iran see Farrokh Gaffary, 'Cinema: i. History of Cinema in Persia', *EIR*, vol. 5, fasc. 6, 567–572.

76 For Ẓahīr al-Dawla and the Society of Brotherhood see L. Ridgeon, 'Revolution and a High-ranking Sufi.

11

Two Khāksār Treatises of the 19th Century

The Fourteen Families (*Chahārdah khānawādah*)
translated by Yaser Mirdamadi

The Booklet of Poverty (*Risāla-yi faqriyya*)
translated by Mehrdad Arabestani

The Fourteen Families (*Chahārdah khānawādah*)

Introduction by Mihrān Afshārī[1]

The Khāksār dervishes believe that they had four spiritual masters (*pīrs*) and that all Sufis are comprised of fourteen chains of transmission (*silsila*). These fourteen chains of transmission are called 'The Fourteen Families'. Hence some of their treatises, written to teach their disciples, bear the title 'The Four Spiritual Masters and the Fourteen Families'. Their belief about the fourteen families however is not compatible with the history of Sufism, and considering the fact that they have been influenced by the Jalālīs, presumably this belief also stems from some Jalālī Qalandars of India; as the author of *Dabistān-i madhāhib* (The School of Religions) points out:

> Be it known that in India, there are groups who consider themselves as Muslim Sufis and they have something in common in terms of rules and beliefs with Sufis. First they like detachment (*tajarrud*). As they have heard that Sanāsīs [Sannyasis] are ten denominations (*firqa*) and Yogis are twelve denominations, they are proud of having fourteen denominations, and as they come across each other they ask: 'Who are the four spiritual masters and the fourteen families?' And the disciples have to serve for years so that they can benefit from the teachings of the four spiritual masters and the fourteen families. They would say: 'the master of masters (*pīr-i pīrān*) is his holiness *muṣṭafā* ['the chosen',

> i.e. the Prophet Muḥammad], may God bless him and his family and grant them peace, the owner of Muṣṭafā's will is Murtaḍā ʿAlī from whom Ḥasan inherits the caliphate, and then Khwājah Ḥasan Baṣrī, who was the disciple of ʿAlī as well as his caliph. These four people are the four spiritual masters. Then, it is said that from Khwājah Ḥasan Baṣrī, two denominations emerged. The first caliph of Ḥasan Baṣrī was Ḥabīb ʿAjamī and from him nine families emerged as follows: the Ḥabībīs, Ṭayfūrīs, Karkhīs, Saqaṭīs, Junaydīs, Kāzirūnīs, Ṭūsīs, Firdawsīs, Suhrawardīs. The second caliph of Ḥasan Baṣrī was Shaykh ʿAbd al-Wāḥid Zayd and from him five families were constituted whose names are: the Zubayrīs, ʿAyyāḍīs, Adhamīs, Hubayrīs and Chishtīs. These are the fourteen families.[2]

Also Ḥājj Zayn al-ʿĀbidīn Shīrwānī (d. 1253/1837), who himself met the Jalālīs in the Indian city of Uch [present-day Pakistan], said about them:

> It is said we have four spiritual masters, fourteen families and nine lineages (*dūdah*). The first is the master of masters, the Prophet Muḥammad; the second is the prince of heirs (*sayyid-i awṣiyā'*) ʿAlī Murtaḍā; the third is Ḥasan Mujtabā'; the fourth is Shaykh Ḥasan Baṣrī. They are the four spiritual masters and unique professors. Consequently, for what concerns the fourteen families, it is said that from Ḥasan Baṣrī, two denominations were constituted. The first caliph of Shaykh Ḥasan Baṣrī was Shaykh Ḥabīb ʿAjamī, out of whom nine families emerged as follows: first Ḥabībīs, second Ṭayfūrīs, third Karkhīs, fourth Saqaṭīs, fifth Junaydīs, sixth Kāzirūnīs, seventh Ṭūsīs, eighth Suhrawardīs, ninth Firdawsīs. The second caliph of Ḥasan Baṣrī was Shaykh ʿAbd al-Wāḥid Zayd and out of him five families emerged: first Zubayrīs, second ʿAyyāḍīs, third Adhamīs, fourth Chishtīs, fifth Amīrīs. From the eighteen lineages the lineage of Ḥaqā'iq[3] [Truths] and Garyāl are famous and the rest are not known to me.[4]

In one way or another, fourteen families of Sufis are famous in the Indian subcontinent, as the author of *Khazīnat al-aṣfiyā'* pointed out about Makhdūm Jahāniyān: 'Makhdūm Jahāniyān is the caliph of the fourteen families who travelled the populated quarter of the world (*rubʿ maskūn*) twice and met hundreds of poor men (*fuqarā'*) and spiritual masters (*mashāyikh*)'.[5]

A Qādirī dervish of India called Shāh Ḍiyā' Allāh wrote a book entitled *Nasab-nāmah-yi kalān wa bayān-i chahārdah khānawādah wa ḥālat-i haftād wa du millat* (The General Genealogy and the Explanation of the Fourteen Families and the States of the Seventy-two Sects). A chapter of this book contains a treatise on the Fourteen Families, the content of which is quite close to the treatise that will be presented after this introduction.[6] The book of *Nasab-nāmah* was published in 1309/1891–2 in Lahore.

The fourteen families are also more or less mentioned in the writings of the Khāksārīs and it is worth pointing out that in the two treatises called *Maṭlūb al-fuqarā'* (The Ideal of Poor Men) and *Faqr-nāmah* (Treatise on Poverty), both edited and published by Muḥammad Taqī Dānish-Pazhūh, the fourteen families are mentioned.[7] Thus it is almost certain that both of the above-mentioned treatises belong to the Khāksārīs, as their other contents are similar to what is mentioned in the Khāksārī treatises.

The manuscripts written solely about the fourteen families, that I have seen, are:

> The fourth treatise, MS 4419, available in the central library of the University of Tehran; the third treatise, MS 5206, available in the central library of the University of Tehran; the fifth treatise, MS 1783, available in the library of the parliament (*Bahāristān*); the forty-fourth and the sixty-first, MS 860, available in the library of the faculty of Islamic theology at Ferdowsi University of Mashhad.

The most detailed treatise is MS 4419 in the central library of the University of Tehran, that will be presented in edited form after this introduction. The manuscript is inscribed by Muḥammad ʿAlī Sharīf Yazdī Shāhrūdī who was himself a Khāksārī dervish of the Qajar period and a disciple of Surkh-ʿAlī Shāh. Most of what is written in this manuscript is about the beliefs and rituals of the Khāksārīs. It was written between 1315–1317/1898–1900.[8]

Although treatises on the fourteen families – unlike Khāksārī treatises in the form of questions and answers – are not similar to *futuwwat-nāmahs* (treatises on spiritual chivalry), they are useful sources for acquiring knowledge of the beliefs and lifestyle of the Khāksārīs. What the treatise shows is that Khāksārīs in the Qajar period would travel to India, probably in order to meet their Jalālī leaders and get to know the Indian denominations, and also that what is mentioned in it about wearing animal skins, and fastening a ring and chain around the waist, holding a sawfish saw [bill] (*arra-yi pusht-i nahang*), begging and so on, is true of the Khāksārīs themselves.

The Fourteen Families (*Chahārdah khānawādah*)

In the name of God, the Compassionate, the Merciful

On the explanation of the fourteen [sic] spiritual masters and the fourteen families based upon a claim whose credibility is from (. . .)[9] that is mentioned. Four individuals became committed disciples of the Holy one. The first one is Maḥmūd Fāṭīlī, whose signification (*murād*) is Salmān [al-Fārsī];[10] the lineage of all Khāksārīs goes back to him. The second disciple was Kumayl b. Ziyād;[11] the lineage of all those who are lowly and destitute (*masākīn*), from Niʿmat Allāhīs[12] to Dhahabīs, goes back to him. The third disciple was Uways Qaranī;[13] the lineage of ʿUlyāʾīs goes back to him. The fourth disciple was Ḥasan Baṣrī;[14] the lineage of all ʿAjamīs,[15] Qādirīs, Rifāʿīs and Madārīs goes back to him in such a way that the caliph of Shaykh Ḥasan Baṣrī was Ḥabīb ʿAjamī. Nine families emanated from Ḥabīb: first Ḥabībīs, second Kāzirīs,[16] third Ṭayfūrīs, fourth Karkhīs, fifth Ḥasanīs, sixth Junaydīs, seventh Ṭūsīs, eighth Firdawsīs, ninth Suhrawardīs.

Kumayl b. Ziyād had one caliph who was Shaykh ʿAbd al-Wāḥid Zayd[17] and five families emanated from him: first Zaydīs, second Ayyāzīs,[18] third Adhamīs, fourth Yāsirmīs,[19] fifth Ḥasanīs.

But nine families give sermons on the name and title (*rasm*) of the same caliph [Ḥabīb], and it is necessary to know their paths (*ṭarīqa*):

It is obvious that Ḥabīb ʿAjamī was the caliph of Shaykh Ḥasan; but the Kazirīs, whose meaning is from Abū Isḥāq Kāzirūnī,[20] had two caliphs: Shaykh Fatḥ Allāh and Khwājah ʿAbd Allāh, who, according to a claim, was none other than Fatḥ Allāh himself. However no chain of transmission (*silsila*) remained of them.

[The third family is the one of] Ṭayfūrīs, whose meaning is from Sulṭān Bāyazīd Basṭāmī who lived quite a long time and was still alive in the time of Imam Jaʿfar al-Ṣādiq.[21] Dāwūd ʿAṭṭāʾī [sic][22] and Khwājah ʿAbd Allāh Khafīf[23] were among Ṭayfūrī caliphs; their path (*ṭarīqa*) was to fast during the day and practise remembrance of God (*dhikr*) during the night. They would never tell a lie or eat to repletion. According to a claim, four other individuals became disciples of Ṭayfūr: Shaykh Masʿūd, Shaykh Maḥmūd, Shaykh Ibrāhīm and Shaykh Aḥmad Muṣannif. Shaykh ʿUthmān and Majd al-Dīn, who were also the caliphs of Shaykh Aḥmad Muṣannif, are called Ṭayfūrīs as well.

[The fourth] group [is the one of] Karkhīs, whose meaning is from Shaykh Maʿrūf Karkhī who was doorkeeper of Holiness [Imam] Riḍā.[24] Khwājah Najm and Ibn Najīb served Shaykh Maʿrūf for twelve years, and Shaykh Aḥmad was also his disciple. All are called Karkhīs. Their path was to abandon ambition (*jāh*) and property (*māl*) and to seek solitude, discipline (*riyāḍa*) and contentment (*qinaʿat*). Everyone who intends to become a disciple of this family must behave like this.

The fifth [family] is the one of Saqaṭīs, whose meaning is from Sirrī Saqaṭī.[25] He had five disciples: Shaykh Zhindahpūsh, Sihām al-Dahr, Ḥisām al-Dīn, Shaykh Maḥmūd and Junayd Baghdādī.[26] Shaykh Junayd Baghdādī became caliph. They are altogether called Sakhṭīs.[27] They don't accept any alms from anyone. Every three days one of them would go out for sustenance. They were highly pious and virtuous. Their disciples must pursue this way of life.

The sixth [family] is that of the Junaydīs, whose meaning is from Shaykh Junayd Baghdādī. Seven individuals became his disciples: first, Muḥammad Shāh Bādkūbaʾī; second, Abū Bakr ʿAbd Allāh, whose meaning is from Shiblī;[28] third, Abū ʿAlī Rūdbārī;[29] fourth, Shāh Muḥammad Rūmī; fifth, ʿUthmān Maghribī;[30] sixth, Yaḥyāʾ al-Dīn [sic][31] Manṣūr; seventh, ʿUthmān Daqqāq. They are altogether called Junaydīs. They abandoned worldly limitations, treated people kindly and did not disturb anyone. If anyone oppressed them, they would react with patience. Anyone who wants to become their disciple must follow their path.

The seventh [family is the one of] Ṭūsīs, whose meaning is from Shaykh Abu'l-Naṣr Sarrāj Ṭūsī.[32] Shaykh ʿAbd al-Wāḥid Nahīb, Shaykh Abū Saʿīd Mubārak al-Makhdūmī, Shaykh ʿAbd al-Qādir Yaḥyā al-Dīn Kalīlānī,[33] were three [individuals] who considered themselves as Ṭūsīs. [They were people of] mercy, chivalry (*muruwwat*), acquiring knowledge, seeking understanding (*fahm*) and perfection (*kamālāt*). Anyone who intends to become the disciple of this family must follow this way.

The eighth [family is the one of] Firdawsīs, whose meaning is from Shaykh Najm al-Dīn Kabīr [sic].[34] He also had two disciples: Shaykh

Ḍiyā' al-Dīn Abū Najīb [sic] and Shaykh Abū Sharīf Bukhārā'ī. [They were people of] discipline, contentment, and they were always fasting. This is their way of life.

[The ninth family is the one of] Suhrawardīs, whose meaning is from Shaykh Abū Najīb.[35] He was caliph for twelve years. He would fast frequently for a period of three days and break his fast with a date. He also had some disciples: Shaykh Shihāb al-Dīn, Shaykh Zakariyyā', Shaykh Mumtāz Nūrī. This is their state: they would sit toward the direction of the Ka'ba (*qibla*) and constantly practise remembrance of God (*dhikr*), they always kept their ablution (*wuḍū'*) and would read the Qur'an. Anyone who intends to become their disciple must follow their path.

The five families of Kumayl b. Ziyād are:

First the Zaydīs, whose meaning is from Shaykh 'Abd al-Wāḥid[36] b. Zayd. Shāh 'Abd al-Razzāq, 'Abd Allāh 'Awf[37] and Amīr Kulāl[38] are all disciples of Shaykh ['Abd] al-Wāḥid b. Zayd and Faḍl b. Ziyād Ayyāz[39] was a disciple of Amīr Kulāl. These four families are called Zaydīs. They were not settled in cities, rather they were always settled in the mountains. They would always have ablution, they read the Qur'an extensively and were firm in practising the religious law (*sharī'a*). They were nominal Shi'is (*shī'a-nāmī*). Anyone who intends to become their disciple must adopt this way of life.

Second the Ayyāzīs,[40] whose meaning is from Faḍl b. Ayyāz.[41] He had two disciples: Shāh 'Abd Allāh and Ibrāhīm Adham. Shāh 'Abd Allāh has no chain of transmission (*silsila*). Their path was to read the Qur'an always and they would fight with their carnal soul (*nafs*). If someone gave them a gift, they would give it to the poor. They would not wear. . . [text missing]. Anyone who wants to become their disciple must adopt this way of life.

Third are the Adhamīs, whose meaning is from Sultan Ibrāhīm Adham.[42] He used to be a sultan (prince) then abandoned his sultanate and wore the clothes of poverty (*faqr*). He had two disciples: Shāh Yaḥyā' al-Dīn [sic][43] and Ḥudhayfa. Ḥudhayfa[44] had one disciple who was Ayyūb Ṭūsī. They are called Adhamīs and they would wear cloaks (*khirqa*). They would donate everything that they had for God's sake. If they received food, they would eat only three bites from it and would give the rest to the poor. They would eat desert plants and forest fruits most of the times. They would not neglect prayer for a moment. They always had ablution. They would not respond before being asked a question. Anyone who wants to become their disciple must adopt this way of life.

Fourth are the Yāsirmīs, whose meaning is from Shaykh Abu'l-Fatḥ. He had two disciples: ʿAmīd al-Dīn and ʿAlāʾ al-Dīnawarī,[45] who is also called Mumtāz Nabūdhī [sic].[46] The Yāsirmīs [were] very well dressed. They were hospitable towards the poor and needy. They would wash the hands of the poor, eat the leftovers of their food and wash their clothes. They would take care of strangers and build many mosques, buildings devoted to religious ceremonies (*takiyyas*) as well as bridges. They would go on pilgrimage to the holy shrines and Mecca, and their food was barley bread.

Fifth are the Chishtīs, [whose meaning is from] ʿAlāʾ al-Dīn Mumtāz Nūrī. He had one caliph who was Shāh Quṭb al-Dīn. Nāṣir al-Dīn, Abū Muḥammad, Nāṣiḥ al-Dīn, Abū Yūsuf and Shāh Abū Aḥmad were altogether called Chishtīs. They would live in the cities as well as the villages. They were men of constant obedience and piety. They would invite people to God (*ḥaqq*). They would respect and hold in high regard the poor and needy. Those who want to become their disciples must adopt this way of life.

There are some other groups that are subdivisions of the fourteen families but they are not called *ʿajam*. One of these groups is Awliyāʾ-Shāhī whose meaning is from Ṣandal-Shāh. He lived in Bengal of India and wore fourteen rings and *qayza*.[47] His invocation (*dhikr*) was 'O Truth!' (*yā ḥaqq*). They are the subdivision of the family of Kāzirīs.[48]

Then there is the group of the Shikārīs, whose meaning is from Shāh ʿAbd Allāh Shikāriyya. He was a disciple of Bahlūl Bard-Daryā [sic] who was a disciple of Shaykh Masʿūd. Shaykh Masʿūd was a disciple of Shaykh Muḥammad Maghribī[49] who was a disciple of Ṭayfūr. They went naked from head to toe, did not associate with anyone, wore animal skins, their food was game meat and their homes were in shops. Their invocation was 'God, the Self-sufficient One' (*Allāh al-ṣamad*). They are a subdivision of the family of Ṭayfūrīs.

Then are the groups of Qalandarīs, whose meaning is from Mīr Ḥayāt Qalandar, of the Shaykhīs, whose meaning is from Shaykh Abu'l-Ḥasan Kharaqānī,[50] and of the Ghazālīs, [meaning from] Aḥmad Ghazālī.[51] They are a subdivision of the Karkhīs. They wear woollen clothes. Their food is barley bread and their invocation [is] 'O the

Living, the Eternal One!' (*yā ḥayy yā qayyūm*). [Then is the group of] Maḥmūd-Shāhī, whose meaning is from Maḥmūd Maghribī and Shāh ʿAbd Allāh Qummī. They were skilled in mathematics and geography. They would wear a thin string tied at the neck and hold a high fire in their hands. They would wear a lion skin. Their invocation was 'O loving, and O adored!' (*yā wadūd wa yā maʿbūd*). They are a subdivision of the family of Sakhṭīs (*Sakhṭiyān*).[52]

Then is the group of Niʿmat Allāh, whose meaning is from Shāh Niʿmat Allāh.[53] Shāh Niʿmat Allāh was disciple of Shāh ʿAbd Allāh Yāfiʿī,[54] Shāh ʿAbd Allāh Yāfiʿī was disciple of Ṣāliḥ Barbarī and Ṣāliḥ Barbarī was [disciple of] Hāshim Shāhī who was Mīr-Hāshim. The genealogy of both goes back to Abū ʿAlī Rūdbārī. Bektāshīs, Rifāʿīs, whose path is from sultan Sayyid Aḥmad Kabīr,[55] and Dhahabīs, whose path is from ʿAmmār Yāsir,[56] go back to Aḥmad Dīnawarī, to the family of Junaydīs and from them to the Holy Seal (*ḥaḍrat-i khātam*) [of the prophets, Muḥammad], peace be upon him. They have secret invocations (*dhikr-hā-yi khafī*).

The group of Qādirīs, whose meaning is from Shaykh ʿAbd al-Qādir; of Wahhābīs, [whose meaning is from] Shāh ʿAbd al-Wahhāb b. ʿAbd al-Qādir; of Mīm-Shāhīs, [whose meaning is from] Shāh Muḥammad Qadḥī; and of Qadḥīs, whose meaning is from Shāh Muḥammad Qadḥī; altogether are Qādirīs. They are a subdivision of the Ṭūsīs. Sayyid ʿAbd al-Razzāq, who was the son of Qaws Aʿẓam, was also Qādirī. Their path is performing public invocation (*dhikr-i jalī*) and playing the *daf* [large frame drum]. They usually have beads around their necks and wooden prayer beads in their hands.

The group of Madanī-Shāhī, whose meaning is from Shāh Shams al-Dīn. His title (*laqab*) was 'the gate of God' (*bāb al-ḥaqq*) who was honoured to have received the initiatory cloak (*khirqa*) through Shāh al-Nahār, which is the name of Zayd b. Ḥanẓala. He was in the service of Sayyid Jalāl and some would say they were those who killed and ate the camel of Shāh Sayyid Jalāl.[57] Their path is that they would wear a hand chain, anklet, necklace and nose-ring (*khizama*)[58] and the group of Madārīs is also a subdivision of the family of Firdawsīs.

The group of Nawākhāhīs, whose meaning is from Shāh Makhdūm;[59] of Shāhbāzīs, whose meaning is from Laʿl Shahbāz;[60] of Bahāʾī, whose meaning is from Shaykh Bahā' al-Dīn Zakariyyā';[61] and from Junūn Shāhī, who would wear a coloured cloth (*chil-band*), dance in India and wear female ornaments, and whose meaning was from Afqān Khān Jūkī. This is a subdivision of the family of Suhrawardīs. However, La'l Shahbāz became separated from this family, opted for Shāh Jamāl Mujarrad [and] was guided to the path of Khāksār and guides [sic].

The group of Karam Allāh Shāhī is a subdivision of the family of Zaydīs. Although Salīm Shāhīs, Ibrāhīm Shāhīs, Dīn Panāhīs, Karīm Shāhīs, Shāh Maḥmūda [sic] and Nūrī Shāhīs are subdivisions of Zaydīs, they are subdivisions of Zaydīs, but following the path of Shāhbāzīs, they converted to Khāksārīs.

The group of Pīrān Shāhīs, Sulṭān Shāhīs, Razzāq Shāhīs and Ḥabīb Shāhī went back to Shāh Ismā'īl Jūkī. They are a subdivision of the family of Ayyāzīs.

The group of Sayyid Shāhīs, whose meaning is from Sayyid Amīr Khān Gujarātī, and Naqshband, is a subdivision of the family of Adhamīs. Sayyid Sādat Khān used to be a king, but he left kingship, opted for poverty, became a disciple of Sulṭān Ibrāhīm Adham and received the initiatory cloak from two individuals: one is Sulṭān Ibrāhīm Adham and the other is Bāb al-Ḥaqq. However, he burnt both of the cloaks. When the committed disciples learnt about this incident, they all gathered and drew a line on their own foreheads with the ashes of the burnt cloaks.

The group of Jabrāna would tear up the top of their *gamucha*, which is Shāh Niẓām al-Dīn b. Baddānī [sic]. They would wear a bell on their waist, hold a sawfish saw and apply perfume. They are a subdivision of the family of Yāsirmīs.

[Finally,] the group of Qalandarīs, whose meaning is from Abū Qalandar[62] and Ṣābirīs, is a subdivision of the family of Chishtīs.

The Booklet of Poverty (*Risāla-yi faqriyya*)[63]

Introduction by Mihrān Afshārī[64]

It should first be mentioned that the manuscript is kept in the Library of Frankfurt University. There is a microfilm copy, number 7104, in the Central Library of Tehran University. The second part of this manuscript contains a collection of short treatises composed by the Ḥaydariyya and dervishes from the Khāksāriyya. The first, entitled 'On Poverty' (*faqriyya*), is translated below.

Parts of this epistle take the form of questions and answers, as is common in the treatises of spiritual chivalry or guild treatises (*futuwwat-nāma-hā*), which suggests the influence of the *futuwwat* ritual on the Khāksār. The text begins with expressions, in prose put into rhyme (*musajja'*), of praise and gratitude towards the Creator. After other expressions of praise to God and greetings to the Prophet, a story is reported from the Prince of the believers (*amīr al-mu'minīn*), 'Alī, about the celestial journey (*mi'rāj*) of the Prophet. According to this story, during his celestial journey, the Prophet saw the form of poverty, and after this, chose poverty and detachment (*mujarradī*). In this treatise, *faqr* (poverty) and *tajrīd* (detachment) are synonymous. It is worth recalling that 'active deprivation' was the most important principle in the path (*ṭarīqa*) of the *qalandar*s.

After mentioning the famous *ḥadīth*: 'Poverty is my pride' (*al-faqr fakhrī*), explaining and clarifying the status (*maqāmāt*) of poverty and the dervish's dignity (*darwīshī*), the author of this epistle says that it is entitled 'On Poverty'. Then different topics about the cloak of investiture (*khirqa*) are mentioned. The author of the epistle considers the 'wearing of the cloak' (*khirqa pūshīdan*) as a sign of the will to be blamed by people (*malāmat-i khalq*). Does this not show that the Khāksār ritual has been influenced in some way by the ritual of the 'people of blame' (*ahl-i malāmat*)? Just like the term *khāksārī* (lit. 'dust-like'), the terms *khwārsarī* (lit. despised) and *malāmat-kashī* ('who comes in for blame') are used to refer to Malāmatīs.

This epistle, after developing some interesting topics on the crown (*tāj*), the beggar's bowl (*kashkūl*), the staff (*'aṣā*), the chest-piece (*sīnah pūsh*), the earring (*ḥalqa-yi gūsh*), the yoke (*ṭuq-i gardan*) and the sarong (*tanūrah*), deals with the explanation of the meaning of poverty and the dervish's dignity. Then, an appendix entitled 'On the Clarification of the Cloak' (*dar bayān khirqa*) speaks about the four masters of the order, the bridle (*pālhang*), the wearing of the belt (*miyān-bastan*), as well as the etiquette and rules of it all. The last part concludes with two verses describing the master of the dervishes (*mawlā-yi darwīshān*) 'Alī.

The Booklet of Poverty (*Risāla-yi faqriyya*)

In the name of God, the Compassionate, the Merciful.

[All] praise is due to God who made the darkness and the light.[65]

Infinite praise, from the earth to the heavens, to the creator of the seven skies and the stars, the maker of the universe, the provider of daily bread for all beings, the remover of the shining sun from the darkness of the night who 'made the night as clothing' (*ja'ala al-layl libāsan*).[66]

After praising God and saluting his holiness Muḥammad 'the chosen' (*muṣṭafā*), may God bless him and grant him peace (*ṣalla allāhu 'alayhi wa sallam*), it is narrated from the Commander of the Faithful (*amīr al-mu'minīn*) 'Alī, may God glorify his face (*karrama allāh wajhahu*), that his holiness the Prophet, peace be upon him (*'alayhi al-salām*),[67] said: 'I reached the zenith of the seven skies; the Lord of lords greeted me and said: 'Greet me!' And I greeted him. Then he told me: 'Look upward!' And I looked upward. I saw a wonderful, indescribable shape. The shape amazed me, and I became unconscious because of wonder. Then I entered the 'no-place' (*lā makān*), and my soul gained a drop of the *subhān*[68] of Life Sea (*daryā-yi ḥayāt*). I became conscious. I looked around, and I did not see the shape. Once again I prayed and asked the court of honour: 'O God the Creator, show me the vision again!' I heard the reply: God, exalted be He, told me: 'Detach yourself (*tajarrad*)!' Meaning, what you have seen was the image of poverty (*faqr*). If you want [to see it again], detach yourself, choose seclusion (*khalwa*), practise discipline (*riyāḍa*), seek solitude (*'uzla*), and keep vigil. So, the stages of the religious law (*sharī'a*), the mystical path (*ṭarīqa*) and the spiritual truth (*ḥaqīqa*)[69] will be revealed to you'.

The Prophet, peace be upon him, said: 'Poverty is my pride, and I will be proud of it among other messengers, saints and prophets on the Day of Judgment.'[70] And his holiness, peace be upon him, said: 'This poverty is my pride, and my poverty is God's will.' For that reason, people of poverty (*ahl-i faqr*) call the wayfarers 'the people of sight' (*ahl-i dīdār*). And the holy Messenger, peace be upon him, also said: 'Annihilation (*fanā'*) is the first stage of poverty (*faqr*)'. It means that [the person] detaches himself from all that is carnal, human and animal so the dignity of the dervish (*darwīsh*)[71] will be established on him. And the messenger, peace be upon him, also said: 'In the station (*maqām*) of poverty, the beginning step is the obvious (*ẓāhīr*), the second is the hidden (*bāṭin*), the third is the meaning (*maʿnā*), the fourth is the chivalry (*jawānmardī*), and the fifth step is the station of the prophets.'

The wayfarers of the spiritual path (*ṭarīqat*) call this book *faqriyya* (On Poverty or Destitution); let it [guide] the wayfarers of the path of Muḥammad the Chosen, and let them follow it to prevent them from darkness and heresy.

> What is 'wearing the cloak' (*khirqa*)? And what does it mean to wear a cloak?
> What is the sarong (*tanūrah*)?[72] And what does it mean?
> What is the meaning of the staff (*ʿaṣā*)? What is the meaning of barefooted and bareheaded?
> What is the meaning of detachment (*tajrīdī*), and what is 'wearing the yoke' (*ṭuq andākhtan*)?[73]

Know that thus say the seekers of the path of poverty and argue in this way.

Now, the meaning of wearing the cloak is to die; then be dressed in poverty's attire, resisting greed for the world, accepting to be the subject of people's criticism, and walking in the path of annihilation, until poverty appears. When one is wounded by friends and foes, and withstands the disasters of both worlds, he deserves to wear the cloak.

Only those deserve to wear the crown (*tāj*)[74] who do not mind if millstones drop down onto their heads.

Those who do not sacrifice their own desire, and deal not with the desires of others, do not deserve to carry the hanging bowl (*kashkūl*).[75]

Those who explain the secrets of poverty and demonstrate the quality of the masters (*mashāyikh*) deserve to hold the staff (*ʿaṣā*).[76]

Those who realise the details of the meaning deserve to wear the chest-wear (*sīnah pūsh*).

Those who are persistent in obedience deserve to wear the belt (*maras*),[77] otherwise it is a *zunnār*.[78]

Whoever listens only to the exalted God in obedience to him and keeps listening to the godly word deserves to put the ring (*ḥalqa*)[79] on his ear. When he recites God's name and remembers him in his mind, he must set his heart on following the way of truth.

If one breaks his own heart, and adopts annihilation and bows down to the lord, he deserves to wear the yoke.

Whoever burns existence in the fire of non-existence deserves to wear the sarong (*tanūrah*).

It is narrated that whoever is not aware of this idea, has nothing to do with the world of poverty (*faqr*) and his robe is actually a *zunnār*. These are all about the form of poverty and if a dervish is not aware [of them] he is not a dervish but an enemy of the saints' path.

Thus say the wayfarers of the path of certainty that poverty is a tree of God's gardens, its root is God's guidance, its ground is love, knowledge is as water to it, its branches are wisdom, its leaves are good deeds, and its shadow is enthusiasm. Whoever receives a leaf of this tree, will be a companion to the exalted God forever. *Būrda bir hads wārdir.*[80]

Then, if they ask: 'What is being a dervish?' Tell them: 'Leaving the others and joining Truth [or God] (*ḥaqq*)'.

And if they ask: 'How many stages does the spiritual path have?' Answer them: 'Forty-four stages; and one must pass through them to become a [true] dervish'.

Explication of the Cloak

If they ask: 'How many are the rules of the spiritual path and the cloak?' Tell them: 'There are twelve rules.'

If they ask: 'What are these twelve rules?' Tell them: 'First is repentance, second is inculcation, third is truthfulness, fourth is full confidence in God (*tawakkul*), fifth is detachment (*tajrīdī*), sixth is acceptance (*taslīmī*), seventh is God-fearingness (*taqwā*), (. . .),[81] ninth is contentment, tenth is seclusion, eleventh is discipline (*riyāḍat*), and twelfth is generosity.

If they ask: 'How many types are the masters (*pīr*)[82] of the spiritual path?' Tell them: 'There are four types.'

If they ask: 'Who are these masters?' Tell them: 'First is the master of shaving (*tarāsh*), second is the master of the sermon, third is the master of the cloak, and fourth is the master of guidance (*irshād*).'

And if they ask: 'How long is the bridle (*pālhang*)?'[83] Tell them: 'The bridle of the spiritual path (*ṭarīqa*) is seven metres.'[84]

[And if they ask:] 'Why is it seven metres?' Tell them: 'Because the body has seven organs.'

If they ask: 'Why is the accuracy of prayer based on seven organs?'[85] Tell them: 'Because they turn to seven ropes, each of them yields a certain purpose. The first ties stinginess and releases generosity. The second ties satiety and releases hunger. The third ties greed and releases contentment. The fourth ties anger and releases forbearance. The fifth ties lust and releases discipline. The sixth ties ignorance and releases knowledge. The seventh ties Satan and releases the Merciful (*raḥmān*). In this way they deserve to wear a belt.'

If they ask: 'What are the twelve words that are recited while a belt is worn?' Tell them: 'First, solidarity (*tawallā'*) with the Prophet's descendants; second, dissociation (*tabarrā'*)[86] from the Prophet's enemies; third, enjoining what is right; fourth, forbidding what is wrong; fifth, being fair; sixth, not being oppressive; seventh, observing chivalry (*futuwwa*); eighth, behaving chivalrously; ninth, obeying the master (*pīr*); [text missing];[87] eleventh, being lowly in dominance; twelfth, being dominant in lowliness. Whoever realises these words, knows the spiritual path; otherwise, he is not the master of the spiritual path.'

Then, when a master is dressing a disciple in a belt, he whispers in the disciple's ear: 'Be firm in observing religious laws! Be resolute in the spiritual path, and be vigilant in truth, so you will be established as a disciple.' Then the belt will be put on him.

ʿAlī has the traits mentioned in *qul huwa Allāh* [Say: 'He is God']
(*mawṣūf-i ṣifāt-i qul huwallāh ʿAlīst*)
ʿAlī is the king of the world of knowledge
(*dar ʿālam-i maʿrīfat shāhanshāh ʿAlīst*)
The light that emanates from him brings forth creation
(*nūrī ki azū shud āfarīnish paydā*)
Swear to God that [the light] is ʿAlī, swear to God [the light] is ʿAlī.
(*wallāh ki ān ʿAlīst, wallāh ʿAlīst*)

NOTES

1 From Mihrān Afshārī, ed., *Futuwwat-nāmah-hā wa rasā'il-i khāksāriyya* (Tehran, 1382 Sh. /2003), pp. 205–218.

2 Kaykhusraw Isfāndiyār, *Dabistān-i madhāhib bā yāddāsht-hā-yi raḥīm-zādah-yi malik* (2 vols., Tehran, 1362 Sh./1983–4) vol. 1, pp. 189, 191.

3 In the Khāksārī treatises what is mentioned is the 'Ḥaqqān', not the 'Ḥaqā'iq', lineage.

4 Zayn al-ʿĀbidīn Shīrwānī, *Bustān al-siyāḥa yā siyāḥat-nāmah* (Tehran, n.d.), pp. 122–123; compare: ʿAlīm Mudarrisī, *Ganjīnah-yi awliyā' yā ā'īnah-yi aṣfiyā'* (Tehran, 1338 Sh. /1959–60), pp. 78–79. On this, see in this volume Alexandre Papas, 'The Khāksār Shiʿi Sufi Order: An Updated Introduction', n.8.

5 Ghulām Sarwar Lāhūrī, *Khazīnat al-aṣfiyā'* (2 vols., Nawlkishwar, 1281/1864–5), vol. 2, p. 59.

6 Shāh Ḍiyā' Allāh, *Nasab-nāmah-yi kalān wa bayān-i chahārdah khānawādah wa ḥālat-i haftād wa du millat* (Lahore, 1309/1891–2), pp. 67–72.

7 Muḥammad Taqī Dānish-Pazhūh, '*Maṭlūb al-fuqarā*'', in Mahdī Muḥaqqiq, ed., *Humā'ī-nāmah, Majmūʿa-yi maqālāt ihdā'ī bih ustād Jalāl al-Dīn Humā'ī* (Tehran, 1355 Sh. /1976–7) pp. 101–102 and 115–116.

8 See Muḥammad Taqī Dānish-Pazhūh, *Fihrist-i nuskhah-hā-yi khaṭṭī-yi kitābkhānah-yi markazī-yi dānishgāh-i Tihrān*, vol. 13, pp. 3380–3382.

9 This is missing in the original manuscript.

10 *Fāṭīl* is the Arabised form of *Pāṭīl*; *Fāṭīl* is also the slang pronunciation of *Pāṭīl*. Salmān al-Fārsī is referred to by Khāksārīs as 'Sulṭān Maḥmūd Pāṭīlī', see ʿAbd al-Ḥusayn Zarrīnkūb, *Jūstujū dar taṣawwuf-i Īrān* (Tehran, 1363 Sh./1984–5), p. 377.

11 Kumayl b. Ziyād b. Nahyak al-Nakhāʿī (d. 82/701–2) was from the followers of the Prophet (*tābiʿūn*) and the companions of ʿAlī b. Abī Ṭālib. He was present with ʿAlī at the battle of Ṣiffīn. He lived in Kufa and was engaged in narrating *ḥadīth*. He was killed by Ḥajjāj b. Yūsuf. Khayr al-Dīn al-Ziriklī, *al-Aʿlām* (8 vols., Beirut, 1980) vol. 5, p. 234. On him, see also the article of Mathieu Terrier in this volume.

12 In the original manuscript it is written: *Ilāhī*.

13 Uways b. ʿĀmir b. Juz' b. Mālik al-Qaranī, one of the early ascetics, an ascetic and pious man and one of the elder followers (*tābiʿūn*). He was originally from Yemen and lived in the desert. He was a contemporary of the Prophet but did not meet him. He fought for ʿAlī in the battle of Ṣiffīn and it is said that he was martyred in this battle. Ziriklī, *al-Aʿlām*, vol. 2, p. 32. See also the chapter of Mathieu Terrier in this volume.

14 Abū Saʿīd Ḥasan b. Yāsir al-Baṣrī (d. 110/728–9) was from the 'followers' and was the spiritual leader of the people of Basra. He was born in Madina and was a scholar, jurist and an eloquent speaker. He was one of those who resisted Ḥajjāj b. Yūsuf. Ziriklī, *al-Aʿlām*, vol. 2, p. 226.

15 Ḥabīb ʿAjamī was a disciple and companion of Ḥasan Baṣrī. It is reported that it was Ḥasan Baṣrī who led him to repent and to become interested in asceticism (*zuhd*). Since he could not speak Arabic fluently, he became famous as ʿAjamī (from *ʿajam*, non-Arab). When Ḥajjāj's agents were pursuing Ḥasan Baṣrī, ʿAjamī hid him in his hermitage (*ṣawmaʿa*). See Abu'l-Ḥasan ʿAlī al-Hujwirī al-Qaznawī, *Kashf al-maḥjūb*, ed. V.A. Zhukovsky (Leningrad, 1344/1304 Sh./1926), p. 107.

16 Apparently *Kāzirūniyān*, i.e. the followers of Shaykh Abū Isḥāq Ibrāhīm b. Shahriyār Kāzirūnī who are famous as *murshidiyya* (Murshidīs).

17 ʿAbd al-Wāḥid Zayd was a disciple of Ḥasan Baṣrī and a man of wisdom. He is considered the religious leader of the people of Basra. Shaykh al-Islam Abū Ismāʿīl ʿAbd Allāh Anṣārī Hirawī, *Ṭabaqāt al-Ṣūfiyya*, ed. M. Sarwar Mawlāyī (Tehran, 1362 Sh./1983–4), p. 130.

18 Apparently it refers to *ʿAyyāḍiyān* (ʿAyyāḍīs), since in other sources *ʿAyyāḍiyān* are considered as one of the fourteen families. See the introduction.

19 Probably *Yāsirbiyān*, it is not legible in the original manuscript. This group is not known. It is probable that *Yāsiriyān* is more appropriate here.

20 In the original manuscript: Kāzirūni. Abū Isḥāq Kāzirūnī: Abū Isḥāq Ibrāhīm b. Shahriyār Kāzirūnī (d. 426/1034–5). He was born in Naward (Kāzirūn) and grew up

there. His father, Shahriyār, converted to Islam. In Sufism Abū Isḥāq was one of the disciples of Abū ʿAlī Ḥusayn Fīrūz-Ābādī, he benefited from traditionists (*ahl-i ḥadīth*) in Kazirun, Shiraz, Basra and Mecca and he knew a lot of *ḥadīth*s and narrations. Nūr al-Dīn ʿAbd al-Raḥmān Jāmī, *Nafaḥāt al-uns min ḥaḍarāt al-quds*, ed., introduced and annotated, Maḥmūd ʿĀbidī (Tehran, 1370 Sh./1991–2), pp. 260–261.

21 Abū Yazīd Ṭayfūr b. ʿIsā al-Basṭāmī (d. 261/874–5) was a well-known ascetic from Bastam and he died there. His followers are known as Ṭayfūriyya or Basṭāmiyya. Ziriklī, *al-Aʿlām*, vol. 3, p. 235. On his alleged contemporaneity with Jaʿfar al-Ṣādiq (d. 148/765), see the chapter of Mathieu Terrier in this volume.

22 Probably what is meant is Dāwūd Ṭā'ī. Abū Sulaymān Dāwūd b. Naṣīr al-Ṭā'ī was one of the pioneers of Sufism. Being originally from Khurasan he was born in Kufa and travelled to Baghdad and was student of Abū Ḥanīfa (d. 150/767) and others. Then he returned to Kufa and was inclined to reclusiveness (*ʿuzlat*). He lived in the era of Mahdī ʿAbbāsī and died in 165/781–2. Ziriklī, *al-Aʿlām*, vol. 2, p. 335.

23 What is probably meant here is Abū ʿAbd Allāh Muḥammad b. Khafīf al-Shīrāzī who was *shaykh al-mashāyikh* (the master of masters) in his era. He benefited from a huge number of Sufi masters such as Ibn ʿAṭā', Shiblī, Ḥusayn b. Manṣūr Ḥallāj, Jurīrī, Ruwaym, Kattānī, Yūsuf b. Ḥusayn Rāzī and Abu'l-Ḥusayn Darrāj. He was a Shāfiʿī and a scholar of his era. He died in 331/942–3. Hujwīrī, *Kashf al-maḥjūb*, p. 199; Jāmī, *Nafaḥāt al-uns*, p. 240.

24 Abū Ḥāfiẓ Maʿrūf b. Fayrūz al-Karkhī was a well-known ascetic and Sufi who was famous for being the companion of Imām ʿAlī b. Mūsā al-Riḍā. He was born in Karkh of Baghdad, grew up there and died in 200/815. Ziriklī, *al-Aʿlām*, vol. 7, p. 269. See also the chapter of Mathieu Terrier in this volume.

25 Abu'l-Ḥasan Sirrī b. al-Maghlis al-Saqaṭī was a great Sufi. He was born in Baghdad and died there. He was the leader of ascetics and Sufis of Baghdad and the uncle of Junayd. He died in 253/867–8. Ziriklī, *al-Aʿlām*, vol. 3, p. 82.

26 Abu'l-Qāsim Junayd b. Muḥammad b. Junayd al-Baghdādī. His father was originally from Nahavand, but he was born in Baghdad and died there in 297/909–10. Junayd is famous as 'Qawārīrī'. In his spiritual journey (*sayr wa sulūk*) he was strictly committed to the observance of religious duties. It is reported that he was first to talk of the science of *tawḥīd* (the unity of God) in Baghdad. Ziriklī, *al-Aʿlām*, vol. 2, p. 141.

27 Apparently *Sakhṭīyān* is the slang pronunciation of *Saqṭīyān*.

28 Abū Bakr Dulaf b. Jaḥdar al-Shiblī (d. 334/945–6). He is famously attributed to be from Shibla, a village of Transoxiana. His name and title are debatable. He was born in Samarra and died in Baghdad. It is reported that he was first the governor of Damawand and then joined the path of the Sufis. Ziriklī, *al-Aʿlām*, vol. 2, p. 341.

29 Abū ʿAlī Muḥammad b. Aḥmad Rūdbārī was one of the great masters of Sufism and the son of a statesman and minister. He was originally from Baghdad, but lived in Egypt and died in 322/933–4. Ziriklī, *al-Aʿlām*, vol. 5, pp. 308–309.

30 Apparently it means 'Abū 'Uthmān al-Maghribī', one of the great masters of the 4th/10th century.

31 Yaḥyā' al-Dīn seems not to be correct and apparently 'Muḥyī al-Dīn' is meant here.

32 In the original manuscript: Abu'l-Naṣraj Ṭūsī. Abu'l-Naṣr Sarraj: Abū Naṣr ʿAbd Allāh b. ʿAlī Ṭūsī (d. 378/988–9), known as Abū Naṣr Sarrāj was one of the ascetics and spiritual masters of Sufism. His famous book is called *al-Lumaʿ fī'l-taṣawwuf*. He died in 378/988–9. Ziriklī, *al-Aʿlām*, vol. 4, p. 104.

33 Apparently 'Shaykh 'Abd al-Qādir Gīlānī' is meant here. Abū Muḥammad ʿAbd al-Qādir b. Mūsā b. Muḥyī al-Dīn Gīlānī or Jīlānī (d. 561/1165–6) is the founder of the path of the Qādirīs. He was a great ascetic and Sufi. He was born in Gilan, and at a young age he travelled to Baghdad where he joined the great masters of knowledge and Sufism. He taught and issued *fatwa*s in Baghdad. He wrote various works such as: *al-Fatḥ al-rabbānī wa'l-fuyūḍāt al-rabbāniyya*. Ziriklī, *al-Aʿlām*, vol. 4, p. 47.

34 'Najm al-Dīn Kubrā' is meant here. Abu'l-Jannāb Aḥmad b. 'Umar al-Khaywaqī, nicknamed as 'Kubrā' or 'Shaykh Walī Tarrāsh', is a famous Sufi of the 6th/12th century. At a young age he studied the science of *ḥadīth*. He was one of the disciples of Shaykh 'Ammār Yāsir Badlīsī. Many of his own disciples were well-known great masters of Sufism, such as: Majd al-Dīn Baghdādī, Sa'd al-Dīn Ḥamāwī, Raḍī al-Dīn 'Alī Lālā, Sayf al-Dīn Bākharzī and Najm al-Dīn Rāzī. Najm al-Dīn Kubrā was killed in the Mongol invasion in 617/1220–1.

35 Abu'l-Najīb 'Abd al-Qāhir b. 'Abd Allāh b. Muḥammad Suhrawardī (d. 563/1167–8) is one of the spiritual masters of Sufism. He was a Shāfi'ī jurist and a preacher of his time. He was born in Suhraward in 490/1096–7. He travelled to Baghdad and settled there and died in this city. He was for a period of time the head of the Niẓāmiyya school. Among his works are: *Ādāb al-murīdīn* and *Sharḥ al-asmā' al-ḥusnā*. Ziriklī, *al-A'lām*, vol. 4, p. 49.

36 In the original manuscript: Shaykh Wāḥid.

37 'Abd Allāh 'Awf: Abū Muslim 'Abd Allāh b. Thawb ('Awf) al-Khūlānī, was a jurist, devout and ascetic, from the followers (*tabī'ūn*). He was originally from Yemen. He lived before the rise of Islam. He converted to Islam before the death of the Prophet but he did not meet him. During the caliphate of Abū Bakr he travelled to Madina and then to Syria and died in Damascus in 62/681–2. Ziriklī, *al-A'lām*, vol. 4, p. 75.

38 Amīr Kulāl: he was a Sufi of the 8th/14th century, one of the masters of the order of Khwājagān and he was the caliph of Khwājah Muḥammad Bābā-yi Samāsīyi and Khwājah Bahā' al-Dīn Naqshband was one of his *murīds*. Jāmī', *Nafaḥāt al-uns*, p. 387.

39 Presumably Fuḍayl 'Ayyāḍ (d. 187/802–3) is meant here.

40 'Ayyāḍī is probably meant here. See the introduction to this treatise.

41 Fuḍayl 'Ayyāḍ is probably meant here.

42 Ibrāhīm Adham: Abū Isḥāq Ibrāhīm b. Adham Balkhī, a well-known ascetic, whose father was a statesman from Balkh. Ibrāhīm made many trips to Iraq, Syria and the Ḥijāz and benefited from the scholars of his time. His job was farming and gardening. He was always fasting and died in Sophene (a province of the Byzantine Empire) in 161/777–8. Ziriklī, *al-A'lām*, vol. 1, p. 31.

43 Apparently: Muḥyī al-Dīn.

44 In the original manuscript: Khudhayfa. What is apparently meant here is Ḥudhayfa Mar'ashī who was one of the ascetics of the 2nd/8th century and a contemporary of Ibrāhīm Adham. As *Nafaḥāt al-uns* puts it: 'Ibrāhīm Adham, 'Alī Bakkār, Ḥudhayfa Mar'ashī and Silm Khawwāṣ were friends of each other.' Jāmī, *Nafaḥāt al-uns*, p. 38.

45 'Ilw Dīnawarī: Khwājah 'Ilw Dīnawarī, nicknamed Karīm al-Dīn. He memorised the whole Qur'an and was the caliph of Khwājah Ḥubayra Baṣrī. He died in 298/910–11. He is one of the pioneers of the chain of Chishtīs. See: Lāhūrī, *Khazīnat al-aṣfiyā'*, vol 1, p. 238.

46 Probably Mumtāz Nūrī; as the name of 'Alā' al-Dīn Mumtāz Nūrī is mentioned in the following lines, probably the very same Khwājah 'Ilw Dīnawarī is meant here. Compare: Zarrīnkūb, *Jūstujū dar taṣawwuf-i Īran*, p. 377.

47 In the original manuscript: *Qayḍa*. *Qayza* is an Indian word meaning *longuta* [lungi, *gamucha*] (Muḥammad Mu'īn, *Farhang-i Fārsī-yi Mu'īn* (6 vols., Tehran, 1363 Sh./1984–5): entry *Qayza-band* (*entry longuta*): 'a *gamucha* that dervishes, poor people and commoners would wear'.

48 Kāzirūniyān. What is meant here are the followers of Shaykh Abū Isḥāq Kāzirūnī.

49 What is apparently meant here is Abū 'Abd Allāh Muḥammad al-Maghribī (d. 279/892–3 or 299/911–12), who was the teacher of Ibrāhīm Khawwāṣ and the disciple of Abu'l-Ḥusayn 'Alī Razīn Hirawī. It is said that he lived for one hundred and twenty-two years and his tomb is on Mount Sinai. Jāmī, *Nafaḥāt al-uns*, pp. 89–90.

50 Abu'l-Ḥasan 'Alī b. Aḥmad Kharaqānī, a well-known mystic (*'ārif*) of the 4th/10th and 5th/11th centuries, a contemporary of Shaykh Abū Sa'īd Abi'l-Khayr and Imām Abu'l-Qāsim Qushayrī. He was from the village of Kharaqān in the city of Basṭām. His job was

to rent properties (*khar-bandagī*). In his spiritual journey (*sayr wa sulūk*), he was influenced by the spirituality of Bāyazīd Basṭāmī. He died in 425/1033–4. One of his devotees collected his speeches and virtues (*manāqib*) in a book called *Nūr al-ʿulūm*, a selection of which has been published. *Kashf al-maḥjūb*, pp. 204–205; Jāmīʿ, *Nafaḥāt al-uns*, p. 303; Mīnawī: *Aḥwāl wa aqwāl-i Shaykh Abu'l-Ḥasan Kharaqānī*, with a selection from *Nūr al-ʿulūm*, pp. 5–7.

51 Abu'l-Futūḥ Aḥmad b. Muḥammad Ghazālī (d. 517/1123–4) brother of Abū Ḥāmid Ghazālī, originally from Tus, and died in Qazwin. He taught in the Niẓāmiyya school for a while on behalf of his brother. Then he abandoned teaching and turned to asceticism. He was proficient in preaching and several treatises are attributed to him. Ziriklī, *al-Aʿlām*, vol 1, p. 214.

52 Saqṭīs (*Saqṭīyān*) by which is meant the followers of Sirrī Saqaṭī.

53 Shāh Niʿmat Allāh: Sayyid Niʿmat Allāh was the son of Sayyid ʿAbd Allāh, known as Shāh Niʿmat Allāh Walī, one of the mystics of the 8th/14th century. He was born in Kuhbanan of Kirman. His noble lineage (*siyāda*) goes back to Imam Muḥammad Bāqir. He travelled widely and visited the scholars and the mystics of his time. In the Ḥijāz he visited Shaykh ʿAbd Allāh Yāfiʿī and under his supervision he became involved in *murāqaba* (meditation) and *riyāḍa* (discipline) and then became his caliph. He returned to Iran and settled in the city of Yazd but due to the rejection and persecution inflicted upon him by the people of this city he left Yazd for Shiraz. He lived there for a while and also lived for a period of time in the village of Mahan in Kirman and died and was buried there. He was respected by Shāhrukh Taymūrī and some of the famous mystics such as Khwājah Isḥāq Khatlānī, Sayyid ʿAlī Hamidānī, Sayyid Muḥammad Nūrbakhsh and Pīr Jamāl Ardistānī were his contemporaries. The Niʿmat Allāhī dervishes are attributed to him and his order in Iran has the most followers. Shāh Niʿmat Allāh left several treatises and a collection of poems. Shīrwānī, *Būstān al-siyāḥa*, pp. 525–528.

54 ʿAfif al-Dīn ʿAbd Allāh b. Asʿad al-Yāfiʿī (d. 768/1366–7), a Shāfiʿī historian and Sufi from Yemen. He was born in Aden; later he settled in Mecca and died there. He wrote several books including: *Mir'āt al-jinān* and *ʿAbrat al-yaqẓān fi maʿrifat ḥawādith al-zamān*. Ziriklī, *al-Aʿlām*, vol. 4, p. 72.

55 Sayyid Aḥmad b. Abi'l-Ḥasan al-Rifāʿī a descendant of Imam Mūsā al-Kāẓim (d. 183/799). The lineage of his *khirqa* goes back to Shiblī. He lived in Umm ʿUbayda in Baṭā'iḥ. Subtle poems are quoted from him. He died in 578/1182–3. See Jāmī, *Nafaḥāt al-uns*, pp. 533–535.

56 ʿAmmār Yāsir Bidlīsī, a mystic of the 6th/12th century. He was a disciple of Abu'l-Najīb Suhrawardī and spiritual master (*pīr*) of Shaykh Najm al-Dīn Kubrā. Some treatises are attributed to him such as *Ṣawm al-qalb* and *Bahjat al-ṭā'ifa*. He died in 582/1186–7. As mentioned in the treatise of the Fourteen Families, he is considered one of the masters of the order of the Dhahabiyya. Jāmīʿ, *Nafaḥāt al-uns*, p. 421; and Iḥsān Allāh ʿAlī Iṣṭakhrī, *Uṣūl-i taṣawwuf* (Tehran, 1338 Sh./1959–60), pp. 188–196.

57 Sayyid Jalāl Bukhārī, a mystic of the 7th/13th century who lived in the Indian subcontinent. He was a disciple of Bahā' al-Dīn Zakariyyā' Multānī (d. 661/1262). See: Abu'l-Qāsim Firishtah, *Tārīkh-i Firishtah yā Gulshān-i Ibrāhīmī*, lithography (1247/1831–2), vol. 2, p. 59. In *Khazīnat al-aṣfiyā'* some titles such as 'lion king' and 'red' have been attributed to him.

58 *Khizāma* is a camel's nose-ring to which a halter is attached. (*Farhang-i Fārsī-yi Muʿīn*, entry 'Khizāma').

59 Probably what is meant here is 'Shāh Makhdūm Jahāniyān Sayyid Jalāl al-Dīn Ḥusayn Bukhārī' (d. 785/1384). He was the son of Sayyid Aḥmad Kabīr and the grandson of Sayyid Jalāl Bakhtyārī. He did not accept anyone as his disciple and instituted brotherhood between his followers. *Tārīkh-i Firishtah*, vol. 2, p. 418; in *Khazīnat al-aṣfiyā'*, he was considered the caliph of the fourteen families, a belief which is probably taken from the sayings of the Jalāliyya about him: 'Makhdūm Jahāniyān was

the caliph of the fourteen families who travelled twice to the populated quarter of the world (*rubʿ maskūn*) and visited hundreds of fakirs and masters (*mashāyikh*)'. Lāhūrī, *Khazīnat al-aṣfiyā'*, vol. 2, p. 59.

60 Shaykh ʿUthmān Marandī, known as Laʿl Shahbāz Qalandar (d. 673/1274). He was originally from Marand and his lineage would go back to Ismāʿīl b. Imām Jaʿfar al-Ṣādiq. He lived in Sehwan in India and was a disciple of Shaykh Bahā' al-Dīn Zakariyyā' Mūltānī, but since he was taken by exaltation (*shūr*) and the spiritual state (*ḥāl*) of ecstatic mystics (*majdhūbān*), he embraced the way of the people of the blame (*malāmat*) and consequently would drink wine, smoke hashish publicaly and wear red clothes most of the time. It is said by some that after becoming a disciple of Shaykh Bahā' al-Dīn Zakariyyā' Mūltānī, he later became a disciple of Jamāl al-Dīn Mujarrad. Lāhūrī, *Khazīnat al-aṣfiyā'*, vol 2, pp. 46–47.

61 Shaykh Bahā' al-Dīn Zakariyyā': his grandfather is Kamāl al-Dīn ʿAlī Shāh Qurayshī who travelled from Mecca to Khwarazm and from there to Multan and settled there. Bahā' al-Dīn Zakariyyā' was his grandson and the son of Wajīh al-Dīn who was born in 578/1182–3. He travelled to Khurasan and visited religious grandees. He went on pilgrimage and lived in Madina for five years and learnt *ḥadīth* from Shaykh Kamāl al-Dīn Muḥammad Yamanī. He visited Shaykh Shihāb al-Dīn ʿUmar Suhrawardī in Baghdad and received the initiatory cloak from his hand. From there he returned to Shaykh Bahā' al-Dīn Zakariyyā' and was engaged in the guidance of his *murīds*. He had many *murīds* among whom are: Fakhr al-Dīn ʿIrāqī and Sayyid Jalāl al-Dīn Bukhārī. Shaykh Bahā' al-Dīn Zakariyyā' died in 661/1262 or 666/1267–8. *Tārīkh-i Firishtah*, vol. 2, pp. 404–409.

62 Probably 'Sharaf al-Dīn Abū ʿAlī Qalandar Pānī Patī' is meant here. He was one of the *qalandar*s of the Indian subcontinent. It is said that he died in 724/1323–4, which seems not to be true. His pen-name (*takhalluṣ*) was '*qalandar*' and significant points regarding the tradition and ritual of *qalandar*s can be found in his *dīwān*.

63 From Mihrān Afshārī, ed., *Futuwwat-nāmah-hā wa rasā'il-i khāksāriyya* (Tehran, 1382 Sh./2003), pp. 144–149.

64 Ibid., pp. 143–144. Translated by Mathieu Terrier.

65 Q 6:1.

66 Q 78:10.

67 Words of praise *karram allāh-u wajhah* for ʿAlī, and *ʿalayhi salām* and *ṣalla-llāhu ʿalayhi wa sallam* for the Prophet Muḥammad are commonly used by Sunnis. This gives a Sunni tone to the text. However, nowadays the Khāksār has a Shiʿi character. The Shiʿa usually use *ʿalayhi salām* for ʿAlī and other Shiʿi imams and the prophets, and *ṣalla-llāhu ʿalayhi wa ālihī wa sallam* (may God bless him and his family and grant them peace) for the Prophet Muḥammad.

68 Meaning 'glorious'. Maybe it has replaced *subuḥāt* (divine radiation) or perhaps *saḥbān* (water left over in a waterskin).

69 Three stages of religion according to Sufi exegesis.

70 It seems that the famous *ḥadīth* 'I am proud of *faqr*' (*al-faqr fakhrī*) is not mentioned in Sunni *ḥadīth* books (according to *al-Muʿjam al-mufahras li-alfāẓ al-ḥadīth al-nabawī*). However, it is narrated in the important works of Sufi predecessors, who were mostly Sunnis, and in Shiʿi *ḥadīth* books such as *Biḥār al-anwār*. For more information see Badīʿ al-Zamān Furūzanfar, ed., *Aḥādīth mathnawī* (Tehran, 1361 Sh./1982–3).

71 *Darwīsh* (dervish) is a Persian word and literally means 'the one who goes to door (to beg), i.e. poor'.

72 *Tanūrah*: a sarong that the *qalandar* and dervishes used to tie around their waist.

73 In the past, criminals were yoked and tied up in chains. In the Qajar era, the Khāksār wore the yoke and chains to show that they see their ego (*nafs*) as sinful and they are against it. Seemingly, wearing the yoke implies this meaning. On the other hand, it seems that such customs were common among Sufis formerly; as it is said of Shaykh

Abu'l-Ḥasan Kharaqānī: 'It was the shaykh's custom to come home at night, put a yoke and chain on his neck, wear a coarse carpet, and put a chain on his legs. He had a whip (*khāmīn*), and if his ego disobeyed, he would chastise it with the whip.' *Muntakhab nūr al-ʿilm*, ed. M. Mīnuwī (Tehran, 1363 Sh./1984–5), p. 144.

74 *Tāj*: the felt hat of the dervish. Some are simple and some others include embroidery. The Khāksār usually wrap a shawl or ornamental halter around their felt hat.

75 *Kashkūl* is a bowl, with a chain for hanging on the shoulders, that the mendicant dervishes carry for collecting charity.

76 The staff along with a jar, bowl, scissors, needle, thread, razor blade, tooth-brush, comb, nail-clippers and kohl container were the equipment that the Sufi must have with him, especially when travelling.

77 Literally the rope that is used for binding dogs and lions (from the dictionary of *Muʿīn*). The Khāksār called the rope which they tie to their neck, or wear on their waist, *maras*.

78 A certain kind of belt that had to be worn by Christians under the rule of Muslims to distinguish them from Muslims.

79 The Khāksars and the *qalandar*s used to put a ring with a pearl on their ears. The pearl was called the 'unique pearl' or the 'ear pearl'.

80 A Turkish phrase that means 'there is a guess'. The relevance of this phrase is unclear.

81 Eighth rule does not exist in the original text.

82 Literally means 'the aged'. In Sufi discourse implies the spiritual guide.

83 It seems that the Khāksār sometimes wear the bridle on their waist and at other times put it on their neck, as is the case with the belt (*maras*).

84 Originally: '*gaz*'. Each *gaz* is roughly equal to one meter.

85 Accurate position of prostration in prayer (*sujūd*) requires that seven parts of the body touch the ground: knees, hands, toes and forehead.

86 *Tawallāʾ* (solidarity with the imams) and *tabarrāʾ* (dissociation from their enemies) are considered two religious duties according to the Shiʿi creed.

87 The tenth word is missing in the original text. However, the footnote reads 'being obedient to the master (*pīr*)', which is only the repetition of the ninth word.

Index of Names and Subjects

ʿAbbās, the Prophet's uncle 78, 86
ʿAbbās al-Qummī 60 n.72
Abbasid 5, 14, 65, 72–3, 75–6, 78, 81–2, 84–7, 90, 91–94. 96–8, 100–4, 112 n.79, 113 n.82, 113 nn.85–6, 113 n.90, 114 n.105, 116 n.126, 116 nn.128–9, 118 n.168, 119 n.175, 205–6, 226
Abdāl, Ṣādiq 262–3
ʿAbd Allāh b. ʿAlī 86–7, 113 n.84, 113 n.92, 114 n.106, 340 n.32
ʿAbd Allāh ʿAwf, Abū Muslim ʿAbd Allāh b. Thawb (ʿAwf) al-Khūlānī (d. 62/681–2) 330, 341 n.37
ʿAbd Allāh Burzīshābādī (d. *ca* 856/1452) 11
ʿAbd Allāh b. Yaḥyā (d. 130/748) 92
Abraham 271–2, 276, 286 n.47, 318
Abū ʿAbd Allāh Muḥammad b. Khafīf al-Shīrāzī, Khwājah ʿAbd Allāh Khafīf (d. 331/942–3) 340 n.23
Abū ʿAlī Ḥusayn Fīrūz-Ābādī (4th–5th /10th–11th century) 340 n.20
Abū ʿAlī Rūdbārī (d. 322/933–4) 329, 332
Abū Ayyūb 86
Abū Bakr (r. 11–13/632–634) 5–6, 36, 102, 341 n.37
Abū Dāwūd [Khālid b. Ibrāhīm] 87, 113 n.91
Abū Dharr al-Ghifārī (d. 32/653) 35–6
Abū Ḥāmid Ṭūsī Marwazī 80
Abū Ḥanīfa (d. 150/767) 340 n.22
Abu'l-Ḥasan Kharaqānī (d. 425/1033) 293, 331, 344 n.73
Abū Hāshim b. Muḥammad b. al-Ḥanafiyya (d. 98/716) 79, 100
Abū Ḥumayd Ṭūsī 87
Abu'l-Ḥusayn ʿAlī Razīn Hirawī 341 n.49
Abu'l-Ḥusayn Darrāj (4th/10th century) 340 n.23
Abū Isḥāq Ibrāhīm b. Shahriyār Kāzirūnī (d. 426/1034–5) 339 n.16, 339 n.20
Abū Muḥammad (Chishtī) 331
Abū Muslim, Jurmān, Abū Mujrim (d. 137/755) 14, 65–119
Abū Muslim Khawlānī (d. 62/682) 97
Abū Muslim-nāmah 262
Abu'l-Najīb Suhrawardī (d. 563/1167–8) 342 n.56
Abu'l-Naṣr Sarrāj Ṭūsī (d. 378/988–9) 329
Abu'l-Qāsim Qushayrī (d. 465/1072) 341 n.50
Abū Saʿīd Abi'l-Khayr (d. 440/1049) 341 n.50

Abū Salama Khallāl 79, 80, 81, 91, 95
Abū Yūsuf (Chishtī) 331
ādāb 118, 237
Adam 34, 87, 187, 265–72, 286 n.43, 286 n.49, 287 nn.55–6, 287 n.69, 318
Adhamīs 326, 328, 330, 333
ʿĀdil Shāh sultans of Bijapur (894–1097/1489–1686) 159, 172 n.3, 233
ʿadl 307, 319
ʿAḍud al-Mulk, ʿAlī Riḍā Khān (13th/19th century) 180–1
Afandī, al-Mīrzā ʿAbd Allāh al-Iṣbahānī (d. *ca* 1130/1718) 32, 71, 76, 82, 110 n.42
Afghanistan 192 n.27, 294
Afshārī, Mihrān 11, 18–19, 291, 306, 315–17, 322 n.27, 323 n.47, 325–8, 333–4
Aga Khan 227–8, 243–4, 254 n.58
ahl al-bayt 6–7, 18, 36–8, 72, 78–9, 81, 94–5, 98, 103, 163, 254 n.67, 255, 262–71, 275, 277
Ahl-i Ḥaqq 195 n.88, 295–7
ahl al-sunna wa'l-jamāʿa 2, 37
Aḥmad b. ʿAlī al-Najāshī (d. 450/1058) 117 n.153
Aḥmad Dīnawarī 332
Aḥmad Shāh (d. 1348/1930) 180
Aḥmad Zamchī (2nd/8th century) 91, 92, 94, 101, 104
al-Aḥsāʾ 31
Ahwaz 209, 299
Aigle, Denise 142, 154 n.44
ʿAjam, ʿAjamī 13, 19, 140, 293, 299–300, 305–24, 326, 328, 331, 339 n.15
akhbār 8, 23 n.40, 72, 94, 183, 186
Akhbāriyya, *akhbārī* 8, 23 n.40, 55, 59 n.47, 108 n.24
Ākhirat-nāmah 257
ʿAlāʾ al-Dawla al-Simnānī (d. 736/1336) 3
ʿAlāʾ al-Dīn Mumtāz Nūrī 331
ʿalam 163
Alamut 228
al-ʿAlawī al-ʿĀmilī, Sayyid Aḥmad (d. between 1054/1644 and 1060/1650) 14, 65, 76–86, 90, 94, 97, 100, 104–5, 112 n.72, 113 n.85, 118 n.166
Alevi 255–6, 261, 264, 266–8, 278–9
Alevi-Bektashi [faith, community, creed, tradition, theology, religiosity] 17–18, 255–89
Algar, Hamid 11
ʿAlī Akbar 232, 239, 243, 248
ʿAlī Aṣghar 151 n.12, 243, 248
ʿAlī b. ʿAbd Allāh b. ʿAbbās b. ʿAbd al-Muṭṭalib 79, 100
ʿAlī b. Abī Ṭālib, Imām ʿAlī, al-Murtaḍā, Abū Turāb (d. 40/661) [the first imam] 5, 33, 35–7, 39, 48, 262, 277
ʿAlī b. Hammād 258
ʿAlī b. al-Ḥusayn, Zayn al-ʿĀbidīn (d. *ca* 95/714) [the fourth imam] 37, 41
ʿAlī b. Muḥammad al-Hādī (d. 254/868) [the tenth imam] 43
ʿAlī b. Mūsā al-Riḍā, Imām Riḍā (d. *ca* 203/818) [the eighth imam] 40, 42, 73, 95, 98, 310
ʿAlid family 227
Āl-i Kāshif al-Ghiṭā, Ayatollah Muḥammad Ḥusayn (d. 1373/1954) 180
ʿAlī Khān (r. 1175–1218/1761–1803) [Niẓām] 15, 165, 173 n.35
ʿAlī al-Madanī, Sayyid (d. 1120/1708–9) 71

ʿAlī Shāh (d. 1302/1885) 227
All India Shiʿa Conference 246
Amal al-āmil 110 n.42
Amasya 69, 285 n.41
ʿAmīd al-Dīn 331
Amīna, the daughter of Imam ʿAlī 88
Amīr Fīrūz Shāh 141
Amīr Ghanā (Ghunā) Shīrīn
152 n.20
Amīr Kulāl (8th/14th century) 143, 330, 341 n.38
Amir-Moezzi, Mohammad Ali 50, 52, 205, 280, 282
Amīr Nūr Allāh 139
Amīr Pīr *dargāh* 227
Amīr Sulaymānī, Amīr Muṣṭafā [Mushīr al-Salṭana Sābiq] 180–6, 188–9, 194 n.71
Amīr Sulaymānī Khān Qājār Madrasa 181
Amīr Ẓahīr b. Nūr Allāh 139
Amīrī 326
Āmīrzā Muḥibb Allāh (d. *ca* 911/1505–6) 147
ʿAmmār b. Yāsir (d. 37/658) 35–6
ʿAmmār Yāsir Badlīsī (d. 582/1186–7) 341 n.34, 342 n.56
al-amr bi'l-maʿrūf wa nahy ʿan al-munkar 308
Amroha 249
Āmul 29
Āmulī, Sayyid Ḥaydar (d. after 787/1385) 3–4, 28–32, 34–8, 41, 43–8, 52–4
Anatolia 6, 12, 18, 138, 262
Anīs al-abrār 93, 98–9, 117 n.139
Anīs al-mu'minīn 68, 107 n.6
anjuman 246, 319
Anjuman Shiʿa Conference 246
anjuman-i ukhuwwat 319
Anṣārī, Khwājah ʿAbd Allāh (d. 481/1089) 136
Anṣārī, Shaykh Murtaḍā (d. 1276/1860) 177, 179, 191 n.18
Anwār al-ḥaqīqa wa aṭwār al-ṭarīqa wa asrār al-sharīʿa 29, 45
Anzali, Ata 11
Āqāsī, Ḥājj Mīrzā (d. 1265/1849) 176, 191 n.10, 192 n.27
ʿaql 14, 90
Arabia, Arabian Peninsula 31, 173 n.30
Arabic xv, 10, 14, 18, 66–8, 70, 73–4, 76, 78, 80, 82–3, 88–90, 92, 94–5, 97–9, 103, 107 n.6, 109 n.33, 111 n.56, 221 n.21, 225, 229, 238–9, 251 n.1, 257–60, 264, 283 n.4d, 311–13, 339 n.15
Arbaʿīn ḥadīth fi radd al-ṣūfiyya 70
Ardabil 69, 311
Ardabīlī, Mullā Aḥmad, *also known as* Muqaddas Ardabīlī (d. 993/1585) 23 n.40, 59 n.47, 258
ʿārif (pl. *ʿārifūn*, *ʿurafā'*) 45, 55, 194 n.63, 341 n.50
Arisṭū Jāh (d. 1219/1804) 166, 168
ʿaṣā 287 n.69, 315, 334, 336
Asad b. Junayd 100
Ashʿarī 31, 98
ashbāḥ (*ashbāḥ nūr*) 268
Ashkiwarī, Quṭb al-Dīn (d. between 1088/1677 and 1095/1684) 13, 28, 32–4, 38–42, 44, 46, 48–51, 53–5
ashrāf 94, 101, 115 n.124, 162
Ashtūr tomb complex 133
ʿĀshūrā 181, 184–5, 189, 195 n.80, 298
ʿāshūr-khānah 163, 165, 173 n.30
Asrār al-ʿarifīn 276
āstāna 139–40, 147

Astarābādī, Faḍl Allāh (d. 796/1394) 257
al-Astarābādī, Muḥammad Amīn (d. 1036/1626–7) 108 n.24
ʿatabāt 29, 177
Aṭṭār Nayshābūrī, Farīd al-Dīn (d. 618/1221) 9
Aubin, Jean (d. 1998) 5, 123, 143, 145, 163
Aurangzeb (d. 1118/1707) 232, 250
Awadh 225, 233
ʿAwālī al-laʾālī 32
awliyāʾ 38, 43, 47–8, 159
Awliyāʾ-Shāhī (ʿajam) 331
awqāf 124, 146, 190 n.4
Āyat-hā-yi tarāsh 292
ʿAyyāḍī(s), Ayyāzī 326, 328, 330, 333, 339 n.18, 341 n.40
Ayyūb Ṭūsī 330
ʿazādārī 181–2
Āzād Khān (d. 1195/1781) 309–10, 322 n.31
Azerbaijan 295
Azeri 311
Azrael 276

Bāb al-Ḥaqq 332, 333
Bābā Ḥusayn 154 n.59
Bābā Ṭāhir (d. *ca* first half of the 5th/11th century) 192 n.22, 194 n.63
Babayan, Kathryn 7, 106 n.1
Baghdad 2–3, 5, 42, 228, 281
Bāgh-i Aharistān 152 n.16
Bahāʾ al-Dīn Muḥammad al-ʿĀmilī, Shaykh Bahāʾī (d. 1031/1621) 76, 85, 93, 99, 104, 108 n.24, 110 n.42, 110 n.43
Bahāʾ al-Dīn Naqshband, *see* Khwājah Bahāʾ al-Dīn Naqshband
Bahāʾ al-Dīn Zakariyyāʾ Multānī, Shaykh Bahāʾ al-Dīn Zakariyyāʾ (d. 661/1262) 333
Bahār ʿAlī Shāh Yazdī (d. 1936) 300
Bahawalpur 253 n.39
Bahlūl Bard-Daryā 331
Bahmanī, Aḥmad Shāh (r. 825–839/1422–1436) [Aḥmad Shāh Abu'l-Maghāzī] 130, 133, 135, 136, 143
Bahmanī, ʿAlāʾ al-Dīn Aḥmad Shah (r. 839–862/1436–1458) [Sulṭān ʿAlāʾ al-Dawla wa'l-Dīn wa'l-Dunyā Aḥmad Shāh] 130, 133
Bahmanī, Muḥammad Shāh (r. 867–887/1463–1482) 147
Bahmanid dynasty (r. 748–933/1347–1527) 158, 162
Baḥr ʿAlī Shāh Thānī 300
Baḥrayn 31
Bakhtyārīs 298
Baktāshī *see* Bektashis
Baku 295
Balkh 341 n.42
Baltistan 172 n.17
Baluch 238, 250
Baluchistan 130
Bam 153 n.38
Banū Hāshim 101
Banū Maʿqil 89, 100
baqāʾ 312
Barīd Shāh (r. *ca* 897–1028/1492–1619) 159
Barīdī kings 140
Baṣāʾir al-darajāt 109 n.34, 117 n.141
Basra 310
al-Baṣrī, Ḥasan, Ḥasan-i Baṣrī, Khwājah Ḥasan Baṣrī (d. 110/728–9) 37–8, 313, 326, 339 n.14

Basṭām 41
al-Basṭāmī, Abū Yazīd, *also known as* Bāyazīd-i Basṭāmī, Sulṭān Bāyazīd Basṭāmī, Ṭayfūr (d. 234/848 or 261/874–5) 35, 40–2, 44, 49, 52–5
Basṭāmiyya 340 n.21
bastan 293, 334
Baṭā'iḥ 342 n.55
bāṭin 3, 30, 35, 46, 51, 336
Bausani, Alessandro (d. 1988) 5
Bayān al-saʿāda fī maqāmāt al-ʿibādā 184
Bayān-i arkān 292
bayʿ 308, 320
bayʿat 73, 187–8
Bayḍā'ī 316
Baydukht 176–9, 181, 184–5, 192 n.33
bazaar 12, 19, 181, 188, 298, 306, 309–10, 312–13, 316, 318
Bekās (d. 1299/1882) 244
Bektāsh, Ḥājjī (d. 669/1270–1) 263
Bektāsh Khān 130
Bektāshiyya, Bektashis 4, 13, 256, 283 n.2, 332
Bengal 241, 331
Berar 165
Bhai Rām Singh (d. 1916) 253 n.39
Bībī Khānūm 243
bidʿa 8, 27
Bidar (*also known as* Muḥammadābād) 124, 125, 130, 136–7, 140–1, 143–5, 147, 150 n.3, 152 n.14, 152 n.15, 158–60, 162–5, 169
Biḥār al-anwār 71
Bihbahānī, Āqā Muḥammad ʿAlī (d. 1216/1801) 191 n.8
Bijapur 159, 233, 242
Bīland 177
Bishr al-Ḥāfī (d. 227/841–2) 40, 42
Bombay 228
Buddhism 2
Bulri 233
buqʿa 127, 146
buqʿa-yi Shāh Khalīl Allāh-i Thānī 127
Burhān al-Dīn Khalīl Allāh (d. 864/1460) 138–41
Burhān al-Mulk (d. 1143/1731) 233
Burhanpur 242
Bursī, Ḥāfiẓ Rajab (d. 813/1411) 10, 20, 28, 62 n.122
Buyid (334–447/945–1055) 3, 281
Buyruq 257, 279, 283 n.3
Byzantine Empire 341 n.42

Calcutta 241, 246
Calmard, Jean (d. 2017) 5, 22 n.30, 33
Caucasus 295
Chahārdah khānawādah 292, 295, 325–44
Chardin, Jean (d. 1713) 69
Chaukhandi 133, 152 n.14
Chishtiyya, Chishtīs 295, 326, 331, 333, 341 n.45
Chittick, William C. 4
Christianity 2, 76
Christians 44, 344 n.78
coffee-houses 317
Corbin, Henry (d. 1978) 3–4, 7, 18, 29–30, 49–50

Dabistān-i madhāhib 325
daf 332
Dakanī, Maḥmūd ʿAlī Shāh 171
Dakanī, Maʿṣūm ʿAlī Shāh (d. *ca* 1211/1797) 157, 158, 171, 176
Dakanī, Riḍā ʿAlī Shāh (d. 1215/1800–1) 157, 190 n.7, 195 n.91
Dalpat Ṣūfī (d. 1842) 243, 251

Damascus 341 n.37
Damawand 340 n.28
Dānish-Pazhū, Muḥammad Taqī (d. 1996) 327
dār al-islām 227
darb-i āb qanāt 146
dargāh 15, 144, 160–6, 168–71, 226–7
Darvīsh Khusraw (9th/16th century) 69
darwīsh 177, 193 n.61, 202, 208–10, 294, 335, 343 n.71; *see also* dervish
darwīshī 334
Dastghayb Shīrāzī 109 n.36
Dawlat City Gate (Tehran) 300
Dāwūd Ṭā'ī, Abū Sulaymān Dāwūd b. Naṣīr Ṭā'ī, *also known as* Dāwūd 'Aṭṭā'ī [sic] (d. 165/781–2) 340 n.22
Deccan 15, 123, 133–8, 140, 142–5, 148–9, 150 n.2, 150 n.3, 153 n.35, 154 n.52, 157–64, 167–71, 176, 190 n.7, 225, 233, 249–50
dede [*ocak-zāde*] 268, 278, 283 n.4
Dehkordī, Sayyid Aḥmad (d. 1339/1920) 322 n.39
Delhi 166–7, 242
dervish, dervishes 6–8, 11, 18–19, 39, 51, 68–9, 139–40, 147, 197, 201, 202, 209, 218, 242, 262, 292–3, 295–301, 305, 309–10, 312–20, 321 n.5, 323 n.47, 323 n.62, 324 n.67, 325, 327, 334–5, 337, 342 n.53, 343 n.71; *see also* darwīsh
desī 235
Devī 229
Dhahabī order 119 n.182, 305
al-Dharī'a 'alā taṣānif al-Shī'a 257
dhikr (*dhikr-i jalī, dhikr-i khafī, dhikr-i khayr, dhikr-i khudā, dhikr-i lisānī, dhikr-i qalbī*) 182, 186–7, 211, 297, 313, 316, 329–32
Dhu'l-fiqār 239, 253 n.35, 287 n.69
Dhu'l-Fiqār 'Alī Shāh (12th/18th century) 165
Dhu'l-janāḥ 252 n.31
Die schiitischen Derwischorden Persiens 10, 154 n.43, 291
Dihlawī, Asad 'Alī Shāh 171
Dīn Panāhī 333
dīwān 166, 211, 246
Ḍiyā' Parsrām (d. 1377/1958) 245
Dizfūlī, Shaykh Ismā'īl (d. 1941) 180
djem 264
du'ā 166, 248
Du'ā Kumayl 194 n.66
Duldul 236, 239, 252 n.31
Durrānī, Aḥmad Shāh (r. 1159–1185/1747–1772) 232
duwaz-imām, duwāzdah imām 262–4

Eaton, Richard Maxwell 144–5
Egypt 3, 5
Elias 276
Empedocles 46
En Islam iranien 3, 7
Enoch 271–2
Ethiopian language 318
Eve 265, 268–70, 318

Faḍlī, Faḍal 'Alī (12th/18th century) 230
Faizi Mahal 240
Fakhr al-Dawla Ḥasan b. Shāh Kay-Khusraw b. Yazdgird (d. 750/1349) 29
fanā' (*fanā' fi'llāh, fānī thiya*) 63 n.129, 211, 238, 243, 250, 312, 335

faqīh (pl. *fuqahā'*) 7, 32, 48, 51, 55, 71, 90, 179
faqīr (pl. *fuqarā'*) 187–9, 237
Faqīr Qādir Bakhsh, *also known as* Bedil (d. 1288/1872) 244–5, 249
faqr 330, 334–5, 337, 343 n.70
Faqr-nāmah 327
farmān 147
Farmītan 154 n.59
Fars 3, 68–9, 125
Farzām, Ḥamīd 142
fatā 253 n.35
Fatḥ ʿAlī Shāh (r. 1211–1250/1797–1834) 176, 239
al-Fatḥ al-rabbānī wa'l-fuyūḍāt al-rabbāniyya 340 n.33
Fāṭima 6, 49, 88, 90–1, 227, 248, 258, 260, 263. 266–70, 272, 286 n.47, 286 n.51
Fatimids 3, 90, 115 n.114
Fawā'id al-mu'minīn 83, 91, 96–8
Fayḍ al-Nisā' Begum 174 n.50
fikr 217
fiqh 9, 32, 179
Firdawsī, Abu'l-Qāsim (d. 411/1020) 229
Firdawsīs 326, 328–9, 332
Firishtah, ʿAbd al-Majīd (d. 864/1459–60) 257, 259
Firishtah, Muḥammad Qāsim (11th/17th century) 152 n.15
firmān 67, 87
fitna 40
Friday prayer 66, 68, 105, 165
Fuḍayl ʿAyyāḍ (d. 187/802–3) 341 n.39, 341 n.41
Furūghī, Muḥammad ʿAlī (d. 1321 Sh./1942) 180
Fuṣūṣ al-ḥikam 29
futuwwa, *futuwwat* 18, 262, 296–7, 318, 324 n.72, 334, 338
futuwwat-nāmah 18, 262, 291–2, 327, 334
Futuwwat-nāmah-yi Ṣulṭānī 108 n.19

Ganj-i Shakar, Farīd al-Dīn (d. 664/1265–6) 169, 295
Gawharshād 135, 152 n.20
Gāzurgāh 136
Geoffroy, Éric 4
Ghadīr Khumm 279, 308
ghalaba 63 n.132
ghālī (pl. *ghulāt*) 6, 251 n.6
ghazal 152 n.26, 252 n.23
Ghazālī, Abu'l-Futūḥ Aḥmad b. Muḥammad (d. 517/1123–4) 331, 342 n.51
al-Ghazālī, Abū Ḥāmid (d. 505/1111) 29, 57 n.13, 59 n.44, 342 n.51
Ghaznī, Maḥmūd (r. 387–420/998–1030) 228
ghilmāns 266
ghinā' 8
ghoṭ (pl. *ghoṭan*) [Sindhi] 237
Ghulām ʿAlī Shāh Hindī (13th–14th/19th century) 172 n.16, 294, 323 n.48
Ghulām ʿAlī Shāhī 18, 299–301
ghulām-bachah 180
Ghulām Ḥusayn Khān 159, 165–6, 168
ghulūww 32, 43, 50, 54, 163, 289 n.94, 307
ghusl 187, 293
Gilan 33, 68, 144
Gīlānī, ʿAbd al-Qādir (d. 561/1165–6) 340 n.33
Gīsū Darāz 144, 154 n.52
Golconda 173 n.22, 173 n.30
Goldziher, Ignaz (d. 1921) 5
Gramlich, Richard (d. 2006) 10, 18, 291

guilds 20 n.12, 70, 108 n.19, 292, 293, 309, 310, 313, 317, 324 n.67
Gunābād 177–9, 192 n.32
Gunābādī, Āqā Ḥājj Mullā Sulṭān Muḥammad ʿAlī Shāh, *also known as* Sulṭān ʿAlī Shāh Gunābādī (d. 1327/1909) 177–8, 183–4
Gunābādī, Āqā Ḥājj Shaykh Muḥammad Ḥasan Ṣāliḥ ʿAlī Shāh, *also known as* Ṣāliḥ ʿAlī Shāh Gunābādī (d. 1386/1966) 178, 201

Ḥabīb Barqānī [or Baraghānī], Ḥabīb-i ʿAjamī 309
Ḥabīb Shāhī 333
Ḥabībīs 326, 328
ḥadd 205
Ḥadīqat al-shīʿa 83, 104
ḥadīth 7, 30–2, 36, 44–6, 49, 51, 53, 66, 70–2, 74, 83–4, 88, 90, 94–100, 106, 212, 265, 308, 334
ḥadīth-i kisāʾ 266
Ḥāfiẓ al-Shīrāzī (d. *ca* 793/1390–1) 194 n.63
Ḥafṣ b. Sulaymān 79
ḥajj 308
Ḥajj Muṭahhar ʿAlī Shāh 298, 299
Ḥājj Zayn al-ʿĀbidīn Shīrwānī (d. 1253/1837) 326
Ḥajjāj b. Yūsuf (d. 95/714) 40
ḥakīm (pl. *ḥukamāʾ*) 71, 72, 87
Hala 239, 253 n.37
ḥāla 202–3
al-Ḥallāj, Manṣūr (d. 302/922) 236, 244, 251
ḥalqa (ring) 336
Hamadan 68, 79
Hamadānī, Sayyid ʿAlī (d. 786/1385) 152 n.18
Hamza b. ʿAbd al-Muṭṭalib (d. 4/625) 258
Ḥanafī [juridical school] 142
Ḥaqāʾiq or Ḥaqqān [Khāksār lineage] 339 n.3
ḥaqīqa 13, 28, 44–7, 49–50, 335
Harātī, Jalāl al-Dīn 314
al-Ḥasan b. ʿAlī (d. 49/669) [the second imam] 206
al-Ḥasan b. ʿAlī al-ʿAskarī [the eleventh imam] 43, 284 n.23
Ḥasan ʿAlī Khān (d. 1324/1907) 245, 252 n.10
Ḥasan ʿAlī Shāh (d. 1298/1881) 243
Ḥasanābādī, Sayf Allāh (9th/15th century) 137
Ḥasanīs 328
Hāshim, Muḥammad 230, 252 n.18
Hāshim Shāhī, Mīr-Hāshim 332
Hasht maqām-i qaṭārkish 292
Ḥaydariyya 18, 294–5
Herat 136, 140, 141
Hidāyat-nāmah 257
Hidāyat, Riḍā Qulī (d. 1288/1871) 167
Hijaz 341 n.42, 342 n.53
al-Ḥillī, al-ʿAllāma (d. 726/1325) 29, 32, 41, 71, 77
al-Ḥillī, Fakhr al-Muḥaqqiqīn (d. 771/1370) 29
al-Ḥillī, Warrām b. Abū Farās (d. 605/1208) 112 n.74
Hindī, Ḥaydar ʿAlī Shāh 171, 294, 323 n.48
Hindu, Hindus 229, 232, 243, 245, 253 n.39, 294
Hinduism 2
Hindustani 253 n.51
Hindūstānī, Aḥmad ʿAlī Shāh 171
Histoire de la philosophie islamique 7

Hubayrī 326
Ḥudhayfa al-Marʿashī (2nd/8th century) 330, 341 n.44
ḥujja 280
ḥujra 127, 148, 178
al-Hujwīrī, Abu'l-Ḥasan ʿAlī (d. 465/1071) 52
ḥulūl 8, 66, 73, 75, 82, 87, 91, 97, 100, 102, 104–5, 114 n.110, 115 n.123
Ḥumayd b. Qaḥṭaba (d. 159/776) 94, 102
al-Ḥurr al-ʿĀmilī, Muḥammad b. ʿAlī b. al-Ḥusayn (d. 1104/1693) 8, 34, 71, 76
Ḥurūfī, Ḥurūfiyya 3, 18, 68, 257
al-Ḥusayn b. ʿAbd al-Ṣamad (d. 984/1576) 11, 98
Ḥusayn b. ʿAlī b. Abī Ṭālib, Imām Ḥusayn, al-Ḥusayn (d. 61/680) [the third imam] 72, 101, 141, 147, 181–2, 194 n.62, 206, 230, 235–7, 243, 245, 250, 263, 266–70, 278–9, 286 n.51, 307, 311
Ḥusayn Kāshifī (d. 910/1404–5) 108 n.19
Ḥusaynī ʿAlam 165
Ḥusaynī, ʿAlī Riḍā (d. 1215/1801) 164, 174 n.50
Ḥusaynī, ʿAẓīm al-Dīn 164
al-Ḥusaynī, ʿImād al-Dīn Maḥmūd, *also known as* Mīr Maḥmūd (d. 1100/1689) 159–60, 164
al-Ḥusaynī, Irtiḍā 164
Ḥusaynī, Muḥammad ʿAlī 164
ḥusayniyya 164, 184–5, 188, 189, 190 n.3, 195 n.76
Ḥusayniyya Amīr Sulaymānī 16, 175–95, 216, 221 n.16
Ḥusayniyya Ḥāʾirī 184, 188, 195 n.74
Hyderabad 15, 157–71, 225, 238–9, 243, 245, 249–50

ibāḥiyya 8, 50, 62 n.116
Ibn Abī Jumhūr al-Aḥṣāʾī (d. after 901/1496) 10, 28, 57 n.5
Ibn Abū ʿUmayr 74
Ibn ʿArabī, Shaykh Muḥyī al-Dīn (d. 638/1240) 257
Ibn ʿAṭāʾ 340 n.23
Ibn Bābawayh, Muḥammad b. ʿAlī, *also known as* al-Shaykh al-Ṣadūq (d. 381/991) 78, 94–8, 265–6, 268, 272, 274, 277
Ibn Ḥanbal (d. 241/855) 321 n.19
Ibn Idrīs, Muḥammad b. Idrīs (d. 598/1202) 77, 111 n.48
Ibn Khaldūn (d. 808/1406) 38
Ibn Khallikān (d. 681/1282) 227
Ibn Shahr Āshūb, Muḥammad b. ʿAlī, (d. 588/1192) 90
Ibn Ṭāwūs, ʿAlī b. Mūsā b. Jaʿfar (d. 664/1266) 116 n.131
Ibn Turka Iṣfahānī, Ṣāʾin al-Dīn ʿAlī (d. 830/1427) 3
Ibrāhīm b. Adham, Abū Isḥāq Ibrāhīm b. Adham Balkhī (d. 161/777–8) 40–1, 341 n.42
Ibrāhīm b. Muḥammad 73, 78–9, 91
Ibrāhīm b. Mūsā al-Kāẓim 49, 71
Ibrāhīm Shāhīs 333
Idrīs b. Maʿqil al-ʿIjlī (2nd/8th century) 78, 100
ʿīd ghadīr 248
Iḥqāq al-ḥaqq 33
ijāza 29, 76, 110 n.42, 179, 315
ijāzat-nāmah 288 n.88, 300
ijtihād 32, 179–80
ikhtiyār 315
Ikhtiyārī 310, 312
Ilkhans, Ilkhanate, Ilkhanid era/rule 3, 5, 28, 30, 154 n.44

ʿIllat al-iftirāq 93, 100
ʿIlw Dīnawarī, Khwājah, *also known as* ʿAlāʾ al-Dīnawarī (d. 298/910–1) 331, 341 n.45, 341 n.46
imamate 72–3, 75, 77–9, 82, 87, 89–92, 100, 102, 204, 226, 241, 256, 284 n.23, 307–8, 319
Imāmbārā(s) 238, 240, 246, 248, 253 n.34
Imami Shiʿism 1–2, 4, 6–9, 13, 31, 50–1, 56 n.1, 261
Imāmzāda-yi Ḥusayn 322 n.35
Imārat-i ʿAbbasiyya *Imāmzāda* (Shiʿi shrines) 152 n.16, 298
India 10, 12, 15, 32–2, 123–4, 138, 140, 144, 147, 149, 154 n.61, 157–9, 161–71, 225, 232, 235, 242–3, 246, 249–51, 294–5, 325–8, 331, 333
Indian language 225–6, 318
Indus 226, 228–9, 232, 242
al-insān al-kāmil 269
ʿIrāq-i ʿAjam 150
ʿIrāqī, Shams al-Dīn (d. 932/1526) 172
ʿirfān 47
Irshād al-adhhān 90
Irshād-i kiswa 292
ʿĪsā b. Mūsā 88–9
Isfahan 14, 66, 69–72. 75–6, 96, 103–4, 110 n.39, 119 n.182, 179, 191 n.16, 192 n.32, 295, 298, 309, 311
Iṣfahānī, Nūr ʿAlī Shāh (d. 1211/1797) 176
Isḥāq Kuttalānī (d. 826/1423) 11
ʿIshq-nāmah 257
Ishrāq 31
Iskandar Mīrzā [Iskandar Sulṭān] (r. 812–817/1409–1415) 125, 135
Ismāʿīl b. Imām Jaʿfar al-Ṣādiq (d. *ca* 145/762) 5, 40–1, 49, 61 n.78, 74, 80, 88, 173 n.30, 284 n.18, 314, 328, 343 n.60
Ismailiyya, Ismailis 35–6, 67–8, 227–9, 253 n.33, 253 n.33, 277, 281
Iṣṭilāḥāt al-ṣūfiyya 46
ittiḥād 54
ittiṣāl 312
Iẓhār al-ḥaqq wa miʿyār al-ṣidq 14, 65, 76–9

Jabal ʿĀmil 7–8, 31
Jabrāna 333
Jaʿfar b. Abī Ṭālib 258
Jaʿfar al-Ṣādiq, Imam Jaʿfar (d. 148/765) [the sixth imam] 5, 40–2, 44, 49, 51, 55, 61 n.78, 74–5, 80–2, 88, 91, 95, 98, 102, 109 n.36, 115 n.124, 173 n.30, 205, 253 n.33, 269, 275, 277, 284 n.18, 314, 286 n.47, 286 n.51, 287 n.56, 314, 328, 343 n.60
Jaʿfar b. Muḥammad b. Ḥasan Jaʿfarī 116 n.128
Jahāngīr (r. 1014–1037/1605–1627) 32
Jalāliyya 18, 294–5, 343 n.59
Jamāl al-Dīn Mujarrad 343
Jambet, Christian 50
Jāmiʿ al-asrār wa manbaʿ al-anwār 28–30
Jāmī, Nūr al-Dīn ʿAbd al-Raḥmān (d. 898/1492) 340 n.20
jamʿ-i ḥaqīqat 295
jang 248
jang jo maydān 248
Jang-nāmah 243, 251
jannat khātūn 248
jawānmard, jawānmardī 324 n.72, 336

Jāwidān-nāmah 257
al-Jazā'irī, ʿAlī b. Hilāl (9th/15th century) 31
Jesus 45, 272
Jews 272
Jhok, village 242
Jhok Sharīf 243
Jibrā'īl 78, 97
jihād 308
jinns 272
Jodhpur 253 n.39
Joseph 271
Judaism 76
Junayd al-Baghdādī (d. 298/911) 36, 43
Junaydīs 326, 328–9, 332
al-Jurjānī, ʿAlī b. Muḥammad Sayyid al-Sharīf, *also known as* Mīr Sayyid Sharīf (d. 816/1413) 41, 52
Jurmāniyūn 79
Justujū dar taṣawwuf-i Īrān 306

Kabul 322 n.31
kāfir 48, 74, 100, 307
kalām 31, 33, 289 n.94
Kalhorās, rulers of Sindh (1112–1196/1701–1782) 233, 242
Kalhoṛo, Yār Muḥammad 242
Kamāl al-Dīn ʿAlī Shāh Qurayshī 343 n.61
kapṛā 235
Karachi 226, 250
al-Karājakī, Muḥammad b. ʿAlī (d. 449/1057) 117 n.140
Karak Nūḥ 31
al-Karakī, ʿAbd al-ʿAlī (d. 940/1533–4) 8, 31, 34, 67–8, 93, 105, 107 n.6, 108 n.24, 111 n.68
al-Karakī, al-Ḥasan (10th/16th century) 68, 99
Karam Allāh Shāhī 333
karb wa balā 307
Karbala 41, 72, 93, 102, 105, 116 n.136, 141, 163, 206, 220 n.11, 227, 230, 232, 234, 235–9, 241, 243, 245, 247, 248, 250, 252 n.17, 252 n.31, 262, 307
Karīm Khān 322 n.32
Karīm Shāhīs 333
Karkh 340 n.24
Karkhī(s) 40, 42–3, 49, 326, 328–9, 331, 340 n.24
Kashan 68–9, 178, 192 n.28
Kāshānī, Muḥtasham (d. 996/1588) [Kāshī] 230
al-Kāshānī, Muḥsin al-Fayḍ (d. 1090/1679) 32, 34, 54, 257
kashf 14
Kashf al-maḥjūb 295
Kāshifī, Ḥusayn Wāʿiẓ (d. 910/1505) 17, 230, 232, 242–4, 250
kashkūl 213, 298–9, 315–6, 334, 336, 344 n.75
Kashmir 172 n.17
Kasr Aṣnām 70, 74
Kattānī 340 n.23
Kawthariyya 191
Kaysaniyya, Kaysanites 93, 99–100, 118 n.166, 227
Kāzirī(s), Kāzirūnī 326, 328, 331, 339 n.16, 339 n.20, 341 n.48
khādim 165
Khairpur 238, 240, 246, 249–50
khāk 294, 309
Khāksār, Khāksāriyya 10–11, 13, 18–19, 195 n.88, 291–304, 305–6, 308–9, 313–16, 319, 321 n.5, 322 n.42, , 323 n.47, 323 n.48, 325–44, 334
khalīfa 73, 162, 167, 171, 174 n.42, 323 n.47

Khalīl Allāh II, Khalīl Allāh-i thānī (d. 925/1519–20) 127
Khalwatiyya 5
khānaqāh (lodge) 15, 123–35, 137–8, 148–9, 150 n.3, 176, 184–5, 189, 190 n.6, 200, 209, 215–16, 295
Khānish Begum 137
kharāj 141
Kharaqān 341 n.50
Khardla [battle of] 166, 173 n.34
khātam al-awliyā' 47–8
khātam al-mujtahidīn 8
Khāwarī, Asad Allāh 11
Khawārij 72
Khawjagān 143
Khayrābād 127
Khazīnat al-aṣfiyā' 326
khidmat bih khalq-i Allāh 187
khilāfa 160, 171
khirqa 29, 45, 49, 167, 174 n.42, 292–3, 330, 332, 334, 336
Khojas 228, 243, 253 n.46
Khojki 243, 253
Khomeini, Rūḥullāh (d. 1989) [Ayat Allāh Khomeini] 179, 217
Khulāṣat al-fawā'id 14, 65, 82–5, 109 n.34
khums 188, 277, 308, 320
Khurasan 3, 6, 11, 14, 32, 65, 68, 72–3, 75, 78–80, 84, 87, 90–3, 100–1, 140, 144, 177–9, 181, 229
Khurāsānī, Ākhūnd Muḥammad Kāẓim (d. 1330/1912) 181
Khurāsānī, Muḥammad ʿAlī Mu'adhdhin (d. 1078/1667) 11
Khurramiyya 90, 115 n.113
khurūj 72, 84, 85, 103
khuṭba 248, 258, 261
Khuṭba al-ithna ʿashariyya, Kitāb-i khuṭba-yi dawāzdah imām 18, 256–8, 283 n.4
Khuzistan 6, 68
Khwājagān order 143 and 341 n. 38
Khwājah Bahā' al-Dīn Naqshband 341 n.38
Khwājah Isḥāq Khatlānī (8th/14th century) 342 n.53
Khwājah Maḥmūd Gāwān (d. 886/1481) 147
Khwājah Muḥammad Bābā-yi Samāsīyi 341 n.38
Khwarazm 343 n.61
Kifāyat al-barāya 87, 90
Kirman 126–7, 136–8, 145–6, 150, 209
Kirmānī, Mullā Quṭb al-Dīn 136
Kirmanshah 295, 299, 300
Kirmānshāhī, Mawlā Muḥsin 257
Kitāb al-Milal wa'l-niḥal 46
Kitāb al-Kāfī 51, 95, 286 n.47
Kitābkhāna-yi Ṣāliḥ 189
Kitāb Sulaym b. Qays, Kitāb al-saqīfa 60 n.59, 117 n.140
Kot Diji 240
Kubrā, Shaykh Najm al-Dīn, *also known as* Abu'l-Jannāb Aḥmad b. ʿUmar al-Khaywaqī, Shaykh Walī Tarrāsh (d. 617/1220–1) 5–6, 260, 274, 341 n.34
Kubrāwiyya 5–6, 11
Kufa 72, 78, 80, 100, 116 n.128, 300–1
kufr 98, 266, 307
Kuhbanan 342
Kūh-i Mīr Maḥmūd 160
al-Kulaynī, Muḥammad b. Yaʿqūb (d. 329/940–1) 37, 51, 114 n.98, 269, 288 n.72
Kumayl b. Ziyād al-Nakhaʿī (d. 82/701–2) 35, 37, 39–40, 60 n.72, 328, 330, 339 n.11
Kurds 69

Ladakh 172 n.17
Lahijan 33–4, 69
Lāhījī, Shams al-Dīn (d. 918/1512) 28
Lahore 32, 327
Laʿl Shahbāz Qalandar, *also known as* Shaykh ʿUthmān Marandī (d. 672/1274) 229, 237, 239, 243, 253 n.33, 295, 343 n.60
lānat 239
Laṇḍāor 253 n.46
Lawāmiʿ-i Rabbānī 76, 110 nn.44–5
Lebanon 7, 32, 248
Leibniz, Gottfried Wilhelm (d. 1716) 46
Les voies d'Allah 4
Levi Della Vida, Giorgio (d. 1967) 59 n.51, 59 n.55
Lewisohn, Leonard (d. 2018) 10–11
L'Imagination créatrice dans le soufisme d'Ibn ʿArabi 3
lisān 296, 298, 300, 315, 320
lubb, pl. *albāb* 46, 61 n.100
Lucknow 225, 232, 246, 249
Lughat Laṭīfī 248
Luqmān 101
Luristan, Lurs 68
lūṭī 323 n.43

maʿād 307, 319
Mabāhij al-muhaj fi'l-manāhij al-ḥujaj 90
madadkārī 188
Madā'in 88
al-Madanī, Sayyid ʿAlī (d. 1120/1708–9) [Ibn Maʿṣūm] 71
Madanī-Shāhī 332
Madar ʿAlī Shāh 239
Madārīs 328, 332
madhhab 79, 99, 163, 314
maddāḥ 239, 253 n.36
Ma'dhūnīn-i namāz 189–90
Madina 80, 88, 236
madrasa 147, 181
Maghribī, Abū ʿAbd Allāh Muḥammad, Shaykh Muḥammad al-Maghribī (d. 279/892–3 or 299/911–2) 331
al-Maghribī, Abū ʿUthmān, ʿUthmān al-Maghribī (4th/10th century) 329
Mahan 15, 124–7, 130, 133, 135–41, 144–50, 151 n.9, 153 n.29, 154 n.59
Maḥbūb al-qulūb 13, 28, 34, 51
mahdawiyya 200
Mahdi, *see* Muḥammad b. al-Ḥasan
Māh Laqā Bāī (d. 1240/1824) 165
Maḥjūb, Muḥammad Jaʿfar 306, 316–18
Majālis al-mu'minīn 13, 28, 33, 38
Majd al-Dīn Baghdādī 341 n.34
majdhūb 15, 157–74
al-Majlisī, Muḥammad Bāqir (d. 1111/1699) 32, 34, 48, 71, 268, 275
al-Majlisī, Muḥammad Taqī (d. 1070/1659) 110 n.42
Makhdūm Jahāniyān, Shāh Makhdūm Jahāniyān Sayyid Jalāl al-Dīn Ḥusayn Bukhārī (d. 785/1384) 326, 342 n.59
Makhdūm Tharo (d. 1160/1748) 232
malāmat, *ahl-i malāmat* 334, 343 n.60
Mālik b. Haytham (2nd/8th century) 87
Malkāpūrī, ʿAbd al-Jabbār Khān (14th/19th–20th century) 159
manāqib 248 342 n.50
Manāqib-i Shaykh Ṣafī [Qizilbash *Buyruq*] 256, 283 n.4
al-Manṣūr, caliph, *also known as* Abū Jaʿfar Dawānīqī (r.

136–158/754–775) 73, 75, 84, 86, 91, 101, 112 n.79, 226
Manz, Beatrice Forbes 142
Maqālāt 34, 263
maqām 53, 293, 316, 336
maqtal-nāmah 227
maras 336, 344 n.77, 344 n.83
Marʿashī (r. 760/1358–9 to second half of the 10th/16th century) 6
Marathas 166, 232
Marḥūm, Maulvī Aḥmad 230
marjaʿiyyat 191 n.18
marjaʿ-i taqlīd 179, 191 n.18
marthiya 17, 225–54
Marthiya Thābit ʿAlī Shāh jā 246
Maʿrūf al-Karkhī, Abū Ḥāfiẓ Maʿrūf b. Fayrūz Karkhī (d. 200/815) 40, 42–3, 49
Maʿrūfiyya 142
Marw 73, 78
Marwān (2nd/8th century) 73, 75, 80, 84
Marwān II (2nd/8th century) 110 n.40
Maryam 47
mashāyikh-i maʾdhūnīn 182
Mashāʾīn 93, 96–7
Mashhad 31–2, 69, 71, 74–5, 104, 136, 177, 181, 292–3, 298–300, 310, 327
Mashhadī Muḥammad Mahdī Tabrīzī (13th/19th century) 306, 314
Massignon, Louis (d. 1962) 2, 9, 52, 55
Mast ʿAlī Shāh (d. 1253/1837–8) 167
al-Masʿūdī, ʿAlī b. al-Ḥusayn (d. 345/956) 77, 80–2, 90–1, 100
maʿṣūm 206
Maʿṣūm ʿAlī Shāhī 299
Maṭāʿin al-mujrimiyya 67
Mathālib al-ʿAbbāsiyya 93, 102
mathnawī 232, 243
Maṭlūb al-fuqarāʾ 327
Mauritius 180
Mawlānā Khālid (d. 1242/1827) 172 n.16
al-Maysī, Luṭf Allāh (d. 1032/1622–3) 107 n.18
Mazandaran 6, 82, 144
Māzandarānī, ʿAbd Allāh Ḥāʾirī [Ayatollah] (d. 1355/1937) 179
Mazdeans 44
maẓhar (pl. *maẓāhir*) 51
Mecca 29, 165, 331
mendī 243
Merāṇī [family] 243
Mevleviyya 318
Mīm-Shāhī 332
Minhāj al-hidāya 93, 102
al-Miqdād b. Aswad (d. 33/653–4) 35, 36
miʿrāj 49, 334
mīr 238–9, 241, 245–6, 249
Mīr ʿĀlam, Abu'l-Qāsim Mīr ʿĀlam Bahādur (d. 1809) 168, 174 n.46
Mīr ʿAlī Murād (r. 1257–1311/1842–1894) 240
Mīr ʿAlī Nawāz Khān Ṭalpūr (d. 1935) 246
Mīr Ānīs *also known as* Mīr Babar ʿAlī Ānīs, (d. 1290/1874) 230, 249–50
Mīr Dāmād, Muḥammad Bāqir b. Muḥammad al-Ḥusaynī (d. 1041/1630) 7, 33, 55, 76, 82, 83, 85, 90, 95–100, 104–5, 110 n.42, 111 n.68, 112 n.69, 117 n.153
Mīr Fayḍ Muḥammad (r. 1311–1326/1894–1909) 240

Mīr Jalāl al-Dīn Miṣbāh Muṭahharī (d. 2008) 300
Mīr Kawthar (d. 2015) 299–300
Mīr Lawḥī, Sayyid Muḥammad b. Muḥammad al-Ḥusaynī (11th/17th century) 14, 65–66, 70–2, 74–5, 82–3, 93, 96–7, 100, 103–5, 108 n.28, 110 n.39, 110 n.42, 119 n.185
Mīr Maḥmūd (d. 1100/1689) 158–65, 169, 171, 174 n.50
Mīr Murād ʿAlī Khan (12th–13th/18th–19th centuries) 241
Mīr Nāṣir Khān Ṭalpūr, *also known as* Jaʿfarī (d. 1260/1845) 241, 245
Mīr Nūr Allāh b. Khalīl Allāh (d. 834/1430–1) 137, 149
Mīr Sābir ʿAlī (d. 1264/1868) 242
Mīr Ṭāhir 300
Mīr Taqī Mīr (d. 1224/1810) 249
Mirpur Khas 238–9
Mīrzā ʿAlī Aṣghar Khān Atābak (d. 1325/1907) 152 n.12
Mīrzā Maẓhar Jān-i Jānān (d. 1195/1781) 166
Mīrzā Qalīch Beg (d. 1929) 245–50
Miṣqal-i ṣafā' 77
Miyākhākī 295
Muhājir 249–50
Molé, Marijan (d. 1963) 6
Mongol court 152 n.27
Mongol Ilkhanate 3
Mount Sinai 341 n.49
Moses 45, 259, 271, 275–6, 287 n.69, 318
Mudarrisī, ʿAbd al-Karīm 294
mufrid 315
Mughal period (932–1274/1526–1857) 166–7
al-Mughīra b. Saʿīd al-Ijlī (d. 119/737) 40, 60 n.76
Muḥammad b. ʿAlī b. ʿAbd Allāh b. ʿAbbās 78, 100
Muḥammad b. ʿAlī al-Bāqir (d. *ca* 114/732) [the fifth imam] 40, 205, 286 n.49, 292, 342 n.53
Muḥammad b. ʿAlī al-Jawād [the ninth imam] (d. 220/835) 43
Muḥammad ʿAlī Shāh Qājār (r. 1324–1327/1907–1909) 152 n.12
Muḥammad b. ʿAlī, Ibn Shahr Āshūb (d. 588/1192) 115 n.117
Muḥammad b. al-Ḥanafiyya (d. 81/700) 79, 100, 104, 118 n.166, 227–8
Muḥammad b. al-Ḥasan, the Mahdi, Imān Mahdī, Muḥammad al-Mahdī [the twelfth imam] 2, 7–8, 48–9, 142, 212, 227, 232, 267, 272, 284 n.23
Muḥammad b. Isḥāq al-Ḥamawī (d. after 938/1531) 68
Muḥammad b. Makkī (d. 786/1384) 115 n.118
Muḥammad, Muḥammad Muṣṭafā (the Prophet) 29, 33, 45, 49, 87, 227, 263, 264–77, 279, 286 n.43, 286 n.51, 287 n.69, 308, 312, 314, 326, 335–6
Muḥammad al-Muṣṭafā al-Ḥusaynī al-Mūsāwī al-Sabziwārī, Amīr Sayyid (10th/16th century) 100
Muḥammad b. Qāsim 226
Muḥammad Riḍā Shāh Pahlawī (d. 1980) 179
Muḥammad Shāh Bādkūba'ī 329

Muḥammad Shāh Bahmanī (r. 867–887/1463–1482) 147
Muḥammad Shāh Qājār, Muḥammad Shāh (r. 1250–1264/1834–1848) 146, 152 n.12, 176
Muḥammadābād 147; *see also* Bidar
Muḥammadiyya 226
Muḥarram 163, 181, 182, 183, 185, 190 n.5, 194 n.63, 195 n.80. 230, 236, 239, 248, 250, 252 n.32, 253 n.35 and n.39, 300
al-Muḥīṭ al-aʿẓam wa'l-baḥr al-khiḍamm fī taʾwīl kitāb Allāh al-ʿazīz al-muḥkam 29, 57 n.4
Muḥsin, Muḥammad (d. 1163/1750) 232
mujaddid 15, 157–74
Muʿjam al-buldān 41
al-Muʿjam al-mufahras li-alfāẓ al-ḥadīth al-nabawī 343 n.70
muʿjiza (pl. *muʿjizāt*) 289 n.93, 308
Mujlī mirʾat al-munjī fi'l-kalām wa'l-ḥikmatayn wa'l-taṣawwuf 28, 31
al-Mukhtār b. Abī ʿUbayd al-Thaqafī (d. 67/687) 111 n.57, 227
Mullā Ṣadrā, Ṣadr al-Dīn Muḥammad al-Shīrāzī (d. *ca* 1050/1640–1) 7, 70
Multan 227–9, 239, 251 n.4
muʾmin mumtaḥan 30
munājāt 239, 253 n.36
Munawwar ʿAlī Shāh (d. 1301/1884) 177
Munawwar ʿAlī Shāhī, Mūnis ʿAlī Shāhī, *also known as* Dhu'l-Riyāsatayn 180
al-Munqidh min al-ḍalāl 29
Munshī, Qādir Khān (13th/19th century) 166
muqallid 191 n.18
Murād ʿAlī Ṭāliʿ 159
murīd 201, 320
murshid 38, 312, 320
al-Murtaḍā, al-Sharīf (d. 436/1044) 289 n.94
Murūj al-dhahab wa maʿādin al-jawhar 77
muruwwat 329
Mūsā b. Jaʿfar al-Kāẓim (d. 183/799) [the seventh imam] 40, 42, 71
Mūsā Khān 180
mushāhada 47
mushāʿira 233
Mushaʿshaʿ, Mushaʿshaʿyān (r. 840–1092/1436–1681) 3, 6, 67
Mushtāq ʿAlī Shāh (d. 1206/1792) 191 n.8
Muslim League 246, 254 n.59
mustakhdima 147
al-Mutawakkil (r. 232–247/847–861) 93, 102
mutawallī 146–7, 181–4, 194 n.65
Muʿtazili 31, 37, 111 n.48, 289 n.94

Nādir Shāh (r. 1148–1160/1736–1747) 232, 309
nafs 330, 343 n.73
nafs-i ʿammāra 243
Nafs al-Zakiyya, Muḥammad (d. 145/762) 226
Nahavand 340 n.26
Nahj al-balāgha 90
Nahj al-ḥaqq 112 n.74
nāʾib al-imām 67
nāʾib-i khilāfa 171
Nain 69
Najaf 11, 31, 93, 102, 163, 258, 300
Najm al-Dīn Rāzī 341 n.34
Napier [General] 245
Naqd al-nuqūd fī maʿrifat al-wujūd 30

naqīb 298, 315, 323 n.55
naql 14
Naqshband, Naqshbandī, Naqshbandiyya 5, 143, 166, 333
Nasa 78
Nasab-nāmah-yi kalān wa bayān-i chahārdah khānawādah wa ḥālat-i haftād wa du millat 327
Nāṣiḥ al-Dīn (Chishtī) 331
Nāṣir al-Dīn (Chishtī) 331
Nāṣir al-Dīn Shāh Qājār (r. 1264–1314/1848–1896) 152 n.12, 154 n.59, 177, 180, 306, 317
Naṣr Sayyār (d. 131/748) 72, 84
Nasr, Seyyed Hossein 9–10, 33, 49
Naṣṣ al-nuṣūṣ fī sharḥ al-fuṣūṣ 29
naʿt 248
Nawākhāhīs 332
Naward (Kāzirūn) 339 n.20
Nayyir al-Dawla 178
nāẓir 181
Neoplatonism, Neoplatonist 2, 46
Niʿmatābād 137
Niʿmat Allāhī 15–16, 123–55, 157–74, 175–95, 197–221, 294, 299, 305, 319, 321 n.1
Niʿmat Allāh-i Thānī Ḥusaynī 146–7
Niʿmat Allāhiyya 10, 12–14, 158, 171, 175, 298–9
Nimrod 271
Nishapur 90–2
Niẓām 159, 164, 168, 170
Niẓām ʿAlī Khān (r. 1762–1803) 15, 165–6, 173 n.35
Niẓāmiyya school 341 n.35, 342 n.51
Niẓām Māfī, Muḥammad ʿAlī 195 n.78
Nizārī Ismailis 67
Noah 271–2, 289 n.93
nubuwwa 47, 297
nuḥās 246–7
al-Nuʿmānī, Ibn Abī Zaynab (d. *ca* 345/956 or 360/971) 288 n.72
Nuqṭawī 68, 69, 107 n.10, 299
Nūr al-Dīn Jaʿfar al-Badakhshānī 61 n.81
Nūr al-Dīn Niʿmat Allāh II (d. after 906/1500) 160
Nūr ʿAlī Shāh Thānī, Āqā Ḥājj Āqā Mūllā ʿAlī Nūr (d. 1337/1918) 178–9, 183, 186
Nurbakhsh, Javad (d. 2008) 16–17, 174 n.43, 197, 200–2, 209, 211, 213, 216
Nūrbakhsh, Muḥammad (d. 869/1464) 59 n.35, 342 n.53
Nūrbakhshī, Nūrbakhshiyya 10, 39, 172 n.17, 200, 213
Nūrbakhshiyya Nūrāʾī 299
Nūr Nahāl 295
Nūrī Shāhī 333
Nuṣrat al-islām fī ʿilm al-kalām 93, 100

Ottomans, Ottoman rule 6, 31, 69, 257, 261–3, 282, 311

Pahlavi [period] 9, 16, 175–95, 300
pahlawān 323 n.43, 324 n.67
Pakistan 240, 243, 249, 253 n.33, 300, 303 n.8, 326
panjāh-yi āl-i abāʾ 263
Pāygāh Khūrshīd Jāhī 169
Pāzūkī, Shahrām, or Pazouki, Shahram 142, 190 n.1
Persian (language) 66, 68, 70, 74, 76–8, 80, 90, 103–5, 112 n.73, 226
Pharaoh 271
pīr 4, 69, 176, 201–3, 213, 229, 293–4, 296, 337–8, 342 n.56, 344
Pīrān Shāhīs 333

Pīr Jamāl Ardistānī 342 n.53
Pīr Muḥammad 145
pīr-i pīrān 325
Pīr Shams 229
piṛu 248
Popper, Karl (d. 1994) 44
Potter, Lawrence G. 142
Prince Ḥusayn, Ḥusayn b. ʿAlī al-Riḍā 311
Proclus (d. 485) 46
Pseudo-Aristotle 46–7
Punjab 253 n.46
Pūryā-yi Walī (d. 722/1322) 323 n.43

Qadḥīs 332
Qādirī, Qādiriyya 242, 244–5, 327–8, 332, 340 n.33
Qādirī, Ghulām ʿAlī (d. 1258/1842) 159–60, 163
Qaḥṭaba b. Shabīb (d. 132/749) 72, 94, 113 n.85
Qajar [period] (1200–1344/1786–1925) 9, 12, 18–19, 175–6, 230, 294, 297–300, 309, 313, 327
qalandar 18, 68, 237, 253 n.33, 294–5, 334, 343 n.62
qanāt 146–7, 179–81, 183, 192 n.35, 194 n.69
qanāt-i Ṭāhirābād 146
Qandahar 294
al-Qāshānī, ʿAbd al-Razzāq (d. 730/1329–30) 46
qaṣīda 252 n.23
Qāsim 237, 243–4, 252 n.14
Qaṭār ʿAlī Shāh 300
al-Qaṭīfī, Ibrāhīm (10th/16th century) 111 n.68
Qaws Aʿẓam 332
Qazwin 69, 309, 311, 322 n.36
qibla 189, 330
qishr (pl. *qushūr*) 46
qiṣṣa-khwānān 68, 72
Qizilbash 6–7, 18, 67–9, 257, 261–2, 264, 276, 278–9
Qulī, Sulṭān Muḥammad (r. 988–1020/1580–1612) 173 n.30
Qumm 70
al-Qummī, Aḥmad b. Muḥammad b. ʿĪsā al-Ashʿarī (d. 299–301/911–4) 98, 109 n.34
al-Qummī, Muḥammad Ṭāhir b. Muḥammad Ḥusayn (d. 1098/1686) 59 n.47
Qurʾan 29, 46, 74, 98–9, 102, 109 n.35, 118 n.154, 182–3, 186, 212, 269, 281, 297, 313, 330
quṭb 2, 4, 8, 16, 139, 145, 150 n.2, 177–9, 181–9, 191 n.20, 192 n.23, 193 n.41, 194 n.63, 197, 201, 212–14, 216–17, 298, 300
quṭb-i silsila-yi ʿilahiyya 184
Quṭb al-Dīn Ḥaydar Zāwiʾī (d. 618/1221) 294
Quṭb al-Dīn Kaydharī Nayshābūrī 87
Quṭb al-Mulk, Sulṭān Qulī (d. 950/1543) 160
Quṭb Shāh sultans of Golkonda (924–1098/1518–1687) 160, 233
Quwānlū 180

Raḍī al-Dīn ʿAlī Lālā (d. 642/1244) 341
Raei, Shahrokh 291
Rafʿ al-munāzaʿa waʾl-khilāf 29
rāga 235
Raḥmat ʿAlī Shāh (d. 1278/1861) 177
Raḥmat ʿAlī Shāh Dihkurdī 299

Rakhiyyal Shāh (d. 1358/1940) 244
Ramaḍān 182–3, 185, 194 nn.64–3, 275, 300, 317
rawḍa khwān 182, 193 n.59, 324 n.67
Rawḍat al-shuhadā' 17, 229–33, 236, 243, 245, 250, 252 n.14, 252 n.18
Rayy 87, 181, 311
rāz-ḥāfiẓ 207
rāz-pūshī 204, 207–8
Razzāq Shāhīs 333
rend 237
Riḍā Shāh Pahlavī (r. 1925–41, d. 1944) 176
Riḍawī, Mīr Muḥammad Zamān b. Muḥammad Ja'far (d. 1041/1631) 14, 65, 71–6, 81–2, 84–6, 91, 94–5, 98, 104–5, 108 n.26, 109 n.36
al-Rifā'ī, Sayyid Aḥmad b. Abī al-Ḥasan (d. 578/1182–3) 342 n.55
Rifā'ī 328, 332
risāla 47
Risāla dar ṭarīqat 292
Risāla-yi faqriyya 325–44
Risāla-yi ṭarīqat-i Sayyid Jalāl al-Dīn Ḥaydar 292
riwāq-i 'Abbāsī [*Dār al-ḥuffāẓ*] 127, 130, 137
riwāq-i wakīl al-mulkī [*ṣaḥn-i wakīl al-mulkī*] 152 n.12
Riyāḍ al-'ulamā' 32, 71
riyāḍa 329, 335, 337, 342 n.53
rubā'īyyāt 248
Rūdakī (d. 329/941) 229
Rūmī, Jalāl al-Dīn (d. 672/1273) 9, 55, 138, 194 n.63
Russian language 318
Rustam Ābād Ikhtāriyya 183
Ruwaym (d. 303/915–6) 340 n.23
Sa'ādat 'Alī Shāh, *also known as* Ṭawūs al-'Urafā (d. 1293/1876) 177, 191 n.16
Sa'adī (d. *ca* 690/1291) 9
Sābiq Khwārizmī 80
Ṣābirīs 333
Sabziwar 71, 109 n.28, 110 n.39, 177
Sabzawārī, Ḥājj Mullā Hādī (d. 1290/1873) 177
Sa'd b. 'Abd Allāh al-Ash'arī al-Qummī (d. between 299 and 301/911 and 914) 98, 109 n.34
Sa'd al-Dīn Ḥamūya, Sa'd al-Dīn Ḥummawī (d. 650/1252) 6
ṣadr-i a'ẓam 152 n.12
Ṣafar 181–3, 185, 194 n.62
Safawids, Safawid period (907–1135/1501–1722) 3, 11, 14, 27, 29, 32, 34, 39, 50, 67, 71, 123, 136, 142, 148, 190 n.7, 215, 257, 308
Ṣafawiyya 6–7, 31
al-Ṣaffār al-Qummī, Muḥammad b. al-Ḥasan (d. 290/902–3) 109 n.34
Saffarid (r. 246–393/861–1003) 116 n.128
Ṣafī 'Alī Shāh (d. 1316/1899) 177–80, 305
Ṣafī 'Alī Shāhī 177–80
Ṣaḥīfat al-rashād 14, 65, 70–6
Ṣaḥn-i Atābakī 152 n.12
Ṣaḥn-i Muḥammad Shāhī 128, 151 n.12
sajjāda-nishīn 165, 171, 174 n.50
Sakīna 243, 252 n.14
Sālār Jang (family) 165
ṣalāt 308
ṣalawāt 260, 264, 283 n.4d
Ṣāliḥ 318
Ṣāliḥ 'Alī Shāh (d. 1386/1966) 178–9, 184, 202–3, 216

Ṣāliḥ Barbarī 332
Sālik 314
Salīm Shāhīs 333
Salīṭ b ʿAbd Allāh b. al-ʿAbbās 101, 114 n.105
Salmān the Persian, Salmān al-Fārsī, *also known as* Maḥmūd Fāṭīlī, Pātīlī or Pāṭilī (d. 35 or 36/655–7) 5, 35–6, 296, 328, 339 n.10
Salṭanat Ābād 183
Salwat al-Shīʿa 104, 112 n.73, 115 n.115
samāʿ 8, 316
Samarqand 135, 152 n.18
Samarra 43, 340 n.28
al-Samhūdī (d. 911/1506) 277–8, 288 n.85
Sanāsīs [Sannyasis] 325
ṣandal 162, 172 n.14, 174 n.50
Ṣandal-Shāh 331
Sangī, Mīr ʿAbd al-Ḥusayn (d. 1342/1924) 245
Sangilaj 181, 182, 185
Saqaṭī(s) 326, 329, 342 n.52
Saqīfa 36, 60 n.59
saqqāʾī 300
Sarbadār 6, 22 n.26
Sarmast ʿAlī Shāh Ṭurughī 299
Sarmast, Sachal, *also known as* Manṣūr Thānī (d. 1241/1826) 242–5, 251, 253 n.51
Sava 69, 72
Sawdā, Muḥammad Rafīʿ (d. 1195/1781) 233
Sawijī, Aḥmad 257
ṣawm 308, 320
Sayf al-Dīn Bākharzī 341 n.34
al-Sayfī, Mīrzā Qawām 257
sayr wa sulūk 340 n.26, 342 n.50
sayyid 28, 159, 160, 277, 278–9, 286 n.43, 288 n.84
Sayyid ʿAbd al-Razzāq 332
Sayyid Abū ʿAlī b. Sayyid Muḥammad Bāqir 258
Sayyid Aḥmad Kabīr 332, 342 n.59
Sayyid ʿAlī Hamadānī 152 n.18
Sayyid ʿAlī Sulṭān 262
Sayyid Amīr Khān Gujarātī 333
Sayyid Amīr Kulāl (d. 772/1370) 143
Sayyid Jalāl Bakhtyārī 342 n.59
Sayyid Jalāl al-Dīn Bukhārī, Shāh Sayyid Jalāl (7th/13th century) 294, 332, 343 n.61
Sayyid Mīr Jān Muḥammad (d. 1167/1754) 242
Sayyid Muḥammad 71–2, 167
Sayyid Sādat Khān 333
Sayyid Shāhī 333
Sayyid Ṭāhir al-Dīn 153 n.38
Sāzmān-i awqāf wa umūr-i khayriyya 154 n.58, 195 n.74
Shāh ʿAbbās (r. 996–1038/1588–1629) 66, 69, 70, 76, 107 n.15, and n.18, 109 n.38, 130
Shāh ʿAbd Allāh 330
Shāh ʿAbd Allāh Shikāriyya 331
Shāh ʿAbd al-ʿAẓīm (d. *ca* 252/866) 311
Shāh ʿAbd al-Karīm (d. 1032/1623) 233
Shāh ʿAbd al-Laṭīf (d. 1165/1752) 17, 231, 233–8, 243–5, 250
Shāh ʿAbd al-Wahhāb b. ʿAbd al-Qādir 332
Shāh Abū Aḥmad (Chishtī) 331
Shāh Akbar (r. 964–1014/1556–1605) 32
Shāh ʿAlī Riḍā Ḥusaynī Thānī (d. early 1940s) 174 n.50
Shāh Ayāzī (ʿAlī) 296
Shāh Chirāgh 311
Shāh Ḍiyāʾ Allāh 327
Shāh-i mardān 242

Shāh Ghāzī, ʿAbd Allāh (d. 156–773) 226–7
Shāh Ghulām ʿAlī (d. 1240/1824) 172 n.16
Shāh Ḥabīb al-Dīn Muḥibb Allāh 140
Shāh Ibrāhīmī (Ḥasan) 296
shahīd 16, 91, 191 n.8, 192 n.24
Shahīdān jo gham 245
Shāh ʿInāyat (d. 1130/1718) 236, 242–4, 250–1, 253 n.41
Shāh Ismāʿīl I [Shāh Khatāʾī] (r. 906–930/1501–1524) 3, 7–8, 31, 142, 258, 262, 264, 283 n.8, 322 n.31
Shāh Ismāʿīl II (r. 984–985/1576–1577) 68
Shāh Ismāʿīl III 322 n.32
Shāh Ismāʿīl Jūkī 333
Shāh jo risālo 17, 233, 235, 246, 249, 250
Shāh Kalīm Allāh (d. 1142/1729) 167
Shāh Khalīl Allāh (d. *ca* 850/1445–6) 124–7, 133–4, 136, 138–41, 144–5, 149, 150 n.2, 153 n.35, 158, 164–5, 169, 243
Shāh Mīrān (d. 1230/1814) 159, 161, 168, 171
Shāh Muḥammad Khudābanda (r. 985–996/1577–1588, d. 1003/1595–6) 69
Shāh Muḥammad Qadḥī 332
Shāh Muḥammad Rūmī 329
Shāh Muḥibb al-Dīn Ḥabīb Allāh 140
Shāh al-Nahār, or Zayd b. Ḥanẓala 332
Shāh Naʿīm al-Dīn Niʿmat Allāh II [Thānī] (d. after 906/1500–1) 146
Shāh Niʿmat Allāh Walī (d. 834/1431) 15, 123–7, 135–40, 142–4, 146–7, 150 n.1, 151 n.3, 151 n.9, 152 n.26, 153 n.30, 153 nn.38–9, 158, 314, 322 n.33, 342 n.53
Shāh Niẓām al-Dīn b. Baddānī 333
Shāh Nūr Allāh Ḥusaynī 140
Shāh Qāsim 59 n.35
Shāh Quṭb al-Dīn (Chishtī) 331
Shāh Rājū (d. 1092/1681–2) 161
Shahādat 17, 225–54
Shāhbāzīs 332–3
al-Shahrastānī, Abuʾl-Fatḥ Muḥammad b. ʿAbd al-Karīm (d. 548/1153) 46
Shāhrūdī, Mīrzā Muḥammad ʿAlī Sharīf Yazdī (13th–14th/19th–20th centuries) 293, 327
Shāhrukh (r. 807–850/1405–1447) 135–6, 138–41, 144–5, 152 n.20, 153 n.30, 342 n.53
Shāh Ṣafī (r. 1038–1052/1629–1642) 70
Shāh Shams al-Dīn 140, 332
Shāh Shams al-Dīn Muḥammad 140
Shāh Sharīf al-Dīn 167
Shāh Sulaymān (r. 1077–1105/1666–1694) 34, 48
Shāh Sulṭān Ḥusayn (r. 1105–1135/1694–1722) 11
Shāh Ṭāhir [Shāh Ṭāhir Dakanī] 15, 167, 171, 176
Shāh Ṭahmāsb (r. 930–984/1524–1576) 258
Shāh Walī Allāh (d. 1176/1762) 166
Shāh Yaḥyā al-Dīn 329–30
Shāh Yūsuf al-Dīn 167
Shām, Syria 86
shām walāyat 248
Shams al-Dīn Ḥusaynī (d. 1161/1748) 160, 161, 163–4, 171, 332

Shamsiyya 191 n.13
Shaqīq al-Balkhī (d. 194/809–10) 40, 49
*shar*ʿ 45–6
Sharaf al-Dīn Abū ʿAlī Qalandar Pānī Patī (d. 724/1323–4) 343 n.62
sharīʿa 13, 28, 43–7, 50–1, 217, 311–12, 314, 330, 335
shaṭḥ, *shaṭaḥāt* 13, 52, 54, 62 nn.125–6, 63 n.129
Shaṭṭ 89
al-Shaybī, Kāmil Muṣṭafā (d. 2006) 9, 24 n.46, 32–3, 43
Shaykh ʿAbd Allāh 153 n.38
Shaykh ʿAbd Allāh Yāfiʿī 342 n.53
Shaykh ʿAbd al-Qādir 329, 332, 340 n.33
Shaykh ʿAbd al-Wāḥid Nahīb 329
Shaykh ʿAbd al-Wāḥid Zayd 326, 328
Shaykh Abu'l-Fatḥ 331
Shaykh Abū Saʿīd Mubārak al-Makhdūmī 329
Shaykh ʿAmmār Yāsir Bidlīsī 342 n.56
shaykh-i maʾdhūnīn [*shaykh-i majāzī*] 188
Shaykh Kamāl al-Dīn Muḥammad Yamanī 343 n.61
Shaykh Masʿūd 329, 331
Ṣhaykh al-Mufīd, Muḥammad b. Muḥammad b. Nuʿmān (d. 413/1022) 115 n.122, 289 n.94
Shaykh Mumtāz Nūrī 330
Shaykh Nūr al-Dīn Abu'l-Futūḥ 41
Shaykh Ṣafī, Ṣafī al-Dīn Isḥāq al-Ardabilī (d. 735/1334) 6, 311
Shaykh Zakariyyāʾ 330
Shaykh Zayn al-Dīn b. Muḥammad b. al-Ḥasan b. al-Shahīd al-Thānī 71
Shaykhī(s) 9, 331
shaykhs, *mashāʾikh* 34, 125, 127, 143, 148, 151 n.4, 168, 179–80, 184–6, 188–9, 195 n.82, 195 n.91, 212
Sherwani, H. K. 142
Shibla 340 n.28
al-Shiblī, Abū Bakr Dulaf b. Jaḥdar (d. 334/945–6) 340 n.28
Shikārīs 331
Shiraz 12, 69, 119 n.182, 152 n.18, 295, 299, 310–11, 322 n.32, 340 n.20, 342 n.53
Shīrāzī, Maʿṣūm ʿAlī Shāh (d. 1344/1926) 167–8
Shīrāzī, Mīrzā Muḥammad Ḥasan (d. 1312/1895) 179
Shūshtar 32, 168
Shūshtarī, Qāḍī Nūr Allāh (d. 1019/1610) 10, 28, 111 n.56
Shūshtarī, Sayyid Riḍā (d. 1780) 168
Ṣiffīn 35, 39, 97, 339 n.11, 339 n.13
Sikandar Jah (r. 1218–1244/1803–1829) 159
sikka 311
al-Ṣila bayna'l-taṣawwuf wa'l-tashayyuʿ 9
silsila 5, 40, 125, 142, 198–9, 201, 203, 294, 296, 299, 310, 325, 328, 330
Simnan 71, 209
Simnānī, Khwājah ʿImād al-Dīn 137
Sindh 17, 226–30, 232–3, 235, 237–40, 242–51, 251 n.4, 252 n.30, 253 nn.33–4, 253 n.37, 253 n.40
Sindhi 17, 225–54

Siraiki 245, 251 n.4, 253 n.51
al-Sirjānī, ʿAbd al-Aḥad b. Burhān al-Dīn b. ʿAlī (10th/16th century) 258
sirr 207, 220 n.2
Sirrī al-Saqaṭī, Abu'l-Ḥasan Sirrī b. al-Maghlis al-Saqaṭī (d. 253/867–8) 340 n.25
Sivas 285 n.41
Solomon 271, 287 n.69
Sophene 341 n.42
Strauss, Leo (d. 1973) 31
Suʿālāt-i waṣla wa khirqa 292
Subḥānī, Ayat Allāh 206
Suhrawardī, Shaykh Shihāb al-Dīn Abū Ḥafṣ ʿUmar (d. 632/1234) 5
Suhrawardī, Shihāb al-Dīn Yaḥyā (d. 587/1191) 6, 51
Suhrawardī 228, 294
Suhrawardiyya 5, 11, 228–9, 233, 242
Sukhan [journal] 306
sukhanwarī 19, 293, 300, 306–7, 309, 311, 313, 316–19
sukr 53
Sulaymān b. Kathīr 88, 116 nn.126–7
Sulṭān ʿAlī Shāhī [Gunābādī, Mūllā Sulṭānī or Tāwūsiyya] 177
Sulṭān Muḥammad Shāh [Aga Khan] 254 n.58
Sulṭān Shāhīs 333
sulūk 202
Sumrās 228
Sunbād 90–2, 115 n.120
Sunnism 1, 10–11, 22 n.30, 31, 284 n.23
'Supreme Name' of God (*al-ism al-aʿẓam*) 36, 274
sur (Sindhi) 235, 237–8
Sur Kedāro 17, 233–8, 243, 248–50
sura 268
Tābanda, Ḥājj Āqā Sulṭān Ḥusayn (d. 1992) 179, 183–4, 189
ṭabaqāt 33–4, 42
al-Ṭabarī, Muḥammad b. Jarīr (d. 310/923) 113 n.82
Tabaristan 29
tabarrā 77–8, 99, 109 n.33, 338, 344 n.86
tabarzīn 299, 301, 309, 315–16
Ṭabātabā, ʿAlī 136, 153 n.35
Ṭabātabāʾī, ʿAllāma Sayyid Muḥammad (d. 1981) 204–6,
Tabriz 7–8, 31, 67, 69, 144, 258, 295, 310
tadhkirat 159, 170
Tadhkirat al-awliyāʾ 38, 43
tafrīd wa tajrīd 312
tafsīr 29
Tafsīr Imām al-ʿAskarī 117 n.146
Taft 15, 124–7, 135–7, 141, 144–6, 148–50, 150 n.2, 151 n.3, 151 n.9
ṭahārat 308, 320
Taheri, Zahra 306, 308
tāj 267, 309, 315, 334, 336
Tāj nāmah-yi pīrān 292
Tajik 14, 66–70
tajrīd 312, 334
ṭālib (pl. *ṭallāba*) 9, 278
Ṭālib al-Mawlā, Makhdūm Muḥammad Zamān (d. 1993) 239
talip 278
Ṭāliqānī, ʿAbd al-Muṭṭalib b. Yaḥyā (11th/17th century) 14, 65, 82–102, 105, 109 n.34, 111 n.68, 112 n.69, 112 n.72, 114 n.102, 114 n.105
Ṭalpūr, Mīr George ʿAlī Murād Khān (13th/19th century) 249
Ṭalpūrs 238–9, 241, 250, 253 n.39

Tānā Shāh, Abu'l-Ḥasan (r. 1083–1098/1672–1687) 161
tanāsukh 281
Tantric sects 294
tanūrah 334, 336, 337, 343 n.72
taqiyya 16, 33, 37, 43–4, 52, 142, 197–221, 309
taqlīd 191 n.18
Ṭarā'iq al-ḥaqā'iq 167–8, 294
tarāsh 337
Tārīkh-i Yazd 116 n.128
ṭarīqa 13, 28, 43–51, 125, 142, 145, 237, 314, 316, 328, 334–5, 338
tarjī'-band 232, 252 n.23
tashayyu'-e ḥasan 22 n.30
Tāsū'ā 298
tawajjuh 166
tawallā 338, 344 n.86
Tawḍīḥ al-Mushribīn 112 n.72
tawḥīd 288 n.93, 307, 312, 319, 340 n.26
ta'wīl 29
Ṭayfūrī, Ṭayfūriyya 326, 328–9, 331, 340 n.21
ta'ziya 147, 241
Tehran 16, 146, 175–95, 216–17, 292–3, 295, 299–300, 311, 317
Tehran University, Central Library of 292–3, 334
Thābit 'Alī Shāh (d. 1224/1810) 238–9, 246, 250
Tharo, Makhdūm (d. 1160/1748) 232
Thatta 242
thawāb 260, 271
Theology of Pseudo-Aristotle 46–7
al-Ṭihrānī, Āqā Buzurg (d. 1389/1970) 257
Tīmūr (r. 771–807/1370–1405) 135, 142–3
Timurids (771–912/1370–1507) 126–35, 138, 148
Tobacco Concession 324 n.73
Tokat 285 n.41
Transoxiana 340
Trimingham, John Spencer (d. 1987) 2, 4
Tuḥfa-yi 'Abbāsī 11
Tuḥfa-yi darwīsh 294
Tuḥfah-i imāmiyya 246
Tūnī, Quṭb al-Dīn Ḥaydar (d. *ca* 830/1426) 295
Turābī, 'Allāma Rāshid (d. 1392/1973) 249
Turkey 5, 17, 255
Turkish language 18, 257, 259–60, 262, 264, 311
Tus 41, 342 n.51
al-Ṭūsī, Naṣīr al-Dīn (d. 672/1274) 18, 90, 257–8, 284 n.11
al-Tūsī, Muḥammad (d. 460/1067) 289 n.94
Ṭūsī 87, 258–61
al-Tustarī, Sayyid Āqā 258

'Ubayd Allāh b. al-Ḥusayn al-Aṣghar b. 'Alī al-A'raj (2nd/8th century) 92–3
Uch 228, 326
ūlū'l-amr 280, 288 n.93
'Ulyā'īs 328
'Umar al-Ashraf b. Zayn al-'Ābidīn (2nd/8th century) 115 n.124
'Umar, caliph (r. 13–23/634–44) 6, 38, 102
'Umdat al-maqāl fī kufr ahl al-ḍalāl 68, 99
Umayyads 73, 84, 101, 104
Umm 'Ubayda 342 n.55
Urdu 17, 159, 173 n.32, 225–6, 230, 232–3, 239, 245, 249–51, 251 n.1, 251 n.4, 252 n.14, 252 n.17
'urf 194
'urs 162, 168–9, 171, 174 n.50, 237

Ustajlu 69
uṣūlī 8, 55, 179, 191 n.18
ʿUthmān Daqqāq 328
ʿUthmān b. Nahīk 88
Uways al-Qaranī (d. 37/657) 35, 37–8
Uwaysiyya 38
Uzbeg 67

Varamin 71
vāvīlās 243

waḥdat 312
waḥdat al-wujūd 322 n.40
Wahhābīs 332
Waḥshī [ʿAjam dervish] 309–10
Wakīl al-Mulk, Muḥammad Ismāʿīl Khān (r. 1274–1283/1858–1866) 152 n.12
walāya 2, 47, 204, 269, 274, 286 n.51, 288 n.72, 307
walī 136, 143, 203
waqf (*waqf-i ʿāmm*, *waqf-i khāṣṣ*) 16, 135, 175–95, 210, 221 n.16
waqf-nāmah 146–8, 153 n.29, 154 n.59, 175–7, 181, 185, 188–90
waqf-nāmah-yi rasmī 181
waqif 176, 182–6, 193 n.58, 194 nn.72–3
Wasīlat al-najāt 19, 293, 299, 306–7, 309–13, 315–16, 319–20, 322 n.32, 323 n.47, 324 n.73
waṣiyya 272
Weber, Max (d. 1920) 8
wilāyat 308
wilāyat al-faqīh 7
Wittgenstein, Ludwig (d. 1951) 60 n.74, 62 n.123

al-Yaʿqūbī, Aḥmad b. Abū Yaʿqūb (d. after 292/905) 113 n.82
Yāsirmīs, Yāsiriyān 328, 331, 333, 339 n.19
yawm al-ḥashr 117 n.146
Yazd 15, 92, 116 n.128, 135, 342 n.53
Yazīd b. Muʿāwiya (r. 60–64/680–683) 93, 101–2, 104, 116 n.136, 141, 248
Yemen 92
Yogis 325
Yūsuf b. Ḥusayn Rāzī 340 n.23

Ẓafar al-Dawla, Iḥtishām-i Jang (13th/19th century) 165
Zāhid Gīlānī (d. 700/1301) 300
ẓāhir 3, 35, 46, 51, 336
Ẓahīr al-Dawla (d. 1924) 319
zakāt 188, 277, 308, 320
Zand [era] 195 n.91
zandaqa 48
Zarrīnkūb, ʿAbd al-Ḥusayn (d. 1999) 11, 306, 308, 323 n.48
Zaydis 35–6, 281, 328, 330, 333
Zayn al-Dīn b. Muḥammad b. al-Ḥasan b. al-Shahīd al-Thānī (d. between 1062/1652 and 1064/1654) 71, 108 n.24
ziyāra 2, 72, 92–3, 102, 168
Zubayrīs 326
zuhd 339
zunnār 336–7
zūrkhānah 318, 324 n.74

www.ingramcontent.com/pod-product-compliance
Lightning Source LLC
Chambersburg PA
CBHW050134240426
43673CB00043B/1660